Sixty Years *of* Independence

Sixty Years *of* Independence

Achievements, Challenges and the Road Ahead for Trinidad and Tobago

EDITED BY

BHOENDRADATT TEWARIE

ROGER HOSEIN

REBECCA GOOKOOL-BOSLAND

The University of the West Indies Press
Mona • St Augustine • Cave Hill • Global • Five Islands

The University of the West Indies Press
7A Gibraltar Hall Road, Mona
Kingston 7, Jamaica
www.uwipress.com

A catalogue record of this book is available from the
National Library of Jamaica.

ISBN: 978-976-658-026-1 (paper)
978-976-658-051-3 (cloth)
978-976-658-027-8 (ePub)

Cover concept by Bhoendradatt Tewarie
Cover design by Marketing and Communications, The UWI, St Augustine
Book design by Robert Harris
Set in Minion Pro 11.2/14.5 x 24.

Printed in the United States of America

Contents

List of Figures

List of Tables

Foreword

As chancellor of The University of the West Indies, which is celebrating its seventy-fifth anniversary this year, it gives me great pleasure to write this foreword for a book that reflects on sixty years of independence in the life of the nation-state of Trinidad and Tobago.

The editors of this book have given much to The University of the West Indies as, indeed, the University has contributed to their life and personal development. Dr Bhoendradatt Tewarie was a former principal of the St Augustine Campus of our regional university and pro vice-chancellor for Planning and Development. Professor Roger Hosein has distinguished himself as an economist in the region and now heads the Trade and Development Unit. Dr Rebecca Gookool-Bosland recently graduated from UWI with a PhD in economics and now works for a small microfinance company in the southwest peninsula of Trinidad. All of the authors of chapters, either graduated from UWI at some level, taught there or are teaching and researching there now. It is with a sense of pride, therefore, that I write this foreword to *Sixty Years of Independence: Achievements, Challenges and the Road Ahead for Trinidad and Tobago*. It is an appropriate point at which to reflect, to assess and to recalibrate, as may be required.

In 2022, the Trinidad and Tobago government, like many others in the world, began to relax its COVID-19 restrictions which no doubt negatively impacted economic and social outcomes in the period 2020–22. For the Trinidad and Tobago economy, though, the impact of COVID-19 was preceded by several years of low to negative growth, thereby seeding not just a recession but an economic depression. Notably, the rise in energy and energy associated prices such as fertilizers did not translate to real growth; and as the year closed, the Russia-Ukraine war remained a worrisome matter in the global conversation, and the geopolitical environment remained uncertain, with the battle for hegemonic power still hanging in the balance.

On these, and other, uncertainties, food prices soared, eroding food security for this small, highly open economy.

Amidst this global turmoil, the government of Trinidad and Tobago continues to argue that an economic turnaround is imminent with improved government revenues, foreign exchange inflows, lower debt indicators and improved trade balances. These improvements are correctly attributed to higher energy prices, but that very fact emphasizes just how vulnerable we are as an economy to the nuances of the international energy markets. On the other hand, no clear vision for articulating precise development strategies beyond this narrative is fully developed. The average person in the street, who now faces higher transport fares, rising fuel costs at the pumps, worsening ease of doing business factors and declining real income, as inflationary trends persist, are also faced with wage negotiations, currently ongoing, the resolution of which may bring peace and some order, but hardly, worker satisfaction.

Against the backdrop of a deteriorating economic situation, the deficiencies of the education system have also been exposed due to the shocks of the past few years. In the first instance, the clear lack of effective remediation for different types of learners has been worsened by social and economic inequalities. A "one size fits all" at the SEA and CXC levels continues to churn out individuals who are not well adapted to assimilating into a transforming globalized world without needed numeracy, literacy and technical-vocational skills. This means that thousands fall through the cracks annually. Even those doing well at the tertiary level may not find jobs that offer a foundation for building a life.

In the recent past, the impact of climate change and indiscriminate environmental degradation has been observed with flooding in particular resulting in increasingly distressed conditions to the nation's physical infrastructure base and the massive dislocation of people. Crime, too, remains a constraining factor, not just for businesses but also a critical challenge to citizen security. The murder toll for 2022 was the highest up to that year at 612; 2024 was the deadliest year with a murder count of 614. This reflects an inherent structural issue which requires urgent policy and governance attention.

This book brings to the fore a few of the main developmental conversations that we cannot avoid, as we reflect on how best to position the economy to grow in the medium-term period. Indeed, the priority list includes a reflection on building a comprehensive programme for sustainable economic growth by which poverty can be meaningfully ameliorated. The programme must also therefore include a focus on the national infrastructure base as well as reform for the public services, including education, and health and state enterprises.

As the nation positions itself on its development path for the next sixty years, there is much to contend with in terms of the legacy of challenges such as those highlighted above, and ventilated with detailed consideration in this publication, no doubt emanating from the quality of governance and the supporting institutional infrastructures, from independence to the present time. While it is realistic to acknowledge, that hindsight brings some clarity, we must also find a way to bring the learnings of the past into the contemporaneous approach to policymaking and capacity building at all levels in the economy and society as we pursue development goals. Indeed, governments must embrace the relevant thought leadership for growth and practical management for sustainability.

It is my sincere hope that many will read this book because of the sound historical record that it provides in important areas, because of its analytical perspective and because of the proposals that it makes for going forward and doing better. It is an important book for Trinidad and Tobago, but it is also of great value for the rest of our future generations as they reflect on the last sixty years of independence.

ROBERT BERMUDEZ
CHANCELLOR
THE UNIVERSITY OF THE WEST INDIES
2017–24

Introduction

This book examines the performance, achievements, errors of judgement and acts of redemption in Trinidad and Tobago's socio-economic history as an independent nation. Sector by sector, it outlines progress made and things yet to be achieved and where that leaves the country sixty years after independence secured in 1962, as it comes face to face with an uncertain future, in a world caught up in the throes of technologically driven, economic, social, political transformation and geopolitical realignment.

It begins with an assessment of oil and gas and its significant contribution to Trinidad and Tobago's economic development, and how this country is positioned after years of overdependence on energy in a changing energy environment in terms of our own production, the cyclicality of price changes, the world shift in focus to renewable energy and the changing economic environment around us with new oil finds in Suriname and Guyana and possibly, in other territories region-wide. The transforming ideological alignments affecting countries in the hemisphere as geopolitics plays itself out globally is considered. At the same time, Trinidad and Tobago is making shifts in policy; the pertinent question is whether we are doing this fast enough or well enough. Kevin Ramnarine brings a reflective but practical point of view on this subject of energy. Mr Ramnarine, as a former energy minister, may have valuable insights and perspectives, but regardless of his views, the facts and figures offer an essential glimpse of reality. Throughout the book, various authors strive for accuracy, objectivity and balance to bring a clear perspective on their particular area of expertise.

This energy chapter is followed by a chapter on food (agriculture). Several years ago, the United Nations, in one of their reports, spoke about the challenge of the food, water, energy stress nexus. Overtime, this has become real. The global population, now surpassing 8 billion, is facing increasing demands for food and water amidst the intensifying impacts of climate change. Extreme weather patterns, including heavy rains, floods, severe droughts, forest fires and declining agricultural productivity, have brought the stress nexus the UN warned about years ago into a sharp reality that demands attention. Access to food and water, once a concern for the future, is now an urgent challenge. Energy exploration, of course, makes its own significant demands on water. In their chapter on agriculture and food security, Wendy Ann Isaac, Omardath Maharaj and Michael Joseph critically re-examine the issue of food security, along with agricultural strategy and policy, against the backdrop of the persistent underdevelopment of the agricultural sector. They highlight how the challenges have intensified in a post-pandemic world, where climate change compounds the issues that must be addressed both in the short and long term.

What is development of a country for if not for the human beings who live there and the sustainability of the environmental conditions that surround them? So, the chapters which immediately follow focus on education, health, human capital, development and the environment.

Jerome De Lisle, Cheryl Bowrin-Williams and Tracy Lucas identify the critical interventions in education over the period and assess success and failure in the context of genuine, documentable achievements elsewhere. The authors argue in the chapter "The Development of Education in Trinidad and Tobago after Independence – Losses, Gains, Missed Opportunities" that the recent COVID pandemic gives us another opportunity to take stock, to recalibrate and create a system, where a significantly larger number of students each year can show genuine achievements. They argue that the goal must be a high performing, more equitable system, focused on equity, well-being and excellence and that an education system which benefits a few can never be considered world class.

The school system provides the basic human capital for development and lays the foundation for individual well-being, but people must be in good health to personally make the most of life opportunities and to make a valuable contribution to society. Chapter 3 focuses on health.

In looking at the sixty-year period under review, the authors, Anjanie Sharma, Keshan Ramnarace and Surujpaul Teelucksingh identify a drop in infant mortality and maternal mortality and an increase in life expectancy as genuine achievements. They also point to a decline in births, a rise in the crude death rates and the prevalence of heart disease, diabetes, stroke, chronic kidney disease and the rise of mental health problems as challenges that require concentration, focus and dedicated attention.

Chapter 6 which focuses on "The Challenge of Human Capital Formation and Effective Deployment in Trinidad and Tobago" views human capital formation as essential for making development happen. How does a small country of 1.4 million optimize the value of each citizen and leverage the contribution of citizens for deployment and how do you get effective outputs from the tertiary sector, finance this sustainably and deploy citizens meaningfully to quicken the pace of development? Bhoendradatt Tewarie makes the case for synergies in policy, planning and execution; for the recognition of merit; for the commitment to building a knowledge economy; and for facilitating the development not just of intellectual capital, but social capital as well. He argues the case for an integrated approach in the harnessing of human and social assetsfor structural economic transformation that can deliver shared prosperity in a more productive society.

The next chapter takes a comprehensive view of environmental management in Trinidad and Tobago. Judith Gobin, La Daana Kanhai and Hamish Asmath thoughtfully explain the natural environment and its ecosystems, the impacts of anthropogenic activities, agriculture, industrial and other activities that demonstrate the challenges that Trinidad and Tobago faces as a small country of formidable natural assets. They also reflect on institutions, legislation and the level of public awareness, and how these impact the trajectory going forward for more effective and sensitive management of the environment.

The remaining chapters focus first on crime as a pivotal issue on which economic, prosperity and sustainability depend. Following the chapter on crime, the hard economic issues are examined – trade, manufacturing, macro-economic development. In the chapter on crime, Garvin Heerah identifies some of the structural problems of law enforcement, and the justice system, as well as some of the missing ingredients that need to be brought together in place, and puts forward an integrated, interconnected approach to an effective solution strategy.

In their chapter on trade and development, Roger Hosein, Regan Deonanan, Rebecca Gookool-Bosland and Mark Roopchan trace the trajectory of trade over the period and suggest strategies for expanding non-energy exports. The authors identify specific products that can benefit from a focused thrust towards export expansion and itemize desirable actions that the Ministry of Trade and other government agencies can together take to make the expansion of export trade a reality. Here the focus is on non-CARICOM exports and favourable markets in the wider region and on tradable goods for exports rather than the generation of non-tradable goods which the authors statistically identify as the inclination and trend at the present time in the Trinidad and Tobago economy.

The chapter on the manufacturing sector seeks to rethink internationalization of the manufacturing sector by looking at how digitalization and data analytics create an opportunity for Trinidad and Tobago's manufacturing sector to integrate into the global value chain and be part of the global production and distribution process. The author, Nigel Williams, argues that this is what the logic of the current phase of internationalization demands to take the manufacturing sector in Trinidad and Tobago forward. He draws from the example of Ireland to make a case for a coherent national strategy in manufacturing for Trinidad and Tobago.

The chapter on Tobago outlines the current comparative labour market conditions in Tobago and Trinidad, including trends in labour productivity and GDP per capita. GDP per capita is a leading indicator of the living standards an economy can support, and the level of development of an economy and labour productivity are its leading cause. Thus, the chapter documents the resulting characteristic empirical relationship that has existed between labour productivity and living standards since 1970 and extracts an implied explanatory theory of the relationship between the average level of education of workers and living standards as well as associated policies aimed at accelerating development in both Tobago and Trinidad. This chapter is by Vanus James, Carlos Hazel and Kenneth Bissoon.

Chapter 11, authored by Roger Hosein, Regan Deonanan, Rebecca Gookool-Bosland and Mark Roopchan, provides a rigorous economic analysis of trends and challenges over the past sixty years. This chapter specifically addresses the steps necessary to achieve sustainable economic growth in a country that experienced over a decade of consistent growth, but from 2015 to 2022, faced a shift from negative growth to decline, and eventually recession. After a significant drop in GDP, the country only began to show signs of recovery and growth in 2023. This chapter makes several recommendations for improved performance, including: 1) the effective deployment of Venezuelan immigrant labour, 2) fiscal targets, and fiscal responsibility legislation, 3) improved, non-energy revenue collection, 4) liberalization of the foreign exchange market, 5) significantly reduced transfers to state enterprises and to statutory boards, all of which will cumulatively result in increased fiscal discipline, reduced government, expenditure, diversification of revenue sources and containment of political arbitrariness in financial and economic management.

The final chapter by Bhoendradatt Tewarie draws on the value of the eleven other chapters in the book to focus on what to do next, given this objective assessment of where Trinidad and Tobago finds itself economically, politically, and socially after six decades of independent self-governance, and suggests an agenda that we might pursue as a country and some actions that we might take, to unite purposefully behind a coherent strategy to develop Trinidad and Tobago, with purposefulness inclusivity and shared prosperity. This last chapter identifies a number of interventions to address corruption, to improve governance, to reform the constitution, to put Trinidad and Tobago on a sustainable development path, to deepen democracy, to facilitate greater equity, and to improve the climate of trust between an elected government and its citizens.

The authors of each chapter are knowledgeable professionals or experts in their particular field and stand by their perspectives articulated in this volume. At the same time, the editors have sought to align these perspectives so that complementarities, supplementation of information, synergies and coherence readily emerge.

There is no doubt that a book of this nature, which not only reflects on the achievements and missteps of the past sixty years but also explores the potential opportunities of the unfolding future, is essential.

The authors, featured in this book, all have considered opinions and strong points of view backed up by facts, figures and solid arguments and a deep history of involvement in ideas as well as actions. This makes these reflections on the sixty-year history of Trinidad and Tobago well worth reading, not just for the history and information but also because of what the substance of this work can do to provoke the reader's own thoughts.

BHOENDRADATT TEWARIE
ROGER HOSEIN
REBECCA GOOKOOL-BOSLAND

[CHAPTER 1]

Sixty Years of Oil and Gas in Independent Trinidad and Tobago, 1962–2022

KEVIN RAMNARINE

This chapter takes us through major interventions, facilitating the development of the oil and natural gas industry from independence to the present time. It is optimistic about the future based on the knowledge, skills and experience of Trinidad and Tobago acquired over the last sixty years and longer because of the potential for a circle of fossil fuel energy producing-countries, such as Guyana, Suriname, Brazil, and in better times, Venezuela, around Trinidad and Tobago. The author sees possibilities for the development of a maritime industry to service the regional energy sector growing around us, based on formidable skills and capacity already developed in the service sector.

Notwithstanding, the chapter takes us through the cycles of booms and busts in Trinidad and Tobago because of the vagaries of the energy industry globally, its central role in geopolitical manoeuvres, and how these factors have affected national decisions and economic fortunes over time, the chapter acknowledges the precarious position that Trinidad and Tobago is in because of inadequate production, volatile prices and lack of diversification. Still, it is optimistic about Trinidad and Tobago's potential for navigating the way forward in energy recalibration in spite of identifiable challenges and uncertainties.

INDEPENDENCE TO BOOM: 1962–73

In 1962, Trinidad and Tobago already had a well-developed oil industry with commercial production starting in 1908. In 1962, the production of oil was in the hands of foreign companies. Trinidad and Tobago's oil industry and its refineries played a crucial role in supporting the Allied war effort in the Second World War. By the time independence was attained, oil production was 133,907 barrels of oil per day (bopd), of which 70.2 per cent came from land and 29.8 per cent came from the offshore area in the Gulf of Paria. Natural gas production was 274 million cubic feet per day (mmcfd). This supported a power plant in Penal and one ammonia plant at Savonetta. At independence, there were two operating refineries, one at Point Fortin operated by Shell and another at Pointe-a-Pierre operated by Texaco. At the time of independence, the Pointe-a-Pierre refinery was the largest in the Commonwealth and represented the largest investment for Texaco outside of the United States.

THE MINISTRY OF PETROLEUM AND MINES

The Ministry of Petroleum and Mines (now the Ministry of Energy and Energy Industries) is one of the most important Ministries in Trinidad and Tobago with responsibility for managing the industry, which Dr Vernon Mulchansingh has described as the *sine qua non* of Trinidad and Tobago's economic life.[1] The Ministry of Petroleum and Mines was established in May 1963. The recommendation for the establishment of a dedicated ministry to oversee the petroleum sector came out of the Second Five Year Development plan for 1964 to 1968.[2] Prior to the establishment of the ministry, the administration of petroleum operations was with disparate government departments. The head office of the Ministry of Petroleum and Mines was first located at the corner of Park and Fredrick Streets in Port of Spain. This location is referred to as "the transfer station" because it was a central point for the electric trams that worked different routes in and around Port of Spain up to 1950. The ministry later moved to the Salvatori Building and then to Riverside Plaza. The ministry is presently located at Tower C of the International Financial Centre in Port of Spain. The early permanent secretaries of the Ministry of Petroleum and Mines were Doddridge Alleyne and Roderick Gene Thomas.

As Dr Eric Williams's policies sought to take control of the commanding heights of the Trinidad and Tobago economy, it was Dodderidge Alleyne who would be the lead negotiator in many of the government's acquisitions. He led negotiations in 1968 with British Petroleum for the purchase of their service station network. In the 1970s, he led talks with Shell to purchase its assets, which led to the creation of Trintoc. In 1969, the Trinidad and Tobago Parliament passed the Petroleum Act into law. The act consolidated and amended laws relating to petroleum operations. The Petroleum Act remains the main piece of legislation governing petroleum operations in Trinidad and Tobago.

One of the notable initiatives of the government of the newly independent Trinidad and Tobago was the establishment of the Mostofi Commission of Inquiry into the petroleum sector. The recommendations of the Mostofi Commission led to major changes in the legislative framework governing the oil industry. The terms of reference of the commission were:

- To examine the present situation and prospects of the oil industry in Trinidad and Tobago in the context of the economics of the world oil industry.
- To recommend a legal framework for the oil industry in Trinidad and Tobago which would stimulate the operations of foreign investors while safeguarding the interests of the nation.
- To make recommendations designed to ensure the greatest possible stability compatible with growth in the industry, including the level of employment.

Before the "oil boom" of the 1970s, the petroleum sector was already the most dominant in Trinidad and Tobago. In 1962, oil revenue accounted for 30 per cent of government revenue. For the period 1928 to 1968, oil revenue as a percentage of government revenue ranged from 15.9 per cent to 41.5 per cent. The highest rate, 41.5 per cent, was attained in both 1957 and 1958.[3] According to the Five-Year Development Plan for 1969 to 1973, in 1963 (one year after independence), the oil and asphalt sector contributed around 27.6 per cent of GDP.

OIL PRODUCTION, 1962–73

From 1962 to 1965, oil production was stagnant. However, from 1964 to 1967, production experienced a significant increase as it rose from 133,860 bopd to 182,798 bopd. This increase in three years arose mainly from land-based production and successful drilling programmes undertaken by Texaco Trinidad in southeast Trinidad in the Guayaguayare-Navet area. Land-based production in Trinidad would peak in 1967 at 112,000 bopd. After this peak, oil production from land experienced a secular decline. Table 1.1 below references these trends.

Table 1.1: Oil Production, 1962–73

Year	Land-based Oil Production (bopd)	Marine-based Oil Production (bopd)	Total Oil Production (bopd)
1962	94,040	39,867	133,365
1963	85,890	47,475	135,877
1964	84,246	51,631	133,860
1965	84,295	49,565	152,340
1966	97,037	55,303	178,634
1967	112,089	66,545	182,798
1968	106,342	76,456	157,311
1969	81,414	75,897	139,855
1970	69,519	70,336	129,172
1971	66,340	62,832	139,920
1972	60,075	79,845	166,219
1973	55,229	110,990	133,365

Source: Ministry of Energy of Trinidad and Tobago

In 1968, facing declining production in Trinidad and Tobago and considering its discoveries in the North Sea, Prudhoe Bay in the Alaskan North Slope and Libya, British Petroleum decided to exit Trinidad and Tobago. The government and a new entrant to the Trinidad and Tobago oil business, the American company Tesoro, took its place. At the eleventh People's National Movement (PNM) convention in September 1968, Dr Eric E. Williams announced his government's plans to buy the assets of British Petroleum in Trinidad and Tobago. This decision was seen to be based on the government's desire to save jobs, mainly in the county of St Patrick. The decision was historic from two points of view. Firstly, it was the state's first foray into the petroleum business. Secondly, the entry of Tesoro brought with it a major corruption scandal that would have ripple effects for decades. Trinidad Tesoro would eventually exit Trinidad and Tobago in 1985 when it sold its assets to the government for 3.23 million barrels of fuel oil.[4] The new company formed to hold the assets of Trinidad Tesoro was named Trintopec.

In 1969, the Trinidad and Tobago Parliament passed the Petroleum Act into law. The act consolidated and amended laws relating to petroleum. The Petroleum Act remains the main piece of legislation governing petroleum operations in Trinidad and Tobago. By the end of the 1960s, certain foundational elements of the Trinidad and Tobago energy sector were beginning to take shape. There was a dedicated ministry for the petroleum sector and governing legislation, and the government had started to assert itself as an owner of oil companies. Most importantly, by the end of the 1960s, a historic exploration campaign was taking place off the East Coast that would fundamentally alter the trajectory of the Trinidad and Tobago economy.

EAST COAST EXPLORATION – PATOC/AMOCO

The exploration programme led by Pan American Trinidad Oil Company (PATOC) in the early to late 1960s was the most important drilling campaign in Trinidad and Tobago's history. It laid the foundation for two post-independence hydrocarbon based booms. The first "boom" was premised on oil production from the Teak, Samman and Poui fields (TSP), and the second was premised on natural gas from the Cassia and Mahogany fields. In 1969, PATOC renamed itself Amoco Trinidad Oil Company.

The early plants established at Point Lisas were supplied natural gas from Amoco's Teak D and B platforms and associated gas from TSP. Amoco Trinidad's first entry into the Gas business in July 1974 was to supply T&TEC with gas for electricity.

When Cassia was brought into production in 1983, it supplied the demand from new plants at the Point Lisas Estate, such as the first methanol plants TTMC 1 and Tringen II. Natural gas from Amoco was also sold to T&TEC

to meet the growing demand for electricity as the Trinidad and Tobago economy expanded and more people entered the middle class.

As will be demonstrated later, natural gas from Mahogany (which was discovered in the East Mayaro wells) was the supply for Atlantic LNG's Train 1 when it started operations in 1999. The natural gas supply to justify LNG Trains II, III and IV would have been discovered mainly in the mid- to late 1990s, during a period when Amoco Trinidad was very successful with its exploration efforts.

The story of this economic transformation began on 10 January 1961, when the government of Trinidad and Tobago granted an exploration licence to a consortium of three companies: the aforementioned PATOC, Trinidad Sun Oil Limited and Pure Oil Company of Trinidad Inc. PATOC was a subsidiary of the American company AMOCO, which was originally Standard Oil of Indiana.

The consortium was granted rights to two million acres of offshore acreage on Trinidad's east coast. The licence departed from the prevailing onshore licences and offshore 1952 vintage lease held by TNA for acreage off the West coast in the Gulf of Paria (now Trinmar). The licence emphasized performance and early appraisal and also made provisions for the relinquishment of acreage. Due to an early disappointment with a dry hole, Sun Oil and Pure Oil exited the exploration campaign, and between 1962 and 1965, PATOC purchased the entire working interest. Prior to this, the consortium had drilled its first well, OPR 1, in 1962. OPR 1 (Offshore Point Radix 1) was drilled approximately twenty miles off the east of Point Radix in water depths of 172ft. OPR1 was a dry hole.[5]

There was a hiatus in drilling until 1967 when PATOC resumed exploration drilling in the Southeast Galeota (SEG), East Mayaro (EM) and Offshore Point Radix (OPR) areas. In total, from 1967 to 1969, PATOC drilled nine wells in these areas. The first seven wells of the 1967 to 1969 campaign were a combination of dry holes and natural gas. In its eight wells in the 1967 to 1969 campaign, OPR3, PATOC found both oil and natural gas. Its ninth well, OPR4, found oil. The OPR3 well discovered the Teak oil field, while OPR2 discovered the natural gas horizons of the Teak field.

Exploration in the SEG area in the late 1960s would eventually lead to the SEG 9 well, which discovered the Cassia field in 1973. While natural gas may not have been what PATOC was looking for when they drilled the early SEG wells in the late 1960s, the discovery of Cassia in 1973 laid the platform for Trinidad and Tobago's leap towards a natural gas-based economy. In 1983, natural gas production began from the Cassia field. The EM 1 well drilled in 1968 by PATOC led to the drilling of EM 2 in 1973 when the Mahogany field was discovered. In 1971, Amoco returned to the site of OPR 1 and drilled OPR 14, just three miles north-northeast. Both oil and gas were found, and the area became the Samaan Field. The first oil from Samman came ashore in late 1972. In 1972, Amoco discovered the Poui Field with the West Tournaline 1 well. The role of PATOC and Amoco in the development of Trinidad and Tobago and the significance of their contribution to the oil and gas industry in Trinidad and Tobago cannot be understated.

BOOM TO BUST: 1973–83

In delivering the 1970 budget, Prime Minister Dr Eric Williams noted that the decade of the 1970s has begun, "most propitiously with the prospects of a high level of offshore production of natural gas and low sulphur crude petroleum". He added that "there are very few developing countries in the world which begin the decade with such assets".[6]

Many people did not share Dr Williams's optimism in 1970, and in that year, there was civil unrest and an army mutiny, which is referred to as the Black Power Revolution. Dr Williams was, however, correct in his assessment of the situation regarding the potential of the oil and gas sector and would have obviously been aware of the extent of what Amoco Trinidad had discovered. He could not have, however, predicted the events of October 1973, which remains one of the most significant points of inflexion in the history of Trinidad and Tobago.

In October 1973, war broke out in the Middle East when Egyptian and Syrian forces launched an attack on Israel on Yom Kippur, the holiest day in the Jewish calendar. The war has since been called the Yom Kippur War. This is relevant to Trinidad and Tobago because the Yom Kippur War and the geopolitical events that followed changed the oil industry and the trajectory of our economy.

One outcome of this war was the Arab oil embargo of the United States and other countries that had supported Israel. The embargo led to the energy crisis of the early 1970s, with oil prices increasing from an average of US$3.29 in 1973 to an average of US$11.58 in 1974. At the same time, oil production from Amoco's Teak and Samaan fields commenced, pushing oil production upwards. In 1972, oil production in Trinidad and Tobago averaged 139,920 barrels of oil per day (bopd), and in 1974, that figure was 186,673 bopd.

The year 1973 is, therefore, a major point of inflexion for Trinidad and Tobago and signals the birth of the modern Trinidad and Tobago economy driven by oil and natural gas. The confluence of the price shock and boost in production led to a tripling of government revenue from TT$494.4 million in 1973 to TT$1,386.7 million in 1974. Revenue would steadily increase, and the period would become known as the "oil boom". Prior to the events of October 1973, Trinidad and Tobago's economy was in a slump. Unemployment in 1973 was around 17 per cent, and at the end of 1973, foreign reserves were just six weeks of import cover.

The Arab embargo precipitated an increase in oil prices of almost 352 per cent in the space of a few months. During the eight years from 1973 to 1980, the price of oil increased by nearly 1100 per cent.

Table 1.2: Oil Production and Prices

Year	Land Production	Marine Production	Total Production /bopd	WTI Oil Price ($US)
1973	20,158,449	40,511,511	166,219	3.29
1974	18,787,674	49,348,144	186,673	11.58
1975	15,095,302	63,525,636	215,400	11.53
1976	16,345,682	61,326,953	212,220	12.38
1977	16,506,057	67,113,020	229,093	13.3
1978	16,589,963	67,187,540	229,527	13.6
1979	17,134,768	61,114,706	214,382	30.03
1980	17,102,907	60,510,053	212,057	35.69
1981	15,797,640	53,309,649	189,335	34.28
1982	15,284,972	49,333,815	177,038	31.76
1983	13,776,304	44,567,290	159,845	28.77

Source: Ministry of Energy of Trinidad and Tobago and BP Statistical Review of World Energy, 2021.

Because of the rapidly changing economic fortunes brought about by increased production and higher prices, in 1974, the government passed the Petroleum Taxes Act (PTA), which introduced the Petroleum Profits Tax (PPT), the purpose of which was to capture more economic rent from the oil companies. The government also passed the Petroleum Production Subsidy and Levy Act that same year, which introduced the controversial fuel subsidy and the levy on oil companies. The PTA separated petroleum operations for tax purposes into E&P, refining and marketing. The rate of PPT applicable to the production of petroleum was 47.5 per cent on every dollar of taxable income.

In 1981, war broke out between OPEC members Iran and Iraq, pushing oil prices above $US40 per barrel. The government introduced a new tax in 1981, the Supplemental Petroleum Tax (SPT).

In 1974, Trinidad and Tobago entered into its first Production Sharing Contracts (PSCs) when four blocks were awarded to bidders out of the 1973 Competitive Bidding Order (CBO). On Independence Day in 1974, the government celebrated the acquisition of the Shell refinery in Point Fortin. The Shell acquisition in 1974 was in keeping with the prevailing economic philosophy of the day, namely, the state taking control of the commanding heights of the economy. The new company that took ownership of Shell's assets was called Trintoc. In 1985, the Trinidad and Tobago government acquired the much larger Pointe-a-Pierre refinery from Texaco. In a recent public forum, it was said that the main rationale for the 1985 refinery acquisition was the preservation of jobs or, as one veteran media personality opined, "preservation of votes". The acquisition was, after all, completed in 1985, and the following year, there would be a general election.

In his book *Trinidad and Tobago Industrial Policy, 1959 to 2008*, former Finance Minister Wendell Mottley wrote that from 1973 to 1983, the state spent TT$7.32 billion or US$3.75 billion acquiring corporate assets. Mottley writes that the government was committed to a state-led approach rather than a private-sector approach to industrialization. The swing towards "Statism" therefore accelerated after 1973 since "money was no problem", and Dr Eric Williams seized the opportunity to implement his vision of industrial Trinidad and Tobago. In the 1970s and into the 1980s, the role of the state was that of investor. After the NAR period and structural adjustment, the role of the state would become essentially that of facilitator.

The thrust into natural gas–based development will be dealt with in a later section. Whatever his political failings, Dr Eric Williams had a vision for industrial Trinidad and Tobago. To achieve that vision, he assembled Errol Mahabir, Professor Ken Julien and Ben Primus around him. Credit must also go to the pioneering businessmen of the South Chamber of Industry and Commerce headed by Robert Montano. The year 1973 was, therefore, a watershed in the history of Trinidad and Tobago that saw the efforts of an American oil company (Amoco), a war in the Middle East and the ambitions of a prime minister come together to birth the modern economy of Trinidad and Tobago. This period is not, however, without its failings and corruption scandals, which are metaphorically captured by Trevor Farrell in his work that details the period, *Worship of the Golden Calf.*

BUDGET SPEECHES OF DR ERIC WILLIAMS 1974, 1975 AND 1976

Williams's thinking on the period is captured in his many speeches on the oil and gas situation. The prevailing economic thinking about the sudden increase in oil revenue is captured in the budget speeches of Prime Minister and Minister of Finance Dr Eric Williams in 1974, 1975 and 1976.

Speaking about the rise in the oil revenues from 1973 to 1974 in the budget address of 1974, the then prime minister, Dr Eric Williams, cautioned the country about the possibility of oil prices reverting to pre-Arab oil embargo prices. Williams cautioned that there was; "the real possibility of oil prices reverting to lower levels and markets becoming difficult in the future". He further cautioned that "prudence and foresight, therefore, require us to plan our affairs on the assumption that the present situation may not be of long duration and to apply the income from this wasting asset as a defensive shield, to develop the foundation for long term economic viability, whatever the vicissitudes we might face".[7]

A year later, in his 1975 budget speech, Williams again cautioned the nation against the possibility of a fall in the oil price when he stated that:

> This very large increase in expenditure will present us with considerable difficulty if the revenue base is weakened. Consider a hypothetical situation. Suppose that the price of oil falls to a level of $7.25 U.S. per barrel, this being the target expressed by one authoritative spokesman on U.S. economic affairs; then our current revenues would be barely adequate to meet current expenditures at

their projected 1975 levels and pay our debt charges. There would be no surplus left to finance the development programme and, what is more, our planned investments in energy-based industries would be put in jeopardy. Merely to mention this possibility is to show how unthinkable it would be.[8]

In his 1976 budget speech, Williams again continued in the vein of caution, noting that:

> We cannot afford to build up recurrent expenditure in a situation in which there is always the possibility that there will be a sudden turn of events that reverses the favourable revenue position created by the energy crisis of late 1973; or, as we originally put it, to encourage new consumption and expenditures which are unsustainable under normal conditions.[9]

The record shows that, far from being cautious and conservative, Dr Williams's government did the exact opposite. From an expenditure of $606.8 million in 1973, by 1982, the government's expenditure was $9473 million, a factor of almost sixteen times. This prompted Jamaican Prime Minister Michael Manley to make his famous "dose of salts" comment as a way of describing the flow of cash through Trinidad and Tobago.[10]

Table 1.3: Government Fiscal Operations, 1973–83

Year	Govt Revenues ($TT)	Govt Expenditure ($TT)	Oil Revenue ($US m)[11]	Oil Production Bopd	Oil Prices $US / bbl	Oil Revenue as a % of Total Revenue
1973	494.4	606.8	96.1	166,219	3.29	21.7
1974	1386.7	959.2	410.1	186,673	11.58	64.8
1975	1874.4	1201.1	514.8	215,400	11.53	67.1
1976	2302.9	1870.6	593.4	212,220	12.80	62.8
1977	2991.4	2263.1	737.7	229,093	13.92	59.2
1978	3126.5	2892.5	722.3	229,527	14.02	55.4
1979	4059.3	4190.9	988.1	214,382	31.61	58.4
1980	6198.8	5466.3	1723.5	212,057	36.83	63.7
1981	7064.8	6674.9	1772.1	189,335	35.93	60.2
1982	7117.8	9473.1	1364.3	177,038	32.97	46.0
1983	6614.3	9333.8	1025.6	159,845	29.55	37.2

Sources: Accounting for the Petrodollar 1973–83 and BP Statistical Review of World Energy, 2021

Table 1.3 above shows that oil production in Trinidad and Tobago peaked in 1978 at 229,527 bopd. After reaching its peak, there was a steady decline to the present day, with a brief reprieve from the commencement of production from the Angostura field in 2005–6. The major event of the sixty years, 1962 to 2022, as far as oil production goes, was realized by the production from TSP, which took the national production to its peak in 1978. Once more, we see the importance of PATOC and Amoco Trinidad in the story of the sixty years of oil and gas production since independence.

FETE OVER BACK TO WORK

In the early 1980s, after the intoxication of oil money in the 1970s, Trinidad and Tobago came crashing down to earth again. Writing in 1980, Jeremy Taylor wrote that,

> Nowhere else in the Caribbean is the split between social wealth and underdevelopment so evident as Trinidad. The country is awash with oil money. But apart from the traffic snarls and inflation there are no real signs of its impact. 'Money is not the problem' Trinidad and Tobago's austere Prime Minister Dr. Eric Williams once remarked in an unguarded moment he would probably rather forget.[12]

"Money is no problem" would be immortalized in calypso by Lord Shorty, who later became Ras Shorty I. In 1981, Dr Williams died, and the new prime minister, George Michael Chambers, was left to pick up the pieces of an economy in free fall after the heady days of the 1970s. An understanding of the Trinidad and Tobago economy in the 1980s requires an understanding of the factors that led to the contraction of the economy in the 1980s. From 1983 to 1989, the Trinidad and Tobago economy experienced seven consecutive years of contraction.

The main reasons put forward for the sharp contraction of the Trinidad and Tobago economy from 1982 to 1987 are:

1. The fall in oil prices in the early to mid-1980s.
2. Declining levels of oil production in the early to mid-1980s.
3. Unsustainable growth in government expenditure 1973–83.
4. The failure of projects/investments at Point Lisas.

From 1985 to 1986, the price of oil fell due to an increase in production by Saudi Arabia in response to quota cheating and discounting by other OPEC members, which caused it to lose market share. The net result was a glut of oil and a collapse in the price of West Texas Intermediate Crude Oil by 70 per cent from late 1985 to early 1986.[13]

In his 1985 budget address, Prime Minister George Chambers lamented that Trinidad and Tobago had experienced a reduction in economic activity for the third consecutive year. Chambers would begin his budget address by calling on the national community to "adjust its expectations and behaviour to take into account the reality of an unfavourable international economic situation".

The main reason posited by Prime Minister Chambers for the decline in economic activity was the weakness of the oil price. Chambers noted that the decrease in the oil sector had also impacted negatively on the non-oil sector.[14] Earlier in 1985, the government of Trinidad and Tobago had also acquired the Texaco oil refinery at Pointe-a-Pierre and the 49.9 per cent of shares held by the Tesero Petroleum Corporation in the Trinidad Tesero Petroleum Company Limited. The acquisition of the Texaco refinery at Pointe-a-Pierre in 1985 was meant to preserve three thousand jobs for citizens who mainly lived in South Trinidad.[15] The 1985 national budget would also see the devaluation of the Trinidad and Tobago dollar from TT$2.40 to the US dollar to TT$3.60 to the US dollar. Chambers's admonition of "fete over back to work" was manifested through these new economic realities that should have shocked the country to the vulnerabilities of a monocultural economy.

In 1986, the myth of PNM invincibility was shattered, and Trinidad and Tobago changed the ruling political parties for the first time since independence. The new government was the National Alliance for Reconstruction (NAR), and the new prime minister, ANR Robinson, led a multi-ethnic, multi-party coalition which included members of the United Labour Front (ULF). The circumstances of the economy inherited by the NAR caused Robinson to declare "the treasury is empty" The NAR later entered into an IMF-administered programme and made other drastic changes to reduce expenditure, such as cutting public servants' salaries and divesting loss-making state enterprises. The medicine was bitter, but the patient needed it. The NAR and Robinson paid the ultimate price for administering it when, in 1990, there was an attempted coup and hostage crisis led by the Jamaat Al Muslimeen.

In 1991, the NAR, which had been poorly fractured while in government, lost the general election, and the PNM, now under the leadership of Patrick Manning, came to power. It goes without saying that no historical assessment of the Trinidad and Tobago economy can be adequately done without fully understanding the vagaries of its oil and natural gas industry and how the tides of global affairs impact it.

Table 1.4: Oil Sector Economic Data, 1983–91

Year	West Texas Intermediate Oil Price ($US)	Oil Production/ bopd	Oil Revenue ($US)	Oil Exports ($US)
1983	29.66	159,845	1025.6	1714.46
1984	28.56	169,513	1149.9	1764.88
1985	27.31	176,052	1002.9	1706.49
1986	14.23	168,877	469.6	969.83
1987	19.18	150,792	543.9	996.31
1988	15.97	150,842	400.6	827.45
1989	19.68	155,180	471.58	934.99
1990	24.50	149,341	545.15	1275.41
1991	21.54	143,624	639.29	1061.9

Source: Dr Roger Hosein, Growth, changing comparative advantage and changing export structure with reference to Trinidad and Tobago

Table 1.4 above shows that oil revenue fell from US$1.772 billion in 1981 to US$400 million in 1988, or 77 per cent. A drastic revenue decline of this extent was bound to create the social dislocation that set the stage for high levels of migration to the United States and Canada and, ultimately, the 1990 attempted coup.

DECLINING LEVELS OF OIL PRODUCTION IN THE 1980S

Oil production in Trinidad and Tobago peaked in 1978 at approximately 229,000 bopd, after which it fell consistently. By 1986, when the price of oil experienced an almost 70 per cent decline, the production of crude oil in Trinidad and Tobago was approximately 169,000 bopd. The following year, it would fall to 150,000 bopd. This was a decline in production by some 35 per cent from 1978 to 1987. The decline in output was attributed to a failure to promote exploration in the late 1970s and early 1980s. A similar story would repeat itself in the latter part of the first decade of the twenty-first century as a slowdown in exploration and poor bid-round outcomes set the stage for a decline in natural gas production after 2010.

ECONOMIC MISMANAGEMENT, 1973–83

As has been showed earlier in this chapter, the windfall of revenue in 1973/1974 was unexpected. In fact, prior to the "boom", Dr Eric Williams had signalled his intention to resign. In the period 1973–83, fifty-one special funds were created. These funds were project-specific, and drawdowns from them were subject to parliamentary approval. However, in the latter part of the boom, the fiscal policy became expansionary, manifesting itself in the subsidization of consumption and an accelerated capital investments programme. Some of the notable public infrastructure projects of the "oil boom" era were the Mount Hope Medical Complex, the Hall of Justice and the Uriah Butler Highway northbound carriageway.

Ultimately, however, the convergence of subsidies, wage increases, appreciation of the real exchange rate and failed state investment in energy-related mega-projects, such as ISCOTT, undermined the economy. The government of the day was also mired in allegations of corruption related to several projects, including the failed attempt at constructing a horseracing complex in Caroni and a scandal involving the purchase of aircraft from McDonnel Douglas.

Table 1.5: Major Gas-Based Projects 1974–84 with Government Involvement

Project	Ownership	Millions of TT dollars
Iron and Steel Company (ISCOTT)	100% Government	1,217
Tringen	51% Government and 49% WR Grace	267
Fertrin	51% Government and 49% Amoco	840
Methanol Company of Trinidad and Tobago	100% Government	430
Urea	100% Government	425

Source: Trevor Farrell, Worship of the Golden Calf

Between 1977 and 1984, the Trinidad and Tobago government spent US$2 billion to establish an infrastructural base and start production in five natural gas-intensive plants.[16] Trevor Farrel notes in the *Worship of the Golden Calf* that by the end of 1983, none of these projects had turned a profit.

One of the reasons posited for the failure of the ISCOTT initiative in the 1970s was the inability of ISCOTT products to penetrate the United States market due to the actions of the protectionist lobby in that country. Industry experts involved with Point Lisas plants in the late 1970s to early 1980s cite the early Point Lisas experience as part of a wider learning experience, which would eventually begin to pay rich dividends in the early 1990s. In the post-2015 period, Point Lisas would enter a chapter of decline as natural gas prices for gas supplied by the NGC increased and available volumes declined, precipitating plant closure and loss of competitive advantage.

One of the symptoms of the economy's decline in the 1980s was the rising fiscal deficit, coupled with a current account deficit. This was the problem of the twin deficits. Another issue is the failure to recognize the onset of Dutch Disease. For the period 1973–85, Trinidad and Tobago's real effective exchange rate (REER) increased the propensity to import, with such imports supplanting local production.

Looking at the period 1970–80, Velculescu and Rizavi opined that subsidies, price controls and wage increases, together with an appreciation of the real exchange rate and an expansion of the public sector, undermined the non-oil sectors of the economy. They further contend that when oil prices declined after 1982, fiscal policy was slow to adjust. By the end of the oil boom in the early 198s, the economy of Trinidad and Tobago had changed fundamentally. As the economy changed, so did the expectations and the lifestyle of citizens. With the decline in oil prices and the fall in oil production came a diminishing of oil revenues, which had supported the economy.

As noted earlier, attempts to diversify away from oil and towards gas-based industries at Point Lisas had proven unsuccessful. The fiscal challenge was, therefore, to reduce recurrent expenditure. The first target of this reduction was the capital investment programme. In 1987, the NAR administration began a process of fiscal tightening by reducing the public sector wage bill, suspending cost of living allowances (COLA) and reducing public service wages by 10 per cent. The trend in salaries, COLA and other allowances are demonstrated in table 1.6 below.

Table 1.6: Salaries, COLA and Other Allowances, 1983–89

Year	Salaries, COLA and other allowances (Billions of $TT)
1983	1.9
1984	2.0
1985	2.0
1986	2.1
1987	1.9
1988	1.8
1989	1.7

Source: Review of Fiscal Measures in the 1989 Budget

A voluntary severance programme was also introduced to reduce the size of the public sector. The government also reduced its holdings in several energy companies and liquidated many state enterprises. During the 1980s, oil's dominance with respect to its contribution to government revenue declined precipitously, as shown in table 1.7 below.

Table 1.7: Oil as a Percentage of Government Revenue and as a Percentage of GDP, 1980–89

Year	Oil as a % of Government Revenue / 1	Oil GDP as a Percentage of Total GDP (at constant prices) / 2
1980	66.7	39.28
1981	62.3	34.22
1982	48.0	24.1
1983	38.2	20.69
1984	42.1	21.39
1985	38.6	21.83
1986	32.4	17.49
1987	37.4	19.71
1988	33.0	15.53
1989	41.0	19.34

Source: 1/ Central Bank of Trinidad and Tobago, cited in Trevor Boopsingh, *Oil and Gas Development: A View from the South*; 2/ Review of the Economy Various Years, cited in Roger Hosein, *Structural Adjustment and (Lewis's) Industrialization by Invitation in a Hydrocarbon Rich Economy: A Case Study of T&T*.

The consequences of this period of "belt-tightening" would have a radical manifestation in 1990 when there was an attempted coup, which resulted in the prime minister and several senior ministers being held hostage in the Red House for five days.

In the budget address following the 1990 coup attempt, Minister of Finance Selby Wilson noted that,

> The deterioration in the terms of trade which began in 1981 worsened in 1986 due to the precipitous decline in the international price of petroleum and petroleum products; to make matters worse, crude oil production continued to decline and the current account deficit of the balance of payments widened to 15 per cent relative to GDP. The financing of this deficit required a drawdown on our reserves of approximately US$670 million, the equivalent of TT$2.4 billion in 1986.[17]

Interestingly, the 1990 budget was delivered against the backdrop of the Iraqi invasion of Kuwait, which would lead to the first Gulf War in 1991 and gave a brief respite for oil prices. From the NAR period to the first Manning government (1991–95), the government sought to divest its equity in the gas-based industries, particularly in iron and steel, ammonia and methanol.[18] This divestment would play a major role in shaping the development of the economy in the 1990s as it introduced a level of local private sector participation in the downstream petrochemical sector that had not previously existed. It created a window into which a local insurance company, Clico, would enter the energy sector as an investor in methanol and ammonia plants in collaboration with German companies. Clico was at that time being led by Lawrence Duprey, who had taken the helm of the company from his uncle Cyril Duprey, who had died in 1988.

The domination of the State in business was reduced by the NAR during 1986–91 and continued during the first Manning administration. The policy thereafter has been to expand state participation in times of plenty and divest in times of budget constraints. On a personal note, in 2013, when the NGC acquired Conoco Phillips's shares in Phoenix Park for US$600 million, it was immediately announced that all or part of the shares would be made available to the public through public offerings. This is now a reality, and in September 2015, TTNGL became the first energy company listed on the Trinidad and Tobago Stock Exchange. The launch of the IPO happened in

August 2015, shortly before the People's Partnership Government lost the general election on 7 September 2015.

The Petrotrin predicament of 2018 should cause us to question the role of the state in business. Has the state-dominated strategic sectors of the Trinidad and Tobago economy for too long? Are there areas of the economy where state involvement is no longer relevant? The whole saga of the control of the commanding heights for the sake of control has expired. Even Russia and China, once bastions of central planning, have moved on. There are examples of state-owned companies that have done well in our region. In Suriname, Staatsolie stands out. In Colombia, former President Alvaro Uribe successfully reformed Ecopetrol by partial privatization via an IPO.

NATURAL GAS–BASED INDUSTRIALIZATION

The role of natural gas in the economic development of Trinidad and Tobago must be considered. By the mid-1990s, natural gas production had eclipsed oil production on a barrel-of-oil equivalency basis, and that has since become the norm. As noted previously, the natural gas era in Trinidad and Tobago really owes its existence to the PATOC exploration campaign of the late 1960s. However, prior to that, natural gas was used for electricity, ammonia and cement manufacturing.

Early use of natural gas in Trinidad and Tobago was non-commercial and entailed support for oil refining and production operations. In the 1940s, Shell discovered natural gas on land in Penal. In 1953, Shell entered into the first gas supply contract with T&TEC for the supply of natural gas to a new power plant in Penal. This represented the first commercial use of natural gas in Trinidad and Tobago. Shell would later supply natural gas to the WR Grace Fedchem plant at Savonetta.[19]

In 1964, Shell supplied natural gas to the T&TEC power plant at Wrightson Road Port of Spain. This required the construction of a dedicated pipeline for the transmission of natural gas from Penal to Port of Spain. The Wrightson Road power plant is now being decommissioned.

THE ESTABLISHMENT OF POINT LISAS

The establishment of the Point Lisas industrial estate was the result of a confluence of three events. The first of these was the successful lobby by the South Trinidad Chamber of Industry and Commerce (now the Energy Chamber), which had lobbied the government to establish a deep-water port facility in South Trinidad. The closure of the Trinidad Government Rail (TGR) in the late 1960s negatively impacted the economy of South Trinidad, and this was one of the reasons for the lobby for the deep-water harbour in South Trinidad.

This effort manifested itself as PLIPDECO, which the South Trinidad Chamber formed. The second was the third five-year development plan. This plan noted that in the six years from 1963 to 1968, approximately 44 per cent of all the natural gas produced was flared.[20] This wastage was a major concern.

Table 1.8: Natural Gas Flared, 1963–68

Year	Natural Gas Production (million cubic feet per day)	% Flared
1963	99,386	54.3
1964	110,732	48.5
1965	111,503	46.1
1966	118,927	36.5
1967	140,338	38.7
1968	151,445	41.5

Source: Third 5-year Development Plan of Trinidad and Tobago, 1969–73

The third event and the most significant was AMOCO's discovery of the Teak and Samman fields in the late 1960s and early 1970s. This exploration campaign by the predecessor of Amoco Trinidad, PATOC, has been dealt with earlier.

The third five-year plan noted that the future of the country's natural gas production was the drilling activity being undertaken by AMOCO off the East Coast of Trinidad. The report states: "Should further drilling in this area confirm the indications of the presence of gas already manifested, its output could supply the basis for building up a large petrochemical complex as well as the establishment of heavy and other industries requiring very cheap electricity". With these three events occurring at around the same time (1966–71), the stage was set for the Point Lisas Industrial Estate.

ESTABLISHMENT OF THE NATIONAL GAS COMPANY

The National Gas Company (NGC) was established in 1975 via a Cabinet decision. It was established to own all gas pipeline infrastructure and buy, sell and transport all-natural gas produced in Trinidad and Tobago. For clarity on this matter, it should be noted that this position is not legislated but rather flows from government policy as it relates to the NGC. Indeed, the NGC middleman model is not applied to the LNG industry in Trinidad and Tobago, where the upstream companies sell directly to the LNG trains.

In his reflections on the establishment of the NGC, former minister of Petroleum and Mines of Trinidad and Tobago Errol Mahabir noted that a designated agency was needed to enter into contracts on behalf of the government of Trinidad and Tobago as contracts between companies.[21] At the time, the ISCOTT, Tringen I and Fertrin plants were being constructed.

The Fertrin project was a Joint Venture with Amoco Trinidad. Amoco and the government agreed to the project when it was decided that they (Amoco Trinidad) could not establish a refinery in Trinidad and Tobago, nor was their light sweet crude being produced in the TSP fields compatible with the refineries in Trinidad and Tobago. The government held 51 per cent in Fertrin and Amoco 49 per cent. In early 1975, Cabinet agreed that a contract should be entered into between the government or its designated agency and Tringen I relating to the sale of gas to Tringen I. Cabinet also approved the principles to be incorporated into a contract between the government or its designated agency and Amoco relating to the purchase of gas from Amoco.

In January 1975, the government of Trinidad and Tobago sponsored a public consultation on the best uses of petroleum resources. Coming out of this, a task force identified seven possible projects. These included:

- Rapid expansion of the electrical power system.
- Upgrading of the petroleum refinery sector
- Establishment of an aluminum smelter.
- Establishment of an iron/steel complex.

- Expansion of ammonia and urea production through the building of new plants.
- Building of a methanol plant
- LNG for export.[22]

At the ceremony to turn the sod for the start of construction of the Iron and Steel Company of Trinidad and Tobago (ISCOTT), Prime Minister Dr Eric E. Williams gave insight into his government's approach to natural gas monetization when he noted that:

> There have been attempts to persuade us that the simplest and easiest thing to do would be to sit back, export our oil, export our gas, do nothing else and just receive the revenues derived from such exports and as it were, lead a life of luxury – at least for some limited period. This, the Government has completely rejected, for it amounts to putting the entire nation on the dole. Instead, we have taken what may be the more difficult road and that is, accepting the challenge of entering the world of steel, aluminum, methanol, fertilizer, petrochemicals. We have accepted the challenge of using our hydrocarbon resources in a very definite industrialization process.[23]

From this statement, it is clear that in the early mid-1970s, LNG was not considered to be an option that the government of Trinidad and Tobago (GORTT) was willing to pursue with regard to the monetization of its natural gas asset. The idea of an aluminium smelter that had been floated as part of the process of regional economic integration was also shelved. Still, it would be resuscitated in the first decade of the twenty-first century by Prime Minister Patrick Manning. The Manning Aluminum initiative, for various reasons too lengthy and complex to discuss here, has yet to materialize.

Natural gas would be used to expand power generation, and to this end, a new T&TEC power plant was constructed at Point Lisas in 1977 (now Powergen Point Lisas). It was also used for Iron and Steel and two ammonia plants (Tringen 1 and Fertrin). In the 1980s, Trinidad and Tobago expanded its use of natural gas to methanol with the construction of the TTMC 1 plant. In 1979, the National Energy Corporation (NEC) was established. The NEC's mandate was gas-based project development and the promotion of gas utilization via the development of the downstream sector. The NEC is currently involved in gas-based business development and the establishment of industrial estates for gas-based industries. In 2013–15, the NEC, the NGC and the Ministry of Energy and Energy Affairs would lead the project development of a methanol plant and a di-methyl ether plant at La Brea that is owned by a consortium of three Mitsubishi companies, the NGC and Massy. The sod was turned for this plant on 1 September 2015, and it became operational in 2020. This methanol plant, known as Caribbean Gas Chemicals, is the first major gas-based plant outside of Point Lisas. It was cited on the location of the cancelled Alutrint project. Environmentalists and community activists challenged the establishment of Alutrint.

ATLANTIC LNG

In the period 1993–2005, a number of factors converged to increase global demand for natural gas. A consequence of this has been the emergence of a global natural gas trade driven by LNG. These factors include:

1. Environmental benefits of natural gas versus oil and coal.
2. Reduction in cost of delivering LNG to market.
3. Advances in power generation, including more combined cycle plants.
4. Deregulation of natural gas markets.
5. Energy security concerns.
6. Increase in demand for natural gas as a feedstock.

In 1992, Cabot LNG of Boston approached the GORTT about developing an LNG export project. To promote an LNG project, Amoco and British Gas signed a memorandum of understanding (MOU) with Cabot and the National Gas Company of Trinidad and Tobago.

In 1995, Atlantic LNG was set up to own and run the project. Sales contracts were signed with Cabot and with Enagas of Spain in 1995 for a total of 3 million tonnes per annum (mtpa) of LNG. Construction of the first LNG train started in 1996. In 1999, the first LNG cargo was loaded. The project was expanded to include a second train that started operations in August 2002 and a third train that started operations in May 2003. Train IV began operations in late 2005. Regarding Cabot's LNG foray into Trinidad and Tobago, Gerald J. Peereboom reflected, "You mentioned LNG to a banker in the U.S., and they thought you must be crazy". According to Shearer, most people in the industry found the Cabot plan "totally harebrained".[24]

A number of factors can be attributed to the success of LNG in Trinidad and Tobago, especially when it is considered that Trinidad and Tobago was able to develop its LNG industry before countries with much larger proven and probable reserves. Sheppard and Ball have, in their examination of the reasons for the success of Trinidad LNG, noted a number of factors. The first was the combination of low-cost gas, and the second was capturing the vital United States market. Another important factor was Spain's desire to diversify its gas supply away from almost total dependence on Algeria.[25] For many countries, LNG is seen as a vehicle for energy supply diversification, which reduces the political risks. Following this point, it is noteworthy that Trinidad and Tobago LNG in 2021 is finding its way to Lithuania in the Baltic Sea and is aiding that country to reduce its reliance on the Russian natural gas supply. Trinidad and Tobago's LNG would also support Brazil as that country's hydroelectric capacity was compromised by a severe drought in 2014 on the eve of its preparations for the World Cup that year and the Olympics of 2016.

AMOCO'S EXPLORATION SUCCESS IN THE 1990s AND THE RETURN OF BP

In the period 1994 to 1998, Amoco Trinidad discovered some 14 trillion cubic feet of natural gas in Trinidad and Tobago, with an exploration success rate of 71 per cent. The success of Amoco Trinidad in that period is attributable to a combination of strategy and technology.[26] The year 1994 marked the first time 3D seismic was used for exploration drilling. The 3D seismic reduced the risk for trap definition and better imaged the complex faulted structures in the Columbus Basin.[27] As a corollary to these discoveries, in 1998, BP plc, at the time headed by Lord John Browne of Madingly, acquired Amoco for a reported US$53 billion. In so doing, BP plc triggered a wave of merger and acquisition activity in the oil and gas industry. Following its acquisition of Amoco, BP plc acquired Arco. In the period shortly after BP and Amoco announced the acquisition, there was M&A activity involving BP and Arco, Exxon and Mobil, Chevron and Texaco, and Total Fina and Elf Aquitaine. BP's strategic intent behind the acquisition of Amoco was multifold. Lord Browne called these strategic gaps. He listed the first of these strategic gaps as natural gas.[28] In the Amoco portfolio, there was significant natural gas in Trinidad and Tobago, where Amoco was, at that time, having success with finding natural gas in the Columbus Basin. In his biography "Beyond Business", Lord Browne described the assets in Trinidad and Tobago, which it acquired in the Amoco acquisition of 1998, as BP's "crown jewels".[29]

LNG PRODUCTION IN TRINIDAD AND TOBAGO

The first shipment of LNG left Point Fortin, Trinidad, on 30 April 1999. The shipment signalled a fundamental change in natural gas monetization in Trinidad and Tobago. Before LNG, natural gas was monetized mainly as a feedstock for ammonia and methanol and used as a fuel in power generation. The Trinidad and Tobago LNG industry was initially established to serve both the American and Spanish markets. As the global LNG business expanded and more players entered the market, the pattern of sales changed. Today, most of Trinidad and Tobago's LNG goes to markets in Europe, South America and Central America.

The establishment of Train 1 at Point Fortin in 1999 set the stage for the global expansion of LNG. It came at a time when the world was becoming more sensitive to the impacts of climate change. As a result, there was a shift away from coal and oil for power generation towards natural gas. The LNG project in Trinidad and Tobago, which had been initiated via an MOU with Cabot of Boston in 1992, would see a project agreement signed in 1996 and its first cargo exported in 1999 during the administration of Prime Minister Basdeo Panday. In 2000, the Panday government agreed with the Atlantic Partners to an expansion to a second and third train. The management of the energy sector under the Panday administration of 1995–2001 was significant and is often bypassed by some writers and researchers. The LNG baton was passed from Manning to Panday in 1995. To his everlasting credit, Basdeo Panday and his Energy Minister Finbar Gangar carried the LNG baton forward. They saw Train I to commercial start in 1999 and gave their approval for the expansion of the LNG business. Oil fell to as low as US$9 per barrel in 1999, making LNG more imperative as a new source of export earnings.

The major players in the project at the time were Amoco, which was acquired by BP in 1998, and British Gas, which was acquired by Shell in 2015. BPTT (formerly Amoco Trinidad) and Shell are the two suppliers

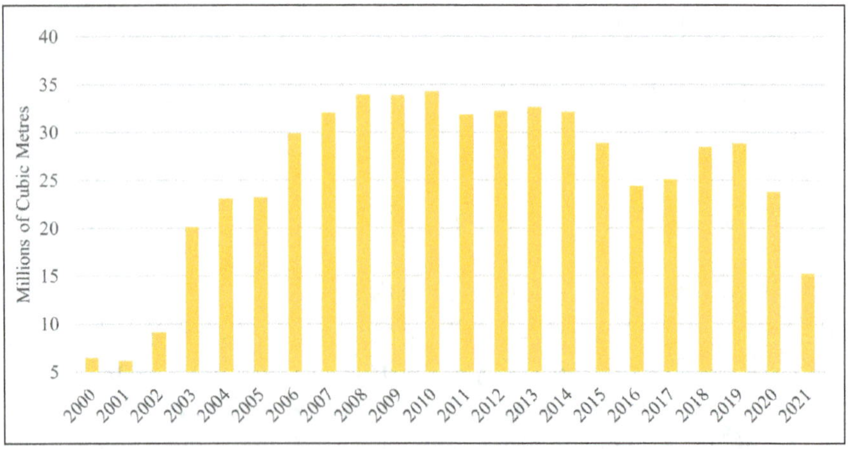

Figure 1.1: LNG Production in Trinidad and Tobago (2000–2021) Millions of Cubic Metres

of natural gas to the four LNG trains. In 2003, Prime Minister Patrick Manning announced the approval of Train IV, and for a while, Trinidad and Tobago even entertained the possibility of a fifth train. The fifth train did not materialize. In 2020, Atlantic LNG shut down Train I operations, and this train has remained closed ever since. The reduction in LNG production in Trinidad and Tobago after the peak in 2010 is directly correlated with falling natural gas supply.

In winding up the debate on the 2005 national budget, the then-prime minister of Trinidad and Tobago, Patrick Manning, stated that the government was going ahead with plans for a fifth LNG train. Manning, in an ebullient state, contended that,

> In 1992, when we talked about LNG, there were those who said to us: "What is wrong with 'all yuh'. You are exporting a natural resource without any value added. Do not do it." We did it. Do you know why we did it? Because we understood the situation far better than they did, and it is the very LNG that today guarantees us of the revenue levels that we are anticipating. I would tell you something else, that the day the prices fall, whether it be gas prices or oil prices, a minimum level of revenue is guaranteed because of the volume of our exports. That is why we are going to Train 5. When we go to Train 5, it means that we would be exporting at LNG, 2.4 billion cubic feet of gas a day, enough volume even at low prices to guarantee you a certain minimum level of revenue.

REFLECTION ON NATURAL GAS

The fifth LNG train never materialized, and Mr Manning never lived to see the closure of Train I in 2020. Admittedly, with the benefit of hindsight, the decision by the Manning administration in 2003 to go ahead with a fourth LNG train was a stretch too far, as it created a demand for natural gas that could not be sustained. In 2004, at the South Trinidad Chamber's annual energy conference, Mr Manning would square off with Chamber President Jim Lee Young on the efficacy of the leap towards a fourth LNG train.

In addition, the much-touted "demand-driven model", which was bandied from conference to conference by one former minister of energy, worked only for a limited period. Logic would dictate that petroliferous basins like the Columbus Basin in Southeast Trinidad and the North Coast Marine Area (NCMA) of Trinidad and Tobago have their economic limits. The natural gas production numbers for seven years, 2015–22, indicate that the Columbus Basin and the NCMA are in decline from a production perspective and that large natural gas and oil discoveries have already been made. The two great hopes for the resuscitation of Trinidad and Tobago's waning natural gas production are natural gas from BHP's deepwater discoveries off the east coast of Tobago and cross-border natural gas from Venezuela. With regard to cross-border gas, the government of Trinidad and Tobago and the government of Venezuela have agreed that Trinidad and Tobago could proceed to develop its side of the large Loran/Manatee field (Manatee is in Trinidad and Tobago's waters). This approach is obviously fraught with political risk, and it is for that reason that the United Nations recommends cross-boundary mineral deposits be developed jointly to minimize conflict.

Table 1.9: Original Ownership Structure of Atlantic LNG

Owner	Train I	Train II & III	Train IV
BP	34%	42.5%	37.8%
BG	26%	32.5%	28.9%
Repsol	20%	25%	22.2%
NGC	10%	–	11.1%
Cabot	10%	–	–

Table 1.10: 2022 Ownership Structure of Atlantic LNG (Now Atlantic)

Owner	Train I	Train II & III	Train IV
BP	34%	42.5%	37.8%
Shell	46%	57.5%	51.1%
NGC	10%	–	11.1%
China Investment Corporation	10%	–	–

PERSONAL REFLECTIONS: 2011–15

In June 2011, I was appointed minister of energy of Trinidad and Tobago. I would hold the portfolio until September 2015, when the People's Partnership administration lost the 2015 general election. My term in office was marked by significant challenges for the energy sector, which saw natural gas production, which had peaked in 2010, start to decline gradually. It was also a period of heightened productivity at the Ministry of Energy with four bid rounds, the licensing of the deepwater, the development of the Mitsubishi/Massy CGCL methanol project, the TTNGL IPO, the construction of the Galeota Port, the expansion of the NGC and reforms to the fiscal regime that stimulated investment in exploration and development drilling.

Reflection on Deepwater Exploration

As a student of Petroleum Engineering, I was made aware of the potential of Trinidad and Tobago's deepwater. As a minister of energy, I made the award of acreage one of the pillars of my tenure in office. During my tenure, I inherited one deepwater bid round and launched and completed another two. We also held a successful bid round for land acreage in 2013/2014. These efforts and their successes must recall the contribution of the public servants of the Ministry of Energy who worked for years behind the scenes to bring Trinidad and Tobago to deepwater success as realized by BHP in the period 2016–20. Table 1.11 below is a summary of deepwater blocks awarded under the Production Sharing Contract (PSC) from 2012 to 2014 under the hand of the minister of energy and the commissioner of state lands. Since the signing of the PSCs in 2014, Trinidad and Tobago has awarded no more acreage in its deepwater provinces. This is one of the most significant failings of energy sector policy post-2015.

Table 1.11: Deepwater Exploration

Block	Area (ha)	Year PSC signed	Operator – Partner
Block 23(a)	259,908	2012	BHP – BP
TTDAA 14	99,808	2012	BHP – BP
TTDAA5	109,559	2013	BHP – Shell
TTDAA6	99,747	2013	BHP – Shell
TTDAA28	101,609	2013	BHP
TTDAA29	100,196	2013	BHP
Block 23(b)	258,405	2013	BHP – Repsol
TTDAA3	109,768	2014	BHP – Shell
TTDAA7	99,827	2014	BHP – Shell
TOTAL	1,238,827		

Source: Ministry of Energy and Energy Industries

Reflection on Natural Gas Shortages

In April 2010, the Macondo Gulf of Mexico oil spill happened when there was an explosion on the Deepwater Horizon drilling rig, which was owned and operated by Transocean. What followed was one of the worst disasters in the history of the oil and gas industry. As a consequence, BP started a planned maintenance programme on its offshore platforms in Trinidad and Tobago, which had an impact on natural gas production. When the government changed, I was accused by persons in the new PNM government of lying about this planned maintenance programme. However, there was overwhelming information in the public space that this was different. The natural gas shortage was one of the major headaches of the period 2011–15, and of course, it continues to the present day in a more acute form. Table 1.12 below shows natural gas production from 2010 to 2015.

One of the major challenges of my tenure happened in September 2013 when BP decided to take down its Cassia B hub for maintenance. Most of BP's natural gas production passed through the Cassia B hub. In addition, in the same window of time, BG Group decided to take down its Dolphin platform. The impact of these shutdowns on the country's economy was not lost on me. I was aware of the effect on GDP and revenue; however, the companies had a duty of care to ensure the safety of operations, and safety

Table 1.12: Natural Gas Production (mmcfd)

2010	4330 (peak)
2011	4169
2012	4122
2013	4145
2014	4071
2015	3835

Source: Ministry of Energy and Energy Industries

always trumped short-term economic benefits. That aside, I requested a meeting with the BP CEO, Bob Dudley, to discuss the impact of the Cassia B hub turnaround. When we met, he assured me that BP would work to minimize the impact of the turnaround and had already designed a bypass system to allow some of the natural gas that would have been knocked out of production to keep flowing. In addition, BP was able to reduce the number of days required for the turnaround. During that period, the ministry was able to perform the role of orchestra conductor and coordinate the turnarounds of the two offshore platforms Cassia B and Dolphin, the turnaround of Atlantic Train 3 and the turnaround of nine plants in Point Lisas, all in the window of mid-September 2013 to mid-October 2013. Unprecedented industry-wide collaboration had to mitigate the impact of what could have been a major problem if not handled well. When it was nearing completion, Bob Dudley came to Trinidad and Tobago (at my suggestion). He gave a speech to the Energy Chamber, where he spoke positively about BP's plans for investment in Trinidad and Tobago. By the time I left office in 2015, BP had four rigs drilling in the Columbus Basin, including one rig drilling the five wells for the Juniper project.

Reflection on Policy Intervention for the Fiscal Regime

From 2011 to 2015, the government recognized that the problem of insufficient natural gas supply was due to a lack of investment in exploration and developmental drilling. In the budget speech of 9 September 2013, the minister of finance, Senator Larry Howai, introduced incentives called "accelerated capital allowances".

The extract from his 9 September 2013, speech is as follows:

> Capital Allowances Capital allowance reliefs provide a mechanism that de-risks and allows for earlier recovery of investments. I propose that capital allowances for the upstream energy sector be simplified and accelerated as follows: For Exploration the existing initial and annual allowances, be replaced by a new allowance of 100 percent of exploration costs to be written off in the year the expenditure is incurred. This incentive will be applicable over the period 2014 to 2017, and from 2018, an allowance of 50 percent in the first year of the expenditure, an allowance of 30 percent in the second year of the expenditure and an allowance of 20 percent in the third year will be applicable.
>
> For development in place of the existing initial and annual allowances, I propose to grant an allowance of 50 percent in the first year of the expenditure, an allowance of 30 percent in the second year of the expenditure and an allowance of 20 percent in the third year. This will be applicable to both plant and machinery (tangible) and the drilling of wells (intangible) expenses.

In April 2014, the government introduced and passed into law these incentives, including the accelerated capital allowances for exploration and developmental drilling, with the intention of stimulating investment. Capital allowances, introduced in 1992, had long been a feature of the Trinidad and Tobago fiscal regime.

The accelerated capital allowances were part of a more comprehensive package of fiscal incentives that had been introduced since 2011. While the industry welcomed these accelerated capital allowances, they were misunderstood by the new PNM government of 2015, although the PNM, while in opposition, in 2014, voted for them. They have been blamed for the decline in government revenue from oil and gas from 2015 to 2016. According to the 2017 Review of the Economy, in 2015, the government collected revenues of TT$57.3 billion. In 2016, this fell to TT$45.0 billion or a 21.5 per cent decline.

Prior to 2013/2014, for many years, public commentators such as the Energy Chamber had spoken publicly about the declining competitiveness of the oil and gas industry due to its underlying fiscal regime. In its commentary on the 2012/2013 budget, accounting firm PWC opined that "Our regime is not sufficiently competitive and requires the introduction of additional capital and investment allowances to encourage exploration" (PWC 2013).

In the period 2011–15, several fiscal incentives were introduced to resuscitate both developmental drilling and exploration drilling. The effect of these incentives was a significant turnaround in drilling. This is reflected in Rig Days. In 2010, there were 1,132 rig days. By 2015, that number had more than doubled to 2,765.[30]

During the same period, the Ministry of Energy was able to attract investment into the deepwater provinces of Trinidad and Tobago by signing nine production-sharing contracts. Investment in deepwater exploration was achieved by offering more attractive terms compared to what was offered in the 2005/2006 bid round, which was a disappointment that resulted in no deepwater acreage being contracted.

The results of all these efforts led to the BP Juniper project (first gas 2017) and the BP Angelin project (first gas 2019). This Juniper project realized its first gas in August 2017 and reached a maximum of 590 million cubic feet per day. The incentivization also led to the Savannah and Macadamia discoveries in the first half of 2017 and the Trinidad Regional Onshore Compression (TROC) project, which started operations in 2017.

Other projects, such as the 2015/2016 BHP Angostura Phase 3 project and the 2016/ 2017 EOG Resources Sercan project, have also helped with the level of natural gas curtailment. As a result, in 2018, natural gas output showed an increase after five years of decline. Of critical importance, too, is the 2011–13 "3D Ocean Bottom Cable (OBC)" seismic survey, which was conducted by BP and is directly responsible for the progression and sanction of the Angelin project and the success of the Macadamia exploration in 2017. From 2019 to 2022, natural gas production in Trinidad and Tobago went into a precipitous decline. From a peak of 4.3 bcfd in 2010, in 2021, natural gas production averaged 2.6 bcfd. This decline has resulted in plant closures at Point Lisas and the closure of Atlantic Train I. The situation with natural gas production seems bleak, but some rays of hope are offered by deepwater gas and Venezuelan cross-border gas. Both have significant risks.

Reflection on Caribbean Gas Chemicals Limited (CGCL)

In April 2012, the Ministry of Energy received a proposal from a consortium led by Mitsubishi Corporation and local conglomerate Neal & Massy for a Methanol to Di-methyl ether facility. Broad Cabinet approval for the project was received in December 2012. After this approval, the Mitsubishi team started living in Trinidad and Tobago as expatriates. In this period, I also sought the advice of former Minister of Petroleum and Mines Errol Mahabir on how to position the project to the ministry, the industry and the public.

This Project Development Agreement was signed in April 2013. It agreed that all parties would work to progress the project to a Project Agreement. In November 2013, the minister of energy of Trinidad and Tobago led a delegation to Japan and visited the Mitsubishi companies to discuss the project. He also visited prospective bankers, such as Japan Bank for International Corporation (JBIC). Prior to leaving for Japan, the minister was successful in getting the Cabinet to agree to remove the requirement for the Japanese to get a visa to visit Trinidad and Tobago. This enhanced the ease of doing business for the Japanese and sent a signal that Trinidad and Tobago was serious about the project. The public servants at the Ministry of Foreign Affairs initially disagreed with granting this visa waiver unless there was reciprocity.

One of the major challenges in getting the project to the stage of Project Agreement was regulatory approvals and other agreements such as EMA clearance, Town and Country Planning Approval, water supply agreement, port user agreements and right of way for pipelines. The project partners formalized a new vehicle that would own and execute the project. This company was named CGCL, or Caribbean Gas Chemicals Limited. It was incorporated in March 2015. The project agreement was signed in April 2015 in La Brea. In early September 2015, the sod was turned for the project at the site in La Brea. On 7 September 2015, there was a general election in Trinidad and Tobago, which resulted in a change in the government.

The investment was valued at US$987 million. It would be the first major downstream investment in Trinidad and Tobago's history outside of the Point Lisas Industrial Estate. It was to be funded in a 70/30 debt-equity ratio. Before the sod-turning ceremony, JBIC and its partner BTMU had approved the loan. However, one document remained, a generic legal opinion from the attorney general, that was outstanding. This legal opinion was one of the condition precedents for drawdowns from the loan.

Despite not being able to access its debt financing, the project progressed in 2015/2016 using equity from the shareholders. The new government used the opportunity to re-negotiate some agreements. The former government had provided a guarantee of gas supply, reducing the risk for the bankers. The new government saw this guarantee as a liability in that it could open the NGC to litigation. The re-negotiated agreements eroded the project's NPV.

The change in government in September 2015 introduced a level of political risk that almost derailed the project. The new government claimed that a legal opinion from the attorney general had been withheld because of objections from the solicitor general. The legal opinion from the attorney general for major investments was a standard and generic legal opinion first introduced in the 1980s. Similar opinions have been given about the far more commercially complex Atlantic LNG project.

The role of the solicitor general is not to opine on the commerciality of any project that the government is involved in, nor is it the role of the solicitor general to make government policy. The role of the solicitor general is to vet contracts entered into by the government. To this day, the reason for the solicitor general's objection to the legal opinion remains a mystery.

To their credit, the Japanese had navigated the issues that were thrown up by the new government in 2015, and by 2016, they received the missing approval. The project is the largest investment by Japan in the Caribbean. Although the PNM administration continues to be critical of it, the fact remains that it is there in La Brea producing methanol. Production at this new methanol plant started in 2020. The CGCL methanol plant will likely be the last methanol plant to be built in Trinidad and Tobago. On reflection, it must be said that attracting an investment of almost one billion US dollars from three of Japan's largest firms to build a methanol plant during a time when natural gas production in Trinidad and Tobago was in decline, and the shale revolution in the United States was in full swing was a significant achievement.

Reflection on the NGC and Petrotrin

During the period 2010–14, the NGC experienced a significant growth in its assets with the acquisition, in 2013, of Conoco Phillips's 39 per cent shareholding of Phoenix Park Gas Processors Limited (PPGPL) at a price of US$600 million. In that same year, NGC acquired Total's upstream positions in Trinidad and Tobago, which included block 2C, where the greater Angostura area was located. These acquisitions took the NGC from total assets of TT$31 billion in 2010 to TT$44 billion in 2014. This was a 42 per cent increase in assets. In 2013, the NGC declared after-tax profits of TT$6.5 billion, the highest after-tax profit for any company in the history of Trinidad and Tobago. When the Conoco Phillips shares were acquired in 2013, there was talk of the nationalization of PPGPL, which had hitherto been 51 per cent owned by the NGC and the National Enterprises Limited (NEL), 39 per cent owned by Conoco Phillips and 10 per cent owned by Pan West Engineers. This talk of nationalization was rebutted by a promise that the shares that were acquired would form part of an IPO. We held to that promise and, in August 2015, launched what was to become the most successful IPO in the history of Trinidad and Tobago. The success of the TTNGL IPO came against the backdrop of a tremendous amount of criticism from the then-PNM Opposition and some persons in the financial sector.

Petrotrin was a behemoth. Prime Minister Patrick Manning cobbled it together in 1993 by merging Trintoc and Trintopec. Its operations spanned most of the deep south of the island, included two refineries and had operations offshore in the Gulf of Paria (Trinmar). In addition, Petrotrin held equity positions in TSP, the NCMA 1 block, and other minority/non-operating positions in different blocks and assets. When the People's Partnership came to office in 2010, it met a runaway horse called the Gasoline Optimization Programme (GOP). The GOP ran up Petrotrin's debt.

In 2002, Petrotrin's total debt was TT$3.3 billion. By 2010, it had increased almost fourfold to TT$12.4 billion. The main driver of the increase in debt burden in that period included two bonds, one in 2007 for US$750 million and the other in 2009 for US$850 million. These bonds were issued to support projects in the refinery, including the Gasoline Optimization Programme (GOP), which experienced significant cost escalation and schedule slippage.[31] The events that led to the closure of Petrotrin and the refinery at Pointe-a-Pierre in 2018 are too extensive to deal with at this point. I will, however, say that it was based on a flawed understanding of Petrotrin's business model and a flawed understanding of the company's accounts. In the end, the executioners of Petrotrin were persons with a limited understanding of the company and little connection to its fence-line communities. It remains one of the most debatable economic decisions in the history of Trinidad and Tobago.

2022 AND BEYOND

The Future of Natural Gas

It is evident that the Columbus Basin, which generated much of the country's production for the last fifty years, has reached its limit based on the exploration of the Pliocene-Pleistocene and younger rocks. This does not, however, consider the potential for hydrocarbons in the pre-Pliocene period. It is, therefore, inaccurate to opine that the Columbus Basin is nearing its economic limit and there may be more oil and gas below the Pliocene that requires deeper exploration wells, such as those that have found giant oilfields in the Upper Cretaceous in the Guyana Basin. Exploration in Trinidad and Tobago has, however, stepped out of the average depth of water and into the deepwater provinces (>1,000 meters).

BHP has had some success in the exploration of waters to the northeast of Tobago in Block TTDAA14 and Block 23(a) and BHP's southern deepwater licence for Block TTDAA5. These discoveries have a potential ten trillion cubic feet of natural gas. However, the issue is whether these projects will make economic sense for the new owners of BHP's petroleum assets, Woodside. Unlike the gas discoveries in Mozambique, Tanzania and the Levant Basin, the ones in Trinidad and Tobago's deepwater are not as large in scale. Time will tell what Woodside does with these assets. However, the government has announced that the Calypso project, which aims to develop the natural gas found in deepwater off Tobago, will realize the first gas by around 2028. The political tension between Venezuela and the United States determines the level of optimism about cross-border gas from Venezuela reaching Trinidad and Tobago. Cross-border gas, however, remains elusive. The government and Shell have made some progress on the development of the Manatee, which is 27 per cent of the overall Loran/Manatee field with the Loran side in Venezuela. They expect the first gas from Manatee by 2027. But there is no real guarantee after 2027.

If Manatee and Calypso offer a ray of light, then what happens from 2022 to 2027? In 2021, natural gas production averaged 2.58 bcfd, the lowest output since 2003. In 2018, a mere four years ago, it stood at 3.63 bcfd, thanks mainly to production from the Juniper project. The sharp fall in natural gas production is the main reason the country cannot celebrate the high natural gas prices and high ammonia prices caused by the Russian invasion of Ukraine.

Renewable Energy

The recognition by the world that it must change the energy system to combat climate change has yielded a new energy system that has moved away from fossil fuels. Trinidad and Tobago has been slow to get off the mark with renewables because of the availability of cheap electricity based on natural gas. Natural gas is, however, no longer cheap in Trinidad and Tobago. At the same time, the cost of electricity from renewables has fallen dramatically in the last ten years and has made wind and solar competitive with natural gas. Inevitably, Trinidad and Tobago will join the renewable energy thrust, albeit almost last in the CARICOM. One motivation for renewables is saving natural gas. When the natural gas supply is falling, it makes sense not to burn natural gas for electricity but to use it to make valuable products for export, like ammonia or methanol. The more renewable energy can displace natural gas-based electricity, the more natural gas is freed up for higher-value economic activity. Faced with a shortage and declining production, this makes a lot of economic sense.

The government has partnered with BP Light Source and Shell to build two solar farms in Trinidad, Golden Grove and Brechin Castle. These will have around 110 megawatts of capacity. The issue with solar is it depends on the sun and requires a large land footprint per megawatt of installed capacity. What has been happening globally is a fight between solar farms and agricultural activity for land. This may also become an issue in Trinidad and Tobago. Trinidad and Tobago does not have any shortage of power generation capacity; however, its power system is 1) totally anchored to natural gas and 2) highly dependent on two large power plants (TGU and Powergen Point Lisas) and therein lays a vulnerability that wind and solar will address.

From a policy perspective, the government also needs to change the T&TEC Act and the Regulated Industries Commission Act to allow for homeowners and commercial businesses to be net-metered. This will encourage a revolution in rooftop solar. This allows homeowners and businesses to utilize their rooftops to install solar panels that supply electricity to their homes and businesses, augmenting electricity from the grid. If there is excess, the homeowner can sell it to T&TEC.

Port and Maritime Logistics

The government of Trinidad and Tobago was slow to recognize the energy revolution in Guyana and Suriname, which was unlocking billions of barrels of oil in upper cretaceous rocks in the deepwater of both countries. To date, Guyana, through ExxonMobil, has discovered 11 billion barrels of oil. It is expected that by 2030, Guyana and Suriname will produce 1.5 million barrels of oil from offshore. This requires a lot of infrastructure and assets to be located offshore, such as FPSOs, drill ships and supply vessels. What is happening in Guyana and Suriname has had spillover effects on Chaguaramas and Labidco port facilities and services. A lot of what ExxonMobil has accomplished in Guyana was staged out of Chaguaramas and Labidco. Apart from Guyana and Suriname, Brazil has a massive offshore oil industry, and there is also the possibility that in the next ten years, Venezuela will revitalize its massive oil industry. The opportunity exists for Trinidad and Tobago to establish a world-scale set of supply bases and free zones to support what is happening in the regional oil and gas sector and to offer services such as rig maintenance and bunkering. This is akin to what has been done in Gran Canaria off the West Coast of North Africa, where they have positioned themselves as the focal point for the West African oil and gas industry or what Aberdeen, Scotland, has become to the North Sea. The potential to do this in Trinidad and Tobago is located in Chaguaramas, La Brea, Point Lisas and Galeota. It will require investment in support infrastructure, but it will lay the basis for the long-sought-after diversification we have been in pursuit of and will create thousands of jobs.

NOTES

1. Vernon Mulchansingh, "The Oil Industry in the Economy of Trinidad," *Caribbean Studies* 11, no. 1 (Apr. 1971): 73–100.
2. Hayden Toney, "Master's Thesis," University of Pennsylvania, 1977.
3. Mulchansingh, "The Oil Industry in the Economy of Trinidad."
4. *New York Times*, "Tesoro Sells Stake in Trinidad Unit," 19 November 1985.

5. Shastri M-Maharaj, The Amoco Trinidad Story, 2022.
6. Dr Eric Williams, Budget Speech, Trinidad and Tobago Parliament, 1970.
7. Budget Speech of the Minister of Finance, 1974.
8. Eric E. Williams, "Budget Speech of Trinidad and Tobago," 1975.
9. Eric E. Williams, "Budget Speech of the Minister of Finance," 1976.
10. Indrani Deolall, http://www.caribbeannewsglobal.com, 10 October 2020.
11. Roger Hosein, "Structural Adjustment and (Lewis's) Industrialization by Invitation in a Hydrocarbon Rich Economy: A Case Study of T&T."
12. Jeremy Taylor, *New Internationalist*, 2 December 1980.
13. Daniel Yergin, *The Prize*, 1990.
14. George Chambers, "Budget Address of the Minister of Finance," December 1985.
15. *New York Times*, "Trinidad to Keep Refinery Going," 15 April 1985.
16. Roger Hosein, "Dutch Disease and Déjà Vu: Policy Advice for the Trinidad and Tobago Economy in the Wake of the Second Oil Boom."
17. Selby Wilson, "Budget Address," 1990.
18. L.A. Barclay, "FDI Facilitated Development, The Natural Gas Industry of Trinidad and Tobago," UN University, 2003.
19. Trevor M. Boopsingh and Gregory McGuire, *From Oil to Gas and Beyond*, 2014.
20. Government of Trinidad and Tobago, *Third 5-year Development Plan 1969–1973*.
21. Errol Mahabir, "Address at the 25th Anniversary of the NGC," August 2000.
22. Trevor Boopsingh and Gregory McGuire, *From Oil to Gas and Beyond*, 2014
23. Dr Eric Williams, speech delivered at sod turning ceremony for ISCOTT, 1976.
24. *Wall Street Journal*, "How Trinidad Became a Big Supplier of Liquefied Natural Gas to the U.S.," 13 March 2001.
25. Rob Sheppard et al., "Liquified Natural Gas from Trinidad and Tobago: The Atlantic Project," Stanford University and the James A. Baker III Institute for Public Policy of Rice University, May 2004.
26. Larry Tiezzi et al., "The History of Exploration by Amoco in Trinidad," Offshore Technology Conference, 1999.
27. Ibid.
28. Forest Reinhardt et al., "BP and the Consolidation of the Oil Industry," Harvard Business School, May 2006.
29. Lord John Browe, *Beyond Business*, 2010.
30. Ministry of Energy of Trinidad and Tobago, "Consolidated Energy Bulletins, 2010 to 2015."
31. Kevin Ramnarine, "Statement to the Senate of Trinidad and Tobago, Hansard," 3 December 2014.

REFERENCES

Barclay, L.A. "FDI Facilitated Development: The Natural Gas Industry of Trinidad and Tobago," UNU-INTECH Discussion Paper Series 2003–7, United Nations University - INTECH, 2003.

Boopsingh, Trevor, and Gregory McGuire. *From Oil to Gas and Beyond: A Review of the Trinidad and Tobago Model and Analysis of Future Challenges*. Lanham: University Press of America, 2013.

———. Budget Speech of the Minister of Finance, 1974.

Chambers, George. "Budget Address of the Minister of Finance," December 1985.

Deolall, Indrani. http://www.caribbeannewsglobal.com, 10 October 2020.

Government of Trinidad and Tobago. Third 5-year Development Plan 1969–1973.

Mahabir, Errol. "Address at the 25th Anniversary of the NGC," August 2000.

Maharaj, M-Maharaj, "The Amoco Trinidad Story," 2022.

Ministry of Energy of Trinidad and Tobago. *Consolidated Energy Bulletins, 2010 to 2015*.

Mulchansingh, Vernon. "The Oil Industry in the Economy of Trinidad." *Caribbean Studies* 11, no. 1 (1971): 73–100. https://www.jstor.org/stable/pdf/25612364.pdf.

Hosein, Roger. 2004. "Dutch Disease and Déjà Vu: Policy Advice for the Trinidad and Tobago Economy in the Wake of the Second Oil Boom." *West Indian Journal of Engineering* 26 (2): 1–21.

———. Structural Adjustment and (Lewis's) Industrialization by Invitation in a Hydrocarbon Rich Economy: A Case Study of T&T.

Reinhardt, Forest et al. "BP and the Consolidation of the Oil Industry," Harvard Business School, May 2006.

Sheppard, Rob et al. "Liquified Natural Gas from Trinidad and Tobago: The Atlantic Project." Stanford University.

Toney, Hayden. Master's Thesis, University of Pennsylvania, 1977.

Tiezzi, Larry et al. "The History of Exploration by Amoco in Trinidad, Offshore Technology Conference," 1999.

Wall Street Journal. "How Trinidad Became a Big Supplier of Liquefied Natural Gas to the U.S.," 13 March 2001.

Williams, Eric. Budget Speech of the Minister of Finance, 1976.

———. Budget Speech of Trinidad and Tobago, 1975.

———. Budget Speech, Trinidad and Tobago Parliament, 1970.

———. Speech delivered at sod turning ceremony for ISCOTT, 1976.

Wilson, Selby. "Budget Address, 1990."

[CHAPTER 2]

Rethinking Agriculture and Food Security:

Trinidad and Tobago's Challenge

WENDY-ANN P. ISAAC, OMARDATH MAHARAJ AND MICHAEL JOSEPH

INTRODUCTION

The agricultural economy of Trinidad and Tobago, especially in its early post-colonial years, remained focused on the metropole, guarantees and markets, relying on existing agricultural and rural infrastructure. Undoubtedly, population growth, cultural diversity, globalization and the rise of a booming energy sector in the subsequent years contributed to a shift in policy and development, focusing away from the national food basket. The resulting deficiencies of outmoded agri-food production and processing sectors made the country unable to compete and satisfy growing tastes and preferences, opening the door to food import dependency.

Trinidad's post-independence experience included a mix of optimism and pessimism regarding prospects for inclusive agriculture development as a catalyst for economic transformation in Trinidad and Tobago. Several situations, both local and abroad, have raised hope that the Malthusian threat could be averted. Recent shocks such as the COVID-19 pandemic, the looming world war threat, pressure on global trade logistics, increasing violence against farm and farming families and climate change, for example, have raised concerns about food security, inflation and other related social and economic implications for the population. These issues impact policy planning and development at the local level. Paired with a shrinking fiscal space, a history of underinvestment and outdated technologies in food production and processing, a clear gap between knowledge and applications has stymied sustained growth and dampened the outlook of the sector in feeding our future needs.

With so many forces reshaping agriculture and with continuing dependence on food imports, a rethink of agricultural development approaches is necessary when examining the reasons for the failure of policy in food security over time. This chapter reflects on snapshots of the evolution of agricultural development planning and strategies from the post-independence period to the present in order to inform a way forward.

An urgent and transformative vision for agriculture is critical in achieving many of the post-2016 Sustainable Development Goals (SDGs) for Trinidad and Tobago if local food production is to survive and compete in this new normal. This can be achieved through strategic planning considering best practices and the prevailing dynamics of the sector as it pertains to existing agricultural and trade policies, infrastructure, transport, land tenure and land management practices, irrigation, research and extension, distribution of inputs and the promotion of producer and marketing organizations that link small and marginal farmers to new market chains and scientific knowledge.

Policy perspectives and other recommendations are proposed. The issues raised are multidimensional and require vision, leadership and political will. Food sovereignty and sufficiency will be secured by involving a diverse group of actors and first acknowledging the downward trajectory and diminishing motivation across the farming population.

BACKGROUND

> Trinidad and Tobago in any year spends approximately US$125 million on French fries, not potatoes, French fries. Can you ask me why we do that, when we have available sweet potatoes, cassava, breadfruit, all of which make – nutritionally and gastronomically – superior fries to Irish potatoes?
>
> – Minister in the Ministry of Finance responding to a question in the Senate: 26 April 2022.

This seemingly simple statement is, in fact, a profound commentary on the current state of agriculture in Trinidad and Tobago. It immediately addresses a commonly overlooked factor in any analysis of the state of agriculture in the nation: the driver(s) of consumption patterns. Whereas tons of data have been generated, for example, the technical and financial constraints to development, relatively little cognizance has been paid to the simple fact that consumption (the market) drives development. What drives consumption, and what accounts for preferences? We need to ask ourselves how what is essentially an imported comfort food item became almost indispensable to the local diet. Other examples may be easily found: apples and grapes, which were once seasonal specialities, are now consumed year-round. One could argue that the desire for the exotic may be a significant driver of consumption patterns.

How did we get here, and, more importantly, can the damage be undone? What are the implications of changing taste patterns that have evolved over time? There have been instances where, in challenging times, the country has had to adopt radical changes in order to survive.

During the latter half of the 1980s, the country experienced a serious recession. As a result, there were acute shortages of foreign exchange, making importation of goods problematic. Food imports were particularly hard hit.

Agriculture in Trinidad and Tobago, especially in the early years of the nation, was generally structured around its colonial past. In that mode, there was essentially a two-tiered system of production. On the top tier was the production of major commodities: cocoa and sugar first, followed to a lesser extent by citrus, coffee, copra and tonka bean. On the lower level were the fresh fruit, vegetables and ground provisions. The commodities were produced on estates, while the food crops were generally the purview of peasant farmers. The commodity crops were focused on satisfying the export market in the metropoles while contributing directly to the gross domestic product (GDP), employment and foreign exchange earnings of the country. The food crops contributed to national food security and sufficiency. This two-tiered structure would have significant and lasting ramifications for both the pre-industrial colony and the industrial, independent nation. Considered a relatively high-income country in the Caribbean, the dominant energy sector has seemingly only propelled the country's dependence on food imports for final human consumption and manufacturing rather than supporting an even-handed national strategy for inclusive agriculture and rural development.

Today, with an open economy in which international trade plays a very important role, agriculture consistently contributes an estimated 0.5 per cent of GDP, and agri-food's share of total exports is only 2.6 per cent. Although agriculture has not been a major contributor to GDP in the energy-driven economy, economic diversification and the reduction of the food import bill have been among the country's development goals across varying governments. Trinidad and Tobago imports an estimated 85 per cent of its food supply. Access to the agri-food commodity markets faced considerable structural changes and challenges in the twenty-first century. Exports of traditional commodities such as cocoa, coffee and sugar (produced in Trinidad and Tobago), as well as rice and bananas (regionally), declined considerably, as did the production of those commodities. Relinquishing the two-tier system, the sector is now comprised of production, processing and marketing activities in the crop, livestock and fisheries subsectors. While Trinidad and Tobago is a net exporter of beverages (including non-alcoholic) and tobacco, the country imports most of its agricultural and food items.

The Food and Agriculture Organization (FAO) (2013) estimated that available cultivation in 2010 was 54,000 ha out of a total area of 513,000 ha, a decline from 77,000 ha in 1990 (Isaac et al. 2019). When the top-tier commodities such as cocoa and sugar production went into decline in the 1990s and the sector focused on the lower-tier production of fruits, vegetables, staples and root crops, the country was still not able to attain self-sufficiency in food production. Trinidad and Tobago's economy has been facing difficulties due to the slowdown in the petroleum subsector, making economic diversification even more pressing. The food import dependency grew by 250 per cent from US$$259million in 2000 to US$756 million in 2014 and US$736 million in 2020, amidst dwindling foreign exchange reserves. Simultaneously, the contribution of domestic agriculture to GDP declined from 3.0 per cent in 1990 to 0.4 per cent in 2010. In 2019, however, the agricultural sector in Trinidad and Tobago contributed about 1.2 per cent of the value added to the country's GDP. This figure represents more than double the contribution of the agricultural sector a decade earlier in 2010. Although the total value of food imports now averages US$750 million, with rising prices in import markets, traditional food exporting countries are revisiting policies to secure their populations and address quality issues; Trinidad and Tobago's delayed response may have more dire consequences in the medium to long term.

The last of the upper-tiered plantation crops, sugar, came almost completely to a halt after 2007, with remaining exports limited to small quantities. Now, sugar processing has stopped completely. The crop is no longer considered a priority for agricultural or economic development. The same is true for coconut production, which fell in the 1990s, as it required more research and investment to support the introduction of new disease-resistant and productive varieties. Coffee and cocoa production had many challenges with pests, diseases and inefficient technology, while rice production has also declined 90 per cent since the 1990s due to low productivity. Cocoa production has, however, made a slight comeback with government and private sector support. In fact, Central Statistical Office (CSO) data indicate that an estimated TT$30 million in cocoa was exported for the period 2016–18, while TT$235.6 million in chocolates was exported for the same period. Production of citrus, vegetables such as tomato and hot pepper, as well as root crops, have seen promising production growth rates in recent years. Livestock production has also been growing slowly but steadily, with some improvement in the national herds over time.

To achieve food security, the country must, therefore, become more self-sufficient by increasing productivity, diversifying the range of crops to focus on the use of indigenous and underutilized foods, reducing postharvest losses, improving the marketing and distribution of farm produce, promoting innovations in agriculture and increasing the participation of youth and women in the food security agenda (Beckford and Campbell 2013).

It was Demas (1987) who first suggested that agricultural diversification should not be interpreted as crop diversification and proposed three components of the process as described by Bridgemohan and Isaac (2019):

1. Product elaboration and transformation (processing),
2. Production of non-traditional export crops and
3. Production of non-traditional export crops for local and regional consumption.

Wilson and Bekele (1998) both elaborated on the Demas model, proposing three different models for agriculture diversification in the Caribbean:

1. Processing house-based diversification
2. Farm-based diversification, and
3. Species-based diversification

Pingali and Rosegrant (1995) shared a slightly different view, describing agricultural diversification as the gradual replacement of farming systems by specialized enterprises for crop, livestock, poultry and aquaculture products. Bridgemohan and Isaac (2019) described the many benefits of agricultural diversification, which can include food security, foreign exchange savings and earnings, employment generation, the creation of economic linkages, the utilization of underutilized resources, and the linkage between agriculture and tourism.

CHALLENGES FACING THE AGRICULTURE SECTOR POST-INDEPENDENCE

Globally, agriculture now faces increased challenges due to the pandemic effects, political and diplomatic threats, and other issues previously mentioned. These issues, combined, further delay food security for import-dependent small island developing states (SIDS) as a national development goal. These effects have arguably further impacted food security by adding another layer of complexity to unstable agri-food systems, especially in Caribbean SIDS (Daley et al., in press).

Wuddivira et al. (2017) described the status of food and nutrition security in the Caribbean region as precarious, citing the region's increasing vulnerability to the high incidence of pests and diseases, poor human resource capacity, limited land resources, reliance on inefficient and outdated technologies in food production and processing, low investments in research, the lack of an enabling environment to foster innovation and entrepreneurship and high occurrence of tropical storms, hurricanes, floods, droughts and earthquakes. These authors go further to say that the volatilities associated with food production and food prices, including a high import bill, unsustainably high energy prices, some barriers to trade and the effects of climate change and its impacts further add to the challenges facing fragile Caribbean territories (Isaac et al. 2019).

It has also been noted that conventional practices in agriculture are associated with excessive use of agrochemicals, which have been proposed as a probable cause for the highest incidence of prostate cancer in CARICOM

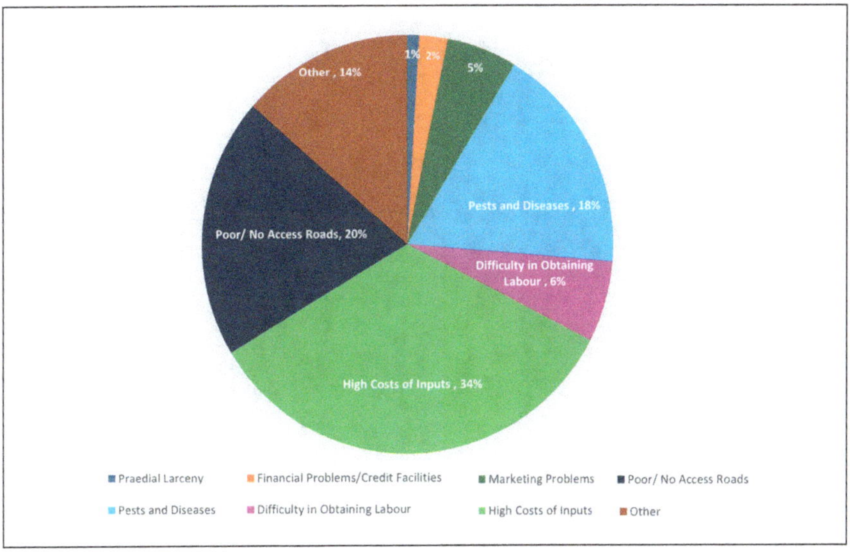

Figure 2.1. Farming constraints (CSO 2015)

countries (Claxton 2009). Isaac et al. (2019 and 2020) point out that the agricultural system requires a change, which can help attain self-sufficiency in food production and produce nutritious and safe food amidst the challenges posed by climate change. One such system which addresses the concerns of agriculture could be the practice of sustainable agriculture.

According to CSO (2015) (See fig. 2.1 above), a survey on farming constraints indicated that the high cost of inputs (34 per cent), pests and diseases (18 per cent), and poor access to roads (20 per cent) were major constraints on farming practices.

Isaac et al. (2019 and 2020) summarized the challenges facing the agricultural production and productivity in Trinidad and Tobago (See table 2.1 below).

Among the myriad of challenges, the current government highlighted land tenure as being the immediate catalyst for growth and investment attraction. There has been some progress in the issuance and renewal of agricultural leases in recent years. However, this does not mitigate the backlog for renewal, and the growing demand for state lands given the economic slowdown of other sectors of the economy and the rising and expressed need across several strata of the population to earn sustainable livelihoods. According to the World Bank (2016), Trinidad and Tobago

Table 2.1: Challenges Facing Agriculture

Policy and Institutional Issues	Lack of transparency in land tenure and land use policy	Poor coordination among national and regional organizations	Agricultural activities spread across ministries with overlapping functions (e.g. Pesticide and Toxic and Chemical Control Board; Pesticide Testing Laboratory under the Ministry of Health)		
Environmental Issues	High use of agricultural chemicals and their disposal, particularly in vegetable growing areas. This is as a result of the high occurrence of pests and diseases in tropical crops (CSO 2015), lack of knowledge in pest and disease diagnosis, poor knowledge on the use of the pesticides.	The hazards such as forest fires and soil erosion, associated with agricultural squatters on forested hillsides.	Climate change and natural disasters		
Economic Issues	Low profitability and competitiveness	High cost of production	Lack of credit to the land under tenure	Lack of specialized credit facility to vulnerable communities.	
Social Issues	Aging farmer population	Farm theft or praedial larceny	Lack of appreciation among youth towards agricultural sector due to history of slavery	Lack of pride towards agriculture sector that lead to scarcity of labour and high labour cost.	Land rights and land rights issues Skills and poor road access to interior farmlands.
Technical Issues	High occurrence of tropical pests and diseases Lack of market information/lack of price analysis	Lack of drainage and poor irrigation management technologies Poor access for small holders/farmer access to high-end markets and agro-industries.	Lack of access to capital Lack of smallholder mechanization	Non-availability of local inputs including seeds. Poor quality seeds and seedlings/no regulation (policy) for seed and seedling production.	Lack of research in the areas of animal and plant breeding. Lack of postharvest technologies and cold storage facilities. Lack of value addition and access to export market due to weaknesses in standards and certification capacity.

ranked 151 out of 189 countries on ease of registering property. Secondly, related to land tenure is a lack of access to capital, which has made it difficult for farmers to provide collateral and obtain credit. Praedial larceny is one of the most serious constraints to agriculture. It is an intractable problem that has catapulted losses to considerable proportions, making it a risky investment (Isaac, Ganpat and Joseph 2017). This crime has been recognized throughout the Caribbean as one of the most significant constraints to food security in the region (Isaac, Ganpat and Joseph 2017; Little 2011). Its proliferation is primarily driven by the increased demand for fresh food by consumers. Isaac et al. (2017 and 2019) pointed out that it simultaneously threatens the quality of life of a productive social class of citizens and the entire economic fabric of a society working toward food security and import substitution.

Table 2.2 provides a typology of farm-related crimes in the Caribbean. The Praedial Larceny Squad, which was formed in 2013, has to date shown no tangible impact.

Table 2.2: A Typology of Rural-Related Farm Crimes in the Caribbean

Farm Crime (predatory/organized/ context-bound)	Wildlife Crime (predatory)	Illegal Rural Enterprise (symbiotic/ entreprencurial)	Village Crime (opportunistic/ context-bound)	Contamination Crime (situational-based)
Theft – farm equipment (irrigation lines, tractors, diesel, water pumps, weed whackers, fertilizer, and pesticides, etc.) Vandalism – to farm and buildings and fences, damage to crops. Fire-raising – buildings and farms. Cruelty to livestock.	Hunting out of season for wildlife – agouti, manicou, lappe, deer. Illegal, unreported and unregulated (IUU) fishing Trapping Theft of turtle eggs, etc.	Theft of livestock (sheep, goat, cattle, poultry), and small stock stealing. Theft of seedlings, fruits, and vegetables. Squatting on private lands. Drug cultivation – cannabis farming.	Petty theft (pipers) – generally opportunistic. Illegal trespassers and shooters. Breaking and entering. Dumping of rubbish on farmland.	Overuse of agricultural inputs (fertilizers and pesticides). Water pollution due to improper storage and disposal of agri-chemicals. Air pollution from drift of agri-chemicals.

Source: Adapted from Smith (2010) and modified by Isaac et al. (2017).

AGRICULTURE POLICIES, PROGRAMMES AND BUDGETARY ALLOCATIONS REVIEW

According to Bridgemohan (2008), agricultural policy frameworks in most Caribbean countries have been reviewed as weak and fragmented due to:

- Lack of strategy and direction;
- Lack of prioritization;
- Understaffing and low budgetary allocations;
- Weak science and technology as well as research and design;
- Over reliance on donors; and
- Marketing and trading system – geared for export and tourist markets.

The agricultural policies introduced in Trinidad and Tobago are a combination of input subsidies, general services support and state-owned enterprises' activities using the following instruments:

- Compensation of production and investment costs (Agricultural Incentive Programme)
- Guaranteed minimum prices
- Subsidized loans (through ADB)
- Training and extension services
- Investments in infrastructure
- Research and development
- Marketing, promotion and information support (NAMDEVCO)
- Border protection

Incentives, subsidies and infrastructure development programmes are also available for the fisheries sector.

A study conducted by the Shik et al. (2018) reported mid-term goals for the development of Trinidad and Tobago which were set in the Medium-Term Policy Framework (MTPF) (2011–14) with agriculture and food security included among the five priority development areas. The next mid-term strategic document, Vision 2030 (2016–30) reported the modernization of agriculture as a crucial factor for the economy's international competitiveness. The Vision 2030 document outlined the public investments in agriculture in Trinidad and Tobago.

For their study, Shik et al. (2018) outlined the main mid-term policy goals:

- Food import bill reduction
- Food inflation control
- Increase in agricultural production
- Increase in employment in agriculture

Citing that the policy goals for the sector had not changed since 2002 at the time of their publication, Shik et al. (2018) identified that this was partly because both agricultural production and employment trends depend on factors that are beyond the potential impact of agricultural policy, as they are a natural consequence of structural transformation of the economy. They further pointed out that areas of potential policy impact, such as agricultural sector profitability, sustainability, competitiveness and actions for the sector's modernization, market integrations or technological advancement, were not among policy priorities.

The 2012–15 National Food Production Action Plan (Agriculture Now) listed actions to achieve four mid-term goals to ensure food security. The Ministry of Agriculture, Land and Fisheries aimed to increase self-sufficiency in twenty-two commodities, grouped in six subsectors (staples, vegetables, fruits, aquaculture, livestock and pulses). Additionally, cocoa and honey were named strategic commodities based on their export potential.

The proposed actions to achieve these goals included the provision of general services, such as research, development of new crop varieties, infrastructure development and assistance with marketing and promotion (through NAMDEVCO). Training and extension services, as well as the introduction of new technologies to farmers in order to address the issue of low competitiveness and the lack of adequate supporting infrastructure (transportation, irrigation, drainage and post-harvest facilities), were highlighted. For specific commodities, proposed actions included increasing acreage under cultivation. At the time, it was believed that these actions would be better achieved by stimulating the private sector rather than direct intervention in areas within the private sector's production choices. Table 2.3 shows the domestic support programmes in Trinidad and Tobago between 2010 and 2015.

Table 2.3: Domestic Support Programmes in Trinidad and Tobago, 2010–15

Programme	Description
Agricultural Incentive Programme	• Compensation of costs • Guaranteed minimum prices
Large Commercial Farms Programme	• Public-Private Partnership for participation in agricultural activities. • Agricultural production at 15 large commercial farms
Employment Encourage Programmes	Encouraging youth participation in the agricultural sector • Farm visits for schools • Agriculture Professional Development Programme (APDP) for university graduates • Unemployment Relief Programme (URP) training in agriculture
Support related to sugar production suspension	• National Adaptation Strategy • EU Assistance
Strengthening of Value Chains	• Establishing and operating packing houses • Establishing and operating wholesale markets for agricultural commodities and fish • Information support and marketing by NAMDEVCO
Subsidized loans	The Agricultural Development Bank (ADB) offers short- and long-term agricultural loans with flexible requirements and terms.
Research and Development	International and local organizations Caribbean Agricultural Development Institute (CARDI), The University of the West Indies, and the University of Trinidad and Tobago provide research and extension services for agricultural producers.
Infrastructure Development	Agricultural access roads and irrigation infrastructure rehabilitation and development are part of annual investment programmes.

Source: WTO 2012, cited in Shik et al. (2018)

Table 2.4 provides a summary of the analysis of commodity-specific policies from 2010 to 2015.

Table 2.4: Commodity-specific Policy in Trinidad and Tobago

Policy	Commodity-Specific Support	Subsector Characteristics
Rice Subsector • Guaranteed prices set above international levels, benefitting rice producers • Subsidized fixed inputs • General services	• MPS positive during the whole period of study and increased in 2015. • Guaranteed prices on average 50% higher than they would be without policy intervention • No product-specific budget support • Rice farmers were supported at the expense of consumers	• Production volume is increasing but in 2015 it was only one third that of 1995 • 90% of consumption is imported • Yields are lower than those of other Caribbean producers
Root Crops Subsector • Stimulating demand through incorporating cassava into the school menu • Support to research and development • Promotion measures to encourage substitution of imported grains with local cassava	• SCT-related policy effect positive for sweet potato farmers: prices about two times higher than in a non-policy intervention situation • SCT-related policy effect nearly neutral for cassava farmers: no price support, budget transfers to the Tobago programme for development of the cassava industry	• Production increased significantly • Measures to increase productivity and improvement of post-harvest management is recommended
Cocoa Subsector • Minimum guaranteed prices set at levels close to international prices • Investment grants: 100% of the costs of cocoa establishment or rehabilitation and 10% of the cost of establishment of cocoa fermentation facilities • Marketing and exports by the state company • Research and development services	• Neutral price support • Positive budget transfers • Total level of support (SCT%) amounts to 35% of gross farm receipts on average in 2012–15	• Production fell significantly • Yields are very low

Table 2.4 continues on next page

Table 2.4: Commodity-specific Policy in Trinidad and Tobago (*cont'd*)

Policy	Commodity-Specific Support	Subsector Characteristics
Hot Pepper Subsector • Subsidized loans from ADB • Investment grants: subsidized machinery and investments in on-farm irrigation • Value chain support: packing houses • Public-private partnerships for production: the state-owned Caroni Greens Limited was a major producer and exporter • Research and development services • 40% import tariff for fresh peppers and a 20% tariff for pepper sauce	• Hot pepper SCT was negative, indicating implicit taxation • There are obstacles to price transmission along the value chain (costly export procedures)	• Highly profitable subsector • High productivity
Pumpkin Subsector • Subsidized inputs: machinery, technical assistance • General services: infrastructure (roads, water supply) • Duty-free imports of inputs since 2016 • Support to the value chain: packing houses that collect and store commodities, marketing infrastructure (wholesale markets)	• Pumpkin SCT was negative in most years, indicating implicit taxation • Negative effect of the policy on export crop farmers is caused by the direct involvement of the government in the production and marketing of those crops: government-owned companies are slow to react to market signals, and increased output drives prices down. • At the same time, low prices contribute to international competitiveness	• Highly profitable subsector • High productivity
Other Export Crops • Incentives to producers for pest management, support to post-harvest infrastructure development. • Investments in infrastructure • Research and development support for productivity improvement and production sustainability	• Pineapple and christophene (chayote) producers were supported by the price policy (positive MPS) • Part of the large price gap may indicate underdeveloped infrastructure • Support was provided at the expense of domestic consumers	• Production is growing • Productivity needs

Table 2.4 continues on next page

Table 2.4: Commodity-specific Policy in Trinidad and Tobago *(cont'd)*

Policy	Commodity-Specific Support	Subsector Characteristics
Dairy Subsector • Guaranteed prices: farmers supply milk to Nestlé Trinidad and Tobago Ltd, under contractual arrangements at prices established by the government. • Research and development services. • Same-day loans for milk farmers from ADB in cooperation with Nestlé Trinidad and Tobago. • An import tariff of 40% for fresh milk imports; the tariff on milk powder imports is only 5%.	• Minimum prices for milk were lower than the actual farm-gate prices received by producers. • Negative price gap for milk was set to zero as it was considered to be reflecting non-policy effects along the value chain. • No budget transfers specific for milk producers in the period of study.	• Production is declining • Productivity is very low
Livestock Subsector • The livestock subsector is a major beneficiary of knowledge generation and transfer services. • The government invests in forage farms and breeding centres. • Imported poultry receives an import tariff of 40%, in addition to which a 15% surcharge was levied in 2013	• Poultry and small ruminant producers were supported by policy. • Price support to poultry producers was the single most important component of national MPS. • Average prices received by the poultry producers were stable despite the volatility of international prices. • The level of protection was moderate as a percent share of gross farm receipts (the highest share was 41% in 2010, and in 2013 it was only 5%), but substantial in absolute terms. • The level of support to sheep producers, provided both in the forms of price support (MPS) and budget transfers, reached an average of 62% of total farm receipts in 2013–15	• Poultry imports are declining and production is stable. • Small ruminant production is expanding, but the export volume is negligible.

Table 2.4 continues on next page

Table 2.4: Commodity-specific Policy in Trinidad and Tobago *(cont'd)*

Policy	Commodity-Specific Support	Subsector Characteristics
Apiculture Subsector • Investment subsidies. • Subsidized loans. • Services to farmers: training in new technologies, and marketing assistance. • Tariff on imports (40%)	• Honey SCT was high (63% of gross farm receipts in 2013–15)	• Export expansion requires quality certification

Source: Shik et al. 2018 / Key: SCT – Single Commodity Transfer (SCT), Market Price Support (MPS)

More recently, Vision 2030 – The National Development Strategy (2016–30) has identified building globally competitive businesses as one of the thematic areas where development efforts will focus on Trinidad and Tobago's economic transformation. As part of this strategy, a strong, modern, competitive agriculture, agro-processing and fisheries sector has the ingredients for successful penetration of regional and international markets. This will allow the country to attain economic diversification while promoting economic growth.

The policy document also identifies the need to reverse decades of poor agricultural land administration and the collapse of land tenure. Current reforms and the government's aggressive approach to modernizing the land administration system will relieve food producers who depend heavily on state land for production. Beyond legislation and regularization, greater activities are required to allow farmers to convert land to food. New techniques, equipment and technology must improve farm efficiency and productivity and lower reliance on manual labour, whether from the farming family or hired help.

The Youth Agricultural Homestead Programme (YAHP) was launched in March 2022. It targets 150 young people between the ages of eighteen and thirty-five and aims to equip them with the training, technical support and access to land to start their agricultural enterprises. The programme, which is led by the Ministry of Youth Development and National Service in conjunction with the Ministry of Housing and Urban Development through the Land Settlement Agency, aims to equip twenty-first-century agri-entrepreneurs with skills for sustainable development in the future.

To promote these objectives, the Minister of Finance has introduced a new Agro-Incentive to be funded in the first year out of an allocation of TT$20Mn targeting agro-producers with the aim of encouraging rational, efficient and methodical applications to agriculture. A key element of this strategy is the transformation of the agriculture sector through increased focus on on-farm investments in protected farming; safe and healthy post-harvest packaging; reduction in post-harvest losses; value-added initiatives; agro-processing; renewable energy; climate-smart agriculture; Good Agricultural Practices (GAP), Good Manufacturing Practices (GMP), Food Safety Management Systems such as Hazard Analysis Critical Control Point (HACCP) and waste reduction. The incentive may also be available to qualified licensed woodcutters who wish to acquire specialized forestry equipment the advice of the Forestry Division and qualified saw millers who wish to improve health and safety in licensed sawmills under the guidance of the OSH Agency.

This agri-incentive is to encourage new and existing farmers who wish, among other things, to invest in modern farming technology or other efficiency upgrades on their farms to resist the effects of changing weather patterns; reduce labour reliance; introduce more efficient use of water; reduce cost of production or improve health and safety as well as food safety. In addition, the Government of Trinidad and Tobago wishes to encourage farmers to improve their breeding stock, pursue value-added initiatives, access research and development support and develop new products. Finally, the Government wishes to encourage younger farmers and provide improved access to the combination of training, land and financing.

Figure 2.2. Recent Proposed Financial Support Strategy

Given the current economic circumstances facing territories in the Caribbean region, policymakers must do more to ensure food and nutrition security at the household level. This will protect and strengthen the citizenry who feed the nation and allow them to act assiduously towards stability and consensus on the way forward in a sustainable manner (Isaac et al. 2019).

Policies must ensure that citizens enjoy safe food in sufficient quantity and quality to satisfy their nutritional needs for optimal health (Isaac et al. 2019, 2020). To achieve this, Wuddivira et al. (2017) recommended the following policy considerations:

- Promote healthy eating;
- Promote low costs and clean energy;
- Foster technological innovation;
- Build human resources;
- International trade issues;
- Strengthen institutional settings;
- Promote sustainable use and management of natural resources.

The Agricultural Policy Framework should also consider:

- Views of all players in the industry;
- Organic farming policies and standards;
- Legislation and regulation on import/export, toxic chemicals and training;
- Budgets for small-scale farming;
- Consultation with stakeholders;
- Farmer Association and clusters.

To confront the challenges facing regional food security, this chapter suggests forward-looking policies emphasizing their interconnectivity and how they would impact sustainable development systems under the ambit of the new climate-smart agriculture, asset-based development and employment opportunities, road and drainage infrastructure, reliable potable water, electrification, healthcare and education. These transformative policies will ensure that all people have continued access to sufficient supplies of a safe and sustainable food supply with a nutritionally adequate diet and, in so doing, achieve and maintain the health and nutritional well-being of citizens (Isaac et al. 2019, 2020).

AGRICULTURE RESEARCH AND EDUCATION – THE GAP BETWEEN KNOWLEDGE AND APPLICATION

The empowerment of food producers in the Caribbean should focus on activities aimed at strengthening local food production and distribution systems while increasing the capacity through innovative education and extension to small producers as well as its general citizenry to increase food production through sustainable systems and practices, thereby increasing incomes and improving livelihoods (Isaac et al. 2019). Such an approach should focus on the development and implementation of an integrated and comprehensive strategy towards building the capacity of small-scale food producers so as to increase productivity and improve livelihoods and income through gender-responsive sustainable agricultural technologies and practices. Isaac et al. (2019) also explained that action research is urgently needed to address the climate risks to food security and the global challenge of reducing greenhouse gas emissions from all sectors, including agriculture in SIDS. This approach fosters impactful connectivity among a range of stakeholders (e.g. different kinds of farmers, local service agencies and development agencies).

Bekele and Ganpat (2015) also supported this approach and stressed that for education, extension and training interventions to be effective, new content must be taught and innovative methods embraced, beginning at the primary and secondary school levels (at the Caribbean Secondary Examination Certificate – CSEC and Caribbean Advanced Proficiency Examination – CAPE curriculum). These authors discuss that, for this type of education to be effective, the following three components are required:

- Locally relevant, adaptive, empowering and science-based curricula;
- A sustainable, enabling educational environment;
- Community-based school activities are driven and founded on the principle of equity.

There is an urgent need to revisit the aim and scope of our national education, training and development programmes and strategies vis-à-vis the social issues that glare in national headlines, health and nutrition, and sustainable livelihoods. Usually receiving the largest allocations and seemingly not growing the citizenry out of poverty and a myriad of inherent issues is untenable. Governments can develop creative ways to engage particular stakeholders to access funds and appropriate actions needed for future research and dissemination of knowledge to promote human capital development for the sector, educate our taste buds and create an appetite for innovation and entrepreneurship in agriculture.

POSSIBLE REASONS FOR FAILURE OF POLICY IN FOOD SECURITY AND SOLUTIONS

The agriculture sector continues to be misunderstood and suffers from a history of underinvestment and failed policy. To systematically reduce our reliance on foreign food products and bolster our own capacity, there must be a fundamental shift in the sector's priority, raising it on the national development agenda, which is to be supported by an overarching national policy framework for sustainable agriculture and rural development. The stakeholders of the sector will then only begin to be motivated through greater consultation, collaboration and coordination of the already limited resources since they have grown accustomed to doing more with less.

Policy includes identifying strategic programmes and projects aligned to measurable outcomes and the required financial, human and technical resources. We must be mindful of the history of neglect of the agriculture and fisheries sector overall and appreciate that we cannot now try to do things in a recession which should have been planned and implemented in better economic times with greater fiscal space.

Higher prices in local markets, increased demand for imported equivalents – which we should be producing in this country – and foreign exchange pressure may prevent food and nutrition security from reaching the men, women, boys and girls who need it most. Certainly, national support for the "local" notion will overwhelm current production in all subsectors. Demand will create supply, but there are significant precursors for growth and development that have not been addressed and discussed previously.

There is perhaps no current incentive for policymakers to act with the required urgency and alarm on issues relating to food and nutrition security planning in this country since the observed position has been to simply advise the population to adjust their lifestyles and expectations.

Although food is available for the population, it remains import-dependent. Rising prices both locally and in traditional import markets, coupled with the increasing cost of living and diminished seed security, continue to loom, causing food and nutrition insecurity. This is the very basis for development work, which educates our taste buds and promotes farmer empowerment.

Trinidad and Tobago imports approximately US$750 million annually, and the value is expected to rise, given the exchange rate pressure. Even if the estimated value does not change, the market for food for final human consumption, intermediary products and concentrates for the food manufacturing industry and other inputs such as agricultural chemicals or vegetable seeds for planting will contract. This is due to international price hikes and diminishing quantities available on the global market. Traditional exporting countries are revising their internal policies to protect their populations, especially now, since the Russian-Ukrainian conflict.

In the absence of such an overarching policy framework, the population cannot gauge the strength of government's intention and whether the goal is food and nutrition security for all, appeasing farmers, wooing a new farming demographic, increasing agricultural crop and livestock production, strengthening the links in the food value chain, providing a fiscal basis for the beneficiaries of the announced public-private partnerships in Moruga and Aripo, the new hatchery and the processing and packing facilities currently supervised by NAMDEVCO in Tabaquite, Couva and Piarco or a combination of all.

While these partnerships represent a significant investment on behalf of this country's taxpayers, it is also important to understand the public benefit, especially how they create quality employment opportunities for university graduates in varying related fields of study. For example, they impact the affordability and availability of food and agricultural products for local consumption or with export potential.

A major national discourse concerning food prices is happening at all levels of society, especially in securing food and nutrition for the most vulnerable among us. This was, however, not acknowledged in the 2021 budget presentation. Local news headlines and across the CARICOM region point to soaring food prices in Trinidad and Tobago. The VAT exemption on a few supermarket items and the addition of VAT to several more do not address the rising cost of production and market prices of primary agricultural commodities which every citizen or household consumes each day.

To date, there has been no coherent plan to rejuvenate or manage the situation through strategic use of the Prices Council or better resources and utilize the Consumer Affairs Division to ensure balance in society, reporting or any punishment for unnecessary profiteering and price gouging. This is in the face of the latest Monetary Policy Announcement by the Central Bank that "On the domestic front, supply-side factors – notably, a surge in international commodity prices such as sugar, wheat and vegetable oils; higher shipping costs; transportation delays; and adverse weather – have led to a discernible increase in food prices. The latest information from the Central Statistical Office shows that food inflation (year-on-year) rose from 3.2 per cent in January to 4.9 per cent in July 2021. The largest increases were recorded for vegetables, fruits, milk, cheese and eggs."

This data and the validity of such a report were disputed by farmers who produce table eggs for domestic consumption and contend that no such price increases took place at the farm gate. A simple, locally produced egg remains one of the most affordable meals in this country. It suggests yet another reason we must be very wary of castigating our productive sector in the face of import prices and dependency, which has been inappropriately dealt with through effective development policy for decades.

Table 2.5 below presents the top five food import categories for the period 2013–17. Despite policy efforts and annual budgetary and development programmes, our food import dependency remains fixated on dairy produce, including eggs, cereals (including rice, wheat, etc.), beverages, meats, fruits and vegetables. Even with the benefit of hindsight, market information and intelligence, crafting appropriate and sustainable interventions are still delayed. Additionally, these five categories approximated 50 per cent of total food imports in those years.

The demise of local rice production also saw the failure of rural infrastructure, agricultural access roads, on-farm roads, farm income, debt service on loans taken by farmers, and the livelihoods of rural and agricultural communities. The loss of agriculture is not simply the loss of food plants, livestock and arable land. This is in addition to the loss of farmer motivation, work effort, financial investment, land preparation and farm architecture, various equipment and machinery, seeds and germplasm and on-farm experiments and rural infrastructure (access roads, bridges, water sources and reserves, etc.). Quantifying the impact on the wider population is a challenge of its own. These are some consequences of policy failure in this country.

The almost two-decade-old offer of land in Guyana formed part of the discussion of the declining role of agriculture in CARICOM, the continuing loss of preferential markets for the region's traditional "tier-one" products, and the rapidly increasing extra-regional food import bill were among the serious and challenging issues highlighted – which persist to this day. It would require labour laws and regulations, financing, infrastructure, and perhaps addressing several of the hurdles that we could not overcome locally. Today, there are issues of intellectual property rights in agriculture, for example, which were not previously considered. The threat of large-scale domestic production has also become a political issue, with fear being brought on by smallholder agriculture and farmers' livelihoods over the years. The problems run very deep in this society; clearly, all farm-to-table public relations have failed, besides awakening the fact that Trinidad and Tobago is facing a crisis that would impact people differently.

Table 2.5: Top 5 Food Import Categories as a Per Cent of Total Food Imports (2013–17)

% Of Food Imports 2013		% Of Food Imports 2014		% Of Food Imports 2015		% Of Food Imports 2016		% Of Food Imports 2017	
Dairy produce; birds' eggs; natural honey; edible products of animal origin, not elsewhere	11.97	Dairy produce; birds' eggs; natural honey; edible products of animal origin, not elsewhere	12.27	Dairy produce; birds' eggs; natural honey; edible products of animal origin, not elsewhere	10.94	Dairy produce; birds' eggs; natural honey; edible products of animal origin, not elsewhere	10.70	Dairy produce; birds' eggs; natural honey; edible products of animal origin, not elsewhere	12.35
Cereals	9.41	Beverages, spirits and vinegar	8.92	Beverages, spirits and vinegar	10.46	Beverages, spirits and vinegar	9.63	Meat and edible meat offal	9.62
Beverages, spirits and vinegar	8.52	Meat and edible meat offal	8.82	Miscellaneous edible preparations	8.98	Meat and edible meat offal	9.48	Beverages, spirits and vinegar	7.69
Miscellaneous edible preparations	7.97	Cereals	8.48	Meat and edible meat offal	8.64	Miscellaneous edible preparations	7.99	Miscellaneous edible preparations	7.43
Meat and edible meat offal	7.73	Miscellaneous edible preparations	7.75	Preparations of vegetables, fruit, nuts or other parts of plants	7.21	Preparations of cereals, flour, starch or milk; pastry cooks' products	7.68	Cereals	7.28

Data Source: ITC TradeMap

Organizing and coordinating the actions of fragmented stakeholders will also compound these issues, as the repercussions of this pandemic will continue to prolong after considering the myriad of challenges confronting agriculture and fisheries previously discussed. If the sector's administrators and experts cannot identify and develop impactful and strategic programmes and projects that collectively advance the national interest in food sufficiency while securing the livelihoods of farming and fishing communities, then the national budgetary trend in terms of agriculture will remain the same.

Responsible and timely data collection and reporting should also be emphasized to inform investment, trade and production decisions regardless of geographical location and technology constraints. This should include coverage of food and agricultural statistics and a focus on building the capacity to inform decision-making in this area.

In 2019, while justifying an increase to the minimum wage, the minister of finance purported that one hundred and ninety-four thousand people would benefit. This, to some extent, exposes the vulnerability of the nation, given the economic outlook. While the government's delivery of one hundred and eighty-five thousand market bags as part of its social strategy was commendable, it highlights the critical need for a more sustainable strategy which will not disproportionately affect the citizenry even amidst the pandemic and other challenges that persist.

There is need for prudent, transparent management and reporting of national affairs and the agriculture sector performance considering there has been a failure to achieve the objectives set out in the Medium Term Policy Framework (2011–14) for Agriculture and Food Security: reduce the food import bill (Target: 10 per cent annually), reduce the rate of food inflation and sustain it within single digits, create sustainable, long-term productive employment in the sector to support a national unemployment level that is under 7 per cent, increase the sector's contribution to GDP (Target: 3 per cent by 2014) and create a food-secure nation.

There is also an urgent need to focus on defining a clear path ahead, with inclusive policy planning and action, detailing the uptake, issues and gains made by a TT$500 million stimulus fund held by the Ministry of Finance and the further allocation of TT$300million in the last fiscal year.

The year 2019 was the fifth budget decided upon by the current government, and despite prompting from stakeholders to the contrary, there was no sign that agriculture, fisheries and rural development held importance in the national development agenda if we consider budgetary allocations to be the yardstick. The development programme runs the same treadmill as similar iterations. Some state enterprises, departments and programmes have been shut down, and allocations reduced, yet the sector held its breath for new dynamism, optimism and growth.

In the 2016 budget statement, the finance minister noted that "consistent with our 2015 Election Manifesto promise, in pursuit of our objective for achieving food security, we will exempt from all duties and taxes, inputs into the agricultural sector, including approved chemicals, pest control, approved vehicles, approved fishing vessels and equipment. These measures will take effect from January 1, 2016."

In the 2017 budget statement, the finance minister stated that in order to:

> stimulate the local agricultural sector, all approved agro-processing operations will now be tax free. A certification process will be put in place at the Ministry of Agriculture, Lands and Fisheries to ensure that only qualified applicants benefit from this tax relief. The qualifying criteria will be that at least 75 percent of the processing of agricultural products must be done in Trinidad and Tobago and 75 percent of the ingredients must be produced or harvested locally. This measure will be implemented in the second quarter of fiscal 2017.

In the 2018 budget statement, the finance minister further stated that "the agriculture sector in Trinidad and Tobago benefits from a myriad of incentives, including exemption from income tax for approved agricultural holdings, tax concessions on vehicles, equipment, raw materials and other inputs, subsidised loan programmes, purpose-built markets, planting materials, access roads, state land leases and the like".

The announcements have somewhat exacerbated ambiguity and confusion as to the intended beneficiaries, considering the registration and recognition issues of practising farmers with the line ministry, the repetition of previous years' proposals and whether there was delay or failure in their implementation.

Nonetheless, similar to the removal of value added tax (VAT) on food items in previous years, the lowering of market prices for these now non-taxable inputs remains to be seen. Hopefully, the tax relief will be passed on to farmers based on their cost of production, asset acquisition, mechanization and technology adoption rather than create a wider profit margin for input suppliers, especially now that COVID-19 is disrupting global trade.

Studies have shown that the Agriculture Incentive Programme (AIP) may have positively influenced some commodities while negatively affecting others. Therefore, from a policy perspective, it may have failed to reduce the cost of production and, by extension, the market price of commodities in general. The critical consideration in assessing its impact on agricultural production is its effectiveness in improving incentives for farmers and the effectiveness and efficiency gains in market development.

Registered farmers who are qualified to benefit from the AIP are caught in a tailspin of disappointment, with some waiting years to collect rebates. At the same time, many languish because of expired leases and land tenure issues despite the 2017 budget proposal that "with the modernization of land records, investors and farmers would now have access to standard agricultural leases which can be collateralized for accessing low-cost credit, in particular through a well-resourced Agricultural Development Bank (ADB)".

Stakeholders agree that agriculture and fisheries are critical to economic recovery. Firm policy positions are needed to directly foster production, build a comparative advantage in value addition, and regain trust and goodwill among the sector's stakeholders. Respecting the circumstances of rural and coastal communities and optimally targeting limited resources must be seen as reciprocal in the struggle for food and nutrition security.

What is needed are accountability mechanisms in agriculture and other portfolios. The population must appreciate how government experts and appointees, ministries, affiliated state agencies and other technical and coordinating bodies have responded to the pandemic and the war crisis and how they would react to any other disasters to ensure food and nutrition security for our people while addressing the perennial issues of the sector – including flooding, praedial larceny, food loss, random quality testing, market development, field sanitation among others.

The government should first be presenting proposals of national interest going forward since they are now maintained more painfully at taxpayers' expense rather than co-opting other bureaucratic committees and processes to respond to issues that require vision and leadership. The approach of the Economic Development Advisory Board and other ad hoc committees failed, resulting in resignations and disbanding.

It is in that discourse that we should be told if we are going to depend on local farmers and agriculture during and after the pandemic, which is causing turmoil in global food systems. The country must be given the status of the industry after almost seven consecutive years of opportunity and one version of political leadership in the sector. Without it, we would not appreciate how serious food security planning becomes for a SIDS with constricted revenue streams in the short term.

New provisions to encourage interest and investment in the agriculture sector for the fiscal year 2023 included an expansion of the grant funding facility for wheat alternative flour producers, increasing from $250,000 to $340,000. This is meant to encourage agro-processing and local alternative commodity utilization. The sum of $300 million was set aside for special projects, albeit in relation to agriculture incentives, infrastructure and other programmes. Additionally, approved agricultural holdings will be offered rebates up to $25,000 for implementing a renewable energy system, such as solar or wind.

With a change in leadership of the Ministry of Agriculture, Land and Fisheries near the mid-term of the current government, stakeholders have recalibrated expectations. A positive sign is that the leadership has taken an approach of greater consultation, collaboration and coordination of the already limited resources since the sector has grown accustomed to doing more with less.

Given the urgency of the many challenges, stakeholders continue to advocate for a fundamental shift in the sector's priority, raising it on the national development agenda, which is to be supported by an overarching national policy framework for sustainable agriculture and rural development. Policy includes identifying strategic programmes and projects aligned to measurable outcomes and its financial, human and technical resources. It is important to emphasize the financing aspect, considering the multidimensional nature of many projects and programmes. These initiatives often depend on other areas of national planning, such as agricultural labour, technical and skills training, market development, product safety and the promotion of exports and organic agriculture. This point is reiterated later as a policy deficit posing a further constraint to agriculture's expansion in the economy.

While consumers are raising concerns about food prices and farmers and fishers about their cost of production, we must also be mindful of the history of neglect of the agriculture and fisheries sector overall and appreciate that we cannot now try to do things in a recession which should have been planned and implemented in better economic times with greater fiscal space.

CHINA AND INDIA: EXPLORING THE IMPORTANCE OF BILATERAL TECHNICAL COOPERATION

China and India are set apart in the global conversation on food and agriculture by aggressively working towards feeding two of the world's most populous countries while creating meaningful and rural employment to slow rural-urban migration. For many years, they have both maintained amicable diplomatic relations with Trinidad and Tobago. More specifically, they have offered scholarships and opportunities for capacity development and training across several sectors, including agriculture and fisheries. The capacity to maintain our affinity for imported food is evaporating, as discussed previously. Our position and dependency on food imports must be understood within a global value chain. In 2016/2017, China set out to invest US$450 billion towards modernizing its agriculture industry by 2020, undoubtedly amassing significant capacity for sustained development and productivity.

The Chinese investment, in line with its government policy, was to protect national food security, support the sector doing business overseas and develop China's seed industry.

According to ITC TradeMap statistics, China was the second largest import market for Trinidad and Tobago, with an estimated value of US$482 million in 2015 or 7.5 per cent of total imports. The main import market was the United States, at an estimated value of US$2.5 billion or 38.9 per cent of total imports. Where ITC data was available, Trinidad and Tobago imported seeds, fruits and spores for sowing (excluding leguminous vegetables and sweet corn) between 2011 and 2015, which was worth approximately $47 million. A few years ago, farmers protested the Ministry of Agriculture over their perceived inaction to assist with restoring a supply of good quality seeds for replanting post-flood, among other issues. Just about

20 per cent of that seed import demand came from China. We clearly require deeper insight into policy thinking and the information which shapes our public sector investment programme and public expenditure in agriculture.

Of all China's exports to CARICOM, food and agriculture products constitute an annual average of 3.21 per cent for the same period, or US$88 million. Overall, food and agriculture products represent an annual average of 18.63 per cent of total CARICOM imports or US$5.33 billion. For Trinidad and Tobago (2014–18), food and agriculture products represented an annual average of 4.09 per cent of total Chinese exports to this country, worth almost US$$17 million. Total Chinese exports to Trinidad and Tobago were estimated to be approximately US$348 million in 2018. Trinidad and Tobago (2014–18) total imports averaged US$7.65 billion. Food and agriculture products imported are estimated to be US$959 million annually or 13.2 per cent of total imports.

The author had the opportunity to visit India on a fully sponsored invitation by the government of India to participate in an international programme on "Financing of Inclusive Agriculture and Rural Development" at the Bankers Institute of Rural Development, Lucknow, Uttar Pradesh, India, in 2018. As the Indian government is 'betting on the farm', this high-level policy planning experience reminds us that their agricultural sector is facing a dilemma. While it has made large strides in achieving the development goals of food security, availability and accessibility, it is still being challenged by a formidable agrarian crisis. This situation has led to fresh thinking on the developmental approach, prompted by foresight and empowered farmers' lobby. The need to focus on the welfare and prosperity of farmers gained prominence. Consequently, the Department of Agriculture and Cooperation was renamed by the Honourable Prime Minister Shri Narendra Modi on Independence Day in 2015 as the Department of Agriculture, Cooperation and Farmers Welfare. In this fresh approach, priority was accorded to making the agriculture and allied sector not only ecologically sustainable in its use of natural resources such as soil, water and forests but also socio-economically sustainable to farmers in terms of prosperity, welfare, and social security. Innovating managerial solutions to maximize farmers' welfare rather than relying solely on modern farming to raise productivity and production, is the clarion call of the day.

Agricultural extension challenges are generally similar, including a shrinking resource base, changes in demand and consumption patterns, productivity and profitability of agriculture, water and energy for agricultural, domestic and industrial uses. Projects, programmes, and performance associated with the industry between India and Trinidad and Tobago can be compared. It was interesting to identify reasons why local efforts such as mobile banking failed while farmers and fishers continued to complain that our institutions and support networks underserved them. This platform is not only rolled out differently but is also multi-purpose as a hub for financial literacy and inclusion. While we have strengths, the methodologies of Trinidad and Tobago pale in comparison in areas such as credit for agricultural purposes, insurance, rationale for equipment acquisition, farm models, subsidy strategy and planting material. Additionally, there appears to be a fundamental difference in organizational and human resource culture, as well as in dedication to the country and a proactive commitment to helping all people fulfil their dreams and aspirations.

On another fully sponsored invitation by the government of China, the author was again invited to participate in an international seminar hosted by the China Agricultural University in 2018, "Development Policy and Planning in Agriculture for Developing Countries"[8]. Additionally, in 2019, a further invitation was similarly extended to investigate "Agricultural Products and Food Safety Management" hosted by the China National Research Institute of Food and Fermentation Industries.

These high-level policy seminars, along with project and programme reviews and field visits across the countries to enterprises and stakeholders in their agri-food systems, allowed for a greater appreciation of the untapped potential and possibilities for technical cooperation.

As explained, for import-dependent countries like Trinidad and Tobago, international crises, especially associated with our major trade partners, can have deep repercussions on our local economy and people whose livelihoods are undoubtedly interconnected. Disruptions in China and India, as well as our major direct trade partners and indirect routes, are cause for concern.

The possibility of a long quarantine should be of major concern for trade partners, not only for direct business with China but with those countries, ports, and freight that are connected via the global trade ecosystem.

The developing world also relies heavily on Chinese technology and human capacity building in their efforts relating to food production and processing.

In these circumstances, traditional food exporting countries (our import markets) may revisit their export strategies and internal policies to build reserves and distribution confidence in order to maintain the food and nutrition security of their populations.

THE WAY FORWARD IN THE CURRENT CONTEXT

Today, international headlines inform of sharp increases in commodity prices. From cars to clothing, the cost of living has jumped for American consumers, for example, since the economy reopened. Average meat prices have risen unusually sharply, with beef up 17 per cent since December 2020, bacon by 17 per cent and fresh fish by 10.6 per cent. Recently, the Chinese government urged people to keep stores of basic goods in case of emergencies. However, it assured them there were sufficient supplies after some panic-buying in cities where COVID-19 pandemic control measures were being implemented.

Repeatedly since the start of this pandemic, the author has urged that we must maintain a sense of urgency and crisis in food security in Trinidad and Tobago. While there may be prompting and anecdotal statements in the public domain, the general mood and thrust is absent in our national discourse. The COVID-19 pandemic has laid bare our food import dependency and reminded policymakers of the need to do more and look closer into this very important sector and industry at all levels. In the short run, as real disposable income falls, policymakers and administrators need to ensure that the social safety nets are responsive, that persons of differing socio-economic circumstances do not fall below the minimum living standard and that any such measure is not abused.

People on the ground are contemplating the cost of feeding their families sufficiently. Current availability should not mask the underlying issues and future access. We have to pay attention to agriculture and food production in this country and start food security planning to avoid price, production and market volatility, resulting in a food chain crisis. Our continued failure and sluggishness to engage and address these issues puts Trinidad and

Tobago and other CARICOM members – more than eighteen million people, in an awkward and exposed position in those dynamics.

Our leaders omitted a major pitch at the COP26 Glasgow Climate Change Conference: We need a fighting chance to feed ourselves fairly. Resourcing such a task should have been the responsibility of developing and vulnerable nations.

Climate change impacts on land-based agriculture are visible, and perhaps we have become complacent and indifferent to the challenges it poses to food production. Warmer oceans not only have more energy to damage coastal infrastructure, fish landing sites and communities, but they cause declining productivity of our aquatic food sources, severity of sargassum seaweed and other similar issues, loss of fish habitats, coral bleaching, ocean acidification and sea level rise. Longer, more dangerous fishing trips fuelled by rising costs, duration or distance to secure food and livelihoods for our population puts this form of food and nutrition out of the hands of many who need it the most.

Climate change and its deleterious impacts and the recognition that agriculture strengthens the national economy provide employment and a social safety net to vulnerable areas and segments of the population, as well as an environmental role, is growing in the Caribbean psyche. Recent trade issues and natural disasters have prompted a global focus on digging deeper into the agriculture and rural sectors – investing in its food, productivity and variety.

Amid all our efforts to sustainably and consistently cultivate a national appetite for understanding where our food comes from, how it is produced and appreciating the circumstances of the men and women who feed us, the focus is shifting. What was once a campaign to promote demand for local food has become an urgent matter of national importance: investigating whether our local food systems have the capacity to sustain a population of 1.3 million. If our goal is true food sufficiency, import cover should not be the starting point of our dialogue.

Planning and advancing food and nutrition security is a clear challenge for Trinidad and Tobago. In the absence of an overarching policy framework for sustainable agriculture and rural development, key stakeholders will continue to misdirect advocacy and resources, jeopardizing the national good. This multidimensional issue demands vision and leadership.

Crop farmers require more inputs – water, labour, agro-chemicals for pest and disease proliferation, changing practices (crop rotation, irrigation, shade and other use of technology) similar to livestock farmers whose management of animals in the changing weather becomes more challenging without appropriate extension support, inputs and financing. Both farmers and fisherfolk are, therefore, caught on a treadmill of having to produce more for less, a situation where they need higher prices to survive while consumers want lower prices. The trade-off, unfortunately for us, is sometimes quality, quantity, lack of diversity of locally produced foods in their natural environment, and agricultural and food safety practices.

Over the years, we have heard all the interconnected issues relating to the north-south model of trade and development and its impact on diet, health, well-being, and the livelihoods of farmers, fishers, and local industries, especially food manufacturing. This historical pattern, political facilitation, and unmanaged capitalism have created a dependence that has left millions of people and CARICOM countries in a globalized world on the periphery of issues that are seemingly beyond our control. Besides global prices, geopolitical and availability issues, flooding, locusts, theft and diseases, for example, make the vulnerability and unsustainability of local food systems more evident. In times of disaster, we depend on canned, processed, and packaged foods – the majority of which are imported. We have to continue the struggle towards our food independence!

After several years of fiscal budget deficits and economic hardship, maintaining our dependency on food imports, coupled with food price inflation and the urgent need to return value and opportunities to rural agricultural and fishing communities, is also a burden. Notwithstanding, this calls for an all-country approach to food security now rather than later.

Strategic partners and assets such as the Faculty of Food and Agriculture (UWI), other research bases, the Food and Agriculture Organization (FAO), the Inter-American Institute for Cooperation on Agriculture (IICA), CARICOM Secretariat and other think tanks must be called to order. The University Field Station and other government-run farms and stations must be guarded and invested in heavily to secure best practices, planting material, germplasm, productive livestock breeds, our ability to engage and influence the pattern of food production and agri-entrepreneurship locally and in the region while tapping the potential of bilateral technical cooperation in the process. We need to safeguard our food security and sovereignty as the world food market is signalling crisis – even worse for the most vulnerable.

On many fronts, food and nutrition security remains challenged for many reasons. Some of these require out-of-the-box thinking, awakening to the new urgency of reality and an understanding that it cannot be business as usual in Trinidad and Tobago, especially if we seek to protect the vulnerable among us, the men and women who literally feed the nation. In many spheres, it is regarded as a national security issue, but our institutional philosophies have not yet evolved to see such an involvement in the happenings of the day. Several state agencies mandated, equipped and resourced to intervene remain in quiet slumber, lacking vision and leadership.

The upcoming reality may be "food diplomacy" for the developing world. Climate change, turmoil in international food markets, global logistics challenges, rising consumer demand in the developed world and among the most populous nations with purchasing power, export strategies revisited to build internal food supplies, cost and availability, foreign exchange pressure and several other factors create the environment for another type of pandemic.

US politician Henry Kissinger left the world to consider, "Who controls the food supply controls the people; who controls the energy can control whole continents; who controls money can control the world." This outcome, directly resulting from our history of underinvestment and failed policy in agriculture, challenges our ability to feed ourselves – inclusively – into the future. The ability of our national and regional psyche in CARICOM to engage, accept and manage such a reality is yet untold.

These conversations and issues affect everyone. They are not only a problem for farmers, fisherfolk, coastal communities or those living in the low-lying areas of our country. We are so distant from understanding the issues that politicians in Trinidad and Tobago mock families who supposedly build houses on riverbanks and farmers who raise crops on swampland.

It is envisioned that we can produce food for the national landscape, bolster the national food basket's diversity and tolerance to our prevailing growing conditions and create sustainable linkages between crop and livestock production and allied industry activities. Prompted by the leadership of Guyana, there is a regional awakening to the stark reality that confronts Caribbean people. We cannot be left behind on this fresh wave of development focus.

This chapter has offered insights into mapping a revitalized agriculture sector utilizing non-traditional methods and other sustainable approaches and technologies. The need for such an approach is broadly recognized; implementation is now imperative for the following:

- Information Communication and Technology;
- Alternate and renewable energy;
- Linkages to the tourism sector;
- Financial support and institutional capability building;
- Appropriate technology.

To this end, it is suggested that policy recommendations must include:

- Reducing the impact of climate change on food production;
- Climate resilient development, which focuses on adaptation as well as mitigation strategies for the food and agriculture sector;
- Enhancing the capacity of relevant institutions to provide climate-related information in collaboration with relevant regional bodies;
- Integration of climate management considerations;
- Promoting extension and capacity building as a key enabler for sustainable agriculture/climate/environmental/gender and economic policy in Caribbean SIDS;
- Improving access to affordable healthy foods, creating supportive environments for healthy eating and adequate access to appropriate health care.
- Education at all levels that promote sustainable food systems
- Realignment of national and regional agriculture research agendas to meet the new demand
- Promotion of agricultural entrepreneurship
- Harnessing the strength of marketing information and intelligence in policy planning and market development
- Exploring the potential of bilateral technical cooperation in agriculture sector development planning

As we prepare to move forward, it may be useful to understand just how we got here. An article published by the *Guardian* on Sunday, 19 August 2012, titled "Develop locally, sell globally" is instructive, as, among other things, it noted that: "The first Buy Local campaign was introduced in the flush of hopes for a newly-independent nation. Our access to foreign goods was limited, and exposure to first world cultural traditions was limited to the American Top 40, cinema, and the imported television that TTT could afford to air."

This single paragraph encapsulates so much of the dynamics of the local economy and also explains perhaps why it has continued to confound all attempts at making it work to date. As Hilaire (1995) observed: "Since their discovery at the close of the fifteenth century, the economic fortunes of the islands of Trinidad and Tobago have revolved around the foreign trade sector." He further noted that the major plantation-based products were geared almost exclusively for export, while domestic needs, in particular, food and raw materials, were serviced by imports. Therefore, by design, we became a nation of imported food tastes. This is evident even today. The importance of this factor must not be underestimated.

As far back as The Second Five-Year Plan (1964–68), this problem had already been identified, and by the Third Five-Year Plan (1969–73), deliberate steps were taken "to reduce the taste for inessential imported goods and services in favour of locally produced goods and services [since] . . . the excessive tendency on the part of the population to import foreign goods and services remains a problem" (Hilaire 1995). "Deliberate steps" were deemed necessary in order to influence the composition of imports *in the absence of voluntary changes by consumers* (Hilaire 1995). The notion of "voluntary changes" would play an important role in subsequent developments.

According to Rampersad (1995): "An increasingly open world economy may challenge policies and institutional frameworks based on high levels of controls and intervention, but it also creates opportunities."

The 'Buy Local' campaign of the later 1960s and 1970s, the Negative List and other governmental interventions at the time were all geared towards "the protection of local economic activity from foreign competition" (Hilaire 1995) and creating opportunities. From a consumer standpoint, however, these did little to alleviate the problem. The early post-independence development efforts were centred on the principle of import substitution

(Hilaire 1995). The problem with this approach was that it fostered inefficient production and produced uncompetitive products. In a local market that was tightly regulated and protected but buoyed up by high prices, this amounted to high-priced inferior merchandise. Consumers felt cheated and showed their displeasure through purchasing behaviour. Many local producers did not fare well, did not grow enough to achieve economies of scale and eventually folded. This was perhaps most evident in the processed food industry during the late 1980s when international oil prices collapsed. Due to the resulting foreign exchange shortage, import restrictions were imposed on non-essential/luxury food items. Many small local processors rushed to fill the gap with substitute products. Unfortunately, as soon as the restrictions had been lifted, consumers returned to the imported fare with gusto.

To understand this phenomenon, one must first distinguish between genuine local product development and import substitution. Building a sustainable development programme on the notion of import substitution is problematic at best. One would compete in a marketplace that major players have defined and controlled. Their standards, to the disadvantage of the new entrants, will certainly judge any new entrants. The imperative must be to create entirely new niches for local products and, it may be argued, based on the uniqueness of local cultural forms. There must be accompanying consumer education drives (recipes, cooking suggestions) to teach consumers how to utilize the new products. There is already a growing trend at some farmers' markets where farmers have been providing consumers with this type of information. The consumers must be sold on the idea of truly local products. As has been previously mentioned, imported foodstuffs have been the go-to option since the inception of this country. To move forward, this mindset must be eliminated. The notion of "make it and the people must buy" has never worked and simply will not work, especially in the present "open" marketplace where the consumer is exposed to and bombarded by a myriad of imported options. "Voluntary changes" in food and agriculture will not be easily achieved under these conditions. Active change management is mandatory.

Local food production is, therefore, not without its challenges, but inclusive policy planning and participation in the process are essential to local brands, products and grassroots initiatives that seek to break the cycle of poverty in rural and fishing communities. Just as important is the need to educate people on the importance of supporting the production, processing and consumption of healthy, wholesome, affordable and available local food and beverages. What else can we, as private individuals, do? These issues call for vision and leadership, as well as harnessing resources, enthusiasm and will.

REFERENCES

Anon. 2017. *The State of Food Security and Nutrition in the World.* https://www.unicef.org/publications/files/. State of Food Security and Nutrition in the World 2017.pdf.

Beckford, C. L., and D.R. Campbell. 2013. *Domestic Food Production and Food Security in the Caribbean: Building Capacity and Strengthening Local Food Production Systems.* NY: Palgrave Macmillan.

Bekele, I., and W.G. Ganpat. 2015. "Education, Extension, and Training for Climate Change." In *Impacts of Climate Change on Food Security in Small Island Developing States*, edited by W.G. Ganpat and W.A.P. Isaac. Hershey, PA: IGI Global.

Bridgemohan, P. 2008. "Incubator Farms as a Sustainable Approach for 'Neo Farmers.'" The 44th Caribbean Food Crop Society Conference, University of Florida, Institute of Agriculture and Food Sciences, 13–17 July 2008

Bridgemohan, P., and W.A.P. Isaac. 2019. "Agricultural Diversification – A strategy out of the Economic Difficulties of the Sugarcane industry." In *Development, Political and Economic Difficulties in the Caribbean*, edited by A. Bissessar. NY: Palgrave Macmillan.

Brown, L.R. 1995. Who Will feed China?: Wake-up Call for a Small Planet. New York: W.W. Norton & Co.

Campbell, B.M., P. Thornton, R. Zougmore, P. van Asten, and L. Lipper. 2014. "Sustainable Intensification: What is its Role in Climate Smart Agriculture?" *Current Opinion in Environmental Sustainability* 8:39–43.

Campbell, B.M., S.J. Vermeulen, P.K. Aggarwal, C.C. Dolloff, E. Girvetz, A.M. Loboguerrero, J.R. Villegas, T. Rosenstock, L. Sebastian, P.K. Thornton, and E. Wollenberg. 2016. "Reducing Risks to Food Security from Climate Change." *Global Food Security* 11:34–43.

CARICOM. 2011. "Food Security in Caricom. Caricom view." Retrieved from http://www.caricom.org/jsp/communications/caricom_online_pubs/caricom_view_jul_2011.pdf.

Claxton, M. 2009. Ensuring Food Security; Mitigating Climate Change – Has CARICOM Made the Right Policy Choices? – Part 1: Food Security. 2009, https://www.alainet.org/images/claxton-has-caricom-made-the-right-policy-choices.pdf.

Daley, O., W.A.P. Isaac, A. John, R. Roopnarine, and K. Forde. 2022. "An assessment of the Impact of COVID-19 on Agri-Food Systems in Caribbean Small Island Developing States (SIDS)." *Front. Sustain. Food Syst.* 6:861570. doi: 10.3389/fsufs.2022.861570.

Demas, W.G. 1987. "Agricultural Diversification in the Caribbean Community: Some Issues." In *Caribbean Development Bank Statement to Board of Governors.* Grand Anse: Caribbean Development Bank.

Food and Agriculture Organization. 2013. "Praedial Larceny in the Caribbean." Issue Brief #3, July 2013.

———. Food and Agriculture Organization. 2018. "Food Loss Analysis: Causes and Solutions Case Study on the Tomato Value Chain in the Republic of Trinidad and Tobago." http://www.fao.org/3/I9592EN/i9592en.pdf.

Ganpat, W. G., and W.A.P. Isaac, ed. 2012. *Sustainable Food Production in the Caribbean*, vol. 1, edited by Wayne Ganpat and Wendy-Ann Isaac. Kingston, Jamaica: Ian Randle Publishers.

———. 2015. *Impacts of Climate Change on Food Security in Small Island Developing States.* Hershey, PA: IGI Global.

———. 2015. *Sustainable Food Production in the Caribbean*, vol. 2. Kingston, Jamaica: Ian Randle Publishers.

———. 2017. *Environmental Sustainability and Climate Change Adaptation Strategies.* Hershey, PA: IGI Global.

———.2019. "Facing Boldly the Scourge of Praedial Larceny on Food Production in the Caribbean." *Journal of International Agricultural and Extension Education* 24 (4): 52–62.

Ganpat, W. G., R. Dyer, and W.A.P. Isaac, ed. 2017. *Agricultural Development and Food Security in Developing Nations.* Hershey, PA: IGI Global.

Hilaire, Alvin D.L. 1995. "Commercial Policy in Trinidad and Tobago." In *Insights into an Emerging Financial Structure: The Experience of Trinidad & Tobago*, edited by Ramesh Ramsaran, 1–52. St Augustine: University of the West Indies, Caribbean Centre for Monetary Studies.

Isaac, W.A.P., W.G. Ganpat, P. Bridgemohan, and M. Attzs. 2020. "Defining a Policy Nexus for Sustainable Agriculture and Food Security in the Caribbean Region." In *Global Climate Change: Resilient and Smart Agriculture*, edited by V. Venkatramanan, S. Shah and R. Prasad, 1–13. Springer Nature Singapore Pte Ltd.

Isaac, W.A.P., N. Felix, W.G. Ganpat, D. Saravanakumar, and J. Churaman. 2019. "Sustainable Climate-smart Agricultural Solutions to Improve Food and

Nutrition Security in Trinidad and Tobago." In *Development, Political and Economic Difficulties in the Caribbean*, edited by Ann Marie Bissessar, PAGE NUMBERS. NY: Palgrave Macmillan.

Isaac, W.A.P., M. Joseph, W.G. Ganpat, and R.A.I. Brathwaite. 2012. "The Caribbean's Windward Islands Banana Industry: A Heritage of Dependency." *The Journal of Rural and Community Development* 7(2): 98–117.

Isaac, W.A.P., W.G. Ganpat, and M. Joseph. 2017. "Farm Security for Food Security: Dealing with Farm Theft in the Caribbean Region." In *Agricultural Development and Food Security in Developing Nations*, edited by W. Ganpat, R. Dyer, and W.A. P. Isaac, 300–319. Hershey, PA: IGI Publications.

Little, D. 2011. "Praedial Larceny: Its Consequences for Caribbean Agriculture: Caricom View." http://www.caricom.org/jsp/communications/caricom_online_pubs/caricom_view_jul_2011.pdf.

Mac Clean, S. 2013. "Trade Policy and Strategy for Trinidad and Tobago, 2013–2017 (Vol. 53)." Retrieved from http://www.publish.csiro.au/?paper=ANv53n1to.

Moya, R., A. Mohammed, and S. Sookram. 2010. "Productive Development Policies in Trinidad and Tobago: A Critical Review." IDB working paper series: 115. Inter-American Development Bank.

Pingali, P.L., and M.W. Rosegrant. 1991. "Agricultural Commercialization and Diversification: Processes and Policies." *Food Policy* 20 (3): 171–86.

Shik, O., R.A. Boyce, C.P. De Salvo, and J.J. Egas. 2018. *Analysis of Agricultural Policies in Trinidad and Tobago*. IDB Monograph. 576.

Wilson, L.A., and I. Bekele. 1998. "Models for Caribbean Agricultural Diversification." *Mimeo*, 24.

The World Bank. 2016. "Doing Business 2016: Measuring Regulatory Quality and Efficiency." Washington, DC. http://doi.org/10.1596/978-1-4648-0667-4.

Wuddivira, M.N., V. de Gannes, G. Meerdink, N. Dalrymple, and S. Henry. 2017. "Challenges of Food and Nutrition Security in the Caribbean." In *Challenges and Opportunities for Food and Nutrition Security in the Americas: The View of the Academies of Science*. IANAS Regional Report, 2017, http://www.ianas.org/docs/books/Challenges_Opportunities.html.

[CHAPTER 3]

Health and Healthcare in the Sixty Years Post-independence in Trinidad and Tobago

ANJANI SHARMA, KESHAN RAMNARINE AND SURUJPAL TEELUCKSINGH

INTRODUCTION

This chapter gives comprehensive coverage of the evolution and expansion of sixty years of healthcare in Trinidad and Tobago. It identifies the significant progress made and shows where Trinidad and Tobago stands in some key indicators when compared with Barbados, Jamaica and Guyana. The chapter looks at investment, structural changes and expansion over the years. It assesses where Trinidad and Tobago stands, the relationship between public healthcare and private healthcare, and the possibilities for mutual value added. It also looks at the evolution of education in supporting healthcare, the research that has emerged related to health issues and the significant impact that both educational institutions and medical research have had on the quality of healthcare. The authors also outline a model of transformative intervention in healthcare delivery for diabetes, beginning with the pregnancy of the mother with the capacity for treating an individual newborn over a lifetime. It closes by identifying healthcare triumphs, as well as areas which can benefit from improvement.

HEALTHCARE ORGANIZATION AND DEVELOPMENT IN TRINIDAD AND TOBAGO

The progress and development of healthcare in Trinidad and Tobago have been steady and quite remarkable over the past sixty years. Since independence in 1962, the landscape for population health has changed for a number of reasons, including economic growth, population shifts internally, migration, influence by other healthcare systems post-colonialism, population heterogeneity and the epidemiologic transition from acute infectious diseases to chronic non-communicable disorders and from under-nutrition to overweight and obesity.

The history of healthcare delivery in Trinidad and Tobago is tied to its colonial history and is worthy of brief analysis as a background. Healthcare in Trinidad and Tobago developed pre-independence as a direct result of the sugar industry, for which this colony of the British West Indies was so valued throughout Europe. The highly profitable industry was served initially by slave labour and, after emancipation in 1834, by the Chinese and later the more dominant Indian indentured labour. Between 1845 and 1917, the ethnic landscape of Trinidad and Tobago was altered dramatically by the introduction of over one hundred and forty thousand immigrant labourers from the Indian sub-continent to the islands (Caribbean Atlas 2013; Hezekiah 1989). These settlers lived mainly in the rural areas (where the sugar plantations were based) while the emancipated local black population shifted to urban areas.

The healthcare system was initially designed to service the healthcare needs of the European settlers and, secondarily, the local population, depending on their social status, with the focus being on curative health (Sastre et al. 2014). The services were extended to the labourers when poor living conditions, high morbidity, mortality and infant mortality began to threaten the workforce. At first, these labourers were looked after by medical practitioners who the plantation owners hired. However, by 1875, attempts were being made to establish a medical service for labourers and the poor. In recognition of the environmental conditions affecting health, including the impact of tropical diseases, public health legislation was passed in 1892 for the Better Protection of Public Health, representing the early roots of this area of medicine (Hezekiah 1989).

Through the early days of colonialism, the social structure in Trinidad and Tobago consisted mainly of two tiers: high-status plantation owners and low-status black and indentured labourers. As the country developed post-emancipation, the differences between the two main ethnic groups became more apparent, with language, culture, religion and social organization being further alienating factors. East Indians remained in the rural areas, receiving medical care from what was provided on the estates by their employers, and the black population migrated to urban areas and received healthcare from what was available in the developing public system (Hezekiah 1989).

By the time of the insurrections in the West Indian colonies in the 1930s, the health and social disparities of the working-class population were in striking contrast when compared to the high profitability of the sugar and oil industries and the health and social welfare of the wealthy landowners/expatriates who benefited from it (Besson 2019). Vector-borne and communicable diseases such as malaria, yellow fever, hookworm and tuberculosis were major causes of death and disability among the working class, who lived in overcrowded housing and under unsanitary conditions. Consequently, the plantation economy began to break down, and trade unions and labour movements began to form to represent the needs of the working class and address their working, social and medical welfare. The post-war period was thus defined by the unification of the population towards independence from colonialism, which intensified to the point of independence in 1962.

There was an enormous task ahead to systematize the country towards social, economic and political progress as an independent nation. The existing structures for governance (civil service, public administration), handed over to the now independent leadership, were developed by the predecessors under the colonial system and reflected a British organizational system. Top positions in the administration were thus filled by local intellectuals, but beyond this, positions of responsibility were generally occupied by personnel who lacked experience and expertise. This also extended to the healthcare system, where demand was exceeded by the available experienced providers, and shortages in human resources, facilities and equipment meant that healthcare delivery was fragmented, unsystematic, not standardized and underprepared (Bahall 2012).

The years following independence saw an overhaul in economic, educational and health planning. Three consecutive five-year economic Development Plans were implemented, paying attention to the historical importance of good healthcare, access to healthcare and living conditions for societal well-being and productivity. The newly independent nation placed emphasis on expanding healthcare facilities and training healthcare professionals and finding a way to fund these endeavours (Hezekiah 1989).

Through membership with the Organization of American States in 1967, there was access to loans from the IADB (Inter-American Development Bank), which financed projects and provided technical assistance in the fields of agriculture, sanitation, education, transport and urban development. Other sources of funds for national development included oil company revenues, the Pan American Health Organization (PAHO) and the Canadian International Development Agency. These funding sources continue to benefit health and social developmental projects to this day, as plans for diversification of the energy and tourism sectors to deal with the loss of revenue from fossil fuel sources evolve.

Through improvements in standards of living, education and access to healthcare, by the mid-1960s, the infant mortality and death rates began to decline (figure 3.1), and chronic diseases such as diabetes, nutritional deficiencies and mental health issues placed a greater demand on the healthcare system (WHO n.d.c.). The period 1964–68 saw the implementation of The Health Plan as designed by the Ministry of Health (MoH), with technical assistance from PAHO/World Health Organization. It involved a national health situational assessment (including identifying technical and administrative problems), criteria for establishing health priorities, development of health policy and an implementation plan that included medical care, epidemiology and environmental health (Hezekiah 1989; Bahall 2012).

To prioritize health access, the MoH could expand coverage by constructing thirty-two suburban and rural health centres from 1974, providing health services to around two hundred thousand citizens who had inadequate access to medical care. The bolstering of primary and secondary healthcare services through training and recruitment of staff (0.45 physicians per 1,000 people in 1975; 4.48 physicians per 1,000 people in 2019; 2.98 nurses and midwives per 1,000 people in 1994; 4.26 nurses and midwives per 1,000 people in 2016) as well as construction of facilities continued throughout the 1970s and 1980s with the MoH and Ministry of Finance having a central role in health planning (7, 8). By 1978, the

Alma Ata declaration was signed, and primary health care was prioritized (promoted by WHO/PAHO) as a means to achieve Health for All by the year 2000 (Hezekiah 1989).

Post-independence growth (and its funding) in its first decade was initially slow, but Trinidad and Tobago saw a great surge in the economy with the increase in oil prices in the 1970s–80s. The oil boom moved the economy forward further from that of the previous sugarcane industry, substantially raising the living standards of the population. By 1982, the crude death rate was 7.7 per 1,000 population, the infant mortality rate was 32.2 per 1,000 live births and the life expectancy of 66.8 years (WHO n.d.c.; WHO n.d.a.; Macrotrends n.d.). By the mid-80s, there were 102 health centres providing healthcare, including health education, immunizations, child and maternal care and promotion of breastfeeding. Other areas of health, including dental, sexually transmitted disease management, Hansen's disease and tertiary healthcare (establishment of intensive care units), were underway using the allocated healthcare budget, which has represented between 3 and 7 per cent of the GDP, with dips for periods of economic recession in the late 1980–90s and 2000s.

Historically, health commissions have been employed to offer critique and evaluation of healthcare services in Trinidad and Tobago (e.g., Moyne Commission 1937; West India Royal Commission 1945). These have largely identified ongoing inequalities in healthcare access, inadequate funding and human resources, poor acquisition and upkeep of equipment, poor implementation of health policies and user dissatisfaction. In an effort to address these issues and improve performance (according to health indicators) and standards of care, the government decided to implement major health sector reforms in the 1990s. This resulted in the decentralization of the system of governance from the Ministry of Health (MoH) into the five Regional Health Authorities (four in Trinidad and one in Tobago) that exist today.

The Regional Health Authorities Act was enacted in 1994, establishing five Regional Health Authorities as independent, statutory bodies accountable to the Minister of Health for managing the healthcare needs of their local population. The RHA territories were divided to coincide with those of local governments (Regional Corporations) to ensure effective communication and synergy between these organizations in providing a range of health services to their catchment populations (PAHO 2001).

This was considered a move to democratize the health service, improve administrative efficiency and accountability, avoid limitations of national as opposed to localized planning, increase awareness and sensitivity to local challenges, reduce corruption and inequitable resource allocation, and improve the political and administrative dissemination of national policies (Bahall 2012). The ownership of publicly financed health facilities was transferred to the RHAs, and the act included provisions for the staff working in public facilities to transfer their employment to the RHAs.

The MoH retained centralized power for setting all matters of national framework, priorities and policy, with oversight for the allocated public funds to meet the population's health needs effectively. The MoH also established standards and monitored the achievement of these. The RHAs were tasked with managing the affairs of each region, with directives from a MoH-appointed board using a national framework based on the principles of health gain and needs assessment (PAHO 2021). The aim is that over time, RHA budgets would be representative of a more equitable allocation based on the population's health needs. This health sector reform transformed the role of the MoH and created new ones with the RHAs consistent with the government's overall strategy for improving public sector performance, particularly for reorganizing the Ministry of Social Development and strengthening local government initiatives. This resulted in massive strides during the 1990s in areas such as food programmes, mental health services, oral health, disability programmes, screening services (for cancer), more beds in hospitals, more out-patient clinics and further development of public health measures and environmental health precautions – all undertaken to improve quality of life in Trinidad and Tobago (PAHO n.d.).

The pre-existing structure of a two-tiered public/private health sector in Trinidad and Tobago also provided a further challenge to decentralization, requiring a robust legal and organizational framework aligned with human resources to prevent unfair competition, monopoly or collusion between the public and private sectors. This was an important consideration as many medical personnel in the public sector also work in the private sector. A feature of decentralization can include delegation of services to the private sector (including via public-private partnerships) in order to bridge the gap in services available in the public sector. An example is the External Patient Programme initiated in 2014 in Trinidad and Tobago.

This can include using the private sector for initiatives to address demands in the public sector (e.g., reducing operation waiting list backlog) or utilization of private services for equipment or expertise that are not available in the public sector. However, unless the services that are lacking in the public sector (which need to be outsourced) can be addressed alongside the outsourcing, a parallel stream of outsourcing will be created, which cannot be terminated due to dependence and which may not be sustainable in the long term.

For all its potential benefits, decentralization has been criticized for increasing management roles, creating conflict or ambiguity in some areas between MoH and RHA, providing a turf for political spoils and promoting a pendulum effect regarding programme development and implementation (Bahall 2012).

In some respects, healthcare development in Trinidad and Tobago may be considered forward-thinking and proactive as it includes a wide range of services for its users, which are all available free at the point of access in the public sector, running alongside private services provided either out of pocket or via insurance. Services available in the public sector include primary healthcare coverage across the twin islands, a national oncology programme, a public health laboratory, the chronic disease assistance programme (CDAP) programme (for accessing prescription drugs), Queens Park Counselling Centre and Clinic (STI management), a national organ transplant unit, national blood transfusion facilities, secondary and tertiary care for adults and paediatric patients, mental health in and outpatient care. Trinidad and Tobago also remains one of the Caribbean countries that has successfully decentralized its healthcare system.

For all the strides forward, in 2000, the WHO commented that the strategies and goals of the Trinidad and Tobago healthcare system were lacking in consistency and delivery, which mainly affected those in lower socio-economic groups (most in need of public services). Later that decade, the Gaffoor Commission in 2008 made several recommendations to align plans with recruitment and training in the health sector and optimize material, financial and human resources (Bahall 2012).

Since then, there has been greater attention paid to coordinating and upgrading services, equipment, management structure, training and human resources and research into the clinical and non-clinical aspects of healthcare. The overall shift over the past sixty years in major causes of morbidity and mortality has moved from communicable diseases and poor living conditions to lifestyle diseases (NCDs). The ongoing strategic planning and programme implementation by the MoH reflects this shift. Alongside measures to continue to improve access to healthcare and standards of care, current and future objectives specifically address the modifiable determinants of NCDs across the life course (population health education on diet and physical activity, programmes to address healthy diet in schools, initiatives to promote physical activity in young people and adults, health in pregnancy, smoking legislation, education and control). Funding for health planning and development continues to come from international sources (IADB, Canada, PAHO) as well as from a percentage of the GDP. However, there may be an opportunity to introduce taxation on unhealthy foods that can be used to subsidize health programmes in the future.

POPULATION HEALTH INDICES FOR TRINIDAD AND TOBAGO COMPARED WITH CARIBBEAN NEIGHBOURS

At the population level, indices like infant and maternal mortality, birth rate, death rate and life expectancy in Trinidad and Tobago have shown steady improvements. As shown in figure 3.1, infant mortality rate in Trinidad and Tobago has fallen from 56 deaths per 1,000 live births in 1960 to 14.8 deaths per 1,000 live births in 2020 and well below the global infant mortality rate of 29 deaths per 1,000 live births (World Bank n.d.c.; WHO n.d.a.). This steady improvement may be tied to medical factors but also to socio-economic and environmental factors (PAHO n.d.).

Improvements in maternal mortality have also been observed. Figure 3.2 outlines the decrease in maternal mortality rate in Trinidad and Tobago from 81 to 67 deaths per 100,000 live births during the period 2000–2017, already well below the desirable global threshold (World Bank n.d.b.; UNICEF n.d.). In so doing, Trinidad and Tobago has successfully managed to accomplish one of the Sustainable Development Goals of 2030, Goal 3.1, which states, "By 2030, reduce the global maternal mortality ratio to less than 70 per 100,000 live births" (United Nations in Trinidad and Tobago n.d.).

Birth rates have been undergoing a steady decline over the period from 1960 to 2019. Figure 3.3 depicts the birth rate of the Trinidad and Tobago population decreasing from 37.4 per 1,000 in 1960 to 12.6 per 1,000 in 2019.

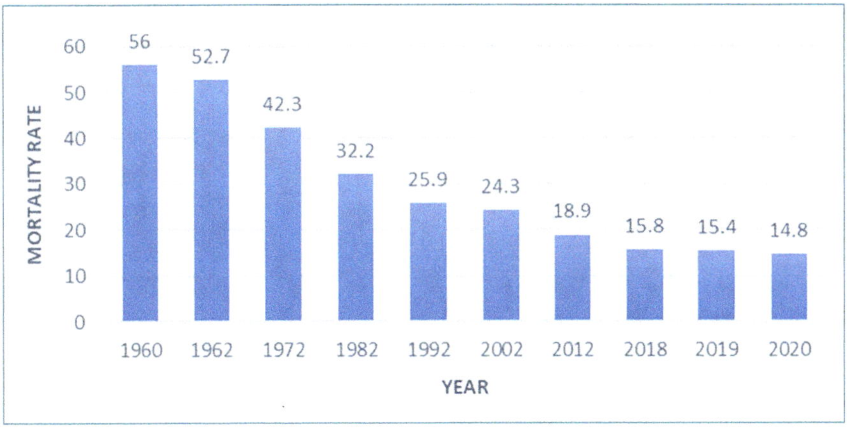

Figure 3.1: Infant Mortality Rate per 1,000 Live Births in Trinidad and Tobago

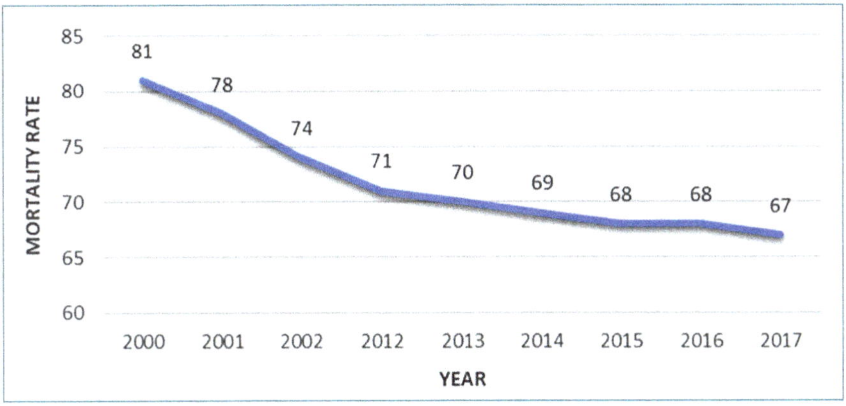

Figure 3.2: Maternal Mortality Rate Per 100, 000 Live Births in Trinidad and Tobago

The local and global trends in falling fertility rates have been attributed to the advancements in educational and employment opportunities for women, leading to delayed choices for pregnancy or postponement of childbearing (Oberhauser 2021).

Life expectancy in Trinidad and Tobago has improved from 61.9 years in 1960 to 73.7 years in 2020, as shown in figure 3.4 (Macrotrends n.d.; Roser et al. 2013). The increase in life expectancy from the 1960s is the consequence of improved medical, socio-economic and environmental factors that have occurred over the years.

The death rates in Trinidad and Tobago are outlined in figure 3.5 from 1960 to present. The trend is best described as starting at a rate of 9.19

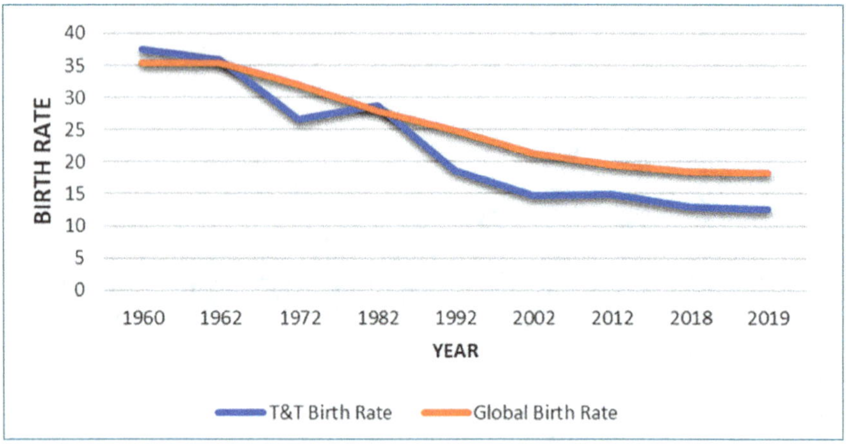

Figure 3.3: Birth Rate per 1,000 people in Trinidad and Tobago vs Global Birth Rate

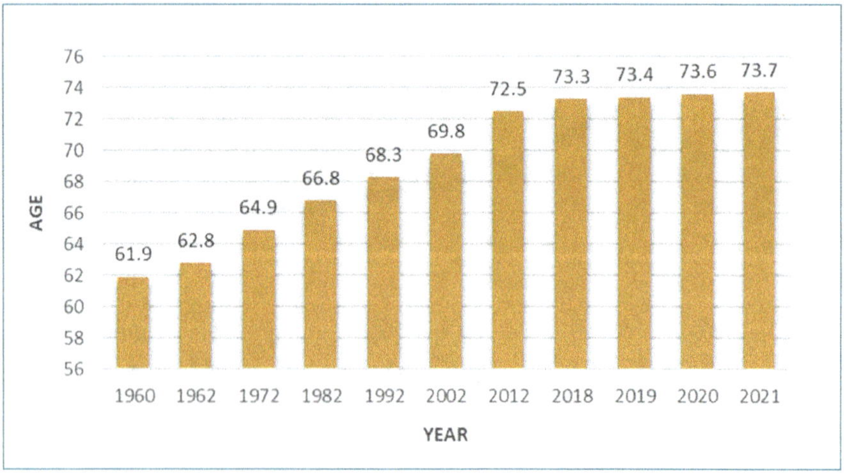

Figure 3.4: Life Expectancy in Trinidad and Tobago

deaths. In 1960, there were 9.19 deaths per 1,000 people, reaching a nadir of 7.47 in 1992, but this number later increased from 8.46 to 8.74 deaths per 1,000 persons during the period 2019 to 2021. More data and greater analysis are needed before firm conclusions, other than the obvious, about the impact of COVID-19 on the death rate in Trinidad and Tobago, given the high degree of uncertainty regarding the accuracy of reported cases both locally and globally (Ritchie et al. 2020).

The data from figure 3.6 were adapted from the *Lancet* 2020 (Vos et al. 2020). The leading cause of death reported in 2009 and 2019 remained

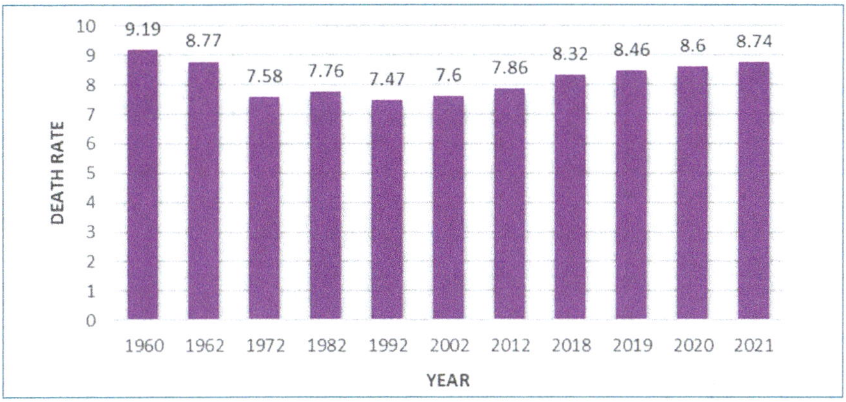

Figure 3.5: Death Rate in Trinidad and Tobago

consistent with ischemic heart disease in Trinidad and Tobago. These data are also consistent with the 2018 study published by the WHO, indicating that the leading cause of death in Trinidad and Tobago was cardiovascular disease. Table 3.1 involved a compilation of data from the "World Health Rankings" website, and, in summary, CHD is still the number one cause of death. In 1994, cardiovascular diseases (39.6 per cent) were the leading cause of death in Trinidad and Tobago, signalling this a longstanding problem burdening the Trinidad and Tobago population (PAHO n.d.).

The former British colonies (Jamaica, Barbados, Guyana) have been selected to compare population health statistical data. They all share the

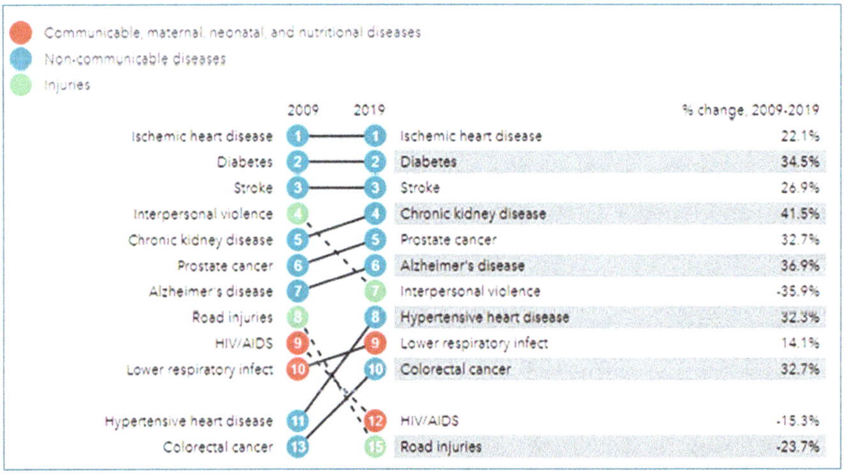

Figure 3.6: Top 10 Causes of Death in 2019 and Percentage Change for 2009–19 for All Ages in Trinidad and Tobago. *Source*: Adapted: Vos T. et al., *The Lancet* journal, published in 2020.

Table 3.1: Cause of Death in Trinidad and Tobago for the Period 2020–21

No.	Cause of Death in 2020	Number of Deaths	Cause of Death in 2021	Number of Deaths
1	Coronary Heart Disease	2,137	Coronary Heart Disease	4,274
2	Diabetes	1,859	Diabetes	3,719
3	Stroke	1,100	COVID-19	2,850
4	Violence	576	Stroke	2,201
5	Prostate Cancer	350	Violence	1,152
6	Influenza and Pneumonia	323	Prostate Cancer	700
7	Hypertension	290	Influenza and Pneumonia	646
8	HIV/AIDS	262	Hypertension	581
9	Kidney Disease	252	HIV/AIDS	525
10	Breast Cancer	235	Kidney Disease	504
17	COVID-19	127	–	–

impact of colonial history and gained independence in the same decade as Trinidad and Tobago (figures 3.7–3.11).

The infant mortality rates for the period 1960–2020 for Trinidad and Tobago, Barbados, Jamaica and Guyana are shown in figure 3.7. All countries show a steady decline in mortality rates, with Barbados depicting the most pronounced drop during the period 1962–2002 and Guyana having the highest rates consistently among the four countries. Birth rates among the four countries exhibit a similar downward trend over the last few decades, as illustrated in figure 3.8. Barbados appears to have the lowest birth rate. In contrast, Guyana has the highest birth rate, with the rates in Trinidad and Tobago and Jamaica fluctuating around their upper and lower counterpart countries.

Moreover, life expectancy in Barbados has progressively increased over the last sixty years, with the highest among the four countries at 79.4 years in 2021. Figure 3.9 shows that the life expectancy rates between Jamaica and Trinidad have been very similar over the years, with Jamaica consistently having a slightly higher rate than Trinidad and Tobago. While Guyana generally shows an increase in life expectancy, it still has the lowest age expectancy among the countries, at seventy years in 2021.

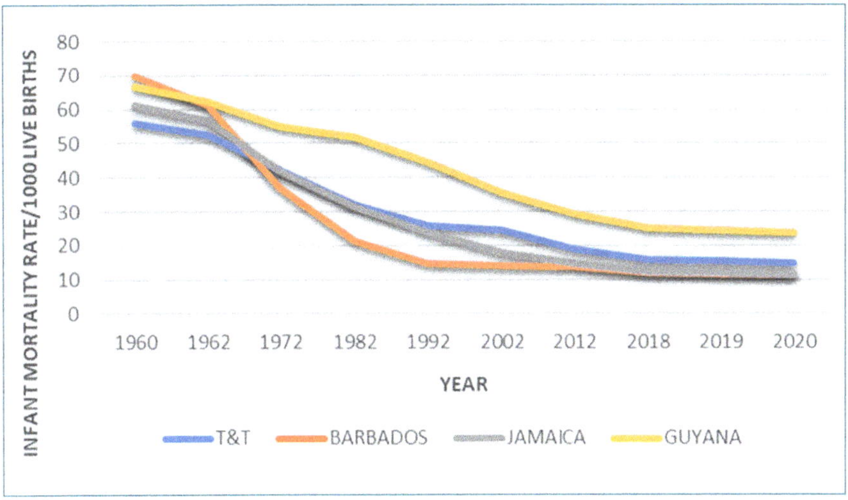

Figure 3.7: Infant Mortality Rate per 1,000 Live Births for Trinidad and Tobago, Barbados, Jamaica and Guyana

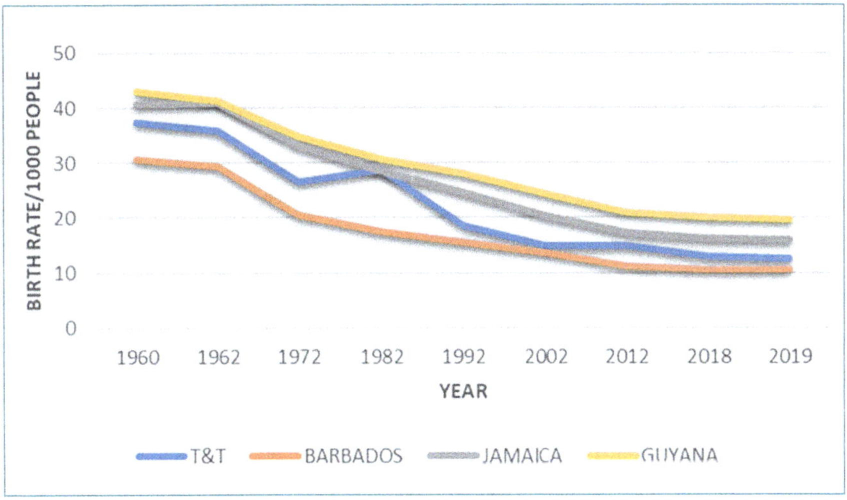

Figure 3.8: Birth Rate per 1,000 People for Trinidad and Tobago, Barbados, Jamaica and Guyana

Furthermore, as seen in figure 3.10, death rates have shown a peculiar pattern of mildly declining during the 1960s and 1990s and a slight increase from 1992 to 2021 for all four countries. Barbados, while having the lowest infant mortality and birth rates and highest life expectancy rates, has the highest crude death rate, at 9.17 deaths per 1,000 persons in 2021.

Perhaps the most striking statistic recorded was that of the maternal mortality rate for Guyana, recording the highest rate of 169 per 100,000

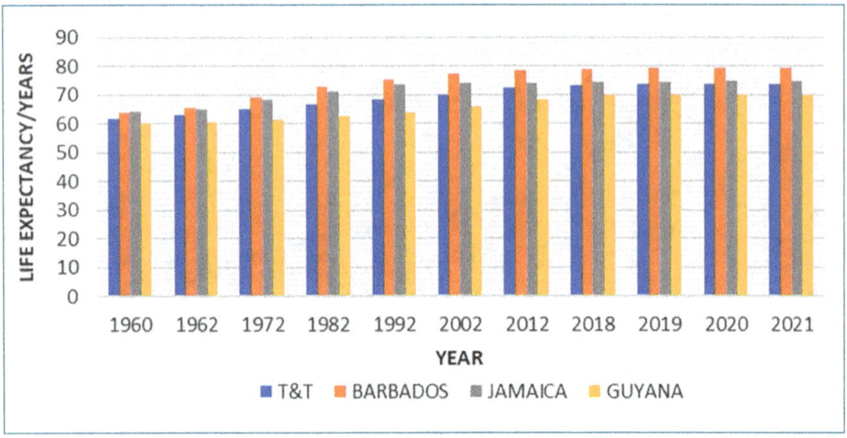

Figure 3.9: Life Expectancy for Trinidad and Tobago, Barbados, Jamaica and Guyana

live births. In contrast, Barbados recorded the lowest rate at 27 per 100,000 live births in 2017 (figure 3.11). As indicated in the SDG 3.1 for maternal mortality rate, Barbados and Trinidad and Tobago are below the threshold of 70 per 100,000 live births, with Jamaica and Guyana still above. The newly found oil in Guyana will impact that country's socio-economic structure and what consequences this will have on improvements is left to be seen. As indicated in the SDG 3.1 for maternal mortality rate, Barbados and Trinidad and Tobago are below the threshold of 70 per 100,000 live births, with Jamaica and Guyana still above the desired landmark (United Nations in Trinidad and Tobago n.d.).

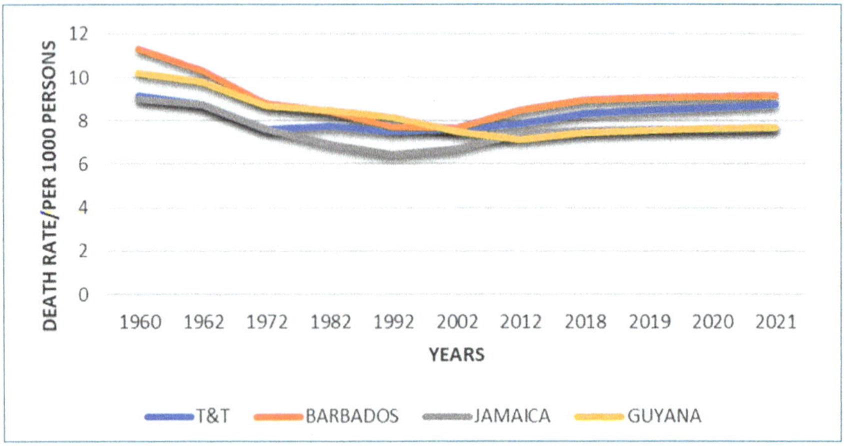

Figure 3.10: Crude Death Rate for Trinidad and Tobago, Barbados, Jamaica and Guyana

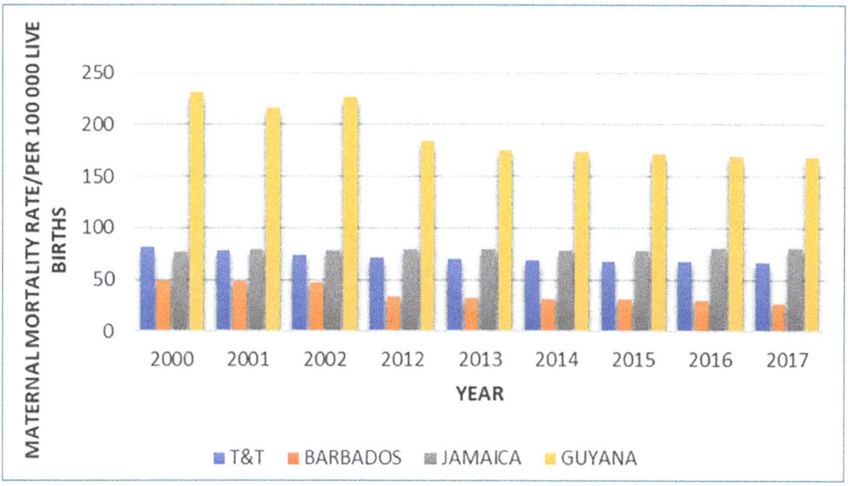

Figure 3.11: Maternal Mortality Rate for Trinidad and Tobago, Barbados, Jamaica and Guyana

The leading causes of mortality and morbidity among Trinidad and Tobago, Barbados, Jamaica and Guyana are quite similar to cardiovascular disease (CVD) in the lead, as shown in table 3.2. This is not surprising given the common antecedents in all territories, including harmful alcohol use, lack of physical inactivity, high salt intake, tobacco use, elevated blood pressure, obesity and diabetes as it has been for the last five decades.

Notwithstanding the similarities in origins and, to a large extent, outcomes, it should be noted that the healthcare system in Barbados compares most favourably against its counterparts in terms of access to healthcare, (lowest) infant and maternal mortality and (highest) life expectancy (Macrotrend n.d.b.).

Table 3.2: Cause of Death for Trinidad and Tobago, Barbados, Jamaica and Guyana for 2016

Disease	Trinidad & Tobago %	Barbados %	Jamaica %	Guyana %
CVD (Cardiovascular Diseases)	33	29	30	34
Cancers	15	23	20	8
Respiratory Diseases	3	4	3	3
Diabetes	15	9	12	8
Communicable Diseases / Maternal / Perinatal / Nutritional Conditions	9	13	11	20

Source: Adapted from WHO

Demographic Changes

The population of Trinidad and Tobago is currently estimated at around 1.368 million (CSO, Trinidad and Tobago from 2011 census). There has been a slow but gradual population growth over time from 1962 to the present despite a declining fertility rate. The population structure of Trinidad and Tobago has also changed in this time, reflecting an overall increase in life expectancy from 62.76 years in 1962 to 73.79 years in both sexes by 2020 (UN projections, Macrotrends 2022). Still, the population pyramid has changed from an expanding population in 1960 to one that is contracting in 2020, with 71 per cent of the population being between fifteen and sixty-four years old. Apart from a decline in fertility rate, emigration (to the United States, Canada and the United Kingdom) may also contribute to this picture.

Currently, approximately 52 per cent of the population live in urban areas, with subtle changes in ethnic diversity over time, but overall, the main ethnic groups consist of African and Indian descent, followed by mixed, White, Chinese and Syrian/Lebanese (table 3.3). This ethnic makeup has a direct impact on the susceptibility of the population to chronic NCDs, such as diabetes, heart disease and hypertension, as do the cultural influences that impact dietary tastes and preferences, engagement in physical activity and propensity for a sedentary lifestyle. The tropical climate in Trinidad also brings with it risks of endemic diseases, such as dengue and influenza, which must also be taken into consideration.

To address vector-borne diseases, the MoH has a dedicated "insect vector control" arm. This arm provides health education to the public regarding protection from bites and the reduction of sources for insects to breed; it also coordinates insecticide spraying in local areas. Due to inconsistencies in access to potable water across Trinidad and Tobago, water collection in tanks or storage containers is commonplace. This provides a source for the vector, and the healthcare system has found a preventative way to manage this issue.

In relation to communicable and vaccine-preventable diseases, the MoH has established the EPI unit (extended programme of immunizations), which supplies, coordinates and educates the public on childhood and adult vaccinations, including the annual flu vaccine.

In March 2019, Trinidad and Tobago joined the rest of the world in recording the presence of COVID-19, marking the beginning of the

Table 3.3: Population Ethnicity over Pre- and Post-independence for Trinidad and Tobago

Ethnic Group	Census 1946 (Number)	Census 1946 (%)	Census 1960 (Number)	Census 1960 (%)	Census 1980 (Number)	Census 1980 (%)	Census 1990 (Number)	Census 1990 (%)	Census 2000 (Number)	Census 2000 (%)	Census 2011 (Number)	Census 2011 (%)
Indian	195,747	35.1	301,946	36.5	426,660	40.3	453,069	40.3	446,273	40	470,524	37.6
African	261,485	46.9	358,588	43.3	434,730	41.1	445,444	39.6	418,268	37.5	452,536	36.3
Mixed	78,775	14.1	134,749	16.3	175,150	16.5	207,558	18.4	228,089	20.5	301,866	24.2
White	15,283	2.7	15,718	1.9	9,850	0.9	7,254	0.6	7,034	0.6	7,832	0.63
Chinese	5,641	1	8,361	1	5,670	0.5	4,314	0.4	3,800	0.3	4,003	0.3
Amerindian	–	–	–	–	–	–	–	–	–	–	1,394	0.1
Syrian, Lebanese, Arab	889	0.2	1,590	0.2	1,010	0.1	934	0.1	849	0.1	1,029	0.2
Other	6,714	0.8	2,900	0.3	1,724	0.2	1,972	0.2	2,280	0.2	5,472	0.4
Unknown	150	0	291	0	2,350	0.2	4,831	0.4	8,487	0.8	5,472	0.4
Total	**557,970**	**100**	**827,957**	**100**	**1,058,320**	**100**	**1,125,128**	**100**	**1,114,772**	**100**	**1,322,546**	**100**

pandemic. As with most countries globally, the approach was kept in the hands of the CMO, and public health measures were used to contain the spread. A "lockdown" of the country was initiated in April 2020, which included the closure of air and seaports. People were asked to stay home in order to prevent contact and movement between individuals; only persons whose jobs or roles were considered "essential" had freer movement outdoors. There was a ban on people going outside of their homes, as well as on people meeting. Businesses and schools were closed, with online access being the main means of communication.

Within a short time, there were health education initiatives on hand washing, sanitizing and mask-wearing. Information was shared with the public via daily state TV and radio updates directly from the MoH and (CMO or representative) and a dedicated telephone "COVID hotline". Protocols were also in place early on to identify and manage potential cases and contacts. In the early stages, this was done by means of state quarantine and testing; it has progressed over time to self-testing and home quarantine. This was chiefly to control infectious spread and to address the pressure placed on health services.

The pandemic had both direct and indirect effects on health and mental health. Persons affected with NCDs who were stable or well-controlled saw their conditions deteriorate. This was due to a number of factors, including reduced access to appointments for chronic care, fear in vulnerable patients to leave their homes, availability and then concern about the COVID-19 vaccinations, inability to source medications (pharmacy shortages, affordability or limitations in the ability of families and care network to continue to offer support), reduced physical activity, isolation. Presentation for other acute or critical conditions may have been delayed due to concerns over exposure to the COVID-19 virus.

The impact of the COVID-19 pandemic on the death rate was profound, with a 2,100 per cent increase in COVID-related deaths in Trinidad and Tobago. The numbers rose further, from 127 in December 2020 to 2,850 in December 2021. There was a 100 per cent increase in both diabetes- and stroke-related deaths between 2020 and 2021. During the pandemic, there was also an increase in violence and cancer-related deaths compared with pre-pandemic levels. While government policies are organized to mitigate the socio-economic, environmental and medical limitations brought on by COVID-19, more needs to be done to reduce the mortality of those diagnosed with chronic diseases like coronary heart disease, diabetes mellitus, hypertension, kidney disease and cancers.

Investments in Trinidad and Tobago Health Sector

For the Fiscal Year 2019/2020, Trinidad and Tobago's health sector received the third-highest allotment of the nation's budget at $6.08 bn TTD ($898.9m USD) (Oxford Business Group 2020). Healthcare in Trinidad and Tobago post-independence has been extremely transformational. Improvements in hospital infrastructure, construction of newer hospitals and enhanced diagnostic equipment are among the developments that showcase the utilization of resources to continually provide quality medical services to Trinbagonians.

In addition to the information presented in table 3.4, the Ministry of Health in Trinidad and Tobago released a Budget Summary for the year 2021 outlining their "Public Sector Investment Programme 2020 – Projections", with the main findings as follows:

Table 3.4: Major Recent Projects and Achievements Made by the Government Towards the Health Sector

INFRASTRUCTURE	BUDGET/$TTD	DETAILS
Arima Hospital	1.5 bn	• Completion by March 2020 • 150 beds • Estimated to serve 250,000 persons
Port of Spain General Hospital	1.1 bn	• Completion by January 2022 • 540 beds • Estimated to serve 400,000 persons • Updated radiology, laboratory and pharmacy services
Point Fortin Hospital	1.2 bn	• Completion by March 2020 • 100 beds • Estimated to serve 75,000 persons
Sangre Grande Hospital	1.2 bn	• Completion by 2021–22 • Better service to persons in the rural areas of eastern Trinidad
Roxborough Hospital Tobago	60 m	• Completion by 2021
St. James Medical Complex	45 m	• Upgrade of facilities with new cancer centre

Table 3.4 continues

Table 3.4: (*cont'd*)

INFRASTRUCTURE	BUDGET/$TTD	DETAILS
Diego Martin Health Centre	8.6 m	• Upgrade of facilities
Couva Medical and Multi-Training Facility	No information	• 230 beds • 30 dialysis chairs • 2 vitreo-retinal machines (eye surgery) • Catheterization lab – angiograms and angioplasty
Medical Equipment Upgrade	34 m	• Update equipment in hospitals across the country: Initiated in 2018
Hospital Refurbishment Programme	25 m	• Refurbishment of hospital infrastructures
Modernization through digitization of medical centres	5 m	• Electronic medical records system in Arima and Point Fortin Hospital

Figure 3.12 depicts a generally increasing trend in the percentage of the national budget allocated to the health sector in Trinidad and Tobago, with 2021 receiving the highest allocation of 9.2 per cent.

A comparison of health expenditure across the English-speaking former British Empire Caribbean countries, as mentioned previously, is shown in figure 3.13 (GDP per capita for health expenditure for Trinidad and Tobago, Barbados, Jamaica and Guyana). Barbados has consistently spent more on health per capita than any other territory, which may, in turn, explain the advantageous position it has held over its Caribbean neighbours, as described earlier in this chapter. Trinidad and Tobago had a steady increase in GDP throughout the years, reporting the highest among the four countries in 2019 at US$1167.93. It remains to be seen if these recent increased investments in health will lead to improved outcomes through efficient use of the increased allocations. Guyana and Jamaica still lag, with Guyana having the lowest GDP for healthcare expenditure in 2019 at US$325.89.

Trinidad and Tobago has seen a massive increase in investments and projects around the country within the healthcare sector (2014–21), as shown in tables 3.5 and 3.6 and figures 3.12 and 3.13. Therefore, increased GDP per capita for health expenditure is strongly associated with increases in capital investments indicated for Trinidad and Tobago. Advocates for increased expenditure in healthcare are well supported by empirical data, which show that an increase in expenditure in the healthcare sector contributes to a

Table 3.5: Public Sector Investment Programme 2020 Summary Projections

PROJECT	ACTIVITIES
New Public Health (PH) Facilities	• $55 m – Continued construction of Sangre Grande Hospital • $4 m – Diego Martin Health Centre completion
Improved PH Infrastructure	• $50 m Budget • Expansion of Toco Health Centre • Expansion of A&E Department at POSGH • Hospital equipment upgrade at Caura Hospital
Medical Equipment Upgrade	• $50 m budget • 3 anaesthetic machines for POSGH • 65 beds for St James Hospital • Bronchoscope System for SFGH • 13 multi-gas monitors and 13 anaesthetic machines for ORs in SFGH

Table 3.6: Major Programmes and Development for the Period 2019–21

Code	Projects	2018 Actual	2019 Actual	2020 Revised Estimate	2021 Estimate
CF 004-07D-003	Special Programme – Renal Dialysis	42,519,150	43,366,410	40,000,000	100,000,000
CF 005-06C-250	Health Services Support Programme	3,752,469	11,353,634	20,000,000	60,600,000
CF 004-07A-001	Medical Equipment Upgrade Programme	37,631,499	18,641,544	55,000,000	50,000,000
CF 004-07D-002	Special Programme – Treatment of Adult Cardiac Disease	19,981,823	19,572,616	18,300,000	35,000,000
CF 005-06C-234	Hospital Refurbishment Programme	23,512,335	26,324,044	25,000,000	35,000,000
IDF-004-07F-007	Construction of the Sangre Grande Hospital	–	–	22,134,726	55,000,000
IDF-004-07F-001	Physical Investments (Hospitals, District Health Facilities, Health Centres)	45,760,591	66,928,687	20,000,000	50,000,000

Table 3.6 continues

Code	Projects	2018 Actual	2019 Actual	2020 Revised Estimate	2021 Estimate
IDF-004-07F-010	Operationalization of the Couva Medical and Multi-Training Facility and the San Fernando General Hospital	–	–	–	45,000,000
IDF-004-07F-004	Construction of the Arima Hospital	118,364,495	86,237,121	76,861,394	36,000,000
IDF-004-07F-005	Construction of the Point Fortin Hospital	41,136,043	51,614,033	47,000,000	20,000,000
IDF-005-06F-003	Re-Development of Port of Spain General Hospital	–	20,313,800	60,000,000	–

Source: Adapted from: Budget Summary 2021, page 56 – A summary of the Ministry's expenditure, divisions and projects – Head 28 – Ministry of Health – Financial Scrutiny Unit – Office of the Parliament of Trinidad and Tobago

promotion of the factors of production. In the final analysis, it is imperative to comprehend that GDP per capita for health expenditure may appear to be inflated as healthcare expenditure increases (as seen in Trinidad and Tobago). However, this concept may be misleading in certain circumstances as it is backed by increased expenditures as opposed to greater efficiency of existing resource utilization, in keeping with the factors of production on GDP (WHO n.d.a.; Raghupathi 2020).

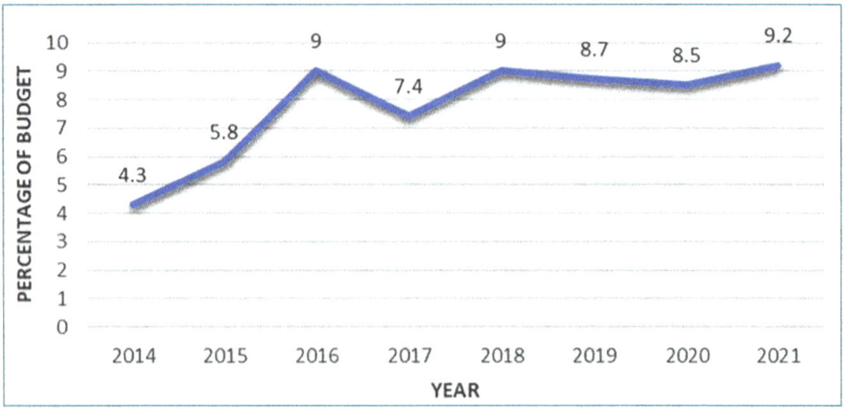

Figure 3.12: Percentage of National Budget Allocated to Health Sector

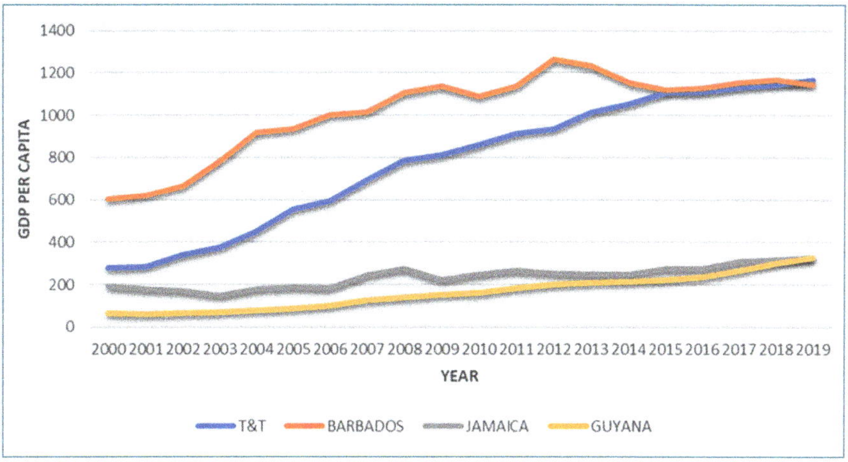

Figure 3.13: GDP per capita for Current Health Expenditure (USD) for Trinidad and Tobago, Barbados, Jamaica and Guyana

Medical Board of Trinidad and Tobago

In 1797, the British took over colonial rule of the island of Trinidad from the Spanish, and soon thereafter, the twin island territory of Trinidad and Tobago became established until Crown rule, with the British governor overseeing the colony. One of the notable legacies of this was the establishment of the Medical Board of Trinidad and Tobago (MBTT) by proclamation of Governor Woodford in 1813, a first for the entire region if not the hemisphere and one that has endured. Indeed, the MBTT announced the establishment of its equivalent in Britain, the General Medical Council of The United Kingdom, by more than half a century. Unfortunately, like many colonial structures, the failure of adaptation has created an illusion of irrelevance in the mind of the public (MBTT n.d.). The MBTT, for a long time, was populated by "members", for which membership for life was obtained once registration was obtained. Up to 2007, it was completely managed by doctors and could have created the impression that it was prone to serve the needs of doctors rather than the public's interest. It is exceptional to identify cases where the MBTT may have appeared to serve a larger public purpose. In this regard, the inclusion of non-medical members on the executive since 2007 and with more recent strategic plans to modernize the operations of the MBTT should serve the profession and the wider public far better in the future (Medical Professionals Association of Trinidad and Tobago n.d.).

Trinidad and Tobago Medical Association: Non-governmental Participation

The Trinidad and Tobago Medical Association (TTMA) was initially an outpost of its British counterpart, The British Medical Association, but became autonomous in 1974 through an act of Parliament. Its core mission is to "teach, treat, mentor and advocate". Over the years, the TTMA has grown into a vibrant organization which has lived up to its tenets of advocacy and continuous professional education of its membership. It is the only fully accredited provider of continuous international professional development credits for local, regional and international courses, as well as scientific and educational meetings. This accreditation is with the American Academy of Continuous Medical Education, the body that accredits WHO and PAHO courses. The TTMA is also accredited by the Accreditation Council of Trinidad and Tobago. The TTMA has five branches throughout Trinidad and Tobago and serves as an important conduit for transferring the latest scientific data into medical practice through its many meetings throughout the year. Its flagship Annual Medical Research Conference is, despite the COVID pandemic, now in its twenty-eight year.

The University of the West Indies

Before 1948, training in the medical profession required distant travel to Europe, America, Canada and even to far-flung places such as India. The establishment of the Faculty of Medicine at Mona, Jamaica, improved access and opportunity for undertaking a long and tedious journey to becoming a doctor. In 1967, there was a huge leap with the introduction of the Eastern Caribbean Medical Scheme, when nationals could return to Port of Spain General Hospital to complete the fifth year and final year of medical education. Soon thereafter, the option of a fourth-year training also emerged. The biggest boon, however, was the establishment of a local medical school in 1989, where the full curriculum could be delivered at the newly commissioned medical training complex and teaching hospital at Mt Hope (The Faculty of Medical Sciences n.d.). Since then, thousands of doctors and an increasing number of nurses, laboratory technicians, pharmacists and scientists interested in healthcare delivery and research have been released into society. It remains an unfortunate reality, however, that retention of the brightest and best is a matter of great concern, as well-trained medical personnel continue to haemorrhage out of the local system for many reasons: financial, social (crime and criminality), academic stimulation and poor recruitment and reward strategies by local health authorities.

COSTAATT

In order to ensure a bank of well-trained professionals to support local services whilst enhancing social equity and economic diversification, The College of Science, Technology and Applied Arts of Trinidad and Tobago was established in October 2000. It is one of the largest providers of tertiary education to the public, providing academic opportunities to all interested citizens, including medical laboratory technology, nursing and radiography. Further communication and alignment of these opportunities with local healthcare bodies in order to promote recruitment and training, allowing for internships, would be beneficial to the training institution, trainees and service providers.

Healthcare and the Private Sector

Healthcare is a commodity that is not exempt from market forces, and the demand for private care has grown exponentially. A number of factors have driven this response. To begin with, quality and quality systems are lacking in the traditional delivery of public care. Attitudes are poor, and morale is low. Communication techniques do not cater for those in pain or fear. Waiting lists for elective procedures can be lengthy, and no amount of energy or initiative has adequately been able to address this ever-widening chasm.

In 2017, there were eleven hospitals, over one hundred nursing homes, a multitude of general practitioners and over three hundred pharmacies, laboratories and diagnostic centres in the private sector. There is an even greater number of unregistered facilities (including herbal, "traditional", or complementary health services), providing layers of care of variable types from clinical consultations to minor and major surgery, laboratory and radiological services to fill the increasing need. Alternative services are culturally acceptable in Trinidad and Tobago, especially considering that patients are willing to pay out of pocket for healthcare. This creates a demand, but if it remains unregulated can lead to clinical harm, misinformation and delayed or protracted courses of management.

In December 2019, when SARS-CoV-2 struck, the need for these services was exaggerated with the near suspension of most routine services. Even in cultures where socialized medicine has been long established, like the United Kingdom, SARS-CoV-2 produced the same consequence (Gov. UK n.d.; GM Journal n.d.).

The emergence of an unregulated private healthcare system emerges from opportunity, but there is danger without controls and standards. For this reason, private sector healthcare has been viewed for a long time with scepticism by officialdom. When, however, citizens choose private healthcare, they actively reduce the burden on the public purse, and this should be viewed favourably. The response of the government could be to strengthen its own systems for quality and standards and then use this referential power to ensure that citizens are well served by equally good systems wherever they may choose to obtain them (Gadsby Wick n.d.).

It is noteworthy that more than 30 per cent of citizens have private health insurance and use this to access healthcare from the private sector in Trinidad and Tobago or internationally. This is likely to remain so or become an area for further growth because cutting-edge tertiary care services are lacking in the government sector. Thus, high-end cardiac, urological, joint, neurosurgical and minimally invasive surgical procedures are routinely performed in private hospitals and are not available or readily accessible to the public. There are more active MRI and CT scanning centres in the private than the public sector, and the only PET scanner in Trinidad and Tobago is privately run. These, taken together, point to a lack of structure, planning or optimization of healthcare resources in the public sector.

MODEL OF A TRANSFORMATIVE INTERVENTION IN HEALTHCARE DELIVERY

Given the increasing scale and complexity of healthcare needs and the natural and perennial competing interests for the national budget, future interventions in healthcare delivery need to be designed in a way that addresses need, is robust enough to be sustained/repeated and provides value for money. Following is a proposed model based on the authors' own area of interest: diabetes mellitus (T2DM). This is a non-communicable chronic disease that stands to undermine many of the public health gains over the last six decades and requires actions through multiple channels across the life course in order to address.

In the simplest of terms, T2DM, being increasingly prevalent in Trinidad and Tobago for the past sixty years, has emerged in our population in synchrony with obesity, which currently affects more than two-thirds of the adult population of Trinidad and Tobago (UWI Today n.d.; Beckles 1986). Together, they accelerate the processes of ageing so that diseases of the elderly, like heart attacks, strokes, kidney failure, blindness and cancers, occur in middle age. Of even greater alarm, recent trends indicate an increasing frequency of disorders of ageing among those in their thirties and forties (CDC 2021). This is a result of the exponential increase in obesity rates among the nation's youth, which has tripled over the last two decades, and now half of all primary schoolchildren are either overweight or obese, with the concomitant increasing prevalence of early-onset T2DM (World Obesity n.d.; Baston et al. 2014; Baston et al. 2013). Taken together, obesity and diabetes contribute to more than half of all the diseases being treated locally. Left unchecked, the pressure on healthcare systems will be relentless and unsustainable.

The tenets of the strategy to target T2DM in Trinidad and Tobago utilize the life course theory, which seeks to identify the many factors from birth to death that shape and influence outcomes in an individual as well as the society (Hutchinson 2011). We now have good evidence that T2DM and obesity may be programmed in fetal life (Catalano 2010). The conceptual framework is, therefore, to identify and treat diabetes in pregnant women as early and aggressively as possible. The following steps were taken to undertake this gargantuan task. They are outlined below with some detail so that this approach may be utilized to deliver integrated care for any number of complex clinical or public health problems.

Step 1: Identify and Define the Target Clinical or Public Health Problem:

In this case, the target condition was HYPERGLYCEMIA IN PREGNANCY – identification and treatment of any degree of disturbed blood sugar during pregnancy.

T2DM was a natural target given its high prevalence, the availability of relatively cheap and safe screening and diagnostic tests, the availability of effective treatment options and the clear and proven benefits of intervention.

Screening for T2DM in pregnancy was much more of a contentious issue when this project was conceived in 2014. There was still uncertainty over the choice of screening test, the standards for diagnosis and even the benefits of treatment. To overcome these barriers, we decided to tackle this problem by convening a group of local experts to obtain CONSENSUS.

Step 2: Consensus

This is not always easy to achieve, so it is helpful to provide high-quality local data to support the proposed interventions. This can then be supported by internationally accepted consensus statements. In this case, the authors convened a consensus group comprising a cross-section of practitioners and interested clinicians, at which data were provided for rational decision-making. Consensus, once achieved, was then shared widely and used to inform public policy (Baird 1970).

Step 3: Policy

Obtaining local consensus was crucial and provided the framework for influencing a policy position on SCREENING FOR, DIAGNOSING AND TREATING HYPERGLYCEMIA IN PREGNANCY and the elaboration of a clinical practice guideline (UWI Today n.d.b.).

Step 4: Execution

This is often the rate-limiting, albeit the most important step in the process. It has been shown that despite the immense value in creating clinical practice guidelines, adoption is all too often hampered if there are no interventions to create environmental changes or if there is a failure to provide the necessary supportive framework vis a vis training, re-training, staffing or technological inputs into the process.

We have found that the elements of a successful campaign to institute systems change should include at least the following key features.

a. *Case Reporting Instrument:* The clinical practice guideline should be accompanied by a clinical case report form. Interestingly, for many public health or clinical issues, such forms may already exist but may be lying fallow somewhere. In this case, the Pan American Health Organization had previously developed a working model of SIPS, a perinatal recording case report form. This allows clinicians, nurses and midwives to enter data in a standardized format in either or preferably a digital template. Having access to such an instrument is essential and, if pre-existing, saves considerable time and costs in rolling out the campaign.

b. *Information and Communication Platform:* This may have to be developed de novo, as in our case. Interestingly, the Ministry of Health has for some time now developed the framework for deploying an ICT system to facilitate healthcare delivery, but once again, adoption and rollout have been far too slow. In time, the hope is that the Hyperglycaemia in Pregnancy initiative may have broken the ice on this and will lead to more widespread adoption and utilization in the near future (Oxford Business Group 2020).

c. *Training/Retraining/Access to continued Professional Development:* In order to facilitate this limb of the intervention, a learning management system (LMS) was built de novo. This allows online and self-directed learning for all members of the medical and allied providers of care to pregnant women. The content is up-to-date, relevant and applicable to local needs. In addition, there is a mix of didactic, multimedia and interactive elements for engagement and learning. Another important aspect of achieving success with interventions is engaging all stakeholders. In this case, a key group is members of the public, so a strategy to engage their participation in the learning process and, thus, content and access has been designed. This is an additional tool to add to other traditional public engagement strategies (e.g., "advertising" via various media, information leaflets, workshops and discussions with healthcare professionals).

d. *Public Engagement and Participation:* As has been amply demonstrated with the rollout of the COVID-19 vaccination programme, here and elsewhere, when distrust or misinformation exists, there is grave danger for underachievement of even the most noble goals! The design and delivery of healthcare messaging using appropriate media and channels are of prime importance to eventual outcomes. This campaign will highlight the use of valid and reliable tests performed as close to the patient's residence as possible, using simple but effective measurement devices which relay data in real time through the ICT network. In addition, patients will be given blood glucose monitoring devices free of charge, from which individual blood glucose control data will become accessible to healthcare providers who can work with patients/clients to achieve blood glucose targets. The mechanisms described here will allow the integration of care among primary, secondary and tertiary levels, from the home to the local clinic and specialized hospital clinics to the delivery suite.

e. *Monitoring, Evaluation and Management Decision-Making*: Deriving timely and valid information will not only integrate care among the various strata of clinical care. Still, it will also provide pooled data for guiding service management decisions and evaluation of impact. Answers to questions like who needs the services and where they are most needed will become obvious, and outcomes for both mothers and babies will be readily ascertained. This provides at once the opportunity to establish a cohort beginning today and for all future generations of citizens for whom data, personal medical records and unique identifiers will exist from birth to the end of life till perpetuity.

HEALTH RESEARCH IN TRINIDAD AND TOBAGO

Health research is critical to making sure that the best care is provided for all in current and future practice. Designing, conducting, analysing and applying research is key to formulating best practices in healthcare on a global scale. Whether through clinical trials, equipment testing, surveys, questionnaires or data analysis, the knowledge gained helps to improve processes, healthcare delivery and standards of care.

In Trinidad and Tobago, inspired and brilliant individuals have had the foresight and motivation to do this in the local setting from an early stage and inspire others to take on the mantle.

Dr Theodosius Poon-King is one such individual. He is known for his groundbreaking work on diabetes, which began in the 1960s. He was also instrumental in eradicating acute nephritis and reducing the high incidence of rheumatic fever in Trinidad. For his world-famous research, he received several honours, including Trinidad and Tobago's Chaconia Medal (Gold) in 1975 (Icons n.d.).

Other notable healthcare professionals mentioned below have either trained and/or conducted seminal research supported by the University of the West Indies. These individuals continued their clinical or field-based practice whilst conducting innovative, internationally recognized research which ultimately defined aspects of healthcare service and delivery: Professor Courtney Bartholomew (medicine and HIV management); Professor Michael Beaubrun (Psychiatry and alcoholism); Professor Dave Chadee (Public Health: Entomology and Parasitology – vector-borne diseases and control – accredited as Most Published Scientist and Most Outstanding Researcher); Professor Vijay Naraynsingh (General and Vascular surgery); Professor Terence Seemungal (Respiratory medicine); Professor Dilip Dan (General surgery including surgical management of obesity) Dr Waveney Charles (General and paediatric haematology); Nita Barrow (Nursing and midwifery) (Icons n.d.).

Their passion, work ethic and dedication set the standards for healthcare professionals and have aided the development of sustainable programmes for continuing and promoting research in clinical practice. They have instilled its importance in both the clinical syllabus and ongoing professional development. Their contributions continue to have applications locally, regionally and globally.

National and international research collaborations between UWI and other researchers/organizations that have provided pioneering research with a role in informing health policy include:

a. Work with MoH and PAHO (Chronic Non Communicable Disease Risk Factor Survey 2012; Global School Health Survey – 3 rounds, last conducted in 2017); (PSI n.d.)

b. Ministry of Health, Anglia Ruskin University (National Eye Survey of Trinidad and Tobago 2014).
c. Johns Hopkins University (Trinidad and Tobago Health Sciences Initiative 2014).
d. MoH, IADB (National Women's Health Survey 2018).

The Health Sciences Initiative was an ambitious collaboration with a great deal of political drive. However, the outcome was not welcomed by some local researchers and healthcare professionals for a number of reasons: a primarily top-down structure with the exclusion of local expertise, a lack of recognition of local assets and programmes without adequate sensitization or integration into existing work or systems and a degree of mistrust with governmental initiatives for healthcare research (McMacken n.d.).

Avoiding collaboration with national and international partners would be detrimental to the progress of local research efforts. Thus, the lessons learned from projects already conducted are important for future collaborations to be successful. Adequate sensitization, with opportunities for local interested parties to participate or share their knowledge, continues to be an invaluable part of project planning.

To support evidence-based practice, UWI medical faculty has incorporated research into its medical, dental and optometry training programmes to encourage uptake in students from their earliest years of training. Medical research became an obligatory course among medical students in the second year of the training programme. Dr Laura McDougal and Professor Donald Simeon in the Community Health Unit were key players in its introduction, and since then, it has taken firm root.

UWI has established an Ethics Committee to vet and ensure that proposed studies are carried out ethically and in accordance with national and international law. The ethics policy was developed in 1998 and revised in 2011, when it was mandated that each campus have a Campus Ethics Committee.

Over the years, local research has moved from a primarily top-down, experimental or interventional clinical science basis towards the inclusion of other study designs and outcomes. This has created more observational, patient-based studies, with a further understanding of healthcare service/delivery impact and effects of health promotion and literacy. There has also been a greater representation of studies using a range of research methodologies by local authors. This is reflected in the studies published by Trinidad and Tobago authors in the scientific community.

MENTAL HEALTH IN TRINIDAD AND TOBAGO

Prior to 1968, any person with suspected or diagnosed mental health disorders requiring inpatient treatment was admitted to St Ann's Hospital for evaluation and care. Constructed in 1965, the San Fernando General Hospital (SFGH) outpatient psychiatric clinic facilitated outpatient care to discharged patients. In 1966, Ward 1 was built at SFGH and utilized as a holding bay for patients to be transferred to St Ann's Hospital for in-patient treatment.

The growth of this department has undergone a significant transformation, extending services throughout the country's district health facilities, namely in Siparia, Princes Town, Barrackpore, Couva, Cedros, Point Fortin and South Oropouche for children, teenagers and adults (PSI n.d.).

As postulated by the Pan American Health Organization (PAHO) in 2018, men are mostly affected by self-harm, suicide, alcohol use and headaches, while women fall victim to headaches, depression and anxiety disorders. Proposed recommendations by PAHO to curb these effects include:

1) Primary healthcare workers should be trained to identify and use effective methods of analysis to detect and treat and/or refer their patients for adequate treatment.
2) Community availability to patients with severe disorders (autism, bipolar disorder, Alzheimer's, etc.) should be adequate for treatment and management of patients.
3) Emergency services in managing acute crisis and high-need patients should be available in hospitals as well as community healthcare services.

Trinidad and Tobago has seen rapid development in its initiative to make community services available to persons suffering from mental health disorders. The incidence of mental health is increasing globally. Therefore, improvements in physician training and promoting awareness of mental health among our population will go further into reducing the impact of this disease.

HEALTHCARE TRIUMPHS

Great achievements in healthcare post-independence include:

- The provision of primary healthcare for all is free at the point of contact.
- Ongoing undergraduate training programmes in the fields of medicine, dentistry, pharmacy, nursing and optometry.
- There are also postgraduate (DM) training programmes in speciality areas of medical training (e.g., surgery, cardiology, paediatrics).
- Trinidad and Tobago have excellent coverage of primary and secondary healthcare services throughout the sister islands, including access to medical imaging, surgery and intensive care facilities.

There is the CDAP medication list available free of charge to members of the population.

i. Significant reduction in infant and maternal mortality through improvements in healthcare training, equipment and services available for women and children.
ii. Improved community mental health services.
iii. Improved community antenatal services.
iv. Queens Park Counselling Centre and Clinic for sexual health screening and support (satellite services available).
v. Dialysis services.
vi. Public-private partnership initiatives to reduce hospital waiting lists (EPP – cataract, orthopaedics programmes).

Create the Extended Programme for Immunizations for children and provide necessary vaccines for adults (annual influenza, pneumococcal, HPV and COVID-19) in the community setting.

NATIONAL ONCOLOGY SERVICES

Culture, Structure and Support for Ethical Research

- Improvements in access to funding and social support for people affected by disability, old age and certain diseases, who may benefit from interventions not available in Trinidad and Tobago, have also significantly improved the quality of life for affected individuals and their families (e.g., Children's Life Fund and EPP).

- Help and support for smoking cessation and substance abuse (Tobacco control unit and policies; community management of alcohol detoxification and support for rehabilitation).
- Improved working between government agencies and departments to sanction or support healthcare policies (e.g., legal ministries, social care).

Areas for Improvement

- Building on the structure and expanding current training programmes to include specialty training in areas that are needed using strategic needs assessment (e.g., geriatrics, psychiatry [old age and adolescent], and allied healthcare professionals, such as community nursing, midwifery, speech and language therapy, psychology and physiotherapy, inter alia) would complement the service provision and sustainability of the existing health service.
- Along with service needs assessment, a review of contractual agreements and policies to attract, train, remunerate and retain healthcare professionals is paramount in health systems planning. There is a high risk of brain drain and the export of well-trained professionals to other countries with better recognition, remuneration and retention programmes. The proposed policy review would also promote consistency of care available to patients and the medico-legal responsibility of healthcare providers.
- Continue to improve primary care services, including recruitment and training of healthcare staff.
- Development of health promotion and health literacy for Trinidad and Tobago (using various media, including written, visual and online).
- Ongoing structuring and integration of services available in the community that complement medical management and support primary and secondary prevention of disease (e.g., physiotherapy, nursing, podiatry, nutrition and physical activity programmes, smoking cessation).
- Regular review of the CDAP medications with strategies to reduce the bureaucracy and simplify the process for practitioners to apply for expansion and review of medications available to patients.

- Support for electronic medical record-keeping programmes with consistency of format, approach and cybersecurity, allowing improved access between services and practitioners involved in patient care and for future consideration of a patient-held record.
- Tackling issues in mental health and promotion of well-being; improved awareness and patient support in primary and secondary care settings in general and targeted areas (antenatal, adolescent, adult, elderly, persons with chronic disease).

APPENDIX

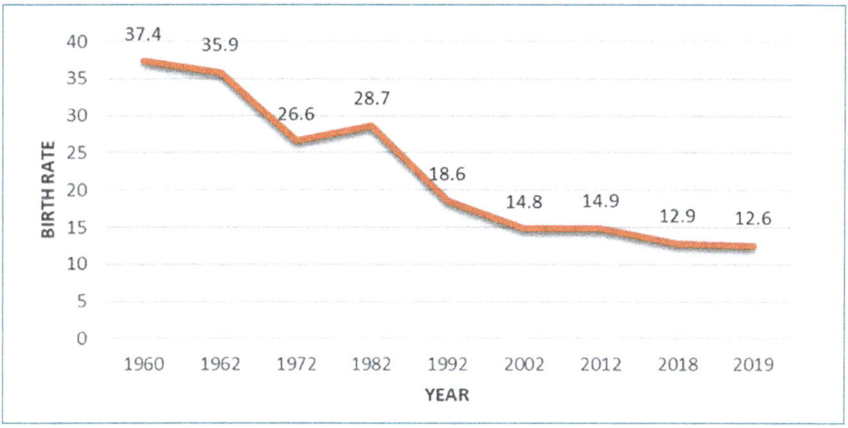

Figure 3. 14: Birth Rate in Trinidad and Tobago

Table 3.7: Demographics for Trinidad and Tobago, Barbados, Jamaica and Guyana

Country	Demographics	1960	1962	1972	1982	1992	2002	2012	2018	2019	2020	2021
Trinidad	Infant Mortality Rate (per 1000 live births)	56	52.7	42.3	32.2	25.9	24.3	18.9	15.4	15.4	14.8	NIL
	Birth Rate (per 1000 people)	37.4	35.9	28.7	28.6	18.6	14.8	12.9	12.6	12.6	NIL	NIL
	Life Expectancy (years)	61.9	63.8	64.9	66.8	69.3	69.8	72.5	73.3	73.4	73.6	73.7
	Crude Death Rate (per 1000 persons)	9.19	8.77	7.58	7.76	7.47	7.26	8.32	8.46	8.46	8.74	8.74
Barbados	Infant Mortality Rate (per 1000 live births)	70.1	61.1	37.1	21.4	15.6	14.2	13.6	12.1	11.7	11.4	NIL
	Birth Rate (per 1000 people)	30.6	29.3	20.6	17.5	18.6	13.6	13	10.6	10.6	NIL	NIL
	Life Expectancy (years)	63.7	65.3	69.5	72.5	73.6	74.4	75.4	79.2	79.3	79.4	79.4
	Crude Death Rate (per 1000 persons)	11.3	10.3	8.81	8.42	7.68	7.67	8.49	8.98	9.01	9.11	9.17

Table 3.7: (*cont'd*)

Country	Demographics	1960	1962	1972	1982	1992	2002	2012	2018	2019	2020	2021
Jamaica	Infant Mortality Rate (per 1000 live births)	61.1	56.9	41.7	31.4	23.9	19.6	14.6	12.2	11.8	11.4	NIL
	Birth Rate (per 1000 people)	40.6	40.8	33.8	28.5	24.6	20.3	17.2	16.1	15.9	NIL	NIL
	Life Expectancy (years)	64.3	65.2	68.3	71.3	73.6	74.1	74.4	74.6	74.6	74.6	74.7
	Crude Death Rate (per 1000 persons)	9.28	7.59	6.93	6.45	6.72	7.39	7.56	7.59	7.61	7.64	7.64
Guyana	Infant Mortality Rate (per 1000 live births)	66.9	62.4	55	44.6	35.4	29.4	25.2	23.8	23.8	NIL	NIL
	Birth Rate (per 1000 people)	43	41.2	34.9	30.8	28.2	25.6	22	19.7	19.7	NIL	NIL
	Life Expectancy (years)	60.2	60.5	61.2	62.6	64.6	65.7	69.7	69.7	69.7	70	70
	Crude Death Rate (per 1000 persons)	10.2	9.85	8.87	8.42	8.14	7.85	7.72	7.52	7.62	7.62	7.72

Table 3.8: Maternal Mortality Rate in Trinidad and Tobago as Compared to Other Economies (rate per 100,000 live births)

Country	2000	2001	2002	2012	2013	2014	2015	2016	2017
Trinidad	81	78	74	71	70	69	68	68	67
Barbados	50	48	47	34	32	31	31	30	27
Jamaica	77	79	78	79	79	78	80	80	80
Guyana	231	216	227	185	175	174	172	170	169

REFERENCES

Bahall, M. 2012. "Reform of the Trinidad and Tobago Health Service: The Limits of Decentralization." *ResearchGate*. https://www.researchgate.net/publication/277957298_Reform_of_the_Trinidad_and_Tobago_Health_Service_The_Limits_of_Decentralisation.

Baird, B. 1970. "Informing Public Policy with Social and Behavioral Science." Issues in Science and Technology. https://issues.org/perspective-informing-public-policy-with-social-and-behavioral-science/.

Baston, Y.A, S. Teelucksingh, R.G. Maharaj, B.N. Cockburn. 2014. "A Cross-Sectional Study to Determine the Prevalence of Obesity and Other Risk Factors for Type 2 Diabetes Among School Children in Trinidad, West Indies." *Paediatrics and International Child Health* 34 (3): 178–83. https://pubmed.ncbi.nlm.nih.gov/24621246/.

———, R.G. Maharaj, V. Singh, S. Balkaran, and B.N. Cockburn. 2013. "Screening for Diabetes in Schoolchildren in Trinidad, West Indies." *Paediatrics and International Child Health* 33 (1): 34–71. https://pubmed.ncbi.nlm.nih.gov/23485494/.

Beckles, G.L., G.J. Miller, B.R. Kirkwood, S.D. Alexis, D.C. Carson, and N.T. Byam. 1986. "High Total and Cardiovascular Disease Mortality in Adults of Indian Descent in Trinidad, Unexplained by Major Coronary Risk Factors." The *Lancet* 327 (8493): 1298–1301.

Besson, G.A. 2019. "Trade Unions." *Caribbean History Archives*. http://caribbean-historyarchives.blogspot.com/2011/12/trade-unions.html. The Borgen Project. 2016. "8 Facts about Poverty in Jamaica and Efforts to Alleviate It." https://borgenproject.org/8-facts-poverty-jamaica/.

Catalano, P.M. 2010. "The Impact of Gestational Diabetes and Maternal Obesity on the Mother and Her Offspring." *Journal of Developmental Origins of Health and Disease* 1 (4): 208.

CDC. 2021. "Diabetes and Your Heart." Centers for Disease Control and Prevention. https://www.cdc.gov/diabetes/library/features/diabetes-and-heart.html. "The Experience of Indian Indenture in Trinidad: Arrival and Settlement." 2013. *Caribbean Atlas*. http://www.caribbean-atlas.com/en/themes/waves-of-colonization-and-control-in-the-caribbean/waves-of-colonization/the-experience-of-indian-indenture-in-trinidad-arrival-and-settlement.html. The Faculty of Medical Sciences. n.d. "About Us." https://sta.uwi.edu/fms/about-us.

Gadsby Wicks. n.d. "NHS vs Private Medical Treatment – Is There Really a Difference?" https://www.gadsbywicks.co.uk/insights/medical-negligence/nhs-vs-private.

GM Journal. "New Data Show the Impact of Covid-19 on Private Healthcare."

https://www.gmjournal.co.uk/new-data-show-the-impact-of-covid-19-on-private-healthcare.

GOV.UK. "List of Medical Providers in Trinidad and Tobago." https://www.gov.uk/government/publications/trinidad-and-tobago-list-of-medical-facilities-practioners/list-of-medical-providers-in-trinidad-and-tobago.

Hezekiah, J.A. 1989. "The Development of Health Care Policies in Trinidad and Tobago: Autonomy or Domination?" *International Journal of Health Services: Planning, Administration, Evaluation* 19 (1). https://pubmed.ncbi.nlm.nih.gov/2925302/.

Hutchison, E.D. 2011. "Life Course Theory." In *Encyclopedia of Adolescence*, 1586–1594.

Macrotrend. n.d. "Barbados Literacy Rate 1970–2022." https://www.macrotrends.net/countries/BRB/barbados/literacy-rate.

Macrotrends. n.d. "Trinidad and Tobago Life Expectancy 1950–2022." https://www.macrotrends.net/countries/TTO/trinidad-and-tobago/life-expectancy.

MBTT. n.d. "General Information." http://www.mbtt.org/GeneralInfo.htm.

McMacken, M. n.d. "Trinidad and Tobago Health Sciences Initiative." Johns Hopkins Medicine International. https://www.hopkinsmedicine.org/international/international_affiliations/latin_america_caribbean/trinidad_tobago_health_sciences_initiative.html.

Medical Professionals Association of Trinidad and Tobago. n.d. "History." http://www.mpattonline.com/history.html.

Niherst. n.d. "Icons." https://icons.niherst.gov.tt/icon/dave-chadee-tt4/.

Oberhauser, A.M. 2021. "Expanding Opportunities for Women and Economic Uncertainty Are Both Factors in Declining US Fertility Rates." The Conversation, 21 March 2022. http://theconversation.com/expanding-opportunities-for-women-and-economic-uncertainty-are-both-factors-in-declining-us-fertility-rates-162494.

Oxford Business Group. 2020. "Trinidad and Tobago Invests in Health Infrastructure." https://oxfordbusinessgroup.com/overview/brick-brick-public-infrastructure-investment-campaign-address-primary-needs-sector-paving-way-future.

"PAHO 2021." Accessed 21 March 2022. https://www.paho.org/english/sha/prfltrt.htm.

PSI. n.d. "Trinidad and Tobago Chronic Non-Communicable Disease Risk Factor Survey." https://www.psi.org/wp-content/uploads/2018/02/TT-STEPS-Survery.pdf.

Raghupathi, V., and W. Raghupathi. 2020. "Healthcare Expenditure and Economic Performance: Insights from the United States Data." *Front Public Health* 8:156.

Ritchie, H., E. Mathieu, L. Rodés-Guirao, C. Appel, C. Giattino, E. Ortiz-Ospina, et al. 2020. "Coronavirus Pandemic (COVID-19)." *Our World in Data*, 5 March 2020. https://ourworldindata.org/excess-mortality-covid.

Roser, M., E. Ortiz-Ospina, and H. Ritchie. "Life Expectancy." 2013. Our World in Data, 23 May 2013. https://ourworldindata.org/life-expectancy.

Sastre, F., P. Rojas, E. Cyrus, M.D.L. Rosa, and A.H. Khoury. 2014. "Improving the Health Status of Caribbean People: Recommendations from the Triangulating on Health Equity Summit." Global Health Promotion. https://journals.sagepub.com/doi/abs/10.1177/1757975914523455.

South-West Regional Health Authority. n.d. "Mental Health." nhttp://www.swrha.co.tt/content/mental-health.

UN in Trinidad and Tobago. n.d. "Sustainable Development Goal 3: Good Health and Well-being." https://trinidadandtobago.un.org/en/sdgs/3.

UNICEF. "Maternal Mortality Rates and Statistics." UNICEF Data. https://data.unicef.org/topic/maternal-health/maternal-mortality/.

Vos, T., S.S. Lim, C. Abbafati, K.M. Abbas, M. Abbasi, M. Abbasifard, et al. 2020. "Global Burden of 369 Diseases and Injuries in 204 Countries and Territories, 1990–2019: A Systematic Analysis for the Global Burden of Disease Study 2019." *Lancet* 396 (10258): 1204–22.

WGO. "Infant Mortality." https://www.who.int/data/gho/data/themes/topics/indicator-groups/indicator-group-details/GHO/infant-mortality.

WHO. n.d. "Countries Are Spending More on Health, but People Are Still Paying Too Much Out of Their Own Pockets." https://www.who.int/news/item/20-02-2019-countries-are-spending-more-on-health-but-people-are-still-paying-too-much-out-of-their-own-pockets.

"UWI Today." n.d. https://sta.uwi.edu/uwitoday/archive/october_2015/article4.asp.

———." n.d. https://sta.uwi.edu/uwitoday/archive/february_2011/article10.asp.

World Bank. n.d.a. "Death Rate, Crude (Per 1,000 People) Data." https://data.worldbank.org/indicator/SP.DYN.CDRT.IN.

———. n.d.b. "Maternal Mortality Ratio (Modeled Estimate, Per 100,000 Live Births) – Trinidad and Tobago Data." https://data.worldbank.org/indicator/SH.MMRT?locations=TT.

———. n.d.c. "Mortality Rate, Infant (Per 1,000 Live Births) – Trinidad and Tobago Data." https://data.worldbank.org/indicator/SP.DYN.IMRT.IN?locations=TT.

———. n.d.d. "Nurses and Midwives (Per 1,000 People) – Trinidad and Tobago Data." https://data.worldbank.org/indicator/SH.MED.NUMW.P3?locations=TT.

———. n.d.e. "Physicians (Per 1,000 People) – Trinidad and Tobago | Data." Accessed 10 April 2022. https://data.worldbank.org/indicator/SH.MED.PHYS.ZS?locations=TT.

World Obesity Federation Global Obesity Observatory. n.d. "Trinidad and Tobago.". https://data.worldobesity.org/country/trinidad-and-tobago-217/#data_prevalence.

[CHAPTER 4]

The Development of Education in Trinidad and Tobago after Independence:

Losses, Gains and Missed Opportunities

JEROME DE LISLE, CHERYL BOWRIN-WILLIAMS AND TRACEY M. LUCAS

INTRODUCTION – CHANGE VERSUS CONTINUITY

Eleven of sixteen Caribbean countries gained independence from their colonizers between 1962 and 1980. For a small island nation-state, independence is sometimes highly valued because it provides opportunities for greater autonomy and sovereignty. All nations have big dreams of independence. Many small countries are able to dream in a big way, perhaps because independence represents an awakening of passions fuelled by the notion of imagined autonomy and greater control over future destinies. Sadly, not all dreams come true, and a reset is often not possible at all. In reality, continuity of structure and practice is the reality of educational development in many nation states. To be sure, most education systems change rather slowly, if at all, and some even degrade when confronted by new internal and external threats.

Education systems function in a state of equilibrium, with change continuously restrained by inherited structural and behavioural tendencies and forces. Radical or transformative education change requires a catharsis followed by a true rebirth (Archer 1982). This rebirth might involve progression to a more complex differentiated system focused upon goals such as equity, well-being, and excellence.[1] One system that has progressed rapidly in the last sixty years is Finland. Although this is not a newly independent or postcolonial state, real progress has occurred only since 1968 and required hard decisions, radical reform and deep restructuring (Darling-Hammond 2010; Sahlberg 2021).

One postcolonial system that has experienced rapid transformation is Singapore. This small nation-state achieved independence in 1965 and has experienced continued transformation and growth, becoming the top-performing country in PIRLS 2016 and PISA 2015. The trajectory of growth and transformation has been described in four phases shown in table 4.1 as *the survival phase*, 1959–79; *the efficiency-driven phase*, 1979–96; *the ability-*

Table 4.1: Trajectory of Education Development in Singapore

Phases of Education Development	Academic Characteristics	Social Characteristics	Governance Structures and Processes	Economic Development Phase
Survival-Driven Education (1965–1978)	Emphasis on languages, science and mathematics	Integration of multicultural population Social Cohesion		Industrialization
Efficiency Driven Education (1979–1997)	System wide emphasis on English, Mathematics and Science Expansion of TVET	Skills focused	Streaming Attrition	Skills/Capital Intensive
Ability and Aspiration Driven Education (1997–2011)	Creativity Mathematics		School Clusters Multiple Pathways Networks Research Driven	Knowledge-based
Student-centric, Values-Driven Education (2011–present)	Excellence Access	Excellence Inclusion Transversal skills	Admission School Improvement	Innovation-Driven

Note. Various sources. For Phases, see S. Gopinathan, *Singapore Chronicles: Education* (Singapore: Straits Times Press: 2015).

based, aspiration-driven phase, 1997–2011; and *the values-driven phase*, 2011 to present. These phases closely match the direction and focus of economic and industrial growth. Both social and academic goals have been the focus during these periods, and the recent turn towards students' processes and outcomes has represented stronger reflexivity and an awareness of the significance of the role of entrepreneurship and innovation.

THEORETICAL CONSTRUCTS FOR EXPLAINING THE TRAJECTORY OF EDUCATION DEVELOPMENT

We frame the analysis of the trajectory of education in Trinidad and Tobago from an explicitly postcolonial perspective (Yeh 2016; Denny 2020). Thus, we argue that the colonial experience was not benign and never terminated. Instead, it has persisted, negatively impacting upon the present. Using a dialectical critical realism[2] lens, we understand current activities and processes through a temporal framework that captures past mechanisms and practices in colonial bureaucracies. Thus, we agree with Campbell (1996, 1997), who traced the conflict between religion and state over schooling in Trinidad and Tobago back to past competition between French and English colonizers. The ability to understand the evolution of these events is fundamental to post-colonial analysis.

The early work on Caribbean administrative systems by Jones (1974, 1975) and Mills and Robertson (1974) is explicitly postcolonial, linking past tendencies and practices in colonial administration to current practices in the civil service. Based on this Caribbean work, we conclude that modern administrators in Caribbean ministries of education have retained values, attitudes and commitments from the colonial administration. This work on the Caribbean civil service is not just theoretical. It has been successfully applied to public service reform in the wider Commonwealth (Draper 2001; Commonwealth Secretariat 2016).

To further increase explanatory power, we include Archer's morphogenetic theory, which has been used successfully to explain the trajectory of education systems in England, Denmark, France and Norway (Archer 2013; Archer et al. 2022; Skinningsrud 2015). Its utility in our analysis is the contrast provided between morphogenesis (transformation) and morphostatis (staying the same). The strength of the explanatory framework is its dependence on time and space. Morphogenetic theory is focused on culture, agency and structure and hints at individual and collective capacities and roles. There is value in understanding the influence of colonial structures, the possibilities of agency and the need for collective reflexivity in education system change within the Caribbean.

Morphostasis is the tendency of an education system to remain stable through self-regulation and feedback. Morphostasis guarantees continuity and stability with the system resisting transformative change. Morphogenesis is true transformative change and involves three phases: (1) structural or cultural conditioning, (2) social or sociocultural interaction and (3) social or cultural elaboration. The propositions of culture may be complementary or contradictory. The latter will create problems for agents of change. Interaction extends the logic of change to the use of and escape from power. Notably, power can trump complementary cultures.

However, under well-ordered sociocultural conditions, cultural elites will accede to demands (Archer 1995, 1996). Reflexivity is a critical concept at both the individual and collective levels. Collective reflexivity involves internal deliberations that people share among themselves to direct their actions according to their interests. We hypothesize that the lack of discourse and transparency over critical education issues in Caribbean societies might limit collective reflexivity, hinder agency and stall the morphogenetic cycle.

A final group of theories explaining how education systems develop comes from systems learning, which explains why some issues are forgotten and why some are remembered. Systems learning may also be used to map and define the way forward, as is done in U Theory (Scharmer 2009). Memory and system learning is critical to understanding the trajectory of educational development because growth and elaboration require gathering information to achieve genuine transformation (Antunes and Pinheiro 2020). In this regard, system memory represents a store of knowledge and shared experiences (norms and stories) that are available to all. This memory is generated through structures and processes that foster standardization and formalization and require strong monitoring and evaluation systems. These two aspects of governance have been notable weaknesses in Caribbean administrative systems and are still nascent or emerging in most states.

System memory includes declarative, procedural and emotional elements. The emotional content may be the key to postcolonial states' inability to

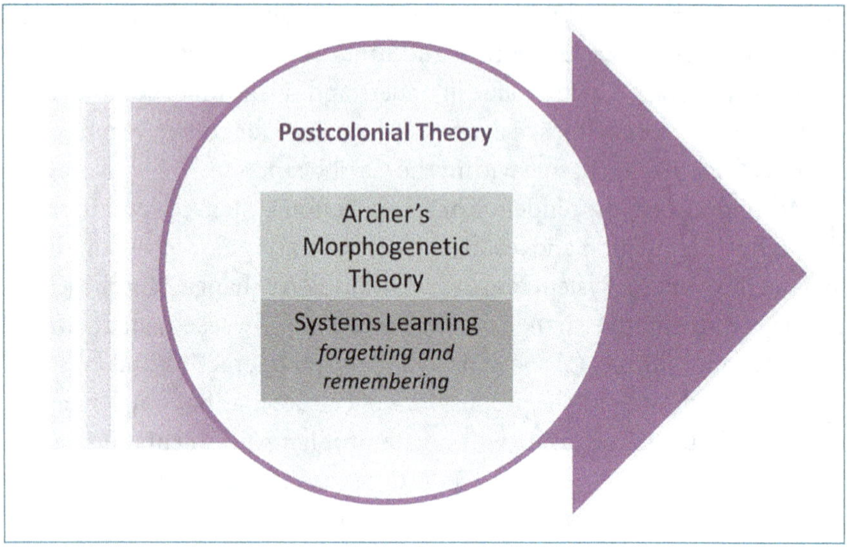

Figure 4.1: The Theoretical Framework Used in this Study

forget. Knowledge and feelings about the past are stored through several cultural elements, such as storytelling and heroes/heroines. Memories are especially strong in systems that rely on folk tales instead of credible data and evidence. The problem of morpho-stasis might lie in the erroneous or misleading stories told in postcolonial states like Trinidad and Tobago.

A POST-INDEPENDENCE TRAJECTORY OF EDUCATION DEVELOPMENT FOR TRINIDAD AND TOBAGO

De Lisle (2009) traced the development of leadership reform in Trinidad and Tobago. He showed that the installation of new leadership and governance systems after independence was strongly influenced by the plans and intentions of funding agencies like the World Bank and Inter-American Development Bank (IDB). Johnson (2006) called this stage of transfer in educational policy compelling, where recipient countries are convinced to adopt the agenda of the donors. De Lisle (2016), in examining the policy trajectory for data-driven actions, pointed to greater local control over policy development and the use of research-based evidence and data from national tests. Such developments were mostly internal to the system and independent of funders' influence. However, for Trinidad and Tobago, these advances in control over policy development did not lead to greater reflexivity. Many reforms in Trinidad and Tobago remained short-lived and strongly resisted even by "planners-practitioners" in the Ministry of Education (London 1997, 317).

London (1997) argued that education planning functions at the intersection of three political forces: the *state, social actors and the planner-practitioner*. In past analysis, we surmise that too much attention has been focused on politicians representing the state. However, the role of the planner-practitioner, who also represents the state, has been largely ignored. Technocrats can be empowered to support the state or function as constraining forces. For many, change in Trinidad and Tobago is about somebody else. Even some technocrats have continued to declare themselves powerless in the face of an imaginary entity called the ministry. This illusion might free them from personal responsibility. Harvey (1981) spoke of such perceived powerlessness in the creation of the comprehensive new sector schools. However, the historical records[3] are clear that various individuals and bodies have had a significant say in the decisions reached by the government.

Interestingly, there is insufficient written about the historical constraining role of technocrats like C.V. Gocking in redirecting the government's intentions in the 1970s and 1980s. The weakness in the analysis by Ryan (2009) and Parris (1983) is the failure to peer beyond the power of the throne and to explore the machinations of princes and pawns. In this regard, Walker (2002) wrote:

> Perhaps the most important 'traditionalist' was Dr Charles Vernon Gocking. In 1961, Dr Gocking, a Queens Royal College (QRC) and Oxford University graduate, was handpicked by Eric Williams, also a graduate of QRC and Oxford University, to be Chief Education Officer (CEO) of the Ministry of Education. As the first local CEO, Gocking's appointment was initially heartily welcomed. However, it soon became apparent that Gocking represented the traditionalists in the T&T education system as he vehemently opposed Williams' readiness to open up the system (personal interview with Ministry officials, August 1992). When QRC graduate and Gocking's former student, Dr Ralph Romain, was appointed Permanent Secretary of the Ministry of Education, the Gocking-Romain team was said to have deliberately obstructed the over-ambitious policies of Williams and Minister of Education at the time, Donald Pierre. (172)

Some of Walker's assertions are supported by primary and secondary sources, such as Alleyne (1996) and Campbell (1997). These sources document the multiple perspectives of politicians, technocrats and stakeholders on the way forward during the reorientation of the plan.[4] Additionally, these sources also acknowledge the role of micropolitics within the Trinidad and Tobago Ministry of Education, which led to changing alliances, posturing and positioning among both technocrats and politicians. In terms of the general functioning of postcolonial bureaucracies in the Caribbean, Jones (1975) theorized on the personal nature of decision-making and noted "conflictual interpersonal relations between Ministers and administrators" (251). Jones and Mills (1976) suggested that implementation failure in the Caribbean might also be attributed to administrators prioritizing routine actions over problem-solving, with successful implementation requiring compromise, contextualization and adaptation of policy plans.

Ryan (2009) missed some of these complexities completely. For example, he treats Gocking as a neutral political antagonist struggling only with the truthfulness of Williams's retirement decision. We stress these internal organizational events only to note an important difference in the trajectory of educational development in Trinidad and Tobago and Singapore. Namely, the capacity of Singapore to transform its education system might lie not in the transformative words or even actions of the then premier, Lee Kuan Yew, but in the unrelenting capacity of the technocrats to translate with fidelity politicians' words and vision into working implementation protocols acceptable to all policy actors (Tan 2011).

Leipziger and Thomas (1993) noted this technocratic capacity within some East Asian systems: "First, there is something to be learned from East Asia's style of policymaking that translates policies on paper into practice. Many of the features associated with such effectiveness, consensus building, policy flexibility and pragmatism are replicable. Most clearly, countries need to develop a mandate for development and also to continually reassess their strategies" (28).

Clearly, the situation was not the same in Trinidad and Tobago, and so the reason for reform failure may be the absence of both collective capacity and reflexivity. Additionally, cultural conflict and retained colonial administrative practices are likely notable impediments to change (Jones 1974, 1975).

THE MAJOR EXTERNAL FUNDED PROGRAMMES

The trajectory of educational development in Trinidad and Tobago is complex, and the phases are often ill-defined, with periods of brief redirection and multiple regressions. This pattern may be related to the weak governance and evaluation systems, which often fail to direct and monitor change, allowing implementation drift. However, distinct phases can still be identified, although these appear to be only vaguely related to historic education policy plans and specific funding programmes. These phases are not associated with specific ministers nor with the political parties, as they often extend across administrations.

There were four major programmes funded by international agencies since independence in Trinidad and Tobago. Each programme consisted of multiple projects, ranging from new school buildings to new curricula and new governance structures. All funding programmes came with external consultants and training, although the quality of both remains in question. Some of these programmes had separate executing units commissioned to coordinate the programme. This was true in the case of the Inter-American Development Bank (IDB) Secondary Education Modernization Programme (SEMP) and the World Bank Fourth Basic Education project. However, few programmes have had the impact hoped for, even when the intentions appeared legitimate or defensible. For example, the introduction of SEMP magnet secondary schools into the system remains one noticeable failure. The logic of such a strategy is still unavailable for the records. As shown in table 4.2, the costliest programme was the SEMP, which was meant to improve quality and equity in the secondary sector.

EDUCATION PLANS FROM INDEPENDENCE TO THE PRESENT

Surprisingly, these externally funded programmes are only loosely linked to national plans either in education or in multiple sectors. This, perhaps, is one of the significant problems in education development in Trinidad and Tobago – the lack of coherence between various system goals and policy strategies. Fullan and Quinn (2016) reminded us that coherence between policies is more than alignment; it is best considered a shared deep understanding of the nature and intent of a transformation. De Lisle

Table 4.2: Major Programmes Funded by External Agencies in Post-independence Trinidad and Tobago

Name of Reform	Reform Period	Primary Purpose	Funder	Funding (USD Million)
15 Year Education Plan	1968–1983	Expansion	World Bank	38.7[a]
Fourth Basic Education Project	1996–2003	Quality	World Bank	51.1
Secondary Education Modernization Programme	1999–2009	Quality and Relevance- Secondary Sector	IDB	105.0
Seamless Education Reform Project	2009–2019	Quality and Efficiency	IDB	55.0

Note. De Lisle, 2009; IDB = Inter-American Development Bank.
[a] Estimated

(2012) theorized that a significant weakness in the implementation of the SEMP was the perceived ambiguity and lack of clarity in the goals, with that ambiguity experienced by managers and practitioners alike.

Table 4.3: Key Policy and Planning Documents on Educational Development

Name of Reform	Reform Period	Primary Purpose	Outcomes
Maurice Plan	Prior to 1962	School Building	Modern Secondary Schools
15 Year Education Plan	1968–83	Expansion/ Radical Reform	New Sector Schools
Education Plan 1985–90	1985–90	Maintenance	Minimal
White Paper	1993–2002	Radical Reform-Quality and Efficiency	Population Acceptance
Education Plan 2002–6	2002–6	Equity and Quality	Improved Low Performing Schools
Vision 2020	2007–20	Relevance, Equity, Quality	Awareness
Strategic Plan 2011–15	2011–15	Relevance and Values	Awareness
Education Plan 2017–22	2017–22	Maintenance and Relevance	Awareness
Vision 2030	2016–30	Relevance	Ongoing

Note. Data sourced from multiple National and Education Development Plans between 1968 and 2016.

This lack of coherence between policies continued into the seamless education reform era. The goals in this externally funded reform did not fully capture all the issues generated prior to and during 2010–20. For example, there was no clear direction on identifying and turning around low-performing schools, an issue made clear in the 2002–6 Education Plan. The perceived lack of local relevance may have failed to energize key stakeholders. Although the work of the Ministry of Planning is of high quality, as evidenced in the Vision 2020 and Vision 2030 plans, the required coherence between economic goals and the education strategy is not made explicit. For example, in Vision 2030, transversal skills[5] are not prioritized as critical tools for achieving an innovation-driven economy. The mention of training systems and skills development and the emphasis on instilling positive values and behaviours speak to a more traditional education strategy.

All of the proposals and plans put forward since 1962 have not led to successful reform. However, some incremental changes at lower levels might have had a significant impact. More alarmingly, across the key periods, there also appears to be quiet periods for policy implementation,[6] with little improvement attempted. Unbelievingly, there are several instances of policy reversals,[7] where new systems are installed, then removed, and old systems are reinstalled. One example is the comprehensive school model contained in the 1975 proposals by the prime minister. Although planners expected all schools to accommodate the Junior Secondary and Comprehensive Model, in the end, denominational schools reverted to a traditional Grammar school model with attached multiple lower-tier schools. Even with the introduction of secondary education modernization schools, which were installed in 1990, such processes have continued, so several models of secondary schools now exist together. Overall, the nation-state has a poor implementation history, but that is true elsewhere in the Global South.[8]

Reversals have also been observed for education policies on decentralization, use of continuous assessment, and grade-level student retention. Some successful reforms have even been halted and extinguished, sometimes without explanation to the public. For example, the period of national testing at the primary school lasted from 2004 to 2016 but was halted in 2017. The local data had been used to direct attention to reducing the high variance in reading scores noted in PIRLS 2016 (De Lisle 2016).

The presence and frequency of policy reversals and stoppages suggest a degree of unintentional forgetfulness and severe limitations in system learning. Part of the problem relates to the absence of knowledge from formal evaluations and the necessary policy discussion that leads to deeper insights and sustainable change among all stakeholders.

Taylor's (2005) framework for implementation appears useful here for explaining the different pathways of change for projects. Taylor listed the following possibilities organized into pairs: (1) non-reform, (2) momentary reform, (3) nominal reform, (4) resident reform, (5) transient reform, (6), temporary reform, (7) sustained implementation and (8) sustained implementation with dynamic equilibrium. Table 4.4 lists definitions for

Table 4.4: Multiple Outcomes in Education Change Applied to Trinidad and Tobago's Educational Development after Independence

<table>
<tr><th>Nature of Reform</th><th>Description</th><th>Examples in Trinidad and Tobago</th></tr>
<tr><td>Non-reform</td><td>The innovation never takes hold and ends quickly</td><td rowspan="2">Decentralization
School-based Management
School Development Planning</td></tr>
<tr><td>Momentary Reform</td><td>The change flourishes briefly but soon dies or is overtaken by another reform</td></tr>
<tr><td>Nominal Reform</td><td>Establishes itself in name only and is finally abandoned</td><td rowspan="2">Comprehensive schooling
Performance Management Appraisal (PMAP)
Single Sex Classrooms in coeducational schools</td></tr>
<tr><td>Resident Reform</td><td>Establishes itself but persists in name only</td></tr>
<tr><td>Transient Reform</td><td>Establishes itself, changes the system and then passes away as if it never existed</td><td rowspan="2">National Learning Assessments
Secondary Education Modernization Programme Curricula
Primary School Rewrite 2013
Continuous Assessment</td></tr>
<tr><td>Temporary Reform</td><td>Establishes itself, changes the system, but gives way to inertia and persists in name only</td></tr>
<tr><td>Sustained Implementation</td><td>Is sustained and overtakes prior systems so that it becomes the status quo</td><td rowspan="2">TVET in schools
New Sector Schools
SEMP Model schools
Modern Secondary Schools</td></tr>
<tr><td>Sustained implementation without single sustained reform effort</td><td>Is sustained and achieves dynamic equilibrium so that adjustments are continuously made</td></tr>
</table>

Notes. Based upon Taylor (2005)

these changes with examples in Trinidad and Tobago. It is noticeable that several reforms have not persisted. As discussed earlier, a most unusual pattern is seen in the case of school-based management, which has been attempted in several reform plans without sustained implementation. School-based management as a component of decentralization was mentioned in the white paper, the "Secondary Education Modernization Programme, the 2002–2006 Education Plan and the 2011–2015 Education Plan".

FORGETTING AND REMEMBERING AS A KEY EXPLANATION

The patterns of change observed in Trinidad and Tobago may be related to the unique nature of forgetting and remembering in postcolonial spaces. Forgetting and remembering are features of the memory used for system learning (Casey and Oliviera 2011). Both learning and unlearning (intentional and unintentional) are required for real system change (transformation). For systems to improve, they must learn from past attempts to improve, including past failed attempts at change (Greene and McShane 2018).

There are different levels of learning[9] within systems, starting with (1) incremental change occurring within existing frameworks, (2) changes to mental frameworks and (3) changes to paradigms and traditions that govern the mental frameworks (Tosey et al. 2012). More importantly, in a postcolonial setting, an improving system requires members to unlearn past routines and metapatterns[10] in pursuit of innovation and change (Level 2). Such unlearning must then extend to beliefs and perspectives that frame the definition of the issue (Level 3). Level 3 requires collective reflexivity.

Such intentional forgetting of the past is not as easy as it appears (Holan and Phillips 2004). The past carries with it positive memories of childhood and schooling, even if, in reality, such positivity did not really exist. The penchant not to forget that which is unworthy or undesired for future progress might explain the firm belief in early test-based selection and the strong resistance to changing the stratified structure of the school system (Payne and Barker 1986). Although data has been shown to trigger change in some high-performing education systems, such as Germany, no such PISA shock effect has been observed in the Trinidad and Tobago education system (Davoli and Entorf 2018; De Lisle et al. 2014).

AN OVERVIEW OF TRINIDAD AND TOBAGO'S EDUCATIONAL TRAJECTORY

Table 4.5 shows the trajectory of educational development in Trinidad and Tobago post-independence. As shown, we interpret the existence of seven distinct phases. The first phase involved an extended period of post-independence planning in which the World Bank and technocrats were involved. Michael Alleyne recorded this experience in some detail (Alleyne 1996). Implementation of this plan in the second phase led to an extended period of growth and school differentiation as different power groups negotiated for position and influence. The third phase is crystallization and hardening as the reality and permanence of the differentiated and stratified system become fully evident. At the end of this third phase, three models of schools emerged (London 1991).

Table 4.5: The Trajectory of Education Development in Trinidad and Tobago

Phases of Education Development	Academic Goals	Social and Affective Goals	Governance Structures and Processes	Economic Development Phase
Post-Independence Planning (1962–70)	Second tier of Government schools		Centralization	Industrialization
Implementation and Expansion (1970–80)	Comprehensive schooling Expansion of TVET	Diversity and Social Cohesion	Multiple School Models	Skills/Capital Intensive
Changing Directions and Planning (1980–90)	Comprehensive/ Grammar Schooling	Inclusion	Decentralization amidst Differentiation	Skills/Capital Intensive
Rebirth with opportunity lost (1990–2000)	Quality Access	Holistic Learning	School Improvement	Skills/Capital Intensive
Poverty concentration amidst differentiation (2000 –2009)	Equity	Diversity	School Based Planning	Skills/Capital Intensive
Accountability and Growth (2010–19)	Quality	Transversal skills	Centralization	Knowledge-based
Confronting a pandemic and futuring (2020 onwards)	Equity	Well-being	Centralization	Knowledge-based

Prior to the crystallization phase in Stage 3, it might have been possible to restructure the school system either through stronger but fair competition or through administrative action, as in Guyana (Lutchman 1970, 1971). This is considered a major lost opportunity. Stage 4 is a period of rebirth, starting with the well-constructed modern white paper, 1993–2003, which was developed through a series of public consultations. This period was more clearly focused on quality, even though issues of universal access to secondary schooling were still to be resolved.

Stage 5 represented an awakening, a growing awareness of the extent of inequity through data from large-scale assessments. It became clear that inequity existed not only among individuals and groups but also in schools. The response of the Ministry of Education was to institute a system of accountability that led to significant improvement in system performance in Stage 6. This was evident, for example, in the improvement in PIRLS between 2011 and 2016. Unfortunately, socio-economic and gender gaps remained significant issues even during this time. This stage led to the current situation of the pandemic crisis and the need to build back better (Fernandez and Ahmed 2019).

THE TRAJECTORY PERIODS

Post-independence Planning – 1962–70. The attempted expansion of the education system during this period must first be put in context. Although it is easy now to claim that access does not necessarily equate to quality, analysts must consider that quality cannot exist if there is no access. The period of expansion was critical because access to secondary schooling was minimal. For example, Andrews (1978) noted that in 1959, 171,774 students were enrolled in primary school, and only 9,932 were in secondary school. These figures remind us that the education system at the time was incapable of fulfilling the will and desires of the people of an emerging nation.

Mahabir (1973) provided data on this period (from 1963 to 1970) for the 11+ examination. He showed that large numbers did not receive any places in secondary school at all, with rural children being severely disadvantaged. As shown in figure 4.2, in 1970, only 18 per cent of students received places on sitting the Common Entrance Examination. Cross and Schwartzbaum (1969) also provided data for this period confirming the urban-rural disparity (urban students 2.8 times more likely to be selected) and pointing out an advantage of socio-economic status (High SES 3 times more likely to be selected).

The 1968–83 plan begins with a strong expression of hope and great expectations. It includes the right words, linking radical change with independence, although there is inadequate logic for action. As Yeh (2016) has argued, "after a colonial government leaves, a new government often overthrows its education system in order to declare the official beginning of post-colonialism" (890). Of course, for Trinidad and Tobago, self-government was already in place; however, the broad concept described by Yeh applies considering the vestiges of dominance that continued through self-government. The document begins this way:

> This Draft Plan was prepared in response to a local problem. Full national independence and identity will be achieved and secured only on the basis of an education system which does not rely on foreign assumptions and references for its existence and growth. The educational revolution which is required is a thorough one – not merely a substitution of a local examination in place of a foreign one nor the replacement of tropical architecture, locally produced books and such things in place of foreign equivalents. (5)

Michael Alleyne was said to be the architect of the fifteen-year plan. He was not shy in describing the ambitious attempts by a new government to plan radical restructuring of the education system with limited resources and unproven stakeholder support. Alleyne's (1996) words have been recorded for posterity:

> The implementation of the 15-Year Plan for Educational Development (1968–83) was the most ambitious and far-reaching educational project ever executed in the history of Trinidad and Tobago. . . . With the breakup of the colonial empires in Africa, Asia and the Caribbean, national governments were burdened with the task of providing adequate and appropriate education to their peoples to equip them to exercise their rights and undertake their responsibilities in these young democratic societies. . . . Due to the poor economic state of the colonial governments, the need for international technical and financial assistance was urgent. International funding agencies such as the World Bank stressed the need for planning in all sectors of development as a prerequisite for loans or any technical assistance. (85)

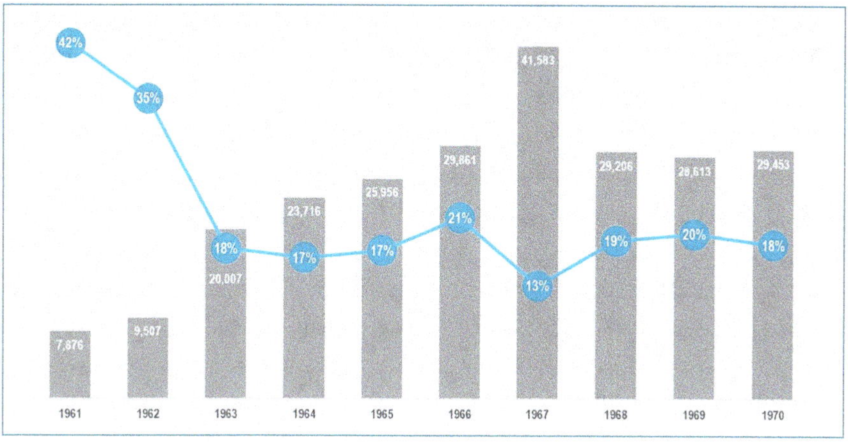

Figure 4.2: Percentage of Students Receiving Places in the Common Entrance Examination
Note. Data abstracted from Mahabir (1973).

Perhaps, then, Alleyne's (1996) analysis suggested that the plan might have been doomed at the start. This is not a negative comment, recognizing that in these post-colonial arenas of conflict, doubt and pretence, hope is necessary to drive any sincere efforts at change. The question is, to what extent was the plan simply wishful thinking[11] since the economic boom that inspired independence was beginning to peter out (Robinson 2001). Ramsaran (1999) noted that the external economic environment was changing radically in the 1970s and 1980s. The problem with the proposal, then, was the failure to acknowledge the risks involved in planning such radical change with so many external threats. There were also internal threats, such as the lack of collective reflexivity and agency.

One of the riskier goals, as identified by Alleyne (1996, 87), was "that the denominational organizations . . . should be requested to adopt the national model" and "assume full responsibility for all costs of education structured along the lines of the national model". This was a subtle invitation to fall upon one's sword, unlikely to be acted upon. In reality, the denominational groups were being asked to give up the advantage of the school model and public choice and accept the threat of economic risk. By 1976, it was clear that the denominational boards were not going to integrate into "a national model".

Reliance on the funding agency to support all aspects of technical change was also foolhardy. Funders and consultants do not translate and enact change protocols; local technocrats do. Despite the quality of technocrats that existed, Trinidad and Tobago did not have the capacity or will to implement this extensive change. Moreover, Walker's (2002) analysis of developmental administration in Trinidad and Tobago suggested that not everyone had the same values about educational development and the lack of shared values and intent would become the fuel that led to the unexpected redirection.

Implementation and Expansion – 1970–80. Despite the pretence of rationality, indeterminacy is the reality of most planning situations (Eisenberg 1995). However, in this case, indeterminacy might have worked for implementation efforts. The school expansion project appeared doomed because of the lack of resources. Opportunely, the 1970 OPEC oil crisis resulted in much-needed funds directed towards the expansion yearned for but still unimagined. This increased funding led to the 1975 prime minister's proposals that redirected the plan. We hypothesize that an expanding education infrastructure was being confronted and constrained by inherited beliefs and perspectives (Margaret Archer's culture), which were still focused upon achievement through innate ability.

We are convinced from the documentation that the then-prime minister clearly understood the opportunities presented. In minutes to Cabinet, one year after implementing the plan, it was recognized that the redirection of the 1968–83 plan and the proposal for all-age comprehensive schools provided several possibilities and opportunities for schools, communities and the nation. Perhaps this is most evident in the last of the seven listed:

> The possibility of attracting to the whole secondary educational system the management, the dedication and traditions of discipline of the denominational schools – through deliberate attempts to involve these organizations in this new secondary school programme.[12] (Note for Cabinet-Implementation of Cabinet's Decision on Education – PM 1976, 138)

During this period, several democratic concessions were made to allow all students to progress onto the later stages of secondary school. The original proposals were perhaps foolhardy in the first place in defining basic education as essentially at 14+. Moreover, the idea of vocational schools for the age group 14–18 years of age proved unviable. It was more appropriate to conceptualize an "integrated comprehensive programme embracing the academic, pre-technician, commercial, general industrial, and limited specialized craft training" (Government of the Republic of Trinidad and Tobago 1975, 12).

This period provided another source of opportunity – riding the social change to build greater awareness of social justice and advocacy for a fairer solution to the wastefulness of stratified schooling. Although Black Power as a social movement advocated for greater social justice in society, there was surprisingly limited awareness of the way in which schooling structures, agency and social mobility were connected (Lowenthal 1972). These issues were only hinted at in a meeting between Prime Minister Eric Williams and Minister of Education and Culture Carlton Gomes. The meeting was held on Thursday, 24 July 1975, at Whitehall with the six teachers' unions. The unions noted (1) the lack of publicity about the plan, (2) continued resistance to the limited course in the Junior Secondary school, (3) the absence of viable pathways from this level of schooling, (4) poor quality staffing of the new schools and (5) resistance to the Form 3 transition point.

Changing Directions and (Dis) Quiet – 1980–90. An assessment of the plan for educational development 1968–83 was published in 1984. The document clearly stated the initial principles of the 1968–83 plan and the redirection or re-profiling provided by the 1975 modifications of the prime minister. The evaluation dealt with many ticklish issues, including funding and joint management of the emerging dual structure. It is also honest in assessing the failure to enact high-quality curricula and effective pedagogy.

At the end of this period, large-scale evaluation data would be gathered through the IEA Literacy survey. This led to several valuable reports from the World Bank that highlighted the extent of inequity[13] in the local school system. These findings would provide important comparative data on the performance of the school system in terms of comparative or benchmarked quality and equity. This decade was critical, too, because it included significant political revolutions. However, documentation and analysis of events suggested limited overall progress in educational development.

The 1985–90 Education Plan was developed during this period. Several new focal points were created in this plan, including a system of professional development under the governance of a "controlling body" (86) and with provisions for a teacher resource and curriculum development centre. The plan also considered special education, technical vocational education and education research. Some comments are very conservative, such as the one on the 11+, which talks about replacing test-based selection with a placement function when universal secondary education was achieved. This was a reversal of statements in the 1968–83 Education Plan, which promised the removal of the examination on achieving universal secondary education.

By the end of this period, the stratified structure of the school system had become fully crystallized. Brathwaite (1981) described it as "a system designed to keep people in their places" (5). Taylor called it "a caste system with strong apartheid characteristics" (5). He described the new sector schools as an appendage not naturally integrated into the system. As Taylor (1982) had discerned, the stratified education system was not pre-planned but had evolved, resulting from both action and inaction by the government and stakeholders. Brathwaithe (1981) marvelled at the way the evolved school structure so closely resembled the 1944 system structure proposed by the Norwood plan for secondary schooling in the UK (UK Board of Education 1943). From another perspective, we argue that the stratified system that emerged represented implicit beliefs about people and learning fixed within the minds and hearts of most stakeholders in this postcolonial state. These are persistent imaginings left behind by the colonial experience, one that creates social pyramids mimicking the local societies (World Bank 1999). These are not the dreams of an independent future.

Rebirth with Opportunity Lost – 1990–2000. Locally, the results of the 1990–91 IEA were still not widely known in Trinidad and Tobago. Nevertheless, its findings put Trinidad and Tobago on an international stage with thirty-two other countries (Elley 1992). Trinidad and Tobago was one of the countries with low achievement, like Venezuela, the Philippines and Thailand. The fourteen-year-olds (mean standard score of 479) did comparatively better than the nine-year-olds (mean standard score of 451).

The overall low performance of the education system in Trinidad and Tobago is significant because it reflects the intense local competition between the government and the religious boards, which has not led to excellence or equity. Perhaps, then, this was another lost opportunity – *the failure to recognize that the system was working for only a few and, therefore, could never be world-class.* As policy actors competed mindlessly over power and resources, countries like the Netherlands[14] and Singapore progressed up the ladder without contention or muted dissent.

Sadly, this was not the only lesson to be learnt from this data. The World Bank education experts quickly picked up a dominant weakness of the system, although the subsequent funded programmes proposed were often less than effective. The Fourth Basic Education project might be regarded as a lesson in failure and teaches that external funding and guidance cannot change the education provision in a dependent country if local capacity is low. The mistranslations and awkward implementation of multiple reforms by local technocrats were simply astounding. When does a system for national learning assessment become a continuous assessment?[15] How and why should special and inclusive education be included within a protocol for continuous assessment? From this perspective, the local Continuous Assessment Programme (2008) was a foolhardy strategy that offered much and delivered little even when implemented with trueness (De Lisle 2015). Such mistranslations have frequently led to lost opportunities in the arena of improving quality.

The evidence gathered from the IEA and other studies showed that equity was a significant issue across multiple areas, such as gender, poverty and marginalized groups (World Bank 1993, 1995, 1996). Elley (1992) documented large differences across gender and geographic location, and these do not appear to have diminished over time (De Lisle 2018). We regard these gaps as relevant to policy because they are comparatively large and practically significant. For example, using the IEA data, Yang (2003) concluded that Trinidad and Tobago was one of the countries with a high socio-economic status effect. She observed:

> A number of countries have a low or medium school SES effect in all three SES-Achievement Studies, and the differences in the school SES effect are not so large. For the Nordic countries, Canada and Italy, for example, the school SES effect is at a low or medium level in all SES-Achievement Studies. Another group of countries is formed by those who have rather high school SES effects in all the three studies: Belgium, East Germany, Trinidad-Tobago, Hungary, the Netherlands, New Zealand, Singapore and the U. S. The school SES effect in the rest of countries is at an intermediate level, *e.g.*, Greece, France, Ireland, Hong Kong, Slovenia, and Switzerland. (69) [Emphasis Ours]

Yang also found high variation between classrooms and higher variation between in the fourteen years of age group compared with the nine-years of age group. Of course, this was because, at that time, the secondary school stratification was much larger than the differentiation of primary schools.

It is unclear whether these findings were (1) clearly understood by local technocrats, (2) fully acknowledged by stakeholders or (3) taken into account by planners. It could be that the Trinidad and Tobago education system is generally much less responsive to data, perhaps because of weak media and other factors, such as perceived lack of validity (De Lisle et al. 2014). This, then, was another opportunity lost, the chance to respond to specific diagnosed weaknesses and make real changes in policy that might improve equity and excellence. However, planning continued, and this period saw the development of a ten-year education plan through multiple consultations and discussions by local experts.

The White Paper, 1993–2003, does have its critics despite strong local support. For example, London (1996) argued that the plan took decentralization as a panacea for the many ills facing the system without clearly defining what decentralization meant. Time has shown us that decentralization is no silver bullet for improving an education system; however, the model and configuration of accountability and autonomy relationships must be clearly defined for success (di Gropello 2007). Nevertheless, the White Paper, 1993–2003, was focused on improving quality, although it politely ignored the issue of secondary school differentiation. Through the SEMP initiatives, this issue would return to trouble an already deeply troubled and inequitable school system.

One of the major events during this period was the formation of the National Task Force to remove the Common Entrance Examination in 1998. This act should be regarded as an attempt at radical reform since it would have likely led to a redistribution of students or a reformulation of choice criteria. In this instance, the then prime minister was able to clearly discern the opportunity for change, with universal secondary education eminent by 2001. The task force chose to retain the examination, claiming the problem of heterogeneity prohibited radical change (Trinidad and Tobago Task Force 1998). The Common Entrance Examination became the Secondary Entrance Assessment in 2001, with a prominent placement function. Further adjustment was attempted in the succeeding period.

Poverty Concentration and Differentiation – 2000–2009. The SEMP reform was initiated by the Inter-American Development Bank (IDB) and launched a slew of reforms targeting the critical secondary school sector. The project focused on four components: (1) improved educational equity and quality, (2) deshifting, rehabilitating and upgrading school infrastructure, (3) institutional strengthening and (4) studies and measures for improved sector performance. The project was inefficiently managed by a coordination agency run by mostly locals. Although the reforms claimed to target the secondary school sector and included an explicit focus on quality and equity, the logic of some of the initiatives remains unclear to this day. However, some reforms have impacted the system and have lasted even when fidelity was low.

Several new secondary schools were built during this period. At the direction of the government of the time, public funds were used to fund a new suite of schools for denominational groups without traditional grammar schools (Meighoo 2010). This policy action might have further weakened and diluted the responsibility and possible impact of the state on education and strengthened the potential for conflict and competition alluded to by Campbell (1997). A magnet school project was launched but without the necessary training, resources or marketing, as if the magic of the word would be sufficient. Technology Education with a problem-solving and innovation focus was launched as part of what is called the SEMP curriculum. This curriculum and accompanying examinations were not integrated into the existing system. At the same time, some denominational schools were allowed to minimize the SEMP/National Certificate of Secondary Education (NCSE) system. However, data from 2015 show that performance in the NCSE mimics that in the SEA (Jackson 2015).

During this period, then, Trinidad and Tobago failed to harness the potential of the SEMP reform through administrative ineptitude and bungling. If implemented with fidelity, the country might have experienced an improved secondary education sector with implications for innovation and economic competitiveness. Unfortunately, by 2006, the project had failed to meet its key goals, and by 2009, it was still floundering at the end of the extended implementation cycle. As table 4.6 shows, several projects were still being initiated ten years after the programme and after the 2006 redirection.

The consultant for the SEMP Curriculum provided a glimpse into the failure of implementation. Gift (2005) noted:

Table 4.6: Implementation and Completion of Projects in the SEMP

Component	AREA	Adoption Status	Implementation Issues
SEMP Curriculum	Component 1	Part 1 was completed and revised. Part 2 was not completed.	Product was evaluated but insufficient information on implementation fidelity.
NCSE	Component 1	Programme closed while ongoing	There is a lack of marketing and limited training at school site.
Teaching using Technology/ICT	Component 1	Mostly Completed	Several Instances of good practice. But requires further support at school sites
Technology Education	Component 1	Completed	Naïve change strategy resulted in strong resistance.
Reading Intervention-Monitoring Unit and Training in Reading	Component 1	Programme closed while ongoing	Need for Coherent implementation-evaluation link
Classroom Collaborative Systems	Component 1	Partially Completed	Limited by failure to complete laboratories
Teacher Professional Development Institute	Component 1	Closed during Initiation	Support and staffing needed
Teaching and Learning Systems	Component 1	Programme closed while ongoing	Need for information on implementation quality
Teaching and Learning – Physical Environment	Component 2	Programme closed while ongoing	NA
School Conversion (Deshifting)	Component 2	Programme closed while ongoing	Time delays with limited evaluation and dissemination of best practice.
School Upgrading	Component 2	Completed	2006 baseline study indicates improvement in laboratories and centres
School Based Management and Decentralization	Component 3	Programme closed while ongoing	Some delay in implementation
Quality Assurance Systems	Component 3	Programme closed while ongoing	Information sketchy
Public Awareness Campaign	Component 3	Not initiated	NA
Sector Studies	Component 4	Only partially completed	NA

Note. Internal Evaluation and close out of the SEMP.

> Teachers have not been sufficiently prepared for delivering the SEMP curricula. The problem is more acute in Technology Education which is a new subject to this country. The Diploma in Technology Education had serious limitations which seriously affected the capability of teachers to deliver the curriculum effectively. Some teachers were assigned to Technology Education laboratories where they were expected to supervise students in the use of equipment for which the teachers themselves were not adequately trained. . . .Teachers felt insecure about reports concerning the replacement of home economics and agricultural science by technology education. There is a view that the subjects to be replaced are vital for economic and social development of this country and their replacement is not in the best interest of the nation. (46–47)

The 2002–6 Education Plan provides the clearest pathway forward for the system built upon the 1993–2003 White Paper and the growing evidence of inequity and organizational inefficiency. For example, the document hinted at the need to redress the issue of low-performing schools, calling for "a mechanism to identify underperforming schools and to render them more effective". It proposed an "introduction of a programme of systematic inspection and evaluation of schools by December 2003" (54). The system for identifying primary schools was developed during this period with local expertise (De Lisle 2016). However, little progress was made in installing an inspection system, even by the end of the period. This was a significant shortcoming because school evaluations are a critical component of accountability and governance systems for schools (Cassano et al. 2019).

A centralized system of national learning assessments was finally developed and installed in 2004. Standard-based performance levels were established in 2005 and 2008, and a system for classifying schools using an accountability index was established in 2007. The driving force for these installations was not just the education plan but data from National and International Learning Assessments showing large variations in performance across geographic regions and schools (De Lisle 2010). The number of low performers in the PIRLS 2006 was noticeable at 36 per cent, and the gender gap favoured females by 0.31 Standard Deviations. By 2010, this low performance in Reading was confirmed with 44.8 per cent of students aged fifteen below Level 2. Level 2 was designated as the minimum acceptable level. From 1990 to 1991, the level of inclusion was higher in the primary school system. This suggests that stratification by secondary school models had a significant effect.

Accountability and Growth – 2010–19. The accountability system employed to reduce the variation in achievement in primary school had a significant effect on PIRLS 2011 schools, and the number of low achievers declined to 22 per cent. This reduction was also reflected in school and student performance on the National Tests, as shown in table 4.7 (De Lisle 2015). Therefore, there was another opportunity to make equity the centrepiece of reform. Although several initiatives, such as Literacy Coaches targeting low-performing schools, were launched, the 2011–15 plan did not have a similar focus. Instead, it supplanted a values-based improvement agenda. Although this approach was welcomed, values teaching cannot negate the gross achievement inequity evident in the Trinidad and Tobago education systems. Some stakeholders made several attempts to end the system of National Testing. These were only successful in 2017 when attempts at installing a system of national learning assessments were abandoned in Trinidad but not in Tobago.

This period is interesting, but the story again suggests many lost opportunities and some reversals. There was evidence that overall performance in the CSEC results was on the rise. This was clearly not time

Table 4.7: Changes in School Performance by District, Based on Accountability Index from National Tests

District/ Division	Mean Rate of Improvement	No. Schools with Improvement	No. Schools with Low, No Improvement, or Decline	Percentage Schools Improving
North Eastern	5.91	28	15	65.1
Tobago	5.60	33	8	80.5
Victoria	4.78	61	16	79.2
Caroni	3.97	41	20	67.2
South Eastern	3.76	36	14	72.0
St George East	3.47	68	39	63.6
Port of Spain	3.41	57	33	63.3
St Patrick	3.24	36	24	60.0

Note: Data sourced from the IDB funded Technical Assistance in the Statistical Analysis of the Performance of Trinidad and Tobago in the PIRLS, PISA, CXC and National Tests, with specific reference to Lessons Learned and Policy Implications: Unpublished Report 2 – Exam Analysis Judging Quality and Inequality in Outcomes using Large Scale Assessments

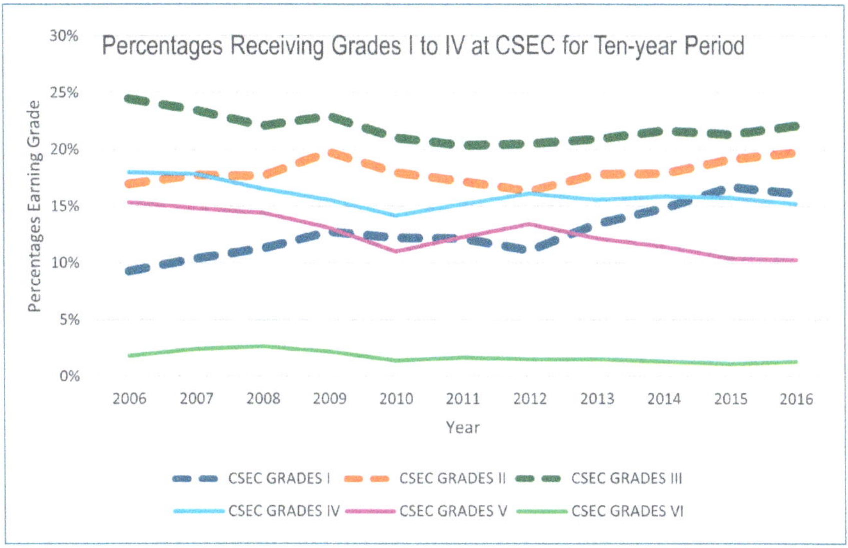

Figure 4.3: Percentage of Students Receiving Grades I to IV in Trinidad and Tobago from 2006 to 2016
Note: Data sourced from the IDB funded Technical Assistance in the Statistical Analysis of the Performance of Trinidad and Tobago in the PIRLS, PISA, CXC and National Tests, with specific reference to Lessons Learned and Policy Implications: Unpublished Report 2 – Exam Analysis Judging Quality and Inequality in Outcomes using Large Scale Assessments; Grades 1 to III are passing levels.

for maintenance or reversals but an opportunity to plan for the future and positioning of Trinidad and Tobago. Some decisions made were based upon evidence, but the data-generating systems of the Division of Educational Research and Evaluation (DERE) and the Planning Division were severely scavenged in the latter part of the decade. The 2019 introduction of the SEA focused upon higher-order thinking appeared pragmatic, except there was little parallel development of aligned and supportive pedagogical systems. The Ministry of Education did not always learn from its innovations, such as the Primary School Rewrite (PCR) and Student Transition and Remediation Support (STARS) programme, because large-scale data from national and international learning assessments were no longer available, and evaluation data was scarce.

For PIRLS scores, there was a significant jump between 2006 and 2011 but a flattening from 2011 to 2016. This implies that the coordinated planning from 2002 to 2006 and the roll-out of Vision 2020 in the 2007–10 operational plan did have some impact. However, examination of the National Test data from 2005 to 2016 and CSEC scores from 2005 to 2016 also confirm improvements in the performance of students in primary school over this period. National Test data shows improvement in all districts, including those that have been underperforming, such as the Tobago Education Division and the South Eastern Education District. Improvement in these areas demonstrates the value of monitoring learning and intervening in instances of chronic low school performance. Figure 4.4 shows the data for CSEC, which indicates a rise in Grades I (10 per cent to 15 per cent) and II (16 per cent to 20 per cent) and a decline in Grades IV and V.

Confronting a Pandemic 2020 onwards. Despite the apparent improvement by 2020, Trinidad and Tobago found itself impacted by school closures during the COVID-19 pandemic. As an analytical framework for planning, we might consider the COVID-19 crisis as a Black Swan Event. A Black Swan event is unpredictable beyond what is usually expected and has potentially severe consequences (Valeras 2020). Few schooling systems are able to plan effectively for such unexpected events. At the same time, research, new protocols and strategies are needed for these times. For example, the development of new models for hybrid learning pedagogy (Zancanella and Rice 2021). We agree, however, that there is no future-proofing of current education plans. However, as the system is reinvigorated, it can be built back better so that it becomes sustainable and resilient (Fernandez and Ahmed 2019).

An education system can be made more adaptable and flexible, making it more ready for future Black Swan events. Planners should undoubtedly work on the clear weaknesses evident during the pandemic period, including the over-reliance upon public examinations (Cairns 2021). The concept of multi-systemic resilience is applicable here as it raises the question of designing interventions, programmes and policies for remediating complex, multi-sectoral issues like literacy, low-performing schools and community poverty (Ungar 2021). Some schools in Trinidad and Tobago have traditionally not sought strong partnerships with all families and communities. Perhaps this reflects the culture of low expectations for academically marginalized youth (Anderson et al. 2017).

Figure 4.4, COVID-19 closures will have different impacts depending upon the context. Considering the high level of inequity in Trinidad and Tobago, it is likely that school closures across 2020 and 2022 will have a much more severe impact on some groups, widening the existing performance gap.

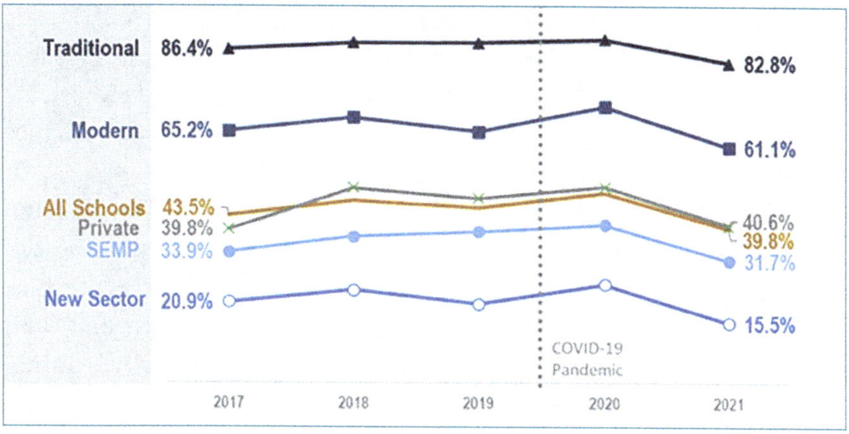

Figure 4.4: Attainment of Full CSEC Certificates in Trinidad and Tobago from 2017 to 2021
Note. Data sourced from the Trinidad and Tobago Ministry of Education, Division of Educational Research and Evaluation and reanalysed; CSEC = Caribbean Secondary Education Certificate; SEMP = Secondary Education Modernization Programme.

One of the weaknesses in such a scenario is that Trinidad and Tobago does not monitor learning and the curriculum, believing that every standardized test is an examination (Ferrer and Fiszbein 2015). Therefore, there is no way now to monitor or measure learning. Moreover, there is a missing focus on formative assessment (Yang and Xin 2022). If we are to take the gold standard of school completion from public examinations at 16+, five CSEC passes in English and Mathematics, the performance of the system has severely declined after 2020, as shown.

In figure 4.4, the pattern of performance across the four secondary school models is very clear, with two points to be noted. Firstly, the performance of all schools declined during the pandemic. Secondly, it is noteworthy that the different school models are performing differently prior to and during the pandemic. This is not a consequence of the particular school or school model; it is the consequence of a system which chooses to allocate different achievers from different contexts to different schools, restrict choices in some schools and expose some students to lowered expectations and inappropriate practices of teachers and parents.

In *building back better*, if these structural weaknesses are retained, resilience and adaptability will be further reduced (Zhao 2021). This is a simple truth, even if one school were to get all one hundred scholarships at CAPE. A singular focus on localized excellence cannot build a population for a true knowledge economy. Nevertheless, there remains very strong resistance to attempting any kind of change in the structure of the school system. Meanwhile, high-performing systems in Germany and Sweden are experimenting with different strategies to enhance system performance (Davoli and Entorf 2018).

Still, there is a word of caution regarding the future of Trinidad and Tobago's policy. Germany's experience shows that despite the success of attempts at structural reforms in some Landers, ingrained systems continue to give an advantage to parents with high social capital (Apple and Debs 2021). Therefore, the journey towards developing a high-performing, equitable education system might be never-ending (Ainscow et al. 2013; Perry 2009). After COVID-19, well-being might be considered an equally critical system goal as students must return to a higher level of psychological, cognitive, social and physical functioning (Rappleye et al. 2020).

THEMES ON LESSONS LEARNED

The analysis of the trajectory from independence to now provides four key policy lessons. These are (1) policy learning, (2) credible hope vs. wishful thinking, (3) the impossibility of morphogenesis in a postcolonial state and (4) adding up lost opportunities. As illustrated in the trajectory of education development from independence, the system does not now have an efficient memory to learn from the present and unlearn the past. The system quickly forgets valuable events but remembers and retains practices and patterns from the colonial era. The memory developed in the Trinidad and Tobago system constructs and distorts even single-loop learning and prevents efficient planning.

Building a more efficient system memory will require greater collective mindfulness, presencing[16] and attention to the development of systems for generating and using high-quality data. Evidence-informed and participatory policymaking systems are embryonic, and there is still over-reliance on the views of a few elites in policy formulation rather than widespread consultation, although this appears to be changing. In reality, there is no such thing as "policy by vamps"; however, policymaking might appear chaotic and capricious when it is directed primarily by elite goals and intentions. Structural violence is said to exist when some students do not have high-quality schooling (Williams 2013). Therefore, policy decisions that maintain the structure and functioning of a stratified system hint at malfeasance and mischief if the actions are deliberate.

There is a vast difference between hope and wishful thinking. Forecasts for the future are often biased in favour of preferences. These will result in inflated estimates for desired outcomes (Rose and Aspiras 2019). Real hope is based upon credible evidence, even if these propositions are simply conjectures based upon the best available evidence (Sanderson 2002). The initial education plans of the 1960s and 1970s were more wishful than pragmatic. Being pragmatic requires planners to deal with policy issues sensibly and realistically, based on practical considerations and reduced risks. Pragmatic plans will identify not just goals but the scaffolding needed to reach these goals. The goal of future planning in the small island states of the Caribbean is to ensure collaborative rationality. This approach can avoid the trap of wishful thinking.

Collaborative rationality requires inclusive collaboration, informed and grounded in authentic dialogue, which results in wise and durable outcomes (Innes and Booher 2018). This is different from the kind of planning that has been attempted in the past. During the 2010–20 period, not all consultations on education were genuine and meant to learn and generate information on stakeholders' perceptions. There is also a need for more evidence to be used in the wider public debate on the education system (Davoudi 2015). As such, we need more data on Trinidad and Tobago from international learning assessments, not less (Braun and Singer 2019). We also need data from robust impact evaluations of improvement projects and continuous data from monitoring and evaluation. In gathering data from stakeholders, there is a challenge in balancing the voice of elite groups and the state against the marginalized majority (Fox-Rogers and Murphy 2014)

This chapter has considered the process of system change using Archer's morphogenesis perspective. Archer's work has its roots in the social origins of educational systems (Archer 1979). Archer (1995) sees morphogenetic processes elaborating or changing a system's given form, state or structure. The structure of schools is a causal mechanism for equity and quality outcomes. School structure and associated processes determine who gets access to what education and how they are taught. Archer and Skinningsrud (2022) argued that change is activity and concept dependent. This means that there must be agents of change who know what to do. Interestingly, Archer and Skinningsrud's work has a temporal dimension with the historical transformation of the education systems in Norway and Denmark compared to structural changes, political influence and responses to external forces.

Morphostasis processes will preserve or maintain a system's given form, organization or state. Homeostatic properties act to return a system to its original state, a phenomenon which may have occurred in the Trinidad and Tobago education system between 2015 and 2020. Positive transformation requires human actions-intentionality, commitment, reflexivity and agency and takes place over time through structural conditioning, social interaction and structural elaboration (Archer 2020). The problem in Trinidad and Tobago is that subcultures (ways of thinking and seeing education and the education system) and agency have become deeply intertwined and are strongly influenced by structure. There is insufficient reflexivity or agency to resist the rules and outcomes demanded by the structure (Some children go to these schools, and others do not – It is good for you.). Although technocrats and officials claim to be powerless through inaction, they still ensure that the system perpetuates and reinforces its hold.[17] Collective reflexivity in planning (Why are we doing this?) is rare, so the system has been able to maintain its integrity literally for decades.

From 1962 to 2022, there have been several losses and a few gains, as is true for most education systems. It is fair to say that the system has made some progress in terms of student performance and expansion. Still, the frequent reversals and lack of monitoring and evaluation continue to create continuous risk. The evolved school structure has become a major source of inequity, reinforcing differences and creating new gaps. In terms of reform, a major concern in this analysis is the failure to act upon the many opportunities that presented themselves. These opportunities included (1) the chance to create a high-performing, equitable secondary education sector from 1970 to 1976, (2) the chance to remove test-based early selection in 1998 and (3) the chance to build upon gains in the 1990s and foster real improvement during the period 2000 to 2019.

The problem of morphostasis does not appear to lie with the politicians but upon the lack of reflexive capacity among major stakeholders, including some education planners. *Building back better* after COVID-19 now presents yet another opportunity for the education system of Trinidad and Tobago to jumpstart to world-class status. Will elite interests win out again? Will technocrats implicitly or explicitly work toward these elite interests? Or will there be a united action to foster equity, well-being and excellence? It is more than likely that homeostatic forces will pull the system back to its original point. It might be possible even now to employ path-dependent policy interventions to prime the system. This might be achieved through incremental and progressive change that targets key weaknesses. Planners working with the super wicked problems of climate change have found success using such an approach (Levin 2012). It might still be wishful thinking, however, to hope that this time, sixty years on, specific policy strategies will be adopted to help Trinidad and Tobago jumpstart its education system.

NOTES

1. Equity, Well-Being and Excellence is a modern reframing of system reform but these goals are consistent with the education philosophy espoused in the 1968 to 1983 Education Plan. In part this reads, "1.7. What are we educating for? We are supposed to produce citizens who are intellectually, morally and emotionally fitted to respond adequately and productively to the varied challenges of life in a multi-racial developing country and to the changes which are being brought about rapidly in the economic foundations of civilization, particularly the challenges of Science and Technology. And we are supposed to anticipate and cater for such inevitable situations, such as the disappearance of the totally unskilled labourer, the rapid increase in the body of highly specialized knowledge upon which the world society progresses (in other words the barest educational demands of effective citizenship will be increasing rapidly as well), and the rapid increase in population which will mean (in addition to other influences working towards the same end) and a greater degree of urbanization of life in the country?" (6).
2. Dialectical critical realism (DCR) is a philosophy of natural and social science that conceptualizes structures to be real outside the researcher's perception. Explanations for inequalities seek generative mechanisms and events with change considered spacio-temporal-causal. Archer's morphogenetic theory captures DCR.
3. (1) Trinidad and Tobago National Council or Parent-Teacher Associations (1975) Memorandum to the Prime Minister of Trinidad and Tobago on

Education System in Trinidad and Tobago. (2) Meeting with Teachers' Unions on Thursday 24 July 1875 at Whitehall to discuss proposals for secondary education. (3) Trinidad and Tobago Chamber of Industry and Commerce, Paper on Education. (4) Discussions in respect of secondary education – Meeting with heads of religious denominations on Thursday, 31 July 1975 at Whitehall.

4. Perhaps it is inaccurate or even simplistic to consider Romain and Gocking to be like minded. Gocking's writings certainly confirm that he was supportive of colonial perspectives (see Parfitt 2009). However, the shared view of technocrats on the fifteen-year plan often did not mesh with that of politicians and key stakeholders and significant sparring occurred during the 1975 reorientation. As Harvey (1981) suggested, intended changes might have acquired special meanings. Alleyne (1996) highlighted the conflicting views of parents and politicians (see pages 85–96). Likewise, Campbell (1997) discussed the many public debates between key stakeholders on the reorientation of the plan in 1975 (117–29).
5. Transversal competences are the skills, knowledge and attitudes relevant to a broad range of occupations and sectors. They are also defined as the basic, essential, cross-thematic, cross-curricular or twenty-first-century skills and competences.
6. As in punctuated equilibrium policy theory. See C. Koski and S. Workman, "Drawing Practical Lessons from Punctuated Equilibrium Theory," *Policy and Politics* 46, no. 2 (2018): 293–308.
7. Policy reversal as used in this chapter refers to a complete change, dismantling or redirection in the agenda and implementation pathway.
8. See, for example, P. Engelbrecht, M. Nel, S. Smit, and M. van Deventer, "The Idealism of Education Policies and the Realities in Schools: The Implementation of Inclusive Education in South Africa," *International Journal of Inclusive Education* 20, no. 5 (2016): 520–35.
9. These have been described as single loop, double loop and triple loop learning.
10. Metapatterns are recurring tacit patterns of relationships. G. B Adams, "Organizational Metapatterns: Tacit Relationships in Organizational Culture," *Administration and Society* 25, no. 2 (1993): 139–59.
11. We use the word wishful thinking here to mean more than superficial recommendations that do not hold any implications for society except on the paper on which they are written. J. Amzat and J. Amzat, "Beyond Wishful Thinking: The Promise of Science Engagement at the Community Level in Africa," *Journal of Developing Societies* 36, no. 2 (2020): 206–28. We juxtapose this approach with a pragmatic logic that captures context and consequences. C.H. Cherryholmes, "More Notes on Pragmatism," *Educational Researcher* 23, no. 1 (1994): 16–18.

12. Retrieved from Vernon Gocking, *Historic Education Documents of Trinidad and Tobago*, vol. 27 (The University of the West Indies 1979).
13. World Bank, Latin America and the Caribbean Regional Office and J. Baker, *Trinidad and Tobago: Poverty and Unemployment in an Oil Based Economy* (Washington DC: World Bank, 1995).
14. Pillarization is the politico-denominational segregation of society promoted in Netherlands but effectively managed. See Y. Leeman, "Education and Diversity in the Netherlands," *European Educational Research Journal* 7, no. 1 (2008): 50–59.
15. The Assessment of the 1968 to 1983 Education Plan had called for an educational testing or measurement service to construct national tests for the new educational system (2).
16. Presencing is the blending of sensing and presence. It means to connect from the source of the highest future possibility and to bring it into the now. Presencing happens when perception occurs from the source of our emerging future. C.O. Scharmer, "Presencing: Learning from the Future as It Emerges: On the Tacit Dimension of Leading Revolutionary Change." Retrieved from http://www.dialogonleadership.org/Presencing-TOC.html on 2 February 2005.
17. For example, they move poor performers from denominational schools to head government schools.

REFERENCES

Adams, G.B. 1993. "Organizational Metapatterns: Tacit Relationships in Organizational Culture." *Administration and Society* 25(2): 139–59.

Ainscow, M., A. Dyson, S. Goldrick, and M. West. *Developing Equitable Education Systems*. New York: Routledge, 2013.

Alleyne, M.H.M. 1996. *Nationhood from the Schoolbag: A Historical Analysis of the Development of Secondary Education in Trinidad and Tobago*. Washington, DC: Organization of American States.

Amzat, J., and J. Amzat. 2020. "Beyond Wishful Thinking: The Promise of Science Engagement at the Community Level in Africa." *Journal of Developing Societies* 36(2): 206–28.

Andrews, V. E. 1978. *An Analysis of the Planning Process in Secondary Education in Trinidad and Tobago*. Doctoral dissertation, Andrews University.

Antunes, H.D.J.G., and P.G. Pinheiro. 2020. "Linking Knowledge Management, Organizational Learning and Memory." *Journal of Innovation and Knowledge* 5(2): 140–49.

Apple, L., and M. Debs. 2021. "'I am not a guinea pig': Parental Opportunity Hoarding and Tracking Reform in Germany." *Research in Comparative and International Education* 16(1): 64–82.

Anderson, K.T., O.G. Stewart, and D. Kachorsky. 2017. "Seeing Academically Marginalized Students' Multimodal Designs from a Position of Strength." *Written Communication* 34(2): 104–34.

Archer, M.S. 1979. *Social Origins of Educational Systems.* Thousand Oaks: Sage Publications.

———. 1982. "Morphogenesis versus Structuration: On Combining Structure and Action." *The British Journal of Sociology* 33(4): 455–83.

———. 1995. *Realist Social Theory.* Cambridge: Cambridge University Press.

———. 1996. *Culture and Agency: The Place of Culture in Social Theory.* Cambridge: Cambridge University Press.

———. 2013. *Social Origins of Educational Systems.* New York: Routledge.

———. 2020. "The Morphogenetic Approach: Critical Realism's Explanatory Framework Approach." In *Agency and Causal Explanation in Economics*, edited by P. Rona and L. Zsolnai, 137–50. Unknown: Springer, Cham.

———, and T. Skinningsrud. 2022. "The Structures of State Educational Systems and Why They Matter: Norway and Denmark Compared." In *The morphogenesis of the Norwegian Educational System*, edited by M.S. Archer, U.D.K. Bæck and T. Skinningsrud, 13–37. New York: Routledge.

Archer, M.S., U.D.K. Bæck, and T. Skinningsrud, ed. 2022. *The Morphogenesis of the Norwegian Educational System: Emergence and Development from a Critical Realist Perspective.* New York: Routledge.

Braithwaithe, R.H.E. 1981. "Plus Ca Change." *Tobago Education Forum: Journal of Association of Principals of Public Schools* 2(1): 5–13.

Braun, H. I., and J.D. Singer. 2019. "Assessment for Monitoring of Education Systems: International Comparisons." *The ANNALS of the American Academy of Political and Social Science* 683(1): 75–92.

Cairns, R. 2021. "Exams Tested by COVID-19: An Opportunity to Rethink Standardized Senior Secondary Examinations." *Prospects* 51(1): 331–45.

Campbell, C.C. 1996. *The Young Colonials: A Social History of Education in Trinidad and Tobago, 1834–1939.* Kingston: The University of the West Indies Press.

———. 1997. *Endless Education: Main Currents in the Education System of Modern Trinidad And Tobago, 1939–1986.* Kingston: The University of the West Indies Press.

Cassano, R., V. Costa, and T. Fornasari. 2019. "An Effective National Evaluation System of Schools for Sustainable Development: A Comparative European Analysis." *Sustainability* 11(1): 195.

Casey, A. J., and F. Olivera. 2011. "Reflections on Organizational Memory and Forgetting." *Journal of Management Inquiry* 20(3): 305–10.

Cherryholmes, C. H. 1994. "More Notes on Pragmatism." *Educational Researcher* 23(1): 16–18.

Commonwealth Secretariat. 2016. *Key Principles of Public Sector Reforms: Case Studies and Frameworks*. London: Commonwealth Secretariat.

Cross, M., and A.M. Schwartzbaum. 1969. "Social Mobility and Secondary School Selection in Trinidad and Tobago." *Social and Economic Studies* 18(2): 189–207.

Darling-Hammond, L. 2010. "What We Can Learn from Finland's Successful School Reform." *NEA Today Magazine* 29(2): 1–9.

Davoli, M., and H. Entorf. 2018. *The PISA Shock, Socioeconomic Inequality, and School Reforms in Germany* (No. 140). IZA Policy Paper.

Davoudi, S. 2015. "Planning as Practice of Knowing." *Planning Theory* 14(3): 316–31.

De Lisle, J. 2009. "An Institution Deeply Rooted in the Status Quo: Insights into Leadership, Development and Reform in the Education Sector of Trinidad and Tobago." *Social and Economic Studies* 58(1): 69–93.

———. 2012. "Explaining whole System Reform in Small States: The Case of Trinidad and Tobago Secondary Education Modernization Program." *Current Issues in Comparative Education* 15(1): 64–82.

———. 2015. "Installing a System of Performance Standards for National Assessments in the Republic of Trinidad and Tobago: Issues and Challenges." *Applied Measurement in Education* 28(4): 308–29.

———. 2016. "Evolving Data Use Policy in Trinidad and Tobago: The Search for Actionable Knowledge on Educational Improvement in a Small Island Developing State." *Educational Assessment, Evaluation and Accountability* 28(1): 35–60.

———. 2018. "The Development of Theory on Gendered Patterns of Achievement in the Anglophone Caribbean: Insights, Contradictions, and Silences." *Gender and Education* 30(4): 450–66.

———, P. Smith, and V. Jules. 2010. "Evaluating the Geography of Gendered Achievement Using Large-scale Assessment Data from the Primary School System of the Republic of Trinidad and Tobago." *International Journal of Educational Development* 30(4): 405–17.

De Lisle, J., R. Mohammed, and R. Lee-Piggott. 2014. "Explaining Trinidad and Tobago's System Response to International Assessment Data." *Journal of Educational Administration* 52(4): 487–508.

Di Gropello, E. 2007. "Education Decentralisation and Accountability Relationshipsin Latin American and the Caribbean Region." In *International Handbook of School Effectiveness and Improvement*, edited by T. Townsend, 503–22. Unknown: Springer.

Denny, S. 2021. "Edutocracy: A Model of the New West Indian Plantocracy in Barbados." *SAGE Open*, April–June, 1–14.

Draper, G.M. 2001. "The Civil Service in Latin America and the Caribbean: Situation and Future Challenges: The Caribbean Perspective." Draft Working Paper. Inter-American Development Bank.

Eisenberg, J. 1995. "The Limits of Educational Research: Why Most Research and Grand Plans in Education Are Futile and Wasteful." *Curriculum Inquiry* 25(4): 367–80.

Elley, W.B. 1992. *How in the World Do Students Read? IEA Study of Reading Literacy.* Amsterdam: International Association for the Evaluation of Educational Achievement.

Engelbrecht, P., M. Nel, S. Smit, and M. van Deventer. 2016. "The Idealism of Education Policies and the Realities in Schools: The Implementation of Inclusive Education in South Africa." *International Journal of Inclusive Education* 20(5): 520–35.

Ferrer, G., and A. Fiszbein. 2015. "What Has Happened with Learning Assessment Systems in Latin America." In *Lessons from the Last Decade of Experience.* Washington DC: World Bank.

Fernandez, G., and I. Ahmed. 2019. "Build Back Better" Approach to Disaster Recovery: Research Trends since 2006." *Progress in Disaster Science* 1, 100003.

Fullan, M., and J. Quinn. 2016. "Coherence Making." *School Administrator* 73(6): 30–34.

Fox-Rogers, L., and E. Murphy. 2014. "Informal Strategies of Power in the Local Planning System." *Planning Theory* 13(3): 244–68.

Gift, E. 2005. "The Consultancy to Advise on the Management of the Current Writing Process for the Core Curricula for Forms Four and Five." Port of Spain: SEMPCU.

Government of the Republic of Trinidad and Tobago. 1975. *Prime Minister's Proposals to Cabinet on Education, September 18, 1975.* Port of Spain: Government Printery.

Greene, J. P., and M.Q. McShane. 2018. "Learning from Failure." *Phi Delta Kappan* 99(8): 46–50.

Harvey, C. 1981. "Practitioners' Perceptions of an Innovative School System in a Developing Country: A Qualitative Analysis." Unpublished doctoral dissertation. Department of Educational Theory, University of Toronto.

Holan, P. M. D., and N. Phillips. 2004. "Remembrance of Things Past? The Dynamics of Organizational Forgetting." *Management Science* 50(11): 1603–613.

Innes, J. E., and D.E. Booher. 2010. *Planning with Complexity: An Introduction to Collaborative Rationality for Public Policy.* Abingdon: Routledge.

Jackson, K. 2015. *Draft Report on Education Sector Diagnosis.* Port of Spain: Ministry of Education.

Johnson, D. 2006. "Comparing the Trajectories of Educational Change and Policy Transfer in Developing Countries." *Oxford Review of Education* 32(5): 679–96.

Jones, E. 1974. "Some Notes on Decision-making and Change in Caribbean Administrative Systems." *Social and Economic Studies* 23(2): 292–310.

———. 1975. "Tendencies and Change in Caribbean Administrative Systems." *Social and Economic Studies* 24(2): 239–56.
———, and G.E. Mills. 1976. "Institutional Innovation and Change in the Commonwealth Caribbean." *Social and Economic Studies* 25(4): 323–46.
Koski, C., and S. Workman. 2018. "Drawing Practical Lessons from Punctuated Equilibrium Theory." *Policy and Politics* 46(2): 293–308.
Leeman, Y. 2008. "Education and Diversity in the Netherlands." *European Educational Research Journal* 7(1): 50–59.
Leipziger, D.M., and V. Thomas. 1993. *The Lessons of East Asia: An Overview of Country Experience.* Washington DC: World Bank.
Levin, K., B. Cashore, S. Bernstein, and G. Auld. 2012. "Overcoming the Tragedy of Super Wicked Problems: Constraining Our Future Selves to Ameliorate Global Climate Change." *Policy Sciences* 45(2): 123–52.
London, N.A. 1991. "An Experiment in Education Provision during Economic Hardship: A Third World Example." *Educational Management Administration and Leadership* 19(3):150–58.
———. 1996. "Decentralisation as and for Education Reform in Trinidad and Tobago." *Educational Studies* 22(2): 187–202.
———. 1997. "Educational Planning and Its Implementation in Trinidad and Tobago." *Comparative Education Review* 41(3): 314–30.
Lowenthal, D. 1972. "Black Power in the Caribbean Context." *Economic Geography* 48(1): 116–34.
Lutchman, H.A. 1970. "Administrative Change in an Ex-colonial Setting: A Study of Education Administration in Guyana, 1961–64." *Social and Economic Studies* 19(1): 26–56.
———. 1971. "Some Administrative Problems of the Co-operative Republic in Guyana." *Public Administration and Development* 10(2): 87–99.
Mahabir, H.G. 1973. *A Study of Elementary Students Coming from Varying Socioeconomic Backgrounds in Urban and Rural Areas of Trinidad And Tobago and the Effect These Backgrounds Have on Performance in the Eleven Plus (11+) Examinations.* Doctoral dissertation, Boston University.
Meighoo, K. 2010. "Religion and Politics in Trinidad and Tobago: Reality vs. Rhetoric towards a Research Agenda." In *Conference 'Religion in the Caribbean: Addressing the Challenges of Development and Globalism,' Trinidad and Tobago,* The University of the West Indies, St Augustine, Trinidad and Tobago, 16–18 September.
Mills, G.E., and P.D. Robertson. 1974. "The Attitudes and Behaviour of the Senior Civil Service in Jamaica." *Social and Economic Studies* 23(2): 311–43.
Parfitt, G. 2009. *Being Anglo-Caribbean.* Lulu.
Parris, C.D. 1983. "Personalization of Power in an Elected Government: Eric Williams

and Trinidad and Tobago, 1973–1981." *Journal of Interamerican Studies and World Affairs* 25(2): 171–91.
Payne, M.A., and D.O. Barker. 1986. "Still Preparing Children for the 11+: Perceptions of Parental Behaviour in the West Indies." *Educational Studies* 12(3): 313–25.
Perry, L. 2009. "Characteristics of Equitable Systems of Education: A Cross-national Analysis." *European Education* 41(1): 79–100.
Ramsaran, R. 1999. "Aspects of Growth and Adjustment in Post-independence Trinidad and Tobago." *Social and Economic Studies* 48 (1/2): 215–86.
Rappleye, J., H. Komatsu, Y. Uchida, K. Krys, and H. Markus. 2020. "Better Policies for Better Lives'?: Constructive Critique of the OECD's (Mis) Measure of Student Well-being." *Journal of Education Policy* 35(2): 258–82.
Robinson, A.N.R. 2001. *The Mechanics of Independence: Patterns of Political and Economic Transformation in Trinidad and Tobago.* Kingston: University of the West Indies Press.
Rose, J.P., and O. Aspiras. 2020. "To Hope Was to Expect": The Impact of Perspective Taking and Forecast Type on Wishful Thinking." *Journal of Behavioral Decision Making* 33(4): 411–26.
Ryan, S. 2009. *Eric Williams: The Myth and the Man.* Kingston: The University of the West Indies Press.
Sahlberg, P. 2021. *Finnish Lessons 3. 0: What Can the World Learn from Educational Change in Finland?* New York: Teachers College Press.
Sanderson, I. 2002. "Evaluation, Policy Learning and Evidence-based Policymaking." *Public Administration* 80(1): 1–22.
Scharmer, C.O. 2009. *Theory U: Learning from the Future as It Emerges.* Oakland: Berrett-Koehler Publishers.
Skinningsrud, T. 2015. "Realist Social Theorising and the Emergence of State Educational Systems." *Journal of Critical Realism* 4(2): 339–65.
Tan, C. 2011. "Framing Educational Success: A Comparative Study of Shanghai and Singapore." *Education, Knowledge and Economy* 5(3): 155–66.
Taylor, E. 1982. "The Comprehensive School System: The Illusion of Size." *Trinidad and Tobago Education Forum: Journal of Association of Principals of Public Schools* 2(3): 9–13.
Taylor, J.E. 2005. "Sustainability: Examining the Survival of Schools' Comprehensive School Reform Efforts." Paper presented at the annual meeting of the American Educational Research Association, Montreal, Canada.
Tosey, P., M. Visser, and M.N. Saunders. 2012. "The Origins and Conceptualizations of 'Triple-loop' Learning: A Critical Review." *Management Learning* 43(3): 291–307.
Trinidad and Tobago, Ministry of Education. 1984. Draft plan for educational development in Trinidad and Tobago 1968–1983. Port of Spain, Trinidad and Tobago.

———. 1985. *Education Plan 1985–1990*. Port of Spain, Trinidad.
———. 1993. *Education Policy Paper 1993–2003. National Task Force on Education* (White Paper). Port of Spain, Trinidad and Tobago.
———. 2002. *Strategic Plan 2002 – 2006*. Government of the Republic of Trinidad and Tobago. Port of Spain, Trinidad. Retrieved from https://planipolis.iiep.unesco.org/sites/default/files/ressources/trinidad_and_tobago_strategic_plan_2002-2006.pdf.
Trinidad and Tobago, Task Force for the Removal of the Common Entrance Examination. 1998) *Report*. Port of Spain: Ministry of Education.
Ungar, M., ed. 2021. *Multisystemic Resilience: Adaptation and Transformation in Contexts of Change*. Oxford: Oxford University Press.
UK Board of Education (BoE). 1943. *Curriculum and Examinations in Secondary Schools*. Norwood Report. London: HMSO.
Valeras, A.S. 2020. "COVID-19: Complexity and the Black Swan." *Families, Systems, and Health* 38(2): 221–23.
World Bank. 1993. *Caribbean Region: Access, Quality, and Efficiency in Education*. Washington DC: World Bank.
———. 1995. *Trinidad and Tobago: Poverty and unemployment in an oil*-based economy. Report No. 14382-TR. Latin American and Caribbean Region. Washington DC: World Bank.
———. *Educational change in Latin America and the Caribbean*. Washington DC: World Bank.
Walker, J. 2002. *Development Administration in the Caribbean: Independent Jamaica and Trinidad and Tobago*. Unknown: Springer.
Williams, H. 2013. "Postcolonial Structural Violence: A Study of School Violence in Trinidad and Tobago." *International Journal of Peace Studies*, 43–70.
Yang, Y. 2003. *Measuring Socioeconomic Status and Its Effects at Individual and Collective Levels: A Cross country Comparison*. Acta Universitatis Gothonburgenis. *Gothenburg Studies in Educational Science 193*.
Yang, L.P., and T. Xin. 2022. "Changing Educational Assessments in the Post-COVID-19 Era: From Assessment of Learning (AoL) to Assessment as Learning (AaL)." *Educational Measurement: Issues and Practice* 41(1): 54–60.
Yeh, C.R. 2016. "Post-colonialism Perspectives on Educational Competition." *Policy Futures in Education* 14(7): 889–909.
Zancanella, D., and M.F. Rice, ed. 2021. "Framing Policies and Procedures to Include Digital Literacies for Online Learning During and Beyond Crises." *Journal of Adolescent and Adult Literacy* 65(2): 183–88.
Zhao, Y. 2021. "Build Back Better: Avoid the Learning Loss Trap." *Prospects*, 1–5. Retrieved https://doi.org/10.1007/s11125-021-09544-y.

[CHAPTER 5]

Environmental Management in Trinidad and Tobago, 1962–2022

LA DAANA K. KANHAI, HAMISH ASMATH, JUDITH F. GOBIN

THIS CHAPTER IS LIKELY TO BE THE ONLY place where one can get a comprehensive assessment of Environmental Management in Trinidad and Tobago from Independence to the present. The chapter considers anthropogenic activities and impacts, transboundary issues, multilateral environmental agreements, environmental policies, action plans, legislation and protected areas concerning species, structure, education and public awareness. While the chapter covers a comprehensive range of pertinent issues, it is also pointed and succinct. Therefore, the chapter, with its supporting photographs, provides an insightful account of Trinidad and Tobago's custodianship and management of its environment and what we have done right, what we have done wrong, and what we can improve upon. As a result, it makes a valuable contribution to a topic that seems to be dominating global knowledge concerns, where climate change and its impacts are severely affecting human populations and their ability to cope. Moreover, it is very specific to Trinidad and Tobago and, therefore, ideal for this volume.

THE NATURAL ENVIRONMENT

Trinidad and Tobago, the most southerly islands in the Caribbean archipelago, is located on the continental shelf of the South American mainland (figure 5.1). Seawater from the adjacent North Brazil Shelf,

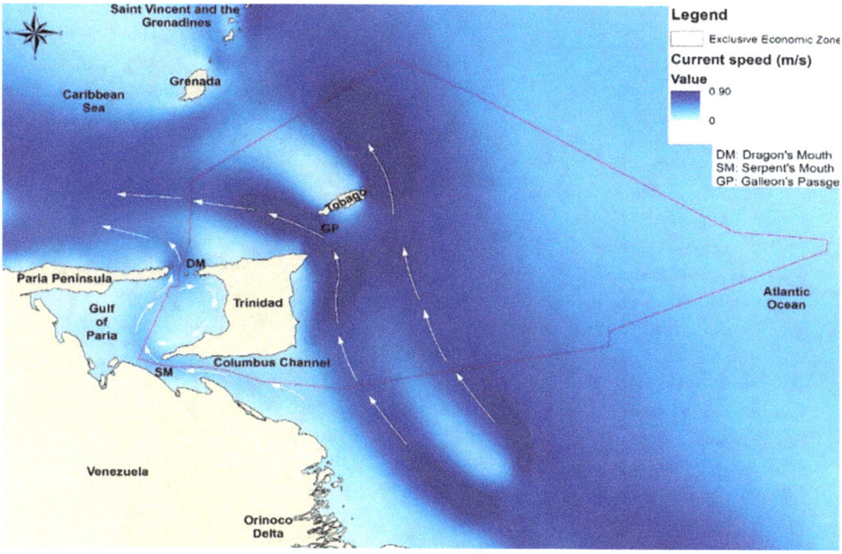

Figure 5.1: Sea surface currents around Trinidad and Tobago

especially the outflows of the Orinoco and Amazon rivers, influences the coastal and marine conditions of both islands (Kenny 2000). Sea surface currents transport seawater from the Atlantic Ocean as well as riverine outflows from South American rivers to the Exclusive Economic Zone (EEZ) of Trinidad and Tobago (figure 5.1). Outflow from these rivers impacts the coastal waters around Trinidad and, to a lesser extent, Tobago. Along the south coast of Trinidad, seawater flows in a westerly direction along the Columbus Channel. It enters the Gulf of Paria (a shared body of water between Venezuela and Trinidad), where there is a clockwise movement of sea surface currents, with seawater eventually exiting via the Dragon's Mouth into the Caribbean Sea (figure 5.1). Along the east coast of Trinidad, sea surface currents transport seawater in a northerly direction through the Galleons Passage, eventually exiting into the Caribbean Sea (figure 5.1). Sea surface currents, therefore, transport substances into, within and out of the EEZ of Trinidad and Tobago, making both islands susceptible to transboundary issues (see section 5.3).

It has been long recognized that the natural ecosystems of Trinidad and Tobago are important habitats for numerous species of plants and animals, and it is the natural resources of both islands that underpin several important sectors (energy, fisheries, tourism, etc.) that humans depend upon.

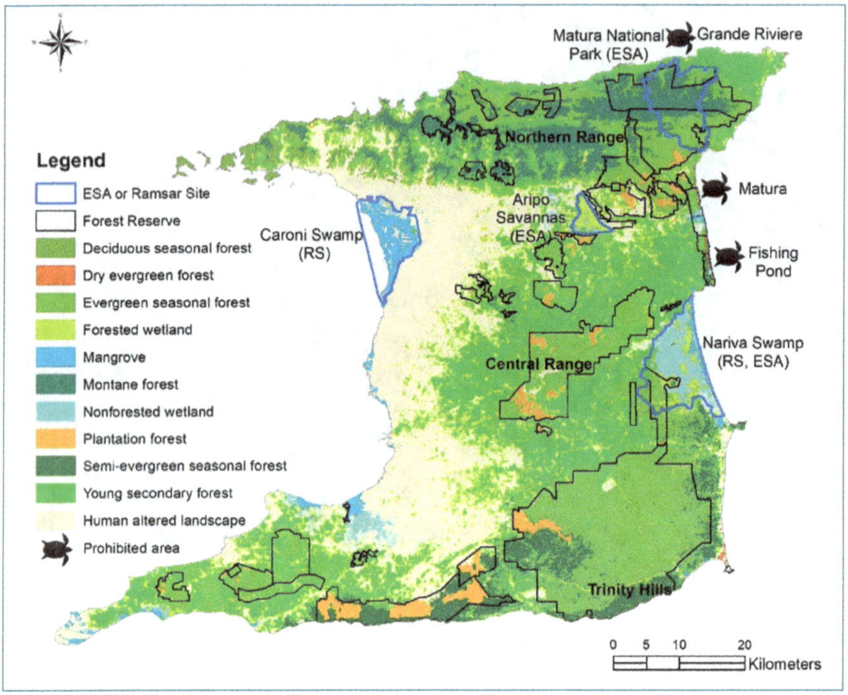

Figure 5.2: Ecosystems in Trinidad
(Based on data from Helmer et al. 2012)

In Trinidad, the Northern Range (highest peaks being Cerro del Aripo at 940 m, El Tucuche at 936 m), Central Range (most prominent hill being Mt Tamana at 330 m), and Southern Range (most prominent hills being the Trinity Hills at 325 m) are elevated ranges separated by the alluvial flats of the northern and southern basins (Kenny 2000; figure 5.2). In Tobago, the Main Ridge (the highest peak is 604 m) is the most prominent elevated region (Kenny 2000; figure 5.3).

On both islands, the dominant ecosystems are terrestrial (forests and savannahs), freshwater (rivers, lakes, freshwater marsh), coastal (mangrove swamps, seagrass beds, coral reefs, beaches, rocky shores) and marine (deep sea). There are several offshore islands, the most prominent around Trinidad include the Bocas Islands (Chacachacare, Monos, Huevos, Gaspar Grande, Gasparillo Island), Five Islands (Caledonia, Craig, Lenagan, Nelson, Pelican, Rock), San Diego Islands (Cronstadt, Carrera) and Saut d'Eau, while those around Tobago include Little Tobago, St Giles Island, Goat Island and Sister's Rock.

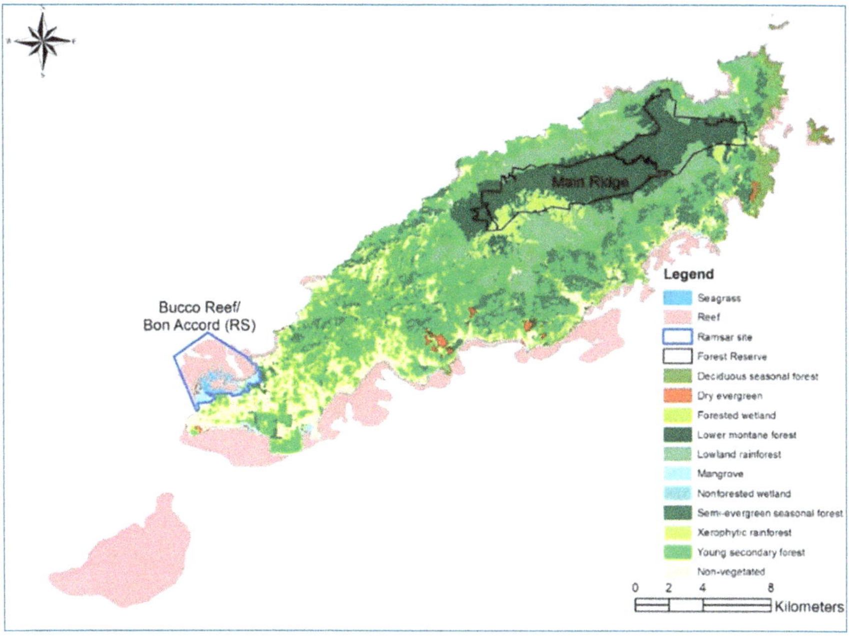

Figure 5.3: Ecosystems in Tobago
(Based on data from Helmer et al. 2012)

Trinidad and Tobago are "continental islands" whose biodiversity reflects what is present on the adjacent South American mainland. Both islands collectively have numerous species of mammals (110 species), amphibians (37 species), reptiles (100 species), birds (484 species), freshwater fish (66 species), marine fish (1013 species), invertebrates (1,128 species), cnidaria (57 species) and vascular plants (3,639 species), with several species being identified as endemic (142 species) and globally threatened (112 species) (FAO 2018). Trinidad has fifty-four watersheds, with approximately 108 rivers (photo 1), the largest of which is the Caroni River. By contrast, Tobago has 15 watersheds and several rivers. Of the emergent wetlands in Trinidad and Tobago, the largest is Nariva Swamp (11,343 hectares), which is comprised of freshwater marsh, palm forest, swamp forest, upland forest, mangrove forest and littoral woodland (Juman 2010). The Nariva Swamp is home to numerous fauna, of which some of the most iconic include the West Indian Manatee (Trichechus manatus), Red Howler Monkeys (Alouatta macconnellii), (photo 2), and Blue and Yellow Macaws (Ara ararauna), (Juman 2010). The Caroni Swamp is the second largest wetland in the country, with its mangrove forest coverage being the largest in the country (Juman 2010). Aripo Savannah is one of two natural savannah ecosystems in the country. Within the Aripo Savannah Environmentally Sensitive Area (ESA), one can find stands (photo 3) of Moriche Palm (Mauritia flexuosa), a keystone species, the seeds of which many parrots and macaws forage upon (Hosein et al. 2017). The prominent vegetation types on both islands include (i) forests, such as montane, evergreen seasonal, semi-evergreen seasonal, dry evergreen and woodlands, deciduous seasonal, forested wetland, young secondary forests, (ii) herbaceous wetlands and (iii) various plantations (See figures 5.2 and 5.3).

The coastlines of both islands have numerous beaches and bays, their characteristics and fauna being influenced by their location; for example, wave energy on the east coast beaches is typically higher than those located on the more sheltered west coasts (IMA 2013; Lee Lum and Duncan 2018). Sea turtles utilize many of the beaches on both islands for nesting from March to August (photo 4). Corals have been documented in northeast Trinidad as well as around some of the offshore islands in the Chaguaramas Peninsula (Belford et al. 2019). However, the island of Tobago has the most extensive coverage of fringing reefs (figure 5.3), of which the most popular are the Buccoo Reef in the southwest (photo 5) and Speyside in the northeast. The Maritime Ocean Collection offers the most comprehensive glimpse of coral reefs in Tobago (photo 5) (The Maritime Ocean Collection 2010). Tobago is also home to the largest remaining expanse of seagrasses (figure 5.4). Specific sites in the deep sea off the east coast of Trinidad, that is, the chemosynthetic communities associated with the El Pilar methane seeps, were recently explored following the initial expeditions in the 1980s (Amon 2017). To date, numerous studies have documented the biological diversity on both islands; however, it is beyond the scope of this chapter to comprehensively summarize these.

Natural ecosystems in Trinidad and Tobago are associated with a diverse array of supporting (e.g., habitat, soil formation, nutrient cycling, etc.), regulating (e.g., erosion control, water purification, carbon sequestration), provisioning (e.g., food, timber, genetic resources, etc.) and cultural services (e.g., recreation, tourism, etc.), many of which are integral to human well-being. When one considers the Northern Range in Trinidad, for example, (i) its tropical forest ecosystems provide an important habitat (supporting

Figure 5.4: **Photo 1**, Marianne River, Blanchisseuse, Trinidad
(Photo Credit: Nandani Bridglal)

service) to numerous species, of which there are three faunal island-endemics; Golden Tree Frog (Phyllodytes auratus), Luminous Lizard (Proctoporus shrevei), Pawi or Trinidad Piping Guan (Pipile pipile), (ii) its ecosystems are a source of timber products, non-timber forest products (e.g., wild meat from wild hog, lappe, tattoo, agouti, iguana, deer), freshwater and fish (provisioning services), (iii) its tropical forests aid in soil/water retention and carbon sequestration (regulating services) and (iv) its forests, riverine and coastal ecosystems provide opportunities for people to engage in recreation (e.g., river limes, beach outings, hiking, etc.) and eco-tourism activities (e.g., turtle-watching), (cultural services) (EMA 2004).

Within the past few decades, attention has been directed to the valuation of ecosystem services in Trinidad and Tobago. Burke et al. (2008) estimated that for 2006/2007 in Tobago (i) the economic impact of reef-related tourism and recreation in Tobago was between US$101 and US$130 million, (ii) the economic impact of coral-reef associated fisheries was between US$758,000 and US$1,148,000 million and, (iii) shoreline protection services provided by coral reefs were valued at between US$18 million and US$30 million. The fringing coral reefs around Tobago offer protection to approximately 50 per cent of the island's shoreline, and it was estimated that over a period of

Figure 5.5: **Photo 2:** Red Howler Monkey (Alouatta macconnellii)
(*Photo Credit:* Nandani Bridglal)

Figure 5.6: **Photo 3**: Moriche Palms (Mauritia flexuosa) in the Aripo Savannahs, Trinidad
(*Photo Credit:* Nandani Bridglal)

twenty-five years, potentially avoided damages were between US$450 and US$$825 million (Burke et al. 2008). The Project for Ecosystem Services-Trinidad and Tobago (ProEcoServe-T&T) estimated that (i) the forests of the Northern Range prevented the erosion of approximately 6.7 million tonnes of soil, (ii) soil retention services of the Northern Range forests were valued at between US$374 and US$622 million, (iii) pollination services provided by the Nariva Swamp were worth between US$193,387 and US$1,022,121 (calculated for cucumber production in 2012) and US$1,003,578 and US$2,181,692 (calculated for hot pepper production in 2012), (iv) annual carbon sequestration by the Nariva Swamp was approximately 1.53 million tonnes of carbon per year which was approximately 11 per cent of carbon dioxide emissions from Trinidad and Tobago (UNEP 2015; Agard et al. 2019). Based on a Choice Experiment (CE) and Contingent Valuation (CV), Cazabon-Mannette et al. (2017) also highlighted the economic benefits of sea turtles in the marine environment of Tobago.

Figure 5.7: **Photo 4:** Leatherback Turtle (*Dermocheyls coriacea*) at Grande Riviere Beach, Trinidad (*Photo Credit:* Michelle Cazabon-Mannette)

Figure 5.8: **Photo 5:** Coral Gardens, South-West Tobago (*Photo Credit:* Underwater Earth, The Maritime Collection)

Figure 5.9: **Photo 6:** Green Iguana (Iguana iguana)
(*Photo Credit*: Nandani Bridglal)

Divers indicated that they were willing to pay approximately US$62 per two-tank dive for a turtle encounter and US$31 for turtle conservation efforts (Cazabon-Mannette et al. 2017). These studies have all attempted to emphasize the economic value of natural ecosystems and their services.

ANTHROPOGENIC ACTIVITIES AND IMPACTS

Since 1962, the growth in domestic, agricultural and industrial activities in Trinidad and Tobago has contributed to a deterioration of environmental quality. Numerous studies have investigated the impact of human activities on the natural environment throughout the years.

Domestic

Human settlements, regardless of location, need access to adequate disposal facilities for human excrement. In Trinidad and Tobago, human excrement is deposited into a variety of collection facilities, some of which offer no treatment (e.g., pit latrines, in-lot septic tanks with soakaways) and others that do, that is, sewage treatment plants (STPs). The Population and Housing Census of Trinidad and Tobago indicated that by the year 2000, 27 per cent of the population utilized pit latrines, 50 per cent had in-lot septic tanks with soakaways, and only 20 per cent had disposals to sewage treatment plants (CREW 2010). Domestic sewage can enter surface waters due to non-functional STPs and runoff from pit latrines and septic tanks/soakaways (IMA 2016). Such activities lead to the introduction of pathogenic (disease-causing) organisms into the natural environment that can pose a threat to human health (IMA 2016). Since 1981, the Institute of Marine Affairs (IMA) has monitored the bacteriological water quality of beaches in Trinidad and Tobago. It has reported that some beaches are contaminated by sewage, making them unsafe for recreational users (IMA 2016). Recreational activities were also shown to have negative impacts on the bacteriological quality of both riverine (Phillip et al. 2009) and coastal environments (IMA 2016). In southwest Tobago, nutrient-enriched conditions due to improperly treated domestic sewage led to sewage-driven eutrophication, which has adversely affected both seagrasses (Juman 2005) and fringing coral reefs (Lapointe et al. 2010) in the area.

There are four major waste disposal sites in Trinidad: Beetham Landfill (61 hectares), Forres Park Landfill (8 hectares), Guanapo Landfill (7 hectares), Point Fortin, and one in Tobago, Studley Park Integrated Facility (0.5 hectares) (Riquelme et al. 2016). It is estimated that these sites receive approximately two thousand tons of municipal solid waste (MSW) per day and that approximately seven hundred thousand tons of solid waste ends up in them every year (Riquelme et al. 2016). Environmental monitoring studies have reported that waste disposal sites in Trinidad have negatively affected the surrounding environment. Environmental compartments (sediments, biota) around the Beetham Landfill have been reported to be contaminated with both inorganic (heavy metals) and organic (Polychlorinated dibenzo-p-dioxin (PCDDs), Polychlorinated dibenzofurans (PCDFs), Polychlorinated biphenyls (PCBs), organochlorine pesticides) contaminants (Mohammed et al. 2009; Mohammed et al. 2011; Mohammed et al. 2012). It has also been reported that the Guanapo Landfill has contaminated the surrounding surface waters, sediments and groundwater with chemical contaminants such as heavy metals and polycyclic aromatic hydrocarbons (PAHs) and that these contaminants pose a potential threat to human health and ecosystem well-being (Beckles et al. 2016).

The construction of infrastructure for various sectors in Trinidad and Tobago has led to the loss, fragmentation and degradation of habitats. For example, an increase in built development has resulted in a change in the coverage of freshwater marsh and mangrove vegetation around and within the Caroni Swamp (Juman and Ramsewak 2013a). Throughout the decades, the phenomenon of "coastal squeeze", that is, where built developments adjacent to mangrove forests prevent their landward migration, has occurred on both islands (Juman and Hassanali 2013; Juman and Ramsewak 2013b). Seagrass beds on both islands have also been impacted by human-induced disturbances (Juman and Alexander 2006). Multi-year data from International Coastal Clean-Up (ICC) events conducted in Trinidad and Tobago between 1994 and 2020 have revealed that marine debris densities on beaches ranged between 0.08 and 4.56 items/m, with the most commonly found items originating from land-based activities (Kanhai et al. 2022).

Agricultural

Trinidad and Tobago's agricultural sector can be best described as dynamic, as there have been changes in the dominant crops from decade to decade. From the 1980s to the present, however, organochlorine pesticides (OCPs) have been used for agricultural purposes and in controlling mosquitos (Mohammed et al., 2011). Several studies have, therefore, detected the presence of organochlorine pesticides (OCPs) and other persistent organic pollutants in the water, sediments and biota of the Caroni Swamp (Deonarine 1980; Sampath 1982) and Gulf of Paria (Mohammed et al. 2009; Mohammed et al. 2011). Recent laboratory-exposure studies have shown that locally used organophosphate pesticides (Malathion and diazinon) can alter the growth and behaviour of the Neotropical crab Poppiana dentata (Singh et al. 2021; Singh et al. 2022). Agricultural activities, such as animal husbandry operations and the use of fertilizers, can lead to the release of high concentrations of nutrients (nitrates and phosphates) into adjacent freshwater and coastal ecosystems, which can result in eutrophication (IMA 2016). Clearing of land to facilitate agriculture may increase sediment runoff into adjacent waterways.

Industrial

Trinidad and Tobago has a long history in the oil and gas sector that dates as far back as 1857 when the first well was drilled in Trinidad (Ministry of Energy and Energy Affairs, GORTT 2022). Since then, the country has ranked among the largest producers of oil and gas in the world, with these resources being fundamental to the growth of numerous downstream industries (Ministry of Energy and Energy Affairs, GORTT 2022). While the oil and gas sector and the associated petrochemical industries have been integral to the economic growth of the country, the natural environment has been negatively affected. Throughout the years, there have been numerous oil spills, with the most significant ones being the collision of two supertankers (Aegean Captain, Atlantic Express) off the east coast of Tobago in 1979 and ruptured infrastructure along the west coast of Trinidad (2013 and 2017) garnering national attention. Due to the presence of natural oil seeps as well as oil spills, tar has been detected on various coasts (Georges and Oostdam 1983), and petroleum hydrocarbons have been reported in the water, sediment and fish at multiple locations in Trinidad and Tobago (Agard 1985; Agard et al. 1988; Singh 1992; Rajkumar and Persad 1994; Persad and Rajkumar 1995; Norville and Banjoo 2011). Polycyclic aromatic hydrocarbons (PAHs), derived from petrogenic and pyrolytic sources, have been detected in the sediments, shellfish and fish from the Caroni Swamp (Kanhai et al. 2015) and the Gulf of Paria (Guppy 2001; Banjoo 2006; Balgobin and Singh 2018; Balgobin and Singh 2019). More recently, PAHs have been detected in road dust (Mohammed et al. 2018; Pragg and Mohammed 2018) and Sargassum (Seepersaud et al. 2017).

Inorganic pollutants have also been released into the natural environment as a result of anthropogenic activities (e.g., transportation, industrial activities, etc.). Heavy metals, in particular, have been detected in multiple environmental compartments of terrestrial (Bernard 1979; Mohammed et al. 1996; Mohammed 2000; Pragg and Mohammed 2020), riverine (Ramsingh 2009; Surujdeo-Maharaj 2010; Nelson 2015; Mohammed et al. 2017; Mohammed et al. 2018b), estuarine (Klekowski et al. 1995; Astudillo 2002; Astudillo et al. 2002; Astudillo, Chang Yen and Bekele 2005; Norville 2005; Kanhai et al. 2014) and coastal ecosystems (Hall and Chang Yen 1986a; Hall and Chang Yen 1986b; Shrestha and Morales 1987; Hall and Chang Yen 1988; Rajkumar and Persad 1994; Persad and Rajkumar 1995; Rajkumar,

Persad and Kumarsingh 1995; Guppy 2001; Mohammed 2005; Norville 2005; Ragbirsingh and Norville 2005; Norville and Banjoo 2011; Mohammed et al. 2012; Balfour et al. 2012; Nelson and Cohen 2014; Mohammed and Mohammed 2017; Seepersaud et al. 2018; Balgobin and Singh 2018; Nelson 2020). Of concern is the detection of both inorganic and organic pollutants in shellfish and fish and the potential risks that are posed to human consumers. Industrial effluents can also lead to nutrient loading in freshwater and coastal ecosystems. Kumarsingh et al. (1998) reported high concentrations of phosphorus in the coastal sediments in South Trinidad were influenced by domestic and industrial effluents.

Other

All of the anthropogenic activities (domestic, agricultural, industrial) discussed above can lead to the loss, fragmentation and degradation of habitats that can subsequently affect the organisms that either permanently or seasonally utilize them. Of note, however, is the fact that other anthropogenic activities pose threats to specific species. For example, the primary threats to sea turtles in Trinidad and Tobago are poaching and their incidental capture as by-catch during fishing activities (Eckert and Lien 1999; Lee Lum 2003; Lee Lum 2006; Eckert and Eckert 2005; UNEP 2010; Eckert 2013; Cazabon-Mannette 2021). Based on interviews with fisher folk, estimates for the year 2000 suggested that the gillnet fishery was responsible for the incidental capture of approximately three thousand sea turtles off the north and east coasts of Trinidad (Lee Lum 2006). Although fisher folk indicated that the majority of sea turtles (north coast – 73 per cent, east coast – 66 per cent) entangled in gillnets in 2000 were released, the concern is that this practice continues to contribute to annual sea turtle mortality (Lee Lum 2006). Based on the IUCN Red List of Threatened Species, the sea turtles that can be found in Trinidad and Tobago are listed as Vulnerable (Dermochelys coriacea, Caretta, Lepidochelys olivacea), Endangered (Chelonia mydas) and Critically Endangered (Eretmochelys imbricata, Lepidochelys kempii). Similar to sea turtles, over thirty species of sharks are incidentally captured in artisanal and commercial fisheries (Shing 2005; Shing 2006). Based on the IUCN Red List of Threatened Species, several shark species that are landed in Trinidad and Tobago are

Endangered (n = 3), Vulnerable (n = 9) and Near Threatened (n = 11) (Ali et al. 2020). Despite this, locals still consume sharks, and the shark fishery in Trinidad and Tobago remains unmanaged (Shing 2005; Ali et al. 2020).

TRANSBOUNDARY ISSUES

In addition to being impacted by local anthropogenic activities, the natural environment of Trinidad and Tobago is also affected by multiple transboundary issues that are driven by activities occurring outside of its EEZ. Among the most prominent issues are climate change, abnormal influxes of Sargassum, marine debris, alien invasive species (AIS), and the influx of Saharan dust. Small island developing states (SIDS) like Trinidad and Tobago are on the frontline of the devastating impact of greenhouse gas (GHG) induced climate change. Potential impacts such as rising sea levels, saltwater intrusion, coastal erosion, coral bleaching and changes in temperature and rainfall are all projected to have adverse effects upon many of the sectors (agriculture, fisheries, tourism, maritime transport, energy) that humans depend upon (Singh 1997; Hassanali 2017). To date, coral reefs in Tobago have experienced massive bleaching events as recently as 2005 (where the majority of sites surveyed were reported as having extensive bleaching >85 per cent) and 2010 (Wilkinson and Souter 2008; Alemu and Clement 2014; Buglass et al. 2016). Coral reefs are examples of ecosystems that are under threat from multiple natural and anthropogenic stressors. For example, in addition to being negatively affected by human activities, these ecosystems have (i) experienced coral bleaching events, (ii) been afflicted with several diseases, for example, Yellow Band Disease, etc., (iii) populations of specific species (e.g., grazing sea urchin (Diadema antillarum), a keystone herbivore) have not yet recovered following their die-offs, (iv) had coral recruitment being affected following extreme weather events such as hurricanes (Hoetjes et al. 2002; Mallela and Crabbe 2009; Mallela et al. 2010; Alemu and Clement 2014).

Oceanic currents are responsible for the transport of substances into, within and out of the EEZ of Trinidad and Tobago. Alien invasive species such as the Indo-Pacific Lionfish (Pterois spp.), first reported off the south-eastern coast of Florida in 1985, spread throughout the Caribbean via oceanic currents, with Trinidad and Tobago being the last (2012) of the Caribbean SIDS to be invaded (Alemu 2016). Surveys conducted on Tobago's reefs (2013–15) revealed that the highest densities of lionfish were reported in the northeast region (326 lionfish/ha) while the lowest were reported in the southwest region (11 lionfish/ha), (Alemu 2016). Based on Choice Experiments (CE), Alemu et al. (2019) indicated that lionfish presence in Tobago's reefs may potentially be associated with negative economic impacts due to the preferences indicated by recreational snorkelers and divers. Another AIS with a longer history in Trinidad is the Asian Green Mussel (Perna viridis), first sighted in the Point Lisas Industrial Estate in 1990 and possibly introduced as a result of maritime transportation (Gobin et al. 2013). Oceanic currents have also transported pelagic Sargassum from the Atlantic Ocean to the Caribbean Region, with abnormal influxes commencing around 2011 and persisting to date (Wang et al. 2019). The coasts of Trinidad (particularly the northeast, east and south) and Tobago (particularly the east) have been affected by Sargassum, with particularly large quantities stranding on beaches in 2011, 2015 and 2018 (CRFM 2019; Juman 2020). Sargassum strandings on beaches and its presence in coastal waters can have biological, ecological, economic and social impacts. In Trinidad and Tobago, Sargassum has disrupted fishing activities, impacted navigation of marine vessels, posed a problem for the nesting of sea turtles and negatively impacted recreational use of beaches (CRFM 2019; Juman 2020). In 2015, The Tobago House of Assembly spent approximately TT$3 million on clean-up operations, thus highlighting the economic impacts of these abnormal influxes of Sargassum on Caribbean SIDS (Juman 2020). Another transboundary issue that has a long history in the Caribbean region (1980–2020) is that of marine debris, in particular plastics, which may be transported by oceanic currents and enter the EEZs of Caribbean SIDS such as Trinidad and Tobago (Kanhai et al. 2022). The proximity of Trinidad and Tobago to major oil-producing nations (Venezuela, Guyana), as well as the intensity of maritime traffic associated with oil transportation in the Caribbean region, is also of concern since oil spilt during exploration, refining and transportation can be transported by oceanic currents, enter the country's EEZ and adversely affect its natural environment (Singh et al. 2015). Such a spill actually occurred off the coast of Tobago in 2024.

For several decades, the North Atlantic Trade Winds have transported aerosolized soil and particulate matter (collectively referred to as dust) from the African continent (especially from the Sahara Desert and the Sahel) across the Atlantic Ocean to the Caribbean region. Influxes of Saharan dust to the Caribbean generally increase particulate matter (PM) concentrations in the atmosphere. For example, Rajkumar and Chang (2000) reported elevated levels of respirable suspended particulates (PM10) along the East-West Corridor in Trinidad during Saharan dust events. During dust episodes in the Caribbean, persistent organic pollutants (POPs), airborne pollen and culturable microorganisms, some of which were pathogenic, have been detected in air samples, suggesting that Saharan dust is a carrier of these substances (Garrison et al. 2006; Garrison et al. 2014; Sullivan et al. 2012; Gowrie 2016). Of concern is the impact of Saharan dust episodes on human health, especially those of vulnerable groups (children, elderly, health compromised). Influxes of Saharan dust in Trinidad were shown to exacerbate paediatric asthma, with some studies reporting increased paediatric asthma admissions to public hospitals following dust episodes (Gyan et al. 2005; Gowrie et al. 2016).

Organisms on both islands are susceptible to various diseases that can pose potential threats to their health. For example, the causative agent (Batrachochytrium dendrobatidis) of amphibian chytridiomycosis has been reported in a critically endangered frog in Tobago (Mannophryne olmonae) and a vulnerable stream frog (Mannophryne trinitatis) in Trinidad (Alemu et al. 2008; Alemu et al. 2013). Although there was no evidence of the disease, such findings are a cause for concern as chytridiomycosis has caused the decline of amphibian populations in the Wider Caribbean Region (Alemu et al. 2008; Alemu et al. 2013). Sea turtles stranded on beaches in Trinidad and Tobago have been diagnosed with Fibropapilloma Tumours (associated with the herpes virus) and Floating Syndrome (collective term for positive buoyancy disorders) (Cazabon-Mannette and Phillips 2017; Savage and Cazabon-Mannette 2020). Major reef-building corals in Tobago have also been reported to have been afflicted with diseases, e.g., Yellow Band Disease (Mallela et al. 2010).

ENVIRONMENTAL MANAGEMENT IN TRINIDAD AND TOBAGO

Trinidad and Tobago has declared its intention to engage in sustainable development, that is, "development that meets the needs of the present without compromising the ability of future generations to meet their needs". To this end, the country has employed multi-pronged approaches to manage its natural environment and engage in sustainable development.

Multilateral Environmental Agreements (MEAs)

To date, Trinidad and Tobago is a signatory to several multilateral environmental agreements (MEAs) related to (i) biodiversity The United Nations Convention on the Conservation of Biological Diversity 1975, Cartagena Protocol on Biosafety (2003) to the UN Convention on Biological Diversity, Protocol Concerning Specially Protected Areas and Wildlife (SPAW Protocol) 1990 to the Cartagena Convention; (ii) environmentally sensitive areas (Convention on Nature Protection and Wildlife Preservation in the Western Hemisphere 1942); (iii) environmentally sensitive species (Convention on International Trade in Endangered Species of Wild Fauna and Flora (CITES) 1973); (iv) coastal and marine areas (Convention on Fishing and Conservation of the Living Resources of the High Seas 1958, Convention for the Protection and Development of the Marine Environment of the Wider Caribbean Area or "Cartagena Convention" 1983, Geneva Convention on the Continental Shelf 1958, Convention on the High Seas 1958, Convention on the Territorial Sea and Contiguous Zone 1958, United Nations Convention on the Law of the Sea-Montego Bay 1982); (v) land management (United Nations Convention to Combat Desertification (UNCCD) 1994); (vi) forests (International Tropical Timber Agreement 2006, International Plant Protection Convention 1951); (vii) wetlands (Ramsar Convention on Wetlands 1971); (viii) ozone-depleting substances (Vienna Convention Protection of the Ozone Layer 1985, Montreal Protocol on Substances that Deplete the Ozone Layer (1987) to the Vienna Convention); (ix) greenhouse gases (Paris Climate Change Agreement 2016, United Nations Framework Convention on Climate Change (UNFCCC) 1994, Kyoto Protocol 2005); (x) hazardous waste (Basel Convention on the Control of Transboundary Movement of Hazardous Wastes and their Disposal 1992); (xi) hazardous substances and spills (Oil Spills Protocol (1983) to the Cartagena Convention, Protocol Concerning Pollution from Land Based Sources and Activities (1999) to the Cartagena Convention, Lome IV Convention Control of Hazardous Wastes 1989, Stockholm Convention on Persistent Organic

Pollutants 2004, Rotterdam Convention for Certain Hazardous Chemicals and Pesticides in International Trade 1998, International Convention for the Control and Management of Ship's Ballast Water and Sediments 2004); (xii) sustainable development (United Nations 2030 Agenda for Sustainable Development 2015). As a signatory to multiple MEAs, Trinidad and Tobago has committed to tackling global environmental issues at the national scale. In meeting its obligations for many of these MEAs, the country has developed relevant environmental policies and action plans.

Environmental Policies and Action Plans

In order to achieve environmental sustainability and, by extension, sustainable development, six priorities were identified in Trinidad and Tobago's National Environmental Policy: (i) protecting environmental and human health through pollution control, (ii) sustainably managing natural assets, (iii) improving the local environment, (iv) evolving a greener economy, (v) fostering an environmentally responsible society and (vi) addressing climate change and environmental and natural hazards (GORTT 2018). In addition to this, several issue-specific policies focus on (i) waste (Municipal Waste Policy 2008, Integrated Solid Waste/Resource Management Policy 2012, National Waste Policy 2015); (ii) natural resources and ecosystems (National Policy and Programmes on Wetland Conservation for Trinidad and Tobago 2002, National Integrated Water Resources Management Policy 2005, National Forest Policy 2011, National Protected Areas Policy 2011, National Wildlife Policy 2013, National Minerals Policy White Paper 2015); (iii) climate change (National Climate Change Policy 2011); and (iv) specific sectors (National Tourism Policy 2010, Green Government Policy 2011, National Policy on Imported Used Goods 2015, Yachting Policy 2016–21, Northern Range Hillside Development Policy, Upstream Effluent Management (UEM) Policy (GORTT 2018). To date, several policies drafted but not yet finalized are the (i) Integrated Coastal Zone Management (ICZM) Policy, (ii) Renewable Energy Policy, (iii) Green Enterprise Development Policy for Micro and Small Enterprises and Cooperatives, (iv) Comprehensive Disaster Management Policy (Framework), (v) Critical Facilities Protection Policy Framework for Trinidad and Tobago (2010), (vi) Hazard Mitigation Policy, (vii) National

Relief Policy, (viii) Shelter Management Policy (2012) and (ix) Volunteer Policy. Similarly, Trinidad and Tobago has also developed several action plans (e.g., National Oil Spill Contingency Plan (2013), National Biodiversity Strategy and Action Plan for Trinidad and Tobago: 2017–22) related to specific environmental issues.

Environmental Legislation

In Trinidad and Tobago, several pieces of primary and subsidiary legislation focus on environmental affairs. Some of the most important primary legislation are the (i) Environmental Management Act (2000), (ii) Planning and Facilitation Development Act (2014), (iii) Fisheries Act (1975), which is in the process of being updated and (iv) Forests Act. Relevant subsidiary legislation includes the (i) Certificate of Environmental Clearance Rules (2001), (ii) Environmentally Sensitive Areas (ESA) Rules (2001), (iii) Environmentally Sensitive Species (ESS) Rules (2001), (iv) Noise Pollution Rules (2001), (v) Certificate of Environmental Clearance Designated Activities Order (2006), (vi) Air Pollution Rules (2014), (vii) Water Pollution Rules (2019), (viii) Waste Management Rules (2021). Protected Areas on both islands have been designated under the (i) State Lands Regulations (Chap. 57:01), (ii) Conservation of Wildlife Act (Chap 67:01), (iii) Environmental Management Act (Chap 35:05) and (iv) Marine Preservation and Enhancement Act (Chap. 37:02), (FAO 2018).

Protected Areas and Species

Conservation measures in Trinidad and Tobago have been largely in-situ, with protection being afforded to natural ecosystems and specific species. To date, protected areas on both islands are within forest reserves (n = 36), wildlife sanctuaries (n = 13), environmentally sensitive areas (n = 3) and marine protected areas (n = 1) (FAO 2018). The legacy of affording protection to natural ecosystems commenced with the declaration of the Main Ridge in Tobago as a Crown Reserve in 1776, making it the oldest legally protected forest reserve in the Western Hemisphere. In 1973, under the Marine Area (Preservation and Enhancement) Act (1970) and the Marine Area (Restricted Area) Order (1973), Buccoo Reef, a fringing reef in southwest Tobago, was designated as a marine park. More recently, under the Environmental Management Act (2000) and the Environmentally Sensitive Areas Rules (2001), Matura National Park, Nariva Swamp and Aripo Savannahs have been recognized as environmentally sensitive areas (ESAs). Under the Convention on Wetlands of International Importance (Ramsar Convention), three wetlands in Trinidad and Tobago have been recognized as RAMSAR sites: Nariva Swamp (declared in 1993), Caroni Swamp (declared in 2005), Buccoo Reef/Bon Accord Lagoon (declared in 2006). Most recently (that is, 2021), North-East Tobago was declared as a UNESCO Man and Biosphere Reserve. Species-specific behaviour has also guided conservation efforts dedicated to protecting specific areas. In Trinidad and Tobago, sea turtle nesting occurs from 1 March to 31 August. During this period, human activities are restricted at three turtle nesting beaches (Matura, Fishing Pond, Grande Riviere) due to their designation as prohibited areas under the Forests Act (chapter 66: 01).

In addition to recognizing the importance of specific ecosystems, under the Environmentally Sensitive Species (ESS) Rules (2001), the following species have been recognized as being Environmentally Sensitive Species (ESS), Trinidad Piping Guan (Pipile pipile), West Indian Manatee (Trichechus manatus), White-tailed sabre-wing hummingbird (Campylopterus ensipennis), Golden Tree Frog (Phytotriades auratus), Ocelot (Leopardus pardalis), Olive Ridley Turtle (Lepidochelys olivacea), Hawksbill Turtle (Eretmochelys imbricata), Green Turtle (Chelonia mydas), Loggerhead Turtle (Caretta caretta), Leatherback Turtle (Dermochelys coriacea) and Scarlet Ibis (Eudocimus ruber). Currently, the Environmental Management Authority (EMA) is in the process of designating the Red Howler Monkey (Alouatta macconnellii) and the White-Fronted Capuchin Monkey (Cebus albifrons) as ESSs.

Sea turtle conservation efforts in Trinidad and Tobago have had a long history (1960s to present), with organizations such as the Trinidad and Tobago Field Naturalists' Club (TTFNC), Pointe-a-Pierre Wild Fowl Trust (WFT), Institute of Marine Affairs (IMA), Forestry Division and several community-based organizations (CBOs); Nature Seekers, The Turtle Village Trust (TVT), Fishing Pond Turtle Conservation Group, Grande Riviere Nature Tour Guide Association, Save Our Sea Turtles (SOS) Tobago, Matura 2 Matelot Network, playing an integral role in co-management, monitoring and the provision of eco-tourism opportunities (Barrow 2021; Cazabon-Mannette 2021). In an attempt to reduce sea turtle by-catch in the gillnet fishery, research has been conducted on the use of marker lights on gillnets, low-profile gillnets, modified mid-water set gillnets and alternative fishing techniques (handline fishing) (Gearhart and Eckert 2007; Gearhart and Eckert 2008; Eckert and Gearhart 2008; Eckert and Gearhart 2009; Eckert et al. 2008; IMA 2013).

There have also been efforts to restock wild populations of the locally extirpated Blue and Yellow Macaws (Ara ararauna) in the Nariva Swamp. The Forestry Division and The Centre for the Rescue of Endangered Species in Trinidad and Tobago (CRESTT), in collaboration with the Cincinnati Zoo and Botanical Garden, sourced Blue and Yellow Macaws from Guyana and later released these into the Nariva Swamp (Oehler et al. 2001; Plair et al. 2002; Plair et al. 2008). Additionally, the Pointe-a-Pierre Wild Fowl Trust (WFT) has also conducted releases of locally bred Blue and Yellow Macaws to Nariva Swamp and Aripo Savannahs. Other waterfowl, e.g., Wild Muscovy Duck (Cairina moschata) and Black-Bellied Whistling Tree Ducks (Dendrocygna autumnalis), which have been locally bred, have also been released to Nariva Swamp by the Pointe-a-Pierre Wild Fowl Trust.

Numerous natural ecosystems in Trinidad and Tobago currently lack formal protection (FAO 2018). For instance, several mangrove swamps in Trinidad, such as the Godineau Swamp/Oropouche Lagoon, Point Lisas, and Los Blanquizales, as well as Kilgwyn in Tobago, are unprotected (Juman and Hassanali 2013). Additionally, marine areas in Trinidad and Tobago are significantly underrepresented within legally protected regions.

Environmental Management Tools

Trinidad and Tobago is one of several countries across the world that utilizes environmental impact assessments (EIAs), an environmental management tool that facilitates a "look before you leap" approach. EIAs allow decision-makers to carefully consider the potential impacts of a proposed development on the biophysical and social environment prior to granting permission for a development to commence. In Trinidad and Tobago, proponents of development engaging in any of forty-four designated activities (as listed in the CEC Designated Activities Order 2006) must apply to the regulatory authority, that is, the Environmental Management Authority (EMA), for a Certificate of Environmental Clearance (CEC). For certain types of development, these applications are submitted to the Town and Country Planning Division (TCPD) of the Ministry of Planning prior to being forwarded to the EMA. Upon receipt of the CEC applications, the EMA performs a case-by-case screening of the application. Prior to issuing a CEC, the EMA may request that the developer submit an EIA. If such is the case, scoping follows, whereby the EMA provides detailed guidelines regarding the EIA that is to be conducted in the form of terms of reference (TOR). Developers usually hire environmental consulting companies to conduct EIAs. Close attention must be paid to the TORs when preparing the EIAs for a proposed development. Once EIAs are submitted to the EMA, they are reviewed by multidisciplinary teams and within a specific timeframe, a decision is issued (CEC granted, CEC not granted, etc.). Decisions made by the EMA may be appealed and brought before the Environmental Commission.

Environmental Education and Public Awareness

Over the years, numerous organizations have undertaken concerted efforts to promote environmental education and public awareness. The Trinidad and Tobago Field Naturalists' Club (TTFNC), one of the oldest NGOs in the country (founded in 1891), has a long history of engaging persons about the natural history of the country through field trips, lectures as well as the publication of Living World, a journal of the TTFNC published between 1892 and 1896 and 1956 and the present. The Pointe-a-Pierre Wild Fowl Trust, another NGO, also has a long history in environmental education. Its audio-visual Environmental Education Programme, the first of its kind to be developed in Trinidad and Tobago in 1977, was taken to primary schools, secondary schools and community groups across the country. Organizations such as the Pointe-a-Pierre Wild Fowl Trust and Asa Wright Nature Centre have also facilitated on-site Environmental Education programs for schools across the country. The Environmental Management Authority (EMA) is another organization whose operations under the Environmental Management Act (chapter 35:05) include the development of "public awareness and education programmes to enhance the understanding of environmental protection and natural resource management issues within Trinidad and Tobago". The Institute of Marine Affairs (IMA), formed under the Institute of Marine Affairs Act (chapter 37:01), also has a specific mandate "to promote public understanding of and appreciation for all aspects of the marine and related environment".

Besides the organizations mentioned above, numerous other organizations have also focused their attention on educating the public about environmental matters. Many local scientists who study the natural environment and investigate human impacts on the environment have also made concerted efforts to communicate their findings to the public through written (newspaper articles, blogs, etc.), verbal (lectures, panel discussions, etc.) and visual media (videos, social media, etc.). More recently, there have been numerous scientific studies that have utilized Knowledge, Attitude and Practice (KAP) surveys to assess what Trinbagonians know (knowledge), how they feel (attitude) and what they do (practice) as it relates to specific environmental issues such as climate change, tsunamis, sharks, natural environment (Rawlins et al. 2007; Kanhai et al. 2016; Ali et al. 2020; EMA 2020). Such surveys are useful for diagnosing, designing appropriate interventions and evaluating the effectiveness of existing programmes (Vandamme 2009).

Specially Appointed Task Force and Councils

For certain matters, the government of Trinidad and Tobago has deemed it necessary to appoint specific groups to oversee certain environmental matters. For example, the Cabinet appointed a National Wetlands Committee in 1995. In order to better coordinate sea turtle conservation and management in Trinidad and Tobago, the Cabinet more recently appointed the National Sea Turtle Task Force (NSTTF) for the periods 2014–18 and 2020–present. The current NSTTF comprises members from governmental and non-governmental sectors. Working groups of the current NSTTF include (i) the Sea Turtle Recovery Action Plan (STRAP), (ii) tourism, (iii) fundraising and (iv) by-catch. This approach is multisectoral and thus provides a foundation for increased dialogue and collaboration between stakeholders. Another example of such an approach is the recently appointed National Council for Sustainable Development (2021–present).

Specific Projects to Address Anthropogenic Activities

Over the years, numerous projects have focused on addressing environmental challenges in Trinidad and Tobago. Although it is beyond the scope of this chapter to document all such projects, attention is drawn to a few projects that have been successful in involving diverse groups of stakeholders. Sea turtle conservation efforts, for example, have had a long history of successful co-management arrangements between the government and community-based organizations (CBOs) (Barrow 2021; Cazabon-Mannette 2021). Such co-management arrangements have led to the acquisition of long-term datasets regarding nesting sea turtles on both islands, the development of eco-tourism opportunities, capacity transfer and positive changes in practices (e.g., reduction of poaching, etc.) (Cazabon-Mannette 2021). Another project that has focused on an integrated approach to water resources management in Trinidad and Tobago is the Adopt-a-River Programme. This project first commenced in 2012 and is currently still operating (Mahabir et al. 2018). The overall goal of the Adopt-a-River Programme was to improve the status of rivers on both islands by developing projects with diverse groups of stakeholders (Mahabir et al. 2018). There is also the Recyclable Solid Waste Collection Project (also known as iCARE), which commenced in 2015 and promotes recycling at a national scale (EMA 2021). For SIDS, such as our twin-island republic, solid waste that can be recycled must be diverted away from landfills. The iCARE project relies on the voluntary participation of the citizens in addressing this challenge of waste management (EMA 2021). Recently, the government of the Republic of Trinidad and Tobago committed approximately $2.6 million to a latrine eradication programme in the capital city of Port of Spain and Mayaro/Rio Claro (*Trinidad Express* 2018). Within the past decade, Trinidad and Tobago also committed to a wastewater rehabilitation programme based on the acquisition of a loan from the Inter-American Development Bank in 2013 (Water Technology 2013). Most recently, funding ($63 million) from this loan was used for the commissioning of the Trincity Wastewater Treatment Plant (Loubon 2022). Environmental samples from unique environments in Trinidad (e.g., natural oil seeps, mud volcanoes, etc.) are currently being studied to detect naturally occurring microorganisms that may potentially be used for bioremediation (Ramoutar et al. 2019; Ramdass and Rampersad

2021a; Ramdass and Rampersad 2021b; Ramdass and Rampersad 2021c; Ramdass and Rampersad 2022a; Ramdass and Rampersad 2022b). The projects highlighted above provide a snapshot of some of the strides that are being made in the environmental sector in Trinidad and Tobago.

Relevant Actors

Beyond a doubt, numerous individuals, community-based organizations (CBOs), non-governmental organizations (NGOs), government ministries, research institutions, and universities have all been involved in the environmental sector of Trinidad and Tobago. Some of these entities are involved in the (i) collection of baseline data that supports environmental management, (ii) regulation of environmental affairs, (iii) development of environmental education and public awareness campaigns and (iv) development of interventions aimed at tackling emerging environmental issues. Listing all these actors is beyond the scope of this chapter. However, some of the key government entities with responsibility for the environment are the (i) Ministry of Planning and Development with its various divisions (Town and Country Planning, Environmental Policy and Planning, Green Fund Executing Unit); (ii) Ministry of Agriculture, Land and Fisheries with its various divisions (Forestry, Fisheries, Horticultural); (iii) Environmental Management Authority (EMA); (iv) Institute of Marine Affairs (IMA); (v) Chaguaramas Development Authority (CDA); (vi) Caribbean Industrial Research Institute (CARIRI); (vii) Ministry of Health, Public Health Department; (viii) Ministry of Works and Transport, with its Coastal Protection Unit; (ix) Ministry of Public Utilities; (x) Water and Sewerage Authority (WASA); and (xi) Tobago House of Assembly, Division of Food Security, Natural Resources, The Environment, Sustainable Development.

Among the tertiary level institutions that focus on environmental education and research at the undergraduate and postgraduate levels are (i) The University of the West Indies (The UWI), St Augustine Campus, established in 1960; and (ii) The University of Trinidad and Tobago (UTT), established in 2004. The Department of Life Sciences of the UWI houses two important collections (i) The National Herbarium of Trinidad and Tobago and (ii) The UWI Zoology Museum. The Asa Wright Nature Centre and the William Beebe Research Station continue to be important bases for conservation-related research. Some of the long-standing non-governmental organizations (NGOs) that have focused on environmental affairs on both islands include (i) Trinidad and Tobago Field Naturalists Club (TTFNC), (ii) Pointe-a-Pierre Wild Fowl Trust, (iii) The Cropper Foundation, (iv) Fishermen and Friends of the Sea (FFOS), (v) Nature Seekers, (vi) Turtle Village Trust, (vii) Save Our Sea Turtles (SOS) Tobago, (viii) Environmental Research Institute (ERIC) Tobago, (ix) Fondes Amandes Community Reafforestation Project, (x) Environment Tobago, (xi) Animal Welfare Network, (xii) Caribbean Natural Resources Institute (CANARI), (xiii) Council of Presidents of the Environment and (xiv) UWI Biological Society. Over the years, countless individuals have made significant contributions to the environmental sector of Trinidad and Tobago.

THE WAY FORWARD

The various ecosystems in Trinidad and Tobago provide its people with fundamentally important services (supporting, regulating, provisioning, cultural). Over the years, numerous anthropogenic activities occurring at the national scale, as well as transboundary issues, have negatively impacted these ecosystems. Within the past six decades, however, it must be acknowledged that significant strides have been made in managing the natural environment. We must build upon the work undertaken in the decades preceding this one.

For 2022 and beyond, Trinidad and Tobago envisions a future where:

i. All Trinbagonians (especially children and youths) recognize that our natural environment is one of our greatest assets. Understanding nature's contribution to people (NCP) in Trinidad and Tobago must be a priority. The valuation of ecosystem services research that began within the past decades must be extended. More importantly, the findings of such investigations must be considered when making decisions about new proposed developments. As a nation, we must continue to prioritize and support environmental education and public awareness programmes that focus on children and youth. We must also spearhead initiatives aimed at influencing changes in Trinbagonians' behaviour regarding environmental issues.

ii. We continue to strive for sustainable development. Developments that we engage in to meet the needs of the present generation should not compromise the ability of future generations to meet their needs. It is, therefore, imperative that we continue to utilize environmental management tools that allow us to "look before we leap", such as environmental impact assessments (EIAs), amongst others. Trinidad and Tobago must continue to implement environmental policies and action plans that have already been developed and work towards the enforcement of existing environmental legislation.
iii. We are action-oriented and take a human-centred approach to designing solutions. The evidence is clear that numerous anthropogenic activities negatively affect the natural environment and human well-being. Regardless of the issue, diverse groups of stakeholders must be meaningfully engaged when crafting solutions to emerging and existing environmental problems. Local communities, in particular, must be engaged from the onset when designing potential solutions. To date, there have been local examples of successful co-management arrangements and integrated approaches, upon which we must build.
iv. We join regional and international efforts to tackle transboundary issues. While we must act locally to address environmental issues, it is important to recognize that Trinidad and Tobago is facing several transboundary issues. To effectively address these, we cannot stand alone; we must work together with our regional neighbours and the international community.
v. We continue to build local capacity to manage our natural environment effectively. We must also continue to create opportunities for young people to learn about, understand and ultimately manage the natural environment of Caribbean SIDS, such as Trinidad and Tobago.

Table 5.1: Snapshot of Cases Where Decisions Made by the Environmental Management Authority (EMA) Were Challenged by NGOs

Applicant	Respondent	Case Number	Issue
Fishermen and Friends of the Sea (FFOS)	The Minister of Planning, Housing and the Environment	Privy Council Appeal No. 0028 of 2016	Water Pollution (Fees) (Amendment) Regulations 2006. Method used to calculate annual permit fees did not consider the type of anthropogenic activity nor the concentration of pollutants that would be released into the environment. Applicant requested that the flat/fixed fee system used to calculate annual permit fees be revisited, given the "Polluter Pays Principle". Outcome: Water Pollution Rules 2001 (amended 2019).
Bhadose Sooknanan-First Applicant, Fishermen and Friends of the Sea (FFOS)-Second Applicant	Environmental Management Authority (EMA) The Ministry of Energy and Energy Affairs (Interested Party)	CV2014-00813	EMA granted a Certificate of Environmental Clearance (CEC) (CEC3963/2013) to Petrotrin to conduct a three-dimensional seismic survey to cover an area of approximately 510 square kilometres within Soldado Fields and the North Marine Field located in the Gulf of Paria off the West Coast of Trinidad. Applicants challenged issuance of CEC, especially since no EIA was requested by the EMA. Outcome: EMA decision upheld

REFERENCES

Agard, J. B. R. 1985. "Total Petroleum Hydrocarbons in Surficial Sediments from Port-of-Spain Harbour, Trinidad." *Marine Pollution Bulletin* 16 (8): 334–35.

Agard, J. B. R., M. Boodoosingh, and J. Gobin. 1988. "Petroleum Residues in Surficial Sediments from the Gulf of Paria, Trinidad." *Marine Pollution Bulletin* 19 (5): 231–33.

Agard, J., L. Dempewolf, M. A. Rawlins, C. Obst, C. M. Brenes, S. M. Ulate, and K. Garcia. 2019. "Integrating Natural Capital and Ecosystem Services into Policy and Decision Making in Trinidad and Tobago." In *Mainstreaming Natural Capital and Ecosystem Services into Development Policy*, edited by P. Kumar, 149–81. London: Routledge.

Alemu, I. J., M. N. Cazabon, L. Dempewolf, A. Hailey, R. M. Lehtinen, R. P. Mannette, K. T. Naranjit, and A. C. Roach. 2008. "Presence of the Chytrid Fungus *Batrachochytrium dendrobatidis* in Populations of the Critically Endangered Frog *Mannophryne olmonae* in Tobago, West Indies." *Ecohealth* 5 (1): 34–39.

Alemu, J., M. Cazabon-Mannette, A. Cunningham, L. Dempewolf, A. Hailey, R. Mannette, K. Naranjit, M. Perkins, and A. Schmidt-Roach. 2013. "Presence of the Chytrid Fungus *Batrachochytrium dendrobatidis* in a Vulnerable Frog in Trinidad, West Indies." *Endangered Species Research* 20 (2): 131–36.

Alemu I, J. B., and Y. Clement. 2014. "Mass Coral Bleaching in 2010 in the Southern Caribbean." *PLOS ONE* 9 (1): e83829.

Alemu I, J. B. 2016. "The Status and Management of the Lionfish, *Pterois* sp., in Trinidad and Tobago." *Marine Pollution Bulletin* 109 (1): 402–08.

Ali, L., E. Grey, D. Singh, A. Mohammed, V. Tripathi, J. Gobin, and I. Ramnarine. 2020. "An Evaluation of the Public's Knowledge, Attitudes, and Practices (KAP) in Trinidad and Tobago Regarding Sharks and Shark Consumption." *PLOS ONE* 15 (6): e0234499.

Amon, D. J., J. Gobin, C.L. Van Dover, L.A. Levin, L. Marsh, and N.A. Raineault. 2017. "Characterization of Methane-Seep Communities in a Deep-Sea Area Designated for Oil and Natural Gas Exploitation Off Trinidad and Tobago." *Frontiers in Marine Science* 4.

Astudillo, L. L. R. d. 2002. *Chemical Investigations on Oysters and Green Mussels from Trinidad and Venezuela*. PhD diss., The University of the West Indies.

———, I. C. Yen, J. Agard, I. Bekele, and R. Hubbard. 2002. "Heavy Metals in Green Mussel (*Perna viridis*) and Oysters (*Crassostrea* sp.) from Trinidad and Venezuela." *Archives of Environmental Contamination and Toxicology* 42: 410–15.

Astudillo, L. R. d., I. C. Yen, and I. Bekele. 2005. "Heavy Metals in Sediments, Mussels, and Oysters from Trinidad and Venezuela." *International Journal of Tropical Biology and Conservation* 53 (Suppl. 1): 41–53.

Balfour, S., N. Badrie, I. C. Yen, and L. Chatergoon. 2012. "Seasonal Influence and Heavy Metal Analysis in Marine Shrimp (*Penaeus* spp.) Sold in Trinidad, West Indies." *Journal of Food Research* 1 (1): 193–99.

Balgobin, A., and N. Ramroop Singh. 2018. "Impact of Anthropogenic Activities on Mussel (*Mytella guyanensis*) in the Gulf of Paria, Trinidad." *Marine Pollution Bulletin* 135:496–504.

Balgobin, A., and N. Ramroop Singh. 2019. "Source Apportionment and Seasonal Cancer Risk of Polycyclic Aromatic Hydrocarbons of Sediments in a Multi-use Coastal Environment Containing a Ramsar Wetland, for a Caribbean Island." *Science of The Total Environment* 664: 474–86.

Banjoo, D. 2006. "Assessment of Biota Quality in the Gulf of Paria: Hydrocarbon Component." The Institute of Marine Affairs (IMA).

Barrow, L. 2021. "Leatherback Turtle Conservation in Trinidad and Tobago 1963–2021: Brief Overview." The Institute of Marine Affairs. Accessed 14 September 2021. https://www.ima.gov.tt/2021/09/14/leatherback-turtle-conservation-in-trinidad-and-tobago-1963-2021-brief-overview/.

Beckles, D. M., L. Cox, G.-A. Bent, V. Cooper, K. Banerjee, D. Dawkins, N. Hosein, A. Samaroo, M. Davis, R. Clarke, X. Chadee, S. Mahabir, and M. Allong. 2016. "The Impact of the Contaminants Produced by the Guanapo Landfill on the Surrounding Environment." St Augustine, Trinidad and Tobago: The University of the West Indies (UWI).

Belford, S. G., D. A.T. Phillip, M. G. Rutherford, S.S. Roach, and E.J. Duncan. 2019. "Biodiversity of Coral Reef Communities in Marginal Environments along the North-Eastern Coast of Trinidad, Southern Caribbean." *Progress in Aqua Farming and Marine Biology* 2 (1): 1–23.

Bernard, G.I. 1979. "A Study of Lead Pollution Resulting from Automotive Exhaust Emission." MPhil thesis, University of the West Indies.

Buglass, S., S.D. Donner, and J.B. Alemu I. 2016. "A Study on the Recovery of Tobago's Coral Reefs Following the 2010 Mass Bleaching Event." *Marine Pollution Bulletin* 104 (1): 198–206.

Burke, L., S. Greenhalgh, D. Prager, and E. Cooper. 2008. *Coastal Capital: Economic Valuation of Coral Reefs in Tobago and St. Lucia.* World Resources Institute (WRI).

Cazabon-Mannette, M., and A.C.N. Phillips. 2017. "Occurrence of Fibropapilloma Tumours on Green Sea Turtles (*Chelonia mydas*) in Trinidad, West Indies." *Living World*, 14–20.

Cazabon-Mannette, M., P. W. Schuhmann, A. Hailey, and J. Horrocks. 2017. "Estimates of the Non-Market Value of Sea Turtles in Tobago Using Stated Preference Techniques." *Journal of Environmental Management* 192:281–91.

Cazabon-Mannette, M. 2021. "The Impact of the COVID-19 Pandemic on the Conservation of Sea Turtles in Trinidad and Tobago." *Living World.*

Caribbean Regional Fund for Wastewater Management (CREW). 2010. *Situational Analysis: Regional Sectoral Overview of Wastewater Management in the Wider Caribbean Region.* CEP Technical Report 66.

Caribbean Regional Fisheries Mechanism (CRFM). 2019. *Fact-Finding Survey Regarding the Influx and Impacts of Sargassum Seaweed in the Caribbean Region: Final Report.* Belize: Caribbean Regional Fisheries Mechanism (CRFM) and Japan International Cooperation Agency (JICA).

Deonarine, G.I.A. 1980. "Studies on the Bioaccumulation of Some Chlorinated Hydrocarbons in a Neotropical Mangrove Swamp." MPhil thesis, University of the West Indies.

Eckert, S.A. 2013. *Preventing Leatherback Sea Turtle Gillnet Entanglement Through the Establishment of a Leatherback Conservation Area Off the Coast of Trinidad.* WIDECAST Information Document No. 2013-02.

Eckert, S.A., and J. Gearhart. 2008. *Promoting the Survival of Leatherback Turtles in the Greater Atlantic Ocean by Eliminating Capture and Mortality Associated*

with Coastal Gillnets in Trinidad: Final Report 2008. Wider Caribbean Sea Turtle Conservation Network (WIDECAST).
———. 2009. *Final Report 2009: Reducing Leatherback Sea Turtle Bycatch by Trinidad's Artisanal Fishing Industry.*
Eckert, S. A., J. Gearhart, C. Bergmann, and K. L. Eckert. 2008. "Reducing Leatherback Sea Turtle Bycatch in the Surface Drift-Gillnet Fishery in Trinidad." *Bycatch Communication Network Newsletter* 8: 2–6.
Eckert, S.A., and J. Lien. 1999. *Recommendations for Eliminating Incidental Capture and Mortality of Leatherback Turtles, Dermochelys coriacea, by Commercial Fisheries in Trinidad and Tobago: A Report to the Wider Caribbean Sea Turtle Conservation Network (WIDECAST).* WIDECAST Information Document 1999–001.
Eckert, S.A., and K.L. Eckert. 2005. *Strategic Plan for Eliminating the Incidental Capture and Mortality of Leatherback Turtles in the Coastal Gillnet Fisheries of Trinidad and Tobago: Proceedings of a National Consultation.* WIDECAST Technical Report No. 5. Port of Spain: Ministry of Agriculture, Land and Marine Resources, Government of the Republic of Trinidad and Tobago, in collaboration with the Wider Caribbean Sea Turtle Conservation Network (WIDECAST).
Environmental Management Authority (EMA). 2004. *State of the Environment Report 2004.* St. Clair: Environmental Management Authority.
———. 2020. *National Environmental Literacy/Awareness Survey.* Environmental Management Authority.
———. 2021. "iCARE." Accessed 14 October 2024. https://www.ema.co.tt/our-environment/ema-icare/.
Food and Agriculture Organisation of the United Nations (FAO). 2018. *National Protected Area Systems Plan for Trinidad and Tobago.* Port of Spain: Government of the Republic of Trinidad and Tobago.
Garrison, V. H., W. T. Foreman, S. Genualdi, D. W. Griffin, C. A. Kellogg, M. S. Majewski, A. Mohammed, A. Ramsubhag, E. A. Shinn, S. L. Simonich, and G. W. Smith. 2006. "Saharan Dust: A Carrier of Persistent Organic Pollutants, Metals and Microbes to the Caribbean?" *Revista de Biología Tropical* 54:9–21.
———, M. S. Majewski, W. T. Foreman, S. A. Genualdi, A. Mohammed, and S. L. Massey Simonich. 2014. "Persistent Organic Contaminants in Saharan Dust Air Masses in West Africa, Cape Verde and the Eastern Caribbean." *Science of The Total Environment* 468–69:530–43.
Gearhart, J., and S.A. Eckert. 2007. *Field Tests to Evaluate the Target Catch and Bycatch Reduction Effectiveness of Surface and Mid-Water Drift Gillnets in Trinidad.* WIDECAST Information Document No. 2007-01. Wider Caribbean Sea Turtle Conservation Network (WIDECAST).
———. 2008. *Report on the Effect of Net Marking Lights on the Interaction Rates of*

Leatherback Sea Turtles (Dermochelys coriacea) in Trinidad's Artisanal Mackerel Gillnet Fishery. NOAA Fisheries.

Georges, C., and B. L. Oostdam. 1983. "The Characteristics and Dynamics of Tar Pollution on the Beaches of Trinidad and Tobago." *Marine Pollution Bulletin* 14 (5): 170–78.

Gobin, J., J. Agard, J. Madera, and A. Mohammed. 2013. "The Asian Green Mussel *Perna viridis* (Linnaeus 1758): 20 Years After Its Introduction in Trinidad and Tobago." *Open Journal of Marine Science* 3 (2): 62–65.

Government of the Republic of Trinidad and Tobago (GORTT). 2018. *National Environmental Policy of Trinidad and Tobago.*

Gowrie, M. 2016. "Airborne Pollen Sampling on the Caribbean Island of Trinidad and Tobago, WI." *Aerobiologia* 32 (2): 347–52.

———, J. Agard, G. Barclay, and A. Mohammed. 2016. "Forecasting Emergency Paediatric Asthma Hospital Admissions in Trinidad and Tobago: Development of a Local Model Incorporating the Interactions of Airborne Dust and Pollen Concentrations with Meteorological Parameters and a Time-Lag Factor." *Open Journal of Air Pollution* 5 (4): 109–26.

Guppy, M. 2001. "Chemical Investigations on the Green Lipped Mussel (Perna viridis) in the Gulf of Paria, Trinidad." PhD diss., University of the West Indies.

Gyan, K., W. Henry, S. Lacaille, A. Laloo, C. Lamsee-Ebanks, S. McKay, R. M. Antoine, and M. A. Monteil. 2005. "African Dust Clouds Are Associated with Increased Paediatric Asthma Accident and Emergency Admissions on the Caribbean Island of Trinidad." *International Journal of Biometeorology* 49 (6): 371–76.

Hall, L., and I. Chang-Yen. 1986a. "Metals in Sediments off Trinidad, West Indies." *Marine Pollution Bulletin* 17 (6): 274–76.

———. 1986b. "Metals in Seawater off Trinidad, West Indies." *Marine Pollution Bulletin* 17 (7): 332–33.

———. 1988. "On the Bioavailability of Heavy Metals in the Gulf of Paria." *U.W.I. BioSpectrum* 1: 25–27.

Hassanali, K. 2017. "Challenges in Mainstreaming Climate Change into Productive Coastal Sectors in a Small Island State – The Case of Trinidad and Tobago." *Ocean and Coastal Management* 142:136–42.

Helmer, E. H., T.S. Ruzycki, J. Benner, S.M. Voggesser, B.P. Scobie, C. Park, D.W. Fanning, and S. Ramnarine. 2012. "Detailed Maps of Tropical Forest Types Are Within Reach: Forest Tree Communities for Trinidad and Tobago Mapped with Multiseason Landsat and Multiseason Fine-Resolution Imagery." *Forest Ecology and Management* 279:147–66.

Hoetjes, P., A. Kong, R. Juman, A. Miller, M. Miller, K. Meyer, and A. Smith. 2002. *Status of Coral Reefs in the Eastern Caribbean: The OECS, Trinidad and Tobago,*

Barbados and the Netherlands Antilles. In *Status of Coral Reefs of the World.*

Hosein, A., D.S. Narang, L. Rostant, and A. Hailey. 2017. "The Abundance of Red-Bellied Macaws (*Orthopsittaca manilata*) and Orange-Winged Parrots (*Amazona amazonica*) in Relation to Fruiting Moriche Palms (*Mauritia flexuosa*) at the Aripo Savannahs, Trinidad." *Revista Brasileira de Ornitologia* 25 (1): 40–46.

Institute of Marine Affairs (IMA). 2013. *A Guide to Beaches and Bays of Trinidad and Tobago.* Chaguaramas: Institute of Marine Affairs (IMA).

———. 2016. *State of the Marine Environment Trinidad and Tobago 2016.* Chaguaramas: Institute of Marine Affairs (IMA).

Jobity, A. M., and R. Shoy. 2013. *Characterisation of Handline Fishing in Grande Riviere Fishing Village and Its Use as an Alternative to Net Fishing During the Turtle Nesting Season.* Chaguaramas: Institute of Marine Affairs (IMA).

Juman, R. A. 2005. "The Structure and Productivity of the *Thalassia testudinum* Community in Bon Accord Lagoon, Tobago." *Revista de Biología Tropical* 53:219–27.

———. 2010. *Wetlands of Trinidad and Tobago.* Chaguaramas: The Institute of Marine Affairs (IMA).

———. "Sargassum – A Visitor to Our Beaches." Accessed 10 April 2020. https://www.ima.gov.tt/2020/04/10/sargassum-a-visitor-to-our-beaches/.

———, and K. J. Alexander. 2006. *An Inventory of Seagrass Communities Around Trinidad and Tobago.* Chaguaramas: Institute of Marine Affairs (IMA).

Juman, R.A., and K. Hassanali. 2013. "Mangrove Conservation in Trinidad and Tobago, West Indies." In *Mangrove Ecosystems: Biogeography, Genetic Diversity and Conservation Strategies,* edited by T. R. V. Gerard Gleason. Nova.

Juman, R., and D. Ramsewak. 2013a. "Land Cover Changes in the Caroni Swamp Ramsar Site, Trinidad (1942 and 2007): Implications for Management." *Journal of Coastal Conservation* 17 (1): 133–41.

———. 2013b. "Status of Mangrove Forests in Trinidad and Tobago, West Indies." *Caribbean Journal of Science* 47 (2–3): 291–304.

Kanhai, L.D.K., J. F. Gobin, D.M. Beckles, B. Lauckner, and A. Mohammed. 2014. "Metals in Sediments and Mangrove Oysters (*Crassostrea rhizophorae*) from the Caroni Swamp, Trinidad." *Environmental Monitoring and Assessment* 186 (3): 1961–76.

———. 2015. "Polycyclic Aromatic Hydrocarbons (PAHs) in *Crassostrea rhizophorae* and *Cathorops spixii* from the Caroni Swamp, Trinidad, West Indies." *Environmental Science and Pollution Research* 22 (2): 1366–79.

Kanhai, L. D. K., D. Singh, B. Lauckner, K. L. Ebi, and D. D. Chadee. 2016. "Knowledge, Attitude and Practices of Coastal Communities in Trinidad and Tobago About Tsunamis." *Natural Hazards* 81 (2): 1349–72.

Kanhai, L.D.K., H. Asmath, and J. F. Gobin. 2022. "The Status of Marine Debris/

Litter and Plastic Pollution in the Caribbean Large Marine Ecosystem (CLME): 1980–2020." *Environmental Pollution* 300: 118919.

Kenny, J. 2000. *Views from the Ridge: Exploring the Natural History of Trinidad and Tobago.* Port of Spain, Trinidad: Prospect Press.

Klekowski, E.J., S.A. Temple, A.M. Siung-Chang, and K. Kumarsingh. 1999. "An Association of Mangrove Mutation, Scarlet Ibis, and Mercury Contamination in Trinidad, West Indies." *Environmental Pollution* 105:185–89.

Kumarsingh, K., L.A. Hall, A. M. Siung-Chang, and V. A. Stoute. 1998. "Phosphorus in Sediments of a Shallow Bank Influenced by Sewage and Sugar Factory Effluents in Trinidad, West Indies." *Marine Pollution Bulletin* 36 (3): 185–92.

Lapointe, B.E., R. Langton, B. J. Bedford, A.C. Potts, O. Day, and C. Hu. 2010. "Land-Based Nutrient Enrichment of the Buccoo Reef Complex and Fringing Coral Reefs of Tobago, West Indies." *Marine Pollution Bulletin* 60 (3): 334–43.

Loubon, M. 2022. "New Wastewater Plant to Benefit 17,000." *Trinidad Express*, 6 April 2022.

Lum, L. L. 2003. *An Assessment of Incidental Turtle Catch in the Gillnet Fishery in Trinidad and Tobago, West Indies.* Chaguaramas: The Institute of Marine Affairs (IMA).

———. 2006. "Assessment of Incidental Sea Turtle Catch in the Artisanal Gillnet Fishery in Trinidad and Tobago, West Indies." *Applied Herpetology* 3 (4): 357–68.

———, and J. Duncan. 2018. *Life Along the Seashore.* Chaguaramas: Institute of Marine Affairs (IMA).

Mahabir, S. A., J. David, A. Miller, D. Samlal, K. Ray, D. Fraser, L. G. Pierre, D. Porter, C. Garcia, A. Cudjoe, A. Brizan, W. Etienne, N. Etienne, K. McKay, and K. Bishop-Mills. 2018. "The Adopt a River Programme as a Vehicle for Progressing Integrated Water Resources Management in Trinidad and Tobago." Adopt a River Conference 2018, The Water Resources Agency, The Water and Sewerage Authority (WASA).

Mallela, J., and M.J.C. Crabbe. 2009. "Hurricanes and Coral Bleaching Linked to Changes in Coral Recruitment in Tobago." *Marine Environmental Research* 68 (4): 158–62.

Mallela, J., R. Parkinson, and O. Day. 2010. "An Assessment of Coral Reefs in Tobago." *Caribbean Journal of Science* 46 (1): 83–87.

Ministry of Energy and Energy Affairs, Government of the Republic of Trinidad and Tobago. 2022. "Historical Facts on the Petroleum Industry of Trinidad and Tobago." Accessed 14 October 2024. https://www.energy.gov.tt/historical-facts-petroleum/.

Mohammed, T. I., I. Chang-Yen, and I. Bekele. 1996. "Lead Pollution in East Trinidad Resulting from Lead Recycling and Smelting Activities." *Environmental Geochemistry and Health* 18:123–28.

———. 2000. "The Evaluation, Characterization, and Treatment of Heavy Metal Contaminated Soils in East Trinidad." PhD diss., University of the West Indies.
Mohammed, A. 2005. "Investigation of Heavy Metals and Butyltin in Chaguaramas, Trinidad." MPhil thesis, University of the West Indies.
———, C. Orazio, P. Peterman, K. Echols, K. Feltz, A. Manoo, D. Maraj, and J. Agard. 2009. "Polychlorinated Dibenzo-p-Dioxin (PCDDs) and Polychlorinated Dibenzofurans (PCDFs) in Harbor Sediments from Sea Lots, Port-of-Spain, Trinidad and Tobago." *Marine Pollution Bulletin* 58 (6): 928–34.
Mohammed, A., P. Peterman, K. Echols, K. Feltz, G. Tegerdine, A. Manoo, D. Maraj, J. Agard, and C. Orazio. 2011. "Polychlorinated Biphenyls (PCBs) and Organochlorine Pesticides (OCPs) in Harbor Sediments from Sea Lots, Port-of-Spain, Trinidad and Tobago." *Marine Pollution Bulletin* 62:1324–32.
Mohammed, A., T. May, K. Echols, M. Walther, A. Manoo, D. Maraj, J. Agard, and C. Orazio. 2012. "Metals in Sediments and Fish from Sea Lots and Point Lisas Harbors, Trinidad and Tobago." *Marine Pollution Bulletin* 64 (1): 169–73.
Mohammed, A., and T. Mohammed. 2017. "Mercury, Arsenic, Cadmium, and Lead in Two Commercial Shark Species (*Sphyrna lewini* and *Carcharhinus porosus*) in Trinidad and Tobago." *Marine Pollution Bulletin* 119 (2): 214–18.
Mohammed, F.K., J. Sieuraj, and M. Seepersaud. 2017. "A Preliminary Assessment of Heavy Metals in Sediments from the Cipero and South Oropouche Rivers in Trinidad, West Indies." *Environmental Monitoring and Assessment* 189 (8): 396.
Mohammed, F.K., D.M. Beckles, and J. Opadeyi. 2018a. "Characterization, Source Apportionment, and Human Health Risk Assessment of Polycyclic Aromatic Hydrocarbons (PAHs) in Road Dust of a Small Island State in the Caribbean." *Human and Ecological Risk Assessment: An International Journal* 24 (7): 1852–71.
Mohammed, F.K., D. L. Deonarine, and M. Seepersaud. 2018b. "An Assessment of Contamination and Ecological Risk of Metals in Sediments of the Guaracara, Caparo and Couva Rivers in Trinidad, West Indies." *Chemistry and Ecology* 34 (3): 241–58.
Nelson, W., and N. Slinger-Cohen. 2014. "Trace Metals in the Sponge *Ircinia felix* and Sediments from North-Western Trinidad, West Indies." *Journal of Environmental Science and Health, Part A* 49 (8): 967–72.
Nelson, W. 2020. "Fractionation of Trace Metals in Coastal Sediments from Trinidad and Tobago, West Indies." *Marine Pollution Bulletin* 150:110774.
Nelson, W. A. 2015. "Trace Metals in Water and Sediment from a Tropical Watershed Subject to Anthropogenic Inputs." *Environmental Earth Sciences* 74:621–28.
Norville, W. 2005. "Spatial Distribution of Heavy Metals in Sediments from the Gulf of Paria, Trinidad." *International Journal of Tropical Biology and Conservation* 53 (Supplement 1): 33–40.
———. 2007. *Environmental Monitoring of the Gulf of Paria: Assessment of Biota*

Quality in the Gulf of Paria: Heavy Metals Component. Chaguaramas, Trinidad: Institute of Marine Affairs.

Norville, W., and D. Banjoo. 2011. "Water and Sediment Quality in a Tropical Swamp Used for Agricultural and Oil Refining Activities." *Journal of Environmental Science and Health, Part A* 46 (2): 149–56.

Oehler, D. A., D. Boodoo, B. Plair, K. Kuchinski, M. Campbell, G. Lutchmedial, S. Ramsubage, E. J. Maruska, and S. Malowski. 2001. "Translocation of Blue and Gold Macaw (*Ara ararauna*) into Its Historical Range on Trinidad." *Bird Conservation International* 11 (2): 129–41.

Plair, B.L., D. Boodoo, S. Malowski, M. Campbell, S. Johnston, K. Kuchinski, I. Craig-Clarke, G. Lutchmedial, and D. Oehler. 2002. "Reintroduction of Blue and Gold Macaws to Trinidad." *American Federation of Aviculture Watchbird Magazine* 29 (4): 56–59.

Plair, B.L., K. Kuchinski, J. Ryan, S. Warren, K. Pilgrim, D. Boodoo, S. Ramsubage, A. Ramadhar, M. Lal, B. Rampaul, and N. Mohammed. 2008. "Behavioural Monitoring of Blue and Yellow Macaws (*Ara ararauna*) Reintroduced to the Nariva Swamp, Trinidad." *Ornitologia Neotropical* 19:113–22.

Pragg, C., and F. K. Mohammed. 2018. "Pollution Status, Ecological Risk Assessment, and Source Identification of Heavy Metals in Road Dust from an Industrial Estate in Trinidad, West Indies." *Chemistry and Ecology* 34 (7): 624–39.

———. 2020. "Distribution and Health Risk Assessment of Heavy Metals in Road Dust from an Industrial Estate in Trinidad, West Indies." *International Journal of Environmental Health Research* 30 (3): 336–43.

Persad, D., and W. Rajkumar. 1995. "A Synoptic View of the Levels of Dispersed/Dissolved Petroleum Hydrocarbons (DDPH) and Heavy Metals in the South-Eastern Caribbean Sea." Marine Pollution Bulletin 30 (7): 487–89.

Phillip, D.A.T., P. Antoine, V. Cooper, L. Francis, E. Mangal, N. Seepersad, R. Ragoo, S. Ramsaran, I. Singh, and A. Ramsubhag. 2009. "Impact of Recreation on Recreational Water Quality of a Small Tropical Stream." *Journal of Environmental Monitoring* 11: 1192–98.

Ragbirsingh, Y., and W. Norville. 2005. "A Geographic Information System (GIS) Analysis for Trace Metal Assessment of Sediments in the Gulf of Paria, Trinidad." *Revista de Biología Tropical* 53 (Suppl. 1): 195–206.

Rajkumar, W., and D. Persad. 1994. "Heavy Metals and Petroleum Hydrocarbons in Nearshore Areas of Tobago, West Indies." *Marine Pollution Bulletin* 28 (11): 701–03.

Rajkumar, W., D. Persad, and K. Kumarsingh. 1995. "Baseline Heavy Metal Levels in Shelf Waters of Northern Trinidad and Tobago Using Ion Chromatography." *Caribbean Marine Studies* 4: 76–77.

Rajkumar, W. S., and A. Siung Chang. 2000. "Suspended Particulate Matter

Concentrations along the East–West Corridor, Trinidad, West Indies." *Atmospheric Environment* 34 (8): 1181–87.

Ramdass, A.C., and S.N. Rampersad. 2021a. "Diversity and Oil Degradation Potential of Culturable Microbes Isolated from Chronically Contaminated Soils in Trinidad." *Microorganisms* 9 (6): 1167.

———. 2021b. "Biodiversity and Biocatalyst Activity of Culturable Hydrocarbonoclastic Fungi Isolated from Marac–Moruga Mud Volcano in South Trinidad." *Scientific Reports* 11 (1): Article number 19466.

———. 2021c. "Molecular Signatures of *Janthinobacterium lividum* from Trinidad Support High Potential for Crude Oil Metabolism." *BMC Microbiology* 21 (1): Article number 247

———. 2022a. "Detection and Diversity of the Mannosylerythritol Lipid (MEL) Gene Cluster and Lipase A and B Genes of *Moesziomyces antarcticus* Isolated from Terrestrial Sites Chronically Contaminated with Crude Oil in Trinidad." *BMC Microbiology* 22 (1): Article 43.

———. 2022b. "Naturally-Occurring Microbial Consortia for the Potential Bioremediation of Hydrocarbon-Polluted Sites in Trinidad." *Bioremediation Journal*: 1–10.

Ramoutar, S., A. Mohammed, and A. Ramsubhag. 2019. "Laboratory-Scale Bioremediation Potential of Single and Consortia Fungal Isolates from Two Natural Hydrocarbon Seepages in Trinidad, West Indies." *Bioremediation Journal* 23 (3): 131–41.

Ramsingh, D. C. 2009. "Identification and Quantification of Trace Metals in the Caroni Arena Watershed, Trinidad; A Chemical and Spatial Approach." MPhil thesis, University of the West Indies.

Rawlins, S., A. Chen, J. Rawlins, D. Chadee, and G. Legall. 2007. "A Knowledge, Attitude and Practices Study of the Issues of Climate Change/Variability Impacts and Public Health in Trinidad and Tobago, and St Kitts and Nevis." *West Indian Medical Journal* 56 (2): 115–21.

Riquelme, R., P. Méndez, and I. Smith. 2016. *Solid Waste Management in the Caribbean: Proceedings from the Caribbean Solid Waste Conference.* Technical Note Number IDB-TN-935, Inter-American Development Bank (IDB).

Sampath, M. 1982. "An Investigation of Levels of Organochlorine Pesticides and Polychlorinated Biphenyls in the Caroni Swamp." MPhil thesis, University of the West Indies.

Savage, A. C. N. P., and M. Cazabon-Mannette. 2020. "Sea Turtle Conservation: Tackling 'Floating Syndrome' A Caribbean Perspective." *Living World* (December): 59–71.

Seepersaud, M. A., A. Ramkissoon, S. Seecharan, Y.L. Powder-George, and F.K. Mohammed. 2018. "Environmental Monitoring of Heavy Metals and Polycyclic

Aromatic Hydrocarbons (PAHs) in *Sargassum filipendula* and *Sargassum vulgare* Along the Eastern Coastal Waters of Trinidad and Tobago, West Indies." *Journal of Applied Phycology* 30 (3): 2143–54.

Shing, C.C.A. 2005. "Sharks: Overview of the Fisheries in Trinidad and Tobago." 47th Gulf and Caribbean Fisheries Institute (GCFI) Conference, Gulf and Caribbean Fisheries Institute (GCFI).

———. 2006. "Shark Fisheries of Trinidad and Tobago: A National Plan of Action." 57th Gulf and Caribbean Fisheries Institute (GCFI) Conference, Gulf and Caribbean Fisheries Institute (GCFI).

Shrestha, K.P., and E. Morales. 1987. "Seasonal Variation of Iron, Copper and Zinc in *Penaeus brasiliensis* from Two Areas of the Caribbean Sea." *Science of The Total Environment* 65 (0): 175–80.

Singh, B. 1997. "Climate-Related Global Changes in the Southern Caribbean: Trinidad and Tobago." *Global and Planetary Change* 15 (3): 93–111.

Singh, J. G., I. Chang-Yen, V. A. Stoute, and L. Chatergoon. 1992. "Hydrocarbon Levels in Edible Fish, Crabs and Mussels from the Marine Environment of Trinidad." *Marine Pollution Bulletin* 24 (5): 270–72.

Singh, A., H. Asmath, C.L. Chee, and J. Darsan. 2015. "Potential Oil Spill Risk from Shipping and the Implications for Management in the Caribbean Sea." *Marine Pollution Bulletin* 93 (1): 217–27.

Singh, D.S., M. Alkins-Koo, L.V. Rostant, and A. Mohammed. 2021. "Sublethal Effects of Malathion Insecticide on Growth of the Freshwater Crab *Poppiana dentata* (Randall 1840) (Decapoda: Trichodactylidae)." *Nauplius* 29: e2021030.

Singh, D.S., L.V. Rostant, A. Mohammed, A.S. Jairam, J.J. Sahatoo, R. Khan Ali, and F. Mohammed. 2022. "Sublethal Levels of Organophosphate Insecticides Alter Behaviour in the Juveniles of the Neotropical Crab, *Poppiana dentata* (Randall 1840)." *Ethology Ecology and Evolution*: 1–29.

Sullivan, T. S., S. Ramkissoon, V. H. Garrison, A. Ramsubhag, and J. E. Thies. 2012. "Siderophore Production of African Dust Microorganisms Over Trinidad and Tobago." *Aerobiologia* 28 (3): 391–401.

Surujdeo-Maharaj, S. 2010. "Heavy Metals in Rivers in Trinidad and Tobago." PhD diss., The University of the West Indies.

The Maritime Ocean Collection. 2020. "The Maritime Ocean Collection." Accessed 30 April 2022. https://maritimeoceancollection.com/.

Trinidad Biodiversity. 2020. "Trinidad and Tobago Biodiversity." Accessed 30 April 2022. http://www.biodiversity.gov.tt/index.php/trinidad-a-tobago-biodiversity.html.

Trinidad Express. 2022. "Latrine Eradication Programme Begins...in Port of Spain." *Trinidad Express.*

United Nations Environment Program (UNEP). 2010. *Sea Turtle Recovery Action Plan for the Republic of Trinidad and Tobago*. CEP Technical Report 49.

United Nations Environment Program (UNEP). 2015. *Success Stories in Mainstreaming Ecosystem Services into Macro-economic Policy and Land Use Planning: Evidence from Chile, Trinidad and Tobago, South Africa and Vietnam*. Global Synthesis Report of the Project for Ecosystem Services, Ecosystem Services Economics Unit, Division of Environmental Policy Implementation, UNEP.

Vandamme, E. 2009. *Concepts and Challenges in the Use of Knowledge-Attitude-Practice Surveys: Literature Review*. Antwerp, Belgium: Department of Animal Health, Institute of Tropical Medicine.

Wang, M., C. Hu, B.B. Barnes, G. Mitchum, B. Lapointe, and J.P. Montoya. 2019. "The Great Atlantic Sargassum Belt." *Science* 365 (6448): 83–87.

Water Technology. 2013. "Trinidad and Tobago Seals Off Major IDB Loan for Wastewater Rehabilitation Programme." *Water Technology*.

Wilkinson, C., and D. Souter. 2008. *Status of Caribbean Coral Reefs After Bleaching and Hurricanes in 2005*. Townsville: Global Coral Reef Monitoring Network, and Reef and Rainforest Research Centre.

[CHAPTER 6]

The Challenge of Human Capital Formation and Effective Deployment in Trinidad and Tobago

BHOENDRADATT TEWARIE

THE SHIFT FROM GDP TO HUMAN CAPITAL

In 1995, Mahbub ul Haq published *Reflections on Human Development*[1] after he had founded the Human Development Report and the Human Development Index (HDI) at UNDP.[2] This represented a shift in thinking from measuring the progress of countries on the basis of GDP, per capita income and economic and financial numbers alone. This new approach, which was viewed at the time as an alternative way of treating development, had a profound impact on thinking about development and about the place of human beings in the development process, as well as the role of human beings in the development trajectory.

Human resources and the management of working human beings as an asset in organizations emerged as a concept in organizations and the management of business organizations in the 1980s as the concept of labour (as in land, labour, capital) gave way to human productivity as a factor in organizational efficiency, effectiveness and profitability.[3] Organizations became aware that the quality of human resources could be improved by training, which could consequently improve productivity.

In the contemporary period, terms such as human capital, intellectual capital and social capital have become important indicators of a country's ability to achieve and progress.[4] The major shift, not just from economic and financial indicators to human well-being but further, to the human being as a factor in development; of the value of education and intellectual application and brain power as formidable assets and of social cohesion and cooperation as valuable context and cultural assets in the development process, have gained increased prominence and potency in the business of policymaking.[5]

THE RISE OF INTANGIBLES

Human capital development became so important for organizational and societal development that significant theories were developed to understand, explain and apply the concept. Human capital refers to a set of tangible and intangible skills and assets that can be developed through education, training, and experience.

Gary Becker, who eventually won a Nobel Prize in economics for his work, is credited with developing a theory of human capital.[6] But Theodore Schultz, also a Nobel laureate, made the case for investment in education to boost human capital in a country because Schultz argued that human capital was necessary to manage physical capital and when physical and human capital develop together, economic growth is stronger and faster because human capital is the most important factor in economic growth.[7] This positions the human being as the central actor in the development process, whatever the physical assets and whatever the technologies in an economic context. Brain power drives productivity, and this is where education becomes the critical factor in development, and investment in education becomes a strategic consideration for development.[8]

INTELLECTUAL AND CREATIVE CAPITAL AND THE ROLE OF TERTIARY EDUCATION

The concept of human capital morphed into intellectual capital as it became clearer that it was more than education and the application of what you know in the workplace or in society that made a difference; that, together with brain power, creativity was important because innovation was necessary to do things differently and to generate solutions. Linsu Kim, for instance, made it clear that for industrial development to take place, secondary education alone was not sufficient. Tertiary education output became critical to the development process. He illustrates this by showing how the electronics and automobile industries were developed in South Korea and by showing how explicit learning and tacit learning worked together to facilitate the necessary intellectual capital formation that made acceleration of development possible in the country.[9]

Paul Romer connected technological innovation to long-term economic growth. He also stressed the need for research and application linked to development and the importance of intellectual property laws to protect innovation. He developed the concept of endogenous growth, theorizing that technological innovation driven by research leads to sustainable economic growth.[10] Romer's Nobel Prize only underscores the importance that human capital, intellectual capital, was gaining in the research and theoretical literature in relation to economic growth and prosperity.

The coming together of all of these ideas has led to an appreciation of education and how it facilitates intellectual capital building but also to questions about what kind of education, what type of curriculum, and the vital role of research and intellectual property, not to mention, the role of education, research and intellectual capital on creativity, entrepreneurship, innovation and business and national development.[11]

SOCIAL CAPITAL

But we have also come to realize that it takes more. Education of the individual is one thing; expanding the pool of education is another; understanding the difference between competencies acquired at the tertiary or further post-secondary and technical vocational levels is yet another because these make a difference to the individual, to industry or a generation; but how can society as a whole benefit? That is a question in another realm altogether. Questions like these, along with the research required to answer them, have driven theorists to expand their focus beyond the human, the intellectual and the creative, leading to the development of concepts like social capital. Two key figures who developed the concept and illustrated how it works are Robert Putnam and Francis Fukuyama. The latter made the concept of social capital known to large numbers of people with his book *Trust*.[12] In *Trust*, Fukuyama explores how working together for a common purpose can make a big difference to prosperity and development and that such a disposition is rooted in ethical values and cultural habits.[13] But one of the pioneers, if not the pioneer of social capital theory, was Robert Putnam.

Putnam developed a theory of social capital out of an understanding of people working together for common purposes, which can make a difference in achievement and results, whether that is done through interpersonal relations, groups or networks.[14] At the same time, the disposition to cooperation is nurtured by family relations, community and culture, so one might argue that the human capital disposed to collaboration and cooperation, which strengthens social capital, is nurtured in environments in which social capital is rich, leading to mutual reinforcement and social cohesion, a kind of circularity.[15] Hence, there is a cultural dimension to this (which will not be pursued in this chapter) explored by scholars like Lawrence Harrison and Samuel Huntington.[16]

Suffice it to say that education in formal school structures or the education system, learning in the home and habits of behaviour in society and culture, as well as societal norms and/or expectations, do help to determine individual dispositions to levels of cooperation and collaboration in a society and, hence, ultimately, collective performance, community and societal achievement and national prosperity and development.

TERTIARY EDUCATION AND SOCIO-ECONOMIC DEFICITS

Against this background, I want in this chapter to examine some of the deficits which we need to overcome to create the conditions for Trinidad and Tobago to shift from mistakes made over the last sixty years that will assist us with the task of human intellectual and social capital formation and building, to stimulate greater prosperity, higher achievement and more meaningful development. This chapter will, therefore, focus on the tertiary sector as a vital bridge to human, intellectual and social capital formation and as a facilitator of prosperity and national development.

Slow progress in the 1950s, 1960s and 1970s gave way to significant growth of the tertiary sector in the region in the 1980s, and afterwards, privately owned tertiary providers emerged to address demand. Besides the issue of growing demand, there was also, however, the issue of a mismatch of skills between secondary output and employer's needs. Post-secondary and tertiary education were seen as remedying this challenge.[17]

There has always been a problem of a small percentage of students from primary school not moving on to secondary. In addition, only about 50 per cent did well enough at the secondary level to move on to tertiary. There was also a significant loss at the CAPE level.[18] Moreover, a hierarchy of schools and consequently varying school performance was the reality. The meaning of this is that all schools were not equal; the variety affected the university's quality of education as well as the unequal achievements of students and schools.

Despite these trends, which resulted in significant losses of human capital at various stages of student development within the sector, CARICOM had set a modest target of 20 per cent participation by 2015. However, Trinidad and Tobago set an ambitious target of 60 per cent, and with the help of the Dollar-for-Dollar programme and, subsequently, GATE, not to mention the push by the then principal of the University of the West Indies, St Augustine, for a rapid and significant expansion – which had a ripple effect across the tertiary sector – that 60 per cent target was achieved.[19] The question of sustainable funding to maintain achieved targets for tertiary expansion always posed a formidable challenge. That challenge is even more significant today as a reversal of gains in participation rates and graduate outputs is taking place.[20]

The challenges of achieving significant and relevant tertiary education outcomes, supported by a primary and secondary system that effectively prepares the annual cohort of sixteen-year-olds for further education, are substantial. There is also the critical issue of aligning the output of the tertiary education sector with the economy's absorptive capacity. Additionally, financing a system that supports an export diversification agenda for the non-energy sector in a post-COVID world presents another formidable challenge. This world is increasingly shaped by automation, robotics, artificial intelligence, augmented reality, the metaverse, environmental sustainability and a necessary shift to renewable energy. Together, these factors represent significant obstacles to human capital development and sustainable growth for Trinidad and Tobago. As a high-income country, so classified by the OECD and World Bank, attaining some levels of prosperity and growth in the economy, cycles of boom and bust in oil, Trinidad and Tobago post-COVID needs to focus on recovery and growth, committed to the principle of inclusion as the country seeks to restructure, diversify and transform its economy.

FINANCING EDUCATION SUSTAINABLY FOR DEVELOPMENT

At the core of human capital formation lies the education sector, including curriculum reconfiguration and the crucial link between educational outcomes and the national economy's capacity to absorb and utilize those skills. Equally important are the connections between research, solutions, intellectual property, business creation and entrepreneurship, which drive diversification. The ability to finance education, alongside the creation of an attractor pool of human capital to support investment in high-value chains within a transforming global economy, must also be considered an essential element in this process. The need for the education system to shift its strategies in defining knowledge to better facilitate the growth and nurturing of social capital is a critical issue that requires thoughtful consideration.

This chapter assumes, therefore, that the pursuit of comprehensive, inclusive human and intellectual capital formation is desirable and that we have a deficit in this area. This deficit arises from wastage in the primary and secondary education systems, limited absorptive capacity in the economy due to unsuccessful growth and diversification, and the system's inability to effectively deploy talent to maximize the value of intellectual capital within the output value chain and job creation strategies. Another weakness is the seemingly limited capacity for social capital formation. As a consequence, this chapter also assumes that Trinidad and Tobago can benefit from stronger social capital formation initiatives to support cooperative, collaborative and purposeful behaviour for wealth formation and for the public good. It is essential to reform and finance the tertiary system sustainably to fuel a thriving, prosperous knowledge economy that reduces our dependence on fossil fuel energy, accelerates the process of diversification, and is connected to global trends in technological innovation. At the heart of the argument in this chapter is the realization that human, intellectual, creative and social capital combine positively to spur productivity, entrepreneurship, growth, innovation, prosperity and sustainability because it is through the combination of tangible and intangible assets, working together to leverage physical assets, that the most ground-breaking developments happen. Moreover, we contend that this is an absolute necessity since the deficits in alignment, lack of synergy and absence of an overarching sense of mutually supportive actions and sectors are glaringly evident and require a holistic approach.

HOW DO WE MOVE FORWARD?

This chapter will address several recommendations for successful human, intellectual, and social capital formation below, starting with the financial sustainability of the system, and including leveraging the current pool of intellectual capital from the tertiary output of graduates over the last two decades. A discussion of what is required of an economy like Trinidad and Tobago, both within the Caribbean region and the global economy, in terms of curriculum transformation at this critical juncture, will be pursued. This includes the need for diversification and the absorptive capacity of graduates in the economy, as well as the facilitation of industries higher up the value chain to provide quality jobs, decent work, and a sense of satisfaction and fulfilment for workers at all levels. Additionally, the moral responsibility of the government to establish a more meritocratic system within the context of a small economy and country. Finally, it is important to understand that in today's world, there is collaborative responsibility between government, business, and academia to fill the research gap, generate intellectual property assets to boost business creation, and solve societal problems of every dimension.

Countries that rank high on the Human Development Index also rank high in economic performance. Human capital (HCI) is measured under the human development index based on the quality of educational output at secondary and tertiary levels. The top six countries in the HCI are Singapore, Korea, Japan, Hong Kong, Finland and Ireland.[21] All have an HDI score of .80. Trinidad and Tobago ranks 62 in economic performance and has an HDI score of .69. There is still significant work to be done in all these comparator countries, but the formation of social capital remains substantial.[22] The World Bank makes the case for the economic value of the connection between human capital, intellectual capital, social capital and economic development and performance.

SHARED RESPONSIBILITY FOR TUITION FINANCING

Dollar for Dollar was introduced as a policy in 2000 by the government of then Prime Minister Basdeo Panday. The government agreed to match dollar for dollar half the cost of tuition required for access to tertiary education by an admitted student. What this meant was that students were automatically responsible for 50 per cent of the cost of tuition. The view was expressed that dollar for the dollar was inherently unfair because if a student could not come up with 50 per cent, they would not be able to access tertiary education and would not be able to trigger government support. However, such thinking is flawed because an arrangement could have easily been made for any student who was admitted to a tertiary institution to access the initial 50 per cent either by direct subsidy or, by loan, or by some combination of these, thus facilitating the additional 50 per cent government support. However, this approach was not taken. Instead, a new programme called the Government Assistance for Tertiary Expenses (GATE), covering a state grant for full tuition cost, was introduced.[23]

Dollar for Dollar was based on a policy position of shared responsibility for the cost of education between the state and student, family or private support, which could include a private scholarship or loan. As I have said earlier, in cases where students had been admitted but had no means whatsoever of paying for tuition, the state could have arranged loan or grant funding by structuring it as part of a systemic thrust to ensure that inability to pay was not a liability to access tertiary education in policy terms. What this would have meant was that anyone who met the criteria for admission but could not afford the cost would be facilitated. Still, all others would take full responsibility for half the price of tuition, and the government would take direct responsibility for only half in all cases. A policy of no one admitted would be denied access on the basis of inability to pay is superior and fairer than a policy of all shall have free GATE access because it opens the door wide to haves and have-nots alike. GATE support meant that the government made tertiary education tuition free to the student or family by state subsidy, which covers the entire cost to all admitted students, regardless of means. As it turned out, this was abused and eventually had to be rationalized, and a means test was ultimately introduced.[24]

The difference between GATE and Dollar for Dollar in this respect is that, under GATE, if the government administers a means test, all students seeking GATE immediately come under scrutiny, and those who do not pass the test get no government support. Moreover, issues related to transparency, fairness and arbitrariness have arisen. Concerning the administration of the test in the instance of Dollar for Dollar, a student would have had to apply for a grant or loan only if they were unable to raise this privately; this would have reduced the number of loans and grants. It would have also put the onus of responsibility on the ambitions of the students and their families, and only those who applied for financial support would have been assessed to determine need. It is my view that the State cannot continue to carry the burden of full cost for tertiary tuition for all admitted students. Tertiary education is already subsidized at the institutional level for all state tertiary institutions. The notions of ambition, individual and family responsibility or private support are important concepts in society. It is social capital at work, personal drive, family cooperation, and the facilitation of social capital building.

As I have argued in a policy paper on financing tertiary education in small states, adopted as a policy position by UNESCO in 2009,[25] tertiary education offers shared benefits to graduates, their families, the business community that may employ them, and the state, whether through direct employment or deployment of their skills. Ultimately, the entire nation benefits from the increased human and intellectual capital[26] that tertiary education fosters. This inevitably raises the question of how the cost of higher education should be shared, which means determining a reasonable financing formula for tuition costs. I am not addressing here a financing formula for institutions, which is another matter. I am addressing the issues of tertiary access and financing required to ensure that tertiary access is not denied because of inability to pay. The other issue is facilitating personal ambition and drive as well as family aspirations because state support of tuition at the tertiary level becomes the provision of a public good with a private benefit.

In my policy paper for UNESCO, I argue that students, families, businesses and governments should all share the cost since they, as well as the wider society, are all beneficiaries. Beyond the issue of shared responsibility for cost is the question of when the student should pay: at the point of access, throughout the pursuit of tertiary certification, or after graduation.

Roger Hosein, Darren Conrad and I argued in another publication that tuition payment should not be demanded at the point of access but at the point of graduation when the graduate is able to operate as an income-earning citizen.[27] At that point, the student should repay the cost of tuition as a loan out of earnings and contribute as well to a modest graduate tax of not more than 2 per cent, which will be assigned to a revolving fund supported by tertiary graduates who fund tertiary education over generations. The policy position here is that anyone who gains access will be facilitated to secure educational advancement regardless of means, and tuition responsibility falls to the students, but only after graduation when they become earning citizens.

Moreover, educated citizens should willingly embrace the opportunity to contribute via a modest tax to a fund in perpetuity towards education, human capital building and intellectual capital appreciation. It is clear that some new permutation is required to finance tuition for tertiary education and fresh options need to be considered. The approaches outlined above are grounded in key principles – ensuring no one is denied access due to inability to pay, recognizing tertiary education as a public good with private benefits, embracing shared responsibility for financing and acknowledging the obligation of graduates to repay costs and contribute to sustainable funding – can be applied individually or collectively. Together, these strategies not only offer solutions to the challenge of financing tertiary education in Trinidad and Tobago or any small state but also foster responsible citizenship, encourage public-private partnerships, promote individual and social responsibility and help cultivate the development of social capital.

REPARATIONS

Another issue I wish to focus on is the issue of reparations and the value of that initiative now being pursued by the vice chancellor of the University of the West Indies, Sir Hilary Beckles, with some success. Pursuing the principle of reparations has been argued by CARICOM, and Vice Chancellor Beckles has taken the lead on behalf of the University of the West Indies. I think this matter should be pursued as a strategy for building education and knowledge institutions in the knowledge sector of the Caribbean region. Institutions such as the University of Glasglow[28] in Scotland and Harvard University in the United States[29] have acknowledged the need for honouring the principle of reparations for the price that an entire race of people had to pay in the New World and the Caribbean region because of the Transatlantic slave trade. This is a worthy initiative that requires thoughtful execution to bring to fruition. If managed effectively and collaboratively, it has the potential to transfer resources from the industrialized world to the Caribbean region, where they can be put to good use. These resources could support institution building, strengthen research collaboration, enhance capacity in critical areas, create scholarship funds, and foster awareness that promotes better understanding, mutual appreciation and the advancement of Caribbean people, their institutions and their societies. An additional benefit that could be meaningfully pursued would be good, collaborative support from donors and donor institutions on a sustained basis.

The University of the West Indies and any other institutions that benefit from such funds must take care not to racialize the allocation and use of reparations-related funds. Instead, these resources should be directed toward institutional development, human and intellectual capital growth, and community, societal, national and regional benefits. The focus should be on benefiting all in these multiracial societies, as well as advancing the human race as a whole. This includes fostering human, intellectual and social capital accumulation as essential for building a competitive, knowledge-based society, which is a public necessity. The enslavement of African peoples and the subjugation and exploitation that came with it can be turned on its head if reparation funding can support enlightenment and upliftment.

Finally, I wish to explore the surplus of intellectual capital in societies like ours, where economic growth does not keep pace with the need to move up the industrial and technological value chain. As a result, graduates of the tertiary education system often face unemployment or underemployment, leaving them with little choice but to consider migration as an option.[30] This disconnect between the education system and economic opportunities is a critical issue on the human capital front.

GOVERNMENT RESPONSIBILITY

I take the opportunity here to forcefully argue that it is the role and responsibility of the government to provide good governance, economic progress and prosperity to its citizens.[31] This can be achieved by pursuing good economic policy that encourages growth, investment and entrepreneurship. Or else the question needs to be asked, "What do we elect governments for?" Moreover, the government must understand that with a range of other supportive policies for business success and in support of investment, the formation or existence of an intellectual capital pool through tertiary output and research engagement can be managed as a vital asset to attract foreign investment and to encourage local investors to move up the value chain in critical areas that have emerged and are likely to be the mainstay of cutting-edge progress.[32] Trends in the Internet of Things, automation, robotics, artificial intelligence, social media, cybersecurity, augmented reality and the metaverse are calling.[33] We need to take the initiative required to be prepared for an upward and outward journey in these service-focused and skills-intensive industries. Therefore, while we produce graduates, we must also promote growth, investment and export trade expansion to absorb each graduating class. One is the responsibility of education policy and the education sector. The other is the responsibility of the government via good and effective governance for a proprietary agenda. At the same time, we must understand, appreciate and leverage the cumulative value of years of graduating classes as an attractor to higher-value investments connected to technological growth trends in the global industry.

For this to succeed, we need more than just a steady stream of tertiary-level graduates. What these graduates study, how they are taught, how they learn, their willingness to continue learning, their disposition and attitude toward work, their sense of responsibility, appreciation for accountability, level of creativity, entrepreneurial drive, ability to absorb technology, capacity for innovation, skill in identifying problems and finding solutions – all these factors are critical. Equally important are well-honed skills and a spirit of cooperation and collaboration that fosters mutually supported achievement. So, the transformation of curriculum, different approaches to learning, and enhanced teaching methodologies are all essential shifts that are required. The design of the curriculum and the refinement of teaching and learning methodology can fuel an economic transformation agenda.

Trinidad and Tobago consists of eight islands – Tobago, Trinidad, five islands off the coast of Chaguaramas, and one off the coast of Tobago. The environment and the ecology that these islands and this country sustain are important to human well-being. Sustainability is an important concept for islands surrounded by oceans that are located in the tropics, and that can be subject to wind, rain, floods, earthquakes, tsunamis and other disasters. Moreover, every country needs food, energy and water at a cost that they can afford in order to be viable. Trinidad and Tobago has the additional problem of fossil fuel energy dependence for both energy needs and national income. At the same time, the alignment of production, the structure of exports and the resulting structure of the balance of trade and payments all contribute to a continuing and worsening foreign exchange crisis.[34]

KNOWLEDGE-DRIVEN APPROACH

All these problems cited above can be solved by knowledge, critical thinking, creativity, insight, innovation and application of research findings and through solution discoveries. To support a knowledge-driven approach, Trinidad and Tobago needs to think and reposition its knowledge sector for sustainable value and application. This can only be done through transformation and realignment of research, the protection of intellectual property and effective deployment of talent on the basis of merit.[35] This, in turn, requires enlightened government policy, the design of viable projects, public/private partnerships, facilitation of trade and investment via improved ease of doing business measures, the recognition of merit and reward for good work, high achievement and the facilitation of collaborative and cooperative endeavour.[36] For this to happen in society, there must be a cultural shift in methods of learning and teaching to support individual effort, creativity, entrepreneurial initiative and independent thought. Still, there must also be a corresponding emphasis on cooperation, collaborative endeavour, mutual respect and support, and collective achievement. This collaboration must go beyond curriculum, teaching and learning to embrace the research process and system in order to leverage its value for intellectual property formation, application of research findings and business creation.[37]

GOVERNMENT, BUSINESS, EDUCATION SECTOR COLLABORATION

Government, business and tertiary sectors must collaborate to create a learning society, knowledge industries and a knowledge economy. Alliances can be made not just to provide local and regional private sector support but also to draw on findings from international sources relevant to local and regional needs. Establishing such a genuine partnership at the local level – one that is supported in an integrated, collaborative manner both nationally and regionally – would create a community of leaders from academia, business and government, all united in addressing national needs or regional necessities. This cohesive approach would serve as a powerful social capital mechanism, positioning the region to engage more effectively with international research funding agencies.[38] There are too many gaps and deficits in the way we are proceeding with development in the Caribbean and too much disjointedness. Not only are economic policy and foreign policy not coordinated in the region,[39] of the approaches to development are often disjointed even in individual countries, including Trinidad and Tobago.

To highlight some of the most obvious solvable problems, we have massive floods but little or no irrigation infrastructure for farmers, and we cannot provide potable water to four hundred and fifty thousand homes. Neither can we provide water consistently for those homes that do receive, seven days per week, twenty-four hours per day. We have a lake of pitch, yet our roads are among the worst in the region.

Our energy industry has supported the Trinidad and Tobago economy for a century, but this poses a high risk to the environment and our beaches. In the crises we have experienced so far, we have simply moved from crisis to crisis. There is no holistic or comprehensive plan for addressing a rapid response to such disasters, nor have we built sustainable capacity.

We have acres of arable land and entrepreneurs willing to invest in various forms of protected agriculture, but our food import bill has been soaring. We can hardly feed ourselves in a crisis, and we cannot seem to make the lucrative link between agricultural production and tourism. Nor have we progressed in agro-processing and agro-manufacturing at the rate that one would consider desirable.

We want to diversify our economy and encourage non-energy export investment. However, we will not improve the various elements of the ease-of-doing-business matrix that can make a difference, and we perpetually make policy errors that undermine business confidence and create uncertainty.[40]

AVOIDING NEGATIVES OF POLITICAL PATRONAGE BY RECOGNIZING MERIT

On the human capital front, the system of political patronage closes many doors to genuine talent, and this failure to recognize merit drives away talent and contributes to underperformance and underdevelopment. We need to nurture, build and support a merit system in the economy as it obtains in places of transparent competition, such as sports or chess so that the best can contribute their greatest value. Inclusive development is simultaneously a socio-economic issue, a political issue and a national resources management issue, and this must reflect a full appreciation of such realities in policy and action. As we transparently draw on national talent, we must also contain the negative effects of patronage so that we minimize some of the consequences, such as a sense of unfairness and exclusion and a lack of systems of accountability.

The structural foundations of political parties in Trinidad and Tobago have also contributed to divisiveness, discomfort and suspicion in the society. Political patronage, which rewards party loyalty in ethnic based parties, will only reinforce these tendencies of divisiveness and cause dissonance. The evolution of our political party system might be explainable, but reinforcement of its dismissive tendencies is not justifiable. Disrespect for merit is supportive of unfairness, underperformance and underachievement. It dampens enthusiasm and promotes the withdrawal of talent. Ultimately, this means a loss of talent for society. We must govern to give confidence that fairness will be honoured and talent will be recognized. This will do a lot to strengthen social capital. The goals of socio-economic inclusion and equality of opportunity are not contradictory to the need for the recognition of merit. Fundamental to good governance and the build-up of trust in society is the just management of these contending demands on which economic, societal and political success depend.

In the knowledge era where education, knowledge and know-how matter, we need to synchronize what we are doing in education with strategies for economic diversification, growth and prosperity. We must also stay in step with the global trends driving technological and economic progress to ensure that our educational systems contribute meaningfully to our economic future. Necessity demands an upward as well as inward push as we harness intellectual capital inclusively to make development happen. At the same time, we also need to push outward to global connectivity so that we are on board the train of future prosperity as other parts of the world lead disruptions.

This is the essential requirement for the post-COVID era, despite the ongoing threat of COVID re-emerging in various forms, the challenges posed by geopolitical realignments, supply chain congestion, transportation disruptions and the devastation caused by wars and conflicts. Nations must be prepared to navigate these complexities while building resilience and sustainability for the future. Regardless of how the future unfolds, there will always be a world where sustainable, competitive economies remain a key goal for every country, making a decisive difference for their people and their place in the global landscape. We must ensure that we are well-organized, have a clear plan and possess the competence and capacity to execute that plan effectively. The greatest asset any country can cultivate is its human, intellectual and social capital, which can be used to leverage its physical assets or enhance its ability to learn and adapt to emerging trends. These forms of capital are vital for a nation's long-term success and resilience in an ever-changing global environment.

After sixty years of independence, we have reached a stage in our journey where we must achieve significantly more, due to the changes happening now and those yet to come in the world. We must be prepared for any paradigm shifts these changes may demand. The only way we can adapt, survive, succeed and thrive is if both our leaders and our people are fully prepared and ready to meet these challenges head-on. We must design a strategy to develop our human and social capital assets and make it work for us in a competitive and challenging world, whatever the transformations that technology will facilitate, whatever the geopolitical shifts, whatever the nature of the world order. We must make rules for ourselves and abide by them. And we must contribute to the rules that the world will live by and help the world to adhere to them. We must not be spectators of the unfolding of a new world order.

Fairness, transparency, an end to entrenched partisan dispositions and a genuine commitment to equality of opportunity and shared prosperity will help free our society and build confidence. It will unleash talent and generate opportunities for creativity, entrepreneurship, innovation. Moreover, it will strengthen democratic discourse and participation and build trust. These are vital assets that require nurturing over the next sixty years. We must cultivate the human, intellectual and social capital needed to identify opportunities and harness creative options in a world that is rapidly moving beyond traditional precedents. As sustainable development increasingly demands perpetual innovation, we are called to generate original solutions for challenges never before encountered in human history – particularly as climate change continues to affect our islands. This capacity for innovation will be essential in navigatig the uncharted problems we face.

NOTES

1. Mahbub ul Haq, "Reflections on Human Development."
2. UNDP, "Human Development Index (HDI)." This became an innovation in looking at development.
3. Nicholas Bloom and John Van Reenen, "Human Resource Management and Productivity."
4. Tom Schuller, "Integrating Human/Knowledge Capital and Social Capital."
5. Barbara Piazza-Georgi, "The Role of Human and Social Capital in Growth: Extending Our Understanding."
6. Gary Becker, "Human Capital."
7. Theodore W. Schultz, "Investment in Human Capital"
8. Ibid.
9. Linsu Kim, "Imitation to Innovation: The Dynamics of Korea's Technological Learning."
10. Paul M. Romer, "The Origins of Endogenous Growth."
11. ECLAC, "Knowledge Management for Development: Towards a Practical Approach for the Caribbean."

12. Francis Fukuyama, "Trust: The Social Virtues and the Creation of Prosperity."
13. Bagrat Harutyunyan and Akbar Valadbigi, "Trust: The Social Virtues"; Francis Fukuyama, "The Creation of Prosperity."
14. Robert Putnam, "The Prosperous Community: Social Capital and Public Life."
15. Robert Putnam, "The Prosperous Community: Social Capital and Public Life"; Francis Fukuyama, "Social Capital and Civil Society."
16. Lawrence E. Harrison, "Underdevelopment is a State of Mind"; and Lawrence Harrison and Samuel Huntington, "Culture Matters: How Values Shape Human Progress."
17. Kapur and Crowley, "Beyond the ABCs."
18. Bhoendradatt Tewarie, "The University of the West Indies: Regional Tertiary Education in the English-Speaking Territory" *in Thinking it Through, Making it Happen.*
19. Ministry of Tertiary Education and Skills Training, "The Future of Tertiary Education and Skills Training 2015–2025"; Bhoendradatt Tewarie, "Chapter: Thinking Through Sustainable Funding," in *Thinking it Through, Making it Happen.*
20. Anand Dass and Halima-Sa'adia Kassim, "Impact of Changes to G.A.T.E on the UWI: Considerations for Enrolment and Funding Prospects," The University Office of Planning, UWI, Mona.
21. World Development Report, "The Changing Nature of Work."
22. Ibid.
23. Janine Mendes-Franco, "Will Trinidad & Tobago Students Be Last Out of the Gate if the Government Stops Funding Tertiary Education?"
24. Office of the Prime Minister, Republic of Trinidad and Tobago, "Here's how Changes to GATE Affect You."
25. Bhoendradatt Tewarie, "Thinking through Sustainable Funding" in UNESCO IIEP Policy Brief.
26. Ibid.
27. Roger Hosein, Bhoendradatt Tewarie and Daren Conrad, "Cost Sharing in Higher Education Financing: A Model for the Caribbean."
28. WIC News, "UWI signs £20 million Caribbean Reparations Agreement with Glasgow University."
29. The New York Times, "Harvard Details Its Ties to Slavery and Its Plans for Redress."
30. Francesca Castellani, "International Skilled Migration: The Caribbean Experience in Perspective."
31. Charles C. Snow, "Organizing in the Age of Competition, Cooperation, and Collaboration."

32. Edward S. Mason, "The Role of Government In Economic Development."
33. Forbes, "13 Cutting-Edge Technologies That May Soon Be Making A Big Impact."
34. IMF, "2022 Article IV Report."
35. Emilio J. Castilla, "Achieving Meritocracy in the Workplace."
36. IDB, "Nurturing Institutions for a Resilient Caribbean."
37. Natália de Lima Figueiredo, Cristina I. Fernandes and José Luis Abrantes, "Triple Helix Model: Cooperation in Knowledge Creation."
38. OAS, "Transforming Lives Through Partnerships."
39. J.F Hornbeck, "CARICOM: Challenges and Opportunities for Caribbean Economic Integration."
40. Rohan Longmore, Pascal Jaupart and Marta Riveira Cazorla, "Toward Economic Diversification in Trinidad and Tobago."

REFERENCES

Becker, Gary. *Human Capital*. 2nd ed. New York: Columbia University Press, 1964.

Bloom, Nicholas, and John van Reenen. "Human Resource Management and Productivity." NBER Working Paper No. 16019, National Bureau of Economic Research, 2010.

Castellani, Francesca. *International Skilled Migration: The Caribbean Experience in Perspective*. Washington, DC: Inter-American Development Bank, 2007.

Dass, Anand, and Halima-Sa'adia Kassim. "Impact of Changes to G.A.T.E on the UWI: Considerations for Enrolment and Funding Prospects." The University Office of Planning, UWI St Augustine, 2016. https://uwi.edu/uop/sites/uop/files/Impact%20of%20Changes%20to%20GTE%20on%20The%20UWI.pdf.

ECLAC. "Knowledge Management for Development: Towards a Practical Approach for the Caribbean." United Nations, 2010. https://www.cepal.org/en/publications/38264-knowledge-management-development-towards-practical-approach-caribbean.

Castilla, Emilio J. "Achieving Meritocracy in the Workplace." *MIT Sloan Management Review*, 2016. https://ideas.wharton.upenn.edu/wp-content/uploads/2018/07/Meritocracy-and-Privilege_Castilla-2016.pdf.

Figueiredo, Natália de Lima, Cristina I. Fernandes, and José Luis Abrantes. "Triple Helix Model: Cooperation in Knowledge Creation." *Journal of the Knowledge Economy* 13, no. 1 (2022).

Forbes. "13 Cutting-Edge Technologies That May Soon Be Making a Big Impact." *Forbes*, 4 February 2021. https://www.forbes.com/sites/forbestechcouncil/2021/02/04/13-cutting-edge-technologies-that-may-soon-be-making-a-big-impact/.

Fukuyama, Francis. "Social Capital and Civil Society." The Institute of Public Policy, George Mason University, 1999.

———. *Trust: The Social Virtues and the Creation of Prosperity*. New York: Free Press, 1996.

Haq, Mahbub ul. *Reflections on Human Development: How the Focus of Development Economics Shifted from National Income Accounting to People-Centered Policies*. New York: Oxford University Press, 1995.

Harrison, Lawrence E. *Underdevelopment Is a State of Mind: The Latin American Case*. Lanham, MD: University Press of America, 1985.

———, and Samuel Huntington, ed. *Culture Matters: How Values Shape Human Progress*. New York: Basic Books, 2001.

Harutyunyan, Bagrat, and Akbar Valadbigi. "Trust: The Social Virtues and The Creation of Prosperity by Francis Fukuyama." *Studies of Changing Societies: Comparative and Interdisciplinary Focus* 1, no. 1 (2012): 80–95.

Hornbeck, JF. "CARICOM, Challenges and Opportunities for Caribbean Economic Integration." *Congressional Research Service*, 7 January 2008. https://www.everycrsreport.com/files/20080107_RL34308_293283f2953ab7609fb5fe6bf2bff1a3bb1fe649.pdf.

Hosein, Roger, Bhoendradatt Tewarie, and Daren Conrad. "Cost Sharing in Higher Education Financing: A Model for the Caribbean." *Caribbean Journal of Education* 29, nos. 1&2 (2017): 66–94.

IMF. "2022 Article IV Report." International Monetary Fund, 2022. https://www.imf.org/en/Publications/CR/Issues/2022/03/09/Trinidad-and-Tobago-2021-Article-IV-Consultation-Press-Release-Staff-Report-and-Statement-514118.

Kapur, Devesh, and Megan Crowley. "Beyond the ABCs: Higher Education and Developing Countries." *Center for Global Development*, Working Paper 139, 2008.

Kim, Linsu. *Imitation to Innovation: The Dynamics of Korea's Technological Learning*. Boston: Harvard Business Press, 1997.

Longmore, Rohan, Pascal Jaupart, and Marta Riveira Cazorla. "Toward Economic Diversification in Trinidad and Tobago." *World Bank*, 2014. https://openknowledge.worldbank.org/bitstream/handle/10986/18330/WPS6840.pdf?sequence=1&isAllowed=y.

Mason, Edward S. *The Role of Government in Economic Development*. Cambridge, MA: Harvard University Press, 1960.

Mendes-Franco, Janine. "Will Trinidad & Tobago Students Be Last Out of the Gate if the Government Stops Funding Tertiary Education?" *Global Voices*, 21 July 2016. https://globalvoices.org/2016/07/21/will-trinidad-tobago-students-be-last-out-of-the-gate-if-the-government-stops-funding-tertiary-education/.

Ministry of Tertiary Education and Skills Training. *The Future of Tertiary Education and Skills Training 2015–2025: A National Policy Framework*. 2015. http://parlcloud.ttparliament.org:8081/PapersLaidViewer/TempFiles/Report%20of%20the%20GATE%20Task%20Force.pdf.

New York Times. "Harvard Details Its Ties to Slavery and Its Plans for Redress." *New York Times*, 2022.

OAS. *Transforming Lives through Partnerships*. Organization of American States, 2018. https://www.oas.org/en/ser/dia/perm_observers/Documents/Transforming-Lives-Through-Partnerships.pdf.

Office of the Prime Minister, Republic of Trinidad and Tobago. "Here's How Changes to GATE Affect You." 2017. https://www.opm.gov.tt/heres-how-gate-changes-affect-you/.

Piazza-Georgi, Barbara. "The Role of Human and Social Capital in Growth: Extending Our Understanding." *Cambridge Journal of Economics* 26, no. 4 (2002): 461–79.

Putnam, Robert D. "The Prosperous Community: Social Capital and Public Life." *The American Prospect*, no. 13 (1993): 35–42.

Romer, Paul M. "The Origins of Endogenous Growth." *Journal of Economic Perspectives* 8, no. 1 (1994): 3–22.

Schuller, Tom. "Integrating Human/Knowledge Capital and Social Capital." OECD/DfES/QCA/ESRC Seminar Knowledge Management in Education and Learning, 2002. https://www.oecd.org/education/innovation-education/2074416.pdf.

Schultz, Theodore W. "Investment in Human Capital." *The American Economic Review* 51, no. 1 (1961): 1–17.

Snow, Charles C. "Organizing in the Age of Competition, Cooperation, and Collaboration." *Journal of Leadership & Organizational Studies* 22, no. 4 (2015): 433–42.

Tewarie, Bhoendradatt. "Thinking through Sustainable Funding." In *Tertiary Education in Small States: Planning in the Context of Globalization*, edited by Michaela Martin and Mark Bray, 233–46. Paris: UNESCO IIEP, 2011.

———. "Thinking Through Sustainable Funding." In *Thinking It Through, Making It Happen*, 83–96. London: Hansib Publication, 2015.

———. "The University of the West Indies: Regional Tertiary Education in the English-Speaking Territory." In *Thinking It Through, Making It Happen*, 69–81. London: Hansib Publication, 2015.

UNDP. "Human Development Index (HDI)." United Nations Development Programme, 2022. https://hdr.undp.org/en/content/human-development-index-hdi.

WIC News. "UWI Signs £20 Million Caribbean Reparations Agreement with Glasgow University." *WIC News*, 2019.

World Bank Group. *World Development Report 2019: The Changing Nature of Work*. Washington, DC: World Bank, 2019.

[CHAPTER 7]

A Review of Sixty Years of Crime Management

Trinidad and Tobago

GARVIN HEERAH

INTRODUCTION

It might be helpful for us to examine the approaches over the past sixty years as management strategies for crime evolved on the island and so peek into the modus operandi of the Trinidad and Tobago Police Service (TTPS) over the years. There is value in scrutinizing what the obvious policing and policy failures were and what the wins were in policing and policy endeavours. A "temperature check" on Trinidad and Tobago's present crime-fighting capabilities and how much the environment has shifted over the years can bring some valuable leads on what could be sensible and successful strategic approaches on the way forward.

THE EVOLUTION OF THE TRINIDAD AND TOBAGO POLICE SERVICE

Sixty years seems like a long time, but when one talks about nationhood and independence, sixty years is considered relatively young. Searches suggest that the TTPS has been in operation for over 430 years. Currently, TTPS has approximately 5,949 police officers and is headquartered at Edward and

Sackville Streets, Port of Spain.[1] According to Ottley (1962), between 1592 and 1792, the human capacity of the then "Police Force" never exceeded six! At that time, the police headquarters was housed at the corner of Abercromby and Hart Streets. The police were Trinidad and Tobago's first postmen, and the police stations were the courthouses. The four-foot-long baton or truncheon was the only weapon carried by the police in the early days. Violence was quelled by the weight of the baton and not by the popping of a gun.

Outlined in the history of the TTPS on its website is the admission that the institution [TTPS] "was responsible to the people of Trinidad and Tobago for their deeds and misdeeds." The Police Service Act (assented to in 1965 and its Regulations of 1966) guides the procedural actions of the TTPS, as well as ensures efficient and transparent management of the service. The act and regulations introduced the change from police force to police service, which the TTPS is referred to today. According to the TTPS's history on its website, the change was expected, not only in name but also in operation, shifting the militarized force to a "service-oriented" organization.

TYPES OF CRIME INTERVENTIONS

Crime prevention, as we know it, is the main focus of the TTPS. The mandate for deterring and detecting crimes and bringing persons before the courts to receive their just due is part of the responsibility of the TTPS. In his writings on crime mediation methods for the Calumet City project in Cook County, Illinois, USA, Robert Ottley (1962, 1972) employed specific interventions. The first mode of intervention was the collection of data on the types of crimes and the rates of crime between persons ages twelve to twenty-five; the second was to survey community members regarding the needs of the community; and the third step was to identify the community assets that are currently addressing crime in the environment. Assets can be community organizations or even individuals with social influence in the community. The first programme would involve a collaboration of services that offer education, team-building and sports, while the second would include persons between the ages of eighteen and twenty-five. The highlight of the second programme was on education, job training and life skills. The goal of both the first and second steps of the programme was to decrease the crime rates in youth by implementing productive curricula that benefited each participant. It is useful to note the age ranges of the participants: twelve, junior age, to twenty-five, young adult. In Trinidad and Tobago's society, the age ranges of offenders are similar and may be lower than the twelve-year age group.

Ottley referenced Kirst-Ashman and Hull's (2015) Ecosystems theory on the importance of understanding the different systems in an environment and the perspective or opinions that the community members hold regarding social systems, such as law enforcement, schools, employers and the availability of recreational facilities. The reality for Kirst-Ashman and Hull is that obtaining the opinions of community members will help identify what programmes are needed in the community and, more importantly, to identify community assets that are currently addressing crime. In our communities, we know of programmes with corresponding intentions, but results do not seem to be forthcoming. Let us take a glimpse into the assessment of one of our local authors.

In Professor Ramesh Deosarans writing on *Inequality, Crime and Education in Trinidad and Tobago: Removing the Masks*, the publication draws on data from reports dating back to the 1960s. Similarly, this chapter examines approximately sixty years of crime management practices. Is there a correlation between our persistent dilemmas in crime and its management and the management of our education systems? If so, how is this influencing the current wave of physical and psychological combats we observe among our secondary school population upon the "physical" re-opening of our schools? Deosaran examined the issues that surround the academic under-performance of the government secondary schools compared with the denominational assisted schools, as well as the corresponding tireless challenge of placement in the secondary schools and the inequalities that are viewed as inherent in the entire process.

In Deosaran's research, he corroborated that the unequal opportunity and its related unequal outcomes are "embedded in the country's education system – a legacy from the colonial past that institutionalized a system of schools run by the government and those run by religious denominations but supported by the state". Deosaran contended that "the structural inequity in the education system and its outcomes amount to discrimination against the most disadvantaged groups with serious debilitating implications for the country's social and economic progress and its status as a modern democracy". Even at the time of his writing, Deosaran appealed for the removal of the "masks of inequality and discrimination" and pleaded for sustained, "carefully planned and data-driven reforms in Trinidad and Tobago's education system".

APPROACHES TO DISCIPLINING OFFICERS – THEN AND NOW

August Vollmer was described as a pioneer in police professionalism and labelled as "the father of modern policing". Vollmer advanced that the public expects "Police Officers to have the wisdom of Solomon, the courage of David, the strength of Sampson; the patience of Job; the leadership of Moses; the kindness of the Good Samaritan; the strategic training of Alexander the Great, the faith of Daniel, the diplomacy of Lincoln; the tolerance of the Carpenter of Nazareth and an intimate knowledge of every branch of the natural, biological, and social sciences." In essence, perfection is expected from a police officer. That view of the role of the police may be so all across the world, but the police officer, like everyone else, is a human being and is prone to mistakes, misdeeds and poor judgement. The police are held to a higher standard and should be. However, in some quarters, integrity remains the greatest training and leadership challenge facing police management in this era. The TTPS cannot be exempt from this challenge.

If you have an opportunity to converse with policemen and women with regimental numbers ranging from eight thousand to twelve thousand (mostly retired), you may recognize that the observance and adherence to the rule and conduct of policing, as well as lawful instructions from a senior officer, were solemn. At that time, "anti-slopers" (a common term used in law enforcement for persons who display laziness, tardiness, delinquency) were few and far between, as a senior officer writing in your pocket diary or the likelihood of losing your employment or the possibility of the senior officer taking "you", as an anti-sloper before a tribunal was real, especially if the tribunal officer before whom you would appear was Mr Cyracious Liverpool, who developed something of a reputation for high standards in this sphere. What is the probability of officers from the TTPS and other law enforcement authorities in Trinidad and Tobago who lack self-control or are recurrent abusers of the rule of law having disciplinary actions taken against them? This is seen as the beginning of the breakdown of order and system in the TTPS.

There was a time when police officers were arrested and charged by the Professional Standards Bureau of the TTPS, and investigations into transgressions by officers were generally investigated by the Police Complaints Division of the TTPS. The Professional Standards Bureau is a department of the TTPS that treats alleged criminal conduct perpetrated by police officers. At the same time, the Police Complaints Division of the TTPS manages the investigations of internal breaches of police regulations. The alleged offenders in matters are brought by the Police Complaints Division before a tribunal (led by senior/first division police officers). While charges are still proffered against officers, which means that poor conduct is considered, the perception currently is that there are too many recalcitrant officers in the field in a profession where the expectation is for the highest standards of exemplary conduct.

At the Twelfth Meeting of the Joint Select Committee (JSC) on National Security in February 2022, on the safety and security of citizens and public concerns about the performance of the TTPS, which officers of the Professional Standards Bureau of the TTPS were interviewed, it was highlighted that one of the issues facing the Police Service is indiscipline amounting to unprofessional behaviour. The TTPS does not address this from a human resource perspective. Indiscipline in a police service could easily lead to further criminal conduct. While matters of police indiscipline are brought before the Professional Standards Bureau, a deeper examination of the facts in the matter, as well as discussions with the DPP, may lead to the matter being referred to the Police Complaints Division.[2]

The JSC was informed that the Professional Standards Bureau welcomes the introduction of the Whistle Blower legislation, as it will encourage persons, including police officers, to come forward if they know that there is some level of protection. Under such conditions, they are more likely to provide information to expose unsavoury behaviours to their very own colleagues. With an estimated four hundred police officers currently under investigation, the Professional Standards Bureau provided statistics on the number of TTPS officers under investigation for the years 2018–21 and the number of matters completed. It appears that there is a 62.2 per cent increase in the number of officers under investigation from 2018 to

2021, also noting an estimated 10 per cent increase between 2018 and 2019, a 38 per cent increase between 2019 and 2021, and a 7.3 per cent increase between 2020 and 2021. The figures for the matters completed also tell another story, and that story may not be so for only this feature but for several arenas of justice.

Table 7.1 suggests that from 2018, there is a consistent increase in the number of police officers whose actions were egregious, and investigations commenced. In some matters, however, no further action was the recommended outcome. It was also suggested that the figures for the years are not cumulative and that not all the officers against whom charges were proffered are on suspension. The nature of the offences in the period may include, but is not limited to:

1. Misbehaviour in public office (this could involve almost any offence and is one of the main offences for which charges are proffered against officers).
2. Corruption under the Prevention of Corruption Act Chapter 11:11.
3. Perverting the course of justice.

The TTPS Disciplinary Procedure is articulated in Part XIII, Regulation 151 through 174 of the Police Service Regulations, 2007. It includes the process for suspension, interdiction and disciplinary tribunals and goes as far as the commissioner removing an officer in the public's interest. There are structures established to hold officers to account; however, whether those structures are tested or applied when there is dissension is another matter. The public is notified via media of arrests and charges proffered against police officers. Vollmers' proposition of the public's view of the police officer, to be as close to faultless as can be, opens the door of concern

Table 7.1: Professional Standards Bureau Statistics on TTPS Officers under Investigations and Matters Completed – 2018–21

Year	No. of TTPS Officers Under Investigations	Matters Complete (Police Officers Charged and Before the Courts)
2021	133	18
2020	124	16
2019	90	23
2018	82	19

based on the Police Complaints Authority's (PCA) picture of allegations of criminal offences for October 2020 to September 2021. The alleged ninety-nine criminal offences carried out by police officers for that period include fraud and corruption, firearm-related offences and fatal/non-fatal shootings. The small percentage of matters brought to completion is another reason for concern.

The PCA is an independent agency established as a police oversight body to protect citizens' rights and hold the police accountable to the highest standard of conduct. We may surmise that not all misdemeanours experienced by members of the population are reported to the PCA; nevertheless, this means that there may be even more acts of misconduct (see figure 7.1).

In 2021, PCA recorded 104 complaints made by members of the population against police officers for alleged misconduct. Figure 7.2 shows the numbers by police divisions for October 2020 to September 2021.

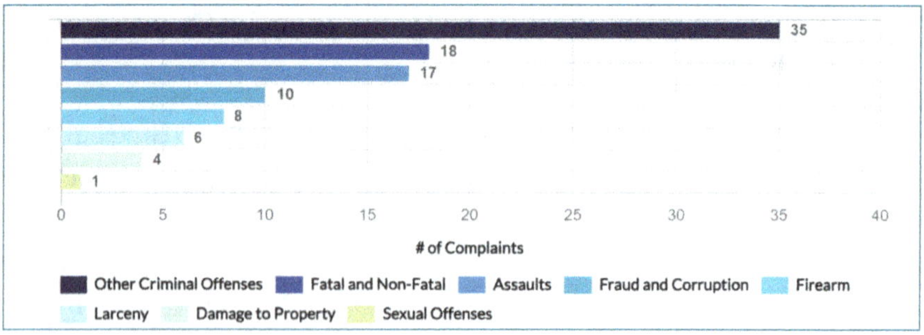

Figure 7.1: Allegations of Criminal Offences for the Period 2020–21
Source: PCA website

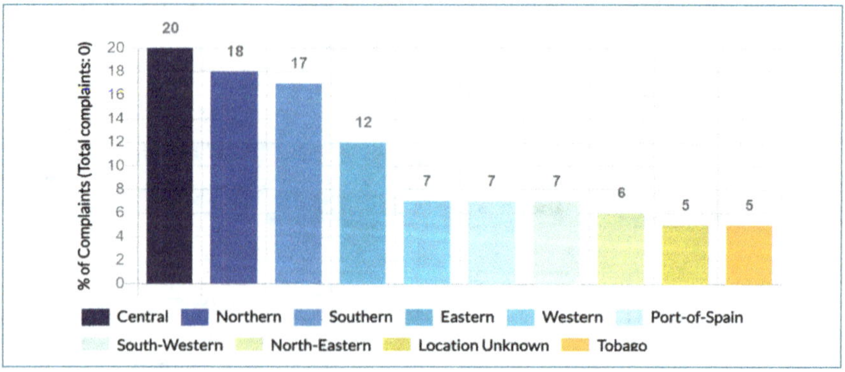

Figure 7.2: Complaints Made to the PCA for the Period 1 October 2020 to 30 September 2021
Source: PCA website

We must conclude, therefore, based on available evidence, that there is a problem of discipline and a lowering of the standard of behaviour in the TTPS and that escalation of these presents a growth danger.

In the TTPS Operating Plan – 2022,[3] the human resource distribution shows that the actual strength[4] consist of 5,949 officers of the Trinidad and Tobago Police Service (TTPS) "regular"[5] police officers. The 5,949 officers of the regular officers are further broken down into 1,781 females and 4,168 males. The actual strength of the Special Reserve Police contingent is 3,172 officers, further broken down into 1,014 female and 2,158 male officers. The Special Reserve Police Officers (SRPs) are governed by the Special Reserve Police Act 15:03. There is a distinction between the SRPs who are governed by the SRP Act 15:03 and the regular police officer, whose direction is found in the Police Service Regulations 11, Chapter 15:01. The regular police officer undergoes 1,100 contact hours of training in the rudiments of policing. In comparison, the SRP is afforded 420 contact hours. The SRP is afforded what can be considered an introduction to the rudiments of policing. All the distinctions between the two groups, however, are of no consequence to the public whom the officers serve, as it is only for the insignia on the shoulder, which reads TTPS or SRP, which makes the distinction from the citizen's point of view.

In addition to the PCA's submissions, having assessed the information available from open source on the status of police officers against whom charges were proffered, it can be deduced that there may be more SRPs who were charged for alleged misconduct. One recent example is a female SRP in the Eastern Division against whom a report was made to the Mayaro Criminal Investigations Department (CID) of an alleged report of Larceny by Trick. The SRP officer was formally charged with one count of money laundering following advice from the director of public prosecutions (DPP).

One may have heard of other incidents of SRPs performing acts that are unbecoming of the office of the noble profession of policing. In Tobago in May 2021, an SRP allegedly falsely reported that a vehicle for which he was still paying its owner was stolen. That SRP was charged with larceny of a motor vehicle, false pretence and wasteful employment of the police. Then, in June 2021, an SRP was arrested and charged for the offences of shooting with intent to do grievous bodily harm, wasteful employment of the police and discharging a firearm within forty metres of a roadway after the SRP was involved in an exchange between himself and another person, who he [the SRP] said pointed a gun in his direction after giving him a "bad drive". These are some examples of matters involving SRPs which sometimes come to the attention of the public.

In the early days, the SRP body was traditionally set up to supplement the TTPS's manpower capacity. This was satisfied by taking on board prominent members of the community, such as teachers and county councillors. These prominent citizens were asked or appointed as special police to assist the Police Service in cases of emergency and on special occasions. Today, more is expected of the SRP, notwithstanding some debilitating processes, and that means higher standards of professionalism are being demanded.

The recruitment of the SRP is not as rigorous or detailed as the "regular" police officer. The regular police are exposed to more rigid vetting and background checks, and the regular officer must pass a polygraph examination, which has formed part of the recruitment process since 2006. Could the inference be made that because of this deficiency in recruitment, inclusive of lack of polygraphing, SRPs are prone to being vulnerable to criminality? Additionally, the training for the SRP is not as demanding and comprehensive as the experience of the approximately six and a half months of training in the Police Academy and the two-year probationary period, as is required for the regular police officer.

As part of the crime management strategy, retired police officers proficient in policing who retired at age fifty-five are given the opportunity to continue serving based on their competencies. While this category of officers is returned to the TTPS manpower as SRPs, misdemeanours are rare among this group of personnel.

More importantly, the terms and conditions of employment between the two portfolios (regular and SRP) are very different. The public's expectation from the SRPs is almost equivalent to that of the "regular" police officer. This notwithstanding, SRPs seldom proffer charges for serious crimes. Indeed, the public, to whom the job of the police is to protect and serve, does not expect the SRP to carry out the roles, functions and responsibilities of policing to a lesser degree than the regular police. So there is a gap between expectations and performance. While the public looks to the SRP as a police officer, the objectives, terms and conditions to which they were employed are only for support to the regular police. Could the superficial nature of the SRPs' recruitment, the sketchy training period and the issue of terms and conditions of employment contribute to the delinquency we observe in the policing space? Consideration should be given to the approach of recruiting, training and the terms and conditions of employment for this most essential field of policing. These elements can impact the sustainability of the crime management system. The case being made here, therefore, is for professionalism in every facet of policing, supported by exacting recruitment standards and competitive terms and conditions.

The objective should be to raise performance standards in every sphere to improve the quality of service delivery and output throughout the police service.

In scrutinizing crime management, the work of the Immigration Division, the Board of Inland Revenue, The Customs and Excise Division, the Trinidad and Tobago Coast Guard, the Municipal Police and intelligence agencies should not be ignored. They, too, should be held to account for deficiencies within the overall crime management infrastructure. In support of the crime management system, municipal police also proffer charges from time to time when crimes occur in markets and cemeteries, among other places within the cities and boroughs. Port police perform their functions within a specific jurisdiction. Similarly, officers within the employ of the Trinidad and Tobago Airport Authority may arrest and lay charges when a crime occurs at the airports.

These postings supplement and support the work of the regular police. It appears that while these groups are often overlooked, they contribute to critical crime management infrastructure in human trafficking, tax crimes, breaches relating to import duties and taxes, among others. Could it be that more focus and attention need to be paid to the Customs and Excise, Immigration, and others and their contribution to crime management because of the important roles that they play? Over 80 per cent of the violent crimes in Trinidad and Tobago are done with guns, and Trinidad and Tobago does not manufacture firearms. This suggests that Customs and Excise and the Coast Guard do have a critical role in the detection of illegal firearms and ammunition entering the jurisdiction at legal and illegal ports of entry. This would mean significant responsibility in the reduction of illegal firearms and ammunition entering the jurisdiction. By extension, the level of violent crime, as well as transnational crime, falls to these institutions.

Because of technology and its fast pace, there are intelligence agencies that support law enforcement in dealing with electronic intelligence. The right persons must be appointed to these intelligence-led positions. In Trinidad and Tobago, it is perceived that individuals who bear allegiance to a person or group may be appointed to influential positions, even if they possess limited knowledge of the requirements for the post and the actions to be taken. The public's concern about not having the right persons in such critical agencies should be quelled, and a resilient faith should be placed in the intelligence infrastructure. Could those appointed to manage such esteemed positions currently claim success in their performance? If the return on investment is at a low level, then the recruitment and appointment system should be reviewed. A recent clean up of the Security Services Agency (SSA) from director down to the suspension of the commissioner of police raises serious concerns about effective scrutiny by the National Security Council, the Police Service Commission and the Parliament itself.

Setting Examples

Social learning theory-deferential association learning theory by Edwin Sutherland (1947)[6] proposes that through interactions with others, individuals learn the values, attitudes, techniques and motives for criminal behaviour. Sutherland also suggests that the more you are exposed to a certain thing, the more likely you are to engage in that activity. If a child is exposed to obscene language, then it is expected that the child will form a habit of using profane language. The level of defiance may not be as pervasive as it appears. However, the policing profession and the significance of its impact on the proper functioning of society cannot be underestimated. It is, therefore, critical that waywardness in the police service, as well as other oversight, enforcement and policing institutions, be contained to a minimum.

There are societal and other benefits which accrue when police actions and procedures are perceived or regarded as unbiased and reasonable. This has to do with both the manner in which the police discharge their duties and the manner of living in their own communities. Realistically, when authorities treat people in ways that harmonize with typical expectations, the population is more likely to view the authorities as authentic. They may more openly cooperate with the authorities and operate in conformity with the law out of an innate sense of obligation rather than out of force or intimidation. Some strengthening of approaches to law enforcement and a more integrated management approach are necessary.

Stephen D. Mastrofski and Cynthia Lum (2008), in their discourse on "Meeting the Challenges of Police Governance in T&T", articulated that in response to a crisis of heightened crime and lowered public confidence, Trinidad and Tobago embarked upon a package of modifications in which the required outcome was the transformation in governance, and ultimately the performance, of its Police Service. One factor of governance that was viewed as an issue for Trinidad and Tobago was its colonial heritage and conflicts between cultural groups in its society. Noteworthy was the insight that the "old system of governance created the appearance of governance, but dysfunctional results". And so, if the old system was unsatisfactory, new methodologies must be embraced to ensure that the required transformation takes place.

One such approach was the Model Station Initiative, which involved both physical and behavioural changes implemented by the TTPS. A key element was the transformation in the behaviour of officers working in the reception room. They adopted a more welcoming attitude toward those seeking assistance. Members of the public were greeted warmly upon entering the station, their concerns were taken seriously, and officers demonstrated genuine concern for the issues raised, taking prompt action to address them. The physical and behavioural changes were rewarded with recipients of the service recognizing the changes and responding appropriately as officers of the TTPS changed their general comportment. Physical changes were also made in each station to make these areas more comfortable and accommodating. Previously imposing desks were lowered to allow the police and the residents to meet eye-to-eye, and water coolers and chairs were added to the space for even greater ease for the public. Such initiatives are acceptable and necessary, but given the surge in crime, increasing fear and seeming lack of control of the authorities, much more than symbolic gestures or improvements are needed.

WHAT WERE THE OBVIOUS POLICING AND POLICY FAILURES?

All the policing and policy failures cannot be articulated in this chapter;

however, some policing methodologies which require reflection include:

Hot Spot Policing – 2015: Trinidad and Tobago was considered a leader in this style of policing. The hot spot policing model is based on the Koper Curve theory.[7] Hot spots were identified, and targeted patrols were conducted in the designated areas, typically lasting between ten to sixteen minutes. In Trinidad and Tobago, the patrols were set for fifteen minutes. Even after the patrols left, a residual impact remained for a certain period. This model was technologically advanced, as the vehicles used for the initiative were equipped with geographic information system (GIS) capabilities. The operating centre closely monitored the duration of the patrols in each area, using geo-fencing to ensure that all designated areas were effectively covered, with signals tracked to maintain oversight over the patrol zones. In late 2013, the TTPS conducted the first randomized experiment ever to test a hot spots patrol strategy (HSPS)[8] across large areas, as distinct from testing extra patrols, one hot spot at a time. The HSPS experiment required and helped to refine a formal theory of both the causes and effects of direct patrols in hot spots.

Twenty-first-century Policing Project Initiative: 2010–11: This was another initiative pursued by the TTPS between 2010 and 2011 by the then deputy commissioner of police, Jack Ewatski. The assessment of this initiative showed that the report's outcomes were poor management and slothful cops, and no legislative provision was in place to facilitate such a model. For instance, while booking stations were proposed, no legal authority was in place to enforce their operation or carry out the intended responsibilities.

Detection and Conviction Rates: Inter-American Development Banks' series on "Crime and Violence in Trinidad and Tobago" (2016)[9] submitted that the trends in detection rates for serious crimes for the period 1990–2013 showed that the murder detection rates were fairly stable, with a high from 1990 to 1999 (a detection rate of 64.8 per cent during this period). However, after 1999, the detection rate consistently declined until data was available in 2013. In 2013, the detection rate for murder was 13 per cent. Similar to murder trends, detection rates for wounding and shootings remained relatively stable between 1990 and 1998 and, after that, began to decline until data was available in 2013. The detection rates for rape, incest and sexual offences remained relatively stable between 1990 and 2005. During this period, the overall detection rate stood at 70.9 per cent. The Inter-American Development Bank's report emphasized in the introduction that "crime is one of the leading social problems in Trinidad and Tobago and one of the most important threats to public safety. Concerns about crime and violence are expressed daily in the news media and rank high among citizens' concerns in public opinion polls".

Notwithstanding the detection rate in the report, there is another element to consider, which is the justice system. A matter is not completed until it is determined at the court, and one matter may take upwards of seven years to complete. During this time, there may be numerous failures to attend court by officers. The non-attendance at the courts by officers is a burgeoning issue, but it may appear easier to be fined a few days' pay as opposed to going before the court to give evidence in a case.

Here, we observe ambitious initiatives undermined by poor performance and declining success due to structural weaknesses, inadequate management, ineffective execution and negative attitudes.

DID WE HAVE WINS?

Is it conceivable that Trinidad and Tobago could have been worse off as it relates to crime and violence than the country is at this time? There were some areas of good success that, if strengthened, may provide ongoing gains for the jurisdiction. In or around 1989, the then commissioner of police, Kenny Mohammed, introduced the community policing model. The preceding commissioners considered or wanted all police officers to be community policing officers,[10] and therefore, the community policing approach was expected to be in all police stations. While community policing has been around for some time, why is there no change in the age groups that are observed perpetuating crime?

The reality of the TTPS structure suggests that the officers who are expected to function in the Community Policing Unit will not remain there for any length of time as promotion to the next higher rank, an opportunity to be absorbed into a commuted/specialist section may appear to be of greater value for an officer.

In *Crime, Violence and Security in the Caribbean*, Derek Chadee, Mary Chade and Simon Alexis, in their study "Fear of Crime", highlight that research conducted over the past decade in Trinidad shows a significant disparity between the fraction of citizens who fear becoming victims of crime and the actual proportion of individuals who fall victim to violent crimes. The authors suggested that although fear of crime is not inherently negative, it is significant that excessive reflection, discourse and concern about the possibility of being a victim of crime generate several social and psychological outcomes. Among these outcomes are anxiety, stress, stereotyping, prejudice and social responses. Social responses include political debates and media hype, which create a collective impact that adversely affects individual and community life.

WHAT IS THE "TEMPERATURE CHECK" ON OUR PRESENT CRIME FIGHTING CAPABILITIES?

Trinidad and Tobago can be assessed as having a "high" crime rate. William Wells, in his writing on "Firearm Possession among arrestees in Trinidad and Tobago", concluded that "a comprehensive approach of prevention, intervention and suppression strategies that are intended to prevent gun-related incidents should be focused on gangs, drugs and guns. Wells's writings aim to describe the sources that active offenders in Trinidad and Tobago use to acquire firearms and to report their motivations for obtaining them. Additionally, his work seeks to estimate the relationships between gang involvement, drug trafficking and firearm ownership or possession. The conclusions suggested comprehensive approaches to prevention, intervention and suppression strategies intended to prevent gun-related incidents should be focused on gangs, drugs and guns. Also, searches for high-risk firearms should focus on public areas where gang members live and socialize. The study further showed the value of collecting data from offender-based populations in the region for the purpose of directing violence-prevention strategies.

In the United Nations Spotlight Initiative[11] on Trinidad and Tobago gender-based violence, the dreadfulness of the report that Trinidad and Tobago experienced a surge in reported domestic abuse incidents, with forty-seven women killed in 2019–20, during the COVID-19 pandemic added to the prevailing disquiet on the island nation.

There is an opportunity to test the level of criminality reported annually to the police and examine the detection of crimes. Table 7.2 illustrates statistics of all reported crimes in the nine police divisions by month for offences in 2021, 2020, 2019, 2018 and 2017. It is estimated that 30 per cent of the annual crimes reported were detected for the five-year period, 2017–21.

Table 7.2: Annual Crimes Reported and Annual Detections

Year	Annual Crimes Reported	Annual Detections
2021	8,549	2,482
2020	8,336	2,416
2019	10,810	2,685
2018	13,334	4,507
2017	13,113	4,091

In 2021, 29 per cent of the annual reported crimes were detected, a figure consistent with 2020, where 29 per cent of crimes in the two categories were also detected. In 2019, the detection rate dropped to 25 per cent for these categories, while 2018 – recording the highest number of reported crimes over the five-year period – showed a 39 per cent detection rate. In 2017, there was a 31 per cent disparity in detection across the two categories.

In 2021, the assessed crime rate in Trinidad and Tobago was calculated at 610.86 per 100,000. In 2020, 595.65 per 100,000; 2019, 772.42 per 100,000; 2018, 952.77; and 2017, 936.98 per 100,000 of the population. How is Trinidad and Tobago viewed in the Caribbean and the Americas region as it relates to violent crimes in particular? An open-source search suggested that Jamaica, Venezuela and Honduras (46.5, 45.6 and 37.6, respectively) stood above Trinidad and Tobago in homicides per 100,000 inhabitants in 2020. It is useful to take a look at figures 7.3–7.12, which shows the annual crimes reported and the annual detections for 2017–21. The data presented may point to possible solutions and alternative approaches.

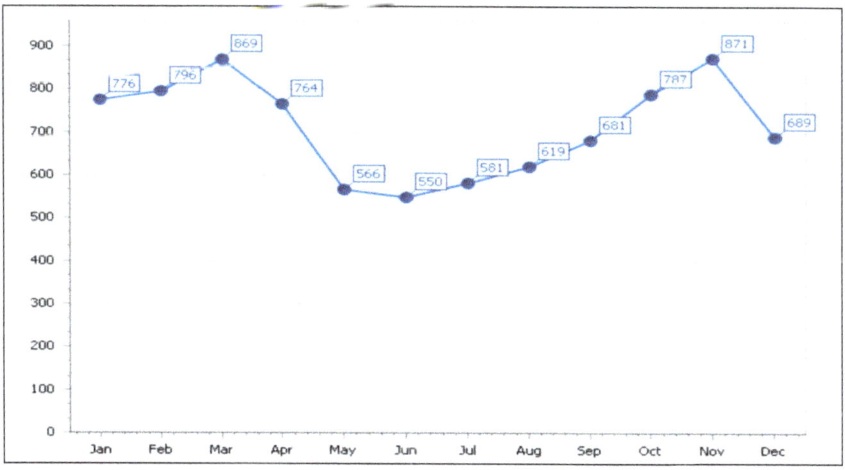

Figure 7.3: Annual Crimes Reported – 2021

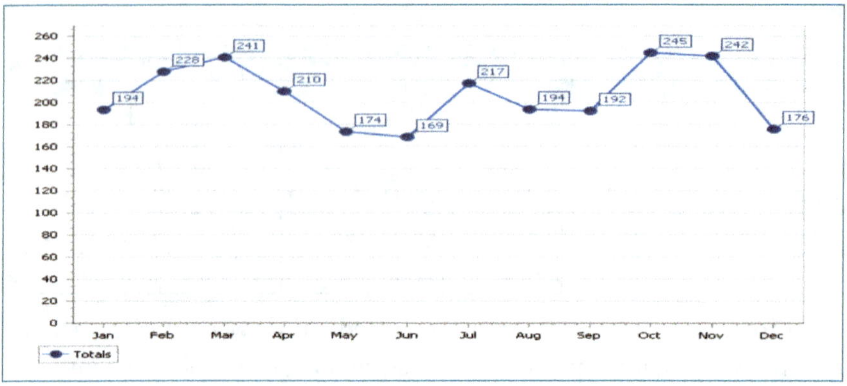

Figure 7.4: Annual Detection – 2021

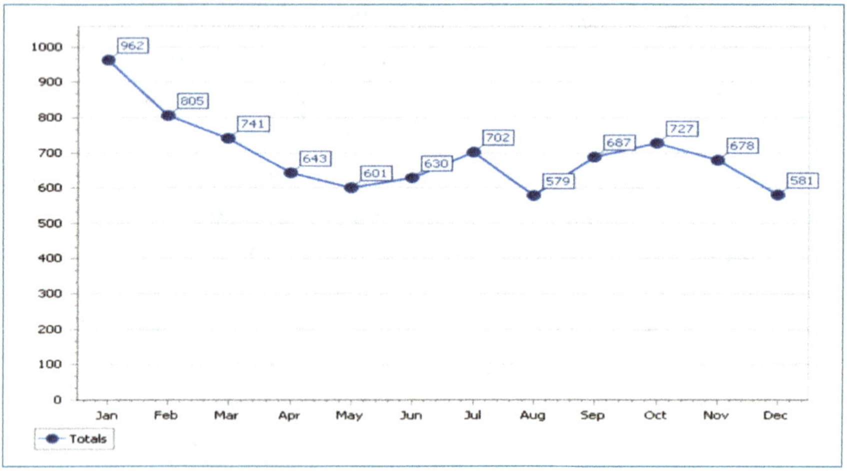

Figure 7.5: Annual Crimes Reported – 2020

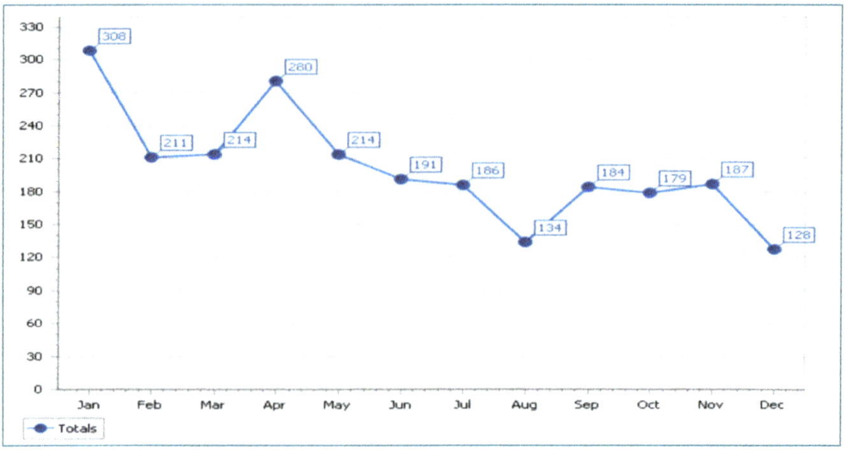

Figure 7.6: Annual Detection – 2020

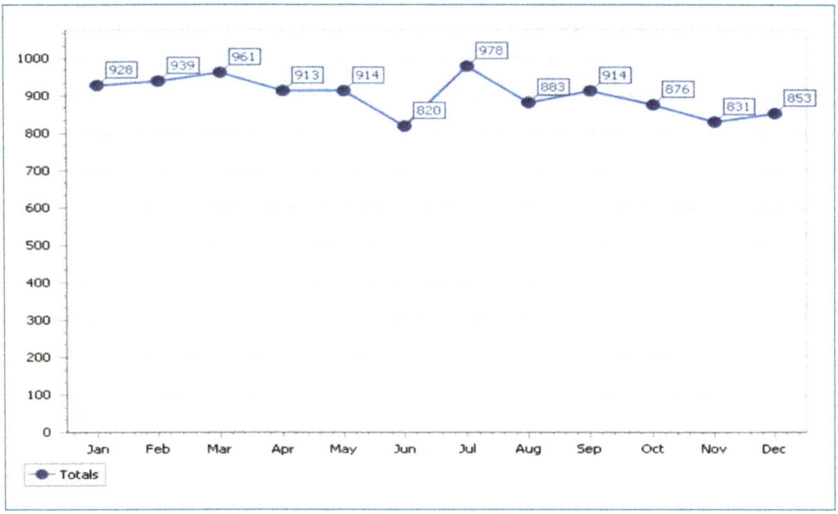

Figure 7.7: Annual Crimes Reported – 2019

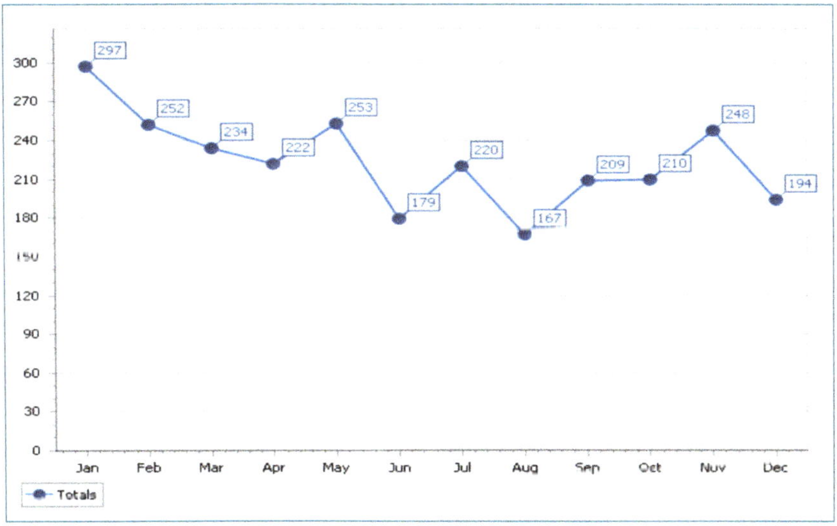

Figure 7.8: Annual Detection – 2019

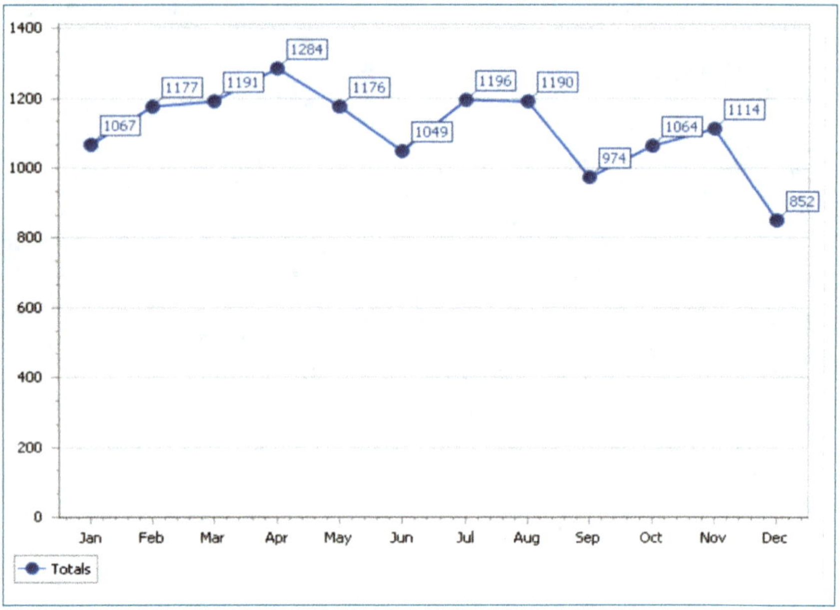

Figure 7.9: Annual Crimes Reported – 2018

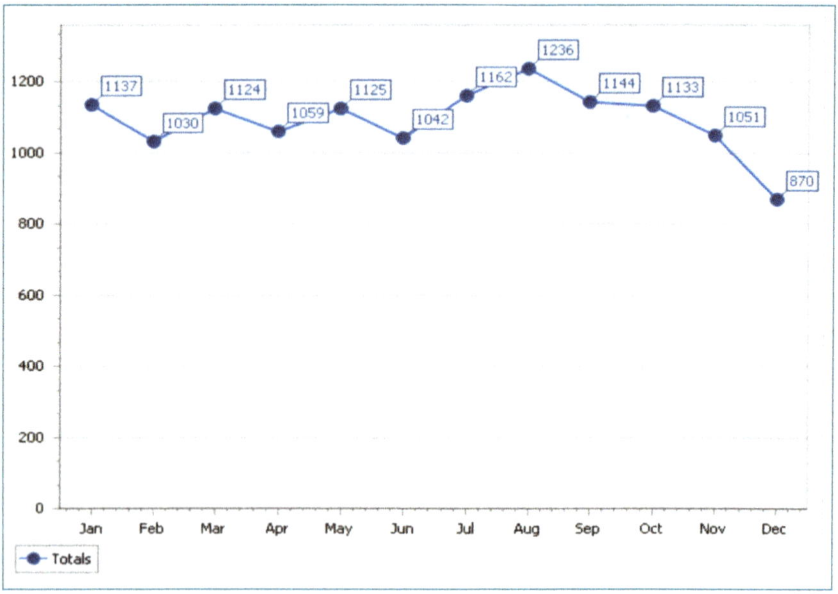

Figure 7.10: Annual Detection – 2018

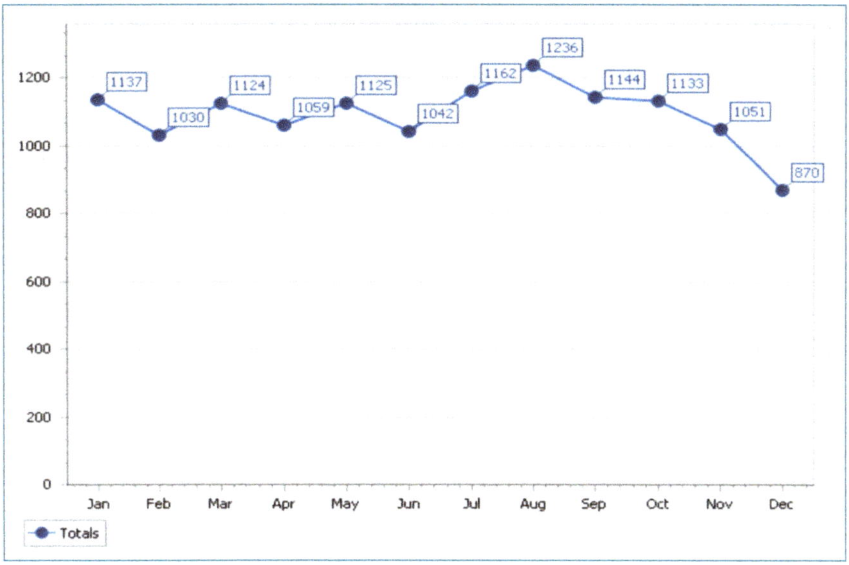

Figure 7.11: Annual Crimes Reported – 2017

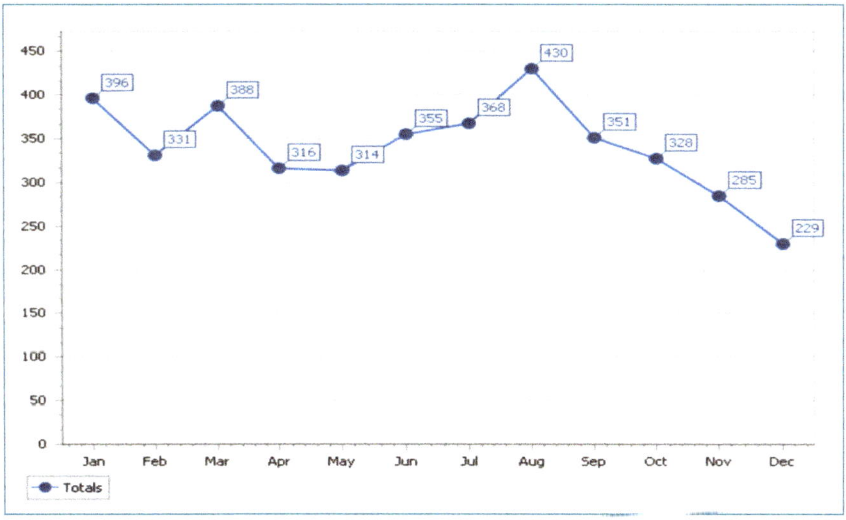

Figure 7.12: Annual Detection – 2017

Escalating crime and a persistently low detection rate are formidable problems. These two facts alone require a rethinking of the TTPS infrastructure, training and organization to achieve results.

HOW HAS THE ENVIRONMENT SHIFTED OVER THE YEARS?

Crime has been a part of human existence since the beginning, but in Trinidad and Tobago, it has reached a point where we find ourselves hoping for its reduction and wishing it were less frequent. If our environment were limited to minor crimes instead of serious offences like murder, it might be easier to manage and cope with. As with everything else, the consciousness of space and time adds context to thought or assumption. There was a six-man police service in the early days compared to the over nine thousand functioning police officers, with possibly more needed. Serious crimes from 1962 to 2022 have been a story of escalation, and in spite of varied initiatives and interventions, the authorities find it difficult to cope. In 2024, Trinidad and Tobago again crossed six hundred murders in a small population of less than 1.5 million.

We may admit that there may be dark figures in crime (crimes that are not reported but occur). For example, sexually driven crimes are sometimes not reported based on the situation. The dark figures suggest more crimes could be happening, though we may not have factored these into any assessment. Also, "false crimes/reports" put forward the idea that there may be incidents/crimes that have not occurred but are, in fact, reported as crimes. An example is a gambler who has gambled away all his salary at month-end but reports a robbery, giving the police a description of an individual who robbed him. Are these false crimes offsetting the dark figures? Such practices skew the statistics of crime reporting. It is difficult to factor these into the data or speculate on how much, but they are raised here as part of the complexity. Our reality is that 2022 was a record-breaking year for murders, repeated in 2024. Based on intelligence on gang violence, a State of Emergency was declared until March 2025.

Whether police officers wish to work alongside domestic or international law enforcement partners, the changing face of crime pushes them to do so. Cyber criminality, forensic technology, money laundering, financing of terrorism and other phenomena may not have been present in 1962, but they are now on the lips of all law enforcement worldwide. The change in crime prompts the thought of whether police officers are required to be in police stations as much as they do and whether an entire rethinking of policing is required for a country of 1.5 million people with identifiable gangs and gangsters with corrupt connections across the society. The discussion further extends to whether officers should be field officers.

The non-appointment of a commissioner of police from 2012 to 2017 may have had its own unique challenges to the morale, operations, composure, vision and dexterity of the TTPS. While there are senior officers in divisions, branches and units of the TTPS, the notion that it was not important enough to appoint a leader may have had unforeseen impacts on the overall functioning of the organization. This is one identifiable issue that may have had a negative impact. There may be a legion of others which help to make law enforcement and the justice system dysfunctional.

GIVEN THIS ASSESSMENT AND THESE GAPS, WHAT IS THE SENSIBLE, STRATEGIC WAY FORWARD?

Predictive policing,[12] which is currently in place, should be assessed to predict the crime environment five to ten years ahead and consign adequate interventions for what may occur. The increased integration of information technology, along with leveraging the insights from past strategic and operational plans, can significantly enhance law enforcement's crime management efforts. The ability to deploy officers more effectively or identify potential offenders and victims could lead to greater efficiency in the allocation of human resources. However, for the successful implementation of any policy, the availability of adequate resources – both human and technological – is essential. Without these, even the best strategies may fall short of their goals.

Airborne Law Enforcement Support

A provoking thought for some citizens might be why there has not been an induction of airborne law enforcement support to crime and crime management in the jurisdiction. Ultimately, the great majority of the population yearns for a safe Trinidad and Tobago, a space with a reasonably low level of exposure to criminality and a high level of confidence in law enforcement authorities, the legal system and all public structures in general. The TTPS has been frequent users of helicopters for law enforcement activity, which dates back to the 1980s. These activities have been primarily relegated to marijuana eradication and anti-kidnapping exercises throughout Trinidad and Tobago. Airborne law enforcement is an integral part of most police organizations around the world and has proven to be a great deterrent and a force multiplier in the fight against crime. A well-operated aircraft can add great value to any organization or region and works best when correctly synchronized with units on the ground and by officers who know the operation.

Aerial assets in support of TTPS law enforcement activities have been provided by various state entities such as National Helicopter Services Limited (NHSL), the Special Anti-crime Unit of Trinidad and Tobago (SAUTT), National Operations Centre (NOC) and most recently, the Strategic Services Agency (SSA). This dependence on other organizations to provide this critical law enforcement tool has, however, crippled the ability of the TTPS to develop its own aerial capability and has greatly reduced its operational effectiveness. This dependency has stifled law enforcement initiatives, operational flexibility and the development of competencies within the TTPS that would enable it to provide its own aerial support.

The Air Support Unit was established in 2003 under the former SAUTT, where it conducted missions related to activities as seen in figure 7.13.

When SAUTT was disbanded in 2005, the Air Support Unit underwent significant changes in name and command structure. The National Operation Centre was established, and the personnel of the Air Support Unit were absorbed into this new organization. This would occur again

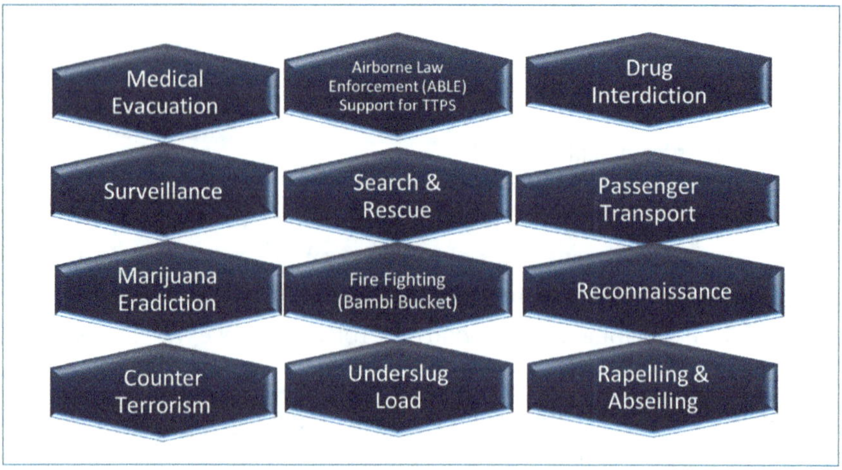

Figure 7.13: Air Support Activities Conducted by Former Sautt

in 2016 and 2020. The Air Support Unit was placed under the Strategic Services Agency and then the Trinidad and Tobago Air Guard (TTAG).

The Air Support Unit is currently manned by a combination of Air Guard personnel, ex-service aviation personnel and civilians. The Pilot and Tactical Flight Officer (Flight Crew) body are professional aviators trained in various aviation disciplines, such as Crew resource management, first aid, helicopter underwater egress training, as well as flight operations.

The government of Trinidad and Tobago currently owns eight military and law enforcement aircraft. Throughout these many iterations of law enforcement airborne support, the TTPS has never been given the opportunity to control an air support unit.

The TTPS frequently utilizes the aircraft from the former SAUTT/NOC and SSA for law enforcement operations on an as-needed basis. However, excessive bureaucracy complicates the planning and coordination of these police exercises, often resulting in the loss of both operational initiative and the element of surprise.

The operational cost of these aircraft is managed by the TTAG, which dictates the availability of the plane and the number of sorties/raids flown per month. This has prevented the use of aircraft for day and night airborne law enforcement patrols, which have proven to be a significant deterrent to criminals in the past. At this time, two of the airborne law enforcement helicopters are unserviceable due to a myriad of issues ranging from certification to maintenance. The Air Guard helicopters are all currently unserviceable and have been handed over to NHSL.

Aircrew Personnel

Over the many years that the TTPS has had access to helicopters, it has never developed the expertise necessary to operate or crew its own aircraft. Like the aircraft used, the TTPS is dependent on another agency to provide trained crews for their operations. This poses many problems, such as:

- chain of evidence
- prosecution
- confidentiality
- institutional incompetence
- loss of professional development for TTPS personnel
- loss of unit pride

The TTPS has sufficient staffing to provide personnel for these roles if given the opportunity. At present, a small cadre of police officers operates with airborne law enforcement helicopters, but this is insufficient and leaves little room for organizational growth and development.

One of the main concerns of law enforcement is that the current aircrew personnel of the TTAG are not in the TTPS chain of command and are not precepted. The commissioner of police, therefore, has no operational control of these personnel and cannot task them to conduct any operation for the TTPS. All operational and administrative control resides with the TTAG. These personnel are, in fact, contracted civilians and cannot perform the duties of a law enforcement officer.

Facilities

Currently, the TTPS does not possess any facilities that can house, maintain and operate helicopters. This is not acceptable if the TTPS is to promote twenty-first-century policing and offer the public of Trinidad and Tobago a relevant, effective and professional airborne law enforcement service. Facilities such as those held by the TTAG at Cumuto Air Base are very suitable for the airborne law enforcement mission and currently serve as the launching pad for police operations. The issues of organizational bureaucracy between the TTPS and the TTAG mentioned earlier are even more predominant in this situation and are a major hindrance to police operations.

The TTPS's ability to plan, conduct and review law enforcement operations within its own facilities will greatly enhance its operational effectiveness. This would allow frequent and sustained operations in the fight against crime throughout Trinidad and Tobago. The former SAUTT hanger facility at Arthur Napoleon Raymond Robinson's International Airport in Tobago is grossly underutilized and should be used to conduct airborne law enforcement operations in the sister island.

Training

The TTPS has traditionally depended on other agencies to provide pilots and tactical flight officers for its airborne law enforcement operations. This has affected the operational effectiveness and efficiency of the TTPS, as well as having a negative impact on the morale of the TTPS. This practice has to be reviewed and eventually stopped. As part of the overall strategy for the development of an effective modern police service, significant human resource investment must be made into serving police personnel to train them for airborne law enforcement missions.

The Airborne Law Enforcement Association of America (ALEA) is one of several organizations that can assist the TTPS in developing its airborne law enforcement capability. Past efforts to liaise with the ALEA by the personnel of SAUTT/NOC Air Division have yielded positive results but have been limited because SAUTT/NOC personnel are not law enforcement officers. Several of the SAUTT/NOC Air Division personnel, primarily pilots and tactical flight officers, have attended courses hosted by ALEA and have significantly benefited from this training. The TTPS has not fully utilized this facility and possesses only a few personnel who have attended these courses.

Maintenance

National Helicopter Services Limited (NHSL) manages maintenance for the law enforcement aircraft owned by the TTAG and used by the TTPS. NHSL is a commercial helicopter operator that provided helicopter services to the Oil and Gas Sector and the TTPS before the establishment of the Air Division of the SAUTT in 2003.

The company, which is 82 per cent owned by the government of Trinidad and Tobago, has long provided logistics and maintenance support for the SAUTT/NOC/SSA aircraft. It applies a 15 per cent markup on all related costs, including salaries and benefits for pilots, aircrew and some support personnel. This arrangement has been scrutinized, with concerns raised about the quality of service and the overall cost.

Tactical Equipment

The Air Division previously operated various tactical equipment, including forward-looking infrared (FLIR) systems, tactical high-definition cameras, real-time video-downlink systems and tactical communications equipment.

Unfortunately, all of this equipment became unserviceable due to a lack of funding for critical maintenance. This critical technical edge has been lost and must be restored as soon as possible if the unit is to significantly impact crime.

Operational Considerations for TTPS' Air Support Unit

The TTPS has been struggling for many years to reduce the level of major crimes, such as murder, rape and kidnapping, and restore public confidence in the service. Bold, positive and proactive measures are required, one of which is the reintroduction of day and night airborne patrols across Trinidad and Tobago. This goal cannot be accomplished if control of the airborne assets remains with another agency that has significantly restricted their use. The following actions are recommended:

1. Formally establish a TTPS Airborne Law Enforcement Unit (see figure 7.14).
2. Establish a separate budgetary allocation for the maintenance of the aircraft.
3. The airborne assets held by the SSA be reallocated to the TTPS.
4. All facilities of the former National Operations Centre Air Division be reassigned to the TTPS.
5. All pilots and tactical flight officers will be assigned to the TTPS and will be made law enforcement officers through the Special Reserve Police.
6. New maintenance contracts are set up between the TTPS and NHSL.
7. Recruit and train additional tactical flight officers from within the TTPS.
8. Reinstitute day and night airborne patrols.
9. NHSL to manage the repair or replacement of all unserviceable tactical equipment on the aircraft.
10. TTPS to manage the repair or replacement of all downlink towers and relay equipment via service contracts.
11. Install a Harris Systems compatible suit of tactical radio equipment on all aircraft.
12. The existing TTPS budget can be used to fund logistical support (non-aircraft support), fuel, and facility maintenance for the unit.
13. Training costs can be added to the existing TTPS training budget.

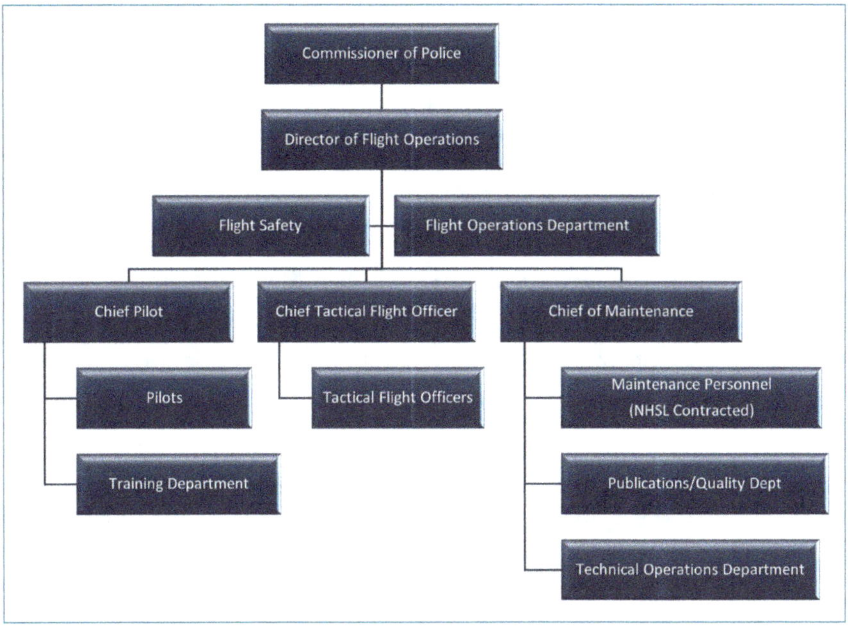

Figure 7.14: Suggested TTPS' Airborne Law Enforcement Unit Structure

The TTPS can manage salaries for pilots, tactical flight officers, and specialists through contracts. It can also recruit and pay all other personnel.

Security, both real and superficial, and exposure to crime are somewhat unevenly distributed across our society. Women's perceived lack of safety is considerably greater than men's. Certain types of crime appear to be falling while others are increasing. Criminality has also become increasingly complex, more varied and more likely to cross borders. People and goods now cross borders in different ways compared to the past, making it easier to import arms and drugs. Distressingly, human beings are trafficked or smuggled more discreetly and by unique methods in and out of the jurisdiction. The novel ways of illegal wildlife trafficking are also agonizing. Organized crime has become more widespread and has changed in nature, and Trinidad and Tobago may now have an international crime presence. Crime targeting different parts of the welfare system is also a major problem. Digital developments, the internet and social media have many positive effects but can also have a negative impact on crime. It is also the case that men's violence against women and honour-related violence and oppression remain serious social problems.

INNOVATIVE METHODS FOR INCLUSION

There can be no meaningful transformation of the current wave of criminality without interaction and inclusion. Some discomfort may be inevitable in achieving the desired outcome. Possible innovative methods of inclusion will encompass some tangibles:

- Review the numerous comprehensive reports and research studies on crime management and related issues in Trinidad and Tobago, with a focus on the recommendations provided. Following this, prioritize the appropriate implementation of these recommendations to address crime effectively.
- Embrace new technologies as they are integral to progress, making it essential to Incorporate technological innovations in both crime-fighting and the administration of justice. This is crucial for staying ahead in modern law enforcement and improving overall efficiency.
- Engage with individuals who have previously been involved in criminal activity and share their experiences within vulnerable communities. By incorporating their insights and emphasizing how past mistakes can help shape and guide those at risk, this approach could foster reintegration and promote social transformation, benefiting both individuals and the wider community.
- Support the reintegration of former inmates into the workforce. The Vision on Mission programme and its team have already initiated efforts to assist individuals re-entering their communities. Strengthening and expanding such a movement is a progressive step towards reducing recidivism and fostering social reintegration.
- Explore and understand the fundamental causes of criminality and underlying issues, with the goal of addressing them effectively.
- Deter potential offenders by ensuring that the consequences of committing a crime outweigh the perceived benefits.

FURTHER RECOMMENDATIONS

The following recommendations are offered with the expectation that, in some capacity, they may be implemented or at least seriously considered. These suggestions are based on a review of sixty years of crime management in Trinidad and Tobago and represent a few key areas for reflection and potential action:

- Focus on equity in our school system. Equity would suggest that each student from Moruga Secondary School or St Joseph Convent is afforded the same opportunities and resources suitable for their needs and unique circumstances. Equity will ensure that the quality of education each student receives will directly impact their quality of life and, more importantly, influence their progressive contributions to a desperate nation. Academic tutelage, together with strong civic induction, will cultivate uprightness, reduce truancy and the attraction of vulnerable minds to criminal gangs. Equity invariably holds one of the many triggers for reducing the dilemma of crime.
- The removal of the Special Reserve Police from the structure of the TTPS is a crucial step toward fostering public confidence, rather than distrust, in law enforcement. One of the primary goals in addressing the current climate of criminality is to stabilize it by ensuring that officers are fully prepared to serve with integrity and competence. Instead of piecemeal induction, consideration should be given to providing men and women with comprehensive, high-quality police training. This approach would ensure that every individual who wears the uniform of the TTPS is fully equipped to perform their duties at the highest standard, thereby strengthening the public's trust in law enforcement.

National coordination in law enforcement will require a police operations centre to manage and monitor all police operations with real-time situational awareness. The E-999 police hotline exists; however, to effectively impact crime, its efficiency in managing daily emergencies, with support by air, foot, mobile or physical interventions, must be bolstered.

Full inclusion of technology as a tool to aid law enforcement. The technology that can support law enforcement officers in their daily functions is almost limitless. The integration of closed-circuit television (CCTV), technologically driven policing tactics, such as global positioning systems (GPS) to track and monitor suspects, cloud computing for the collection, collation and storage of critical data, facial recognition software (inter alia biometrics), and the use of social media and drones can help to identify and apprehend offenders.

The TTPS Air Support Unit needs to be established immediately. As the infrastructure is already present, this action can be accomplished in the short to medium term. The details presented in this chapter articulate the purpose of this recommendation and the methods by which it can be accomplished.

The Judiciary of Trinidad and Tobago must acknowledge its responsibility in crime prevention and management and move from its current lethargic stance to a more assertive one. As a key component of the criminal justice system, alongside law enforcement and other agencies, the Judiciary's role is critical. The interdependency of these entities – law enforcement, the Judiciary and others – is significant, as the decisions made by one directly impact the others within the system. While progress is being made, the Judiciary appears slow in its approach. A more efficient Judiciary would contribute to a more effective crime management infrastructure, ensuring better outcomes across the criminal justice system.

"Genuine harmony" of its people to replace prejudice and suspicion. If there is an overwhelming acknowledgement that the perception of "unity" is but a superficial arrangement among the occupiers in the Twin Islands of Trinidad and Tobago, one that was borne out of the nation's colonial heritage, then the conversation on this issue is overdue. Crime and its management are not only for one sector, as they affect all. Therefore, the voices of the West, East, South and North on prejudices and suspicion are necessary. The conversation on harmony and harnessing our diversity may permit helpful suggestions for reducing the crime situation.

Trinidad and Tobago's temperature on crime is not in the right place, but we are not yet at the point of no return. We are at a point where we must take the bull by its horns.

Can we predict what the future of Trinidad and Tobago may look like if we just took the horn of the bull and determined for ourselves what environment it is desirable to have? Having examined the statistics over the past years, we know what that image is now. However, optimism mixed with grit, patriotism, political will, discipline, a heavy dose of spiritual awakening and tolerance for each other, among other noble actions, can bring us to another space and new perspective. It is essential that we take command of crime, murders and criminality urgently, or else we may find that the government, its institutions and society may be overwhelmed.

Gangs remain central to the crime problem in Trinidad and Tobago. Therefore, we cannot avoid focusing on this element. Even if policing excels in areas such as training, discipline, detection rates, and overall performance, and even if crime-fighting capabilities are aligned with a coherent, integrated strategic approach, two key challenges remain unavoidable: the entrenched presence of over two hundred gangs operating with impunity, and the level of proactive intervention by police to prevent crime. Without effective measures to curtail gang killings and escalating murders, these prevailing conditions on the ground will continue to hinder the success of crime prevention efforts.

There must be a specific strategy for the containment and the reduction of murders. The fight must be taken to the gangs, the communities in which they operate and the value chain which connects them with murders and loot. If we cannot do this, despite all else that we do, we will be "spinning top in the mud". Gangs of criminals must be contained for crime to be reduced. The cost of crime and criminality must be fierce for murderers and criminals to regulate themselves and for citizens to enjoy reasonable conditions of peace and safety.

Moreover, no subsystem that perpetuates crime can exist in a society and thrive and grow without the support of corruption and complicity of elements of police, customs and immigration and the tacit support of elements of the political directorate.

Ultimately, the collective will to implement solutions is crucial in creating a more desirable society. If the power structure itself is a fundamental part of the problem, it becomes exceedingly difficult to sustainably manage the gang crisis and the related issues of guns, drugs and violent crime. Pervasive corruption and complicity within the system undermine efforts to address these challenges; in fact, they actively contribute to the escalation of crime and criminality. Without addressing these systemic issues, any attempt to curb crime will remain ineffective.

This chapter has identified problems in structure, infrastructure, systems operations, strategy, technology and anticipatory preparation and interventions. It has pointed to flaws in the value chain, which can have devastating consequences, and the subversion of solutions that corruption can make possible.

If Trinidad and Tobago is serious about tackling gangs, murders, gun violence, drugs, human trafficking and other forms of criminality, policymakers must adopt a holistic approach to developing integrated solutions. This requires assembling a trustworthy team of law enforcement units capable of working together toward the shared goal of crime reduction, containment and eradication. Strong leadership at the political level is essential, along with legislative support from Parliament and effective governance across all sectors of the justice system. Without this cohesive and collaborative effort, addressing crime and criminality successfully will remain elusive.

NOTES

1. Our History (ttps.gov.tt).
2. Police Complaints Division is a police lead department which conducts non-criminal matter involving police officers. These non-criminal matters are managed based on the directions of the Police Service Regulations.
3. The TTPS Operating Plan – 2022 is a vestige of the TTPS's Strategic Plan 2022–2024. The Operating Plan is a detailed description of what the TTPS will focus on, regarding daily or weekly tasks, for the year 2022.
4. The actual strength can be described as the number of officers who are functioning in the TTPS. The sanctioned strength, however, may not exist and is the number of officers approved for the efficient operations of the TTPS.
5. "Regular" police is a term used to distinguish an officer who would have undergone six and half months (in some cases a longer period) live-in training in the Police Barracks (now called the Police Academy). The term is usually used as a distinction between regular officers and Special Reserve Police officers.
6. Sociological Theories of Crime and Their Explanation on Crime, 2007, Theories of Differential Association Theory | ipl.org.
7. Police Foundation, "Five Things You Need to Know about Hot Spots Policng and the 'Koper Curve' Theory," https://www.policinginstitute.org/wp-content/uploads/2015/07/PF_FiveThings_HotSpotsPolicing_Handout_Rev6.23.15.pdf.
8. Lawrence W. Sherman, Stephen Williams, Barak Ariel, *An Integrated Theory of Hot Spots Patrol Strategy: Implementing Prevention by Scaling Up and Feeding Back.*

9. https://publications.iadb.org/publications/english/document/Crime-and-Violence-in-Trinidad-and-Tobago-IDB-Series-on-Crime-and-Violence-in-the-Caribbean.pdf.
10. https://www.ttps.gov.tt/Branches/Branches-A-E/Community-Policing.
11. The Spotlight Initiative in Trinidad and Tobago held a series of joint virtual dialogues with the government and civil society stakeholders for sixteen days of activism against gender-based violence, in accordance with the global theme: "Orange the World: Fund, Respond, Prevent, Collect".
12. Perry, Walter L. et al, "Predictive Policing: The Role of Crime Forecasting in Law Enforcement Operations." RAND Corporation, 2013, http://www.jstor.org/stable/10.7249/j.ctt4cgdcz. Accessed 23 Apr. 2022.

REFERENCES

"5 Things You Need to Know about Host Spots Policing & the "Koper" Curve Theory." *Policing Institute*. https://www.policinginstitute.org/wp-content/uploads/2015/07/PF_FiveThings_HotSpotsPolicing_Handout_Rev6.23.15.pdf.

Chadee, Derek, Mary Chade, Simon Alexis. "Fear of Crime." In *Crime, Violence and Security in the Caribbean*, edited by M. Raymond Izarali, 135–57, Oxfordshire: Taylor & Francis, 2017.

"Community Policing." *Police Complaints Authority*. https://www.pca.org.tt/statistics.

"Crime Totals by Month." *Trinidad and Tobago Police Service*. https://www.ttps.gov.tt/Stats/Crime-Totals-By-Month.

"FIUTT-Act Chapter 72:01." https://fiu.gov.tt/wp-content/uploads/FIUTT-Act-72-01.pdf. 2012

"History of the Trinidad and Tobago Police Service." https://fiu.gov.tt/wp-content/uploads/FIUTT-Act-72-01.pdf.

"Investigations Completed for the Period October 1, 2022–September 30, 2023." *Police Complaints Authority*. https://www.pca.org.tt/statistics.

Loubon, Michelle. "Inequality, Crime and Education in Trinidad and Tobago: Removing the Masks." *Trinidad Express*, 18 October 18, 2016.

Mastrofski, Stephen D., and Cynthia Lum, "Meeting the Challenges of Police Governance in T&T." *Policing* 2, no. 4 (2008): 481–96.

Perry, Walter L., Brian McInnis, Carter C. Price, Susan C. Smith, and John S. Hollywood. *Predictive Policing: The Role of Crime Forecasting in Law Enforcement Operations*. RAND Corporation, 2013. http://www.jstor.org/stable/10.7249/j.ctt4cgdcz.

"Theories of Differential Association Theory." IPL. https://www.ipl.org/essay/Theories-Of-Differential-Association-Theory-PKLFPD74SCP6.
Wells, William, Charles M. Katz, and Jeonglim Kim. "Firearm Possession among Arrestees in Trinidad and Tobago." 9 July 2010. https://cvpcs.asu.edu/sites/default/files/content/products/Wells%20Katz%20Kim_2010.pdf.

[CHAPTER 8]

Trade and Development in the Trinidad and Tobago Economy

Reflections on the Post-independence Period

ROGER HOSEIN, REGAN DEONANAN, REBECCA GOOKOOL-BOSLAND AND **MARK ROOPCHAN**

INTRODUCTION

The Trinidad and Tobago economy is at a precarious crossroads in its developmental trajectory. The tradable sector is a critical part of the economy, and as a small economy, trade is indeed the umbilical cord for its economic development. This relationship between economic growth and trade has been proposed by classical economists such as Adam Smith and David Ricardo, who have indicated that international trade significantly impacts economic growth. Adam Smith (1776) proposed the notion that broader markets lead to a higher accumulation of capital and technological progress, which in turn improves the division of labour and productivity and fosters economic growth.

However, trade is a broad term that can be segmented into imports and exports. Samuelson and Nordhaus noted that "Free Trade produces a mutually beneficial division of labour among nations: free and open trade allows each nation to expand its production and consumption possibilities, raising the world living standards". Indeed, at one point, Cairn cross-noted that "as often as not, it is trade that gives birth to the wage to develop the knowledge and experience that make development possible". Trade helps to connect nations and provides the material means that drive the economic development processes. Trade is the mechanism through which technical knowledge is partly disseminated. Trade facilitates the transmission of ideas and the importation of know-how. With trade, a country can consume more than it is producing and a different bundle of goods from what it produces. Imports can provide essential machinery to boost a country's output, while international trade creates opportunities to export surplus production.

This chapter is segmented into four sections. The first section investigates the trends in Trinidad and Tobago's trade by utilizing two indexes (the regional orientation index and trade intensity index) to examine the commodities traded by Trinidad and Tobago with various intra-regional and extra-regional partners. The following section provides a deeper look at the export sectors, including opportunities for services trade. The third section provides policy adjustment initiatives that the government of Trinidad and Tobago can implement to improve the trajectory of its economic development. The fourth and final section provides concluding remarks based on the findings from the previous sections.

REFLECTING ON TRENDS IN TRINIDAD AND TOBAGO'S TRADE

Product Composition of Trade

Table 8.1 below shows the trends in Trinidad and Tobago exports. The data clearly show that the strongest export sectors are SITC 3 and 5. Indeed, in the last decade, exports of SITC 3 and 5 exceeded 70 per cent of the total, which indicates a dependence on these sectors.

Table 8.2 provides an overview of Trinidad and Tobago's imports. We note that Trinidad and Tobago imports manufactured goods (SITC 6.7 and 8), but it should be highlighted that food imports (SITC 0, 1 and 2) in the last decade of the data set have increased.

Table 8.1: Trinidad and Tobago's Exports between 1991 and 2021 in US$mn

Year	0	1	2	3	4	5	6	7	8	9	Total
1991	94.32	69.78	22.69	1083.32	3.52	339.75	167.44	17.40	21.94	28.83	1848.99
1992	90.61	111.79	12.70	974.08	2.21	267.73	184.40	24.28	35.95	28.76	1732.52
1993	113.79	105.58	10.94	767.25	3.68	296.22	199.34	27.22	29.88	23.12	1577.04
1994	117.96	109.92	11.61	882.53	4.03	644.22	262.07	35.83	35.96	66.35	2170.48
1995	167.15	95.45	15.73	818.01	5.48	728.95	309.40	33.92	42.20	19.06	2235.34
1996	162.38	116.43	21.32	857.60	5.56	673.54	278.19	61.09	40.47	21.86	2238.43
1997	181.57	191.78	19.49	1031.19	7.89	712.59	350.11	53.79	51.17	25.24	2624.83
1998	176.94	190.46	11.91	862.25	8.42	624.17	343.35	54.12	57.97	16.91	2346.49
1999	205.84	67.20	30.15	1584.62	4.97	627.36	342.61	53.51	68.72	36.59	3021.56
2000	183.60	56.82	10.64	2438.34	2.39	809.49	367.80	57.75	69.10	111.72	4107.65
2001	170.62	74.18	35.53	2254.38	3.73	892.30	413.88	57.44	64.94	135.51	4102.51
2002	171.06	72.79	13.29	2535.44	4.14	900.19	449.91	166.93	61.21	150.46	4525.41
2003	179.70	80.33	30.25	4451.52	5.97	1534.43	447.50	64.10	64.83	201.50	7060.13
2004	178.20	79.48	43.39	5319.35	7.18	1995.54	654.36	78.35	65.45	252.26	8673.56
2005	195.44	112.51	61.78	7915.91	8.21	2769.21	620.81	76.86	85.74	256.95	12103.42
2006	222.01	118.19	68.92	9163.51	1.88	3234.78	649.97	70.11	81.56	336.37	13947.30
2007	216.09	136.17	88.27	9518.56	2.19	3712.61	875.44	72.05	87.57	576.80	15285.76
2008	227.05	149.84	164.21	12636.60	2.98	5122.23	1192.57	86.31	80.09	473.39	20135.27
2009	207.72	152.95	53.68	8544.80	3.35	2737.66	616.51	60.03	71.11	133.58	12581.40

Table 8.1 continues on next page

Table 8.1: Trinidad and Tobago's Exports between 1991 and 2021 in US$mn (*cont'd*)

Year	0	1	2	3	4	5	6	7	8	9	Total
2010	223.66	152.28	129.87	8883.42	2.18	4073.79	1243.84	61.26	69.59	139.23	14979.13
2011	224.02	154.87	130.28	12510.11	2.08	5441.17	1532.61	71.02	79.98	158.09	20304.22
2012	231.88	163.18	106.30	12322.92	3.65	4984.16	1460.74	116.67	76.30	426.00	19891.79
2013	226.04	163.76	92.20	12567.50	3.91	4716.76	1269.66	203.09	78.83	200.38	19522.13
2014	246.59	162.30	77.84	11353.94	4.07	4779.57	1325.16	84.59	80.46	220.27	18334.79
2015	251.79	134.47	60.03	6667.55	3.91	4128.38	888.40	65.72	91.27	365.22	12656.75
2016	263.07	136.91	53.47	4378.01	3.31	2716.15	458.55	158.02	76.97	445.69	8690.15
2017	228.09	116.38	74.11	4899.24	5.05	3376.47	679.09	160.07	64.01	260.32	9862.82
2018	219.52	126.05	91.48	6684.87	5.17	3774.68	751.01	211.66	73.27	459.77	12397.47
2019	237.41	139.13	72.12	5958.77	4.71	3382.91	801.06	409.70	81.51	137.42	11224.73
2020	220.54	94.25	54.71	3475.24	4.35	2520.40	580.37	87.04	36.87	90.93	7164.70
2021	154.04	71.52	29.27	3145.72	1.02	2531.47	888.36	39.21	23.92	230.91	7115.43

Source: Central Bank of Trinidad and Tobago

Table 8.2: Trinidad and Tobago's Imports between 1991 and 2021 in US$mn

Year	0	1	2	3	4	5	6	7	8	9	Total
1991	149.65	8.05	81.18	258.15	4.45	133.53	208.33	313.03	69.41	30.90	1256.69
1992	143.79	9.12	60.69	270.00	3.07	115.30	197.58	363.74	68.13	46.78	1278.21
1993	150.70	5.86	69.88	215.78	3.81	115.97	192.35	337.71	61.24	50.96	1204.27
1994	146.42	5.61	85.89	170.99	6.54	112.63	182.02	379.32	62.20	43.56	1195.18
1995	184.20	8.71	80.94	119.45	7.19	170.89	270.97	527.21	74.68	60.29	1504.54
1996	199.06	18.84	92.65	319.05	8.11	148.47	239.08	541.92	66.61	63.60	1697.39
1997	199.60	27.98	88.31	200.88	12.00	171.04	403.66	948.42	92.33	91.08	2235.29
1998	215.95	27.35	72.04	237.78	22.15	175.98	364.02	844.64	111.24	119.26	2190.39
1999	207.98	17.86	95.84	410.61	13.29	169.16	326.55	731.19	112.09	182.50	2267.08
2000	215.26	17.81	117.98	793.75	7.48	175.78	309.08	983.60	109.22	90.55	2820.50
2001	242.04	20.49	161.03	598.17	7.17	221.21	378.46	897.95	142.66	161.24	2830.41
2002	230.12	21.71	145.31	417.58	6.74	200.91	356.81	854.48	154.73	115.50	2503.89
2003	271.31	28.31	133.18	558.61	12.42	224.25	380.96	1080.79	171.24	226.68	3087.77
2004	326.47	38.17	188.50	455.32	14.46	255.03	567.96	1222.49	196.00	546.36	3810.76
2005	339.22	51.15	238.04	686.75	17.32	316.73	532.39	1421.45	236.55	185.83	4025.41
2006	398.94	57.60	250.31	538.73	15.72	365.43	589.61	1649.61	279.60	155.55	4301.08
2007	503.52	68.42	403.25	703.07	27.00	438.05	727.36	1657.48	329.14	175.06	5032.36
2008	620.17	68.97	561.30	1717.08	39.13	558.56	930.56	2228.83	370.55	377.30	7472.47
2009	568.58	62.48	285.31	1105.14	28.07	406.02	796.35	1441.62	321.55	364.98	5380.10

Table 8.2 continues on next page

Table 8.2: Trinidad and Tobago's Imports between 1991 and 2021 in US$mn (*cont'd*)

Year	0	1	2	3	4	5	6	7	8	9	Total
2010	627.40	62.86	631.65	399.68	35.96	409.76	651.16	1418.78	339.73	225.30	4802.29
2011	718.25	71.43	769.60	1671.06	50.25	642.51	680.32	1448.56	425.65	283.80	6761.42
2012	747.36	79.64	707.36	1301.28	45.46	617.56	696.49	1580.53	467.58	255.62	6498.88
2013	787.00	89.65	659.93	1312.07	39.53	562.29	806.74	1918.91	482.86	264.50	6923.48
2014	796.45	90.28	593.96	706.31	38.98	557.79	817.67	1688.31	485.82	377.76	6153.34
2015	757.68	106.49	361.59	477.04	36.00	529.70	735.00	2210.30	525.53	344.81	6084.13
2016	701.56	99.30	198.17	850.01	35.75	486.58	641.87	1797.88	435.97	261.68	5508.76
2017	709.67	93.55	319.69	1063.73	38.14	608.28	561.66	1526.33	288.41	233.63	5443.09
2018	697.24	76.19	301.73	1187.19	37.98	604.34	581.21	1433.98	232.25	232.53	5384.64
2019	705.25	101.77	412.38	1101.34	29.40	539.43	593.33	1502.73	262.46	283.54	5531.65
2020	675.06	77.31	237.76	646.67	34.38	574.73	571.14	1365.72	235.02	244.09	4661.88
2021	601.01	27.00	193.65	839.91	29.05	438.34	341.77	904.96	149.18	418.89	3943.76

Source: Central Bank of Trinidad and Tobago

Direction of Trade

Table 8.3: Trinidad and Tobago Exports Using SITC Single-digit Data from 1988 to 2021 in US$mn

Year	Total	Canada	CARICOM	United Kingdom	United States	Other Countries	USA as a % of total	CARICOM as a % of total
1988	311	43.3		63.6		–	0%	0%
1989	1,153.7	18.8		61.2		–	0%	0%
1990	1,495.5	21.2		80.2	1,076.3	317.8	72%	0%
1991	1,648.	35.7	96.6	73.2	930.1	512.7	56%	6%
1992	1,618.0	31.6	166.1	62	921.6	436.7	57%	10%
1993	1,559.6	17.9	257.6	64.7	872.8	346.7	56%	17%
1994	2,159.7	12	363.7	74	1,199.1	510.9	56%	17%
1995	2,261.3	13.8	447.5	58.4	1,054.6	687	47%	20%
1996	2,237.1	34.2	501.4	73.5	1,105.6	522.4	49%	22%
1997	2,674.0	19.1	627	103.7	1,227.2	697	46%	23%
1998	2,360.0	23	615.5	65.1	1,071.2	585.2	45%	26%
1999	3,021.6	49.6	848.8	59.1	1,424.7	639.3	47%	28%
2000	4,112.7	48.7	896.7	90	2,228.8	848.5	54%	22%
2001	4,106.2	126	884.2	92.1	2,380.0	623.8	58%	22%
2002	4,531.0	106.3	757.8	101.2	2,667.9	897.8	59%	17%
2003	7,072.9	166.6	1,119.9	157.6	4,722.9	906	67%	16%
2004	8,709.1	120.3	1,094.7	157.1	6,251.8	1,085.2	72%	13%
2005	12,112.5	195.9	1,882.0	150.7	8,354.1	1,529.8	69%	16%
2006	13,957.5	271.1	1,857.7	378.1	8,822.2	2,628.5	63%	13%
2007	15,292.7	386.4	2,062.2	315.3	9,341.8	3,187.0	61%	13%
2008	20,142.3	321.6	2,852.1	426.3	9,471.3	7,071.0	47%	14%
2009	12,611.3	276.9	1,682.2	523.4	5,623.8	4,504.9	45%	13%
2010	14,979.7	446	1,917.2	460.9	7,012.4	5,143.2	47%	13%
2011	20,305.2	393.6	2,662.6	333.8	8,506.0	8,409.3	42%	13%
2012	19,893.7	246.6	2,419.2	116.9	8,158.4	8,952.6	41%	12%
2013	19,535.1	182.4	2,436.3	172.7	6,493.9	10,249.7	33%	12%
2014	18,335.8	504.6	1,893.5	243.7	6,291.7	9,402.2	34%	10%
2015	12,664.1	268	1,515.2	176.1	4,585.3	6,119.6	36%	12%

Table 8.3 continues on next page

Table 8.3: Trinidad and Tobago Exports Using SITC Single-digit Data from 1988 to 2021 in US$mn

Year	Total	Canada	CARICOM	United Kingdom	United States	Other Countries	USA as a % of total	CARICOM as a % of total
2016	8,692.1	143.4	1,435.8	81.7	3,164.4	3,866.8	36%	17%
2017	9,863.4	137.1	1,382.3	156	3,530.6	4,657.4	36%	14%
2018	12,398.0	261.2	1,821.0	208.2	3,874.4	6,233.3	31%	15%
2019	11,225.8	206.7	1,795.4	129.1	3,631.1	5,463.4	32%	16%
2020	7,167.5	227.5	719.2	219.2	2,609.9	3,391.7	36%	10%
2021	7,550.3	282.3	638	140.8	4,430.9	2,058.2	59%	8%

Source: Central Bank of Trinidad and Tobago

Table 8.4: Trinidad and Tobago Imports from Selected Markets Using SITC Single-digit Data from 1988 to 2021 in US$mn

Year	Total	Canada	CARICOM	United Kingdom	United States	Other Countries	USA as a % of total	CARICOM as a % of total
1988	271.7	47.6	0	68.3		–	0%	0%
1989	882.4	49.5	0	71.8	554.7	–	63%	0%
1990	880.4	52.9	0	86.5	424.7	316.1	48%	0%
1991	1,194.30	52.3	32.3	96.9	460.9	551.9	39%	3%
1992	1,248.90	49	50.1	103.7	438.6	607.5	35%	4%
1993	1,215.70	43.4	50.9	106.1	523.1	492.1	43%	4%
1994	1,199.70	50.7	54.1	110.8	531.4	452.6	44%	5%
1995	1,501.60	74.7	59.4	149.7	674.2	543.5	45%	4%
1996	1,696.50	63.5	57.8	123.4	644.8	807	38%	3%
1997	2,238.70	74.1	74	154.5	1,076.00	860.2	48%	3%
1998	2,196.60	87.4	80.1	156.1	955	918.1	43%	4%
1999	2,267.00	109	106	221.5	755.6	1,074.90	33%	5%
2000	2,826.70	54.8	83.7	115.3	1,075.50	1,497.50	38%	3%
2001	2,838.10	105	78.5	132	1,051.20	1,471.40	37%	3%
2002	2,509.30	93.6	70.7	122.1	986.7	1,236.20	39%	3%
2003	3,103.90	92.9	87	170.1	996.8	1,757.20	32%	3%
2004	3,818.80	93.5	104.9	177.3	1,150.90	2,292.20	30%	3%

Table 8.4 continues on next page

Table 8.4: Trinidad and Tobago Imports from Selected Markets Using SITC Single-digit Data from 1988 to 2021 in US$mn (*cont'd*)

Year	Total	Canada	CARICOM	United Kingdom	United States	Other Countries	USA as a % of total	CARICOM as a % of total
2005	4,028.90	116.8	108.7	187.9	1,343.90	2,271.60	33%	3%
2006	4,310.30	157.6	136.7	187.7	1,511.60	2,316.80	35%	3%
2007	5,042.90	196.1	192.5	237.4	1,679.10	2,737.80	33%	4%
2008	7,479.50	248	157.7	216.6	2,146.00	4,711.30	29%	2%
2009	5,441.80	217.6	158.1	166	1,874.80	3,025.30	34%	3%
2010	4,878.00	280.8	140.7	156.1	1,790.90	2,509.50	37%	3%
2011	6,767.70	336.2	168.6	191	2,036.90	4,035.00	30%	2%
2012	6,504.70	330	174.6	180.2	2,296.90	3,522.90	35%	3%
2013	6,924.20	331.8	155.9	201	2,200.70	4,034.80	32%	2%
2014	6,160.70	278.2	199.1	188.6	2,178.70	3,316.20	35%	3%
2015	6,111.80	229.9	114.7	221.9	2,253.90	3,291.40	37%	2%
2016	5,518.90	155	122.8	173.5	2,085.90	2,981.70	38%	2%
2017	5,450.20	224.6	157.8	132.4	1,569.70	3,365.70	29%	3%
2018	5,398.90	261.6	100.1	179.6	1,868.90	2,988.70	35%	2%
2019	5,544.40	201.7	107.1	135.2	2,622.70	2,477.70	47%	2%
2020	4,664.60	153	153.8	186.2	2,147.90	2,023.80	46%	3%
2021	3,774.00	237.8	71.4	142.3	2,498.10	824.4	66%	2%

Source: Central Bank of Trinidad and Tobago

In terms of the direction of imports, the majority of Trinidad and Tobago's imports go to the United States, with CARICOM being a non-trivial market. In 2019, total Trinidad and Tobago exports were US$11,225.8 million, compared to US$1,153.7 million in 1989. The United States is also a major source of imported goods for Trinidad and Tobago. CARICOM, although an important target destination for Trinidad and Tobago's exports, is not a major source from which Trinidad and Tobago obtains imports, as imports from this source average 40 per cent of the total between 1991 and 2019.

Table 8.5: Trinidad and Tobago's Average Propensity to Import

Year	Imports of Goods and Services (BoP, current US$mn)	GDP (current US$mn)	APM	Customs and Other Import Duties / Imports	Customs and Other Import Duties/GDP
1975	855.43	2,442.67	35.02		
1976	1,001.81	2,500.41	40.07		
1977	1,157.00	3,138.67	36.86		
1978	1,412.79	3,562.33	39.66		
1979	1,808.25	4,602.42	39.29		
1980	2,434.42	6,235.83	39.04		
1981	2,478.25	6,992.08	35.44		
1982	3,369.17	8,140.42	41.39		
1983	3,130.71	7,763.75	40.32		
1984	2,554.29	7,757.08	32.93		
1985	2,080.04	7,375.92	28.2		
1986	1,823.03	4,794.44	38.02		
1987	1,551.14	4,797.78	32.33		
1988	1,518.13	4,496.85	33.76		
1989	1,485.01	4,323.06	34.35		
1990	1,426.71	5,068.00	28.15	-	-
1991	1,744.71	5,307.91	32.87	-	-
1992	1,557.48	5,439.55	28.63	-	-
1993	1,419.30	4,669.49	30.4	-	-
1994	1,474.70	4,947.21	29.81	-	-
1995	2,110.36	5,329.21	39.6	-	-
1996	2,189.10	5,759.54	38.01	-	-
1997	3,230.65	5,737.75	56.31	-	-
1998	3,254.22	6,043.69	53.84	-	-
1999	3,005.90	6,808.98	44.15	-	-
2000	3,694.00	8,154.34	45.3	-	-
2001	3,946.40	8,824.87	44.72	3.3	1.48
2002	4,045.50	9,008.27	44.91	3.38	1.52
2003	4,273.90	11,305.46	37.8	3.8	1.44

Table 8.5 continues on next page

Table 8.5: Trinidad and Tobago's Average Propensity to Import (*cont'd*)

Year	Imports of Goods and Services (BoP, current US$mn)	GDP (current US$mn)	APM	Customs and Other Import Duties / Imports	Customs and Other Import Duties/GDP
2004	5,250.10	13,280.28	39.53	3.75	1.48
2005	6,254.40	15,982.28	39.13	3.74	1.46
2006	6,853.60	18,369.36	37.31	4.24	1.58
2007	8,046.40	21,641.62	37.18	3.94	1.46
2008	9,877.10	27,871.59	35.44	3.49	1.24
2009	7,345.90	19,172.17	38.32	3.93	1.51
2010	6,870.50	22,157.95	31.01	4.35	1.35
2011	11,038.78	25,433.01	43.4	3.06	1.33
2012	11,832.33	25,763.22	45.93	3.05	1.4
2013	11,956.31	27,268.48	43.85	3.36	1.47
2014	10,699.45	27,615.84	38.74	4.17	1.62
2015	10,444.38	24,959.86	41.84	4.52	1.89
2016	9,821.73	22,386.26	43.87	4.6	2.02
2017	9,543.81	22,385.43	42.63	4.66	1.99
2018	9,143.64	23,679.92	38.61	4.41	1.7
2019	7,960.43	23,208.33	34.3		
2020	6,614.65	21,588.04	30.64		

Source: Central Bank of Trinidad and Tobago, author calculated

Table 8.5 also presents the economy's average propensity to import (apm), which is calculated simply as the ratio of Trinidad and Tobago's imports to its GDP. In table 8.5 above, the average propensity to import in the Trinidad and Tobago economy is shown for the period 1975–2020, based on available data. In the period of the first economic boom, there was an elevated average propensity to import in Trinidad and Tobago as per capita incomes increased. People used some of their newfound income to import more goods and services from abroad. The average import propensity value for the period 1975–82 was 38.3 per cent. The average propensity to import fell to 32.7 per cent on average per annum for the period 1983–93.

Subsequently, this indicator rose sharply as significant amounts of capital goods were imported for the construction of the four LNG trains, with the apm averaging 48.2 per cent during the period 1997–2002. In the period 2003–10, the apm averaged 36.9 per cent but increased sharply to 42.9 per cent in the period 2011–17. As economic challenges set in and demand fell, there was again a decline in the apm, which averaged 34.5 per cent per annum in the period 2018–20.

REFLECTIONS ON THE NATURE OF TRADE USING TRADE INDICES

Regional Orientation Indices

To obtain a more detailed insight into which component of the Trinidad and Tobago export basket is targeted to the protected intra-regional as compared to the more competitive extra-regional market, we can refer to regional orientation indices.

Regional orientation indices can be calculated using the formula shown below:

ROIj = (Xirj/Xtir)/(Xerj /X ter)

Where:
Xirj: exports of sitc j intra-regionally (ir)
Xtir: total value of Trinidad and Tobago's intra-regional exports[1]
Xerj: exports of sitc j extra-regionally (er)
Xter: total value of Trinidad and Tobago's extra-regional exports.

The theoretical range of this index is from zero to infinity.

Table 8.6: Trinidad and Tobago's ROI-CARICOM

Year	0	1	2	3	4	5	6	7	8	9
1991	2.6	1.7	0.2	0.3	20144.5	0.7	4.1	39.5	8.4	
1992	3.0	0.6	0.5	0.4	2049.1	0.7	3.3	5.0	19.2	0.0
1993	2.1	0.6	0.4	0.8	15.7	0.4	2.2	3.7	9.3	0.0
1994	2.9	1.1	0.3	1.1	140.5	0.3	1.9	1.9	7.7	0.0
1995	1.9	1.7	0.2	1.5	1727.1	0.2	1.2	2.4	5.9	0.0
1996	1.6	1.0	0.1	1.7	823.7	0.2	1.0	0.9	5.6	0.0

Table 8.6 continues on next page

Table 8.6: Trinidad and Tobago's ROI-CARICOM (*cont'd*)

Year	0	1	2	3	4	5	6	7	8	9
1997	2.5	0.8	0.2	1.3	321.5	0.2	1.4	1.3	8.1	0.0
1998	2.5	0.9	0.8	1.3	141.3	0.2	1.3	1.0	6.1	0.0
1999	2.2	3.5	0.3	1.1	322.7	0.3	1.4	1.0	7.4	0.0
2000	3.6	9.4	1.0	0.9	41.7	0.2	1.6	3.2	10.6	1.1
2001	3.9	12.5	0.2	1.0	79.1	0.2	1.4	1.7	8.0	0.3
2002	4.4	13.9	1.7	0.9	197.0	0.3	1.6	0.6	14.0	0.4
2003	4.2	14.9	0.9	1.0	99.7	0.2	1.9	2.9	17.8	0.5
2004	5.4	24.7	1.1	1.0	150.3	0.2	1.7	2.2	20.9	0.6
2005	5.2	15.2	0.4	1.1	134.2	0.1	1.7	2.4	15.8	0.5
2006	5.3	16.9	0.3	1.1	39.2	0.1	2.0	4.3	21.5	0.5
2007	7.0	17.0	0.2	1.2	39.6	0.1	1.4	5.3	19.6	0.3
2008	9.3	15.3	0.1	1.3	23.1	0.1	1.0	4.6	14.7	0.5
2009	10.4	18.5	0.4	1.0	659.6	0.2	1.9	7.3	28.2	0.0
2010	9.8	23.2	0.2	1.2	1083.0	0.1	0.8	9.3	28.7	0.1
2011	10.8	21.6	0.2	1.3	50.9	0.1	0.6	7.0	14.7	0.3
2012	18.0	27.5	0.2	1.2	49.5	0.1	0.7	5.2	34.4	0.2
2013	15.0	23.0	0.2	1.1	61.8	0.1	0.8	15.0	36.1	0.8
2014	12.8	22.3	0.7	1.2	437.8	0.2	0.7	18.1	21.3	0.0
2015	11.2	17.4	1.3	1.3	54.1	0.1	0.9	14.9	10.3	0.0
2016	7.9	7.6	0.6	1.1	26.2	0.2	1.4	27.6	14.7	0.0
2017	12.0	11.7	0.4	1.1	36.4	0.2	1.2	51.8	25.5	0.0
2018	13.9	12.5	1.5	1.0	34.0	0.3	1.3	40.3	30.2	0.0
2019	11.2	12.7	0.5	0.8	27.6	0.2	1.6	46.7	20.8	0.0
2020	13.9	20.8	0.3	0.7	46.5	0.2	1.7	41.8	17.8	0.0
2021	17.9	21.4	0.9	1.4	5.2	0.2	0.7	11.5	41.7	0.0
1991–99	2.4	1.3	0.3	1.0	2854.0	0.4	2.0	6.3	8.6	0.0
2000-2009	5.9	15.8	0.6	1.1	146.3	0.2	1.6	3.5	17.1	0.5
2010–2019	12.2	18.0	0.6	1.1	186.1	0.2	1.0	23.6	23.7	0.1
2020–2021	15.9	21.1	0.6	1.0	25.9	0.2	1.2	26.7	29.8	0.0

Source: author calculated

Table 8.6 above shows Trinidad and Tobago's regional orientation index at the single-digit level between 1991 and 2021. The clear indication is that

Trinidad and Tobago's exports are regionally biased, except for SITC 2 (for which total exports are negligible), and SITC 5, not surprisingly (mainly petrochemicals), are extra-regionally biased. Even more, not only are Trinidad and Tobago's exports regionally biased, but the extent of the regional orientation of Trinidad and Tobago's trade with CARICOM is expanding. This is not necessarily unhealthy if the firms are eventually breaking into extra-regional markets. However, as table 8.7 below shows, Trinidad and Tobago has been experiencing a decrease in the number of sectors, with RCA scores above 1. As such, some of the firms that export to CARICOM may be surviving because of X-inefficiency.[2]

Table 8.7: RCA for Trinidad and Tobago Using Single-digit SITC Data between 1991 and 2021

Year	0	1	2	3	4	5	6	7	8	9
1991	0.66	3.48	0.25	5.82	0.49	1.98	0.56	0.03	0.09	0.83
1992	0.67	5.86	0.16	6.07	0.33	1.65	0.67	0.04	0.14	0.81
1993	0.98	6.25	0.16	5.42	0.60	2.04	0.81	0.05	0.13	0.58
1994	0.74	4.90	0.12	5.17	0.42	3.12	0.76	0.05	0.12	1.31
1995	1.05	4.44	0.15	4.94	0.49	3.24	0.85	0.04	0.14	0.35
1996	1.01	5.21	0.23	4.45	0.55	3.09	0.81	0.07	0.13	0.38
1997	1.03	7.29	0.18	4.59	0.66	2.78	0.88	0.05	0.14	0.37
1998	1.13	7.99	0.14	5.69	0.71	2.65	0.96	0.06	0.18	0.30
1999	1.08	2.24	0.29	7.25	0.39	2.08	0.78	0.04	0.16	0.45
2000	0.83	1.61	0.08	5.76	0.19	2.08	0.66	0.04	0.13	0.69
2001	0.72	1.93	0.26	5.50	0.29	2.13	0.74	0.04	0.12	0.96
2002	0.64	1.66	0.09	5.88	0.24	1.83	0.72	0.10	0.10	1.08
2003	0.44	1.21	0.13	6.09	0.20	1.96	0.47	0.02	0.07	0.78
2004	0.38	1.05	0.14	5.39	0.20	2.08	0.54	0.02	0.06	0.94
2005	0.31	1.12	0.15	4.73	0.18	2.07	0.38	0.02	0.06	0.66
2006	0.32	1.10	0.14	4.43	0.04	2.15	0.34	0.01	0.05	0.65
2007	0.27	1.13	0.15	4.40	0.03	2.20	0.40	0.01	0.05	1.14
2008	0.21	1.00	0.20	3.56	0.03	2.32	0.44	0.01	0.04	0.76
2009	0.26	1.34	0.11	4.63	0.05	1.78	0.39	0.01	0.05	0.32
2010	0.26	1.28	0.19	3.77	0.03	2.37	0.65	0.01	0.04	0.34
2011	0.19	0.98	0.13	3.41	0.02	2.35	0.59	0.01	0.04	0.30

Table 8.7 continues on next page

Table 8.7: RCA for Trinidad and Tobago Using Single-digit SITC Data between 1991 and 2021

Year	0	1	2	3	4	5	6	7	8	9
2012	0.20	1.05	0.12	3.30	0.03	2.24	0.61	0.02	0.04	0.79
2013	0.19	1.05	0.11	3.61	0.04	2.15	0.54	0.03	0.04	0.33
2014	0.22	1.12	0.10	3.76	0.04	2.30	0.58	0.01	0.04	0.40
2015	0.30	1.24	0.12	4.53	0.06	2.75	0.56	0.01	0.06	1.04
2016	0.45	1.75	0.16	5.14	0.07	2.59	0.43	0.05	0.07	1.90
2017	0.34	1.39	0.18	4.36	0.09	2.51	0.58	0.04	0.07	1.24
2018	0.29	1.23	0.18	4.01	0.08	2.24	0.51	0.04	0.06	1.67
2019	0.33	1.45	0.16	4.21	0.08	2.19	0.63	0.09	0.08	0.55
2020	0.44	1.50	0.18	5.27	0.10	2.36	0.72	0.03	0.05	0.57
2021	0.33	1.12	0.12	4.20	0.02	2.40	1.03	0.01	0.03	0.99

Source: Author Calculated

Trade Intensity Index

Corroboration of the evidence from regional orientation indices can be provided through reference to trade intensity indices. Trade intensity indices, Iij, can be defined as:

$Iij = (Xij/Xi) / (Mj/Mw)$

Where
Xij: is exports of country i to country j,
Xi: total exports of country i,
Mj: imports of country j,
Mw: imports of the world.

The table 8.8 below shows that Trinidad and Tobago has a higher degree of trade intensity with CARICOM members.

Table 8.8: Trade Bias between Trinidad and Tobago and Members of CARICOM

Year	ATG	BHS	BAR	BLZ	DMA	GRD	GUY	HTI	JAM	MSR	KNA	LCA	VCT	SUR
1991			191.42			288.34	107.95		29.12			163.28		142.70
1992			220.76	26.08			111.45		23.35			207.70		53.03
1993			260.80	16.33	83.71	346.87			59.79		178.07	199.02	167.90	0.00
1994			218.25	26.45	86.52	359.28			72.96		183.98	123.60	173.11	16.50
1995		0.95	257.76	27.52	80.94	387.06			109.98		251.74	107.60	306.12	28.31
1996			250.55	21.17	195.82	482.62			147.71		339.51	297.02		120.72
1997		0.92	208.52	25.59	174.71	422.53	278.03		123.75		291.98	219.06	139.60	157.93
1998		1.61	298.98	35.72		502.13	296.50		138.77			275.48	183.33	149.35
1999	87.09	1.82	203.09	790.08	190.60	367.93	263.49		125.35	85.97	215.53	238.10	130.26	152.38
2000	84.25	2.34	96.46	21.09	204.82	338.04	249.99		93.96	99.94	254.24	96.88	140.24	155.96
2001		5.04	148.87	30.75	132.99	344.86	267.83		106.42	104.83	224.89	37.14	155.12	183.29
2002		1.86	132.00	18.72	191.27	337.82	293.84		80.66		182.42	36.02	169.41	243.91
2003		1.57	174.47	13.11	141.74	235.61	172.51		68.28		131.32	141.83	115.28	191.38
2004		0.57	64.53	12.94	161.67	282.33	301.57		91.92	114.54	222.93	123.50	204.28	222.43
2005	73.86	0.39	128.74	4.86	142.63	193.40	161.80		71.96	500.63	127.50	29.53	75.37	117.80
2006	59.71	0.56	118.64	6.84	135.39	135.46	157.05		49.93		63.10	39.37	122.20	102.32
2007	18.78	1.31	52.48	9.84	173.84	298.60	202.43		122.47	1109.96	92.19	18.95	130.36	135.96
2008		2.80	78.65	5.17	137.78	219.75	158.03		97.60	547.90	127.76	8.34	96.98	100.86

Table 8.8 continues on next page

Table 8.8: Trade Bias between Trinidad and Tobago and Members of CARICOM (*cont'd*)

Year	ATG	BHS	BAR	BLZ	DMA	GRD	GUY	HTI	JAM	MSR	KNA	LCA	VCT	SUR
2009	15.54	3.23	80.15	2.16	188.74	452.31	275.97		120.12	16.51	153.90	9.38	208.04	187.89
2010	9.63	3.21	19.38	5.76	170.80	428.47	157.31		131.59	0.00	102.00	10.48	214.23	173.03
2011	2.37	6.76	26.08	0.56	0.00	436.68	159.84		115.15	584.08	5.66	11.80	259.49	227.04
2012	5.32	5.20	79.97	7.45	150.02	499.78	189.35		100.49	245.22	101.16	24.97	263.71	165.12
2013	8.30	4.73	116.12	7.83		335.62	138.12		102.76	263.81	64.67	57.93	169.08	177.88
2014	12.67	3.26	146.47	20.23		219.47	196.46		87.55	201.50	34.50	17.20	186.61	147.81
2015	6.89	0.92	188.94	17.92		462.92	376.23		119.70		135.94	23.95	242.90	114.23
2016	23.34	1.17	504.25	26.41		970.67	1050.85		130.54		187.45	38.16	445.98	347.99
2017	22.48	0.27	494.83	19.19		861.91	1118.66		76.19		95.42	23.48	474.03	101.92
2018	17.55	0.30	384.98	14.60		914.00	1345.18		66.48			18.95	434.34	83.41
2019	20.25		360.68	16.40		833.43	1525.50		36.36			19.80	458.53	211.28
2020			240.63	20.45		1011.67	544.91		52.44					
2021			114.96	20.62		586.48	402.62							

Source: author calculated

Table 8.9: Trade Intensity between Trinidad and Tobago and Selected Countries

Year	Barbados	CARICOM	Guyana	Jamaica	United Kingdom	United States	Canada	Costa Rica	Panama
1991		2,873.16	19,483.71	3,635.08		277.54	0.54		
1992		4,558.84	16,892.18	3,474.65		314.41	0.57		
1993		8,002.55		7,542.83	66.05	299.92	0.30		
1994		11,746.16			61.73	339.73	0.17	6.50	
1995		11,448.96			53.59	328.4	0.22	6.77	1.54
1996		14,837.77		19,703.56	61.56	320.05	0.50	0.98	1.17
1997	18,822.63	10,919.20	28,168.88	16,304.90	70.32	282.63	0.21	6.62	2.45
1998	29,684.30	12,565.08	33,009.35	17,869.98	48.42	263.2	0.29	5.12	1.21
1999	21,580.00	14,144.97	24,964.08	18,465.59	34.85	250.07	0.46	5.04	4.67
2000	25,930.57	11,162.07	22,856.06	15,781.10	37.87	288.48	0.34	10.76	0.48
2001	24,729.99	10,380.06	22,952.52	15,948.47	38.93	316.25	0.92	2.56	0.19
2002	16,793.52	8,619.30	22,638.25	11,889.51	39.18	320.28	0.73	2.81	3.90
2003	21,360.74	8,851.11	28,821.33	11,829.88	40	391.36	0.80	2.32	1.28
2004	8,155.03	7,772.69	28,465.32	13,099.06	33.37	437.74	0.50	2.74	1.14
2005	18,297.00	8,530.42	28,800.22	12,997.91	24.66	416.34	0.59	0.81	1.59
2006	19,545.27	7,699.21	29,205.41	10,013.25	53.47	399.71	0.74	4.67	1.08
2007	7,042.66	7,848.89	22,878.75	14,309.24	42.26	422.07	1.01	5.77	1.10
2008	15,818.55	7,991.09	17,629.02	13,939.90	48.27	349.41	0.70	3.29	0.64
2009	15,553.03	7,591.87	19,778.37	10,615.60	93.12	344.79	0.93	5.98	0.18
2010	7,220.73	8,907.58	22,108.86	13,879.79	73.87	358.36	1.27	13.77	0.13
2011	23,305.71	8,462.04	18,663.29	11,347.84	40.87	330.15	0.89	5.82	0.24
2012	26,098.48	7,189.98	13,059.05	9,593.24	15.32	323.94	0.54	4.27	0.01
2013	24,681.33	7,353.51	18,175.86	11,573.68	24.73	269.69	0.42	7.34	0.01
2014	20,684.97	6,460.07	21,237.19	10,291.85	35.37	262.99	1.21	4.59	0.03
2015	20,222.30	7,616.38	29,778.06	12,171.65	35.78	253.9	0.89	4.20	0.04
2016	24,364.91	17,045.08	52,775.82	13,194.00	23.3	255.49	0.71	2.07	0.07
2017	29,969.39	14,427.62	49,113.87	9,179.42	43.49	262.23	0.63	1.28	0.59
2018	27,810.42	15,504.55	53,447.02	8,859.89	48.26	231.04	0.97	1.00	
2019	24,888.24	17,802.81	40,457.74	4,493.85	30.88	234.19	0.83	1.04	
2020	33,129.74	17,429.36	27,175.18	7,014.82	82.72	259.65	1.47	2.41	
2021	19,822.21	13,795.10	12,718.91		32.48	239.77	1.25		

Source: Author Calculated

Table 8.9 above presents the results of the trade intensity index between 1991 and 2021 for various countries that are either intra-regional trade partners (Jamaica, Guyana and Barbados) or extra-regional trade partners (United States, United Kingdom, Canada, Costa Rica and Panama). Mirror data was utilized due to data limitations for recent trade information on Trinidad and Tobago, as the most recent available data from WITS was for 2015.

The Trade Intensity index shows an intense relationship between Trinidad and Tobago and all of the listed trade partners except Panama.

Between 1999 and 2014, the Trinidad and Tobago government collected US$36.74 billion in energy revenues. These revenues were spent in various ways (but especially in T&S). The next section discusses the associated change in the structure of production.

CHANGES IN THE TRADED SECTOR OF THE ECONOMY

Figure 8.1 below provides a closer look at the GDP data since 2012 in the new ISIC rev 4 format.[3] Using this data, one can identify the tradable sector (T) of the Trinidad and Tobago economy as the sum of mining and quarrying, and manufacturing, which accounted for 27 per cent of total GDP in 2020. The non-tradable (NT) sector can simply be defined as a residual. In this regard, and using the available data, the T sector contracted by 46.1 per cent between 2012 and 2020; the NT sector expanded by 10 per cent. Alternatively, we now have an economy whose structure is relatively more inclined towards the production of NT sector goods. This is precisely what is expected in the bust phase of economies characterized by boom-bust cycles.

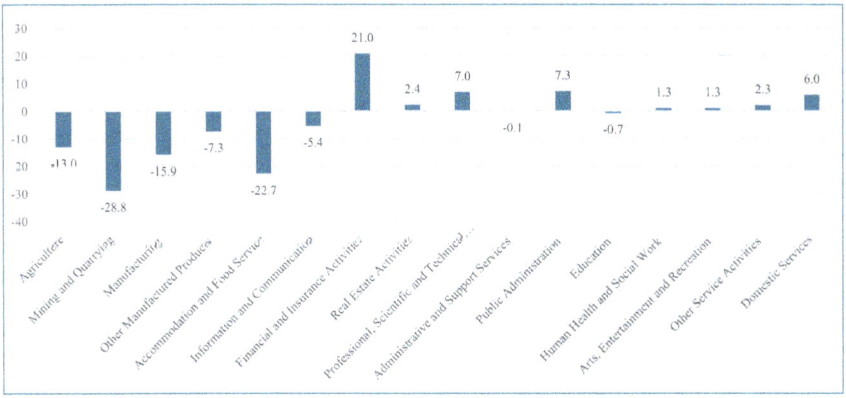

Figure 8.1: Percentage Change in Real GDP by Sector, 2012–20

Table 8.10: Structure of the Economy between 2012 and 2020 Trinidad and Tobago $mn

Year	Mining and Quarrying (Trinidad and Tobago $ Mn)	Manufacturing (Trinidad and Tobago $ Mn)	Other Manufactured Products (Trinidad and Tobago $ Mn)	Total (Trinidad and Tobago $ Mn)	Tradable sector (Trinidad and Tobago $ Mn)	Total Trade (Trinidad and Tobago $ Mn)	Mining and Quarrying (% of total trade)	Manufacturing (% of total trade)	Other Manufactured Products (% of total trade)	Tradable sector (% of total trade)
2012	35927.2	31767.2	2255.8	165766.2	69950.2	167778.2	21%	19%	1%	42%
2013	40530.2	26798.5	2817.2	175848	70145.9	177861	23%	15%	2%	39%
2014	38029.2	28410.9	2584.9	177163.6	69025	179177.6	21%	16%	1%	39%
2015	22145.6	25166.7	2153.5	160657.7	49465.8	162672.7	14%	15%	1%	30%
2016	14955.9	28817.9	2340	149208.6	46113.8	151224.6	10%	19%	2%	30%
2017	19133	27905.7	2883.1	157150.1	49921.8	159167.1	12%	18%	2%	31%
2018	22047.4	30824.9	2801.6	161284.3	55673.9	163302.3	14%	19%	2%	34%
2019	20657.4	29135.1	2823.5	161335.3	52616	163354.3	13%	18%	2%	32%
2020	12718.9	23823.2	2561.6	144422.1	39103.7	146442.1	9%	16%	2%	27%

Source: Central Bank of Trinidad and Tobago

Table 8.11: Decomposition Trinidad and Tobago's Economy

Year	Tradable Sector (Trinidad and Tobago$ Mn)	Non-tradable Sector (Trinidad and Tobago$ Mn)	Energy Balance (Trinidad and Tobago$ Mn)	Non-energy Balance (Trinidad and Tobago$ Mn)	GDP (Trinidad and Tobago$ Mn)
2012	69950.2	95816	58294.2	11656	165766.2
2013	70145.9	105702.1	59251.6	11430.3	175848
2014	69025	108138.6	58228.6	11401.9	177163.6
2015	49465.8	111191.9	56250.1	12978.8	160657.7
2016	46113.8	103094.8	51748.8	11980.5	149208.6
2017	49921.8	107228.3	51805.4	11181.8	157150.1
2018	55673.9	105610.4	49759.2	11786	161284.3
2019	52616	108719.3	47416.4	12914.3	161335.3
2020	39103.7	105318.4	41621.5	12260.8	144422.1
% Change	-44.1%	9.9%	-28.6%	5.2%	-12.9%

Source: Central Bank of Trinidad and Tobago

In translating the variables observed in table 8.11 above, consider figure 8.2 below, which shows the production possibility frontier (PPF) representation for the Trinidad and Tobago economy. In 2015, Trinidad

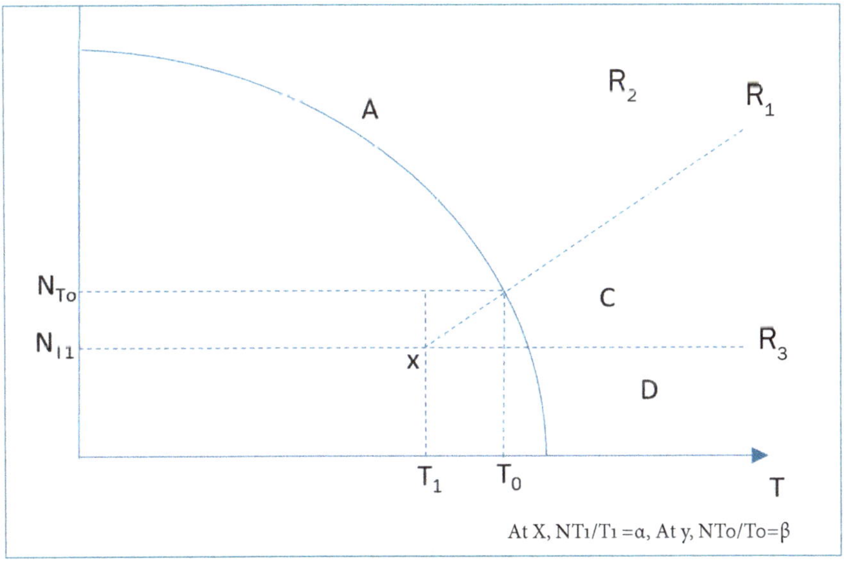

Figure 8.2: Trajectories for Growth

and Tobago produced To units of tradable goods, consisting of EBo units of energy goods and NEBo units of non-energy-based export goods. In 2020, the Trinidad and Tobago economy finds itself in a testing position with a relatively larger proportion of total GDP accounted for by the NT sector.

Building on the logic of figure 8.2, there are three generalized recovery pathways available to the government of Trinidad and Tobago as the economy opens up. For simplicity, we call these R1, R2, R3 (as illustrated in figure 8.2). The recovery pathways are such that one takes us to the left of the point Y, one that takes us to the right of the point Y (R3) and, of course, one that passes through point Y (R1).

Recovery Pathway 1 (R1)

It does not make sense to go back to point Y because at that point, the economy experienced economic contraction (see table 8.12 below). Official reserves were on the decline, the non-energy-based fiscal balance was deepening, transfers and subsidies were elevated, employment in agriculture and manufacturing was declining, and the economy was not thriving. Table 8.12 below provides a basic sketch of some key macroeconomic data and their trends up to the present.

Recovery Pathway 2 (R2)

R2 involves a worse situation than recovery pathway 1 because it involves an increased production of NT goods. This pathway is also not recommended as the economy's stock of reserves is being rapidly depleted, and its capacity to sustain a higher level of non-tradable sector activity is declining.

Recovery Pathway 3 (R3)

The third route here is recommended for the Trinidad and Tobago economy, that is, R3 which consists of zones C and D, however, with zone C being much more practical. With R3, the output level moves to a higher level of tradables and a lower level of non-tradables as compared to the point Y. Any policy intervention must be linked directly to specific objectives. Table 8.13 below compares R1, R2 and R3 using various criteria outlined in column 1.

Table 8.12: The Basic Attributes of the Pre-COVID Economy

Year	Real GDP (2012=100) Growth (%)	Net Official Reserves (US$Mn)	Import Cover (months)	Non-energy Fiscal Balance (Trinidad and Tobago $Mn)	Transfers and Subsidies (Trinidad and Tobago $Mn)	Employment in Agriculture (000)	Employment in Manufacturing (000)
2014	-0.9	11497.1	12.9	-35842.8	35327.7	22.9	50.4
2015	1.8	9933	11.2	-12465.4	30845.1	21.3	51.2
2016	-6.3	9465.8	10.5	-12632.8	26657.9	19.8	48.3
2017	-2.7	8369.8	10.5	-20127.7	25783.1	22.3	48.9
2018	-0.7	7575	9.9	-14800.6	25851.6	24.1	48.4
2019p	-0.2	6929	10.4	-21650.2	26414.2	20.3	44.8
2020	-7.4	6953.8	10.9	-28490	26942.9		
2021	-1.0	6879.6	10	-26845	27246		
2022p	5.5	5925	8.8	-27883	28107		

Source: Central Bank of Trinidad and Tobago, IMF 2022

Table 8.13: Vision of the Trinidad and Tobago Economy after 2022

	R1	R2	R3
Production of NT	Increases	Same as 2016–21	The production of I non-tradables, falls while the proportion of tradable goods, rise
Production of NBT	Falls	Same as 2016–21	Increases
Production of T	Falls	Same as 2016–21	Increases in production of exportable goods and increase production of competitive import substitutes
Production of BT	Remains the same as in 2021	Same as 2016–21	Increases
Consumption of non-essential non-tradable goods	Rises	Same	Falls
Macroeconomic impact			
Stock of foreign exchange	Worsens	Same as 2016–21	Producing less NT and more NBT and more BT
Debt to GDP ratio	Likely to worsen as NT production has a high import content	Same as 2016–21	Producing less NT and more NBT and more BT
Real GDP	Increases from X	Same as 2016–21	Grows thereafter because the greater amount of NBT will enhance productivity and technological spillovers
CAB	Worsens as we earn less foreign exchange	Same as 2016–21	Will improve as the economy's imports fall and exports rise. Note the decrease in NT includes an increase in domestic food production
Inflation	Can rise because of the rise in wage rates associated with the Baumol cost disease and the production of more NT	Same as 2016–21	The supply capacity of the economy likely to improve so inflation will be tempered

Table 8.13 continues on next page

Table 8.13: Vision of the Trinidad and Tobago Economy after 2022 (*cont'd*)

	R1	R2	R3
Economic resilience	Worsens as our stock of foreign exchange falls and import dependence in the economy	Same as 2016–21	A strong vibrant economy trading a wider range of exports and importing and exporting with a wider range of countries and using less foreign exchange for the production of non-tradables
Unemployment	Can fall if output increases but NT sector employment can rise at the expense of other sectors.	Same as 2016–21	Will eventually fall

Source: Author Compiled

SERVICES AS AN OPPORTUNITY TO INCREASE EXPORTS

Table 8.14 below indicates that while the services sector's share of total GDP increased from 2012 to 2023, the sector's size declined. During this period, the labour force in the services sector decreased from 551,000 in 2012 to 513,900 in 2023.

Table 8.14: Selected Service Sector Indicators

Year	Services GDP Trinidad and Tobago $mn	Nominal GDP Trinidad and Tobago $mn	% Share	Services Employment	Total Labour Force	% Share
2012	99216.57	169217.9	58.6	551000	620500	88.8
2013	107213.9	178297	60.1	558000	626300	89.1
2014	114073.8	184456.1	61.8	568200	636800	89.2
2015	115851.1	164481.3	70.4	551700	620900	88.9
2016	110098.3	151720	72.6	547900	**613,200**	89.4
2017	110238.9	157244.5	70.1	540900	**603,500**	89.6
2018	107092.8	159776.3	67.0	549000	**610,300**	90.0
2019	108523.4	154641	70.2	535900	**591,100**	90.7
2020	100498.5	133329	75.4	521700	**569,800**	91.6

Table 8.14 continues on next page

Table 8.14: Selected Service Sector Indicators (*cont'd*)

Year	Services GDP Trinidad and Tobago $mn	Nominal GDP Trinidad and Tobago $mn	% Share	Services Employment	Total Labour Force	% Share
2021	101210.1	157083.5	64.4	509000	**560,500**	90.8
2022	110044.7	198648.2	55.4	517400	**565,300**	91.5
2023P	115898.1	186923.1	62.0	513900	**566,000**	90.8

Source: ROTE (various years).

The Trinidad and Tobago CSI has identified several areas of the services sector in which it tries to capture data. These are:

1. Business and professional service
2. Energy services
3. ICT services
4. Educational services
5. Fashion services
6. Tourism services
7. Creative services
8. Aviation services
9. Health and wellness services
10. Commercial maritime and yachting services.

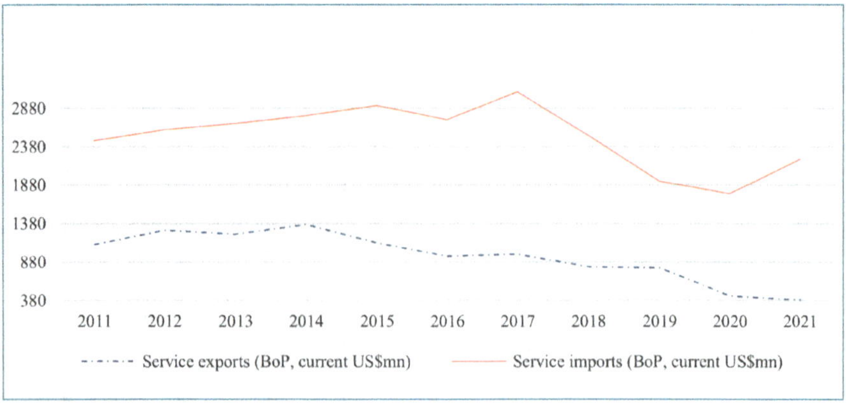

Figure 8.3: Service Exports and Service Imports of Trinidad and Tobago 2011–21, US$mn

Table 8.15: Services Sector Exports in CARICOM

Country	% Change 2011–19	Service Exports (BoP, current US$mn) – 2022
Antigua and Barbuda	138	704.81
Bahamas, The	79	2592.32
Belize	99	620.87
Barbados	17	–
Curacao	6	935.87
Dominica	23	102.03
Grenada	286	345.01
Guyana	-20	284.55
Haiti	-2	110.96
Jamaica	67	2919.91
St Kitts and Nevis	197	363.23
St Lucia	194	624.00
Suriname	-22	95.94
Trinidad and Tobago	-28	385.18
St Vincent and the Grenadines	104	100.18

Table 8.15 above shows that Trinidad and Tobago had the worst performance in the period 2011–19 among all CARICOM member states. In this regard, it is here recommended that Trinidad and Tobago take a deep dive look at the factors that helped the Jamaican economy's service sector exports to increase so quickly and try to set in place some of those same changes in the Trinidad and Tobago economy.

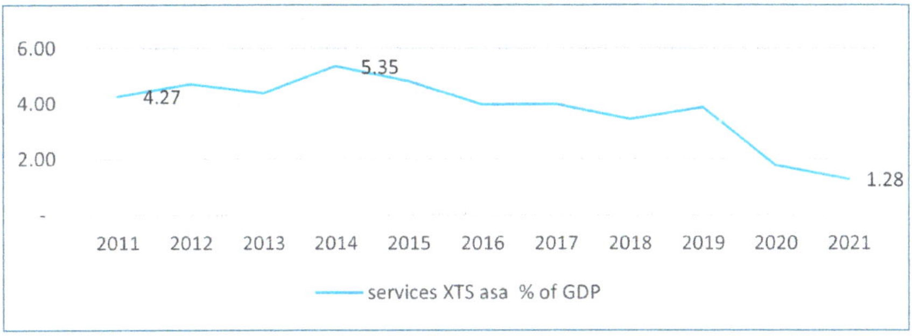

Figure 8.4: Services Exports as a Percentage of GDP

Figure 8.4 above shows the trends in the service exports and service imports of Trinidad and Tobago. Trinidad and Tobago's services sector has a deficit, and policymakers would need to find ways to boost this sector, given the projected deterioration of the economy's gas reserves. Focusing on tourism as a subset of the services sector, note that table 8.16 below shows that as compared to 2010, by 2019, Trinidad and Tobago had a smaller volume of international tourist arrivals. In the same period, Chile, Mauritius and Singapore received 486,400 arrivals, 1,170,400 arrivals and 15,665,550 arrivals, respectively. Given the importance of stimulating export revenues for the wider progress of the Trinidad and Tobago economy, policymakers in Trinidad and Tobago would have to plan carefully ahead to push our tourism numbers up to that of peer comparator states.

Trinidad and Tobago can implement targeted marketing campaigns that showcase the diversity of the island's attractions. China and India are the two fastest-growing markets in the world (for countries with an international departure of over twenty million tourists), and policymakers in Trinidad and Tobago may wish to think ahead and more aggressively target these markets.

To assist the growth and development of its tourism sector, the government of Trinidad and Tobago should consider expanding accommodation options and developing eco-friendly and sustainable tourism initiatives. Ensuring that visitors have a comfortable and enjoyable experience during their stay can also lead to positive word-of-mouth recommendations. Indeed, turtle watching in Trinidad and Tobago offers a remarkable opportunity for tourists to witness one of the world's most important nesting grounds,

Table 8.16: International Tourist Arrivals Various Countries

Country	1995–99	2000–2009	2010–19	% Change 1995–2019	% change 2010–19
Trinidad and Tobago	351400	500700	486400	70.21	-2.04
Chile	–	3685000	5285600	46.1	51.53
Antigua and Barbuda	520200	747000	891000	131.54	31.35
Bahrain	2615400	6252600	10066900	378.62	-7.45
Mauritius	536600	790400	1170400	224.49	48.33
Singapore	6965400	8601400	15665550	167.84	64.20

Source: computed from WDI

Table 8.17: Top 12 Countries: International Tourism, Number of Departures

Country	2019	% change 2010 to 2019
China	154.6	169.5
Korea, Rep.	28.7	129.9
Romania	23.1	111.5
India	26.9	107.2
France	49.3	64.4
Spain	22.8	60.1
Hungary	24.9	54.6
Saudi Arabia	27.2	46.0
United Kingdom	93.1	44.0
United States	170.9	40.6

Source: WDI online

particularly for Leatherback turtles. Turtle watching promotes eco-tourism, supporting local communities engaged in conservation and guiding while also raising awareness about the importance of preserving these endangered species. It provides an authentic and unforgettable experience that not only attracts tourists but also fosters a deeper understanding of the need for environmental conservation.[4]

However, for all of this to work, substantive efforts and interventions must be made in Trinidad and Tobago to reduce crime. As shown in table 8.18, Trinidad and Tobago ranks 7 out of 101 countries, using available WDI data for 2021 on intentional homicides (per 100,000 persons).

Trinidad and Tobago policymakers should promote cultural and ecotourism by organizing and publicizing local festivals, events and cultural activities to attract travellers seeking authentic experiences. Additionally, developing ecotourism initiatives such as guided nature tours, hiking trails and wildlife conservation efforts can appeal to environmentally conscious tourists. Indeed, according to Precedence Research (2023), the global ecotourism market size was estimated at US$195.9 billion (2022), with a forecasted expansion to US$656.19 billion by 2032, translating to a compound annual growth rate (CAGR) of 12.90 per cent over the projected period 2023–32. In addition, in the US, Google online searches for "sustainable travel" increased by 142.6 per cent between April 2019 and April 2022.

Table 8.18: Top 10 Countries, 2021: Intentional Homicides (per 100,000 people).

	Intentional Homicides (per 100,000 People)	2021
1.	Jamaica	52.13
2.	St Lucia	38.96
3.	Honduras	38.34
4.	Belize	31.25
5.	St Vincent and the Grenadines	30.67
6.	St Kitts and Nevis	29.41
7.	Trinidad and Tobago	29.36
8.	Bahamas, The	29.17
9.	Myanmar	28.44
10.	Mexico	28.18

Description of Data: "*Intentional homicides are estimates of unlawful homicides purposely inflicted as a result of domestic disputes, interpersonal violence, violent conflicts over land resources, intergang violence over turf or control, and predatory violence and killing by armed groups. Intentional homicide does not include all intentional killing; the difference is usually in the organization of the killing. Individuals or small groups usually commit homicide, whereas killing in armed conflict is usually committed by fairly cohesive groups of up to several hundred members and is thus usually excluded.*"

Source: WDI Online Database (2023).

Online searches for "eco-tours" also increased by 83.8 per cent during the same period (Radical Storage 2022).

Remittances

From another dimension, Trinidad and Tobago realizes a significantly lower amount of remittances from abroad as compared to most of its CARICOM peer states. Indeed, a close look at table 8.19 below shows that remittances to Trinidad and Tobago in 2022 stood at US$204.4 million. Between 2011 and 2019, remittances grew by 44.6 per cent, with only St Kitts and Guyana experiencing lower growth (note though that Guyana's remittances are more than twice that of Trinidad and Tobago). For the period 2011–22, of all the listed countries, Trinidad and Tobago experienced the slowest growth in remittances from the diaspora abroad with the exception of St Kitts and Nevis.

Table 8.19: Remittances in Various CARICOM Countries, US$mn

Country	2022 US$mn	2011–19% Change	2011–22% Change
Antigua and Barbuda	34.6	123.1	70.5
Belize	142.4	79.7	89.1
Dominica	52.0	184.5	127.4
Grenada	69.4	155.5	139.9
Guyana	540.3	32.9	31.1
Haiti	4532.1	170.5	192.1
Jamaica	3687.6	76.0	75.1
St Lucia	55.2	114.9	87.5
St Kitts and Nevis	33.0	-17.0	-26.2
Suriname	148.2	3691.1	3705.3
St Vincent and the Grenadines	69.6	139.6	137.9
Trinidad and Tobago	204.4	44.6	26.3

Source: WDI Online

Trinidad and Tobago's economy needs to boost its services sector to attract more remittances. The government must promote financial inclusion by expanding access to banking and digital financial services. It should also encourage the use of mobile banking and online remittance platforms, making it easier and more affordable for overseas Trinidadians to send money back home.

Policymakers in the Ministry of Planning should consider deeper collaborative ties with the Trinidad Diaspora Network (TDON), which has a focus on locating and sustaining connections between Trinidad and Tobago and its diaspora. The MOP has identified in its Vision 2030 document that a Diaspora Affairs unit would be created in the Ministry of Foreign and CARICOM Affairs "to ensure that our foreign relations redound to the country's benefit and allow for improved responsiveness to international development".

In addition, the Trinidad and Tobago government should encourage skilled members of the diaspora to return temporarily to Trinidad and Tobago to share their expertise and skills. This could lead to increased remittances, as well as knowledge transfer, that benefit the local economy. Mention has to be made of Inves, Trinidad and Tobago's initiative "Global

Diaspora Business Advocates" (DBAs). This entity represents a dedicated group of Trinidad and Tobago diaspora members who have generously offered their expertise and connections to serve as advisors and liaisons across the globe. They are committed to contributing to Trinidad and Tobago by leveraging their extensive networks and industry insights. DBAs play a pivotal role in fostering connections between international investors and corporations in their contacts and investment prospects within Trinidad and Tobago. With their substantial capabilities, DBAs are poised to drive FDI into Trinidad and Tobago through a strategic advocacy approach.[5]

Moreover, it is possible that Trinidad and Tobago can learn from the experience of France. Specifically, in France, there are active initiatives aimed at supporting diaspora communities as valuable partners in the development process. One such initiative is the Forum of Migrants' International Solidarity Organizations (FORIM), which acts as an umbrella organization uniting various Development Organizations (DOs) in France. FORIM collaborates closely with the French Development Agency (AFD) to provide these DOs with capacity-building programmes. Each year, FORIM sponsors over seventy-five micro-projects in sectors like education, health, water supply, agriculture and diaspora entrepreneurship. These projects receive financial support, with each one benefiting from EUR 15,000.

These are by no means exhaustive but instead are some simple suggestions by which the diaspora can be further embraced.

STEPS IN INCREASING NBT

Increasing Competitive Import Substitution

This chapter recommends that the Ministry of Trade conduct an exercise to identify commodities that Trinidad and Tobago can competitively substitute through imports to boost the output of non-booming tradables. This list should be made publicly available and shared with the commercial banking system and the EXIM Bank, using moral suasion to discourage the use of foreign exchange to import these commodities. This approach follows the methodology of Moore et al. (2015) to determine the areas where Trinidad and Tobago has the potential for import substitution.

In this regard, several commodities stand out as options for import-substituting industrialization (ISI). These are shown in table 8.20 below.[6] The minister of trade should meet with producers in these various areas and try to ascertain their capacity to meet Trinidad and Tobago's import needs in these and related areas. The ETeck theme park logic that guided the formation of the Mayaro Agro-processing plant is here suggested as a good example to follow. The Mayaro Agro-processing plant promotes investments within the agricultural sector and helps develop agricultural commodities through the utilization of the provided park infrastructure. The infrastructure of the Agro-Processing plant will help farmers add value to harvested fresh produce by packaging it, thereby extending its shelf life for both domestic and foreign markets. Additionally, the park offers leasable land for farmers and entrepreneurs, providing easy access to agricultural development agencies like the National Agricultural Marketing and Development Corporation (NAMDEVCO) to support their initiatives. Thus, the construction and utilization of such a park will aid farmers within Mayaro and its environs by enabling them to increase the value of their commodities while promoting growth within the sector as they reap the rewards of utilizing the facility. The construction of ETeck parks specifically oriented to target critical areas within the economy is a necessary investment, as it has the potential to induce economic activity associated with the targeted sector. Table 8.20 shows the top fifty items Trinidad and Tobago can import substitute (at the SITC 5-digit level) for 2018.

Table 8.20: The Top 50 Commodities for Import Substitution

Product Code	Commodities that can be import substituted
67133	Cultured pearls, worked
51576	Heterocyclic compounds with nitrogen hetero-atom(s) only, containing a pyrimidine ring (whether or not hydrogenated) or piperazine ring, or an unfused traizine ring, whether or not hydrogenated, in the structure; nucleic acids and their salts
11244	Rum and other spirits obtained by distilling fermented sugar cane products
59899	Other chemical products and preparations
28239	Ferrous waste and scrap, n.e.s.
66122	Portland cement
11102	Waters (including mineral waters and aerated waters) containing added sugar or other sweetening matter or flavoured, and other non-alcoholic beverages, n.e.s.

Table 8.20 continues on next page

Table 8.20: The Top 50 Commodities for Import Substitution (*cont'd*)

Product Code	Commodities that can be import substituted
53343	Other paints and varnishes (including enamels, lacquers and distempers); prepared water pigments of a kind used for finishing leather
69549	Sets of articles of two or more of Hand tools (including glaziers' diamonds), n.e.s.; blowlamps; vices, clamps and the like, other than accessories for and parts of machine tools; anvils; portable forges; hand or pedaloperated grinding wheels with frameworks
28821	Copper waste and scrap
64243	Toilet paper, cut to size or shape, in rolls or in sheets
4812	Cereals other than maize (corn), in grain form, precooked or otherwise prepared
74494	Parts suitable for use solely or principally with the machinery of other lifting, handling, loading or unloading machinery of subgroups 744.7 and 744.8
3418	Other fish, fresh or chilled (excluding livers and roes)
72393	Parts for boring or sinking machinery of heading 723.37 or 723.44
74395	Parts of the machines and apparatus of subgroups 743.5 and 743.6 of filtering or purifying machinery and apparatus
9849	Other sauces and preparations therefore; mixed condiments and mixed seasonings
27892	Natural barium sulphate (barytes); natural barium carbonate (witherite), whether or not calcined (other than barium oxide of heading 522.65)
28229	Waste and scrap of other alloy steel
4811	Prepared foods obtained by the swelling or roasting of cereals or cereal products and from unroasted cereal flakes or from mixtures of unroasted and roasted cereal flakes or swelled cereals
9842	Tomato ketchup and other tomato sauces
27827	Bentonite, whether or not calcined
77254	Relays
52331	Hydrogen chloride (hydrochloric acid); chlorosulphuric acid
28221	Waste and scrap of stainless steel
87478	Other instruments and apparatus for measuring or checking electrical quantities
27897	Bitumen and asphalt, natural; asphaltites and asphaltic rocks
57541	Urea resins; thiourea resins
52322	Chlorates of sodium
89965	Artificial teeth and dental fittings

Table 8.20 continues on next page

Table 8.20: The Top 50 Commodities for Import Substitution (*cont'd*)

Product Code	Commodities that can be import substituted
89611	Paintings, drawings and pastels
66511	Containers, of glass, of a kind used for the conveyance or packing of goods; stoppers and closures, of glass
87423	Instruments for measuring length, for use in the hand (e.g., measuring rods and tapes, micrometers, calipers), n.e.s
64299	Other paper, paperboard, cellulose wadding or webs of cellulose fibres cut to size or shape; other articles of paper pulp, paper or paperboard, cellulose wadding or webs of cellulose fibres
77411	Electrocardiographs
82125	Mattresses of other materials
52239	Other inorganic oxygen compounds of non-metals
11101	Waters, including natural or artificial mineral waters and aerated waters, not containing added sugar or other sweetening matter nor flavoured; ice and snow.
72442	Machines for preparing textile fibres
89281	Paper or paperboard labels of all kinds, whether or not printed
5676	Potatoes prepared or preserved otherwise than by vinegar or acetic acid, not frozen
69541	Drilling, threading and tapping tools
5996	Mixtures of fruit or vegetable juices
64211	Cartons, boxes and cases, of corrugated paper or paperboard
74491	Parts suitable for use solely or principally with the machinery of headings of machinery of subgroups pulley tackle and hoists (other than skip hoists or hoists of a kind used for raising vehicles); winches and capstans and jacks; hoists of a kind used for raising vehicles
62144	Tubes, pipes and hoses, of unhardened vulcanized rubber, with or without their fittings (e.g., joints, elbows, flanges) reinforced or otherwise combined with other materials, without fittings
25119	Other (including unsorted waste and scrap)
82121	Mattress supports

Source: author generated

Focused Strategy on Dynamic Sectors (Rising Stars and Missed Opportunities)

In order to determine which categories of exportable goods to promote, policymakers can consider the deployment of TradeCAN,[7] as it allows for the analysis of export competitiveness using trends in export values and by the technological patterns of exports. The indicators employed in the TradeCAN analysis include:

Market share: $\frac{M_{ij}}{M_i}$; Percentage of imports $\frac{M_i}{M}$

Where: M – refers to the value of total imports
Mj – refers to import from country j
Mi – refers to imports from sector i
Mij – refers to imports of sector i originating from country j.
Where: ()by stands for base year and ()fy stands for final year.

Table 8.21: The Market Share Formulas

	Formula	Comments
Rising Star	$\frac{M_i^{fy}}{M^{fy}} > \frac{M_i^{by}}{M^{by}}$ and $\frac{M_{ij}^{fy}}{M_i^{fy}} > \frac{M_{ij}^{by}}{M_i^{by}}$	A commodity or sector is considered to be a rising star if market share is being gained in a dynamic sector
Missed Opportunity	$\frac{M_i^{fy}}{M^{fy}} > \frac{M_i^{by}}{M^{by}}$ and $\frac{M_{ij}^{fy}}{M_i^{fy}} < \frac{M_{ij}^{by}}{M_i^{by}}$	A commodity or sector is considered to be a missed opportunity if export share declines in a dynamic sector.

Further to assess the dynamics of comparative advantage, policymakers can use the Balassa (1965) index is outlined as:

$$RCA_{ij} = \left[\frac{X_{ij}}{X_{it}} \Big/ \frac{X_{wj}}{X_{wt}} \right]$$

Where: Xij – refers to a country's (i) exports of a SITC 3-digit commodity (j) to the specific trade partner (t),
Xit – refers to a country's total exports to the specific trade partner,
Xwj – refers to the world (w) exports of a SITC 3-digit commodity to the specific trade partner,
Xwt – refers to the world total exports to the specific trade partner.

The RCA index[8] has a theoretical range from a value greater than zero (0), to less than infinity (∞) which is divided into two groups:
0< RCAj < 1 – the country has a comparative disadvantage in commodity j,
1< RCAj < ∞ – the country has a comparative advantage in the commodity j.

Emphasis is placed in identifying those commodities with RCA more than 1 as it tells you where the Trinidad and Tobago economy simultaneously has capacity.

Tables 8.22–8.27 below provide a snapshot of export commodities in which Trinidad and Tobago exporters can seek to expand market share as a strategy to increase foreign export earnings. These rising stars and missed opportunity sectors are sectors for which demand in the partner country is rising. As such, if the export capacity of these sectors is improved, Trinidad and Tobago exporters can benefit from rising demand, improved market share and increased foreign exchange earnings. Tables 8.22 and 8.23 represent the rising star and missed opportunity sectors within the extra-regional market. It was identified that twenty-three rising stars existed for Trinidad and Tobago exports into the CARICOM market with a revealed comparative advantage (for the period 2000–2015) score of greater than 1. Of these twenty-three categories, fifteen categories were identified as having a strong RCA.[9]

Table 8.22: "Rising Star" Areas Which Currently Possess an RCA for Trinidad and Tobago's Export Market to CARICOM Countries

RCA Category	RCA Score	SITC Rv-3 5 Digit Code	Description
Weak RCA	1.21	84523	Women's or girls' garments made up of fabrics (not knitted or crocheted) of heading 657.32, 657.33 or 657.34
	1.67	9843	Mustard flour and meal and prepared mustard
	1.69	5613	Mushrooms, wood ears, jelly fungi and truffles
Medium RCA	2.14	59818	Wood tar; wood tar oils; wood creosote; wood naphtha; vegetable pitch; brewers' pitch and similar preparations based on rosin, resin acids or on vegetable pitch
	2.46	54139	Other antibiotics
	2.49	64291	Bobbins, spools, cops and similar supports of paper pulp, paper or paperboard (whether or not perforated or hardened).
	2.88	7513	Fruits of the genus Capsicum or of the genus Pimenta, dried or crushed or ground
	3.00	89941	Umbrellas and sun umbrellas (including walking-stick umbrellas, garden umbrellas and similar umbrellas)

Table 8.22 continues on next page

Table 8.22: "Rising Star" Areas Which Currently Possess an RCA for Trinidad and Tobago's Export Market to CARICOM Countries (*cont'd*)

RCA Category	RCA Score	SITC Rv-3 5 Digit Code	Description
Strong RCA	4.57	64215	Other packing containers, including record sleeves
	5.79	5648	Flour, meal and powder of the products of any heading of Fruit and Nut (Not including Oil nuts) Fresh or Dried
	5.84	11249	Spirits and distilled alcoholic beverages, n.e.s.
	5.91	69914	Manufactures of Base Metals ne.s. Castors
	6.09	61183	Patent leather and patent-laminated leather; metallized leather
	6.34	77583	Electrothermic hairdressing or hand-drying apparatus
	8.30	5897	Mixtures of fruits or other edible parts of plants, n.e.s.w
	12.95	64299	Other paper, paperboard, cellulose wadding or webs of cellulose fibres cut to size or shape; other articles of paper pulp, paper or paperboard, cellulose wadding or webs of cellulose fibres
	13.64	9849	Other sauces and preparations therefor; mixed condiments and mixed seasonings
	14.27	5893	Pineapples
	16.12	89815	Other string musical instruments (e.g., guitars, violins, harps)
	34.56	7529	Other spices; mixtures of two or more of the products of different headings of Spices
	38.53	59774	Lubricating preparations containing oils or greases other than of petroleum or bituminous minerals
	41.76	4812	Cereals other than maize (corn), in grain form, precooked or otherwise prepared
	47.73	67643	Bars and rods of iron or steel, not further worked than cold-formed or cold-finished of iron or non-alloy steel, not further worked than forged, hot-rolled, hot-drawn or hot extruded but including those twisted after rolling

Table 8.23: "Missed Opportunity" Areas Which Currently Possess an RCA for Trinidad and Tobago's Export Market to CARICOM Countries

RCA Category	RCA Score	SITC Rev-3 5 Digit Code	Description
Weak RCA	1.15	84562	Spray-guns and similar appliances
	1.24	5459	Other vegetables, fresh or chilled
	1.57	65215	Other pile and chenille fabrics, woven, of cotton (other than terry towelling or similar terry fabrics of headings 652.12 and 652.13 and subgroup 656.1)
	1.63	84521	Dishwashing machines (other than household-type)
	1.89	65839	Blankets and travelling rugs (other than electric) of other materials
Medium RCA	2.03	59227	Glues based on starches, or on dextrin or other modified starches
	2.66	1612	Bellies (streaky) and cuts thereof of Bacon, ham and other salted, dried or smoked meat of swine
	2.80	84692	Other gloves, mittens and mitts
	3.12	66339	Ceramic articles, n.e.s.
	3.94	64293	Trays, dishes, plates, cups and the like, of paper or paperboard
Strong RCA	4.95	67912	Line pipe of a kind used for oil or gas pipelines, of iron (other than cast iron) or steel
	5.21		Imitation jewellery of base metal, whether or not plated with precious metal
	5.64	4815	Germ of cereals, whole, rolled, flaked or ground
	6.34	4811	Prepared foods obtained by the swelling or roasting of cereals or cereal products and from unroasted cereal flakes or from mixtures of unroasted and roasted cereal flakes or swelled cereals
	6.96	7111	Coffee, not roasted, not decaffeinated
	7.56	4849	Other Bread, pastry, cakes, biscuits and other bakers' wares, whether or not containing cocoa in any proportion; communion wafers, empty cachets of a kind suitable for pharmaceutical use, sealing wafers, rice-paper and similar products.
	7.74	3418	Other fish, fresh or chilled (excluding livers and roes) Fish, fresh (live or dead) or chilled (excluding fillets and minced fish

Table 8.23 continues on next page

Table 8.23: "Missed Opportunity" Areas Which Currently Possess an RCA for Trinidad and Tobago's Export Market to CARICOM Countries (*cont'd*)

RCA Category	RCA Score	SITC Rev-3 5 Digit Code	Description
Strong RCA (*cont'd*)	7.78	5456	Cucumbers and gherkins, fresh or chilled
	8.91	4842	Sweet biscuits, waffles and wafers, gingerbread and the like
	9.01	5677	Sweet corn prepared or preserved otherwise than by vinegar or acetic acid
	10.07	9891	Pasta, cooked or stuffed; couscous, whether or not prepared
	10.34	9844	Vinegar and substitutes for vinegar obtained from acetic acid
	10.84	5995	Juice of any other single fruit or vegetable
	11.03	11211	Grape must in fermentation or with fermentation arrested otherwise than by the addition of alcohol.
	11.78	2213	Cream of a fat content, by weight, exceeding 6% Milk (including skimmed milk) and cream, not concentrated or sweetened
	17.27	69919	Other mountings, fittings and similar articles; base metal hatracks, hat-pegs, brackets and similar fixtures; automatic door closer
	18.05	68231	Copper bars, rods and profiles of copper alloys
	18.52	89729	Imitation jewellery of other non-precious materials

For the CARICOM market, twenty-eight categories (export sectors) were missed opportunities, with eighteen of these categories having a strong RCA (Refer to table 8.23.).

Fifteen rising-star areas were identified, with seven having a strong revealed comparative advantage to the extra-CARICOM market (Refer to table 8.24.).

Table 8.24: "Rising Star" Areas Which Currently Possess an RCA for Trinidad and Tobago's Export Market to Non-CARICOM Countries

RCA Category	RCA Score	SITC Rev-3 5 Digit Code	Description
Weak RCA	1.04	9899	Pasta, cooked or stuffed; couscous, whether or not prepared
	1.26	11101	Waters, including natural or artificial mineral waters and aerated waters, not containing added sugar or other sweetening matter nor flavoured; ice and snow
	1.38	82116	Seats, n.e.s., with wooden frames
	1.43	69129	Aluminium structures and parts of structures, n.e.s.; aluminium plates, fods, profiles, tubes and the like, prepared for use in structures
	1.93	33541	Petroleum bitumen and other residues of petroleum oils or of oils obtained from bituminous mineral
Medium RCA	2.79	64241	Cigarette paper, cut to size, whether or not in the form of booklets or tubes
	3.90	51574	Heterocyclic compounds with nitrogen hetero-atom(s) only, containing an unfused pyridine ring, whether or not hydrogenated, in the structure.
	3.99	8199	Preparations of a kind used for animal food, n.e.s.
Strong RCA	4.51	52237	Silicon dioxide
	4.53	51692	Sugars, pure (other than sucrose, lactose, maltose, glucose and fructose); sugar ethers and sugar esters, and their salts (other than products of subgroups 541.4 and 541.5 or heading 541.61)
	5.84	11245	Gin and Geneva
	24.19	67247	Ingots and other primary forms of stainless steel
	28.81	56214	Double salts and mixtures of calcium nitrate and ammonium nitrate
	54.37	28229	Ferrous Waste and Scrap; re-melting scrap ingots of iron and steel of other alloy steel
	66.00	28793	Cobalt ores and concentrates

Table 8.25: "Missed Opportunity" Areas Which Currently Possess an RCA for Trinidad and Tobago's Export Market to Non-CARICOM Countries

RCA Category	RCA Score	SITC Rv-3 5 Digit Code	Description
Weak RCA	1.77	7528	Saffron
	1.97	7527	Ginger (excluding ginger preserved in sugar or conserved in syrup)
Medium RCA	3.71	4811	Prepared foods obtained by the swelling or roasting of cereals or cereal products and from unroasted cereal flakes or from mixtures of unroasted and roasted cereal flakes or swelled cereals
Strong RCA	4.78	4812	Cereals other than maize (corn), in grain form, precooked or otherwise prepared

Four missed-opportunity areas were identified for the extra-CARICOM market, with only Cereals other than maize (corn), in grain form, precooked or otherwise prepared, to have a strong RCA.

The following section will provide some considerations for policymakers to better leverage the opportunities offered by expanding production and exports in the identified sectors.

POLICY INTERVENTIONS TO SUPPORT EXPANSION OF THE NBT SECTOR

Of course, in order to get exports going in Trinidad and Tobago, it is necessary to improve the Ease of Doing Business (EoDB) situation. Trinidad and Tobago's EoDB performance has been poor, declining from a rank of 66 in 2014 to a rank of 105 in 2020.[10] This must be reversed as a matter of urgency. In this regard, policymakers in Trinidad and Tobago should take a careful look at some of the changes Jamaica has made in the last few years in order to have the best ranking among Caribbean economies. Beyond this, table 8.26 outlines the various pillars of the EODB and suggests interventions, based on experiences from other countries, that could be applied to improve Trinidad and Tobago's EODB environment.

Table 8.26: Interventions in Other Countries That Can be Used to Improve Trinidad and Tobago's EODB Ranking

Trinidad and Tobago EODB Ranking	2014	2020	3 interventions per thematic area to improve EODB ranking
Global Rank	**66**	**105**	
Starting a Business	67	76	Make starting a business less expensive by reducing the fees for business incorporation (Doing Business 2020, Dem Rep of Congo). Make starting a business faster by improving the exchange of information between public entities involved in company incorporation (Doing Business 2020, Antigua and Barbuda). Make starting a business faster by reducing the registration time for the business licence and value added tax and by eliminating the business registration fee (Doing Business 2020, Bahamas).
Dealing with Construction Permits	77	125	Make dealing with construction permits easier by investing in georeferencing and its geographic information system database (Doing Business 2020, Cabo Verde). Make dealing with construction permits cheaper by eliminating fees for building permits (Doing Business 2020, Denmark).
Getting Electricity	10	41	Make improving the review process and increasing the availability of equipment for new electricity connections. (Doing Business 2020, Ghana). Make getting electricity faster by allocating more staff to process applications. Lao PDR also improved the reliability of power supply by deploying an automated Supervisory Control and Data Acquisition (SCADA) system for outage monitoring and the restoration of service (Doing Business 2020, Lao PDR).
Registering Property	178	158	Make property registration easier by streamlining the inspection and registration processes. Kuwait also improved the quality of its land administration system by publishing official service standards on property transfers (Doing Business 2020, Kuwait). Make property registration faster by making it easier to check for encumbrances. Mauritius also improved the quality of its land administration system by publishing official service standards and court statistics on land disputes (Doing Business 2020, Mauritius). Make property registration faster by streamlining deed registration and appraisal. Myanmar also improved the quality of its land administration system by publishing the fee schedule, official service standards, and statistics on property transfers for the previous calendar year (Doing Business 2020, Myanmar).

Table 8.26 continues on next page

Table 8.26: Interventions in Other Countries That Can be Used to Improve Trinidad and Tobago's EODB Ranking (*cont'd*)

Getting Credit	28	60	Strengthen access to credit by automatically extending security interests to the products, proceeds, and replacements of the original assets and by giving secured creditors absolute priority during insolvency proceedings. Kazakhstan improved access to credit information by reporting credit data from retailers. (Doing Business 2020, Kazakhstan). Improve access to credit information by reporting both positive and negative data on individual borrowers (Doing Business 2020, Israel).
Protecting Minority Investors	22	57	Strengthen minority investor protections by requiring shareholder approval when listed companies issue new shares (Doing Business 2020, Egypt). Strengthen minority investor protections by requiring greater disclosure and an independent review before the approval of related-party transactions as well as greater corporate transparency of executive compensation (Doing Business 2020, Greece). Strengthen minority investor protections by requiring shareholders to approve the election and dismissal of an external auditor (Doing Business 2020, Kenya).
Paying Taxes	97	166	Make paying taxes easier by implementing an online filing and payment system for social security contributions (Doing Business 2020, Kenya). Made paying taxes easier by introducing additional features to an online filing system to incorporate income tax and value added tax (Doing Business 2020, The Republic of Korea). Make paying taxes easier by reducing the social security contribution rate paid by the employer and the capital gains basis. The value of the environmental tax and the time for labour taxes and contributions will increase (Doing Business 2020, Moldova).
Trading across Borders	73	130	Make trading across borders faster by streamlining paperless customs clearance, and extending port hours of operation (Doing Business 2020, Morocco).
Enforcing Contracts	174	174	Make enforcing contracts easier by introducing an electronic case management system for judges and lawyers. (Doing Business 2020, Paraguay). Make enforcing contracts easier by publishing court performance measurement reports and information on the progress of cases through the court (Doing Business 2020, Saudi Arabia). Make enforcing contracts easier by establishing financial incentives for the parties to attempt mediation. (Doing Business 2020, Serbia).

Table 8.26 continues on next page

Table 8.26: Interventions in Other Countries That Can be Used to Improve Trinidad and Tobago's EODB Ranking (*cont'd*)

Resolving Insolvency	114	77	Make resolving insolvency easier by introducing a reorganization procedure, by allowing debtors to initiate the reorganization procedure, and by improving the continuation of businesses and the treatment of contracts during insolvency proceedings (Doing Business 2020, Jordan). Make resolving insolvency easier by improving the continuation of the debtor's business during insolvency proceedings (Doing Business 2020, Kenya). Make resolving insolvency easier by introducing a reorganization procedure, allowing debtors to initiate the reorganization procedure, improving voting arrangements in reorganization, improving the continuation of businesses and the treatment of contracts during insolvency proceedings, allowing post-commencement credit, and increasing the participation of creditors in the insolvency proceedings (Doing Business 2020, Saudi Arabia).

Source: Compiled from various EODB reports

Policymakers at the Ministry of Trade and Industry should survey the top fifty non-energy exporters in Trinidad and Tobago and design a "How to Export" manual for them, potentially funded through the Green Fund. This manual should be user-friendly and provide guidelines based on the experiences of successful exporters. It should outline the obstacles they encountered, how they overcame them, and offer practical advice on exporting goods and services.

The Ministry of Trade must also comprehensively examine the current supply chains and, where possible, restructure them to reflect the new normal realities. The ministry should scan the non-energy sector to identify niches that can be leveraged to benefit Trinidad and Tobago exporters, especially those sectors that utilize local content. Integrating more local content can indeed strengthen the linkages between the domestic and external sectors and bring more local productive resources into employment, especially in terms of foreign exchange earnings.

Given the proximity of regional suppliers, special attention must also be paid to creating CARICOM supply chains for essential goods. CARICOM can, therefore, be considered an extension of the "local content" logic, which would also improve regional integration among member states. This type of reasoning is associated with the originally conceived production integration opportunities foreseen by C.Y. Thomas and Norman Girvan with Caribbean integration.

The proximity of suppliers has become a critical factor in maintaining economic activity, especially during global shocks like the COVID-19 pandemic. In 2020–21, logistics bottlenecks, worsened by distance, led to production delays in some economies as public health regulations limited activity in certain sectors. Suppliers located closer to production facilities can be accessed more easily, reducing risks related to potential transport challenges.

The Ministry of Trade should also reform its oversight of industrial parks. Consideration should be given to creating a new holding company with funding to upgrade the parks, which could be leased to local and international investors and promoters to attract business. The goal should be to establish leased, private sector–run industrial parks that generate a rate of return, ensuring the long-term viability of these facilities.

Table 8.27 below provides a summary of the interventions discussed above.

Table 8.27: Non-energy Trade Policies

Current Challenge	Dimensions	Considerations/Action Plan to address	Likely Impact
How to export manual	A joint committee of policymakers at the Ministry of Trade and Industry should undertake a survey of the top fifty non-energy exporters in the Trinidad and Tobago economy and from this survey design a "How to Export" manual funded via the Green Fund. A secretariat should be established for this purpose.	This manual must be one that is easy to use, and offers guidelines based on the experience of existing successful exporters as to what are the obstacles that they encounter, overcome the obstacles encountered and basically how to position/manoeuvre a firm in terms of its decisions, investment and outlook in order to penetrate the export market.	Improved access to new and existing markets.
How to identify potential competitive export sectors	Competitiveness review of sectors and subsectors already established and identification of new ones. Priority listing.	A priority listing for promotion among local and foreign investors.	Enhanced investment in export sectors with potential.

Table 8.27 continues on next page

Table 8.27: Non-energy Trade Policies (*cont'd*)

Current Challenge	Dimensions	Considerations/Action Plan to address	Likely Impact
How to compete in supply chains	Examination of the current supply chains and efforts to restructure them. Identification of niches where Trinidad and Tobago can supply. Special attention to the creation of CARICOM supply chains in essential goods and restructured global supply chains.	The focus of the examination must be on identifying areas of competitive advantage in these chains where Trinidad and Tobago can supply. This should be the basis for a new foreign investment thrust.	Improved local and foreign investment in this sector.
How to create viable industrial parks	A new holding company with funding for upgrading the industrial parks, which should be leased to local and international investors and promoters that could attract business.	The aim should be to develop leased private sector–run industrial parks and GO Trinidad and Tobago getting a rate of return to ensure the long-term viability of these parks.	More vibrant and profitable industrial parks promoting business internationally.
Food production linked to agro-processing for exports	In 2018, the food import bill totalled US$772.38 million.	The Trinidad and Tobago economy can link with regional food producers such as Suriname, Belize and Guyana in this regard as the COVID-19 should have taught us that at a moment's notice, the World can be "closed for business" and plans B and C must be programmed into the way production is undertaken. As part of national food security but from a trade perspective, policymakers should encourage as much processing of local food where possible and use moral suasion to encourage customers to buy local where it is possible.	The agro-processing element is to help crowd in domestic value added to benefit the local economy from backward and forward linkages and also for associated technological spill overs. The bonus is saving foreign exchange.

Table 8.27 continues on next page

Table 8.27: Non-energy Trade Policies (*cont'd*)

Current Challenge	Dimensions	Considerations/Action Plan to address	Likely Impact
Improving Ease of Doing Business	EODB index moved backward from 66 in 2014 to 105 in 2020.	The government of Trinidad and Tobago should form a taskforce to improve the EODB ranking by 50 places between now and the end of next year.	This can help to crowd in both domestic and foreign investments into the Trinidad and Tobago economy.
Improper deployment of Venezuelan workers	Trinidad and Tobago completed a two-week registration process for Venezuelan immigrants from 31 May to 14 June 2019, where 16,523 Venezuelan immigrants were registered under the Amnesty. However, the UNHCR estimates that the country hosts over forty thousand migrants from Venezuela.	Because these workers are mainly employed in the nonessential services sector, they are currently mainly unemployed. Apart from this temporary situation they implicitly and explicitly utilize resources from our scarce stock of reserves to buy goods and this is unsustainable.	It makes sense to design a sectoral labour market strategy so that the Venezuelans are required to work in areas where they produce foreign exchange or where they reduce the demand for foreign exchange.
KPIs for the Minister of trade	It is critical that non-energy exports in Trinidad and Tobago increase.	Describe the trend in the non-energy export balance for Trinidad and Tobago	Can help create foreign exchange, jobs and a greater use of domestic factors of production.

Table 8.27 continues on next page

Table 8.27: Non-energy Trade Policies (*cont'd*)

Current Challenge	Dimensions	Considerations/Action Plan to address	Likely Impact
Need to improve trade with Spanish-speaking countries	Trade between Trinidad and Tobago and Spanish-speaking countries have been increasing over the period 2000–2018. For instance, Trinidad and Tobago's exports to Argentina increased from US$7.2 million in 2000 to US$967million by 2018. Exports to Colombia increased from US$25.4 million to US$246.1 million by 2015. Imports from these countries have mainly been in non-energy trade.	Complementarity does exist between Trinidad and Tobago and these Spanish-speaking countries as these countries exports non-energy commodities to Trinidad and Tobago and Trinidad and Tobago exports mainly energy products to these countries. Higher complementarity index values existed for Guatemala (22.17), Dominican Republic (21.86), Ecuador (18.89), Costa Rica (17.05) and Ecuador (18.84), which is higher than traditional trading partners such as the United States, United Kingdom and China. However, since a language barrier exists, this would inhibit trade due to increased communication cost. It is recommended to adopt Spanish as a second language in order to promote trade.[11] Using both OLS and PPML modelling, it was determined that having a common language does favourably impact total trade. In this regard, further promoting Spanish as a second language would likely assist in deepening trade ties with neighbouring Spanish speaking countries especially since these countries have trade complementarity with Trinidad and Tobago (and Trinidad and Tobago's complementarity with traditional partners have been either declining or very low).	The likely impact of adopting Spanish as a second language would be to increasing trade with these countries where complementarity exists. This would propel trade into new markets as complementarity has been low or declining with traditional trade partners such as the United States, United Kingdom and CARICOM.

Table 8.27 continues on next page

Table 8.27: Non-energy Trade Policies (*cont'd*)

Current Challenge	Dimensions	Considerations/Action Plan to address	Likely Impact
Identifying rising star opportunities and missed opportunities with RCA	It was identified that twenty-three rising stars existed for Trinidad and Tobago exports into the CARICOM market with a revealed comparative advantage, where fifteen categories were identified as having a strong RCA. For the CARICOM market, it was also determined that twenty-eight categories were missed opportunities with eighteen of these categories having a strong RCA. For the extra-CARICOM market, fifteen rising star areas were identified. seven had a strong revealed comparative advantage. Four missed opportunity areas were identified for the extra-CARICOM market with only Cereals other than maize (corn), in grain form, precooked or otherwise prepared having a strong RCA.	How can the number of rising stars and the number of missed opportunities be increased? There should be continued efforts to promote the exports of rising stars which have established themselves in the CARICOM and extra-CARICOM markets. However, missed opportunities can be targeted to increase exports by allowing for tax concessions, loans and subsidized capital equipment and other mechanisms that would promote the production and export of these opportunities especially since the country would have a strong RCA in these categories.	Promoting the rising stars and missed opportunities with RCA can enable Trinidad and Tobago to earn more foreign exchange

CONCLUSION

This chapter sketches a vision for the non-energy sector in Trinidad and Tobago after 2022. It uses good practice application on how to determine sectors that are missed opportunities in which Trinidad and Tobago has a strong comparative advantage. In so doing, this chapter helps to outline how non-energy exports can be strengthened moving forward.

The first strategy revolves around the creation and publishing of a manual, which simplifies export procedures for foreign markets. The provision of such a manual will aid in expanding non-energy exports since domestic firms will be more aware of potential markets and their respective requirements that would have elsewise prevented these commodities from entering and penetrating foreign markets. In addition to this manual, it is necessary to promote innovation and new technology within domestic firms. This compels domestic firms to invest in newer technology, which subsequently results in an improvement in productivity and competitiveness in the export market. It is also necessary to develop leasable industrial parks for private sector or international investors. The provision of such parks not only provides a suitable environment for private and international investors to set up operations for the production of non-energy-based commodities but also provides rental income for the leasing company. Furthermore, as the production of these non-energy-based commodities increases, it is likely that these firms will utilize the aforementioned strategies and seek out foreign markets, which will subsequently increase non-energy exports. Additionally, trade with Spanish-speaking countries should be expanded since these countries exhibit a complementary relationship with Trinidad and Tobago. This can be achieved through the adoption of Spanish as a second language, which reduces the cost of trade between both countries. Lastly, it is necessary to conduct a thorough investigation into the commodities that Trinidad and Tobago can either competitively produce or aim to produce. The results of this investigation must be published as it will aid domestic firms in aligning themselves with the goals of Trinidad and Tobago's government.

Thus far, Trinidad and Tobago has heavily relied on trade, which mainly comprises exports of energy-based commodities, to propel its economic development. This dependence has resulted in the shrinkage of its non-energy sectors, which has compromised its future development. However, the economy can recover from this through various strategies that will encourage the expansion of non-energy exports.

NOTES

1. Theoretically, the ROI ranges from 0 to infinity. An ROI close to 0 indicates an export pattern biased to the extra-regional market, whilst a value of unity indicates an equal tendency to export to both intra- and extra-regional markets. Lastly, a value greater than 1 that is trending towards infinity reveals an export pattern, which is biased intra-regionally. An export pattern that is neutral in terms of the pattern of exports to both the extra- and intra-regional markets attains a value of unity.
2. The inability to fully utilize productive resources, resulting in an output level that is lower than optimal.
3. ISIC revision 4 refers to the fourth iteration of a classification scheme that was published by the United Nations to aid entities in strategically categorizing activities for collecting and reporting statistics. This forth iteration redefines prior classifications of activities from the previous iteration (ISIC 3.1). This new iteration has 21 sections, 88 divisions, 238 groups and 419 classes, where the prior iteration had 17 sections, 60 divisions, 159 groups and 292 classes.
4. Turtle Watching: Destination Trinidad and Tobago | Tours, Holidays, Vacations and Travel Guide (destinationtnt.com).
5. Global Diaspora Business Advocates (investt.co.tt).
6. Data was collected from the International Trade Centre and also UNCOMTRADE for Trinidad and Tobago.
7. Trade Competitiveness Analysis of Nations: The methodology facilitates for the grouping of exports into technological categories. TradeCAN evaluates and analyses trends in post trade data of partner countries importing goods from a given sector and compares the same to the overall import of goods, from all other sources. By comparing these import trends of the partner country, the TradeCAN methodology assigns a competitiveness category to each traded sector. The TradeCAN approach develops the argument that the change in competitiveness is revealed by the evolution of exports (or partner country imports).
8. The RCA index relates the share of country i's exports of commodity j, to the world or a specific market to the share of the world exports of commodity j to that market. The intuition is that if country i is a competitive supplier of commodity k, then the share of k in its exports would be larger than the share of k in total exports for alternative sources of supply (world exports of k). This situation implies that if country i has a comparative advantage in commodity k, the RCA index will yield a value greater then unity. A value less than unity indicates comparative disadvantage.
9. RCA values are classified as follows: comparative disadvantage: 0–1, weak

comparative advantage 1–2, medium comparative advantage 2–4, strong comparative advantage 4–OO+

10. *The Business Report* by the World Bank, which employs the ease of doing business index was discontinued after an internal review and audit by the organization discovered irregularities in the data for its 2018 and 2020 reports (World Bank 2021). These irregularities were revealed by Wilmer Hale, a Washington-based law firm, and included changes made to data on the behalf of representatives of selected countries (Mukul 2021).
11. A Spanish Implementation Secretariat was established in the Ministry of Education launched in 2005 as Trinidad and Tobago was supposed to be the headquarters of the Free Trade areas of the Americas (FTAA). The success of this secretariat was impacted by the fact that the FTAA did not materialize as expected. https://www.moe.gov.tt/spanish-implementation-secretariat-sis/.

REFERENCES

Abrahams, N.H., and J. Jordan. "Joint Production and Averting Expenditure Measures of Willingness to Pay: Do Water Expenditures Really Measure Avoidance Costs?" *American Journal of Agricultural Economics* 82, no. 2 (2000): 427–37.

Adeleye, J.O., and A.O. Adeleye. "Impact of International Trade on Economic Growth in Nigeria (1988–2012)." *International Journal of Financial Research* 6, no. 3 (2015): 163–72.

Ahmed, W., et al. "First Confirmed Detection of SARS-CoV-2 in Untreated Wastewater in Australia: A Proof of Concept for the Wastewater Surveillance of COVID-19 in the Community." *Science of the Total Environment* 728 (August 2020).

Alvarez, P.J. *Nanotechnology-Enabled Water Treatment: A Perspective for Distributed Treatment in Developing Countries.* Bridgetown: FAO Caribbean, 2021.

Asher, M. *Economic Reasoning and Public Policy: Case Studies from India.* Delhi: Delhi School of Public Policy and Governance, 2021.

Baietti, A. *Characteristics of Well-Performing Public Water Utilities.* Washington, DC: World Bank, 2006.

Balassa, B. "Trade Liberalisation and 'Revealed' Comparative Advantage." *The Manchester School* 33, no. 2 (1965): 99–123.

Barnes, B., et al. *The Way Forward: WASA.* Cabinet-Appointed Committee Report. Port of Spain: Government of Trinidad and Tobago, 2002.

Bartholomew, A., et al. *3-Year Action Plan on the Water Industry.* Port of Spain: Government of Trinidad and Tobago, 2003.

Batchelor, D., et al. *Staff Training for Water Supply Projects in the West Indies.* Kingston, Jamaica: Caribbean Water and Wastewater Association, n.d.

CANARI. https://canari.org/who-we-are/. 2022.

CARI-BOIS. "The Cropper Foundation." CARI-BOIS. https://www.caribois.org/about/the-cropper-foundation/2022.

Central Bank of Trinidad and Tobago. https://www.central-bank.org.tt/.

Cosgrove, W.J. *World Water Vision: Making Water Everybody's Business.* London: Earthscan Publications, 2000.

CPG Consultants. *Caroni River Basin Study: Hydrological Study and Storage Option Assessment Caroni Water Treatment Plant Upgrade.* Port of Spain: Water and Sewerage Authority, 2013.

Davis, A.C., N. Skibbe, and M. Müller-Petke. "First Measurements of Surface Nuclear Magnetic Resonance Signals in a Grounded Bipole." *Geophysical Research Letters* 46, no. 16 (2019).

de Miranda, P.E. *Hydrogen Energy: Science and Engineering of Hydrogen-Based Energy Technologies.* London: Elsevier, 2019.

DESALCOTT. 11 April 2022. https://desalcott.com/.

Doria, M.F. "Bottled Water versus Tap Water: Understanding Consumers' Preferences." *Journal of Water and Health* 4, no. 2 (2006): 271–76.

Esfahani, H.S. "Exports, Imports and Economic Growth in Semi-Industrialized Countries." *Journal of Development Economics* 35, no. 1 (1991): 93–116.

Ferrier, C. *Bottled Water: Understanding a Social Phenomenon.* Gland, Switzerland: World Wide Fund for Nature (WWF), 2001.

FFOS. "Fishermen and Friends of the Sea." 2022. https://ffostt.com/about-us/what-we-do/.

Gemechu, D. "Export and Economic Growth in Ethiopia: An Empirical Investigation." Master's Dissertation. Addis Ababa: Addis Ababa University, 2002.

Genivar. *Development of a Water & Wastewater Master Plan & Policy for Trinidad and Tobago.* Port of Spain: Water and Sewerage Authority, 2009.

Gill, I. *Presentation on Water Utility Operator Training: Trinidad and Tobago Perspective.*, n.d.

Government of Trinidad and Tobago. *Regulated Industries Commission Act Chap. 54:73.* Port of Spain: Government Printery, 1998.

———. "Statement by Environment Minister at the Opening of the Point Fortin Desalination Plant." 11 April 2013. http://news.gov.tt/content/statement-environment-minister-opening-point-fortin-desalination-plant#.

———. *Water and Sewerage Act, Chap. 54:40, Section 9(1).* Port of Spain: Government Printery, 1965.

Govia, S. "The Top 3 Risks Facing the Caribbean Water and Sanitation Sector." *Future Proof*, Issue 1, April 2022.

———. "Using Geology to Meet T&T's Water Demand." *Hammer Magazine*, Issue 1, Quarter 1, 2020.

Hamiche, A.M., A.B. Stambouli, and S. Flazi. "A Review of the Water-Energy Nexus." *Renewable and Sustainable Energy Reviews* 65 (November 2016): 319–31.

IDB Invest. *Project Disclosure for Advisory Services Projects*. Washington, DC: Inter-American Development Bank, 2021.

Institute of Marine Affairs. *State of the Marine Environment Report*. Chaguaramas, Trinidad: Institute of Marine Affairs, 2016.

Inter-American Development Bank. *Trinidad and Tobago Wastewater Infrastructure Rehabilitation Program (TT-L1018): Orphan WWTPs in the Maloney Sewerage Region*. Washington, DC: IDB, 2011.

Intergovernmental Panel on Climate Change. *Climate Change 2022: Impacts, Adaptation and Vulnerability*. Geneva: IPCC, 2021.

International Trade Centre. 2024. https://intracen.org/.

Investt. "Investt's Global Diaspora Business Advocates." 2022. https://www.investt.co.tt/how-we-help/investts-global-diaspora/Investts-Diaspora-Business-Advocates-2022.pdf.

Janson, N., Burkhard, L., and Jones, S. *Caribbean Water Study: IDB Technical Note No. IDB-TN-2320*. Inter-American Development Bank, 2021.

Javeed, A. "Green Fund Gets Refreshed Mandate." *Trinidad Express Newspaper*, 8 February 2022.

Julien, K.E. *Report on the Short-Term Programme and the Interim Structure for WASA*. Cabinet-Appointed Committee, 2006.

Lum Lock, A., and T. Geoghegan. *Rewarding Community Efforts to Protect Watersheds: Case Study of Fondes Amandes, St. Ann's, Trinidad and Tobago*, 2006. http://216.119.77.147/documents/rewardingcommunityeffortstoprotectwatershedscasestudyofFondesAmandes.pdf.

Mahabir, S. *IWRM Working in Trinidad and Tobago: A Benefits Analysis of the Adopt A River Programme*. Caribbean Water and Wastewater Association, 2015. https://cwwa.net/wp/wpcontent/uploads/2019/04/IWRM_working_in_Trinidad_and_Tobago_An_analysis_of_the_Adopt_A_River_Programme.pdf.

McTaggart, M., G. Stevens, and K. Singh. "New Beetham Wastewater Treatment Plant – A First Step towards Modernizing Wastewater Treatment in Trinidad and Tobago." *Proceedings of the Water Environment Federation* 2007 (11): 6352–68. Water Env.

Ministry of Education. *Secretariat for the Implementation of Spanish (SIS)*. 2023. https://www.moe.gov.tt/spanish implementation-secretariat-sis/.

Ministry of Finance. *Estimates of Development Programme (2011–2020)*. Government of Trinidad and Tobago, 2011–20.

———. *Estimates of Revenue and Expenditure of Statutory Boards and Similar Bodies and the THA (2011–2022).* Port of Spain: Government of Trinidad & Tobago, 2022.

Ministry of Planning and Development. *Water Resources Management Strategy Study: Main Report*. Government of T&T, 1999.

———. *Water Resources Management Strategy Study: Annex 1 Water Resources Planning 1B Trinidad – Measures and Strategies.* Port of Spain: Government of Trinidad and Tobago, 1999.

———. *Water Resources Management Strategy Study: Annex 17 Action Plan*. Port of Spain: Government of Trinidad and Tobago, 1999.

Ministry of Public Utilities. *State of the Water Sector.* 2016.

———. "Our History." 12 April 2022. https://www.mpu.gov.tt/our-history/.

NewGen. "Newgen Energy Ltd." 2022. https://newgenenergyltd.com/author/newgen-energy-ltd/#:~:text=Trinidad%20and%20Tobago%20is%20already,the%20Point%20Lisas%20Industrial%20Estate.

Office of the Auditor General. *Report of the Auditor General of Public Accounts of the Republic of T&T for the Financial Year 2020.* Port of Spain: Government of Trinidad and Tobago, 2021.

Olson, E. *Bottled Water: Pure Drink or Pure Hype?* New York: Natural Resources Defence Council (NRDC), 1999.

Organisation for Economic Co-operation and Development. *Private Sector Participation in Water Infrastructure: OECD Checklist for Public Action*. Paris: OECD Publishing, 2009.

Pantin, D., and V. Krishnarayan. *Incentives for Watershed Management in Trinidad: Results of a Brief Diagnostic.* Port of Spain: Caribbean Natural Resources Institute, 2003. https://www.canari.org/wp-content/uploads/2016/02/316-Incentives-for-Watershed-Management-in-Trinidad-Results-of-a-Brief-Diagnostic.pdf.

Parliament of the Republic of Trinidad and Tobago. *8th Report of the Joint Select Committee on Ministries, Statutory Authorities and State Enterprises on Water Resources Agency.* Port of Spain: Government of Trinidad and Tobago, 2012.

Particip. *Vulnerability and Capacity Assessment Report Trinidad and Tobago*, 2019.

Peters, E.J., and K.D. Balfour. "Water Losses and the Potential of Reducing System Pressure: A Case Study in Trinidad." *West Indian Journal of Engineering*, 37, 2014.

Presedence Research. "Ecotourism Market (By Activity Type: Land, Marine; By Group: Solo, Groups; By Booking Mode: Direct, Travel Agent, Marketplace Booking) – Global Industry Analysis, Size, Share, Growth, Trends, Regional Outlook, and Forecast 2023–2032." *Presedence Research*, July 2023. https://www.precedenceresearch.com/ecotourism-market.

PWC. *PWC Budget Memorandum*. Port of Spain: PWC, 2013.

Randolph, B., and P. Troy. "Attitudes to Conservation and Water Consumption." *Environmental Science and Policy* 11, no. 5 (2008): 441–55.

Safege. Trinidad and Tobago Corporate Governance Services for the Multi-Phase Wastewater Rehabilitation Program (Phase 1), 2017.

Shiklomanov, I.A. World Water Resources: A New Appraisal and Assessment for the 21st Century. United Nations Educational, Scientific and Cultural Organization, Paris, 1998.

Sitzenfrei, R., and W. Rauch. "Investigating Transitions of Centralized Water Infrastructure to Decentralized Solutions – An Integrated Approach." *Procedia Engineering* 70 (2014): 1549–57.

Smith, A. *The Wealth of Nations*. London: W. Strahan and T. Cadell, 1776.

Sub-Committee of Cabinet. *Report of the Cabinet Sub-Committee Appointed to Review the Operations of WASA and to Determine the Strategy for Enabling the Authority to Achieve Its Mandate, 2020.*

Subcommittee of the Standing Committee on Energy. *Water Sector Strategic Plan: Laying the Foundation, 2004.*

Trinidad and Tobago Parliament. *Debates of the House of Representatives. Hansard Report*. Port of Spain: Government Printery, 6 August 1965.

UN Water. "SDG 6 Data Portal." https://sdg6data.org/country-or-area/Trinidad%20and%20Tobago, 20 April 2021.

UNEP. *Green Infrastructure: Guide for Water Management*. 26 April 2014. https://www.unep.org/resources/publication/green-infrastructure-guide-water-management.

United Nations Food and Agricultural Organisation. *Aquastat Database*, 2017.

Water and Sewerage Authority. *WASA 50 Years and Beyond – Summary Study Guide, 2015.*

———. *National Quiz Secondary Schools Competition: Supplement* 2, 2011.

———. "Wastewater." https://www.wasa.gov.tt/WASA_AboutUs_history1.html#:~:-text=Lock%20Joint%20(America%20Ltd.),and%20Port%2Dof%2DSpain, 2022.

———. "WASA Multiphase Wastewater Rehabilitation Program – Malabar Wastewater Project Details." https://www.wasa.gov.tt/WASA_Wastewater%20Rehab_Malabar2890Details.html, n.d.

———. "WASA Multiphase Wastewater Rehabilitation Program - San Fernando Wastewater Project Details." https://www.wasa.gov.tt/WASA_Wastewater%20Rehab_SanFernando2890DetailsPg2.html, n.d.

Water Resources Agency, Water and Sewerage Authority. "Map of Trinidad's Groundwater Wells." 2018.

Water Resources Agency, Water and Sewerage Authority. "Movement of Water Resources Management Function to the Ministry of the Environment and the Formation of the Water Resources Management Authority: Strategic Issues." n.d.

Water Resources Survey. *Annual Data Report*, 1972.

Winston Moore, J.B. Size. "Structure and Devaluation." Central Bank of Barbados Working Paper, 2015.

World Bank Group. *Doing Business 2020*. https://archive.doingbusiness.org/en/reports/global-reports/doing-business-2020, 24 October 2019.

———. *World Development Indicators*. https://databank.worldbank.org/source/world-development-indicators, 2024.

[CHAPTER 9]

Rethinking Trinidad and Tobago Manufacturing Internationalization

From Intermittent Export to Global Trinidad and Tobago

NIGEL WILLIAMS

INTRODUCTION: COUNTRY LINKAGES AND INTERNATIONALIZATION CAPABILITIES

The state plays a lead role in economic diversification. Recent work has acknowledged that while broad sector neutral policies are necessary, they are not sufficient and have to be supplemented with sector-specific policies that reduce the costs of production, improve organizational efficiency and encourage the creation of organizations in new economic sectors (Navarro, Benavente and Crespi 2016). Countries have sought to develop their manufacturing sector as part of diversification strategies from commodity production. Countries may use fiscal linkages, or the revenue generated from commodity production to invest in newer sectors, consumption linkages from local demand and production linkages (forward and backward) to develop these areas (Hirschman 1981). These linkages can be extended further to transversal Capabilities, which include organizational capabilities, infrastructure and technology created in a domestic extractive sector that can support diversification (Andreoni 2018).

For countries, these options can create pathways of vertical diversification into the upstream and downstream. Upstream diversification relates to the localization of the supply of goods and services required as inputs for commodity exploitation. Downstream diversification entails value addition through processing (adding value before becoming an input to another industry) and beneficiation, which is understood as the process of transformation in which the processed commodity is converted into an entirely different product, generally in unrelated manufacturing activity (Morris et al. 2018) Horizontal diversification towards unrelated and related sectors (often use similar technologies, infrastructure, inputs or production organization to the already established extractive sectors). Sector-specific policies to support these actions can be categorized according to the extent to which the intervention provides public goods (for example, targeted infrastructure) or the extent to which it seeks to influence the actions of economic agents (through subsidies, for instance) or vertical market interventions (VM). The latter are generally intended to be temporary and can be combined with monitoring initiatives to ensure that the policy works as intended.

POLICY INITIATIVES TO DEVELOP TRINIDAD AND TOBAGO MANUFACTURING EXPORTS

For more than fifty years, the Trinidad and Tobago government has implemented Economic, Legal, Soft and Meta Policies in an attempt to change the structure of Trinidad and Tobago's economy. Like most Caribbean economies, Trinidad and Tobago was an exporter of raw and semi-processed commodities for most of its colonial history (Payne and Sutton 2001). For example, in 1920, the local economy was dominated by the export of agricultural and mineral commodities (Mayers 2004).

By independence in 1962, the Trinidad and Tobago export position barely changed, with exports of Petroleum and Sugar accounting for over 70 per cent of revenues. In the early stages of development, vertical policies (Piore et al. 2001) targeting specific sectors were employed using financial and economic instruments to achieve growth. Later, Trinidad and Tobago's adoption of IMF terms and later World Trade Organization membership limited the ability of the government to explicitly target sectors. Some have argued that Trinidad and Tobago shifted from industrial to science and technology policy, incorporating countrywide "horizontal" policies to encourage R&D (Breznitz 2007) and "meta" policies such as foresighting (Rappert 1999). As an externally driven economy, Trinidad and Tobago was also subject to changes in commodity prices (Smith 2004). The commodity price dilemma has persisted. Attempts to shift to science and technology strategies and Foresighting perspectives have not always been smooth or successful.

The non-energy manufacturing sector was targeted for development using policies similar to those of governments in East Asia and Latin America. The origins of these frameworks were rooted in the particular historical circumstances that prevailed at the time: local and international economic conditions and social and political forces. Each policy era resulted in distinctive environments for firms, influencing both the nature and availability of resources. Firms face pressures to adapt in order to survive (Nelson and Winter 1982) or risk failure.

However, without corresponding interventions or measures to ensure performance (Rodrik et al. 1995), firms did not create the knowledge resources to support the optimization of imported technology or evolve new knowledge resources such as engaging in R&D. As a result, the intended outcomes of growing both vertically, to capital goods, and horizontally, into new industries were not achieved. In Trinidad and Tobago, government protectionist policies were part of the mix, but in the period of liberalization, retooling and technological infusion by firms and sectors did take place to meet the challenge of effective competitiveness.

TRINIDAD AND TOBAGO POLICY AND EXPORT ORGANIZATIONAL ADAPTATION

Organizational ecology theorists view environmental change as a source of variation, requiring firms to adopt new forms (Aldrich and Martinez 2001). Firms will experiment with various resource configurations before adopting one that is appropriate to the environment or selection, followed by a period of incremental change or retention (Tushman and Anderson 1986). Firms that do not match the environmental requirements face a higher possibility of failure (Hannan and Carroll 2003).

This process can result in both positive and negative adaptation by firms. A change from open trade to a more restricted approach, for example, can increase the opportunities available for domestic entrepreneurs by protecting the local market, enabling them to improve productivity to the point of exports. In many East Asian countries that have successfully diversified (Bruton 1998), trade protection measures supported knowledge resource creation: technological mastery and technological deepening. In technological mastery, firms build knowledge resources, enabling them to use imported technology. Firms that engage in technological deepening build systemic knowledge resources, including adaptation and innovation. In these countries, an industrial policy promoted an adaptation process, enabling the formation of knowledge resources that eventually supported internationalization.

However, import protection can also result in firms that increase their reliance on the domestic market (Thomas 1988). In this case, industrial policy supports a maladaptive process, supporting the creation of uncompetitive domestic firms. These characteristics may persist even when environmental conditions change as development processes may exhibit path dependency (Sokoloff and Engerman 2000). Actions, events and outcomes are not independent, and particular sequences may emerge over time to indicate an association among them (Araujo and Rezende 2003). History may become embedded in observable structures (North 1994) that may both enable and constrain change

These outcomes are known as spatial and temporal Path dependence (Ha˚kansson and Lundgren, 1997). Spatial path dependency is the persistence of resource structures over time that reflects the firms' origins and preserve historical development (North 1994). Temporal path dependency refers to the sequence of causation that exists in historical processes, which can result in distinct outcomes from a given set of initial conditions (Mahoney 2000).

INTERNATIONALIZATION OF TRINIDAD AND TOBAGO FIRMS

The external development of Trinidad and Tobago firms is an output of an organizational resource development process. Firms initially accumulate a resource profile and deploy them in external markets and further with export-specific investments. The composition of resource combinations, along with the modes by which they were adjusted, is influenced by changing environmental conditions. This process incorporated an adaptive evolutionary process, as domestic conditions changed along with assets externalized by previous entrants or co-evolution, resulting in adjustments in the range, mode, direction and rate of internationalization.

In the relatively closed import substitution policy era of the 1970s, organizations used firm-driven resource development strategies to engage in limited inward and outward internationalization. As the environment became more open, resource development strategies and internationalization outcomes became more varied. Using both firm and network strategies, firms increased the range and sophistication of inward internationalization, importing designs, products and services. Linked by relationships, Trinidad and Tobago firms have entered extra-regional markets as subcontractors, distributors and manufacturers. While networks have been identified as an internationalization-enabling mechanism (Chetty and Blankenburg Holm 2000), no research has identified their ability to constrain firm development. A firm's dependence on customer networks for market access can reduce its ability to act independently, a distinct liability in an uncertain export environment. Firms are unable to respond to changes in the domestic environment, such as labour availability or demand.

TRINIDAD AND TOBAGO FIRMS ADVOCACY AND ALIGNMENT

Organizations are active agents that influence and are influenced by the resource ecosystem, composed of "related businesses, customers and suppliers, as well as economic, cultural and legal institutions" (Middleton-Kelly 2003, 31). These firms can also self-organize to create their structures in order to influence economic outcomes. In this case, the TTMA, established in 1956, is an industry organization that works with the Government to support export industrialization. Due to transversal linkages from the energy sector, there are reduced rates for water and energy and a skilled and educated workforce. They share the goal of reducing domestic economic dependence on the extractive sector, but non-energy manufacturing sector exports have fallen TT$5.8b in 2014 to TT$3.3b in 2018. The sector also experiences persistent challenges:

1. Financial (late payment of VAT refunds, lack of capital and financing options unavailability of foreign exchange)
2. Infrastructure (inefficiencies with the Customs and Excise Division, delays at the ports and the associated costs, inefficient and burdensome government bureaucracy, time and costs required by testing labs)
3. Legal (competition from sub-standard imported goods, crime and theft)
4. Human resource (unavailability/cost of skilled labour, low labour productivity/poor work ethic
5. Informational (insufficient access to manufacturing data, lack of data analytics capability)

The TTMA has developed a strategy for increasing Trinidad and Tobago's manufacturing exports by 2025. Table 9.1 below compares the proposal of the TTMA with the current policy framework of the Trinidad and Tobago government (2019–23).

Table 9.1: Comparing Manufacturing Strategy

TTMA Strategy Pillars	TTMA Actions	Related Items from Trinidad and Tobago Policy 2019–2023 Framework
Public Sector Advocacy	1. Actively lobby the government and public sector agencies to transform trade facilitation and ease of doing business in Trinidad and Tobago (foreign exchange, VAT refunds – cash flow, developed labour pool, ports, CED, IRD, transportation, industrial relations)	1. Develop information systems and analytical methods to inform discussions on non-tariff measures when negotiating new, as well as monitoring the implementation of existing trade agreements
	Monitor successes and issues and actively communicate results to membership	
Private Advocacy Sector	3. Assist large and medium exporting manufacturers to advocate against trade facilitation obstacles	Address gaps in the Single Economic Window
	5. Actively monitor growth results of top 20 large and medium exporting manufacturers toward doubling exports by 2025 (80:20 rule)	Increasing the capacity of exporting MSMEs by establishing warehousing systems
	6. Create an SME Toolkit to address issues and provide support with solutions for members to achieve their growth objectives	

Table 9.1 continues on next page

Table 9.1: Comparing Manufacturing Strategy (*cont'd*)

TTMA Strategy Pillars	TTMA Actions	Related Items from Trinidad and Tobago Policy 2019–2023 Framework
Demand	1. Increase CARICOM penetration	Upgrade and modernize all components of the national standards infrastructure, consistent with the projects
	2. Expand exposure in diaspora markets 4. Improve quality standards in manufacturing Develop Trinidad and Tobago manufacturing brand for competitive target subsectors	Outlined in the Cabinet approved National Quality Policy Develop and publish the priority sectors for national diversification to allow prioritization of standardization of both goods and services in relevant sectors Amendment of the Standards Act and Food and Drugs Act to unify the consensus approach to standards development and address the issue of mandatory standards.
Supply	Promote increased use of local content in the manufacturing supply chain	
	Develop shared procurement, trade logistics and back-office support systems among exporters	
Infrastructure	1. Encourage private sector ownership of fit-for-purpose manufacturing infrastructure	Establish e-Commerce platform to provide producers and promotion facilities, secure and reliable payment facilities, and shipping arrangements in CARICOM.
	2. Encourage shared production and distribution mechanisms for MSMEs	
Labour	1. Improve skills, competencies and productivity across the manufacturing supply chains	2. Investment and development of cooperation initiatives in educating, training and retooling the labour force will also be ramped up. 3. The institution of mechanisms to encourage private sector investment in innovative production activities and fostering innovation and technology creation. 4. Expansion of ICT education and close collaboration with key stakeholders to determine the most appropriate modality for increasing the number of qualified persons available to drive innovations and anticipate skills requirements.
	2. Generate interest for careers in manufacturing	

Table 9.1 continues on next page

Table 9.1: Comparing Manufacturing Strategy (*cont'd*)

TTMA Strategy Pillars	TTMA Actions	Related Items from Trinidad and Tobago Policy 2019–2023 Framework
Technology/ Innovation	1. Actively promote the Increased use of technology throughout the manufacturing value chain	The GORTT will seek to develop a green industrial value chain that would include financing, marketing, regulation and R&D, among other factors.
	2. Promote increased investment in Research and Development	
	3. Encourage 'green' manufacturing across the sector	
Capital	1. Improve access to capital and financing	Increase the capitalization of the EXIMBank to supply affordable trade credit in support of export-centred projects in the distribution, services and creative sectors, across all modes of supply, where there currently is acute excess demand. Upgrade EXIMBank to meet the working capital and overseas investment requirements of exporters as well as their long-term loan requirements to finance new projects, expand, modernize or purchase new capital equipment powered by cutting edge technologies, or conduct research and development. Upgrade credit-guarantee schemes designed to create access to affordable credit by viable MSMEs involved in the trading sector, especially those prioritized by the GORTT. Promote development of the capital market as a basis for providing medium- and long-term financial products to MSMEs involved in the trading sector, including development of Junior and Micro stock exchanges. Undertake awareness-building programmes to upgrade the capacity of the MSMEs to utilize the financial and capital markets.

RETHINKING THE TRINIDAD AND TOBAGO EXPORT MANUFACTURING SYSTEM

> "Purposes are deduced from behaviour, not from rhetoric or stated goals."
> – Donella Meadows (Meadows 2008).

Systems have a function or a goal, which is the outcome that is being produced when the system is operational. 'Systems thinking' applies these ideas to complex issues and seeks to address the limitations of management methods that cannot address emergent phenomena such as path dependence, conflict, and multiple perspectives (Midgley and Pinzón 2013). This approach has been used to enable analysis and develop mutual understanding in public sector health, local development and infrastructure scenarios (Checkland and Winter 2006). Systems thinking enables the application of multiple perspectives to a challenge as a whole. Decomposition of a problem to component elements can work with simple challenges. Still, in complex issues, the entities, scenarios, and interactions evolve in real-time within domains, which can create unpredictable and unwanted outcomes (Cabrera and Cabrera 2015). A systems approach has been used to explore challenges that often occur in policymaking, such as interventions that work in controlled conditions but do not work in others, strategies that are not replicable across contexts and unintended consequences from strategy implementation (Midgley and Rajagopalan 2020).

The approach is valuable in examining manufacturing, which is a dynamic industry with internal and external interactions. In the broadest sense, this manufacturing system can be viewed as elements and relationships within a boundary (Checkland and Poulter 2020). There is some value in utilizing this approach where challenges arise from (1) poor stakeholder coordination, (2) multiple types of participants, (3) persistent problems despite attempts to address them and (4) solutions are not direct (Monat and Gannon, 2015). History matters as past interactions constrain future activities via path dependence. In the case of Trinidad and Tobago, the Trinidad and Tobago manufacturing system has evolved since independence to create regionally oriented and international exporters. Trinidad and Tobago's manufacturing exports present a dynamic problem since the formulation is unclear; there are multiple connected elements, along with participants with differing perspectives. To date, the challenge of increasing exports has evaded traditional approaches to resolving this issue. Economists have viewed this as a policy issue; the TTMA has viewed it as an infrastructural and financial issue, while internationalization researchers have identified gaps in firm capabilities.

At present, both the TTMA and Trinidad and Tobago policymakers present the non-energy sector as a monolith defined by what it is not (not energy). This conceptualization ignores the linkages with the energy sector, which provides lower energy costs and uses some of the same infrastructure, human capital, and operational and project techniques. Further, each subsector of the non-energy sector is embedded in a different global value chain, which has different drivers, governance structures, entry requirements and prospects and processes for upgrading. Finally, Tobago, as a separate island, faces very different logistical and resource constraints from Trinidad, and these constraints should be analysed separately.

The plans presented do not identify ambiguities and uncertainties. Historical data can help identify the range of possible outcomes from each initiative. Plans are simple interventions/effects. They need a systems perspective as both entities and scenarios are evolving in real-time, also creating new ambiguities and uncertainties in the cluster and related sector development. Past internationalization research has taken the environment as a fixed constraint (Zwart 1995). Heavy emphasis has been placed on identifying fixed export "barriers" at the country, firm and individual levels and identifying strategies to overcome them (Zou and Stan 1998). This research supports earlier work that developing countries are volatile resource environments, with changes in both the nature and volume of resources. Responding to this volatility required extensive reconfiguration, not mere adjustments. There was significant variation in the degree of munificence or the resources available activity. Two categories of munificence were identified, production and market munificence, based on their effect on firms' ability to produce or sell their outputs, respectively. Variation in both of these elements presented firms with a shifting resource landscape, an environment requiring extensive reconfiguration by firms. Over time, Trinidad and Tobago firms evolved from property-led to knowledge-led resource portfolios, adjusting their characteristics in response to changing environmental conditions, moving from protected domestic manufacturers to leveraging external resources to serve regional and international markets.

There was also an element of co-evolution between firm characteristics and country manufacturing experience. As organizations evolved, specific internal processes became externalized; that is, they eliminated resources not required for success in the new environment. These resources became available for new entrants to build firm capabilities. Thus, each new group of entrants were also influenced by previous entrants in a feedback or co-evolutionary process.

This indicates a need to rethink the boundaries, interactions, and participants in the Trinidad and Tobago export manufacturing system. Systems thinking encourages the development of inter-organizational responses to complex challenges as it encourages formal examination of the domains of issues that can be ignored in analytical approaches (Ison and Straw 2020).

RETHINKING SYSTEM BOUNDARIES

Systems boundaries are defined as interior (all components in the system and exterior (environment to which the system belongs) elements. Definitions of the boundaries of a problem is critical for examining it as it determines how the problem is specified, how improvement is evaluated, which stakeholders are important and what knowledge is considered relevant. The boundaries of the existing policy solutions and advocacy (table 9.1) have to be expanded to incorporate the characteristics of global value chains. This implies a change in organizational and infrastructural approaches.

TTMA have defined their scope of action to participation organizations, whereas the policy boundary of government speaks to a regional/ international context. A global body chain approach would require an expansion of policy boundaries to incorporate the role of other production and service facilities that serve the same markets as we do and further address the structural and infrastructure requirements of entering and sustaining the presence in these areas, which imply a process of measuring monitoring and upgrading organizational learning.

The persistent issues of finance, operations, human resources, infrastructure, access to working capital and foreign exchange have existed since before Trinidad and Tobago's independence. For Trinidad and Tobago manufacturers, there is a need to align their purposes with those of policymakers and jointly expand the boundaries of this problem. Defining the future of Trinidad and Tobago's manufacturing processes is not merely the creation of a set of targeted policy interventions; it is also not simply a process of increased marketing and promotion by organizations.

Other countries have also attempted to expand the boundaries of their international engagement. Notably, Global Ireland 2025 was launched in 2018 as an integrated government approach to double the global footprint of Ireland in diplomacy, culture, business and tourism. These domains are seen as connected and mutually reinforcing.

This approach seeks to expand the boundaries to export development as part of the Irelands' engagement in multiple areas. As such, relationships formed in one area could be leveraged to provide access in another. This strategy also explicitly recognizes the role of the diaspora as promoters for Global Ireland.

RETHINKING INTERACTIONS IN GLOBAL VALUE CHAINS

The low participation of the Caribbean in Global value chains has been identified as a challenge since the 1960s. There has been no known attempt, however, to map the nature of Trinidad and Tobago's engagement with global supply chains to identify systemic failings. While the term "value chain" describes the entire process of production and delivery of an offering for a customer, a global value chain engages in production activities across multiple countries (Gereffi 2001). Participation in global value chains (GVC) tends to require a high level of specialization to meet customers' cost and delivery requirements. Previous attempts to address this issue via trade agreements and regionalization of production have, to date, failed to resolve the issue.

The current approach that seeks to deploy industrial restructuring (table 9.1) to enable exporters to adopt technologies ignores the characteristics of global value chains. Producer-driven global value chains are ones in which capital-intensive manufacturers own or control multiple levels of a hieratically organized production system. Buyer-driven chains are less structured networks of suppliers and retailers who create items under a single brand or label (Gereffi 2001). The issue of governance in these structures has been further refined in the Global Value Chain research network (see www.

globalvaluechain.org). to incorporate dimensions of transaction complexity, communication processes and supplier capabilities (Gereffi, Humphrey and Sturgeon 2005). The outcome is a typology of GVS as shown that ranges from the market (price-focused, simple interactions, available supply base) to the hierarchy (value-focused, complex interactions from weak/poor supply base). What this systems approach advocates is a movement beyond individual firm strategy and its connectivity with government policy objectives to a more holistic government/business approach involving an integrated national strategy, yoking together complementarities and mutually reinforcing synergies to support a broader export growth result.

The engagement with global value chains in itself is not a single issue. Actually, it has technological, Infrastructure, Human resource and policy interactions, which result in the emergent problem of low participation in global value chains. From a systems environment perspective, the characteristics of the supply chains, global and otherwise, in countries outside of the Caribbean, which Trinidad and Tobago wishes to participate in, are fundamentally different to traditional service supply chains. The latter link suppliers and customers of intermediaries in a very straightforward linear or consecutive plan where one person gets inputs, and it provides outputs. Organizations do not need to integrate processes and simply need to align transactions so one organization delivers at the time that the other person requires it. Disputes can be addressed internally using existing commercial procurement approaches. The limitation of this model is that information and materials do not flow at the rate that happens, and since demand can be unpredictable, this can result in misallocation.

The changing requirements of internationalization indicate that firms that wish to participate in global supply chains need to undergo a digital transformation to meet emerging oversight requirements. Organizations in developed countries are frequently moving towards more complex supply chains with real-time data flow. While these systems are visible in business-to-consumer systems such as Amazon, 90 per cent of digital transactions are between businesses. For these organizations, electronic data interchange can require the application of specific data information acquisition technologies such as radio frequency identification and the Internet of Things. These tools provide real-time information so that production can be adjusted to real-time demand as closely as possible. Data analytics takes a much more decisive role in delivering real-time insights into customer demand, which guides other participants in the supply chain. Algorithms are used not just to provide indicators but to predict, which helps create a robust and responsive supply chain that drives areas such as maintenance. Digital transformation encourages the automation of traditional logistics activities, as well as the use of robotic transportation and digital measuring systems. These systems need to be applied in order to not just join but also participate as long-term partners in global supply chains and contribute to strategies such as customer knowledge or vendor management.

Both TTMA and Trinidad and Tobago policymakers need to align their efforts in order to create an integrated perspective on export development that acknowledges current realities. The process can adopt a systems-based perspective to gain a common understanding of the dimensions and identify joint quantitative indicators from both a macro (policy) and micro (organizational level). The Trinidad and Tobago government and TTMA need to create an environment that includes joint co-creation of business and technical capabilities. Current strategies do not identify the difference between final, desired outcomes and intermediate benefits, which can help provide oversight. For manufacturing firms, intermediate benefits are the actual operational improvements as a result of policy interventions or organizational development activities, which can be measured quantitatively. Intermediate benefits can also be subclassified into Technical and Business Capabilities. Technical capabilities are new operational tools or techniques that create changes in ways of working, processes, or interactions in organizations (for example, the ability to integrate all customer communication data). Business capabilities focus on the value created by applying technical capabilities, such as the increased revenue from the improved ability to communicate with customers, which were created by the technical capability. It is not yet known if TTMA or the Trinidad and Tobago government have identified possible benchmarks for exporters in order to monitor the improved organizational performance from the implementation of these initiatives.

This is particularly important in the emerging category of global value chain requirements for exporters that result from Climate change legislations such as Net Zero in the UK and the Green New Deal in the United States. Exporters will be required to demonstrate efforts to reduce the carbon emissions of production and distribution. This suggests that for Trinidad and Tobago firms, new technical capabilities in the form of data collection and analysis have to be developed in order to obtain business value from exports. Failing that, the existing advantage of Trinidad and Tobago firms (low-cost energy) can become a weakness when low-cost energy is subjected to increasing carbon taxes from customers.

RETHINKING SYSTEMS PARTICIPANTS

Human capital has remained a persistent challenge in Trinidad and Tobago's export development. The aim of the current strategy to develop a skilled and creative workforce at competitive costs to support penetration into foreign markets, while laudable, has been attempted in many guises before. The challenge has been framed by both the TTMA and the Trinidad and Tobago government as resolving gaps in existing capacities. The demands of evolving global supply chains, however, require rethinking how manufacturing is done as a digitally integrated activity. This suggests the creation of new types of workers who are comfortable with data analytics that can link internal production activities to customer demand requirements. An important point to note is that improvement in manufacturing may reduce employment as the requirements of high-skill manufacturing require more capital and less labour. This considers articulated positions by TTMA as well as the government of Trinidad and Tobago for the doubling of exports.

Given the time frame within which such advances need to be achieved (2025), it is unlikely that the education system will make the required changes to respond to this fundamental rethinking of manufacturing employment. Further, no extant institution has been dedicated to developing these required individuals, suggesting that existing enterprises will have to adapt their offerings. Based on the time frame for organizations to create validated courses (three to five years), it may not be possible to have the required individuals before the strategy period has expired.

In addition to its internal production capacity, Trinidad and Tobago needs to increase its market data intelligence collection rate. Diaspora relationships play a critical role in the development of firms providing foreign market knowledge. The TTMA/Trinidad and Tobago government should establish a diaspora council (possible working name "Global TT") to provide independent consumer intelligence on market trends. This approach has been utilized by other export-oriented economies such as Ireland. The real-time nature of digitally enabled businesses requires an increased market data collection and analysis rate. Similar to Ireland, Trinidad and Tobago has a dispersed professional diaspora in influential markets (United States, United Kingdom and Canada), and they can be recruited to provide information on their purchases, interests, and market trends. Particular attention should be paid to professionals who work in global value chains, which are growth opportunities for Trinidad and Tobago products. These individuals can act as product ambassadors for Trinidad and Tobago products, providing introductions and identifying specific market access requirements.

REFERENCES

Aldrich, H., and M.E. Martinez. 2001. "Many Are Called but Few Are Chosen: An Evolutionary Perspective for the Study of Entrepreneurship." *Entrepreneurship Theory and Practice* 25 (4): 41–56.

Andreoni, A. 2018. "The Architecture and Dynamics of Industrial Ecosystems: Diversification and Innovative Industrial Renewal in Emilia Romagna." *Cambridge Journal of Economics* 42 (6): 1613–42.

Araujo, L., and S. Rezende. 2003. "Path Dependence, MNCS and the Internationalisation Process: A Relational Approach." *International Business Review* 12 (6): 719–37.

Breznitz, D. 2007. "Industrial R&D as a National Policy: Horizontal Technology Policies and Industry-state Co-evolution in the Growth of the Israeli Software Industry." *Research Policy* 36 (9): 1465–82.

Bruton, H.J. 1998. "A Reconsideration of Import Substitution." *Journal of Economic Literature* 36 (2): 903–36.

Cabrera, D., and L. Cabrera. 2015. *Systems Thinking Made Simple*. New York: Plectica Publishing.

Checkland, P., and J. Poulter. 2020. *Soft Systems Methodology. Systems Approaches to Making Change: A Practical Guide*. London: Springer.

Checkland, P. and Winter, M., 2006. "Process and Content: Two Ways of Using SSM." *Journal of the Operational Research Society* 57 (12): 1435–441.

Chetty, S., and D. Blankenburg Holm. 2000. "Internationalisation of Small to Medium-sized Manufacturing Firms: A Network Approach." *International Business Review* 9 (1): 77–93.

Hannan, M.T., and G.R. Carroll. 2003. "Cascading Organizational Change." *Organization Science* 14 (5): 463–82.

Ha˚kansson, H., and A. Lundgren. 1997. "Paths in Time and Space: Path Dependence in Industrial Networks." In *Evolutionary Economics and Path Dependence*, edited by L. Magnusson and J. Ottosson, 119–37. Cheltenham: Edward Elgar.

Hirschman, A.O. 1981. *Essays in Trespassing: Economics to Politics and Beyond*. Cambridge: Cambridge University Press.

Ison, R., and E. Straw. 2020. *The Hidden Power of Systems Thinking: Governance in a Climate Emergency*. Abingdon: Routledge.

Mahoney, J. 2000. Path Dependence in Historical Sociology." *Theory and Society* 29 (4): 507–48.

Meadows, D.H. 2008. *Thinking in Systems: A Primer*. Chelsea: Green Publishing.

Midgley, G. and Pinzón, L.A., 2013. "Systemic Mediation: Moral Reasoning and Boundaries of Concern." *Systems Research and Behavioral Science* 30 (5): 607–32.

Midgley, G., and R. Rajagopalan. 2020. Critical systems thinking, systemic intervention, and beyond. Handbook of systems sciences, pp. 1–51.

Monat, J.P., and T.F. Gannon. 2015. "What Is Systems Thinking? A Review of Selected Literature Plus Recommendations." *American Journal of Systems Science* 4 (1): 11–26.

Navarro, J.C., J.M. Benavente, and G. Crespi. 2016. "The New Imperative of Innovation: Policy Perspectives for Latin America and the Caribbean." Inter-American Development Bank. https://publications. iadb. org/en/handle/11319/7417.

North, D.C. 1994. "Economic Performance Through Time." *American Economic Review* 84 (3): 359–68.

Payne, A., and P. Sutton. 2001. Dr Eric Williams and the National Development State in Trinidad and Tobago. In *Charting Caribbean Development*, vol. 1, edited by A. Payne and P. Sutton, 30–64. London: Macmillan Education.

Piore, M.J., J.S. Neil, and B.B. Paul. 2001. "Industrial Policy." In *International Encyclopaedia of the Social and Behavioural Sciences* (1st ed. pp. 7333–7338). Pergamon.

Rappert, B. 1999. "Rationalising the Future? Foresight in Science and Technology Policy Co-ordination." *Futures* 31(6): 527–45.

Rodrik, D., G. Grossman, and V. Norman. 1995. "Getting Interventions Right: How South Korea and Taiwan Grew Rich." *Economic Policy* 10 (20): 55–107.

Smith, B. 2004. "Oil Wealth and Regime Survival in the Developing World, 1960–1999." *American Journal of Political Science* 48 (2): 232–46.

Sokoloff, K.L., and S.L. Engerman. 2000. "History Lessons: Institutions, Factors Endowments, and Paths of Development in the New World." Journal of Economic Perspectives 14(3): 217–32.

Thomas, C.Y. 1988. *The Poor and the Powerless: Economic Policy and Change in the Caribbean*. London: Latin American Bureau.

Tushman, M.L., and P. Anderson. 1986. "Technological Discontinuities and Organisational Environments." *Administrative Science Quarterly* 31(3): 439–65.

[CHAPTER 10]

A Tale of Two Islands

Economic Development in Tobago and Trinidad

VANUS JAMES, CARLOS HAZEL AND KENNETH BISSOON

INTRODUCTION

This chapter examines the comparative labour market conditions in Tobago and Trinidad, focusing on trends in labour productivity and GDP per capita. GDP per capita serves as a key indicator of the living standards an economy can sustain, while labour productivity and the overall level of economic development are primary drivers of this measure. As Lewis (1954) suggests, to understand how the benefits of development are spread and how they are created, it is important to examine how much the economy depends on the output of workers with little capital investment, often linked to low levels of education. As noted by Best (1968) and Best and Levitt (1969), a sign of undercapitalization is that the economy relies heavily on external forces, including a strong dependence on imported inputs for production. These inputs range from capital and skills directly used in production to consumer goods necessary for sustaining the workforce. This chapter presents clear evidence of significant undereducation within the labour force, particularly in Tobago. It also demonstrates that the national economy has been driven by external factors, a condition that has persisted from 1970 to 2022. The key to addressing these conditions lies in increasing labour productivity growth through the expansion of capital production as a share of economic output and the growth of capital stock per worker. This chapter documents the empirical relationship between labour productivity and living standards that has been evident since 1970. It also proposes an explanatory theory, linking the average education level of workers to living standards, along with policies aimed at accelerating development in both Tobago and Trinidad.

Even though informed by earlier theories, especially Lewis (1954, 1955), Best (1968), Best and Levitt (1969, 2009) and Best and St Cyr (2012), the data analysis and theory, and much of the implied policies, have not been previously formulated elsewhere. So the chapter makes three substantive contributions to the existing literature. The first is a previously undocumented evidence-based comparison of the education of workers and related recent trends in productivity and GDP per capita of the economies of Tobago and Trinidad. The second is compelling econometric evidence of external propulsion of the economy. The third contribution is a theoretical explanation of how, through its influence on the wage rate and the real exchange rate, the level of education of workers influences the dynamic nexus of the rate of profit, savings, investment, prices and productivity, which causes growth of GDP per capita.

The chapter contains five other sections. Using data published by the Central Statistical Office (CSO) and other international sources, section 2 documents the current labour market conditions in terms of standard indicators, such as the rate of employment and unemployment, as well as indicators, such as the education of employed and unemployed workers, types of occupations, types of jobs and their industry suppliers, the role of government, the income outturns, especially the average wage. Section 3 provides econometric evidence that the economy is still externally propelled. Section 4 provides comparative data on the relationship between productivity and GDP per capita for both islands as well as evidence of the causal relationship that has existed between productivity and GDP per capita from 1970 to 2022. Section 5 sets out the generalized analysis of the average level of education and the development process implied by the evidence adduced in sections 2 and 3. Section 6 provides a broad summary of the policies implied by the analytical framework and empirical evidence.

LABOUR MARKET CONDITIONS, LABOUR PRODUCTIVITY AND GDP PER CAPITA

This section provides comparative evidence of the current education levels of the labour force in Tobago and Trinidad, along with data on recent trends in the associated levels of labour productivity and GDP per capita. To aid interpretation from a development perspective, the official guideline for the minimum standard of success in Trinidad and Tobago's school system is provided, along with the skill levels and performance capacities of various levels of education defined by the ILO (2012). The data on education cover 2022 and the first two quarters of 2023 (2023Q1&2). The data are presented in a way that allows for the possibility of seasonal effects in 2023Q1&2 relative to the average for 2022, partly to emphasize some of the differences in the underlying behaviour of the two island economies.

Table 10.1 reports comparative data on the general state of the labour markets of Tobago and Trinidad. Of the 594,600 persons in the national labour market in 2022, 32,000 or 5 per cent lived in Tobago, and 562,600 or 95 per cent lived in Trinidad. By the end of the second quarter of 2023 (2023Q2), the national labour force had *increased* by 1.3 per cent to 602,500, while the labour force in Tobago had *decreased* by 1 per cent to 31,700, and the labour force in Trinidad had increased by 1.5 per cent to 570,800.

In 2022, Tobago supplied 6 per cent of the total employment (31,200), and Trinidad supplied 94 per cent (534,100). The national employment rate was 95 per cent, similar to that in Trinidad. The employment rate in Tobago was 98 per cent. At the end of 2023Q2, total employment in Tobago was 31,000, a loss of two hundred or just under 1 per cent, and Tobago's share of total employment had declined to 5 per cent. On the other hand, total employment in Trinidad increased by 2.2 per cent to 545,700, corresponding to an increase in the island's share to 95 per cent. At the end of 2023Q2, the national employment rate had increased modestly to 95.72 per cent of the labour force, that of Tobago had remained virtually the same at 98 per cent, and that of Trinidad had increased to 95.6 per cent. Further, in 2022, 3 per cent of the nation's unemployed lived in Tobago, and 97 per cent lived in Trinidad. That distribution was the same at the end of 2023Q2.

The data, especially the decline in the labour force and the number of employees in Tobago, reflect the fact that while Tobago was losing new jobs, Trinidad was creating new jobs. Accordingly, in the absence of new job creation in Tobago, people who cannot find employment tend to either withdraw from the labour force or migrate to Trinidad and elsewhere to seek better job prospects.

To be correctly interpreted from a development perspective, the data in table 10.1 ought to be complemented by statistics on the education and skills of workers, which are directly related to the capitalization of work, especially in terms of materials, tools and equipment that can be used, and the outputs produced (ILO 2012, 11). These are presented below and assessed against two sets of standards. One is the national minimum standard set for a well-educated worker, which is at least five subject passes at the "Ordinary" (CSEC) level, preferably including passes in English and Mathematics. Achievement of this standard also qualifies a person to matriculate to more advanced studies at the tertiary level. The other is the set of skill levels underlying the International Standard Classification of Occupations, 2008 (ISCO-08) as defined by ILO (2012). Both standards are used by the CSO in its survey and reporting on the available and employed labour force of Trinidad and Tobago.

ILO (2012: 11) defines a skill as "the ability to carry out the tasks and duties of a given job," where a job is "a set of tasks and duties performed, or meant to be performed, by one person, including for an employer or in self-employment". An occupation is defined as "a set of jobs whose main tasks and duties are characterized by a high degree of similarity". In ISCO-08, a skill has two basic dimensions:

Table 10.1: Labour Market Basics, 00's

Year		LF	Island %	Emp	Island %	Emp Rate	Unempl'd	Island %
2022	T&T	5,946		5,653		95.10%	293	
	lobago	320	5%	312	6%	97.50%	8	3%
	Trinidad	5,626	95%	5,341	94%	94.90%	285	97%
2023 Q1&Q2	T&I	6025		5767		95.72%	258	
	Tobago	317	5%	310	5%	97.79%	7	3%
	Trinidad	5708	95%	5457	95%	95.60%	251	97%

Source: CSO

1. Skill level – defined as a function of the complexity and range of tasks to be performed in an occupation and measured practically in terms of (i) the nature of the work performed in an occupation, (ii) the level of formal education required for competent performance of the tasks and duties involved; and (iii) the amount of informal on-the-job training and/or previous experience in a related occupation required for competent performance of the tasks or duties.
2. Skill specialization – assessed in terms of (i) the field of knowledge required, (ii) the tools and machinery used, (iii) the materials worked on or with, and (iv) the kinds of products and services produced.

ISCO-08 identifies four levels of skills (ILO 2012, 12–13):

1. Skill level 1 is used in occupations that involve performance of simple and routine physical or manual tasks and typically require primary or basic secondary education, sometimes complemented by minimal on-the-job training. Level 1 skills can use handheld tools, such as shovels, and simple electrical equipment, such as vacuum cleaners.
2. Skill level 2 is used in occupations that typically involve the performance of tasks and duties that require the ability to read and follow instructions, prepare records of work completed, and accurately perform simple arithmetical calculations. Most occupations at this level require successful completion of basic secondary education as evidenced by the national standard five O-level (CSEC) passes, sometimes complemented by on-the-job training and experience. Level 2 skills can operate general machinery and electronic equipment, drive vehicles, maintain and repair electrical and mechanical equipment, and manipulate, order or store information.
3. Skill level 3 is used in occupations that involve the performance of complex technical and practical tasks that require mastery of an extensive body of factual, technical and procedural knowledge in a specialized field and the ability to share, communicate and apply such knowledge. The knowledge and skills required for competent performance of these tasks are generally obtained from one to three years of tertiary education following successful completion of secondary education. Advanced and complex physical and information capital is usually needed for related tasks, such as medical radiographic and laboratory equipment, various

forms of data, including legal data, and broadcasting and recording equipment.

4. Skill level 4 is used in occupations that involve the performance of tasks that require complex problem-solving, decision-making and creativity/innovation based on mastery of an extensive body of theoretical and factual knowledge in a specialized field. The associated tasks usually involve analysis and research to extend the body of human knowledge in a specific field, sharing and communicating knowledge and results to others, and application to design of advanced problem-solving structures, machinery, equipment, institutions and processes for construction and production (problem-solving capital). Much of this work is usually done in collaboration with, or supervision of, persons having level 3 skills. The knowledge and skills required for competent performance of level 4 tasks are typically acquired in three to six years of tertiary education, leading to a first degree or higher, and often complemented by extensive specialized training.

These assessment standards are linked directly to the development process, including the development of the capacity to adapt rapidly and competitively to ongoing technical change in other economies. It has been shown by James and Hamilton (2022) that, in general, the growth of a country's GDP per capita is caused by simultaneous productivity-enhancing improvement of institutions, growth of the capital share of GDP, and growth of the capacity to innovate and introduce winning solutions to problems thrown up by local and global markets. Such a development process relies primarily on increasing success in undertaking the tasks of (i) continuous extension of the frontiers of theoretical and factual knowledge in specific fields, (ii) use of such knowledge to undertake complex problem-solving and institutional upgrade for decision-making, and (iii) application of the knowledge to design problem-solving capital in the sense of structures, machinery and processes for construction and production. Competent execution of these tasks enables productivity growth and successful competition for development opportunities in the global space, and they all rely on the increasing availability of workers with ISCO-08 level 3 and level 4 skills.

Education Characteristics of the Labour Force

The data in tables 10.2 and 10.3 report the education characteristics of the labour force in both islands. The data show that at the end of 2022, about 12 per cent of the national labour force received no better than primary education. Another 25.4 per cent received secondary education with some supplementary training but passed no subjects. By the end of 2023Q2, the share with no better than primary education had increased to about 15 per cent. The share with only secondary exposure plus training increased marginally to 25.8 per cent. These are workers with level 1 skills, as defined by ILO (2012). So, overall, at the end of 2023Q2, about 40 per cent of the national labour force was too severely undereducated to support the ISCO-08 level 4 occupations that undertake the development of high-technology (problem-solving) capital production in the national production system, a significant increase from 37.4 per cent at the end of 2022.

At the end of 2022, 18.4 per cent of the national labour force had received secondary education, with one to four (CSEC-level) passes, some supplemented by additional training. A further 17.9 per cent had received secondary education with five or more (CSEC-level) passes, sometimes supplemented by further training. By the end of 2023Q2, the share with secondary education and one to four CSEC-level passes plus training was still at 18.3 per cent, and a slightly smaller share of 17.4 per cent had received secondary education with five or more CSEC-level passes, some with additional training. In general, by the end of 2023Q2, about 36.0 per cent of the labour force had received reasonable education, marginally down from the 36.3 per cent at the end of 2022. Such workers could undertake work requiring ILO-defined level 2 skills, such as clerical work, service and sales work, craft and related work, and work in plant and machinery assembly and operation. Overall, then, by the end of 2023Q2, 76 per cent of the national workforce still had insufficient knowledge and skills to undertake the level 3 and level 4 tasks of developing the advanced capital output and institutions that could bring winning solutions to problems thrown up in local and export markets and drive national economic diversification and development.

At the end of 2022, approximately 139,900 persons or 24 per cent of the national labour force had tertiary training, resulting in certificates, diplomas, and university degrees. By the end of 2023Q2, this number had declined somewhat to 130,000 or about 22 per cent of the labour force. The lack of growth in the numbers of such workers, even considering seasonal variation, should be a matter of concern to policymakers since this is the group with ILO-defined level 3 and 4 education and training that embodies much of the national capacity to lead the upgrade of governance, the development of high-tech capital service industries, and the innovation process, all of which underlie productivity growth.

At the end of 2022, Tobago accounted for 5.4 per cent of the labour force, but 16.4 per cent of those with better than primary standard 4 education. At the end of 2023Q2, Tobago's share of the labour force was 5.3 per cent, and the share of the labour force with primary standard 4 education had declined to about 14 per cent. At the end of 2022, this group accounted for 15.6 per cent of Tobago's workforce, compared to only 4.5 per cent of Trinidad's. However, by the end of 2023Q2, the group accounted for 16.7 per cent of Tobago's workforce, compared to 5.8 per cent in Trinidad. It is also interesting that Tobago accounted for only 3.6 per cent of persons without secondary subjects who received additional training for work. This underrepresentation also meant that in 2022 and 2023Q2, only 10.3 per cent and 11 per cent, respectively, of Tobago's workforce got access to additional training to supplement underachievement in secondary school, compared to 15.8 per cent and 16.1 per cent of Trinidad's workforce in corresponding periods.

At the end of 2023Q2, Tobago also accounted for 5,100 or 14.8 per cent of nationals with only 1–4 CSEC-level secondary passes, up substantially from 3,300 or 9.5 per cent at the end of 2022. At the end of 2023Q2, this group accounted for 16.1 per cent of Tobago's workforce, up sharply from 10.3 per cent at the end of 2022. The comparable share of Trinidad's workforce was 5.1 per cent at the end of 2023Q2, down somewhat from 5.6 per cent at the end of 2022. On the other hand, the workforce of each island was broadly similar in terms of the shares of such graduates with supplementary training in the workforce. Tobago accounted for 4,200 or 5.7 per cent of the national pool in 2022, falling to 3,600 or 4.8 per cent of the national pool at the end of 2023Q2. The group accounted for 11.4 per cent of Tobago's labour force at the end of 2023Q2, down from 13.1 per cent in 2022. The comparable share for Trinidad was 12.6 per cent at the end of 2023Q2, up marginally from 12.4 per cent in 2022.

Tobago's underrepresentation among workers with more than five secondary passes, sometimes including A-level passes plus work-specific training, also contrasts sharply with Trinidad's. Tobago's workforce had 3,200 or only 4.2 per cent of the national supply of such graduates at the end of 2022, falling to 2,800 or 3.5 per cent at the end of 2023Q2. Correspondingly, at the end of 2022, about 10 per cent of Tobago's workforce had such level 2 qualifications, falling to 8.3 per cent in 2023Q2. The corresponding estimates for Trinidad were 13 per cent of its labour force at the end of 2022, increasing to 13.5 per cent at the end of 2023Q2. To the extent that the 2023Q1&2 data reflect seasonal effects, they clearly reflect different seasonal forces.

As we have seen, the development of an economy depends on the growth of its capacity to undertake competently the tasks that lead to the production of advanced problem-solving capital and the development of supportive institutions, and hence the growth of the number of workers with level 3&4 skills. It is therefore striking that in 2023Q2, there were only 4,200 or 3.2 per cent of tertiary graduates with diplomas, certificates, and university degrees in Tobago's workforce, down sharply from 6,300 or 4.5 per cent of the national pool at the end of 2022. This translated to only about 13.2 per cent of Tobago's workforce in 2023Q2, down sharply from 20 per cent at the end of 2022. The corresponding estimates for Trinidad were 22 per cent at the end of 2023Q2, down significantly from 24 per cent at the end of 2022. In both islands, some of the decline in numbers was likely the effect of significant seasonal variation, including the result of the emigration of skilled workers.

Even considering seasonal variation, the warranted conclusion is that while the labour force in Trinidad is severely undereducated relative to the needs of a shift to producing high-technology problem-solving capital services, the degree of undereducation is far higher in Tobago.

The data on the education of the employed and unemployed in tables 10.4 and 10.5 also tell a compelling corresponding tale of the undereducation of workers in both islands.

In Tobago, by the end of 2023Q2, a very high share, 73 per cent, of persons with jobs were inadequately educated, relying on one to four secondary (CSEC-level) passes plus training or less. Moreover, this was a sharp increase from 62 per cent at the end of 2022. The corresponding figures for Trinidad were 58 per cent by the end of 2023Q2, up from 55 per cent at the end of

Table 10.2: Education Characteristics of the Labour Force, 2022

	T&T (00's)	Share	Tobago (00's)	Share of Tobago	Trinidad (00's)	Share of Trinidad	Tobago Share of National
Labour Force	5946		320		5626		5.4%
No education (including with training and kindergarten)	15	0.3%	3	0.9%	12	0.2%	20.0%
Primary<Standard 5	21	0.3%	3	0.9%	18	0.3%	14.5%
Primary >Standard 4	305	5.1%	50	15.6%	255	4.5%	16.4%
Primary with training	380	6.4%	19	5.9%	361	6.4%	5.0%
Secondary, no subjects	589	9.9%	30	9.4%	559	9.9%	5.1%
Secondary, no subjects plus training	923	15.5%	33	10.3%	890	15.8%	3.6%
Secondary, 1–4 subjects	348	5.9%	33	10.3%	315	5.6%	9.5%
Secondary, 1–4 subjects plus training	742	12.5%	42	13.1%	700	12.4%	5.7%
Secondary, 5 or more subjects	300	5.0%	26	8.1%	274	4.9%	8.7%
Secondary, 5 or more plus training	764	12.9%	32	10.0%	732	13.0%	4.2%
University education, no degree	104	1.7%	0	0.0%	104	1.8%	0.0%
University degree/diploma/certificate	1399	23.5%	63	19.7%	1336	23.7%	4.5%
Educated in a foreign country	60	1.0%	5	1.6%	55	1.0%	8.3%

Source: CSO

Table 10.3: Education Characteristics of the Labour Force, 2023Q1/2

	T&T (00's)	Share	Tobago (00's)	Share of Tobago	Trinidad (00's)	Share of Trinidad	Tobago Share of National
Labour Force	6025		317		5708		5.26%
No education (including with training and kindergarten)	15	0.25%	0	0.00%	15	0.26%	0.00%
Primary<Standard 5	35	0.58%	0	0.00%	35	0.61%	0.00%
Primary >Standard 4	383	6.36%	53	16.72%	330	5.78%	13.84%
Primary with training	446	7.40%	15	4.73%	431	7.55%	3.36%
Secondary, no subjects	598	9.90%	41	12.93%	557	9.76%	6.86%
Secondary, no subjects plus training	956	15.87%	35	11.04%	921	16.14%	3.66%
Secondary, 1–4 subjects	344	5.71%	51	16.09%	293	5.13%	14.83%
Secondary, 1–4 subjects plus training	756	12.55%	36	11.36%	720	12.61%	4.76%
Secondary, 5 or more subjects	270	4.48%	16	5.05%	254	4.45%	5.93%
Secondary, 5 or more plus training	799	13.26%	28	8.83%	771	13.51%	3.50%
University education, no degree	98	1.63%	0	0.00%	98	1.72%	0.00%
University degree/diploma/certificate	1300	21.58%	42	13.25%	1258	22.04%	3.23%
Educated in a foreign country	25	0.41%	0	0.00%	25	0.44%	0.00%

Source: CSO

Table 10.4: Education Characteristics of the Employed and Unemployed, 2022

	Tobago				Trinidad				T&T			
	Empl'd (00's)	Share	Unemp (00's)	Share	Empl'd (00's)	Share	Unemp (00's)	Share	Empl'd (00's)	Share	Unemp (00's)	Share
All Workers	**322**		**16**		**5336**		**282**		**5708**		**298**	
No education (plus training and kindergarten)	3	0.9%	0	0.0%	12	0.2%	0	0.0%	15	0.3%	0	0.0%
Primary < Standard 5	3	0.9%	0	0.0%	18	0.3%	0	0.0%	21	0.4%	0	0.0%
Primary > Standard 4	47	14.6%	3	18.8%	245	4.6%	12	4.3%	292	5.1%	15	5.0%
Primary with training	15	4.7%	4	25.0%	347	6.5%	15	5.3%	362	6.3%	19	6.4%
Secondary no subjects	27	8.4%	3	18.8%	522	9.8%	38	13.5%	549	9.6%	41	13.8%
Secondary no subjects plus training	30	9.3%	3	18.8%	849	15.9%	41	14.5%	879	15.4%	44	14.8%
Secondary, 1–4 subjects	33	10.2%	0	0.0%	294	5.5%	21	7.4%	327	5.7%	21	7.0%
Secondary 1–4 subjects plus training	41	12.7%	0	0.0%	663	12.4%	38	13.5%	704	12.3%	38	12.8%
Secondary, 5 or more subjects	26	8.1%	0	0.0%	255	4.8%	19	6.7%	281	4.9%	19	6.4%
Secondary 5 or more subjects plus training	32	9.9%	0	0.0%	690	12.9%	42	14.9%	772	13.5%	42	14.1%
University education, no degree	0	0.0%	0	0.0%	97	1.8%	9	3.2%	97	1.7%	9	3.0%
University degree/diploma/certificate	60	18.6%	3	18.8%	1289	24.2%	47	16.7%	1349	23.6%	50	16.8%
Educated in a foreign country	5	1.6%	0	0.0%	55	1.0%	0	0.0%	60	1.1%	0	0.0%

Source: CSO

Table 10.5: Education Characteristics of the Employed and Unemployed, 2023Q2

	Tobago				Trinidad				T&T			
	Empl'd (00's)	Share	Unemp (00's)	Share	Empl'd (00's)	Share	Unemp (00's)	Share	Empl'd (00's)	Share	Unemp (00's)	Share
All Workers	310		10		5457		248		5767		258	
No education (plus training and kindergarten)	0	0.0%	0	0.0%	15	0.27%	0	0.00%	15	0.3%	0	0.0%
Primary < Standard 5	0	0.0%	0	0.0%	29	0.53%	5	2.02%	29	0.5%	5	1.9%
Primary > Standard 4	52	16.8%	2	20.0%	316	5.79%	13	5.24%	368	6.4%	15	5.8%
Primary with training	15	4.8%	0	0.0%	424	7.77%	7	2.82%	439	7.6%	7	2.7%
Secondary no subjects	41	13.2%	3	30.0%	534	9.79%	19	7.66%	575	10.0%	22	8.5%
Secondary no subjects plus training	34	11.0%	0	0.0%	876	16.05%	46	18.55%	910	15.8%	46	17.8%
Secondary, 1–4 subjects	47	15.2%	3	30.0%	274	5.02%	21	8.47%	321	5.6%	24	9.3%
Secondary 1–4 subjects plus training	36	11.6%	0	0.0%	683	12.52%	37	14.92%	719	12.5%	37	14.3%
Secondary, 5 or more subjects	16	5.2%	0	0.0%	244	4.47%	11	4.44%	260	4.5%	11	4.3%
Secondary 5 or more subjects plus training	27	8.7%	2	20.0%	728	13.34%	42	16.94%	755	13.1%	44	17.1%
University education, no degree	0	0.0%	0	0.0%	94	1.72%	4	1.61%	94	1.6%	4	1.6%
University degree/diploma/certificate	42	13.5%	0	0.0%	1215	22.26%	43	17.34%	1257	21.8%	43	16.7%
Educated in a foreign country	0	0.0%	0	0.0%	25	0.46%	0	0.00%	25	0.4%	0	0.0%

Source: CSO

2022. Though better than those for Tobago, the data also indicate significant undereducation of a large share of the employed workers in Trinidad.

At the end of 2023Q2, 46 per cent of persons with jobs in Tobago had passed no secondary subjects at all, up sharply from 39 per cent in 2022. The corresponding estimates for Trinidad were broadly similar at 40 per cent at the end of 2023Q2, up significantly from 37 per cent in 2022.

At the end of 2023Q2, 4,200 or 13.5 per cent of employed persons in Tobago had achieved tertiary diplomas, certificates, or university degrees, down sharply from 6,000 persons or 19 per cent at the end of 2022. The corresponding estimates for Trinidad were 121,500 or 22.3 per cent of employees at the end of 2023Q2, down significantly from 128,900 or 24.2 per cent of employees in 2022. Some of the identified loss of such level 3 and level 4 workers was likely due to unexplained seasonal variation in labour force participation and some to emigration from Tobago to Trinidad and from Trinidad to the rest of the world, most likely the developed economies of the North Atlantic.

Among the pool of 1,000 unemployed workers in Tobago at the end of 2023Q2, 50 per cent held no secondary passes, down from 81.3 per cent at the end of 2022. In 2022, no person with one to four secondary passes was openly unemployed in Tobago, and only 19 per cent of Tobago's unemployed achieved one to four secondary passes or better. However, during the first two quarters of 2023, the situation worsened, as three hundred persons with one to four passes and two hundred persons with five secondary passes plus training joined the ranks of the unemployed and accounted for 30 per cent and 20 per cent, respectively (or 50 per cent collectively) of the pool by the end of the 2023Q2. By comparison, at the end of 2023Q2, 36.3 per cent of the unemployed in Trinidad had no secondary passes, marginally down from 37.6 per cent at the end of 2022. At the end of 2023Q2, 15,800 or approximately 63.7 per cent of the unemployed had one to four secondary passes or better, with 8.5 per cent of the unemployed having one to four secondary passes and 4.300 or 17.3 per cent having tertiary education with diplomas, certificates, and university degrees. This represented only modest improvement in the period since at the end of 2022, 17,600 or 62.4 per cent of the unemployed had one to four passes or better, with 7.4 per cent having one to four passes and 4,700 or 16.7 per cent having tertiary education with diplomas, certificates and university degrees.

Overall, the data on Tobago support the observation that it will prove to be extremely difficult to build a very productive and competitive service economy in Tobago with the labour force in its current state. To enable development, policies and programs will be needed to increase the availability of level 4 workers in the labour force, partly by accelerated education and skills training and partly by attracting appropriately skilled and knowledgeable workers from abroad. Apart from shedding significant light on the high levels of unemployed knowledge and skills available to undertake competing criminal enterprise, the data on Trinidad also signal largescale undereducation of workers. For strong growth-supporting diversification and development initiatives, a significant upgrade of the capitalization of the production process is also needed, starting with an increase in the flow of suitably educated workers with level 4 skills from the education and training system.

Types of Occupations

The data in table 10.6 shed light on the types of occupations created by the large pool of undereducated workers in the country.

The most important consequence of a widespread undereducation of workers in Tobago was that in 2022, 9,700 workers or 31 per cent of workers were in "elementary occupations" demanding level 1 knowledge and skills, such as cleaning, restocking supplies and performing basic maintenance in apartments, houses, kitchens, hotels, offices and other buildings; washing cars and windows; delivering messages or goods; carrying luggage and handling baggage and freight; collecting and sorting refuse; sweeping streets and similar places; performing various simple farming or fishing tasks; providing various street and environmental maintenance services; ground transportation of passengers and goods; and driving basic vehicles or machinery. The numbers in such occupations increased substantially to 10,400 or 34 per cent of workers in 2023Q1&2. In Trinidad, a much lower though still quite high share, 18 per cent or 96,100 workers, were similarly in elementary occupations in 2022, rising to 102,800 or 19 per cent of workers in 2023Q1&2. The data reinforce the general picture of island economies with a large share of undercapitalized, low-productivity and hence low-income workers. As was the practice over the past 140 years, faced with

Table 10.6: Number and Share of Occupations, by Type of Occupation

	Numbers and Shares			Numbers and Shares		
	2022			2023 Q1 & 2		
	Tobago	Trinidad	T&T	Tobago	Trinidad	T&T
All Occupations (00,s) and skill levels	312	5341	5653	310	5457	5767
Legislators, senior officials, and managers (level 4)	25	588	622	18	682	700
Share of Occupations	8%	11%	11%	5.8%	12.5%	12.1%
Professionals (level 4)	16	374	396	11	370	381
Share of Occupations	5%	7%	7%	3.5%	6.8%	6.6%
Technicians and associate professionals (level 3)	47	748	791	24	720	744
Share of Occupations	15%	14%	14%	8%	13%	13%
Clerks (level 2)	34	534	565	38	559	597
Share of Occupations	11%	10%	10%	12%	10%	10%
Service workers and shop sales workers (level 2)	44	855	904	51	817	868
Share of Occupations s	14%	16%	16%	16%	15%	15%
Agricultural, forestry and fishery (level 2)	3	160	170	6	153	159
Share of Occupations	1%	3%	3%	2%	3%	3%
Craft and related (level 2)	41	694	735	50	744	794
Share of Occupations	13%	13%	13%	16%	14%	14%
Plant and machine operators and assemblers (level 2)	9	374	396	8	373	381
Share of Occupations	3%	7%	7%	3%	7%	7%
Elementary occupations (level 1)	97	961	1074	104	1028	1132
Share of Occupations	31%	18%	19%	34%	19%	20%

Source: CSO

such occupation prospects, many persons in the Tobago labour market will continue to choose to leave the island for better employment options in Trinidad and elsewhere.

In 2022, 4,100 workers, or 13 per cent of the total in Tobago, were in level 2 craft and related occupations in construction, maintenance, repairs and self-employment. The number increased to 5,000 workers, or 16 per cent, in 2023Q1&2. In Trinidad, the share of workers with such occupations was 13 per cent in 2022, rising marginally to 14 per cent in 2023Q1&2.

In 2022, approximately 4,400 or 14 per cent were level 2 service and sales workers in areas such as travel, housekeeping, preparation and serving of food and beverages, childcare, rudimentary nursing and related care at homes or in institutions, personal care such as hairdressing or beauty treatment, protection of property and life against fire and unlawful acts and enforcement of law and order, selling goods in wholesale or retail establishments, stalls and markets. The numbers in such occupations increased to 5,100 or 16 per cent of workers in 2023Q1&2. The corresponding estimates for Trinidad were 16 per cent in 2022, declining to 15 per cent in 2023Q1&2 as the number of such workers fell.

In 2022, 4,700 or 15 per cent of workers were in level 3 technical and associated professional occupations, supporting the application of concepts and operational methods in fields such as medicine, primary and preschool teaching, providing support services in trade, finance, administration, including government, social work, artistic and sports entertainment, and even religious tasks. The number of workers in such occupations fell sharply to 2,100 or 8 per cent in 2023Q1&2. In Trinidad, the corresponding estimates were 14 per cent in 2022, declining marginally to 13 per cent in 2023Q1&2. Even though these occupation shares look broadly similar in the two islands, an important difference with Trinidad is that most of the job-creators in Tobago, whether the government or other industries, are not involved in viable export activity.

Overall, in Tobago in 2022, 73 per cent of all workers were in occupations that required only level 1 and 2 knowledge and skills, and this share increased to 83 per cent in 2023Q1&2. The corresponding estimates for Trinidad were 67 per cent in 2022 and 68 per cent in 2023Q1&2. Only 27 per cent of workers in Tobago were in occupations that required level 3 and 4 knowledge and skills, and the share declined to 17 per cent in 2023Q1&2. In Trinidad, the share of such occupations was higher and more stable, nearly 32 per cent. Even considering the presence of significant seasonal variation in Tobago, the undereducation of workers and the corresponding undercapitalization of work in the country is high, but to a much higher degree in Tobago than in Trinidad.

Types of Workers

Considering the perceived obligation of the government to provide work for the undereducated when the private sector cannot do so profitably, the consequences of widespread undereducation show up in the supply structure of paid employment and the industry structure of employment.

The data in table 10.7 show that, in 2023Q1&2, even as total employment declined in Tobago, 74 per cent of paid employees depended on the government for employment. This represented a sharp increase from 65 per cent in 2022. In Trinidad, where a substantial number of new jobs were created in the period, the government's share of paid employees was 33 per cent, down from the 35 per cent it contributed in 2022. So, in Trinidad, by the end of 2023Q2, 67 per cent of paid employees were in the private sector, up from 65 per cent in 2022. In Tobago, that share was 26 per cent at the end of 2023Q2, down sharply from 35 per cent in 2022. Even considering seasonal forces operating in Tobago, this difference in performance is evidence of the continuing weakness and decline of the private sector in Tobago.

In light of that decline and the overall fall in job creation in Tobago, 17 per cent of employed persons sought to create their own jobs in the first two quarters of 2023, up slightly from 16 per cent in 2022. The corresponding

Table 10.7: Types of Workers

	2022			2023Q1/2		
	Tobago	Trinidad	Trinidad and Tobago	Tobago	Trinidad	Trinidad and Tobago
	Employed Persons			Employed Persons		
Total Employed	31875	534286	558571	31000	545700	576700
Paid Employees	25538	385429	409459	24800	397800	422600
Government Paid Employees	16600	134900	151500	18300	130900	149200
Share of all paid employees	65%	35%	37%	74%	33%	35%
Private Sector Paid Employees	9000	254300	263300	7000	264200	271200
Share of all paid employees	35%	65%	63%	28%	66%	64%
Own Account Workers	5100	112200	117300	5200	118200	123400
Share of total employed	16%	21%	21%	17%	22%	21%

Source: CSO

rate of self-employment in Trinidad was 22 per cent in the first two quarters of 2023, up somewhat from 21 per cent in 2022. The data underscore a significantly higher degree of dependence on the state for employment and income in Tobago.

Industry Contributions to Employment

The types of industries that create jobs are indicators of both the availability of educated workers and the direction of development. The key to development is the employment of level 4 skills in job creation in export-capable manufacturing of capital goods and capital services and linked construction activity.

The data in table 10.8 show that, in Tobago, agriculture generated 2 per cent of the jobs in 2022 and 3 per cent of the jobs in 2023Q1&2, less than the 4 per cent in Trinidad in the same periods. Workers in Tobago are more dependent on government-controlled employment in electricity and water than their counterparts in Trinidad.

In the light of claims that Tobago is a "tourism economy", it is instructive that the core of that cluster, "wholesale, retail, restaurants, and hotels", contributed only 14 per cent of jobs in Tobago in 2022, compared to 19 per cent in Trinidad. In 2023Q1&2, the number of jobs created by the sector increased across the economy, causing the share of jobs to increase to 15 per cent in Tobago and 21 per cent in Trinidad. The higher share of jobs created by the sector in Trinidad reflects the fact that the island's specialist export sector can finance a relatively larger wholesale, retail and restaurant subsector. In contrast, Tobago's tourism sector is still underdeveloped.

In 2022, the government-dominated "community, social, and personal services" sector created 14,400 jobs or 46 per cent of all jobs in Tobago. This number increased sharply to 15,500 jobs, or 50 per cent, in 2023Q1&2. The corresponding share in Trinidad was 38 per cent in 2022, declining to 36 per cent in 2023Q1&2 as the number of jobs created by the sector fell.

Tobago created no significant numbers of manufacturing jobs in 2022, while 7 per cent of the jobs in Trinidad were provided by manufacturing activity, mainly in food and beverages. The seven hundred jobs recorded as manufacturing jobs in Tobago in 2023Q1&2 were in local bakeries and fledgling agro-industrial food and beverage production. These amounted

Table 10.8: Industry Employment and Share of Jobs, 2022 and 2023Q1/2

	Employment and Share of Jobs, 2022			Employment and Share of Jobs, 2023Q1/2		
	Tobago	Trinidad	Trinidad and Tobago	Tobago	Trinidad	Trinidad and Tobago
All Industries (00's)	312	5341	5653	310	5457	5767
Agriculture, forestry, hunting, fisheries (00's)	6	214	226	10	203	213
Share of Total Jobs	2%	4%	4%	3%	4%	4%
Petroleum and gas, including production, refining and service contractors (00's)	3	107	113	0	91	91
Share of Total Jobs	1%	2%	2%	0%	1.7%	1.6%
Other mining and quarrying (00's)	3	11	11	0	15	15
Share of Total Jobs	1.00%	0.20%	0.20%	0%	0.27%	0.26%
Other Manufacturing (00's)	0	374	396	7	402	409
Share of Total Jobs	0%	7%	7%	2%	7%	7%
Electricity and Water (00's)	6	53	57	4	53	57
Share of Total Jobs	2%	1%	1%	1.3%	1%	1%
Construction (00's)	62	588	678	60	657	717
Share of Total Jobs	20%	11%	12%	19%	12%	12%
Wholesale, retail, restaurants, hotels (00's)	44	1015	1074	46	1160	1206
Share of Total Jobs	14%	19%	19%	15%	21%	21%
Transport, storage, communication (00's)	12	320	339	10	306	316
Share of Total Jobs	4%	6%	6%	3%	6%	5%
Financing, insurance, real estate, and business services (00's)	31	588	622	23	558	581
Share of Total Jobs	10%	11%	11%	7%	10%	10%
Community, social, and personal services (00's)	144	2030	2148	155	1986	2141
Share of Total Jobs	46%	38%	38%	50%	36%	37%

Source: CSO

to 2 per cent of all jobs in Tobago. The sector contributed more jobs in Trinidad in 2023Q1&2, though the share remained at 7 per cent as total employment grew.

The construction sector in Tobago lost 200 jobs in 2023Q1&2, so its share of jobs declined from 20 per cent in 2022 to 19 per cent in 2023Q1&2. Notwithstanding, the share of jobs contributed by construction in Tobago was much higher than the 11 per cent and 12 per cent contributed by the sector in Trinidad in corresponding periods. Construction in Tobago is also substantially more dependent on government spending than in Trinidad.

Overall, the data reveals a tiny share of jobs in the sectors that either can produce and export capital (manufacturing) or support such activity (construction). It is important to observe that even though the "community, social, and personal services" sector includes education, healthcare, the creative industries, and related professional services, it does not generate a significant development effect since, except for the creative services, most of the sector's output targets domestic demand.

On their face, these data indicate a very weak private sector with low capital production and job-creating capacity in Tobago. They also reveal that the government in Tobago hosts large numbers of undereducated and, therefore, undercapitalized workers. Underneath, the data really reveal the employment characteristics of an economy that depends on transfers from Trinidad to fund more than 80 per cent of the government's budget, and that does too little to create a robust private sector with significant ISCO-08 level 4 capacity to produce and export the capital services competitively. In this case, the data reflect a lack of exportable capital service anchors to support a successful tourism thrust and point in the direction of the type of industrial development policy the island is failing to pursue.

On the other hand, the data on job creation in Trinidad reveal the employment patterns of an economy with a significant but highly specialized export sector that cannot produce capital. The meagre share of jobs (7 per cent) created by its non-energy manufacturing sector reflects its low capacity to compete in the international market for exportable medium- and high-technology manufactured capital goods and services despite the continuing availability of relatively low-cost energy. Exports of food and beverage manufactures, or methanol, urea, and liquified natural gas are not a solution to this problem, and the data point to the need to revisit the industrial policy in Trinidad to consider whether underutilized export potential lies in growing and employing the level 4 knowledge, skills and self-confidence required to produce advanced capital services.

Labour Incomes

The data in tables 10.9 and 10.10 show that the average wage has remained low in the national economy among a large share of the undereducated (level 1 and 2 workers) and has, therefore, stagnated in the economies of both islands.

In table 10.9, the data show that in 2016, undereducated workers accounted for 70 per cent of all workers in Trinidad and Tobago, falling slightly to 68 per cent in 2022. Of these, 13 per cent had income at or below the minimum wage ($17.50/hour), falling slightly to 11 per cent in 2022. However, in 2016, 24 per cent of the undereducated were earning at or below $24/hour, which is within $3 of the current minimum wage ($20.50/hour). This share fell modestly to 21 per cent by 2022. Even in the face of significant inflation, the data suggest the existence of significant surplus labour pressures in the labour market that tend to keep the wage rate relatively stationary across all wage earners. The data in table 10.10 show that between 2016 and 2022, the average monthly wage remained in the neighbourhood of $5,900 in the country and Trinidad ($5,857) and $5,752 in Tobago. Table 10.11 reports

Table 10.9: Share of Undereducated Workers with Low Income

	Level 3 & 4		Level 1 & 2		Number and Share with Low Income (at or less than minimum wage)		Number and Share with Low Income within 20% of current minimum wage	
Year	00's	%	00's	%	00's	%	00's	%
2016	1 831	30%	4 302	70%	543	13%	1 036	24%
2017	1 789	30%	4 243	70%	547	13%	985	23%
2018	1 828	30%	4 275	70%	481	11%	909	21%
2019	1 804	31%	4 106	69%	444	11%	859	21%
2020	1 783	31%	3 917	69%	502	13%	881	22%
2021	1 788	32%	3 816	68%	451	12%	844	22%
2022	1 824	32%	3 828	68%	440	11%	786	21%

Source: CSO

Table 10.10: Average Monthly Wage (TT$), Trinidad and Tobago

Year	Trinidad and Tobago	Trinidad	Tobago
2016	6,077	6,120	5,730
2017	5,897	5,817	5,875
2018	5,836	5,890	5,870
2019	5,634	5,648	5,703
2020	5,922	5,978	5,811
2021	6,037	6,039	5,486
2022	5,895	5,508	5,788
Average	5,900	5,857	5,752

Source: CSO

average incomes by occupation groups since 2016 and table 10.12 reports average incomes by industry groups. The data in both tables support the likelihood of significant wage-suppression effects of comparatively large numbers of workers with only level 1 and level 2 skills engaged in elementary occupations and the like.

THE EXTERNAL PROPULSION OF THE TRINIDAD AND TOBAGO ECONOMY

Another feature of an undercapitalized economy is that it is externally propelled in the sense intended by Best (1968), Best and Levitt (1969) and Best and St Cyr (2012). To identify indicators of external propulsion, it is helpful to contrast the conditions with those of an internally propelled economy. Internal propulsion is a manifestation of the abundance of capital as understood by the classical economists, early neoclassical economists such as J.B. Clark (1899) and Lewis (1954), in which institutional design enables full-information policymaking but the economy is mainly coordinated by market competition among capitalist firms seeking to undertake the tasks of level 4 workers and develop and produce capital, discover and bring winning innovative solutions to market, develop related new industries, raise labour productivity and move capital among industries in search of the highest rate of profit. In such a dynamic process, investment is the driver of domestic production and exports and plays a more important role than imports. Such a process of internal propulsion requires only an appropriate supply of money to grease the process, and hence only the

Table 10.11: Mean Monthly Income by Occupation Groups, 2016–22

Year	Average All	Legislators, senior officials and Managers	Professionals	Technicians and Associate Professions	Clerks	Service/ Sales Workers	Agriculture	Craft and Related Workers	Plant and Machine Operators and Assemblers	Elementary Occupations
2016	6077	8886	12548	8005	5178	5054	4065	5196	6524	3651
2017	5897	7953	12433	7958	5246	5211	3581	5328	6371	3561
2018	5836	7551	12200	7691	5244	5132	3625	5334	6223	3684
2019	5634	6140	11414	7918	5181	5013	3418	5302	5931	3719
2020	5922	6924	12829	8267	5432	5429	3119	5089	6796	3665
2021	6037	7050	14448	8432	5365	5382	3674	5260	6641	3509
2022	5855	7273	11720	7971	5313	5521	2973	5359	6709	3578

Source: CSO

Table 10.12: Mean Monthly Income by Industry Group, 2016–22, TT$

Year	All	Agriculture	Petroleum and Gas, Including Production, etc.	Other Mining and Quarrying	Other manu-facturing (excluding sugar, oil)	Electricity and Water	Construction	Wholesale, retail, restaurants, hotels	Transport, Storage, Comm.	Finance, Insurance, Real Estate, Business Services	Community, Social and Personal Services
2016	6 077	4,203	11,800	5,887	5,837	9,444	5,559	4,525	6,621	7,643	6,078
2017	5,897	3,804	11,417	5,275	5,851	9,815	5,650	4,542	6,333	6,939	6,043
2018	5,836	3,834	10,844	6,186	5,881	9,770	5,465	4,378	6,563	6,912	6,086
2019	5,634	3,550	8,494	4,600	5,551	10,078	5,162	4,208	6,123	6,474	6,190
2020	5,922	3,518	10,128	6,500	6,392	12,117	5,084	4,355	6,257	7,024	6,359
2021	6,037	3,710	11,197	5,392	7,026	11,733	4,872	4,085	6,312	7,482	6,492
2022	5,895	3,118	11,929	4,783	5,862	11,609	5,061	4,517	5,808	7,119	6,354

Source: CSO

monetary policy interventions of a central bank. A Caribbean economy lacks such a high degree of dependence on its capital output to drive market competition, innovation, investment and exports and instead is typically externally propelled. Two indicators of this condition are reported here: (i) the low share of capital in GDP and (ii) the high degree of dependence of exports on imports rather than investment and the capital share of GDP.

Low Capital Share of GDP

Low reliance on domestic production of capital is the baseline measure of likely external propulsion in the form of a structural bias away from the production and export of capital and towards the production of consumer products or the production and export of outputs for intermediate consumption. The latter is the "muscovado bias" discovered by Best (1968) and Best and Levitt (1969), which undermines the development of domestic inter-industry linkages. The condition is one of the consequences of a highly undereducated labour force because the economy does not have the complement of level 3 and level 4 education and skills needed to produce and export problem-solving capital competitively. Then, when the capital share of output is low, there are related consequences for the quality of institutions and the capacity to innovate (James and Hamilton 2022). These, in turn, keep down productivity growth in the sectors of the economy and, thus, economy-wide growth of living standards. The significance of capital production as a cause of productivity growth and development was clarified by Lewis (1954) as well as Leontief (1953, 1970). In the case of Lewis, it enables innovation and is the basis for the growth of the marginal product of labour relative to the wage rate and, hence, for an increase in the rate of profit and savings that validate and motivate labour productivity growth. In the case of Leontief, it is the basis for making the rate of profit, savings rate and capacity growth rate endogenous elements of the inter-industry multiplier process driving the rate of productivity growth.

To examine the evidence on productivity growth and growth of GDP per capita, we use data provided in the national accounting country profiles supplied by the United Nations Statistics Division to create a proxy measure of potential capacity to produce capital as the share of manufacturing, construction, and the set of sectors that produce education, healthcare, financial services, creative output that generate intellectual property products, and other professional capital services classified as ISIC J-P. In the case of Trinidad and Tobago, the data in table 10.13 show that in the decade from 2010 to 2022, the share of real GDP (2015 prices) increased from 43.8 per cent to 44.5 per cent, with an average share of around 42.9 per cent. In 2019, before the start of the COVID-19 pandemic, the capital share was 44 per cent, about 32 per cent below the benchmark of 65 per cent typical of developed economies (James and Hamilton 2022). Considering the data presented above showing an undereducated labour force in Trinidad and more severely so in Tobago, this is evidence of an economy with a low capacity to produce enough of the capital it needs to create innovative solutions to global problems and grow its participation in intra-industry trade.

Table 10.13: Economic Structure of Trinidad and Tobago, 2010–22

	Industries with Capacity to Produce Capital, Constant US$ (2015 prices)					
Year	Manufacturing (US$b)	Construction (US$b)	Other (US$b) (ISIC J-P)	Sum (US$b)	GDP (US$b)	Share of Capital Producing Industries in GDP (%)
2010	4.00	1.60	6.00	12.00	27.40	43.8%
2011	3.90	1.40	6.30	12.00	28.10	42.7%
2012	3.80	1.40	6.40	12.00	27.50	43.6%
2013	3.80	1.50	6.60	12.00	28.20	42.6%
2014	3.70	1.50	6.60	12.00	29.60	40.5%
2015	3.80	1.50	6.60	12.00	30.50	39.3%
2016	3.70	1.40	6.50	12.00	29.00	41.4%
2017	3.60	1.40	6.70	12.00	27.40	43.8%
2018	3.60	1.30	6.70	12.00	27.10	44.3%
2019	3.50	1.30	6.90	12.00	27.30	44.0%
2020	3.00	1.10	6.80	11.00	25.50	43.1%
2021	3.00	1.20	6.80	11.00	24.80	44.4%
2022	3.20	1.20	7.00	11.00	24.70	44.5%
Average						42.9%

Source: Computed from UNSD Country Profiles Database

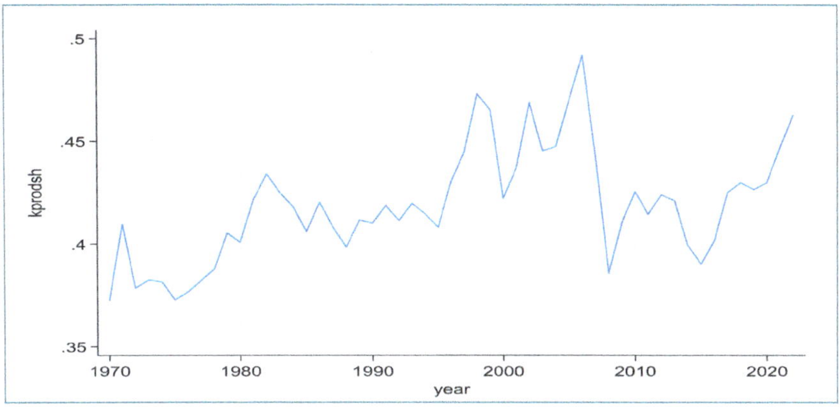

Figure 10.1: Share of Industries That Can Produce Capital in GDP, Trinidad and Tobago, 1970–2020

Figure 10.1 shows how the share in GDP of industries that can produce capital evolved from 1970 to 2022 in the case of Trinidad and Tobago. Relative to the reference 65 per cent standard, the global maximum was 25 per cent lower at 49 per cent, the mean share was 42 per cent, and the graph drifted upwards throughout the period but with an apparent distinct change in the mean in the early 1980s. This change is confirmed by a supremum Wald test for stability of the share with an unknown break date over the period using a constant-only regression model and CUSUM of recursive residuals. The Wald test statistic of 30.8669 has a p-value of 0.0000, implying rejection of the null of a stationary or constant share, and the estimated break date is 1981.

Importing to Export

As suggested by Best (1968), in the context of inadequate production of domestic capital, the economy imports in order to export, with imports being the main input into production and exports, either directly as capital or indirectly as a means of reproduction of labour power for production. So imports are expected to be consistently more important drivers of exports than domestic investment and domestic capital production. This condition makes the growth of import productivity and import displacement compelling challenges of the development process. To present evidence, we adopt the time series modelling strategy of Gali and Gertler (1999) and estimate an instrumental variables 2sls regression of exports *(X)*, on imports

(J), the capital share of GDP (K_{sh}), and expected exports in t+1 $(E(F.X))$ conditional on data available up to t, where F is the forward operator, and where $L.X$ and $L.J$ are used for identification of the exports function. All variables are expressed in natural logarithms so that a self-similar power law with predetermined and instrumented variables represents exports. One should note that if the instrumented variables are, in fact, exogenous, the IV regression results would still be consistent. However, following Pearl (2009), backdoor routes to causal inference would become available.

For the case of Trinidad and Tobago, which depends heavily on energy sector exports, we estimate the following model:

1. $X = \alpha + \beta_1 L.X + \beta_2 E(F.X) + \beta_3 E(F.p_x) + \beta_4 E(F.p_d) + \gamma g(k_{sh}) + \delta_1 M + \delta_2 I + + \delta_3 G + \epsilon_t$

$$F.p_x = z_{1t}\theta_1 + v_{1t+1}$$
$$F.X = z_{2t}\theta_2 + v_{2t+1_1}$$
$$F.p_d = z_{3t}\theta_3 + v_{3t+1}$$

The ϵ_t and v_{it+1} are zero-mean error terms, and it is assumed that the correlations among them is nonzero. In the specification, $g(k_{sh})$ is the rate of growth of the domestic capital share of GDP. With imports, M, as the main causal variable, expected exports, $E(F.X)$, is a confounding variable that cannot be observed, so we instrument $F.X$ with (z_{2t}), identified as the first two lags of the mineral sector share of GDP, NK_{sh} and the domestic capital sector share of GDP, K_{sh}, as well as the first two lags of the investment share of GDP, I_{sh}, and government spending as a share of GDP, G_{sh}. Expected energy sector price $(E(F.p_x))$ is another unobserved confounder, so $F.p_x$ is instrumented by z_{1t} identified as the first two lags of sector price, p_x. Similarly, the expected domestic price level $(E(F.p_d))$ is an unobserved confounder, so $F.p_d$ is instrumented with z_{3t}, identified as the first two lags of the exchange rate and of p_d. By construction, the v_{it+1} are independent of the associated expectations.

The results of the estimation are presented in table 10.14. Figure 10.2 graphs the model residuals. Using the optimal one-period lag recommended by the SIC, a standard augmented Dickey-Fuller (DF) test (Dickey and Fuller 1979) with a 1 period lag decisively rejects the null hypothesis of a unit root in the residuals at all conventional levels of significance (1 per cent, 5 per cent, 10 per cent). At the optimal 1 period lag suggested by the SIC, the

Table 10.14: Coefficient Estimates and Diagnostics of Export Model, Trinidad and Tobago

Instrumental Variables 2SLS regression					Number of obs = 50		
					Wald chi2(8) = 2593.24		
					Prob > chi2 = 0.0000		
					R-squared = 0.9811		
					Root MSE = 0.09016		
	Coefficient	Std. err.	z	P>z	[95% conf. interval]		Approx. beta
	0.587866	0.109353	5.38	0.000	0.373538	0.802193	0.59
	-0.30649	0.106378	-2.88	0.004	-0.51498	-0.09799	-0.37
	0.154016	0.062264	2.47	0.013	0.031981	0.276052	0.26
	0.909041	0.461339	1.97	0.049	0.004832	1.813249	0.06
	0.237382	0.097004	2.45	0.014	0.047258	0.427505	0.19
	0.21029	0.079868	2.63	0.008	0.053752	0.366828	0.27
	-0.25312	0.06973	-3.63	0.000	-0.38979	-0.11645	-0.18
	-0.75516	0.158864	-4.75	0.000	-1.06653	-0.4438	-0.23
_cons	1.694793	2.579882	0.66	0.511	-3.36168	6.751269	

Source: computed

more powerful modified DF (DFGLS) test of Elliott, Rothenberg, and Stock (1996) does the same at the 10 per cent level of significance. We conclude that the estimated model is statistically reasonable, at least in the sense that the parameters have been consistently estimated even if the variables in

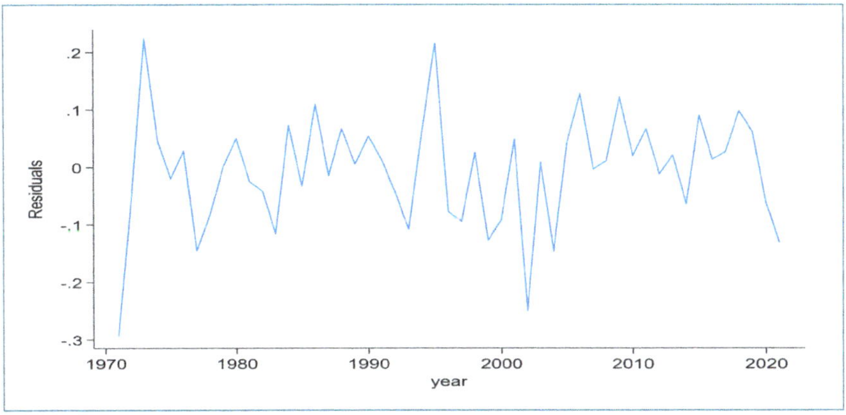

Figure 10.2: IV 2sls Regression Model Residuals, Trinidad and Tobago

the X equation are not all covariance stationary. The coefficient estimates show that the leading positive causes of exports are the expectations and history of exports, expected and current oil prices, expected inflation, and imports. An increasing share of investment and government spending in GDP slows exports, while imports and growth of the capital share of GDP cause exports to grow. After the model coefficients are standardized by the ratio of the covariate standard deviation to the standard deviation of exports, the resulting approximate beta coefficients of the model suggest that the rate of growth of the share of domestic capital in GDP plays a very modest role far outweighed by the influence of imports. Thus, the economy retained the characteristic of importing to export over the period.

Data are not available to provide econometric evidence for Tobago or Trinidad, according to table 10.14. However, the condition of persistent external propulsion of the country is likely to apply to each island's economy. For example, in the case of Tobago, it can be deduced from the data in table 10.15 below that, at the national average tax rate of 29 per cent of GDP, the current taxable capacity of the Tobago economy is approximately TT$600, or about 18 per cent of the total annual government expenditures in Tobago of TT$3.4 billion. This suggests that government transfers and imports from Trinidad and the rest of the world via Trinidad propel the Tobago economy. Then, from the national evidence, one can conclude that the Trinidad economy is also externally propelled.

Productivity and GDP per Capita

Consistent with the description of level 4 tasks by the ILO (2012), it is expected that an immediate counterpart of a persistently low share of capital in GDP (and a related low capacity to produce and export capital and capital-intensive output) will be slow growth of the knowledge, skills, and self-confidence of workers. Some of this slow growth might be associated with the net emigration of skilled workers and some with the slow rate at which graduates with advanced skills are produced by the education and training system. Ultimately, by inhibiting innovation, these conditions keep down productivity growth and cause a slow rate of growth of real GDP per capita and a low real GDP per capita when compared to the developed economies (James and Hamilton 2022).

Table 10.15: Real GDP Per Capita and Productivity, Trinidad and Tobago, 2012–22

	2012	2013	2014	2015	2016	2017	2018	2019	2020	2021	2022	2012–22
Exchange rate	6.43	6.44	6.41	6.38	6.67	6.78	6.77	6.75	6.75	6.78	6.77	
GDP (US$ millions)	25217	26186	27056	26852	25036	23857	23649	23675	21858	21633	22304	
Population	1335194	1340557	1345343	1349667	1353895	1356633	1359193	1363985	1366725	1367558	1365805	
Employment	620500	626300	636800	623300	613200	603500	610300	591100	569800	560500	565300	
Real GDP per capita, T&T (US$)	18886	19534	20111	19895	18492	17585	17399	17357	15993	15819	16330	
Growth of GDP per capita (US$)		3.43%	2.95%	-1.07%	-7.05%	-4.90%	-1.06%	-0.24%	-7.86%	-1.09%	3.23%	-1.4%
Productivity (T&T)	40640	41811	42487	43080	40828	39531	38750	40052	38361	38596	39454	
Productivity Growth (T&T)		2.9%	1.6%	1.4%	-5.2%	-3.2%	-2.0%	3.4%	-4.2%	0.6%	2.2%	-.25%
Real Tobago (TTS millions)	1,694.7	1,959.0	1,939.0	1,997.4	1,896.6	1,812.2	1,741.7	1,708.8	1,610.9	1,678.6	1,645.7	
Population	61203	61449	61668	61866	62060	62186	62303	62523	62648	62686	62606	
Employment	33600	31800	33100	33200	31500	31200	31000	31100	33100	29900	31100	
Real GDP per capita (US$)	4306	4950	4905	5060	4582	4298	4129	4049	3809	3950	3883	
Growth of GDP per capita		15%	-1%	3%	-9%	-6%	-4%	-2%	-6%	4%	-2%	-0.8%
Productivity (Tobago)	7844.1	9565.8	9138.9	9429.9	9026.9	8566.9	8298.9	8140.1	7210.0	8280.3	7816.3	
Productivity Growth (Tobago)		21.9%	-4%	3.2%	-4%	-5.1%	-3%	-1.9%	-11%	14.8%	-6%	0.4%

Sources: UNSD; Division of Finance, THA; CSO (Population for Tobago are own estimates using CSO details)

The data in table 10.15 show that in the decade of 2012-2022, after an initial increase, labour productivity in Trinidad and Tobago, as measured by GDP per worker, declined from US$40,640 to US$39,454. Over the same decade, productivity in Tobago initially drifted upwards from US$7,844 to US$9,429 in 2015 before falling steadily to $7,210 in 2020, recovering to $8,280 in 2021 and falling again to US$7,816 in 2022. It is instructive that over the decade, productivity in Tobago has generally been about five times lower than in Trinidad.

Corresponding to these data, Trinidad and Tobago's somewhat volatile real GDP per capita has been declining at an average rate near 1.4 per cent per annum, below a sixty-one-year trend of 2 per cent growth evident since political independence in 1962 when real GDP per capita was US$4,834. Thus, in 2022, the country's real GDP per capita was US$16,330, about 68 per cent below the benchmark average of US$50,000 characteristic of developed economies (James and Hamilton 2022).

In the case of Tobago, real GDP per capita also tended to decline at just under 1 per cent per year, from US$4,306 in 2012 to US$3,883 in 2022. Thus, in 2022, Tobago's real GDP per capita was 76 per cent below that of the country and 92 per cent below the international development benchmark. Tobago has yet to catch up with the economic conditions in the country sixty-two years ago.

Productivity and GDP per capita in Trinidad and Tobago feature a high correlation of 0.94, and productivity growth and GDP per capita growth are also highly correlated at 0.89. In the case of Tobago, there is a correlation of 0.92 between productivity and GDP per capita and a correlation of 0.88 between productivity growth and GDP per capita growth. Since both the levels and growth rates are similarly correlated, the correlations are not spurious in the sense of being mere reflections of a common stochastic trend (Johnston and DiNardo 1997). The crucial observation is that the growth of GDP per capita is *caused* by the forces driving productivity growth. This was demonstrated by James and Hamilton (2022) using Rubin-causal modelling and data for 128 countries, which will be augmented with the data provided below. The theoretical justification for the correlations is provided by the analytical framework presented in section 4.

With respect to the data reported and the comparisons between the islands, the pattern evident in all previous tables is that the average for

Trinidad tracks closely that of the country. In general, the data on Trinidad and Tobago can be treated as the data for Trinidad in table 10.15. However, here, it is helpful to observe that the indicated significant differences in GDP per capita between the two islands should be interpreted with caution, guided in part by the differences in labour productivity. It is well-known that when the objective is to compare the volumes of goods or services produced or consumed per head, the data captured in the national currency is converted into US dollars by means of the exchange rate without regard to purchasing power parity. In general, the exchange rate does not really reflect the relative internal purchasing power of the Trinidad and Tobago dollar in the two islands. Tobago imports from the world via Trinidad and pays a transport premium for this condition. Because of this and the significant differences in productivity documented, it could be expected that the price levels for local or imported products in Trinidad are generally lower in Trinidad than in Tobago, making real incomes in Trinidad correspondingly higher than are reflected in the constant-price productivity estimates. The subsequent conversion of GDP and GDP per capita into US dollars tends to ignore the resulting differences in real incomes between the islands. So, even though a single currency is used in the country, some of the productivity and related price differences ought to be captured in the conversions and comparisons of Tobago and Trinidad. However, we ignore them when making the comparisons in table 10.15 because of the lack of appropriate data on differences in the purchasing power of the Trinidad and Tobago dollar in the two islands.

A general causal model of the influence of productivity on the evolution of GDP per capita is presented here for Trinidad and Tobago, consistent with ul Haque (1995). It uses data on employment obtained from the CSO for the period 1970 to 2022, with information missing for two years, 1972 and 1976. The missing data for these years were imputed using Bayesian OLS regression-based methods developed in Stata 18 following Rubin (1987) and Schafer (1997). While we considered the results of several rounds of imputations to check for robustness, the results of the first round of imputation were used in the modelling exercise. Here, we treat GDP per capita (y_p) as a function of lagged GDP per capita ($L.y_p$) to capture its dynamic properties, productivity (y_l), and the expected value of GDP per capita in $t + 1$ ($E(F.y_p)$ conditional on data available in $t + 1$. Expected GDP per capita in $t+1$ cannot be directly observed, so it is instrumented with the first two lags of GDP per capita, the government share of GDP, the investment share of GDP, and the share of the output of the traditional export sector in GDP. Productivity is inherently endogenous because shocks to GDP per capita are likely to affect it simultaneously. We instrument it with the capital share of GDP, the stock of capital per worker and its first two lags, and the first two lags of productivity and the export-import ratio. Thus, with all variables measured in natural logarithms, the following model is estimated with instrumental variables 2sls regression:

2.
$$y_p = \beta_o + \beta_1 L.y_p + \theta y_l + \gamma E_t (F \,.\, y_p) + \epsilon_t$$
$$y_l = \delta_1 x_{1t} + v_t$$
$$F \,.\, y_p = \delta_2 x_{2t} + w_{t+1}$$

In the equations of (2), ϵ_t, v_t, w_{t+1} and are zero-mean residuals that might be correlated, x_{1t} is the vector of instruments for y_l, and x_{2t} is the vector of instruments for $F \,.\, y_p$. The forecasted values $E_t(F \,.\, y_p)$ are independent of w_{t+1} by construction. We are also interested in whether the coefficients of the y_p equation have changed over the period. For the measure of the economy's capital per worker, we estimate the capital stock on the assumption that its trend growth, after accounting for depreciation, is equal to the rate of growth of the output of the traditional export sector, Y_T, a proxy for which is the constant price measure of the output of "Mining and Utilities (ISIC C&E)" in the case of Trinidad and Tobago. A more traditional approach would treat the growth of the stock as directly proportional to GDP growth. That is, we estimate *Trend* ($K_t = Y_{Tt} \frac{dK_t}{dY_{Tt}}$). The method avoids the need to estimate a depreciation rate in each year. Procedurally, we first estimate and then extract the trend using the Hodrick-Prescott (1997) high pass filter with a smoothing parameter of eight hundred because we are using annual data. Figure 10.3 graphs the estimated stock of capital, and a table of the complete series is available from the authors.

The results of model estimation are presented in table 10.16. Figure 10.4 graphs the model residuals. Using the optimal one-period lag recommended by the SIC, a standard augmented Dickey-Fuller (DF) test (Dickey and Fuller, 1979) with a 1 period lag decisively rejects the null hypothesis of a unit root in the residuals at all conventional levels of significance (1 per cent, 5 per cent, 10 per cent). At the optimal 1 period lag suggested by the SIC, the more

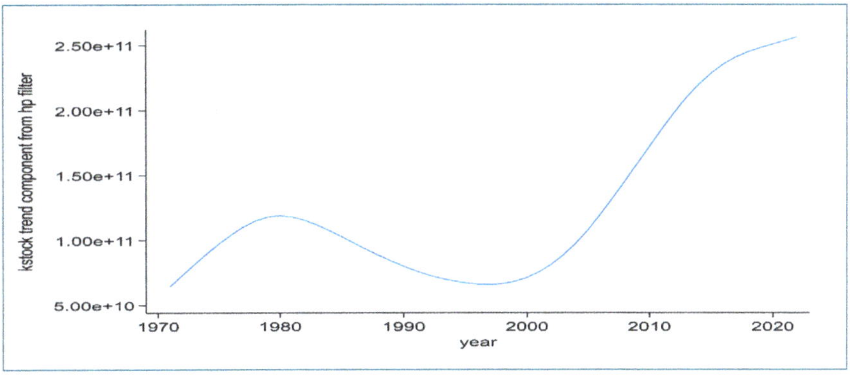

Figure 10.3: Estimated Capital Stock of Trinidad and Tobago, 1970–2020

powerful GLS modified DF (DFGLS) test of Elliott, Rothenberg, and Stock (1996) does the same. We conclude that the estimated model is statistically reasonable in the sense that the parameters have been consistently estimated even if the variables in the equation are not all covariance stationary. The coefficient estimates show that the productivity elasticity of GDP per capita is 0.29 but lies in a 95 per cent confidence band of 0.12 to 0.47. The elasticity measure found by ul Haque (1995) using data from 15 developing countries was 0.41. The general result is that productivity growth decisively drives up GDP per capita under the influence of the capital share of GDP, capital per worker, and an improving balance of trade. Further, a Wald supremum test statistic of 25.2970 with a p-value of 0.0012 revealed that the strength of the influence of productivity increased somewhat around the year 2000.

Table 10.16: Coefficients and Diagnostics of Model of GDP Per Capita

Instrumental Variables 2SLS Regression					Number of obs = 49	
					Wald chi2(3) = 4282.13	
					Prob > chi2 = 0.0000	
					R-squared = 0.9888	
					Root MSE = 0.03082	
	Coefficient	Std. err.	z	P>z	[95% conf. interval]	
F1.	0.510716	0.044458	11.49	0.000	0.42358	0.597851
	0.294348	0.091009	3.23	0.001	0.115973	0.472723
L1.	0.320308	0.072268	4.43	0.000	0.178665	0.461951
_ cons	-1.48919	0.452374	-3.29	0.001	-2.37583	-0.60255

Source: Computed

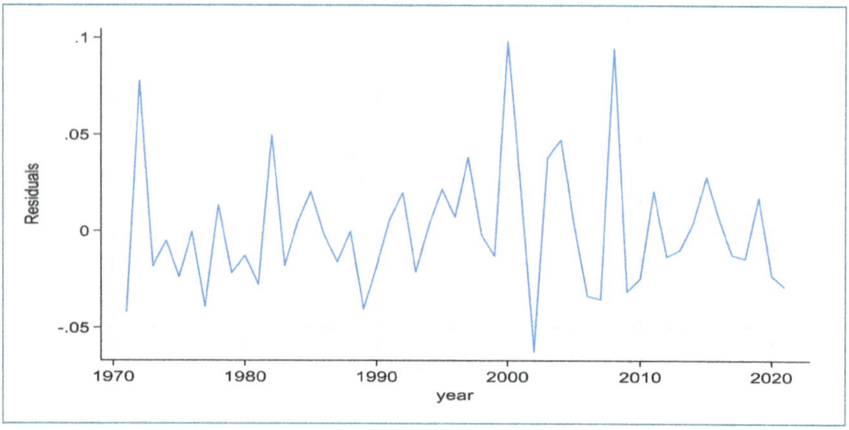

Figure 10.4: Residuals of GDP per capita Model

A SIMPLIFIED FRAMEWORK FOR POLICY DESIGN

The preceding data indicating the current undereducation of workers, the associated undercapitalization of work, the capital share of GDP, the persistence of external propulsion of the economy and the consequent relationship of productivity growth and GDP per capita growth imply a related framework of interpretation of the development process that can be used for policymaking. The framework extracted in this section explains how the average level of education of workers influences the nexus of profits, wages, prices, and productivity that drives the growth of GDP per capita. The framework contains elements that update aspects of the contributions of Lewis (1954, 1955), Best (1968), Best and Levitt (1969, 2009) and Best and St Cyr (2012). However, it is specified at the sectoral level and does not account for the extent of interindustry linkages in the economy. The advantage of the sector-level specification is that it admits the existence of a composite production function for any sector, including those sectors that employ level 4 skills to undertake tasks that result in competitive innovation and production of capital as well as production of knowledge, skills and self-confidence and other forms of human capital.

It is also worth observing here that the ISCO-08 definitions of skills on which the interpretation relies, especially in the tasks and products requiring level 4 skills, admit extension of the production boundaries of SNA 2008 to treatment of part of final consumption on education and health as fixed capital formation, resulting in human capital assets (UN 2009, 8). This also applies to expenditures by firms on staff training, education, and the accumulation of data. The rationale is that acquiring knowledge, skills, qualifications and data enhances the productive capacity of individuals and firms, contributing to their growth and serving as a source of future economic benefits for both them and society as a whole. Specifically, knowledge, skills and qualifications are clearly capital assets in a broad sense, even though they are acquired through learning, studying, and practising activities g that cannot be undertaken by anyone else on behalf of the participating worker. The framework also admits that the knowledge and skills acquired are produced through the education services provided by schools, colleges, and universities, as well as through the research institutions and departments of companies and the process of work itself – learning by doing.

In this updated framework, we assume that production of output in any sector $J(Y_j)$ follows a Lewis (1954, 1955) composite production function in which employment of knowledge, skills and self-confidence, $\tilde{N}_j$, depends on its stock of contributed capital of capitalists, K_j, which in turn is influenced by the underlying policymaking institutions of the sector, h_j and learning time (t). This allows both and to always be a result of production by some sector, either domestically or abroad, in the current period or in a previous one. That is:

3. $$Y_j = f(\tilde{N}_j(K_j\,(h(t))))$$

In equation (3), we define $E_{jn} = N_j$, where E_{jn} is knowledge, skills, and self-confidence (human capital) per worker and N_j is the number of workers in the sector. Knowledge and skills include problem-solving capacity. In capitalism, K_j is used to put $\tilde{N}_j$ to work and the technology of production embedded in (3) is defined by $\phi_j = \frac{\tilde{N}_j}{K_j}$. Both K_j and E_{jn} are produced inputs, some locally and some imported. Thus, if we neglect intermediate inputs, including natural resources, an algebraic form that satisfies equation (3) is:

4. $$Y_j = \psi_j\,(t)\mathrm{K}_j(h_j(t))$$

Both equations (3) and (4) admit Leibnitz's chain rule. The equations are interesting because they suggest that the education characteristics of the employed labour force shed light on the quality of the technology a sector can deploy. In general, the higher is E_{jn} the better the technology a sector can deploy, the more problem-solving and innovative capacities it possesses, and the higher the level and better the quality of output it can produce. The process of development relies on the existence of sectors, especially capital-producing sectors, that employ high and rapidly changing knowledge, skills, and self-confidence, $\frac{d\tilde{N}_j}{dK_j}$, defined as the ISCO-08 level 3 and level 4 skills, and hence high and rapidly changing $\phi_j(t)$ to generate high profit rates driven by high productivity growth rates.

Equation (4) implies that growth of output per worker depends on the rate of growth of the average level of knowledge, skills, and self-confidence of workers employed, which in turn depends on the rate of profit. In particular, it follows from (4) that:

5. $$\frac{dY_j}{Y_j dt} = \frac{dK_j(h(t))}{K_j dt} + \frac{d\phi_j(t)}{\phi_j dt}$$

But, $\frac{d\phi_j}{\phi_j} = \frac{dN_j}{N_j} + \frac{dE_{jn}}{E_{jn}} - \frac{dK_j(h(t))}{K_j dt}$. Thus, equation (5) implies that sector productivity growth depends mainly on the rate of growth of the average level of knowledge, skills, and self-confidence of workers. That is:

6. $$\frac{dy_j}{y_j dt} = \frac{dE_{jn}}{E_{jn}}$$

where, y_j is the productivity of labour in the sector. Now, the rate of growth of the average level of the knowledge, skills, and self-confidence of workers employed by a sector depends on the rate of capital accumulation financed from three sources: (i) retained earnings, $\frac{S}{K}$; (ii) net foreign capital inflows, including technology, knowledge and skills, induced by the excess of the rate of profit over the international cost of financing, i, i.e., $((r_j - i)\frac{dF}{F})$; and (iii) deficit spending by government to develop infrastructure and institutions supporting sector growth, $(\frac{G_j - T_j}{Y_j})$, where T_j is sector taxes and G_j is government spending targeting sector j. That is,

7. $$\frac{dE_{jn}}{E_{jn}} = \left(\frac{G_j - T_j}{Y_j}\right) + \frac{S_j}{K_j} + (r_j - i)\frac{dF_j}{F_j}$$

In equation (7), retained earnings must be $S_j = s_p r_j K_j(1-\tau_j)$, where τ_j is the tax rate on profits and s_p is the rate of savings out of profits after tax. Thus, combination of equation (7) and equation (6), and treatment of as learning time, gives the differential equation for sector productivity growth as:

8. $$\frac{dy_j}{dt} = \left(\frac{G_j - T_j(\tau_j)}{Y_j} + s_{pr} j(1-\tau_j) + (r_j - i)\frac{dF_j}{F_j}\right) y_j;\ y_j(t) = y_{j0}$$

All terms on the right-hand sside of equation (8) depend on the rate of profit, r_j. The dependence of the profit rate on $\frac{d\tilde{N}_j}{dK_j}\frac{dK_j}{dh_j}\frac{dh_t}{dt}$ and the rate of technical progress can be seen if we use an algebraic representation of Lewis's (1954) classical geometry of income distribution. That is, profits are the difference between the value of output and wage costs:

9. $$r_j K_j = p_j Y_j - w_j \tilde{N}_j$$

where, r_j is the sector rate of profit, p_j is sector output price, w_j and is the sector average wage rate for workers based on their knowledge, skills, and self-confidence. Using the total differential of equation (9) gives the sector rate of profit as:

10. $$r_j = \frac{\dfrac{d\tilde{N}_j dK_j dh_t}{dK_j\, dh_t\, dt}}{\left(1 + \dfrac{K_j dr_j}{r_j dK_j}\right)} = [(p_j \frac{dY_j}{d\tilde{N}_j} - w_j) + \{p_j(x_j + y_j^d)\frac{\tilde{N}_j dp_j}{p_j d\tilde{N}_j} - w_j \frac{\tilde{N}_j dw_j}{w_j d\tilde{N}_j}\}]$$

where we have used the decomposition $\frac{Y_j}{\tilde{N}_j} = x_j + y_j^d$, for $x_j = \frac{X_j}{\tilde{N}_j}$ the sector exports per worker and $y_j^d = \frac{y_j}{\tilde{N}_j}$ the per worker supply of sector output that provisions domestic demand. Equation (10) implies that, like equation (4), in contrast to the well-known AK model of King and Rebelo (1990) and Rebelo (1991), the instantaneous rate of profit is neither constant nor simply dependent on the technology of production. Variables like the wage rate, the marginal product Labour, prices and productivity also contribute to a dynamic nexus that involves workers' education and skills.

Consistent with the tasks undertaken by the increasing ISCO-08 level 3 and level 4 skills, it is straightforward that in equation (10), $\frac{d\tilde{N}_j}{dK_j} = \phi_j\left(1 + \frac{K_j d\phi_j}{\phi_j dK_j}\right) = \phi_j\left(\frac{K_j dN_j}{N_j dK_j} + \frac{K_j dE_{jn}}{E_{jn} dK_j}\right)$, which measures the technical change induced by capital accumulation, or equivalently the rate of growth of the sector's capacity to innovate resulting from increasing employment of workers with more advanced knowledge, skills, and self-confidence. Equation (10) can therefore be rewritten as

11. $$r_j = \frac{\phi_j\left(\dfrac{K_j dN_j}{N_j dk_j} + \dfrac{K dE_{jn}}{E_{jn} dK_j}\right)\dfrac{dK_j dh_t}{dh_j\, d_t}}{\left(1 + \dfrac{K_j dr_j}{r_j dK_j}\right)} [(p_j \frac{dY_j}{d\tilde{N}_j} - w_j) + \{p_j(x_j + y_j^d)\frac{\tilde{N}_j dp_j}{p_j d\tilde{N}_j} - w_j \frac{\tilde{N}_j dw_j}{w_j d\tilde{N}_j}\}]$$

In equation (11), under the influence of institutional development, the capacity to innovate raises the rate of profit by rescaling the gaps $(p_j \frac{dY_j}{d\tilde{N}_j} - w_j)$ and $p_j(x_j + y_j^d) \frac{\tilde{N}_j dp_j}{p_j d\tilde{N}_j} - w_j \frac{\tilde{N}_j dw_j}{w_j d\tilde{N}_j}$. The influence was anticipated by both Lewis (1954, 1955) and Best (1971). It is also inherent in the growth and application of the supply of level 4 skills as defined by ILO (2012).

For some sectors, $\boldsymbol{p_j}$ is exogenous, and for some it is determined endogenously with output (Lewis 1954). For reasons of brevity, we do not address the issue in this chapter but refer to James (2023a) for an appropriate explanation of $\boldsymbol{p_j}$ in the endogenous cases, which allows for the role of monetary and credit policy.

One would expect that an economy's high degree of dependence on undereducated workers will tend to keep down $\boldsymbol{w_j}$, so both gaps will increase as the production and employment of capital raises the marginal product of labour in a sector and increases its price making power while increasing $\boldsymbol{x_j}$ and $\boldsymbol{y_j^d}$. This will raise the sector's rate of profit and therefore the savings rate that validates its investment. The wage rate will tend to be suppressed because of the influence of undereducation on the wage determination process. Let $\boldsymbol{\eta}$ be the economy-wide employment rate and $\boldsymbol{p_j}$ the markup on $\boldsymbol{q_s}$, the average product of labour among the undereducated required to encourage movement of workers into high-skilled labour. Then, the rate of growth of a sector's wage rate in equation (11) is appropriately represented as:

12. $$\frac{dw_j}{dt} = w_j \frac{d\eta}{(1+\eta)}; w_j(0) = (1+p_j)\, q_s$$

Equation (12) solves to:

13. $$w_j = (1 + p_j)q_s(1 + \eta)$$

Equation (13) indicates that even if the overt employment rate $\boldsymbol{\eta}$ could be pushed to full employment by contriving low-quality work for the undereducated, an economy's high degree of dependence on large numbers of undereducated workers can tend to keep $\boldsymbol{q_s}$ very low or falling and tend to suppress $\boldsymbol{w_j}$ even as $\boldsymbol{\eta \rightarrow 1}$. This differs from the Lewis (1954) model in which the approach to full employment would automatically raise the wage rate. To raise $\boldsymbol{q_s}$, the wage rate over time takes targeted policy to increase the education of workers and capitalize work in the sectors of the economy that employ the undereducated (Lewis 1954).

Further, the aggregate supply identity allows accounting for the influence of import dependence of the productivity of the knowledge, skills and self-confidence of workers in generating supply to provision domestic demand, y_j^d, as raised by Best (1968, 1971) and Best and St Cyr (2012). That is, a sector's aggregate supply (Y_j^A) is its total supply to provision domestic demand plus the real value of its imports evaluated with the real exchange rate, $\frac{\varepsilon p_m}{p_j} M_j$. Again, as in Best (1968), these imports are factor inputs, either used directly as capital inputs in production or used indirectly as a means of reproduction of labour. This implies that:

14. $$y_j^d \tilde{N}_j = Y_j^A - \frac{\varepsilon p_m}{p_j} M_j$$

Here, the total differential of (14) gives:

15. $$y_j^d = \frac{dM_j / d\tilde{N}_j}{\left(1 + \frac{\tilde{N}_j dy_j^d}{y_j^d d\tilde{N}_j}\right)} = [\left(\frac{dY_j^A}{dM_j} - \frac{\varepsilon p_m}{p_j}\right) + \frac{\varepsilon p_m}{p_j}\left\{\frac{M_j dp_m}{p_j dM_j} - \left(\frac{M_j d\varepsilon}{\varepsilon dM_j} + \frac{M_j dp_m}{p_m dM_j}\right)\right\}]$$

In equation (15), $\frac{dY_j^A}{dM_j}$ is the marginal influence of increasing knowledge, skills, and self-confidence on imports, and $\frac{dY_j^A}{dM_j}$ is the marginal influence of sector imports on its aggregate supply. It is perhaps worth noting here that since $\frac{dY_j^A}{dM_j} = \frac{dY_j}{dM_j} + \frac{\varepsilon p_m}{p_j}$, where $\frac{dY_j}{dM_j}$ is the marginal product of imports in sector j, it must hold that $\frac{dY_j^A}{dM_j} - \frac{\varepsilon p_m}{p_j} = \frac{dY_j}{dM_j}$. Thus, the factor $\frac{dM_j}{d\tilde{N}_j}$ raises the per worker supply that provisions domestic demand, y_j^d, by rescaling the marginal product of imports as well as the gap $\frac{\varepsilon p_m}{p_j}\frac{M_j dp_m}{p_j dM} - \frac{\varepsilon p_m}{p_j}\left(\frac{M d\varepsilon}{\varepsilon dM} + \frac{M dp_m}{p_m dM}\right)$.

As observed by Best (1968), in sectors that are externally propelled and trade in accordance with comparative advantage, both p_m and p_j are determined abroad and $\frac{\varepsilon p_m}{p_j}$ will tend to be very volatile, causing uncertainty about the sector profit rate and lowering the flow of domestic retained earnings to validate investment. However, one would expect that as some sectors of the economy increases their employment of ISCO-08 level 4 skills and thus their capacity to produce and use domestic capital and grow $\tilde{N}_j$, they will acquire monopolistic price-making power and be able to raise p_j relative to p_m in the process of engaging in intra-industry trade. This will lower $\frac{\varepsilon p_m}{p_j}$ while growing $\frac{dY_j^A}{dM_j}$ and hence the gap $\left(\frac{dY_j^A}{dM_j} - \frac{\varepsilon p_m}{p_j}\right)$. It will also increase the gap $\frac{\varepsilon p_m}{p_j}\frac{M_j dp_m}{p_j dM} - \left(\frac{\varepsilon p_m}{p_j}\frac{M d\varepsilon}{\varepsilon dM} + \frac{\varepsilon p_m}{p_j}\frac{M dp_m}{p_m dM}\right)$. Innovation in such sectors will more than offset the demand-reducing effects of the increase in p_j. The overall effect will be to raise y_j^d and the rate of profit of the sector along with the investment-validating savings rate. Moreover, the capacity for intra-industry trade will also grow, raising x_j and producing similar effects. As the capital-producing and using sectors increase their production and employment of advanced knowledge and skills as a share of total employment and increase their share of GDP, the effect will be to increase the rate of growth of output per worker and ultimately of GDP per capita.

For completeness, it is noted that regarding trade, in equation (8), $\frac{G_j - T_j}{Y_j}$ and τ_j can be treated as policy-determined and is exogenous along with the FDI response to $(r_j - i)$. So, for $a(t) = \frac{G_j - T_j}{Y_j} + s_p r_j(1-\tau_j) + (r_j - i)\frac{dF_j}{F_j dt}$, it would hold that $y_j = y_{j0}e^{\int 0 a(s)ds}$ is determined as the solution of equation (8) in a nexus with r_j defined by equations (8) through (15), assuming $a(t)$ is continuous. Further, since y_f^d is determined by equations (14) and (15), the available sector supply of exports per worker, x_j, is the residual $y_j - y_j^d$. Then, bearing in mind the results on aggregate exports in equation (1), the actual growth of sector exports per worker over time can be represented as a result of its key growth factors reflecting both growth of domestic supply capacity supplemented by growth of the capital share of GDP, k_{sh}, and growth of foreign demand, Y_f, to take up the supply offered:

16. $$\frac{dx_j}{dt_j} = \left(\alpha_1 \frac{dy_j}{y_j} - \alpha_2 \frac{dy_j^d}{y_j^d} + \alpha_3 \frac{dk_{sh}}{k_{sh}} + \alpha_4 \frac{dY_f}{Y_f}\right)x_j;\ x_j(0) = x_{j0}$$

where, $\alpha_1 = \frac{Y_j}{x_j}$, $\alpha_2 = \frac{d_j^d}{x_j} dy_j^d$, α_3 transmits the effects of growing innovative capacity created by a rising share of capital in GDP ($\frac{dk_{sh}}{k_{sh}}$), and α_4 transmits the effects of growing foreign income. Equation (16) locates the relevance of productivity growth in the growth of the export capacity of the sector and economy. In general, the higher the rate of productivity growth, the faster the growth of the export capacity of the sector and hence the economy. In some sectors, α_2 is comparatively small because of export specialization reflecting Lewisian comparative advantage (Lewis 1954) and external propulsion with price-taking behaviour as defined by Best (1968). So, domestic output is not designed to satisfy domestic consumer demand and X_j is most of sector output, with α_3 low and the rate of growth of exports influenced heavily by exogenous demand. In the capital-producing sectors evolving under internal propulsion to provision domestic consumer demand, α_2 is comparatively high and $\frac{dx_j}{dt}$ depends heavily on $\frac{dk_y}{k_y}$ and its capacity to create intra-industry trade, with final sales governed by the foreign-demand-creating capacity of sector prices and the problem-solving capacity of sector output (Best 1971; Dixit and Stiglitz 1977; Dixit and Norman 1980; Krugman 1981). Equation (15) solves to $x_j = x_{j0}e^{\int_0^t b(s)ds}$, where $b(t) = \alpha_1 \frac{dy_j}{y_j dt} - \alpha_2 \frac{dy_j^d}{y_j^d dt} + \alpha_3 \frac{dk_{sh}}{k_{sh} dt} + \alpha_4 \frac{dY_f}{Y_f dt}$ is assumed to be continuous. Further, the balances of trade and payments as well as domestic self-reliance can be represented using the imports of equation (14) and exports as determined by equation (16), considering the inflow of foreign savings referenced in equations (7) and (8). The supplementary equations required to represent these conditions are neglected here for brevity (for details, see James 2023a).

It should be clear that equations (11), (13), (15) and (16) update the algebraic representation of the classical geometry of Lewis (1954, 1955) and the related model of the rate of profit and trade, by: (i) making the role of innovation explicit through $\frac{d\tilde{N}_j}{dK_j}$; (ii) adding the influence of the gap between sector price growth and sector wage growth induced by growth of employment of knowledge, skills and self-confidence of workers represented in the term $\{p_j(x_j+y_j^d)\frac{\tilde{N}_j dp_j}{p_j d\tilde{N}_j} - w_j\frac{\tilde{N}_j dw_j}{w_j d\tilde{N}_j}\}$; (iii) accounting explicitly for sector exports per worker, and hence for differences in the pattern of sector specialization in international trade, with some sectors trading according to rationalized comparative advantage, discussed extensively in the open model of Lewis (1954), and some sectors engaged in innovation-driven intra-industry trade, implied by Best (1971) and discussed at length in other literature (Dixit and Stiglitz 1977; Dixit and Norman 1980; Krugman 1981); and (iv) accounting explicitly for the effects of growing knowledge, skills and self-confidence on the marginal productivity of imports and hence on the supply of output that provisions domestic demand, a matter raised by Best (1968) and by Best and St Cyr (2012).

Critical to the framework of interpretation is the observation that economy-wide productivity growth is a multisectoral weighted process, with the key weight being the sector share of GDP. Specifically, economy wide output per worker, y, can be represented as the average of the sectoral output per worker, y_j, weighted by the share of the labour force employed in each sector, l_j. That is:

17. $y = \Sigma_j l_j y_j$

where $\Sigma_j l_j = 1$. It is then straightforward that the total differential of (17) yields:

18. $$\frac{dy}{ydt} = \Sigma_j \alpha_j \frac{dy_j}{y_j dt} + \Sigma_j \alpha_j \frac{dl_j}{l_j dt}$$

where the $\alpha_j \frac{Y_j}{Y}$, the sector shares of GDP, are the applicable weights. The term $\Sigma_j \alpha_j \frac{dy_j}{y_j dt}$ is the weighted average of the rates of growth of the sector output per worker under the influence of the rate of profit, as in equation (8), some increasing and some decreasing. The term $\Sigma_j \alpha_j \frac{dl_j}{l_j dt}$ is the weighted average of the rates of growth of the sector shares of total labour, again with the shares of some sectors increasing and those of others decreasing.

GDP per capita is one of the primary indicators of the level of development achieved by economy, and the relationship between aggregate GDP per capita growth ($\frac{dy_l}{y_l dt}$)and labour productivity growth ($\frac{dy}{ydt}$) is represented by a generalization of the ul Haque (1995) proposition. That is:

19. $$\frac{dy_l}{y_l dt} = \beta_1 \frac{dy}{ydt} + \beta_2 \frac{dn}{ndt}$$

where $\frac{dn}{ndt}$ is the rate of growth of the average level of knowledge, skills and self-confidence of workers relative to population growth. If $\frac{dn}{ndt}$ is treated as unobserved, equation (19) is consistent with equation (1) and underlies the correlations reported based on the data in Table 10.16 above. With equation (16), it indicates that both export performance and living standards improve with sector productivity growth. The ul Haque (1995) hypothesis arises from the strong assumptions that $\beta_1 < 1$, $\beta_2 < 0$, and $\frac{dn}{ndt} = 1$. Here, it is assumed that $\beta_2 > 0$ and $\frac{dn}{ndt} > 0$, so that the average knowledge, skills, and self-confidence of workers might grow faster than the population. Equation (19) also clarifies why the emigration of workers with high levels of knowledge, skills and self-confidence lowers the rate of growth of GDP per capita.

Consistent with equations (16), (18) and (19), we observe that for an economy to compete successfully for development opportunity in the global space, it must achieve continuous growth, up to some limit, of k_{sh}, the share in GDP of sectors that can produce and deploy capital using

ISCO-08 level 4 skills. These are the sectors that can produce and deploy advanced ISCO-08 level 4 knowledge, skills and self-confidence to innovate, produce and export problem-solving capital and capital-intensive output, and thus engage in intra-industry trade (James and Taylor 2021; James and Hamilton 2022; James 2023b).

SUMMARY AND POLICIES TO GROW GDP PER CAPITA

The evidence presented in section 2 clarifies the existence of widespread undereducation and, hence, undercapitalization of workers, employment, and work in Trinidad and, more so, in Tobago. The evidence presented in section 3 indicates that the economy continues to be externally propelled. Together, they amount to evidence that the economy does not produce enough capital to operate as an internally propelled (or developed) economy driven by the dynamic forces of market competition. The evidence presented in section 4 clarifies the consequences of slow productivity growth and related slow growth of GDP per capita. The evidence implies the analysis of the development process presented in section 5, which showed that under the conditions of widespread undereducation of workers, development occurs only when well-informed deliberate policy measures are taken. Such policy measures should foster capital production and accumulation, along with innovation, that together cause the growth of the capital share of GDP and growth of the marginal and average products of labour relative to the wage. They also cause growth of the marginal product of imports relative to the real exchange rate. Import displacement and growth of economic self-reliance are beneficial correlates of the process. Overall, the data and analytical framework outlined imply policies aimed at growing productivity and GDP per capita in Trinidad and Tobago. They also suggest how development in Tobago fits into the national process. These policies are set out in broad terms in this section.

In general, the guiding framework and the available evidence suggest the need for simultaneous efforts to upgrade institutions, restructure the economy towards capital production, and grow innovative capacity. While not revealed by the empirical methods used in this study, estimates produced by James and Hamilton (2022) using data from 128 countries suggest the following impact multipliers (elasticities) that can guide prioritization of this development effort: (i) growth of the capital share of GDP (2.33); (ii) institutional progress (1.72); and (iii) growth of innovative capacity (1.49). All the impact multipliers reflect the fact that the growth of the strategic factors creates backward and forward linkages among the sectors of the economy, reinforced by productivity growth, import displacement and rising domestic consumption per worker.

Consistent with the tasks undertaken by ISCO-08 level 4 skills, the impact multiplier associated with growing the capital share of GDP reflects growing backwards and forward linkages to the other sectors of the economy created by the growing capital sectors, reinforced by productivity growth, import displacement and rising domestic consumption per worker. Here, for Trinidad and Tobago, emphasis must be on the impact of growing the competitive capacity to produce and export the output of the capital services: (i) education (knowledge, skills and self-confidence); (ii) healthcare; (iii) the creative industries; and (iv) linked infrastructure and tourism plant. Production and export of most manufactured capital goods are unlikely to be competitive in the foreseeable future. On the other hand, considering the growing significance of the capacity to collect and transform wide-ranging forms of cultural and sociological data into information and knowledge for use by consumers and producers, the creative industries offer especially important and accessible opportunities to produce innovative problem-solving capital in the form of versatile "knowledge-capturing products" as defined in SNA 2008 (UN 2009, 97). Knowledge-capturing products are used to provide, store, communicate, and disseminate information, advice, and entertainment in such a way that users can accumulate and access information and knowledge repeatedly. The industries that produce them are concerned with the production and distribution of general or specialized information, stories, news, consultancy reports, computer programs, imagery and graphics, movies and video games, music and the like. Ownership rights may be established over knowledge-capturing products, which are typically stored on physical objects such as paper or digital media and, therefore, can be traded like ordinary goods. As capital forms, they can be owned, accumulated, upgraded, traded, and used repeatedly, and would facilitate the rapid emergence of markets in an economy such as Tobago.

The rising rate of profit generated by productivity growth will provide a basis for a sustainable increase in the validating savings rate and for attracting international collaboration, especially foreign direct investment, underpinned by suitable fiscal policies related to both the corporate tax rate and deficit spending. Since much of the exporting of the capital services can best be done on the existing tourism platform of the economy, the approach can be summarized as promoting industrialized tourism with priority attention to attracting sufficient numbers of long-stay visitors as anchors of tourism product development. Monetary policy initiatives to support the growth of the capital share of GDP primarily include growth of the supply of credit targeted at producers of problem-solving domestic capital and investors/entrepreneurs adopting it. Skilled and inclusive development banking institutions typically achieve this.

The impact multiplier associated with institutional progress reflects the spread effects of improved policy and decision-making stimulated by improved institutional production of data and its use to produce, share, and communicate information among stakeholders, including government, and to inform policy. The conditions of extensive undereducation of labour, the undercapitalization of work, and associated external propulsion imply that the growth of GDP per capita cannot be taken for granted – as a natural consequence of the efficient operation of markets ruled by the competitive movement of capital. Deliberate policy interventions are needed, and these could only come from the upgrade of the governance framework to allow (i) full-information joint decision-making, characterized by effective legislative oversight of the executive function, as well as (ii) effective legislative responsibility for the spatial equality of access to development opportunity. In turn, drawing on international capital inflows and faculty upgrades, the education, training and research systems will need to be upgraded to boost the production and distribution of the exportable information, knowledge, and skills typical of high-quality level 3 and level 4 graduates. The emphasis here must be on the technical skills to learn quickly by practice and develop winning solutions to local and global problems. Thus, an essential aspect of the upgrades must be the introduction and development of a full-scope skill-intensive track in the schooling system, from preschool through to advanced tertiary education, converging with the academic track at the tertiary levels. Another important aspect must be a tertiary-level competitive skills training and acquisition programme to respond rapidly to ongoing innovations in the global economy while developing domestic exportable solutions to offset the import costs of adopting foreign innovations. Given the length of time it takes to increase the inflow of level 3 and 4 skills into the labour force, a crucial complement to the upgrade of the school system must be an upgrade of the institutional arrangements for attracting foreign entrepreneurs and their workers, especially start-ups, into the capital production sectors. Such arrangements include favourable and competitive tax/subsidy arrangements, subsidized infrastructure, citizen-by-investment programmes and the like.

The impact multiplier associated with the capacity to innovate points directly to the linkage and import-displacement effects of growing capital production on the capacity to produce winning solutions to problems thrown up by the local and global markets as well as to respond with alacrity to ongoing rapid changes in international technologies, especially information technologies. However, deliberate programming will be required to build a responsive national innovation system based on an expansion of domestic production of exportable capital. Such programming may have to be led by an "innovation czar" managing a competitive search and response process focused on innovation in the capital service industries. The czar will have to be empowered to take necessary steps to identify and remove barriers to innovation at all relevant levels, especially firms, and for identification of enablers to be introduced and targeted to investors in capital production. These identification processes will have to be informed by suitable data collection, processing and reporting, facilitated and amplified by modern and rapidly changing machine learning technologies.

The evidence suggests a stationary average wage. To increase the average real wage as a basis for raising productivity and living standards, it will be necessary to proceed with a two-pronged policy. On the one hand, given that the government is the largest employer, policies will be needed to raise the social wage (the quality of public services) in the first instance without raising the basic monetary wage, allowing room for the growing productivity of labour to increase private sector profits and validating savings. On the other hand, policies must be introduced to raise productivity in all other activities that seek to provide domestic demand, including in sectors such as agriculture and creative services. Such policies should seek to upgrade the capital used in the sectors, especially the domestic capital, such as the education and skills used by undereducated workers.

Assuming that Tobago is properly defined with appropriate boundaries in the Constitution, policies to promote development in Tobago fit naturally into the above scheme, except that they must be designed to foster faster growth in Tobago than in Trinidad. On the evidence and framework, the focus of such policies should be: (i) the introduction of a targeted programme to build Tobago's private sector and displace the THA as the island's leading employer and (ii) optimization of the use of the island's tourism platform to produce and export capital services, underpinned by a significant inflow of foreign investors/entrepreneurs and their level 3 and 4 workers. This industrialized tourism programme should be scaled to attract a growing number of international visitors annually, eventually exceeding one hundred thousand in the medium term.

There are several supporting elements of such a programme. One is an upgrade of the policy-making capacity of the Tobago Island Government to include: (i) an Executive Council that is a tiny minority of the House of Assembly (THA); (ii) legislative oversight of the Executive Council and local law-making by a sufficient majority of elected Assembly representatives large enough to run the oversight committees and complete with mandates to ensure effective public petitioning of the legislature by all relevant stakeholders, including the diaspora and other foreign stakeholders; (iii) introduction of an elected Tobago Senate for the primary purpose of ensuring spatial equity in development across Tobago, but with responsibilities to share legislative law-making and oversight of the Executive Council, and advise and consent on the scale and structure of the Tobago Development Budget. Such reforms would enable full-information policymaking rather than the limited information practices of the current design.

Another element of the programme should be an upgrade of the education and training system in Tobago, with adaptation to address the role of modern machine learning. Such upgrade should include at least the following: (i) a strong publicly funded *continuing education* pprogramme targeting workers with level 1 and 2 education; (ii) introduction of a parallel skill-intensive track through to tertiary education; (iii) strengthening of the STEAM elements of the academic track of the existing system; (iv) a programme of teacher recruitment, training and certification aimed at elevating teachers and researchers to the most productive performers and highest earners in the labour market over time; and (v) reorienting teaching and research skills towards philosophy, epistemology, logic and methodology in the light of rapidly evolving machine learning and quantum computing.

A third element is the establishment of an integrated national development bank based in Tobago, which can (i) serve as banker to the THA and custodian of the THA Fund; (ii) manage the foreign exchange reserve pool Tobago must build to facilitate its accelerated development process; and (iii) promote the production of exportable capital services by the private sector, with international collaboration. In the latter case, the focus of its credit policies should be on (i) affordable (means-tested) financing of acquisition of the knowledge and skills required for competent performance of level 4 tasks and (ii) financing and technical support for institutional units that produce innovative and problem-solving capital by using level 4 skills to undertake analysis and research to extend the body of human knowledge in specific fields, share and communicate knowledge and results to others, and, crucially, apply results to design of advanced problem-solving structures, machinery, equipment, institutions and processes for construction and production. Further, the Tobago development agenda should include national and international collaboration to establish and maintain a publicly funded Tobago Innovation and Entrepreneurship Development Centre embedded in the development banking facility. Financing for this facility should be supplemented by mandated private contributions from the business sector, subject to legislative oversight and charged with the responsibility to manage the development of innovative capacity in the industrialized tourism sector, including rapid adaptation to modern information technologies. This facility should be required to take the necessary steps to do the following: (i) identify and remove barriers to innovation at all relevant levels; (ii) identify and introduce enablers (such as innovation competitions) targeting private sector investors in capital production; and (iii) ensure supporting data collection, processing and reporting, facilitated and amplified by modern machine learning.

ACKNOWLEDGEMENTS

The authors wish to thank the editors of the book, Professor Dillon Alleyne of the Department of Economics at UWI, Mona, and Professor Rosalea Hamilton of the Institute of Law and Economics, Jamaica, for their helpful comments on an early draft of the chapter. Thanks are also due to Dr Shelton Nicholls, former deputy governor of the Central Bank of Trinidad and Tobago for his careful examination of the data, econometric methods and theory. The methods of labour market analysis were learned many years ago from noted labour market analyst Dr Roy Thomas at the Department of Economics at UWI, St Augustine.

REFERENCES

Best, L. A. 1968. "Outline of a Model of Pure Plantation Economy." *Social and Economic Studies* 17(3): 283–326.

———. 1971. "Independent Thought and Caribbean Freedom." In *Readings in the Political Economy of the Caribbean*, edited by N. Girvan and O. Jefferson, 7–28. Kingston: New World.

———, and K. Polanyi-Levitt. 1969. *Externally Propelled Growth and Industrialization in the Caribbean*, 4 Volumes. Mimeograph. Montreal: Centre for Developing Areas Studies, McGill University.

———. 2009. *Essays on the Theory of Plantation Economy: A Historical and Institutional Approach to Caribbean Economic Development.* Mona, Jamaica: University of the West Indies Press.

Best, L.A., and E. St Cyr. 2012. *Transforming the Plantation Economy: Economic Policy and Management Choices – Trinidad and Tobago 1950–2005.* Tunapuna, Trinidad and Tobago: The Lloyd Best Institute of the West Indies.

Clark, J. B. 1899. *The Distribution of Wealth: A Theory of Wages, Interest, and Profits.* New York: MacMillan (1908 Edition). https://oll.libertyfund.org/title/clark-the-distribution-of-wealth-a-theory-of-wages-interest-and-profits.

Dickey, D.A., and W.A. Fuller. 1979. "Distribution of the Estimators for Autoregressive Time Series with a Unit Root." *Journal of the American Statistical Association* 74 (366): 427–31.

Dixit, A., and J. Stiglitz. 1977. "Monopolistic Competition and Optimum Product Diversity." *American Economic Review* 67, no. 3 (June): 297–308.

Dixit, A., and V. Norman. 1980. *Theory of International Trade.* Cambridge: Cambridge University Press.

Elliott, G.R., T.J. Rothenberg, and J.H. Stock. 1996. "Efficient Tests for an Autoregressive Unit Root." *Econometrica* 64 (4): 813–36.

Gali, J., and M. Gertler. 1999. "Inflation Dynamics: A Structural Econometric Analysis." *Journal of Monetary Economics* 44 9(2): 195–222.

Hodrick, R.J., and E.C. Prescott. 1997. "Postwar U.S. Business Cycles: An Empirical Investigation." *Journal of Money, Credit, and Banking* 29 (1): 1–16.

ILO. 2012. *International Standard Classification of Occupations – ISCO-08*. Geneva: International Labour Office.

James, V., and L. Taylor. 2021. *Competing for Development: Perspectives on Self-Sustaining Growth for Caribbean Economies*. Port of Spain: Tapia House Group. https://competingfordevelopment.com.

James, V. and R. Hamilton. 2022. "Strategic Factors in Economic Development Revisited." *Development Essays* 1 (1): 1–23.

James, V. 2023a. "The Essence of Development." Unpublished paper available from the author on request (vanus.james@gmail.com).

———. 2023b. "Intra-industry Trade and Economic Development." *Development Essays* 1, no. 3: 1–19.

Johnston, J., and J. DiNardo. 1997. *Econometric Methods*. New York: McGraw-Hill.

Irfan-ul-Haque, I. 1995. *Trade, Technology, and International Competitiveness*. World Bank: Economic Development Institute.

King, R.G., and S. Rebelo. 1990. "Public Policy and Economic Growth: Developing Neoclassical Implications." *Journal of Political Economy* 98 (5): 126–50.

Krugman, P. 1981. "Intra-industry Specialization and the Gains from Trade." *Journal of Political Economy* 89 (October): 959–73.

Leontief, W. 1953. "Dynamic Analysis." In *Studies in the Structure of the American Economy: Theoretical and Empirical Explorations in Input-Output Analysis, edited by* W. Leontief, H. Chenery, P. Clark, J. Duesenberry, A. Ferguson, A. Grosse. R. Grosse, M. Holzman, W. Isard, and H. Kinstin, 53–90. Oxford: Oxford University Press.

———. 1970. "The Dynamic Inverse." In *Contributions to Input-Output Analysis*, Vol. I, edited by A. P. Carter and A. Brody. Amsterdam: North-Holland.

Lewis, W.A. 1954. "Economic Development with Unlimited Supplies of Labour." *Manchester School of Economics and Social Studies* 22 (2): 139–91.

———. 1955. *The Theory of Economic Growth*. London: Allen and Unwin.

Pearl, J. 2009. *Causality: Models, Reasoning, and Inference*. 2nd ed. Cambridge: Cambridge University Press.

Rebelo, S. 1991. "Long Run Policy Analysis and Long Run Growth." *Journal of Political Economy* 99 (3): 500–521.

Rubin, D.B. 1987. *Multiple Imputation for Nonresponse in Surveys*. New York: Wiley.

Schafer, J.L. 1997. *Analysis of Incomplete Multivariate Data*. Boca Raton, FL: Chapman and Hall/CRC.

UN. 2009. The *System of National Accounts, 2008* (SNA 2008). New York: United Nations.

[CHAPTER 11]

Reflections on Economic Development in Trinidad and Tobago in the Post-independence Era

ROGER HOSEIN, REGAN DEONANAN, REBECCA GOOKOOL-BOSLAND AND **MARK ROOPCHAN**

INTRODUCTION

In understanding the economic development process, Rosenstein-Rodan (1961) proposed that a country can promote economic development through a "big push". Rosenstein-Rodan indicated that economic development is not a smooth and uninterrupted process as it is comprised of a series of discontinuous jumps. In order to overcome the initial inertia that has occurred in a stagnant economy, a "big push" is needed to propel the economy toward higher wages and productivity. The authors proposed that without this "big push", an economy will fail to induce self-sustaining economic development.

Sir Arthur Lewis, the first Black West Indian Nobel laureate, noted that economic development could be achieved through an unlimited supply of labour. Lewis (1954) stated that "if unlimited supplies of labour are available at constant real wage rate, and if any part of the profits is reinvested in productive capacity, profits will grow continuously relatively to the national income." Lewis (1954) expressed the idea of an unlimited supply of labour through a two-sector (traditional and capitalist) model where the combination of shifting labour from the traditional sector and the entry of women into the labour force would provide the capitalist sector with an unlimited supply of labour. The result would be an expansion of the capitalist sector, which would subsequently experience an increase in output and share of profits. As excess labour is consumed, wages and productivity increase, which is the outcome predicted by other growth models. This, at the time of independence, was of relevance to the Trinidad and Tobago economy as there were unlimited supplies of labour available locally to be able to undertake deliberate economic planning towards an industrial development strategy.

Hirschman (1958), unlike the previous authors, proposed unbalanced development within an economy. Hirschman (1958) argued that "To create deliberate imbalances within the economy in accordance with a pre-designed strategy is the best way to accelerate economic development." The author advocated for the development of sectors or industries that have high forward and backward linkages. Thus, some sectors will remain underdeveloped while other sectors are developed. Subsequently, the decision to develop sectors with high backwards and forward linkages also leads to the natural development of the remaining sectors at a slower pace. It thereby helps to temper the pace at which prices increase. This unbalanced economic development will keep the economy moving forward. As Hirschman (1958) noted, "This 'seesaw advancement' moves the economy from one disequilibrium to another." This implies that when both sectors are developed further, investment into the sector with high forward and backward linkages will occur once more, and this induces additional growth in the remaining industries, and thus, the "seesaw" advancement between both occurs.

Indeed, nuances of different development paths can be observed for the Trinidad and Tobago economy since 1962, and in reflecting on the economics of these, the paper is organized into three sections. The first section focuses on examining the economic growth and performance of Trinidad and Tobago. The second section provides policy adjustments for Trinidad and Tobago, and lastly, the third section offers concluding remarks reflecting on the economy in a post-COVID-19 global environment.

ECONOMIC GROWTH PERFORMANCE: DRIVERS AND OBSERVATIONS

Figure 11.1 below shows the production of crude oil in Trinidad and Tobago and its average annual price on the international market from 1955 to 2021. In 1955, the Trinidad and Tobago economy produced 24.9 million barrels of oil. The production of crude oil increased 161 per cent between 1955 and 1967, after which it declined almost continuously until 1971 (the 1971 level of output was 72.5 per cent of what was produced in 1967). After 1971, the production of crude oil increased again and peaked in 1978 at 83.8 million barrels.[1] Since 1978, though, there has been an almost continuous decline in crude oil production in Trinidad and Tobago, except for a short period between 2001 and 2006. By 2021, the production of crude oil in Trinidad and Tobago stood at 20.7 million barrels of oil per annum, or a mere 24.6 per cent of the 1978 level of production.

Regarding oil prices, between 1955 and 1971, the price of crude oil remained moderately constant, but in 1973, on account of the Yom Kippur War, there was a sudden and sharp increase in the price of oil from US$2.70 in 1972 to US$9.80 in 1974. The price of oil remained buoyant until 1978, when the war between Iraq and Iran[2] led to a sharp surge in prices from US$12.70 in 1978 to US$39.60 in 1981. Thereafter, the price of oil fell, and by 1998, the price of oil decreased to US$14.4 per barrel. After 1998, with a commodity price super cycle taking place, the price of oil increased from US$14.4 in 1998 to US$97.9 in 2013 and averaged US$88.7 in the period 2008–2014[3]. Since then, the price of oil has decreased considerably, and in 2020, amidst

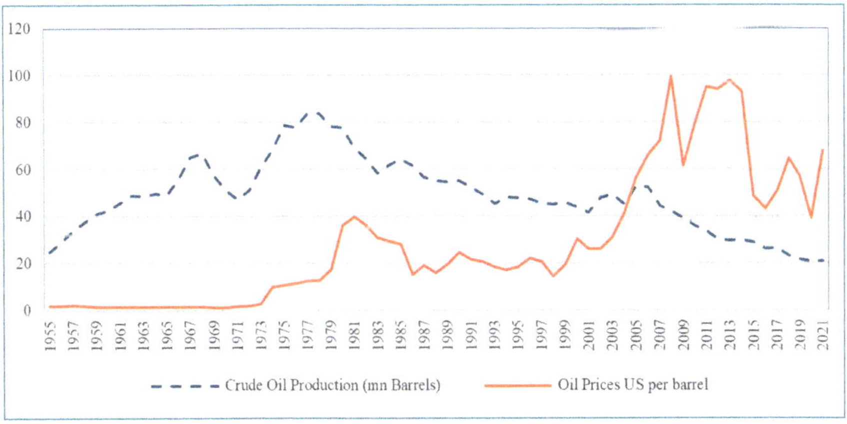

Figure 11.1: Crude Oil, Production in Trinidad and Tobago and International Price US$ per barrel

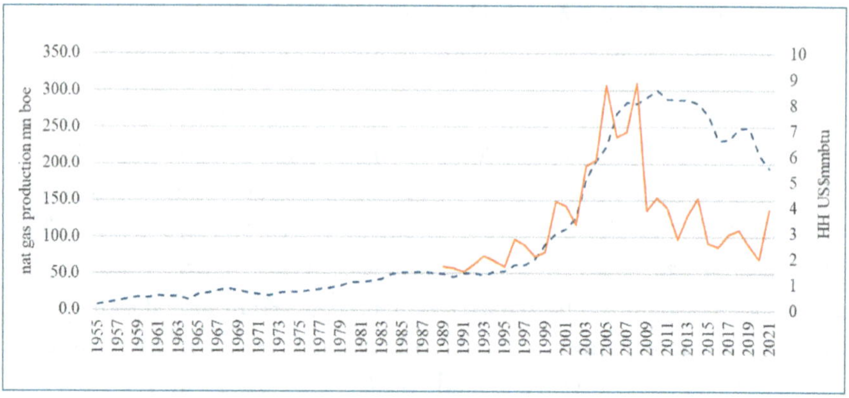

Figure 11.2: Natural Gas Production in Trinidad and Tobago and International Price US$ per mmbtu

the COVID-19 pandemic stood at US$39.3, although by 2021, it recovered to US$68 per barrel (see figure 11.2).

As for natural gas, production levels in 1955 stood at 7.9 million barrels of oil equivalent (boe), and this increased slowly but steadily until 1965, when gas production increased to 21.4 million boe as compared to 14.5 million boe in 1964. Natural gas production continued to increase thereafter, and in 1996, it rose to 61.5 million boe, compared to 52.6 million boe in 1993. After 1999, with the coming on stream of LNG[4], the production of natural gas in Trinidad and Tobago exploded and peaked at 300.3 million barrels of oil equivalent in 2010. After 2010, though, there was an almost continuous decline in the production of natural gas in Trinidad and Tobago, so that by 2021, natural gas production was only 64.6 per cent of that in 2010. Natural gas prices stood at US$1.70 per million British Thermal Unit (mmbtu) in 1987 and averaged US$2.00 per mmbtu between 1987 and 1998. In the context of the energy commodity price super cycle, natural gas prices after 1998 escalated and in 2008 peaked at about US$9 per mmbtu. This means that the Trinidad and Tobago economy was fortunate in that the rise in the price of natural gas and the production of natural gas coincided between 1998 and 2010. After 2008, natural gas prices fell and in 2020 stood at US$1.99 mmbtu, although by 2021, it increased marginally to US$3.9 per mmbtu.

The rapid increase in the production of crude oil and natural gas and, at times, in the prices of crude oil and natural gas led to a massive inflow of natural resource rents. Specifically, natural resource rents increased from US$18.2 million in 1960 to US$43.1 million in 1971, but after that, it increased

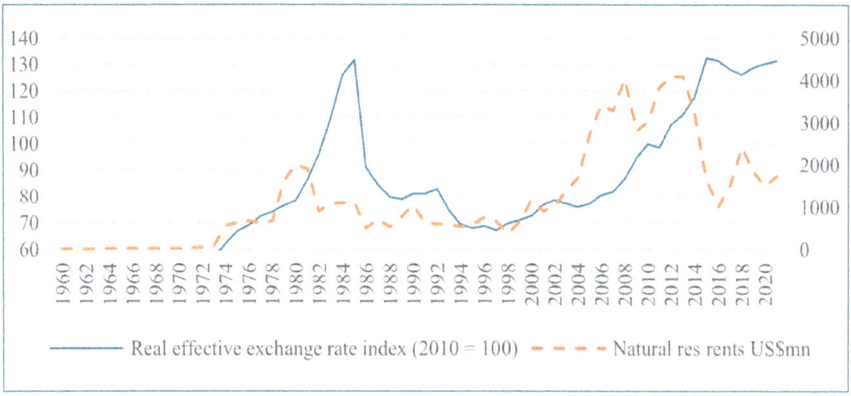

Figure 11.3: Real Effective Exchange Rate and Natural Resource Rents

sharply to US$2,016.1 million in 1980. After 1980, natural resource rents fell to the extent that in 1998, they were only 18.6 per cent of 1981's. After 1998, though, natural gas rents escalated in Trinidad and Tobago, and in 2012, they stood at US$4,084.2 million, averaging US$3,533.7 million per annum from 2006 to 2014. After 2012, natural resource rents declined in Trinidad and Tobago, and by 2021, they stood at US$ 1,721 million, or 48.8 per cent of the annual average for the period 2006 to 2014.

The Trinidad and Tobago economy, in the context of the changes observed in its primary foreign exchange earning sector, made progress. Its per capita GDP, as can be seen in figure 11.4 below, increased considerably between the

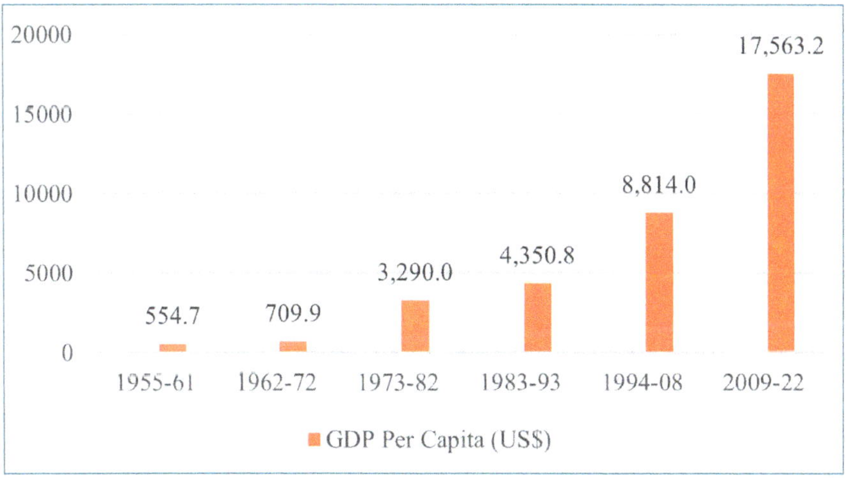

Figure 11.4: GDP per capita between 1955 and 2022

pre-independence period of 1955–61, when GDP per capita averaged US$554.7, and all the subsequent time periods. Note that in the period 2009–2022, the average annual GDP per capita was significantly higher than it was in any of the previously identified periods. In 2022, the GDP per capita of the Trinidad and Tobago economy was approximately US$15,962.5 (using data from the IMF 2022 Article 4 report on Trinidad and Tobago), which, whilst lower than the US$21,410.5 which occurred in 2008, was significantly more than the US$679.2 at the dawn of the economy's independence.

Comparatively speaking, though, the Trinidad and Tobago economy's real GDP growth performance since 1979, relative to other CARICOM member states, has not been outstanding, as shown in table 11.1 below.

Indeed, although between 1979 and 2021, the Trinidad and Tobago economy produced 1.97 billion barrels of oil and 6.23 billion barrels of natural gas, the growth of its real GDP was only 121.4 per cent and in this same time period as compared to Antigua and Barbuda where GDP growth was 226.7 per cent or Belize which experienced real growth of 511.9 per cent. Even more and as the following table 11.2 shows, when compared to the global economy, the Trinidad and Tobago economy moved relatively backwards, in that real GDP in 2021 was 19.7 per cent lower than in 2010 while in that same period, the world economy as a whole grew by more than 30 per cent!

Indeed, a disturbing outcome is also observed in figure 11.5 below, which shows that since 1980, Trinidad and Tobago, except for the years in which

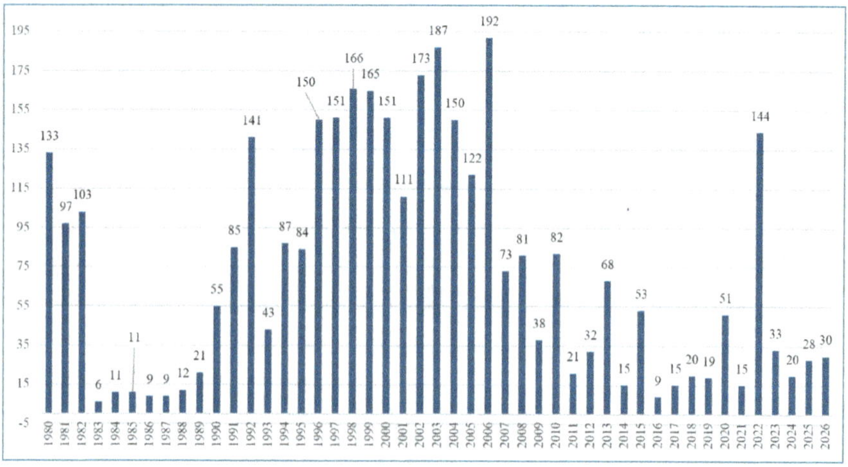

Figure 11.5: Trinidad and Tobago's GDP Rank in the World (195 is optimal, 1 is worst)

Table 11.1: Real GDP Growth of CARICOM Members, 1980–2021

Year	Antigua and Barbuda	The Bahamas	Barbados	Belize	Dominica	Grenada	Guyana	Haiti	Jamaica	St Kitts and Nevis	St Lucia	St Vincent and the Grenadines	Suriname	Trinidad and Tobago
1980	108.2	107.1	104.4	105.0	113.4	115.1	97.9	107.3	96.0	101.3	99.5	102.9	93.5	110.4
1985	140.2	125.9	102.5	113.3	141.8	138.2	81.4	104.9	107.6	126.2	135.1	124.3	81.4	97.1
1990	190.1	141.5	114.6	211.0	183.1	180.2	70.3	103.6	130.7	183.4	219.1	161.5	80.9	86.7
1995	211.1	140.9	108.9	282.4	199.4	184.9	99.0	94.7	144.6	222.3	246.9	193.3	73.4	105.1
2000	273.7	180.0	129.0	378.3	223.9	254.5	113.4	107.3	143.4	291.1	275.5	220.1	88.3	151.2
2005	315.3	195.4	136.7	484.3	239.8	317.8	116.0	113.7	154.9	340.6	297.6	273.6	114.9	217.5
2006	355.4	200.4	144.4	507.7	251.0	305.1	122.0	115.7	159.4	351.3	316.2	294.6	121.6	248.3
2007	388.5	203.3	147.6	510.3	267.0	323.8	130.6	121.2	161.7	353.5	322.3	304.5	127.8	258.9
2008	388.5	198.5	148.7	528.1	286.0	326.8	133.1	124.4	160.4	393.0	338.1	309.3	133.1	267.4
2009	342.0	190.2	141.1	529.3	282.6	305.2	137.6	131.7	154.9	379.7	331.8	302.8	137.1	254.5
2010	315.2	193.2	137.9	545.2	284.5	303.7	143.6	124.3	152.7	379.9	333.5	292.7	144.2	263.3
2015	342.2	200.7	137.5	615.5	283.3	353.7	168.7	142.9	156.7	439.8	344.4	308.6	156.2	268.3
2016	361.0	200.9	140.9	615.3	291.2	366.9	175.2	145.5	159.0	457.0	357.3	314.4	148.5	253.2
2017	372.3	204.2	141.6	626.5	271.9	383.2	181.7	149.1	160.1	461.3	369.9	317.6	150.8	245.7
2018	398.2	209.3	140.8	644.7	281.5	399.9	189.8	151.6	163.0	473.6	380.7	324.4	158.3	245.8
2019	417.1	211.3	139.0	656.1	302.6	402.6	199.9	149.0	164.6	496.4	380.4	326.2	160.0	242.8
2020	333.6	180.6	114.0	564.0	269.4	350.1	286.9	144.1	148.1	424.9	302.9	315.6	134.6	223.7
2021	336.8	184.3	117.7	611.9	278.4	359.4	345.4	143.0	154.9	420.5	313.5	296.4	135.5	221.4

Source: IMF

Table 11.2: Relative Growth Rates of Selected Economies

	1980	1985	1990	1995	2000	2005	2010	2015	2020	2021
Trinidad and Tobago	123.5	108.6	97	117.6	169.1	243.2	294.4	300	250.2	247.6
World	70.7	80.5	97.4	111.4	134.1	163	196.9	235.4	260.3	275.6
Advanced economies	71.2	81.7	98.4	110.2	130.4	145.9	154.5	168.4	174.3	183.4
Euro area				106.1	121.8	131.4	136.8	142.3	144	151.3
Major advanced economies (G7)	72.1	82.8	98.8	109.1	127.5	140.4	145.6	158.1	161.8	170.3
Other advanced economies (Advanced economies excluding G7 and euro area)	60.5	74.5	96.4	121.1	150	179.4	211.8	242.2	263.4	275.6
European Union	79	84.8	98.6	105.9	122.1	134.2	142.1	149.9	154.7	162.6
Emerging market and developing economies	69.8	78.4	95.8	113.1	139.1	186.1	254	326.8	379.8	404
Emerging and developing Asia	49.2	67.2	94.1	141.5	189.7	275.3	426.2	600	759.7	814.6
Emerging and developing Europe	84.8	95.3	106	79.9	90.1	118	139.4	161.2	177.7	188.3
ASEAN-5	52.7	64.8	93.1	133.6	148.9	191.1	247.4	318.2	376.8	387.9
Latin America and the Caribbean	83	86.9	96.3	114.1	132.8	151.7	182.7	205.9	195.4	207.8
Middle East and Central Asia	78.3	76.9	92.5	108.5	130	174.8	218.6	262.7	283.7	295.4
Sub-Saharan Africa	–	–	–	107.4	127.1	168.2	222.7	278.5	304.8	316.1

Source: IMF online database

energy revenues increased, experienced such poor growth performance that it was recorded many times to be among the top 35 worst growth performances in the world.

The poor relative rankings of the Trinidad and Tobago economy require some explanations, and these are discussed hereunder. In the period up to 2006, as energy output expanded (mainly natural gas) and energy prices increased, the economy maintained a reasonable growth performance and particularly in the period 1996–2006, treated here as the golden era of LNG, the economy maintained an excellent growth performance relative to many other countries in the world. However, this growth performance was "geographic" and hovered around changing the level of GDP "above the ground" by bringing energy resources located "below the ground" into production. The failure to sow the rents generated during periods of high performance and to adequately improve the economy's genuine savings meant that as the non-reproducible energy resources of the economy declined, the stock of capital, which was not adequately replaced by a compensating build-up of reproducible capital (for example the highway to Point Fortin only started in 2011 and at the time of this chapter, remains incomplete) resulted in a decline in the economy's growth performance.

The decline in the economy's relative growth performance also came about in part because of a fall in domestic labour productivity, motivated again by the way the energy revenues were used. Indeed, the labour force

Table 11.3: Output per Worker, Labour Force Participation Rate (LFPR) and Murders

Year	LFPR	Output per worker	Murders
2000	61.2	102585.2	118
2005	63.7	131227.5	386
2010	62.1	151900	485
2015	60.6	151064.3	410
2016	59.7	146622.6	463
2017	59.2	145424.1	494
2018	59.1	141016.8	516
2019	57.4	144387.9	538
2020	54.3	–	396
2021	–	–	448

Source: Central Statistical Office of Trinidad and Tobago, Central Bank of Trinidad and Tobago and Trinidad and Tobago Crime (a) 3rd quarter.

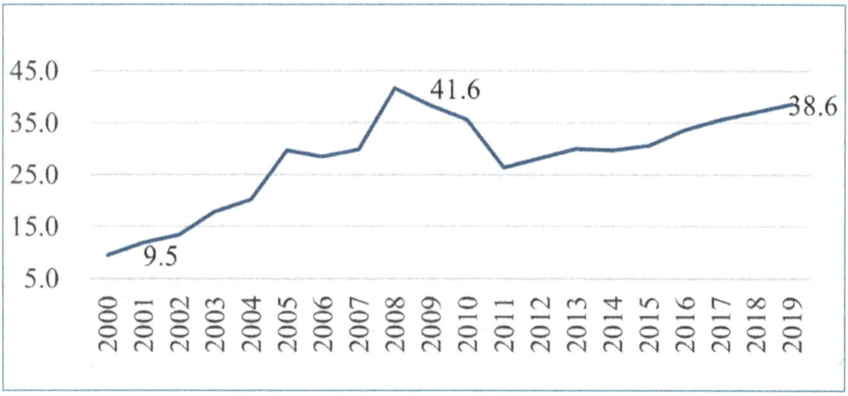

Figure 11.6: Trinidad and Tobago Homicide Rate (per 100K Population)

participation rate (LFPR) in the Trinidad and Tobago economy fell from 63 per cent in 2004 to 57.4 per cent in 2019. Output per worker in 2008 was TT$157,418.7 per person, and by 2019, this was TT$144,387.9 per person. Consider figure 11.6 above, which shows the increasing rate of crime over the period 2000 to 2019.

The Trinidad and Tobago economy also suffered from a decline in institutional capital, reflected in a decline in the economy's Ease of Doing Business ranking and with a similar pathway for the economy's corruption perception index. This meant that any compensation to the growth process that could emerge from a facilitative environment in which entrepreneurs could thrive was partly lost.

The rise in the homicide rate in Trinidad and Tobago also placed a damper on the "animal spirit" of entrepreneurs and no doubt forced them to divert productive resources towards security concerns rather than increasing their actual physical production.

One area of concern that may have led to the poor performance of the Trinidad and Tobago economy has to be linked to the way the economy uses its energy rents. Table 11.4 below shows Trinidad and Tobago's public sector finance position over the period 1955 to 2022. Total revenues from the energy sector escalated sharply from US$22.9 million in 1955 to US$1772.1 million by 1981. As both the price and production of energy products simultaneously fell after 1981, energy revenues plunged, and indeed, by 1998, stood at US$270.9 million or a mere 15.3 per cent of 1981. However, after 1998, energy revenues

Table 11.4: Publ c Sector Revenue and Expenditure (1955–2021) in millions US$ (Unless Otherwise Stated)

Year	Total Revenue	Total Revenue % of GDP	Current Revenue	Of which: Oil	Energy Revenues as a % of Current Revenues	Total Expenditure	Total Expenditure % of GDP	Current Expenditure	Current Expenditure as a % of GDP	Wages and Salaries	Transfers and Subsidies	TS/Oil Revenues (%)
1955	47.9	9.5	47.5	22.9	48.1	52.0	17.6	41.2	13.9	15.0	7.2	31.5
1960	87.7	9.5	86.9	39.8	45.8	91.4	17.0	69.5	12.9	25.5	10.6	26.6
1965	135.9	10.8	120.6	49.9	41.4	146.6	19.9	112.9	15.3	37.1	20.6	41.4
1970	158.8	9.7	156.6	56.4	36.0	195.1	23.7	140.2	17.1	55.2	26.3	46.6
1975	790.3	14.9	774.3	578.2	74.7	553.5	22.7	390.6	16.0	172.4	116.5	20.1
1980	2424.8	16.2	2414.8	1723 5	71.4	2277.5	36.5	1281.3	20.5	505.6	391.8	22.7
1985	2596.4	14.4	2596.4	1002.9	38.6	3152.2	42.7	2480.8	33.6	1126.8	1091.5	108.8
1990	1351.3	6.3	1302.1	545.3	41.9	1594.8	31.5	1279.6	25.2	466.5	442.5	81.2
1995	1413.4	4.5	1421.1	426.2	30.0	1421.0	26.7	1317.0	24.7	484.8	418.0	98.1
2000	2069.3	4.0	2064.6	710.4	34.4	1939.3	23.8	1745.0	21.4	506.4	661.6	93.1
2005	5066.3	5.0	5065.1	2516.0	49.7	4063.8	25.4	3562.5	22.3	841.9	1822.1	72.4
2006	6110.6	5.3	6109.8	3345.6	54.8	5055.5	27.5	4301.4	23.4	870.4	2424.1	72.5
2007	6429.2	4.7	6424.5	3059.2	47.6	6329.2	29.3	4987.8	23.1	1037.0	2801.4	91.6
2008	9192.6	5.2	9186.6	4944.4	53.8	7309.2	26.2	5738.8	20.6	1099.4	3292.7	66.6
2009	6107.3	5.0	6098.6	2345.7	38.5	7140.5	37.2	5815.2	30.3	1057.6	3248.6	138.5
2010	7063.3	5.0	7027.4	3011.9	42.9	6834.9	30.9	5909.1	26.7	1046.4	3398.7	112.8

Table 11.4 continues on next page

Table 11.4: Public Sector Revenue and Expenditure (1955–2021) in millions US$ (Unless Otherwise Stated) (*cont'd*)

Year	Total Revenue	Total Revenue % of GDP	Current Revenue	Of which: Oil	Energy Revenues as a % of Current Revenues	Total Expenditure	Total Expenditure % of GDP	Current Expenditure	Current Expenditure as a % of GDP	Wages and Salaries	Transfers and Subsidies	TS/Oil Revenues (%)
2011	7813.5	4.8	7766.6	3661.6	47.1	7643.3	30.1	6568.6	25.8	1130.4	3976.8	108.6
2012	7319.1	4.4	7314.2	2698.2	36.9	8131.3	31.5	7028.5	27.3	1134.0	4379.7	162.3
2013	8946.9	5.1	12299.3	3235.7	26.3	9063.6	33.2	7815.8	28.6	1470.4	4707.4	145.5
2014	8687.4	4.9	8635.2	3280.1	38.0	9976.7	36.1	8591.2	31.1	1349.9	5511.3	168.0
2015	8730.9	5.4	7812.2	1650.5	21.1	9328.7	37.0	8222.2	32.7	1596.7	4834.7	292.9
2016	6259.7	4.2	5739.4	489.3	8.5	7703.3	34.4	7086.5	31.7	1448.5	3996.7	816.8
2017	5490.2	3.5	5383.8	728.1	13.5	7157.8	30.9	6680.0	28.8	1454.2	3743.1	514.1
2018	6579.0	4.1	6576.3	987.6	15.0	7196.6	30.2	6841.1	28.7	1347.4	3846.9	389.5
2019	6726.3	4.2	6597.1	1773.7	26.9	7520.1	31.5	6962.7	29.1	1364.1	3913.2	220.6
2020	4947.9	3.4	4940.1	1163.3	23.5	7532.3	35.2	6926.4	32.4	1330.8	4047.6	347.9
2021	5283.4	3.3	5214.1	1358.4	26.1	7701.0	32.9	7109.6	30.4	1360.0	4141.3	304.9

Source: Central Bank of Trinidad and Tobago

improved rapidly in Trinidad and Tobago and between 1999 and 2014, the government of Trinidad and Tobago collected US$36.74 billion in energy revenues. Of particular concern is the relationship between transfers and subsidies and energy revenues, as shown below. This relationship towards the latter part of the data period consistently exceeded 100 per cent, showing the inertia in these types of expenses. (This relationship is further developed in a separate section.)

Indeed, from a mere 31.5 per cent of energy revenues in 1955, transfers and subsidies exploded to 304.9 per cent in 2021, and for the period 2009 to 2021, on average per annum, this ratio was 286.4 per cent. In the opinion of the authors of this chapter, the government of Trinidad and Tobago's fiscal indiscipline has contributed to the compromise of the economy's growth trajectory.

As the data in table 11.4 also clearly shows, there was a rapid increase in government expenditure from US$52 million in 1955 to US$9976.7 million in 2019, although it dipped to US$7701 million in 2021. The rapid increase in the government expenditure outlay helped to trigger an appreciation of the economy's real effective exchange rate. The first block of appreciation sharply grew by 150 per cent between 1972 and 1985. A series of devaluations thereafter corrected the value of Trinidad and Tobago's currency[5] to the extent that in 1995, the real effective exchange rate was 52.1 per cent lower than in 1985. After 1996, the currency embarked upon a continuous pathway of appreciation to the extent that by 2021, the real effective exchange rate was 93 per cent more appreciated than in 1995. Attempts were made to control the value of the Trinidad and Tobago real effective exchange rate after 2016 by an internal devaluation.[6] This strategy did not work as in 2021, the real effective exchange rate was just as overvalued in relation to 1995 as it was in 2016 with regard to 1995.

Analysing the mechanics of Dutch Disease[7] revealed significant adverse shifts in the employment structure of the Trinidad and Tobago economy. Table 11.5 below shows that agricultural employment in Trinidad and Tobago is on the decline, and further that the sector has a low level of output per worker. This is in the setting of a food import bill, which stood at US$251.2 million in 1999 and by 2020 stood at US$825.4 million. Further, note that the manufacturing sector has lost workers and indeed operates with almost 35 per cent spare capacity (according to data from the Central Bank of

Trinidad and Tobago). Correspondingly, what has happened in the Trinidad and Tobago economy is that the agricultural sector has lost workers. Still, even more than this, the comparatively stronger manufacturing sector (in terms of output per worker) has also lost workers to the services sector, as seen in table 11.5 below.

Table 11.5: Changes in the Structure of Employment in Trinidad and Tobago, 1999–2019

Real GDP					
	Agriculture	Petroleum	Manufacturing	Services	Total
1999	750.50	13993.90	3511.90	29948.10	48204.40
2008	511.40	36600.30	7626.70	47682.10	92420.50
2019	344.09	27177.49	6842.97	51204.03	85568.58
Employment					
	Agriculture	Petroleum	Manufacturing	Services	Total
1999	40346	14986	51196	382416	488944
2008	23400	18800	50500	494400	587100
2019	21940	11294	44287	515108	592630
Employment Shares					
	Agriculture	Petroleum	Manufacturing	Services	Total
1999	0.083	0.031	0.105	0.782	1.000
2008	0.040	0.032	0.086	0.842	1.000
2019	0.037	0.019	0.075	0.869	1.000
Change in Employment Shares					
	Agriculture	Petroleum	Manufacturing	Services	Total
1999–2008	-0.043	0.001	-0.019	0.060	0.000
2008–19	-0.003	-0.013	-0.011	0.027	0.000
Labor Productivity TT$, 2000=100					
	Agriculture	Petroleum	Manufacturing	Services	Total
1999	18601.6	933798.2	68597.2	78312.9	98588.8
2008	21854.7	1946824.5	151023.8	96444.4	157418.7
2019	15682.9	2406334.2	154514.4	99404.4	144387.9
Change in Labour Productivity					
	Agriculture	Petroleum	Manufacturing	Services	Total
1999–2008	3253.1	1013026.3	82426.6	18131.5	58829.9
2008–19	-6171.8	459509.7	3490.7	2960.0	-13030.8

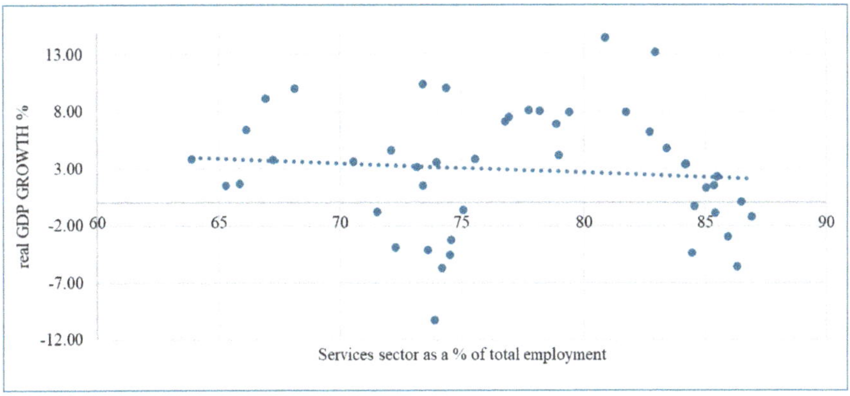

Figure 11.7: Scatterplot of the Relationship between the Share of the Services Sector in Total Employment and Real GDP Growth in Trinidad and Tobago, 1973–2020

Because output per worker in the services sector is lower than in the manufacturing sector (see table 11.5), this has caused a drag on productivity in the economy. Indeed, the scatterplot below illustrates that as the share of workers in total employment increases, there is a decline in the real GDP growth performance of the Trinidad and Tobago economy (see figure 11.7 above).

Given these realities facing the Trinidad and Tobago economy, outlined above, especially as relates to its relatively poor performance globally, the following suggestions are made as possible avenues that can help to improve economic outcomes beyond the country's sixtieth anniversary of independence.

SUGGESTED POLICY CHANGES

Utilize Venezuelan Immigrant Labour

There are a significant number of Venezuelan immigrants in Trinidad and Tobago. Indeed, the former commissioner of police and former Minister of National Security pointed out on 3 May 2021, in a newspaper comment entitled, "We need public help in securing borders," that there are over 120,000 illegal/ unregistered Venezuelans in Trinidad and Tobago. Venezuelans in Trinidad and Tobago tend to be in the age group (sixteen years to sixty-four years) and thus represent a potentially important addition to the economy's ageing labour force. The Trinidad and Tobago labour force in 2020 was 22.7 per cent larger than in 1991. In this same period, the population of the Trinidad and Tobago economy, aged sixty years and older, increased by 68.1 per cent. Table 11.6 below shows that Venezuelan workers are doing increasingly better in the Trinidad and Tobago labour market. In the first instance, the unemployment rate among Venezuelans was down to less than 30 per cent. This is considerably lower than the unemployment rate of 44.5 per cent held in 2020, and it may be because opportunities have been created as the economy has reopened. Note that on 30 March 2020, Trinidad and Tobago went into lockdown, but by 15 May 2020, gradual reopening of the economy began, and, whilst a state of emergency was imposed on 17 May 2021, it was lifted on 24 November 2021. The data from the Displacement Tracking Matrix (DTM) 2021[8] was collected between October 2021 and November 2021, when the economy was already reopening. The data shows that there was a slight increase in the number of informal sector workers to 53 per cent. However, this increase was relatively less than in 2018 and in 2019. The number of informal workers fell in 2021, possibly because the Venezuelans learnt to navigate the local system better and found jobs in other, more formal arrangements. According to the DTM 2022, by 2019, of all the surveyed Venezuelans, 82.5 per cent were already in Trinidad and Tobago. Also, the number of Venezuelans underpaid in both the formal and informal sectors is on the decline, and that's another healthy signal from a labour market perspective. Of concern is that the Venezuelans tend to work in the services sector of the economy. On this basis, the government of Trinidad and Tobago should register all

Table 11.6: Various Attributes of the Venezuelan Immigrant Population in Trinidad and Tobago, 2018–2021

	Unemployment %	% of Venezuelans working in the informal Sector	% of underpaid Venezuelan workers in the informal sector	% of underpaid Venezuelan workers in the formal sector
DTM 2018	32	90	–	–
DTM 2019	32	60	30	25
DTM 2020	44.5	46	54	36
DTM 2021	29.5	53	37	27

Source: Institute of Migration, Data Tracking Matrix (Various Years)

Venezuelan workers and give a proportion of them work permits for the manufacturing sector. Registering the Venezuelans reduces the probability that they would need to work in the less productive informal sector. If the government increases the number of Venezuelans who work in the agriculture sector, that would be a way to reduce agricultural imports and perhaps even reduce the price of some of the goods produced therein as a strategy to improve domestic food security.

Fiscal Targets and Fiscal Responsibility Legislation (FRL)

It is the opinion of the authors of this chapter that the government of Trinidad and Tobago take the necessary steps and establish a rules-based fiscal framework. This suggestion is made against the backdrop of twelve consecutive years of fiscal deficits and a ballooning ratio of transfers and subsidies (TS) to energy revenues, and, transfers and subsidies to capital expenditures. Many countries now use fiscal rules. At the end of 2021, about 105 countries had at least one fiscal rule; this is eleven countries more than in 2015 and ninety-six countries more than in 1985 (Davoodi et al. 2022).

National rules have been adopted many times after a crisis or to help avoid procyclical spending on account of volatile natural resource prices. Davoodi et al. (2022) have noted that the number of fiscal rules per country has increased in the last two decades, up from an average of two fiscal rules in the early 2000s to an average of about three now. As time progressed and fiscal rules were better understood, additional features were introduced to help strengthen the enforcement and monitoring of the fiscal rules. Some of these reforms introduced to help strengthen flexibility include:

a. Escape clause
b. Legal clauses: as of 2021, over 40 per cent of fiscal rules were buttressed by the legal system. A stronger legal basis can make fiscal rules more durable and credible.
c. Some countries have gone as far as to put formal enforcement mechanisms in place. Peru[9] and Panama[10] have corrections that guide the fiscal rules after there has been a deviation.

In setting fiscal responsibility targets, some broad criteria should be followed. These include simplicity, credibility, flexibility and, of course, the

Table 11.7: Possible Fiscal Responsibility Targets

Target	Notes
Simplicity	Lower debt rates by 5% of GDP annually for the next ten years for years with growth rates above 5% and 2% annually when growth rates are less than 5%.
Credibility	Build systems of monitoring into the legislation Ensure that a committee is established to execute interventions and hold public bodies accountable for actions/inactions.
Flexibility	Suspensions of the rule is possible for years which include natural disasters or other justifiable shocks
Idiosyncrasies	Natural disasters or Sharp Falls, e.g., sharp decrease in the price of oil.

country's idiosyncrasies (Wright and Grenade 2018). The anchor chosen depends on the peculiarities of the implementing country. In the Trinidad and Tobago context, it is suggested that a debt target, an overall balance rule and an expenditure rule be established.

A simplicity test for Trinidad and Tobago clearly established the fiscal variables being targeted[11]:

a. Transfer and subsidies (TS) should not exceed 50 percent of total government expenditures by 2027 and should not exceed 40 percent by 2030.
b. Net public sector debt should not exceed 60 percent of GDP. As of 2022, the IMF forecasts it at 88.4 percent.
c. The overall fiscal balance should be zero.
d. Current expenditure must not grow faster than the expected growth of nominal GDP.

The fiscal rule must also be flexible, and the suggestion here is that the fiscal balance should not exceed 0.5 per cent of GDP (Eyrand et al. 2018). Appropriate escape clauses must also exist, as they have become a necessary component of second-generation fiscal rules (Eyrand et al. 2018). These escape clauses cater to the need for urgent countercyclicality.

Anderson and Minarik (2006) have noted that the objective of Fiscal Responsibility Legislation (FRL) is to enshrine the rules and targets into law and can help to promote sustainable economic growth and, at the same time, help to improve accountability, assist in controlling deficits,

Table 11.8: Fiscal Legislation Rules

Intervention	Notes
Public Debt Target	65%
Fiscal Rule	Cannot exceed 0.5% of GDP by 2027
Escape Clauses	Pandemic (or any such global economic shock) Sharp decline in energy revenues
Legislated Fiscal Council	Fiscal Responsibility Council with five members

limiting debt accumulation, and helping to improve fiscal accountability and transparency. Two other approximate goals are to help secure long-term fiscal responsibility and stabilize the economy in the short term.

Credibility would be achieved by enshrining the fiscal rules and the associated targets in law. An independent fiscal council will help monitor the compliance of the government and report on the level of compliance. Note that a fiscal council is just an institutional arrangement, though, and they do not have a role in setting fiscal targets but in monitoring whether fiscal targets are met and in providing parallel forecasts and analysis. Wyplosz (2002) has contended that after fiscal rules, fiscal councils are the next most important intervention for helping to promote fiscal discipline. A fiscal council as part of the fiscal responsibility framework for Trinidad and Tobago will help promote fiscal transparency and accountability and thus reinforce the credibility of the fiscal framework.

Improve Non-energy Revenue Collection

As part of the strengthening of the economy, there must also be measures to improve revenues on the non-energy side so that the fiscal management of the economy can become more independent of energy sector revenues. In this regard, three initiatives in the government pipeline should be mentioned: revenue authority, gambling tax bill, and property tax. As seen in table 11.9 below, non-energy revenue contributed TT$9,247 million or 66 per cent of total revenue in 2001. However, by 2020, non-energy revenue grew to TT$25,940.8 (note that the share fell to 35.6 per cent in 2020) and accounted for 75 per cent of total revenue.

The IMF assessed the Board of Inland Revenue in Trinidad and Tobago in 2017 and found that out of twenty-eight high-level sectors, only twenty-

Table 11.9: Non-energy Revenue Generation, 2001–20

	VAT (TT$Mn)	Non-Energy Revenue (TT$mn)	Non-Energy Revenue / Total Revenue (%)
2001	2154.5	9247	66%
2005	2962.6	15396	52%
2010	6032.3	25153.8	57%
2011	4917	26418.7	56%
2012	6337.4	22608.6	46%
2013	6657.4	25655.2	49%
2014	5744.7	28950.6	50%
2015	7223.3	33583.7	59%
2016	7004.7	34514.5	77%
2017	5050.4	27110.6	75%
2018	7244.8	31300.6	73%
2019	5847.5	29894.5	64%
2020	6682.3	25940.8	75%

five sectors had ratings of either a C or a D. Indeed, in another study by the IMF in 2019, a VAT gap of about 5 per cent of GDP was found. About 50 per cent of the gap is on account of non-compliance, and about 50 per cent is on account of exemptions. If the government addresses these various leakages and weaknesses, then revenue collection can be considerably improved.

The Trinidad and Tobago Revenue Authority (TTRA) has been an institutional goal of the Trinidad and Tobago economy since the early 2000s. The Trinidad and Tobago Parliament approved the Revenue Authority Bill in December 2021. The TTRA will replace the inefficient Inland Revenue Division (IRD) and the Customs and Excise Division (CED) as it seeks to enforce and improve the collection of taxes from the citizens of Trinidad and Tobago. The TTRA aims to achieve these goals through its ability to investigate individuals for tax evasion while enforcing border protection and carrying out audits where applicable. Thus, tax collection will be done by one organization as opposed to two different branches of the Ministry of Finance (MOF).

The government is also establishing the framework for a new property tax, although it has been experiencing some challenges.[12] The Parliament passed in 2021 the Gambling Control Bill. The bill aims to establish the

Gambling (Gaming and Betting) Control Commission, which will regulate the industry and establish a licensing regime.[13]

Implementation of the Public Procurement and Disposal of Public Property Act

In 2020, the Act to amend the Public Procurement and Disposal of Public Property changed. It is expected that the Public Procurement and Disposal of Public Property Act will be operational in 2022. This act has the potential to induce non-energy revenue generation through tax collection. In particular, this act promotes economic activity by encouraging competition among various local contractors and suppliers as they bid for government projects. Subsequently, as these contractors and suppliers complete the project, their revenue will increase, and they will also be liable to pay taxes, which contributes to the growth of non-energy revenue as additional firms are compelled to partake in various projects. The act, therefore, can also contribute to firms improving their outlook in terms of audited finances and other operational systems to meet the standards prescribed by the government as a procuring agency.

Liberalize the Foreign Exchange Market

The government of Trinidad and Tobago must carefully monitor capital outflows from the Trinidad and Tobago economy since it was announced that the Federal Reserve intends to raise its interest rates, which is expected to increase by 2 per cent by the end of the year (BBC 2022). This can result in large capital outflow from Trinidad and Tobago as investors seek to reap the benefits of these higher interest rates in the United States. The greater demand for the USD can, in turn, also lead to an appreciation of the USD-TTD exchange rate. If the Central Bank of Trinidad and Tobago also raises its interest rate in response to the federal reserve, it is unlikely that this response will counter the capital outflow. Furthermore, as the USD appreciates, the price of imports subsequently also rises, which contributes to inflation. While this is likely to impact consumers negatively, the exchange rate would become more appropriately valued (rather than being overvalued) and, therefore, be more reflective of true market rates.

Reduce Transfers to SOEs

Transfers and subsidies grew more than proportionally to the associated increase in GDP from 2001 to 2021. Between 2007 and 2021, they increased by 67 per cent, while GDP increased by a mere 10 per cent.

Table 11.10 below shows the fluctuations in both energy revenues and transfers and subsidies for the period 2001–21. Observe from the data that when energy revenues collapsed, transfers and subsidies did not fall, i.e., they maintained their momentum. (This is reflective of the comment

Table 11.10: Energy Revenue and Expenditure on Transfers and Subsidies and Capital

Year	Energy Revenue (TT$Mn)	Expenditure on Transfers and Subsidies (TT$Mn)	Capital Expenditure (TT$Mn)	TS/ER%	TS/KE%
2001	4583.8	4555.4	929.6	99.4	490.0
2002	3249.4	5186.7	682.4	159.6	760.1
2003	6182.5	5963.4	795.5	96.5	749.6
2004	7641.7	7910.6	1621.1	103.5	488.0
2005	13961.3	10821.6	2798.6	77.5	386.7
2006	21416	14830.4	4615.3	69.2	321.3
2007	20025.9	16780.9	7781.9	83.8	215.6
2008	32463.2	20114.1	9684.5	62.0	207.7
2009	19335.4	21173.6	8414	109.5	251.6
2010	22700.6	20833.3	6399.2	91.8	325.6
2011	27169.8	25099.5	6952.6	92.4	361.0
2012	26625.9	27206.1	6987.7	102.2	389.3
2013	25127.4	30068.4	8439.8	119.7	356.3
2014	28111.3	34663.5	8434.8	123.3	411.0
2015	18660.9	30701.9	7620.8	164.5	402.9
2016	6644.4	27856.1	4398.3	419.2	633.3
2017	7759.3	26030.3	3448.5	335.5	754.8
2018	11031.3	25391.1	3492.1	230.2	727.1
2019	15874.3	26377.7	3790.7	166.2	695.9
2020	7852.5	27321.9	4077.5	347.9	670.1
2021p	9169	27954	3992	304.9	700.3

Source: Central Bank of Trinidad and Tobago

made by James Duesenberry, who effectively noted that consumption has a built-in inertia that is difficult to reverse). This is not good as natural capital such as oil and gas are not reproducible, so when they are extracted, they should be monetized in a way that generates a long-term stream of returns, as compared to a strategy that spends out all of the energy rents as they are received on transfers and subsidies. Also, it was observed that capital expenditures declined after 2007 to the extent that the ratio of transfers and subsidies to capital expenditures actually increased over time. Specifically, this ratio grew from 207.7 per cent in 2008 to 754.8 per cent in 2017 and averaged 709.64 per cent from 2017 to 2021. In the opinion of the authors of this chapter, this was a grave error by policymakers in Trinidad and Tobago.

Note that in 1991, Trinidad and Tobago spent TT$1305.2 million on transfers and subsidies (T&S), which remained moderately dormant until about 1997, when it stood at TT$1828.1 million. Thus, in the period 1992–2001, T&S averaged 10.5 per cent per annum, and in the period 2002 to 2009, it averaged 27.1 per cent on average per annum to the extent that by the end of 2009, T&S were 5.8 times the size in 2002. The growth of T&S declined by 1.6 per cent in 2010, but in the period 2011 to 2014, the average was 13.7 per cent per annum. T&S in 2014 was 1.7 times that in 2009. In the period 2015–20, the average annual growth of T&S was 3.0 per cent, with T&S in 2020 being 81.7 per cent in 2014. It is the opinion of the authors of this chapter that the acceleration of T&S in the period 2002 to 2014, especially 2002–9, has placed the economy on an unsustainable expenditure pathway.

The rest of this section focuses on state-owned enterprises (SOEs) and statutory bodies, which are major recipients of government transfers. In 2022, there were fifty-five SOEs. Of these, forty-three are wholly owned, either majority-owned or minority-owned, and the Trinidad and Tobago government holds a minority stake in the others. These state entities operate in several sectors, including the oil and gas sector, banking and financial services sector, manufacturing, transport and communication, tourism, agriculture information technology and social services provision.

The output from SOEs and statutory boards should be competitively priced according to the market (see figure 11.8 for the case of WASA in Trinidad and Tobago). If market prices create distributional challenges for the poorest and most vulnerable, the government should use a voucher system to assist them. This voucher system has been utilized to provide access to various services, such as education in Chile (Gauri and Vawada 2003) and healthcare in Nicaragua (Meyer, Bellows, Campbell and Pots 2011). In particular, Meyer, Bellows, Campbell and Pots (2011) concluded that the health voucher system in Nicaragua, although new, has been successful in boosting the utilization of its healthcare system by targeting specific populations.

Table 11.11 below shows that SOE debt expanded considerably from TT$7,257.6 million in 2007 to TT$22,519.6 million in 2020. In the same period, transfers to SOEs increased from TT$2,280.1 million in 2007 to TT$3,339.5 million in 2019. Employment in SOEs decreased considerably from 20,500 people in 2007 to 10,800 in 2020.

As regards statutory boards and similar bodies, employment increased from 129,000 in 2007 to 147,900 in 2020. Transfers to these statutory boards averaged TT$6094.8 million per annum from 2007 to 2019, with transfers in 2019 totalling TT$5890.9 million, compared to TT$4436.6 million in 2007.

The aforementioned growth in employment within statutory boards can be seen at the Water and Sewage Authority (WASA), where a report[14] submitted to Cabinet identified that WASA will revert to its approved organizational structure of 1999 so that some 3,152 employees can possibly be sent home. The report indicated that even at the management level, there are 426 employees as compared to an approved 172 employees. The report noted that WASA's staff was cut from four thousand seven hundred to two thousand five hundred but then, within five years, ballooned to over five thousand. So, the problem is likely due to soft budget constraints. It is noted that WASA is not producing a sufficient amount of water to meet population needs, has an insurmountable debt, continues to pay heavy bonuses to staff, and also continues to accrue overtime bills. On a monthly basis, WASA pays close to TT$50 million dollars to Desalcott due to 2,755 leaks per month within WASA's pipelines, as indicated by the report submitted to the cabinet.

The number of WASA employees per connection ratio is thirteen employees per one thousand connections. In contrast, the regional benchmark is eight employees per one thousand connections. This over-employment results in elevated wages and reduces per-worker productivity. Similar issues of overstaffing were also discovered within the Trinidad and

Table 11.11: Fiscal Position of SOEs and Statutory Boards

Year	Nominal GDP TT$bn	Government Guaranteed SOE Debt Outstanding TT$mn	Transfers to SOE TT$mn	Central Gov't Total Debt TT$bn	SOE Debt Outstanding as a % of Total Debt	Employment in SOE	Employment Statutory Boards	Transfers to Statutory Boards TT$m	Debt of Statutory Boards TT$m
2007	136.9	7275.6	2280.1	36.1	38.7	20500	129000	4436.6	–
2008	175.3	10756.8	2326.3	41.7	60.8	20300	138000	5332.4	–
2009	121.3	12558.1	1892.4	43.5	62.6	19500	132500	4693.5	–
2010	141.3	13968.4	1601.3	48.1	56.3	19300	135300	5481.8	9713
2011	163.1	17092.4	3501.4	51.2	62.6	21100	135000	5701	11010.2
2012	165.2	17622.7	4127.2	63.1	43.9	18503	143700	6368.3	9773.9
2013	170.3	18431.7	2231	67.2	43.5	15653	148500	7106.4	10463.9
2014	167.8	19710.1	3572.1	80.7	44.2	21100	150960	7199	10325.6
2015	150.2	19724.2	2079.1	78.6	44.4	19200	147500	7679.3	11090.4
2016p	145.9	19153.5	2330.5	89.3	35.7	17300	141510	6726.1	11243.9
2017	151.1	18739.4	2063.4	91.4	–	18525	13300	6354.4	10461.6
2018	161.2	20229.3	2462.6	94.9	–	19230	135700	6262.3	9524.6
2019	161.3	21558.6	3339.5	91.7	–	14210	140600	5890.9	9257.1
2020	144.4	22519.6	–	101.1	–	13510	147900	–	10273.9
2021p	150.9	–	–	–	–	–	–	–	–

Source: Central Eank of Trinidad and Tobago

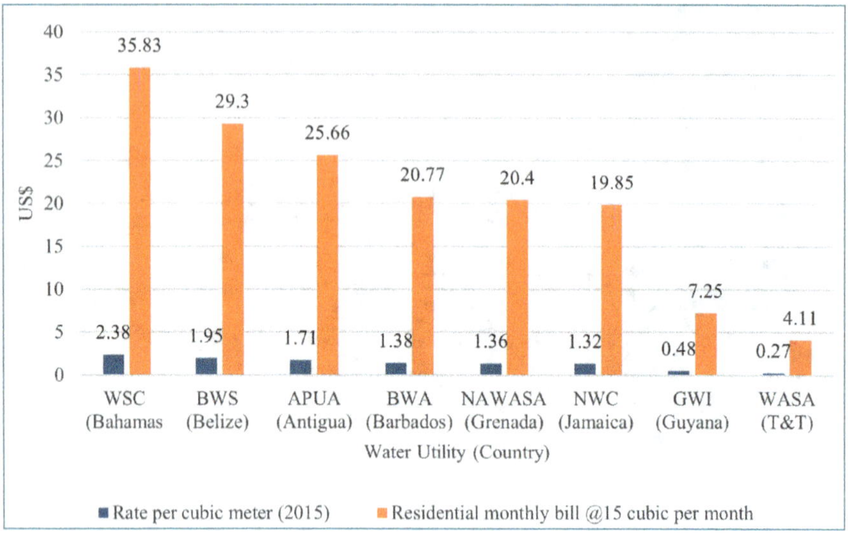

Figure 11.8: Regional Residential Water Rate and Bill Comparison

Tobago Electricity Commission (T&TEC) and Petrotrin, where the latter was forced to cease its operations in 2018.

Using another example, consider the regional price for Liquid Petroleum Gas (LPG). A competitively priced LPG market can result in consumers being unable to purchase LPG, which subsequently creates undesirable effects for consumers. These undesirable effects target both households and businesses alike since the cost of cooked food will eventually increase as LPG prices increase. However, the state can use a voucher system, as indicated above, to reverse the undesirable effect on the poorest and most vulnerable.

Tariff rates at another statutory board, T&TEC, are shown in table 11.13 below. Trinidad and Tobago has the second lowest rate. These subsidies add up and stifle the government's fiscal space.

Transparency and non-restrictive procurement regulations should be implemented to prevent tunnelling. Such policies reduce the likelihood that the majority shareholder (the government in most SOEs) will select a particular contractor or supplier to the detriment of the SOE for a future project. This occurs because such procurement legislation grants access to all contractors or suppliers who can freely bid and compete for their part in the future project, thus reducing the likelihood that the same group of contractors or suppliers will be selected.

Table 11.12: Comparative Prices of 20lb LPG Cylinder

Country	Actual Price	US$ Equivalent
Antigua and Barbuda	EC 33	12.22
Barbados	17.5	8.75
Dominica	EC 33	12.22
Grenada	EC 40	14.82
Guyana	3400 Guy	16.35
Jamaica (25lb)	$3000 Jam	23.83
St Kitts and Nevis	EC 30	11.11
Belize (100LB)	99.02	49.51
Suriname	43	5.77
St Lucia	EC 31.5	11.67
St Vincent	EC 34.5	12.78
Trinidad and Tobago	22TT	3.25

Source: Compiled

Table 11.13: Comparative Average Electricity Tariffs for Residential Customers across Selected Caribbean Countries

Country	USD per kWh (Avg)
Aruba	0.185
Bahamas	0.312
Barbados	0.208
Belize	0.227
Cayman Islands	0.307
Jamaica	0.293
Suriname	0.023
Trinidad and Tobago	0.05

Source: Compiled

It prevents political intervention from influencing the SOE board's operation. In this regard, a nominee from the Confederation of Chambers and a nominee from the opposition should hold positions on each board.

Linking the borrowing capacity of a state-owned enterprise (SOE) to its financial capability, rather than allowing state discretion, can serve as a constraint to limit how much the organization can borrow. This policy approach can act as a check against overborrowing by SOEs, reducing the need for government bailouts. Examples of SOEs that have excessively borrowed include the Urban Development Corporation of Trinidad and Tobago (Udecott), Petrotrin, the National Insurance Property Development Company (Nipdec), and the Telecommunications Services of Trinidad and Tobago (TSTT). Collectively, these entities have contributed to a massive debt burden of TT$44 billion across various SOEs in Trinidad and Tobago. Specifically, government-guaranteed debt for state enterprises stood at TT$19 billion, while non-government-guaranteed debt reached TT$25 billion. This substantial debt resulted from the adoption of inconsistent policies by some SOEs, including poor financial or debt management practices, outdated strategic plans, and irregularities in the approval processes for debt financing.

Additionally, government intervention must be strictly tied to the performance of the organization, which takes two forms. The first form of intervention requires the formation of a specialized monitoring and evaluation unit. This unit will enable the provision of quantitative and qualitative metrics such as return on investment, liquidity ratios and debt coverage that can be used to monitor the performance of SOEs. The second method of government intervention is the enforcement of mandatory updates of SOEs' strategic plans. This, coupled with proper loan decision-making, will prevent issues that have historically plagued SOEs.

CONCLUSION

Since its independence on 31 August 1962, Trinidad and Tobago has heavily relied on its oil and gas industry for the majority of its revenue to finance its operations. In the post-independence period, for many years, this dependence has allowed the country to reap the benefits of its natural resource rents in the presence of high oil and gas prices. This has allowed the country to see initial periods of economic growth. However, this dependence has also resulted in a stop-go growth performance. This is particularly evident when comparing the growth rate of other CARICOM countries with that of Trinidad and Tobago. This lack of relative overall economic progress is most visible when, after 2015, the country consistently ranked among the top 35 worst-performing countries in the world.

Despite the lack of economic growth, especially after 2008, the government of Trinidad and Tobago has continued to increase its expenditures. Of particular concern was that since 2009, the amount the government poured into transfers and subsidies exceeded 100 per cent of energy revenues earned for the period. This type of fiscal indiscipline highlights the dangers of this expenditure pattern, and the inertia behind this expense makes it difficult to stop such behaviour.

Furthermore, as oil revenues and government expenditure increased, various non-energy sectors within the economy, not surprisingly, started to diminish in size. In particular, the agricultural and manufacturing sector saw a decline in the number of employees in 1999 from 40,346 and 51,196, respectively, to 21,940 and 44,287, respectively, in 2019. This decline in employment in the agricultural sector has partly resulted in a rapid growth of the food import bill, which was US$251.2 million in 1999 to US$825.4 million in 2020. Furthermore, the decline in employment in the manufacturing sector has resulted in the sector operating with a 35 per cent spare capacity. In contrast to these two sectors, the service sector has seen significant growth within the same period, such that in 2019, the services sector employed 515,108 workers as compared to 382,416 workers in 1999.

Subsequently, this has contributed to the compromise of the economy's growth trajectory, which has no doubt been stymied by the impact of the COVID-19 pandemic. Notwithstanding that most global economies declined during the pandemic, for the Trinidad and Tobago economy, the Dutch disease-related nuances that occurred during previous years exacerbated the negative impact on growth and resulted in some lethargy in regaining growth momentum.

In the context of the relatively poor growth performance of the Trinidad and Tobago economy, this chapter made several policy suggestions to increase output. Despite this unique situation in which Trinidad and Tobago has found itself, there are a variety of policy changes that can be implemented to help propel economic growth. These policies include the utilization of Venezuelan immigrant labour in sectors that are suffering, such as the agriculture sector. This not only reduces the number of unemployed but also aids domestic food security. Additionally, the government should implement fiscal targets and Fiscal Responsibility Legislation, which will help the government curb its spending habits while rebuilding its buffers.

It is also necessary that the government revise its expenditure on SOEs and strategically develop the facilities and legislation that will aid in expanding its non-energy revenue. Lastly, the government must develop a network that allows for faster and smoother access to data, which can help devise solutions in a timely manner.

NOTES

1. This peak in the production of crude oil occurred because of AMOCO, which successfully discovered its first well, which contained 350 mmbo in Trinidad and Tobago in 1969. Currently, this well is referred to as Teak Field and was the ninth attempt by AMOCO in its exploration programme to discover oil wells. Subsequently, AMOCO discovered two large additional oil wells (Samaan and Poui fields) four years after its initial success in 1969. Following this period of success, AMOCO experienced twenty years of minimal success in oil-well discovery, which led to the development of new strategic plans, which saw its success rate soar from 17 per cent in the twenty years to 71 per cent in the period 1994–98.
2. The Iraq-Iran War occurred between the period 1980 and 1988 after many years of bilateral border disputes between the two nations. In particular, as both nations engaged in various forms of combat, the supply of oil originating from the Persian Gulf was severely interrupted since both nations targeted infrastructure associated with oil production (Mills 2020). This extended well into the post-war period when oil production from both nations continued to suffer from either political sanctions or infrastructural damage that occurred during the war.
3. The period 2008–2014 is within a commodity price super cycle that started in 1999 and saw its peak in 2008, which is the same year as the global financial crisis. After its peak, prices declined in the immediate years that followed the global financial crisis and once again peaked between 2011 and 2012. In the subsequent years that followed, there were continuous declines in prices such that the prices in 2015, by comparison, were still lower than what was observed post-financial crisis (Hosein 2015).
4. Atlantic LNG was formed in 1995 and was the first company that produced LNG in Trinidad and Tobago using Train 1 on 11 April 1999 (Atlantic 2022). Train 1 has a maximum capacity for LNG of 3.0 mtpa and is co-owned by Shell (46 per cent), BP (34 per cent), NGC (10 per cent) and CIC (10 per cent) (Atlantic 2022). Following the success of Atlantic LNG's Train 1, an agreement

was reached in 2000 for the expansion of two additional Trains (Train 2 and Train 3) (Ministry of Energy and Energy Industries 2022). Train 2 began operations in August 2002, while Train 3 commenced its operations in April 2003 (Atlantic 2022).

5. The Trinidad and Tobago dollar experienced seven devaluations within the period 1985–96. The first devaluation occurred in December 1985, when the currency fell from TT$2.45 to TT$3.60 (Crowe 2000). Shortly after, in August 1988, the currency fell again to 4.25 (Crowe 2000). This exchange rate was maintained until April 1993, when the then government decided to liberalize the external account and move to a floating exchange rate regime. This decision resulted in an immediate devaluation of the currency, which fell to TT$5.75 (Crowe 2000). In the subsequent years, there were yearly devaluations to the TTD, which in 1996 had fallen to TT$6.01.
6. This refers to an expenditure reducing strategy which reduces overall aggregate demand and overtime the demand for foreign exchange for imports.
7. The term Dutch Disease was introduced in 1977 (Pettinger 2017) and refers to the issues that are associated with the impact that a booming tradable resource (e.g., oil and gas) has on other traditional export sectors (Hosein 2013). Specifically, the exploitation of a booming tradeable resource often results in a decline in the development of other tradable sectors (commonly the manufacturing sector) as labour is reallocated from these other tradable sectors to the booming tradable sector (Neo 2009). This shift in labour subsequently results in an appreciation of nominal wages and export demand, which triggers an appreciation of the real exchange rate (Hosein 2013).
8. The Displacement Tracking Matrix was annually computed and published since 2018 by the institute of migration for Trinidad and Tobago.
9. The correction mechanism of the Peruvian fiscal rules details that when the rules deviate, the executive must specify the ceilings that must be applied to deficit and expenditure rules (Davoodi et al. 2022). Each respective ceiling sets the maximum funds that the government can borrow or spend, propelling the government back towards the initial fiscal rule by forming these soft anchor points.
10. The correction mechanism of the Panamanian fiscal rules details various soft anchor points in the form of debt ceilings which the government must adhere to during a transitory period that gradually reduce debt to GDP ratio until the goal of the initial rule is achieved. These gradually reducing ceilings help to curb the growth fiscal debt by the Panamanian government as they work towards satisfying its initial fiscal rule.
11. These were generalized from the research on the application of fiscal rules in other economies such as Peru and Panama.

12. The property tax bill has been heavily opposed by the Opposition party, which has voiced concerns about its introduction amidst the COVID-19 pandemic, which has severely affected the income of individuals and businesses alike. Furthermore, the opposition has also voiced concerns that the property taxes fails to target industrial properties while targeting properties which they have classified as vulnerable, such as residential, commercial and agricultural properties. Lastly, the opposition voiced concerns that landowners will have to periodically file valuations for their properties, which can be problematic for elderly individuals.
13. The Bill was introduced in the Senate on 11 June 2021.
14. Joint Select Committee on land and Physical infrastructure, Report of the Cabinet Sub-Committee Appointed to Review the Operations of the Water and the Sewage Authority and to Determine a Strategy for enabling the Authority to Achieve its Mandate, 2020, Parliament of Trinidad and Tobago.

REFERENCES

Atlantic.2022. "Our Trains." https://atlanticlng.com/our-business/our-trains/.

BBC. 2022. *BBC*. Accessed 2023. https://www.bbc.com/news/world-latin-america-36319877.

Crowe, Christopher. 2000. *Second generation Models of Currency Crisis: An Application of T&T.* Bridgetown: Caribbean Development Bank, Economic and Programming Department.

Davoodi, Hamid, Paul Elger, Alexandra Fotiou, Daniel Garcia-Macia, Andresa Lagerborg, Raphael Lam, and Sharanya Pillai. 2022. *Fiscal Rules Dataset: 1985–2021.* Washington, DC: International Monetary Fund.

Eyrand, Luc, Xavier Debrun, Andrew Hodgem Victor Lledo, and Catherine Pattillo. 2018. *Second-Generation Fiscal Rules: Balancing Simplicity, Flexibility and Enforceability.* Washington DC: International Monetary Fund SDN 18/04.

Gauri, Varun, and Ayesha Vawada. 2003. *Voucher for Basic Education in Developing Countries: A Principal-Agent Perspective.* Washington, DC: The World Bank, Development Research Group, Public Services and Human Development Network, Education Team.

Government of Trinidad and Tobago. 2022. "Links to State Enterprises" https://www.ttconnect.gov.tt/gortt/portal/ttconnect/!ut/p/a1/.

Henry Mooney, Allan Wright, and Kari Grenade. 2018. "Fiscal Councils: Evidence, Common Features and Lessons for the Caribbean." DOI:10.18235/0001454.

Hirschman, Albert O. 1958. *The Strategy of Economic Development.* New Haven: Yale University Press.

Hosein, Roger. 2015. "The Collapse of the Commodity Super-cycle and Its Implications for TT." *The Energy Chamber of T&T*, 30 November 2015. https://energynow.tt/blog/the-collapse-of-the-commodity-super-cycle-and-its-implications-for-tt#:~:text=Implications%20of%20the%20End%20of%20the%20Super-cycle%20for,of%20a%20pronounced%20degree%20in%20the%20global%20market.

International Monetary Fund. 2022. "World Economic Outlook Update: Rising Caseloads and Disrupted Recovery and Higher Inflation." https://www.imf.org//media/Files/Publications/WEO/2022/Update/January/English/text.ashx.

Lewis, Arthur. 1954. "Economic Development with Unlimited Supplies of Labor." *The Manchester School*, no. 22:139–91.

Meyer, Carinne, Nicole Bellows, Martha Campbell and Malcolm Potts. 2011. "The Impact of Voucher on the Use and Quality of Health Goods and Services in Developing Countries: A Systematic Review." London: EPPI-Centre, Social Science Research Unit, Institute of Education, University of London.

Mills, Robin. 2020. "How the Iran-Iraq war shaped oil markets regionally and globally." https://www.thenationalnews.com/business/how-the-iran-iraq-war-shaped-oil-markets-regionally-and-globally-1.1084279.

Minarik, Barry Anderson, and J. Joseph. 2006. "Design Choices for Fiscal Policy Rules." OECD Journal on Budgeting 5 (4): 159–208.

Ministry of Energy and Energy Industries. 2022. "Historical Facts on the Petroleum Industry of T&T." https://www.energy.gov.tt/historical-facts-petroleum/.

Pettinger, Tejvan. 2017. "Dutch Disease." *Economics Help*. https://www.economicshelp.org/blog/11977/oil/dutch-disease/.

Rosenstein-Rodan, P.N. 1961. "Notes on the Theory of the Big Push." In *Economic Development for Latin America*. International Economic Association Series, edited by H.S. Ellis. London: Palgrave Macmillan. https://doi.org/10.1007/978-1-349-08449-4_3.

Wyplosz, Charles. 2002. "Fiscal Policy: Institutions Versus Rules." *Available at SSRN: https://ssrn.com/abstract=305596.*

[CHAPTER 12]

Reflections on What to Do Next

BHOENDRADATT TEWARIE

FUNDAMENTAL QUESTIONS

How does a country deliver high growth rates in the economy, improve living conditions in the society and provide higher standards of living for its people so that they can enjoy a good quality of life? How do you do this if growth has been largely non-existent for most of a decade and GDP and per capita income have been falling? And, further, do you depend largely on one commodity and fluctuation in prices of that one commodity for revenue and, ultimately, economic and financial viability? How does such an economy break through to growth to get to the point of sustainability, where it reduces its dependence on production and price of energy and finds new export growth centres?

And what if there have been sudden world changes taking place at the same time with inter-impactive consequences and significant effects COVID-19, a production and supply crisis with supply chain delays, logistical jams, food shortages and higher prices for food, energy and everything else cutting into wages and purchasing power of your citizens.[1] And this, after seven years and twenty-eight continuous quarters of recession, pre-COVID, during COVID and post-COVID? This is where Trinidad and Tobago found itself in fiscal 2022/2023, with further challenges almost inevitable.

Even the tiny growth projected for 2022 and 2023 must be seen against a backdrop of significant, sustained decline, as well as in the context of nominal growth being achieved based on high prices of energy commodities rather than significantly increased production in energy, manufacturing or non-energy sectors. Based on the Central Statistical Office (CSO) figures, the Ministry of Finance claims 4.1 per cent growth for the first six months of 2022[2] and expects growth for 2022 and 2023. However, energy dependence, limited diversification and slow progress in non-energy growth in tradable goods and services persist.

From 2023, recovery was indeed slow. Prospects for increased natural gas production were not progressing either. The minister of finance, in his 2024 budget speech, indicated that production would continue to lag for several years.[3] In 2023 and 2024, any growth, unlikely to be more than 2 per cent, really represents catch up recovery on a 20 per cent fall in GDP in seven years, from 2015. It will take some effort to get back to the GDP level of 2014 and to begin to grow the GDP beyond that.

ECONOMIC COMMISSION FOR LATIN AMERICA AND THE CARIBBEAN (ECLAC) ON CARIBBEAN DEVELOPMENT

Since 2012, in its Development Paths in the Caribbean, ECLAC identified critical challenges for the Caribbean region for which solutions needed to be formed.[4] They spoke of "the need to improve import productivity or the efficiency with which foreign exchange is used, by using local domestic capital to produce high value-added exports of goods and services."[5] ECLAC added, "policymakers must craft policies to deal with both external current account imbalance, including high inflation and high unemployment."[6] They continued, "the systems of governance need to be overhauled to limit the power of the executive and to increase the participation of citizens and decision making."[7] Add to this rising crime[8] and social dysfunction, and we have a formidable challenge throughout the region. Still, Trinidad and Tobago is particularly challenged because it is currently facing significant difficulties in emerging from a recession, with uncertainty about the sources of future growth. The country is heavily reliant on fossil fuel energy, grappling with revenue issues, and its diversification strategy lacks urgency and decisiveness. As a result, Trinidad and Tobago remains stuck in a middle-income trap.

It is not entirely bleak, however. Clearly, as a country, we have made some progress. Trinidad and Tobago has achieved high-income status.[9] This is due to the level of per capita income as well as the extent of social welfare, although the country has had limited growth over close to two decades.[10] It is important to note that the COVID-19 crisis was preceded by the global financial crisis of 2008. While we have managed to achieve universal primary school education, a small percentage of students do not progress beyond this level. Furthermore, post-COVID SEA (Secondary Entrance Assessment) results suggest a decline in student performance.[11] The 2024 results showed some improvement. There has been an increase in high school success rates, although not every graduate is adequately prepared for the workforce or further education. Tertiary education participation has also grown, though it remains below the 60 per cent rate achieved in 2015. Persistent challenges such as unemployment, underemployment, limited absorptive capacity in the economy, and migration[12] continue to affect the nation. It is uncertain whether Trinidad and Tobago is meeting the literacy and numeracy standards necessary for the demands of the workplace. Questions arise about whether enough high school graduates are adequately prepared to enter the economic mainstream and, ultimately, if the country is effectively utilizing the talent pool developed at higher education levels. Suppose a nation is losing its human resource capacity starting at the primary level, experiencing further declines at the secondary level and facing significant challenges with its tertiary graduates; in such a case, the country would face a serious problem. Chapter 10 offers an in-depth analysis of this issue and its implications for the labour market and overall development.

However, weak export capacity and competitiveness remain issues outside the energy sector, as becomes clear in earlier chapters by Roger Hosein et al. CAF has indicated that productivity in Trinidad and Tobago is half of what it is in the United States.[13] Add to this ongoing fiscal deficits and challenging debt servicing requirements, natural disasters and climate change-induced problems and challenges. One finds that Trinidad and Tobago has its hands full. One might say that about other developing countries as well, but it is important not to take comfort from that fact. Instead, one should accept that our situation is severe and resolve to do something about it.

Moreover, Trinidad and Tobago's challenges need to be addressed not only with urgency but also with a solution-driven approach that is cumulative and embraces and includes willing solution partners. While it is beneficial to view the glass as half full rather than half empty, comparing Trinidad and Tobago to countries performing worse might provide some comfort but is hardly inspiring. The country should instead look to examples from nations that are excelling.

Regarding the Caribbean as a whole, the authors of the ECLAC document "Development Paths in the Caribbean" stated the following:

> Sustainable development in the Caribbean entails a multi-dimensional process of progressive change in economic, social, political and environmental conditions that improves the welfare and freedoms of citizens. Sustainable development implies harmonious progress in the economic, social, political and environmental parameters of society. This entails improved productivity in the use of resources, a change in the structure of the economy from lower value added, less competitive to higher value added, more competitive sectors and activities, improved levels of education, healthcare and housing, including freedom of choice and action for citizens within the context of better environmental protection in management.[14]

In this ECLAC publication, the authors emphasize both the achievements and challenges in various sectors, providing readers with a detailed understanding of these areas. They also present a broad overview of the significant challenges facing the region and stress the need for a comprehensive, integrated and holistic approach to harness resources effectively and deploy them in pursuit of development solutions.

Four Recommendations

The authors of "Development Paths" make four recommendations:

- "Address policy inconsistency by optimizing capital-output ratio… deliberate government policy is required to facilitate the growth and restructuring of exports to relieve the balance of payments problem. This requires optimizing the trade and economic benefits that can be achieved under the CSME and the EPA, as well as increasing the productivity of all factors of production through improved systems of research and development, innovation, and management."[15]

- Such a recommendation requires much strategic work and careful attention. ECLAC made more recommendations that go beyond trade and exports such as the follows:
- "ECLAC recommends a focus on restructuring the regional economy growing capital service exports faster than consumer service exports such as education, healthcare, copyright-based services and related products. ECLAC suggests that governments focus on ICT infrastructure development and to encourage private sector participation in the areas mentioned.[16]

Two further recommendations are:

- ECLAC further recommends strengthening the role of the private sector in capital service industries. In the field of education, it advocates for models like the St George's University in Grenada and suggests offshore-style medical education, supported by private sector investment, as seen in Dominica.
- ECLAC also recommends the implementation of existing integration treaties. They stress making the treaties work. They recommend a CARICOM-wide initiative to attract foreign investment and South-South Corporation and Triangular Corporation. They encourage CARICOM to look at high-growth markets such as Brazil, China and India.[17]

COVID-19 BLUES AND OPPORTUNITIES

These recommendations were made in 2013, well before the emergence of COVID-19 in early 2020. Development in the Caribbean has long been a challenge, and sustainability remains uncertain for both high-income and middle-income countries in the region. The COVID-19 lockdown, shifting geopolitical interests, wars, price escalations and unprecedented inflation – resulting in a persistently higher cost of living even as inflation decreases – along with the ongoing restructuring of global production and trade systems, have turned existing challenges into crises, as well as opportunities. Regional countries, including Trinidad and Tobago, cannot afford to be overwhelmed by these crises. Instead, they must seize the opportunities that arise. The key question is: what should be done, and how should they proceed?

In February 2021, the Pew Research Center examined the issue of ideology and how it might evolve over the coming years. They predicted that by 2025, in the post-COVID era – this was before the emergence of supply chain disruptions, logistical challenges, rising energy and commodity prices, food shortages and the Russian invasion of Ukraine – life would be "far more tech-driven, presenting more big challenges".[18] Based on interviews with experts, the Pew Research Center concluded that "A plurality of experts think sweeping societal change will make life worse for most people as greater inequality, rising authoritarianism and rampant misinformation take hold."[19]

Other experts felt that life would be better in a "tele-everything world where workplaces, healthcare and social activity improved". Moreover, this technology would produce enhancements in virtual and augmented reality and AI (artificial intelligence) that would allow people "to live smarter, calmer, safer and more productive lives enabled in many cases by smart systems in such key areas as healthcare, education and community living".[20]

As events have unfolded from 2021 to 2022, we are witnessing the rise of multiple challenges, leading to a kind of policy crisis. These include food shortages, soaring prices that outpace the purchasing power of wages, and extremely high energy costs. There is also the looming possibility of a global financial and economic crisis, exacerbated by various factors, including developments in China. Additionally, the war in Ukraine is reshaping geopolitical alignments and fuelling global tensions. At the same time, escalating distrust between Israel and Iran threatens to ignite a broader conflict in the Middle East. A recent example of this growing tension was the joint FBI/MI5 press conference, which warned about rising temperatures in the Taiwan Strait and the South China Sea that threaten an already strained relationship between the United States and China[21] over Taiwan. The Trump presidency and tariff diplomacy will escalate complexity.

WESTERN HEMISPHERE

The 2022 Summit of the Americas made it clear that geopolitical tensions involving China and Russia, among others, will continue to affect the Western Hemisphere. Cuba, Nicaragua and Venezuela were notably excluded from the summit despite the significant presence of both China and Russia in these countries. During the summit, Venezuela signed a twenty-year cooperation agreement with Iran, a nation with which the United States has longstanding conflicts and which also raises concerns in Europe. Israel has frequently warned about Iran, especially as internal pressures on human rights, including the increased subjugation of women, have been ignored. The influence of Iran on global affairs has intensified due to the Israel-Hamas conflict and growing tensions in the Middle East, alongside its strengthening alliances with Russia and China.

Within the Western Hemisphere, some countries chose not to attend the Summit or send envoys instead of heads of government, expressing the view that no country in the Americas should have been excluded from such a gathering.

Additionally, poverty and inequality remain serious challenges in this region, which is considered the most unequal in the world, according to ECLAC.[22] If some strategic interventions are not made, the divide between the haves and have-nots will intensify as economic and financial pressures mount and as the digital divide and the technological divide escalate.

The immigration challenge in the hemisphere is but one symptom of such developments, which continue to perpetuate huge inequality gaps. Strategies now being pursued will further facilitate geopolitical tensions within the hemisphere as countries seek help from wherever they can get it. China is now the largest trading partner of the South American region, and Chinese government state enterprises and state-sponsored businesses are heavily involved in infrastructure and construction projects across the Caribbean and Latin America.[23] What does a small country, classified as high-income but without growth, do in such circumstances? What does Trinidad and Tobago do in the alignment of forces amidst the swirl of currents? How must it proceed as it watches its standard of living fall and quality of life diminish?

Perhaps the first step is for Trinidad and Tobago to identify the things it can and should do independently and act on them. This may seem like a basic response to the question, "Where does one start?" but it is a crucial one. While external help and partnerships are valuable, self-reliance creates a foundation for sustainability. Developing a mindset and strategy centred on self-help and self-sufficiency should be the beginning of a broader shift in attitude and approach for Trinidad and Tobago. Therefore, the first item on the agenda should be fostering greater self-sufficiency and cultivating the resolve to achieve it.

The second reasonable step is to recognize that Trinidad and Tobago cannot continue operating with a budget that calls on taxpayers to support a system where the country consistently lives beyond its means. The state remains too large, state enterprises are heavily subsidized, social support is irrationally high and rising debt results in an increasing annual repayment burden. Deficits have become the norm, and the persistent perception of corruption only compounds these issues. Additionally, policies often fail to inspire investor confidence, support private sector success or drive the structural and technological transformation needed for productivity, competitiveness, economic growth and shared prosperity.

Trinidad and Tobago cannot continue with policies that have created a formidable crisis. A significant shift is needed – one that promotes a leaner state fosters a thriving private sector and implements strategic, targeted policies to encourage diversified export trade, attract investments and support technologically driven industries. These changes should aim to cultivate a dynamic public service that prioritizes research, entrepreneurship, creativity and innovation.

While this may seem like a daunting task, in the current circumstances, responsible leadership and an engaged citizenry cannot avoid the need to act. If Trinidad and Tobago fails to make these necessary changes, the country will lag in its quest for global competitiveness.

Countries in partnerships like CARICOM must collaborate more effectively to address the challenges that hinder regional growth and prosperity. Strategic cooperation and synergies are vital for sustainable success. As a critical player in CARICOM, Trinidad and Tobago has the potential to influence the region and beyond, depending on its leadership's vision and the interests it balances.

To move forward, Trinidad and Tobago needs greater self-sufficiency, a smaller state, reduced dependence on state enterprises, private sector – led growth, diversification of non-energy exports and a focus on technology-driven industries – all within a framework of regional collaboration.

ECLAC Suggestions

The previously mentioned 2013 ECLAC document, "Development Paths in the Caribbean", recommended that the Caribbean:

1. Address policy inconsistency by optimizing the capital-output ratio
2. Focus on restructuring the regional economy to produce capital service exports
3. Enhance the role of the private sector in capital service industries
4. Implement existing integration treaties
5. Ensure routine legislative oversight of executive function
6. Draw on the advantage of political reforms to revisit outstanding challenges.[24]

This author values the substance of some of these recommendations and appreciates the desirability of policy consistency, economic restructuring and an enhanced role for the private sector. The establishment of a single economic, financial, trade and investment space would clearly make a decisive difference in the region. The link between political reforms and addressing economic challenges, along with reinforcing the role of parliament in resisting executive dominance, are critical for the well-being of the region. Trinidad and Tobago needs recovery, growth, job creation, investment, diversification, export expansion and consistent foreign exchange earnings on a sustainable basis.

How does a government guarantee these? Therefore, some basics must be addressed to make these vital necessities possible.

HIGHLIGHTING SOME BASICS

To put the region on a path to prosperity, a few key actions are essential. For example, improving sea and air transport could make a significant difference by facilitating trade, entrepreneurship, investment, the movement of people and access to new markets and opportunities. There are private sector initiatives in this area, supported by some intergovernmental efforts. However, good intentions have not always led to results in the past – only time will tell if this will be different.

What if a binding agreement could be reached on the rationalization of at least some production, if not all, across the region? Could a good beginning be with the most successful export manufacturers and those that are beginning to export, together with a rationalization of production inputs in a way that makes economic and logistical sense? Focusing on the raw material and value-added inputs that would increase value, enhance outputs and boost exports would make a great deal of difference. What if some university research were strategically aligned to this process in order to build a sustainable system in which research and knowledge would play a key role on a sustained basis? What if an agreement was reached on a regional support framework for agro-processing and agro-manufacturing and a working infrastructure for export success was established? What if the food needs of the growing regional tourism industry were integrated with regional school-feeding programmes as part of a unified social policy on nutrition? This could drive significant local production to support both school nutrition initiatives and a steady food supply for tourists. The outcome could be a well-structured, competitive agricultural supply system with efficient logistics and supply chains. Such an initiative would boost business, agro-entrepreneurship, job creation and the development of service industries to support these efforts. Additionally, what if governments acted to legitimize the CSME and made it work through competition and enhanced capacity? What if a wider regional economic integration with Central America and coastal South American countries were meaningfully pursued and standardized?

Some of these ideas are contained in a distinguished lecture delivered by the author on the occasion of the thirtieth anniversary of CARICOM (2003)[25] in Belize and another presented to CARICOM heads in 2004 in Port of Spain, on the invitation of then prime minister, Patrick Manning.[26] What if sustainable tourism based on an integrated airlift strategy linked to education, health and wellness and outdoor activities in addition to holiday travel were thoughtfully built up for Trinidad and Tobago? What if, across the region, a genuine regional economic and financial space and a world-class ICT-enabled system aligned with focused research at UWI to support entrepreneurship competitiveness, innovation and the creation of new products and services were pursued? What if Trinidad and Tobago made digitalization work to our advantage in the global value chain that is emerging and evolving at a rapid pace as part of the fourth industrial revolution transformation of the global economy? What if Trinidad and Tobago created the value added required to align with success in that sphere? What if we summoned the will and assembled the "do-how" to achieve these things?

What if we developed a regional foreign investment strategy that aligned with current trends in nearshoring and self-sufficiency alongside a robust regional security strategy to combat guns, drugs, crime, human trafficking and terrorism? Such a plan, supported by international partners like the United States and the United Kingdom and other key travel hubs, such as Holland or Guyana, could create a clear path toward making the region a prosperous zone of peace and sustainable development.

Additionally, we must prioritize digital transformation and connect with competitive industries in areas like virtual reality, artificial intelligence, robotics, the Internet of Things, the metaverse, cloud computing, and big data. These technological innovations are reshaping the global economy, and failure to act now on well-thought-out strategies could leave us behind in the global value chain.

Within this framework, we need to see the contrast between what is happening in the rest of the world, how we are responding to that evolving reality and the irony of our lack of response and paucity of action in our economies. We need also to take cognizance of the disaster that our unresponsiveness might facilitate. Both action and inaction yield results. The chapters on trade, the comparison between Tobago and Trinidad, agriculture, manufacturing and the requirements for sustainable economic development make it clear that Trinidad and Tobago, along with the wider region, needs to shift gears.

The second essential step is to develop an economic plan based on greater self-sufficiency, linked to strategies across CARICOM. This plan should include a regional school-feeding and nutrition strategy, also serving as a supply chain for the regional tourism industry. It should adopt an outward-looking approach, focusing on trade in goods and services with the wider Caribbean, Central America and the South American coastal region. Additionally, it must integrate the value-driven approach of fourth industrial revolution technologies, encourage international investments and foster strategic alliances supported by education and research from our universities, strengthened by global research partnerships.

What is proposed here is a holistic and integrated policy action aimed not only at recovering lost time and missed opportunities but also at keeping pace with global progress and securing the Caribbean's place in the evolving global value chain.

In this chapter, I argue that we must act now to prevent a technology-driven world from leaving the Caribbean and Trinidad and Tobago behind.

CHANGES IN ATTITUDES

As 2020 was coming to an end, an associate professor at Texas A&M University, Professor Anthony Klotz, forewarned about a "Great Resignation" coming in the United States and perhaps worldwide in the industrialized world.[27] He indicated that COVID-19 had driven people to evaluate their work situation as well as their life choices and options. There were four trends which he identified:

- A backlog of resignations from jobs
- Widespread burnout of workers
- Re-evaluation of workers of their relationship with work and
- The opportunity of remote work.[28]

Klotz argued that there seemed to be a big disconnect between what workers wanted after experiencing the pandemic and what organizations wanted from workers after the pandemic. The demand for remote work and hybrid work was in the ascendancy. Frontline workers who had to be present every day felt they were being treated unfairly.[29]

With forty-seven million Americans quitting their jobs in 2021 and 4.5 million more quitting in the first three months of 2022, worker choice increasing and better pay coming, the world of work was changing. Moreover, if a worker was being paid less for coming to work on the front line and more for working remotely from home, why would he/she choose the more demanding job with less flexibility and convenience and, perhaps, less pay? Since 2022, we have also seen tech firms such as Twitter and Facebook rethink their strategy. They have restructured and redesigned their organizations to be leaner and more effective by laying off workers in substantial numbers. The pandemic kept people at home, and communications technology was heavily utilized. With the pandemic over, this has lessened somewhat. So social media and related technology firms hired more during the pandemic when demand was high but now need fewer workers because demand for services is down.[30]

CARIBBEAN RESPONSE

In response to the growing trend of remote work, some Caribbean countries have chosen to focus on tourism, which caters to this shift. This approach is particularly appealing for tourists during the winter months, as they can travel to the Caribbean, enjoy sun, sand and sea, and still complete their work. With open spaces, tropical weather and a variety of leisure activities, these destinations offer an ideal combination of productivity and relaxation.[31]

The irony is that in Caribbean countries, no adjustments have been made for work in their own economies, no significant remote working arrangements have been made, no hybrid work has been structured, no pay increases have been made, and no work or demands or increases in work or choices have been made in what are essentially stagnating economies with limited options.

Chances are that the workplace may be viewed differently in the Caribbean. Work may be a way for both men and women to get out of the house; work may present an opportunity for social interaction; it may have to do with issues of identity; it may be a release from domestic violence, and so on. However, none of these things have been researched, examined, or assessed; therefore, the opportunities and challenges presented by a changing world and a transforming work environment are not addressed in the Caribbean. It is somewhat ironic that while some Caribbean societies are adapting their tourism strategies to be more responsive to changes happening globally, they are not also seeking to make accommodations within their regional territories for local workers.

The context for many fundamentals is shifting in the post-pandemic era. Tourism habits and trends are evolving; energy dynamics are changing in the wake of COP 25 and COP 27 as fossil fuels lose favour and renewables take centre stage, and rapid technological advancements – accelerated by the pandemic and driven by artificial intelligence – are reshaping production, competitiveness, innovation and customer expectations. Trinidad and Tobago, along with the region, must not only catch up with what has or has not been done but also keep pace with the direction of the competitive global landscape. This requires aligning with trends, embracing technology and advancing value chains to strengthen our competitive capacity. Realistically, there are multiple gaps to address simultaneously, with the capacity gap being especially critical.

TRINIDAD AND TOBAGO AND SELF-SUFFICIENCY

So, against this background, what does Trinidad and Tobago do? How do we proceed as a country? The way countries are proceeding shows that they have pursued a significant level of self-sufficiency since the pandemic. Asian countries, for instance, feel vulnerable and are looking to generate self-reliance and self-sufficiency.

Ghamz E Ali Siyal of the London School of Economics and Political Science argues that "particularly for the developing countries, it is important to mark a boundary or a threshold of exports and imports dependence to avoid economic vulnerability to unexpected shocks to the global economy."[32] India, for instance, has initiated a movement for self-reliance, also known as Atmanirbhar Bharat (self-reliance engine movement). According to Siyal, "this movement stresses making local products and providing a special package to industries and workers". He encourages other countries like Pakistan and Bangladesh to do the same.[33] The United States, while competing fiercely with China on technology and intellectual property, also prides itself on energy independence and strives for greater self-sufficiency, particularly in food. Many individual states in the United States are also highly self-sufficient. Similarly, China produces a significant portion of its own food, with President Xi Jinping placing a strong emphasis on food self-sufficiency.[34] For decades, China has been a global production hub and is increasingly focused on achieving technological self-sufficiency as well.

Some countries around us are fairly self-reliant. Cuba, for instance, is self-reliant, though this self-reliance was born out of necessity because of embargoes, isolation and sanctions from inception. But so are Argentina, Columbia and Ecuador, and far away Tanzania, Indonesia and India, all of which are fairly self-sufficient or at least largely self-reliant through dedicated and systematic efforts. So the drive towards as much self-sufficiency as possible is legitimate and achievable, as has been demonstrated by several countries, and it is a goal worth pursuing.[35]

A comprehensive approach to economic planning, combined with regional cooperation, the harnessing of synergies, and the rationalization of production, does not require complex solutions. It simply calls for reasonable dialogue supported by knowledge, data and technical expertise. Decisions must be rational, backed by political will, and bolstered by commitment from the public and private sectors. This approach can make growth, profitability and competitiveness a reality, laying a foundation for correcting past mistakes and seizing future opportunities. Clear objectives and commitment will naturally attract finance and investment.

Fix, Transform, Change

In the current context and given the outline of the issues in this chapter, it is reasonable to say that there were things that were really required to be done over the last sixty years of independence that, as a country, Trinidad and Tobago, the government and its people, just did not do, or did not do well. We need to revisit these, repair damage where possible, fix, transform and eliminate as required.

Significant adjustments are needed to address the post-COVID-19 world and the many challenges we face – economic, political, sociological and technological. The urgency has only increased, as countries striving for competitiveness are transforming at an accelerated pace. At the same time, Trinidad and Tobago has done little to restructure or transform its economy even before COVID-19. So as a country that needs to make up for past losses, trying to find a way through the present maze and seeking somehow to build a better future, certain truths cannot be avoided, fundamental realities that cannot be ignored and specific actions that must be taken in spite of the uncertainties and the inevitable unpredictability ahead.

The past cannot be redeemed, but it can be considered, repaired, improved upon and built upon. The future cannot be planned for with certainty. There are too many unknowns, and it is not predictable. We can only seek to stabilize and anchor ourselves in the present, as uncertain as it is, with its many contending and sometimes volatile variables. So, what to do, and how to begin? We need to create a better, more desirable future.

How to Begin

Learning from the lessons of the past is an excellent way to begin, if only to see what can be fixed now based on these lessons.

This volume contains valuable chapters on critical issues that take into account Trinidad and Tobago's historical experiences, achievements, and deficits and point to international and global advances that need to be taken into account. This chapter will not focus too much on fossil fuel energy because energy, which has been a boon as well as a problem and, in fundamental ways, a major source of other problems, does have identifiable challenges going forward. There seems to be a stronger will to address challenges and opportunities in energy than anywhere else in the economy at present. This country will have to operate with less natural gas in the foreseeable future and with limited supplies of oil, and even when this becomes better, the price situation may change and world developments in renewables and the environmental trends and options which emerge may create different demands and different choices. The next ten years are as unpredictable, and the present is uncertain. However, energy was identified many years ago by the United Nations as part of a great stress nexus that would present a formidable challenge for the world: the "food, water, energy" stress nexus. Trinidad and Tobago is not likely to face an energy challenge any time soon in terms of local needs, but energy needs for LNG and to keep chemical plants running cannot be met by current production. Here, Venezuelan gas is critical. Other changes with NGC, Atlantic LNG and a renewables project involving Shell and BP has begun. The United States has lifted Limited sanctions from Venezuela, but detailed Trinidad and Tobago/ Venezuela negotiations are required in a two-year timeframe.

The non-energy sector has made little progress. The real challenges involve energy transformation – deciding what kind of energy to pursue rather than its availability. This impacts foreign exchange earnings from exports, economic rents and revenue for local use. Another key challenge is how to grow the non-energy sector in terms of investment, exports and foreign exchange earnings to make Trinidad and Tobago more sustainable, considering past and current natural gas production shortages. Lastly, the transition towards renewable energy is essential to achieve net-zero carbon emissions.

Food and Water

Trinidad and Tobago has a serious problem with food and water. The history, evolution, and identifiable challenges are well-documented in relevant chapters of this volume. The question is how do we solve the problems of food self-sustainability as far as possible, and how do we manage water more efficiently, effectively and productively? These are problems that we must solve. The Trinidad and Tobago food import bill is unnecessarily high ($6 billion for a country of 1.4 million). We produce too little of the food we consume, and we consume too little of the food we are capable of producing.

Along with this, our pattern of taste has been conditioned for import products, mainly from the United States, and our culinary creativity, in spite of street food successes, is still underdeveloped. Moreover, export potential exists, and while a vibrant agro-processing industry is emerging, it can expand much further. Well-organized local and regional programmes centred on tourism and social nutrition initiatives, such as school feeding, food banks and aid for the poor, could stimulate agricultural production and crop diversification. It is important to recognize that solving one problem often opens up opportunities to address others.

Water is essential not only for homes and industry but also for preventing floods, supporting irrigation and simplifying agricultural production. A well-thought-out action plan is needed, drawing on experts' knowledge and expertise to create a foundation for self-sustainability and national development. The knowledge and expertise exist – are we prepared to use them and implement a plan? So far, the evidence suggests that we have not.

Food and water are basic problems that we must take control of for self-sustainability. With the impact of climate change, stresses from both flood and drought may well be severe. Greater self-sufficiency and self-sustainability is, in principle, being pursued by several countries now, not only in food and water but in almost everything. The principle is to produce as much as you can at home so that you are less dependent on others for what you need. Such strategies have been pursued by a country like Cuba, which has for a long time been isolated, embargoed and sanctioned.[36] But during apartheid, when South Africa was relatively isolated and sanctioned by many countries of the world for its transgressions, that country also pursued a strategy of self-sufficiency.[37] India has pursued self-sufficiency in many areas in which it has indigenous capacity for a long time.[38] But countries such as Argentina, Colombia and Kenya are also pursuing strategies similar to those of the United States. And since Brexit, the United Kingdom has been pursuing its own strategy of self-sufficiency.[39] In countries like Cuba, South Africa and Israel, the drive for self-sufficiency extends beyond food and water. It has also spurred research and scientific and technological advancements, with human and intellectual capital playing a critical role. Recognizing the myriad intangible connections involved in development is crucial. A knowledge-driven push toward self-sufficiency can lead to technological sophistication, foster synergies and create opportunities for entrepreneurship, creativity, innovation, investment and competitiveness. Intangible assets will increasingly play a key role in the development process.

Intangible Assets

The development of these intangible assets begins with human beings. Good health, quality education, and human and intellectual capital formation are absolutely critical for development to take place. We have seen from the earlier chapter on health that while much has been achieved, much more remains to be done to address the issue of health and human welfare, which is the bedrock on which human productivity, creativity, innovation and competitiveness are built. There seems to be a consensus that COVID-19 was relatively well managed, but prior to this, we have been slow off the blocks in the way that we have managed human health and welfare sectors. Health and education go hand-in-hand. If you have a healthy, well-educated population, you are halfway along the journey to prosperous development. Desirable development is about people. It sounds trite, but it is real. Much depends on the people you have and how the system treats them and prepares them for a meaningful role, and ultimately, how human resources and human talent are harnessed and deployed in any society or economy.

Individual, Home, Family, School

So, the problems in our primary school system and the ongoing, escalating challenges in our secondary school system must be solved. How do you deploy 100 per cent of your sixteen-year-olds every year for further education or meaningful participation in the economy, especially when your birth rate is just about twenty thousand per year? This is a most fundamental question that we must answer in the context of 37 per cent of our primary school students achieving 50 per cent in the 2022 SEA and only 50 per cent of our secondary school students achieving at least five CXC passes.[40] The crisis of access and throughput, which is now emerging at the tertiary level, must also be solved. It is not as daunting a task as it may seem at first brush. It is essential to take scale into account. Our birth rate is lower than twenty thousand annually, and those are not unmanageable numbers to work with. The cohort of sixteen-year-olds in any given year, for instance, will be just under twenty thousand.

This is the size of a small university, or about two hundred busloads of children or twenty fully attended shows at Queens Hall. It is fewer people than the number which attends a test cricket match at the oval or an international football match at the stadium. The scale is doable. But imagination is required. It is the same number, fewer than twenty thousand, who are born every year, which we have to track with their mothers and after birth to ensure good nutrition, good health habits, and a sound physical activity regimen to address lifestyle diseases, which proportionately are an epidemic in this country. This can be reversed with smart meaningful, decisive, sustainable interventions. In development, we can begin with the individual at birth, trace it to his or her home, understand the context of parenting, home, and community, and pursue a strategy for sustainability and success in every home. There are only four hundred and fifty thousand homes in Trinidad and Tobago, according to the 2011 census.[41] Even if it is five hundred thousand households now, it is not an insurmountable challenge. In every school, we can assess the circumstances and devise a strategy for the school, its students, its teachers and principals to win. Every school can become a winner if objectives are clearly defined, purposefully pursued and effectively managed and achieved. And every home and their circumstance, of the twenty thousand children born annually, can be assessed and attended to. So individual, home, family, school. Eventually, medical care and attention, as required, can be provided for both prevention and cure. Quality healthcare and fruitful educational experiences can make a world of difference and provide the base for competitiveness and prosperity.

How can the health centre of a community be effectively equipped and integrated into a larger support network and system to serve the health needs of individuals, homes and communities? Technology and training are critical here. The 2011 census identifies four hundred and fifty thousand households and about six hundred communities in this society.[42] We have fourteen municipal regions in Trinidad and one in Tobago. The Ministry of Planning, the CSO and the UNDP mapped out the sociological realities (health, employment, facilities, population profile, etc.) for each of the fourteen regions.[43] TheNational Census due in 2021 is later than planned but is being done now. One anxiously awaits the statistical update. With a bit of dedication, commitment, and focus, it is possible to map out human development and economically sustainable strategies for each household, community, region, and, ultimately, nation and make them work. So, if we take care of food, water, sanitation and preventative health in individual households and communities, we can begin to monitor and evaluate progress. But a critical factor is the environment. I mean this in two ways – the physical environment and how it can be conserved and developed. And the security and safety environment so that businesses, families and citizens can conduct their daily affairs and proceed safely with their lives. Both are critical to support human development and any economic development thrust.

The Need to Shift Gears

Since 1962, groups in domestic, agricultural, land development and industrial activities have all contributed to the deterioration of environmental quality. This includes human settlements, the management of human waste, the way we manage our garbage, and the way we have, sometimes indiscriminately, sometimes not with enough care, built out our infrastructure, resulting in fragmentation and degradation of habitats. Lousy land management of agriculture and the use of pesticides have added to the problems, as well as indiscriminate granting of planning permission, reckless development practices and callous use of land and waterways. Our major industries, oil, natural gas, and petrochemicals, have caused significant problems from time to time, together with ongoing challenges and tensions. This is exacerbated now as we are surrounded by oil-producing nations – Venezuela, Guyana and Suriname. Accidents can happen, and the normal process of drilling, exploration and shipping can take their toll. Recently, in 2024, we had a major spill off the coast of Tobago, not from the drilling but from the transportation of fuel, which was very costly on a number of fronts.

The connection between energy, environmental conservation, sustainability and energy transformation to renewables cannot be underestimated. Trinidad and Tobago faces major challenges in these areas, but there are also significant opportunities for economic transformation, resilience and sustainability. These must be identified and embraced.

As Isaac et al. observe in an earlier chapter, the diversity of actors has to be included and embraced, especially as we need to acknowledge "the downward trajectory and diminishing motivation across the farming population". The truth is that recent shortages in production and bottlenecks in the supply chain must make it clear that we cannot continue to depend on imports for 85 per cent of our food supply. The agricultural challenge must be addressed holistically, from seed to food on the table, through an integrated approach to agricultural production that supports economic integration. Moreover, agriculture makes no sense for a country unless the producers and farmers benefit. So we must have an inclusive approach that includes stakeholder inputs, beneficiaries and connected parties. The gap between agricultural knowledge and applications for food production, agricultural diversification and sustainability must be closed.

Beyond Policy

Beyond policy, action and implementation on key issues such as agriculture (food self-sufficiency, import reduction, forex savings, agroindustry, exports); water resource management (basic needs, water conservation, flood and irrigation management); health (wellness, preventive care, productivity, longevity); education (human capital development, competitive capacity); crime (safety, security, lower costs); and the environment (conservation, sustainability, greener industries), we face challenges in investment, trade, manufacturing and economic development.

This volume covers these subjects in depth, reflecting on our history, current state and future direction. However, after sixty years of independence, if we have only come this far, there is clearly a problem. The challenges lie in governance, policy formulation and execution, politics, constitutional framework, democracy and economic strategy. These seven issues have grown increasingly intractable over the past decade, and it is crucial to address them to move forward.

As we enter the next decade, on the economic front, we have three principal challenges:

1. Transformation of the energy sector while continuing to expand fossil fuel resources and draw on it for revenue.
2. Restructuring of the economy for less dependence on fossil fuel energy and greater diversification of production base, export products and export markets.
3. Digitalization and leveraging of digitalization to align the manufacturing and services sectors to the technological power of the fourth industrial revolution technologies, driving global transformation and competitiveness.

These are fundamental and urgent economic challenges. But we must not be afraid to confront other problems that systematically undermine our capacity for economic progress; for instance, gangs, guns and violent crimes culture which is a major obstacle to progress.

Some Comparisons – Are We in Jeopardy?

Over the last sixty years of independence and our journey as a sovereign nation, we recognize that while we have made significant strides, there remains a gap between our achievements and our full potential. This shortfall extends beyond economic indicators alone.

There are 81 out of 180 countries less corrupt than Trinidad and Tobago in what is essentially a world of corrupt political systems, with 98 countries being assessed as more corrupt than Trinidad and Tobago.[44] In the Legatum Prosperity Index, Trinidad and Tobago has dropped in prosperity by five places since 2011. Fifty-three countries in the world are now more prosperous than Trinidad and Tobago.[45] It is difficult to find the means and wherewithal to provide social support if you are not prosperous. Where we are on the Ease of Doing Business Index, especially since there had been a steep drop in less than three years, has become a sore point for business and academics alike. The 2015 Ease of Doing Business Report ranked Trinidad and Tobago among the ten most improved in ranking, jumping twelve points.[46] Today, the latest report ranks Trinidad and Tobago at 105, the lowest we have ever been.[47] In the last ranking of competitiveness, Trinidad and Tobago was 79, which means more than half of 141 countries are better off than we are.[48] Among fifty-one countries in the high-income group in which Trinidad and Tobago is classified, in the realm of innovation, we are last.[49] Out of eighteen in Latin America and the Caribbean for innovation, we rank fifteenth.[50] These rankings cannot give comfort. We have our work cut out for us, but such performance raises the question of the effectiveness of policy formulation, execution and impact. Is effective policy being implemented, and if it is, is it working?

Are we making good policy? Is that policy understood and internalized by those whose job it is to carry out policy – the public service management and workers, the state enterprise chairmen and boards and the management of state enterprises? Do such people turn policy intentions into action, and is there any alignment between policy intent and execution? What results do we get? In his chapter on education, Professor De Lisle and his team provide some important insights into this challenge. These are serious questions because the government spends taxpayers' money on policy formulation and public service bureaucracy. And state enterprises depend heavily on taxpayers' money transferred by the state. Indeed, recurrent expenditure takes up the bulk of the budget, and a significant part of that is spent on salaries and wages. For instance, recurrent expenditure is 93 per cent, of which 20 per cent is spent on wages and salaries.[51] Only 7 per cent is spent on capital expenditure, and 57 per cent goes to transfers and subsidies.[52] Beyond the obvious challenge of altering the pattern of expenditure, there is the critical issue of value for money, the rate of return of human resources and the cost of operating the Public Service, as well as productivity, outcome, results and real impacts on the citizen/taxpayer. The IMF tells us that Trinidad and Tobago is among the least competitive countries in the world and is likely to perform at a low level over the next two years.

Growth Has Been Elusive

Moreover, since 2008, a period of over a decade, there has been little sustained growth and over a seven-year period from 2016, there have been declines every year, putting Trinidad and Tobago in what is essentially an economic recession. If pre-COVID policies did not make a difference and recovery policies and initiatives post-COVID are not making a difference, then reason tells us that new and different policy interventions might be necessary. Over the last fifteen years, Trinidad and Tobago has not even had "discontinuous jumps", as most countries have, according to Roger Hosein in an earlier chapter of this book. Perhaps, as Professor Hosein also points out, the economy needs a "Big Push" "to propel the economy to higher productivity, self-sustaining economic development and higher incomes". Ultimately, meaningful progress in policy and action requires not just setting agendas but ensuring effective execution. While determining "what needs to be done?" is critical at the planning stage, the true test lies in answering "what has been achieved?" during evaluation.

Implementation – the actual work of getting things done – remains an enduring challenge. Too often, even well-designed initiatives fail to deliver their intended results. Closing this gap between intention and outcome is essential for turning policy into tangible impact.

State Business

One is left to wonder whether policy formulation and its necessary dependence on execution is related to the quality of governance. Specifically, this author refers to how well institutions function according to their mandates and the extent to which corruption in government and politics, apart from being important and longer-term issues, requires urgent and immediate action. One is not talking here about constitutional matters such as where power shall lie and how it is balanced and distributed, nor is one referring to institutional relationships and constitutional provisions for independence or interdependence or separation of powers and roles. One is talking here simply about good business practice – how to make an economic system efficient and effective, how to ensure that businesses under the jurisdiction of the state make a profit and how to ensure there is transparency, accountability and good practice in government business, especially when the state owns or dominates a significant portion of the economy. What happens when a small economy depends on state decisions and actions and so many opportunities are made available only by the state?

Take, for instance, the case of state enterprises, very few of which are profitable and most of which are heavily subsidized with taxpayers' money.[53] This cannot be sustained. The problem begins with the extent of autonomy of these businesses and whether or not there is political interference in decision-making. John Kenneth Galbraith, who once served as the United States ambassador to India for the John Kennedy administration,[54] wrote about this a long time ago in *Ambassadors Journal*. He pointed out that what matters profusely in a state enterprise is not who owns it, but whether or not it operates according to business principles, understanding that the raison d'être of a business is to make a profit. The second thing that matters is whether or not political interference is strong enough to derail its business mandate.

From WASA to Petrotrin

In Trinidad and Tobago, state boards are clearly not driven by profit, nor the effectiveness that profit-making demands. It is also clear that political influence on state companies is significant. Better to give these institutions the freedom to succeed financially and economically and free the taxpayers of the burden of heavy subsidies. A way has to be found. It is not the purpose of this chapter, this book or this author or the authors who have written chapters in this volume to give a prescription of how and why taxpayers cannot carry the burden any longer. It is just not fair to them. The prevailing trend suggests that prices of state goods and services keep increasing even as subsidization of state enterprises continues indefinitely. Taxpayers pay heavily.

Moreover, the state as employer and state enterprises as government-owned institutions have become susceptible to blackmail by unions because politics and political patronage become factors in wage negotiations. When the state is an employer, wage negotiations are not only about wages. Because it involves government, it inevitably involves politics. A way, consequently, to free all state enterprises is to ensure that they are made to operate on the basis of business principles – state enterprises can be fixed, transformed, sold or shut down depending on performance and prospects for economic viability. Selling can be multidimensional: foreign acquisition, foreign-local partnership. Employee share ownership can be part of the arrangement, as well as partial union ownership shares on the stock exchange. Several permutations are possible. The critical issue must be that once a decision is made to fix, transform or sell, from then on, that company must operate on its own with taxpayers and the government having no responsibility whatsoever for its success or failure. The company will rise or fall on the basis of business principles as practised by its board of directors, management, employees and other stakeholders. Accountability must rest with the board and management.

Corruption

Another issue is corruption in government and the conduct of government business. In any democratic country, governments are elected by the people through a system of political party competition. Parties need funds to maintain effective campaigns and to communicate their message to voters. When a political party wins, its task is to govern, manage the state and act as custodian of state funds on behalf of the taxpayer. That means spending as approved by Parliament in a budget and/or other money bills.

Procurement of goods and services accounting for taxpayers' funds and the disposal of state assets may arise from time to time. How are these things to be managed transparently and accountable? How do you get good governance practices and honest government? In other words, given the way political parties, governments and government opportunities connect with business, how do you ensure honesty and root out corruption in businesses? This is a problem not unique to Trinidad and Tobago, but failure to address this and similar challenges have created a monster that grows on greed.

Responsive System, Working Structure of Accountability

Budgetary expenditure is reviewed on an ongoing basis in a budgetary year by a Public Accounts Management Committee (PAMC). However, the committee is chaired by the Speaker. In our system, the Speaker is a member of the ruling party who may or may not be impartial in the management of debates but who is not independent enough to challenge the ruling party or the minister of finance in the way that an independent senator might or an opposition member is likely to do. Since the Senate does not vote on money bills, including the budget, there might be an objection to having an independent senator chair such a committee in the place of the

Speaker. But it makes a lot of sense to have an independent senator preside over the ongoing spending of taxpayers' money, especially in a budget in which they may have had a say in debate even if they had no vote or have any power to approve or deny. In such a situation, an independent senator in the chair can truly exercise independent oversight since they have no direct interest except as an enlightened citizen in how the money is spent. It is assumed that an independent senator would consider it desirable to guard his or her independence.

Alternatively, a member of the Opposition who would have ordinarily voted for the budget, perhaps with criticisms or reservations, may be charged with chairing the oversight committee just as it is done with the Public Accounts Committee (PAC), which scrutinizes accounts after the auditor general audits them. Either of these would be an improvement on what we have now, that is to say, independent senatorial oversight or oversight by an opposition MP. On no account should such a committee be chaired by a minister, government member or government-nominated Speaker or Senate president – also nominated by the government – because inevitably, in the system as it currently operates, such representatives would find themselves in an awkward situation at some point, especially sitting in the chair.

Parliamentary Scrutiny

How should parliamentary scrutiny on matters flagged by the auditor general or issues that come up frontally, indirectly, or obliquely based on the auditor general's report be strengthened? And can the PAC be given more teeth?

In the current system, a member of the opposition chairs the PAC, which is good, and a member of the opposition also chairs the Public Accounts Enterprises Committee. This potentially ensures keen and robust oversight. However, reports of these committees are not debated in Parliament, and recommendations are not fully engaged. Debate on selected reports, or selected items within reports, and recommendations and responses of ministers would add significant value and make the executive branch more responsive to Parliament and accountable to it. That would help to strengthen the accountability system of government and bring the parliamentary scrutiny function alive in Parliament to the benefit of the general public and citizenry.

Auditor General

The Auditor General's Office also needs to be strengthened. For one, the office should have the power to force compliance in terms of reportage requirements and meeting deadlines. The auditor general needs to be independent of the Ministry of Finance and the minister to be able to freely say what needs to be told without fear or favour or worry about offending the minister or the ministry.[55] An independent budgetary allocation would allow that to happen and would also strengthen the will of public service officers and statutory bodies to comply. The process of appointment of the auditor general is currently acceptable – appointed by the president after consultation with the prime minister and leader of the opposition. Still, the office might be much more independent if it had its own budget, if it could force compliance and if it could insist on action in problematic areas. The Auditor General's Office could be strengthened as well by debates on selected PAC reports laid out in Parliament.

Campaign Financing

The other issue essential to ensure transparency in government and corruption-sensitive governance is an accountable system of campaign financing. Campaign financing is hard to monitor in every country, and money has a way of cutting a path to its intended destination. The objective of a transparent campaign and party financing system is to ensure that undue influence is not purchased in secret and away from the public eye.

The reporting system under the Elections and Boundaries Commission (EBC), as it currently exists, has nothing to do with the realities of election spending. Each candidate has an unrealistically small limit; the reporting requirement is ritualistic, and nowhere is a political party required to report or account for election expenditures; only individual candidates are required to report. A transparent system needs to be devised to make donors to the party known, making expenditures in favour of political parties during the year and especially during an election campaign more transparent.

Effective Procurement Law

Procurement is related to party financing but not limited to it. It is meant to ensure transparency, accountability and fair governance practices in the acquisition of goods and services.

Trinidad and Tobago established a strong procurement law in 2014 after various attempts at procurement law had languished for decades in the form of white papers. However, that law assented to in January 2015, has since been amended several times, rendering it weaker and less effective in addressing acts of corruption. The author of this chapter invested at least three years of his life in establishing a solid procurement law in Trinidad and Tobago as a minister of planning and sustainable development.

The January 2015 act was passed with full and vocal support from independent senators, civil society, and business groups. A consensus was built around the legislation, which was generally met with approval from the wider society. Although the law has been amended and weakened, it has now been proclaimed. However, there are increasing exemptions from the scrutiny of the procurement regulator. It is important to appreciate that the voting citizen needs comfort on two matters in any society after a general election is over. First, his vote to elect a government and the collective will of the people as revealed in election results should be more powerful for the public good than the financial contribution of another citizen, individual or corporate entity to a political party that would more likely be committed to a narrower, sectarian interest. That is an essential assurance that a citizen needs.

Second, citizens need to feel assured that personal preferences, partisan preferences or corrupt practices will not affect the procurement process, thereby costing taxpayers more than honest competition and objective assessment of proposals should allow.

Transparent party financing rules and effective procurement law are fundamental to honest government, good governance and reasonable citizen expectations in a democratic society. They are also essential for fairness, transparency, accountability and a reasonable balance of power. An institutionally independent auditor general, a meaningful campaign financing law and a strong procurement law committed to transparency, accountability and good governance would create a desirable framework for more honest governance.

In 2024, the Trinidad and Tobago government passed a whistleblowing law, which should also be helpful. However, existing gaps do need to be bridged.

Democracy

A key issue is what type of democracy and what quality of democratic experience exists in Trinidad and Tobago? The world has long learnt that elections alone do not make a democracy. Democracy demands an ongoing dialogue and consultations, as required, between the citizens who elected a government and those who are elected and nominated to govern. Citizens in their own right and through civil society, trade unions and business organizations through which they act and engage society are stakeholders in a democracy. Essentially, a real democracy involves at least two phases: free and fair election so a government can be clearly chosen by the majority and stakeholder participation in the process of decision-making so that government decision-making can take well-considered views of citizens into account on an ongoing basis. Free and fair elections are not the end of a democratic process; they are the beginning.

The 2015 Procurement Legislation, for instance, though there was much navigation of difficult terrain, saw a worthwhile consensus built around it and achieved honourable results. This had more to do with the fact that the consultative process was so thorough – joint select committee, a unanimous agreement after extensive consultation with any and all stakeholders who wanted to contribute, including citizens, organizations and multilateral institutions, testimony as well as informal talks with the Procurement Regulator of Jamaica, and solid participation and support from independent senators. The deepening of democracy to get the most desirable outcome added significant value. After the assent and partial proclamation, everything came to nought with the change of government in 2015; there was so much for good governance, politics, responsibility, political behaviour, and legislative continuity. So, with the procurement law, over two administrations, we can learn what not to do and how not to do it. This issue of continuous advancement in legislative, executive, parliamentary and policy decision-making for the public good is an important matter in a democracy. The citizenry should not tolerate reversals that are hostile to public interest in fundamental matters of governance. The tragedy of procurement legislation is that while lobbying for good legislation and passage of the bill was strong, resistance to problematic regulations lacked aggression.

While politics, governments and governance constitute one element, what about economic strategy, economic policy and budgets, and what are the dismal results that come from these? Seven continuous years with no growth should demand significant policy shifts in any reasonable environment in which rational discourse is made possible. Windfall revenue from unusually high oil and natural gas prices in 2022 should not mask the reality of no growth since 2016. But there is no meaningful debate, little shifts in policy and no dramatic shifts in results.

Structure of Production and Results of Development

If we look at the Trinidad and Tobago economy critically, its two fundamental problems are the structure of production and inequality. Over sixty years, we have not diversified enough to have the range of options we require to balance trade and payments when energy production or energy prices go down. All our eggs are in one basket, so to speak. However, the energy basket itself is relatively diversified. So, we do well when energy prices are on the upswing. So Trinidad and Tobago has a genuine problem with the structure of production, the structure of investments, the diversity of exports, which reinforce our dependence on oil, natural gas and the energy sector and this creates a problem in terms of balance of payments and in foreign exchange earnings when energy income is down.

The Human Development Atlas (2012) tells us that we have unequal regions, and unemployment and poverty figures tell us that we have wide disparities in income and substantial numbers of poor.[56] Social welfare transfers are also significant.[57] So we need a recovery, investment, growth, jobs, income and prosperity strategy but also an inclusive shared prosperity agenda for the purpose of addressing equity and equality of opportunity issues. Such a holistic strategy is essential to anchor peace and harmony in the society. What would be a good way of addressing this?

One way of addressing this is by policies that put the economy into recovery by stimulating investments, growth, jobs and incomes. However, opportunities must also be created through policy for earned land and property ownership, employee share ownership, and effective engagement of the economic and financial system. It goes without saying that a prosperity agenda must be established and must begin to be achieved before a shared prosperity agenda can be rolled out. The wealth of the whole accumulated through collective productivity deserves to be spread out to citizens. Still, higher levels of productivity and greater wealth creation are prerequisites for making shared prosperity possible.

In 2022, after seven consecutive years of economic decline, with the only bright light being the high price of energy sector commodities because of the Russia/Ukraine war, the immediate challenge was recovery and growth and how to increase production and exports and strengthen the non-energy tradable goods and services sectors to address balance of payments issues and forex gains as energy prices fall and production is reduced. This requires a major comprehensive, integrated effort of economic restructuring and transformation of existing sectors, as well as the creation of technologically driven sectors which can bring significant value added.

If corruption, transparent governance and good governance are concerns, if the quality of democracy is a concern and if economic strategy, policy, the structure of production and inequality are concerns, then three other critical issues demand focused attention. These governance and economic strategy challenges are deeply interconnected.

Coordinating Government, Getting Policy Coherent

The first of these is uncoordinated government action and the need for coherence in governance. The second is the nature of our political party system. And the third is the relevance of the constitution after sixty years of independence and limited progress, and after forty-six years as a republic. Let us take uncoordinated government action and coherence in government.

The manifestos of political parties typically outline a range of promises that collectively reflect a philosophical approach to setting broader priorities. In Trinidad and Tobago, these priorities are usually translated into a three-year medium-term plan when a party assumes government. This was the case between 2011 and 2014, with a basic plan also prepared in 2015. Action 2025, a ten-year programme of action, was designed to facilitate several three-year plans over the decade. However, the succeeding government did not adopt this approach. In 2009, a previous administration developed Vision 2020, which, despite extensive consultation with various sectors, did not receive opposition support.

Similarly, Action 2025 failed to gain the approval of the incoming government in 2015, which opted instead to introduce Vision 2030, marking a departure from the earlier framework. That (Vision 2030) also did not receive the support of the Opposition. So from 2009 to 2022, a government, whichever government, has been guided by documents prepared for national action without the support of the Opposition, whichever Opposition – a period of thirteen years. So, over thirteen years at least, there has been little continuity or commitment to the continuity of broad policy. As a result, policy has taken a turn toward haphazardness.

For thirty years (1956–86), the country was governed by a single party. Government policy, including national five-year plans, was never done in consultation with the Opposition or debated in Parliament. So from inception, a bad precedent was set, in which once elected, executive power, largely on its own, determined policy.

Moreover, when the party that ruled for thirty consecutive years demitted office, it depleted all the country's financial resources. Trinidad and Tobago had to approach the IMF for financial support and a structural adjustment programme. So, in 1988, there was a decisive disruption of policy. However, it may be argued coherently that the policy that had been in force for thirty years needed to be disrupted and a new course needed to be set in motion. In any case, thirty years of policy, 1956–86, had led to financial bankruptcy, and the country, in a sense, had to press a restart button, which had been signalled by the Demas Report of 1983.[58] So, at the technocratic level nationally and at the multilateral level internationally, the agreed position was that Trinidad and Tobago had to change course.

Continuity

The National Alliance for Reconstruction (NAR) government, which succeeded the People's National Movement (PNM) after thirty years and initiated a limited programme of restructuring with the IMF, lost the next elections to the PNM. Initially, the incoming PNM government sought to change the NAR policies but ultimately did not do so. Therefore, Trinidad and Tobago had a continuity of policy from 1988 to 2008 despite changes in party government. This is an important period of policy continuity and economic consolidation. But then, from 2008 to 2009, a global financial crisis, which saw energy prices plummet and real estate markets crash, disrupted the world financial and economic system so severely that government bailouts were required in several major industrialized countries. In Trinidad and Tobago, we had our own issues with the collapse of a major private sector company, CL Financial.

The years 1991–2008 were good years of recovery and growth for the national economy, with continuity of policy from 1988. These policies focused on restructuring, recovery and growth. However, against the background of the 2008 financial crisis, deficit spending was initiated in 2009. In 2010, there was a change of government and some disruption in policy, but the deficit spending continued. The government of 2010 established an Economic Development Board and an Innovation Council. It deployed a strategy of regional growth poles to complement the macro-economic strategy, but these hardly had time to impact. The national state of emergency called in 2012 disrupted whatever momentum that might have been set in motion at both a practical and psychological level.

In 2015, the government changed again, and with it, there were policy reversals. The Economic Development Board became an advisory board and was eventually abandoned. The National Innovation Council was scuttled immediately, and the growth pole strategy was not pursued. Whatever the disruptions, however, deficit spending continued without interruption. As a result, 2015–22 has been one prolonged recession, exacerbated by another disruption, COVID-19. Deficit financing averaged TT$9 billion per year between 2016 and 2023.

As previously mentioned, Trinidad and Tobago had thirty years of continuity with one party, which, by 1986, had taken the country into bankruptcy. During that period, Trinidad and Tobago had lived through a cycle of booms and busts in oil. Following that, we had thirteen years of policy continuity, although we had two different party governments (NAR and PNM). However, this policy continuity led to recovery, growth and buoyancy as natural gas anchored the Trinidad and Tobago energy-driven economy.

In 2015, there was some policy rethinking on the part of the People's Partnership government, with a focus on educational expansion, encouragement of investment, and some emphasis on people and community development and social infrastructure. However, the government walked into an oil crash in 2014 and lost elections in 2015, and with the change of government came policy reversals and shifts in emphasis. These policies from 2015 on, with the additional adversity of the COVID-19 lockdown and the continuing low energy prices from 2014 to 2021, have led to economic decline and a seven-year recessionary period in which recovery was elusive.

The policy issue cannot be ignored. Trinidad and Tobago must clearly identify urgent medium-term and long-term priorities to achieve policy coherence and summon growth and progress, regardless of electoral outcomes. To achieve this, a formula needs to be advanced, negotiated and agreed upon.

One way might be to agree in Parliament on the principle of three-year national plans on a rolling basis, accompanied by a fiscal plan of the same duration. Correctly done, this could support continuity as well as accommodate variations, but a basis will have been established for the collective achievement of longer-term objectives for country and nation through collaborative effort, even if such effort, of necessity, would be led by the duly elected government and its ministers with public service support. Each three-year plan by the sitting government will be debated and approved by Parliament, and each government will be limited to passing just two such three-year plans in a five-year parliamentary term. This will give some coherence and guarantee continuity to policy, and build in some level of predictability as well. One assumes a professional public service with institutional memory and technical competence. If the government changes, they continue with the plan for one year, and subsequently, the new government would bring their own three-year plan early in their term for parliamentary debate and approval. It is hoped that these new plans will build on past gains and prioritize new initiatives that advance the country's economic, financial and development prospects. Parliamentary debate on policy direction and priorities add some significant value.

Coordination

What about the coordination required, though, to achieve implementation for results? Successive governments in Trinidad and Tobago have consistently been associated with an implementation deficit. And one key factor contributing to poor implementation is a lack of synergy because government ministries and other key governmental agencies operate in silos and, often, in contradiction, with each other.

Let us take a simple but easily recognizable example. The Ministry of Works may pave a road today, and tomorrow, the Water and Sewage Authority (WASA) may show up to dig up the newly paved road, which would now once again need repair. Multiply this scenario by several occurrences, and we begin to see the unnecessary headache we are creating for citizens, how development is undermined, how underdevelopment is facilitated and how inconvenience proliferates.

Let us take a slightly more complex problem. Farmers are hit, depending on the season, by droughts and floods. Farmers have irrigation problems in the dry season, particularly. Farmers have access road problems. It seems to me that through cooperation between the Ministry of Agriculture, the local government bodies, the Ministry of Rural Development, the Ministry of Local Government and the Ministry of Works, all these problems can be solved coherently via collaboration and cooperation. Moreover, WASA, with oversight by the Ministry of Public Utilities, has a problem with water capture, storage and effective distribution. It seems to me that several ministries can work together to enhance water capture solutions in the rainy season through dredging, draining and creating water capture opportunities and facilities, from retention ponds to rainwater harvesting.

If farmers were meaningfully supported by the Ministry of Agriculture, and that ministry also pushed technologically driven agriculture, we could be significantly more self-supporting in food production and much more food secure. But we could also then, since we would be embarking on a new enterprise, align food production strategy to some of the problems that are food-related, at least in part.

For instance, a significant problem in Trinidad and Tobago is non-communicable diseases such as diabetes, hypertension and heart disease, all requiring dietary discipline as part of treatment. But a food security plan could easily dovetail with a better health plan in the free market as well as in the hospitals and terms of information sharing and better citizen health guidance and health centres and clinics. Better nutrition strategies in the homes of approximately twenty thousand mothers who give birth to babies every year can make a qualitative difference in health outcomes for the baby, mother, and other members of the family and household. Moreover, there are links between hunger and the ability to concentrate in the classroom. A serious policy of school feeding across the system can address hunger in children, improve nutrition for children in school, boost agricultural production, and help change patterns of taste and food preferences while giving those children a better chance of doing well in school.

A meaningful link involving the hotels and guest houses, supported by culinary advice and training, can change the percentage of tourist dollars that is genuinely earned locally through the consumption of food.

Moving from silo behaviour to synergistic thinking and action and embracing collaborative leadership and behaviour, and practising cooperation can make a world of difference in implementation, impact and results which will contribute significantly to the development process. What is being advocated here is a systems thinking approach to achieve clearly identified desirable results and high, positive impacts on the citizens.

Political Party System

We cannot ignore our political party system. Should we admit that notwithstanding our best intentions, our political party system is too partisan, sectarian, combative and divisive to serve our best national interest in a fair, transparent and just way? Is it legitimate to ask the question: do we end up with national governments or partisan governments? And if we end up with partisan governments, what are the implications for a change of government and continuity of policies for national development? Undoubtedly, the option cannot be a one-party government or a one-party state. Nor can a reasonable answer be the legitimatization of nepotism and political patronage.

And if our political parties are too divisive and combative, what are the implications for parliamentary behaviour and political behaviour? In such a culture as has evolved, and with such an entrenched culture, can we expect cross-party cooperation in or out of Parliament, or is behaviour from one election to another likely to be tension-ridden and warlike? And what can we expect in terms of citizen response if political leadership establish such a tone and disposition? There has to be room for political combat as well as cooperation and collaboration in the national interest. It is one thing to argue about economic or social policy, but it is entirely another to be irretrievably hostile to foreign policy issues and national security issues. It seems to me that these two areas at least require collaboration, cooperation, joint efforts and mutual support in the nation's best interest. The security, safety and well-being of citizens cannot be put at risk. The sovereignty and national interest of Trinidad and Tobago must not be compromised or placed in jeopardy. However, the issues of physical planning to support sustainable development and some reasonable approaches to constructive policy also require cooperation in order to facilitate sustained development and economic progress.

Both major political parties are rooted in ethnic and, to some extent, religious and regional constituencies. Still, both have also crossed ethnic barriers in terms of leadership spread and parliamentary representation, and even the loyal constituencies of both (about 20 per cent each) are perpetually worried about the undue influence of party financiers and personal friends of party leadership personalities. So, the situation is not simple. A large constituency not directly aligned to either party floats and feels largely left out and alienated by the political directorate, no matter which party is in government. This creates another problem: the willingness of talented experts to contribute and the openness of political parties to reach out to potential contributors to the governance process not necessarily aligned to a political party. Room must be made to draw from that pool of citizens for whom party loyalty is not a dominant consideration.

Disenchantment with Status Quo

Yet it has been difficult for a third party to emerge or to evolve with rooted strength. Third parties have had no deep roots in a particular constituency, nor have they had broad reach and appeal. Traditional constituencies remain largely loyal. Third parties have shown that they cannot win on their own, only through coalitions and further after a coalition dissolves or loses power, there is no sustainable life for a third party. What the future holds on this account is left to be seen. However, there is a need for the existing dominant parties to think deeply and take steps to reform and reinvent themselves. The hold of both traditional political parties seems to be loosening, and what each one stands for and what differentiates them seems to be nebulous. The common dominant concern is the quest for power and then the leveraging of the benefits of possession of power and office.

On the other hand, the majority of citizens' alienation from the two existing parties on the political landscape and even from the parliamentary and governance processes raises the question of what citizens can do to change the character and perspective of traditional parties or summon the courage to create an alternative to what has existed in one form or another for sixty years. This is a pending challenge with no easy answer or clear pathway.

The truth is that the force and appeal of each of the two traditional parties has been blunted. Citizens see choices but no real options because the positive results of electoral change cannot be assumed. No matter what is articulated, the question remains whether citizens feel driven enough to create a new option that can have broad national appeal in the face of such alienation and dimming of political lights by traditional parties. And then, what would it stand for? What would be different? How would the country be better off and on a better course? So, there is a political discourse that needs to take place since the quality of governance and the effectiveness of government depend on the disposition, perspective, habits of behaviour and culture of political parties. Maybe political parties themselves need to initiate a rethinking and transformation process. But isn't one element of democracy about citizen participation and influence? What is the role of the non-aligned citizen in the transformation process which the political party system and politics require?

Constitution

The third issue is the constitution and the need for constitutional reform. In 2024, the government established a committee to review the constitution. Whatever their recommendation, there are a few necessities. Separation of powers – legislative, executive, judicial – with accountability. The executive must do what it is supposed to do: manage the state apparatus with which it is entrusted, make policy and execute, lead the parliamentary and legislative agenda, run the government and account to parliament responsibly. The government must account through questions answered, during debate and through committees. The role of the Opposition and back bench of the government must be strengthened. The back bench of the governing party never acts with freedom. The role of the Opposition has become weaker as the strength of the Speaker has grown and as protection of the government by the Speaker and senate president has emerged as an unwritten rule.

On the other hand, the quality of the opposition parliamentarians seems to have diminished on the basis of poor candidate selections, and the level of preparation for parliamentary debates seems to require a boost. Party combativeness, as well as tension-ridden relations between opposition members and presiding officers in Parliament, have escalated. Corrections to ensure democracy and a balance must be reinforced by the constitution and the standing orders. No committee of Parliament should be chaired by a minister. Instead, a committee should be chaired by an opposition member, an independent senator, or a backbencher so that genuine independence of committees is strengthened and the power of executive influence over the parliamentary process is limited. Only joint select committees, to which bills are referred, where it makes sense for the minister piloting the bill and determining policy on behalf of the government to preside, should be chaired by a government minister.

It may well be that we need a full-scale revision of the constitution to alter power relations and strengthen accountability responsibilities, as well as to ensure that those entrusted with power serve the public good. For instance, there is not only a need for a strong executive but also a strong Parliament to keep the executive in check. The issue of term limits for prime ministers might also be desirable in order not to entrench an individual as an institution.

Given the challenges presented for the citizenry by the existing political party system and a win-all or lose-all context, it may be desirable to introduce some form of proportional representation. There are several other issues which have been raised from time to time, which suggest that significant constitutional revision might be in order.

Key areas for reform include a thorough review of the judiciary and the broader justice system. One critical question is the connection between increased lawlessness and improved management and fair outcomes of the justice system. Additionally, there is ongoing debate about whether the current presidential system should be replaced with an executive presidency, a topic that gained prominence in 2005–6. Another critical issue is the role of local government in a decentralized system, where greater devolution of power could enhance governance.

These matters are closely linked to the separation of powers, the determination of constitutional authority and reforms aimed at improving governance, strengthening democracy and increasing accountability. However, for the judiciary, more than just the separation of powers is required. The judiciary must function as an independent entity with a clear mandate, supported by an efficient and effective justice system that ensures law, order and justice. Transparency and accountability in judicial efficiency, effectiveness and outcomes are essential.

When considering broader governance reforms, the effectiveness of the public service also needs rethinking. This includes revisiting the terms and conditions under which it operates and implementing changes that promote greater efficiency, responsiveness and higher levels of citizen satisfaction.

Local Government

The local government entities need to be strengthened and properly resourced, given autonomy over budgets made accountable to Parliament through the Public Accounts Committee, and directly responsible to the people through formalized meetings three or four times per year in each region. There should be no central ministry of local government. The Constitution must set the framework for racial equality before the law. Economic equity, cultural and religious diversity and the guiding ideas behind national sovereignty, nationhood and unity of purpose should set the tone for the relationship between government and people. To bring coherence to this, the justice system must be fixed, made credible and serve justice with an acceptable sense of fairness. Currently, it is dysfunctional, and there is no assurance of justice within a reasonable time or that the result of justice delivered is law and order. The constitution should set the frame, given our history, for Trinidad and Tobago to be a first-class nation of prosperity, democracy, peace, harmony and high levels of achievement. The constitution must reinforce the notion that a system working for a few can never be considered world-class. The contest between merit and equity is a false contest. We have seen worldwide, as well as at home, exacerbated by the COVID-19 experience that democracy and markets are working for the few at the expense, or to the detriment, of the many, and that is the greatest challenge to shared economic prosperity and political stability in the world at large. It is the greatest threat to order and peaceful progress in the world. And it is an ever-escalating threat to peace, harmony and unity in Trinidad and Tobago or any individual country for that matter.

A Guiding Idea

V.S. Naipaul, in an interview with this author in 2006,[59] spoke of the essential need of countries, especially small countries such as ours, to have a guiding idea – of who we are, what we stand for and where we need to be in the world. He elaborated that it is hard to keep talent from being attracted to opportunities abroad when such opportunities and the range of options available elsewhere are not available in a small country. So, at one practical level, the essential task is to build a country of opportunities that can retain homegrown talent and attract talent from elsewhere. The only way to achieve this is to create a prosperous economy that can make an island nation such as Trinidad and Tobago as self-sufficient as possible and outward-reaching. The key to every opportunity is prosperity and sustainable development. That will attract, enrich, renew, sustain. And that means that both democracy and economic competitiveness must evolve to benefit from emerging and evolving global trends for progress.

This must begin with food security, and we must learn from the example of others. A report on food security in Iceland, a country of three hundred and sixty thousand people, prepared by the Agricultural University of Iceland, tells us that horticulture provides 43 per cent of the supply of vegetables, animal husbandry 90 per cent of the meats, 96 per cent of the eggs and 99 per cent of dairy products.[60] This and more are achievable in Trinidad and Tobago. Fishing in Iceland exceeds domestic demand, so an export industry has been built. A growing tourist industry finances agricultural production, and tourists help consume some of the food and promote the growth of agriculture. Iceland is the world's largest green energy producer per capita and is strong on wind and geothermal energy.

Uruguay a country of 3.4 million people, not far from Trinidad and Tobago, provides enough food for thirty million people. Companies from outside Uruguay invest there because of confidence, security and exceptional quality of support and trust. Uruguay exports to 150 countries, including the most demanding markets in North America and Europe and to China. Its domestic production thrust is driven by information systems and other technologies. Uruguay generates 98 per cent of its electricity from renewable resources such as hydropower, wind, solar and biofuels. Although Uruguay's natural resources are limited, sun, water and wind are used with great effectiveness.

Independent Countries Post-1960

From 1960 to 1965, thirty-three countries gained their independence. Among them, Singapore, Malta, Kuwait and Cyprus are doing better than Trinidad and Tobago in terms of per capita income, which is not the best measure, but it does mean something.[61]

The Challenging Issues

Trinidad and Tobago faces several critical issues. First, GDP has declined, and per capita income is also decreasing. Second, inequality is on the rise. Third, the economy is stagnating, and fourth, the country is overly dependent on the energy sector. Inward investment outside of energy is minimal, and even within the energy sector, investments are dwindling. Additionally, export capacity outside of energy is weak, foreign reserves are shrinking, and the national debt has risen significantly, raising concerns about repayment. The country's high food import bill adds to the economic strain, and since 2009, Trinidad and Tobago has been operating on a budget deficit.

So, beyond as much self-sufficiency as possible in food, Trinidad and Tobago will have to grow the economy outside of energy and fossil fuels. That means growing exports in manufacturing, commerce, services, agriculture, and tourism and increasing local and foreign investment in export industries outside energy, with investors bringing markets, know-how and technology. The country needs to stimulate entrepreneurship and innovation within existing industries. A new industry is driven by new investment, but we need to create a climate supportive of start-ups that can take the entrepreneur from idea to innovation and business creation. In addition, small, medium and family businesses, which account for about twenty-five thousand businesses, need to be made to thrive. That means that there is an urgent need for growth and expansion of export markets, a buoyant national economy and healthy consumer demand.

Trinidad and Tobago is missing a considerable opportunity with the pool of tertiary-level graduates that it has generated over the last decade or two, many of whom are unemployed or underemployed and thinking of migration or have migrated. How can this pool of human assets be meaningfully leveraged? First of all, with those who are so inclined, start-up businesses and entrepreneurship ventures can be facilitated and encouraged. Secondly, with the right international companies, this group can be effectively marketed as a talent pool from which educated, trainable, talented recruits can be drawn in IT-based industries, robotics, artificial intelligence and other information and technologically driven businesses. This will allow Trinidad and Tobago to build a category of industries higher up the value chain, connected to cutting-edge technology trends, develop partnerships and alliances internationally and forge business-to-business collaboration in a global value chain. Investment, growth, jobs and income, prosperity and sustainability are where the future is. Technology and digitalization are where the future is. Exporting tradable goods and services and embedding Trinidad and Tobago industries into the global value chain is where the future is. The alternative to these necessities is failure, being left behind. The output of the tertiary sector is about four hundred ICT graduates per year. We have established a Ministry of Digital Transformation, and we have some skills and a consistent throughput of skills. What we need is foreign investment, which connects us to the global ICT value chain.

Renewable Energy and Climate Change

That brings this chapter to the energy transformation question and the imperative for sustainable development. Why can't Trinidad and Tobago jump-start these two essential initiatives?

One requires an energy transformation project which will link world solutions and regional research to our energy transformation agenda. The second area is a climate-change response, mitigation and adaptation project approached holistically. In any society, silo thinking cripples. We need collaborative leadership, integrated strategies and synergies across traditional boundaries.

Renewable Energy

In a small country like Trinidad and Tobago, with a population of 1.4 million, the impact of these challenges can be significant. The country has a manageable number of communities – around six hundred – served by fourteen regional governments in Trinidad and one in Tobago. With approximately four hundred and fifty thousand households, addressing these issues should, in theory, be more feasible compared to larger nations. However, the scale of the economic and social challenges makes it critical to implement targeted, effective policies to mitigate the negative effects on such a compact population. What would it take to bring together a serious team of government officials, energy companies, other private sector entities, university researchers and NGOs to focus on energy transformation? It takes just the will, dedicated collaborative interest and purposeful action to drive progress. A committed group could identify feasible projects and successfully implement them with the backing of the government, the private sector and citizens. These initiatives could include industries centred on renewable energy sources such as solar, wind, geothermal and biofuels. The solar project, currently led by BPTT and Shell in partnership with NGC and the government of Trinidad and Tobago, is a promising step forward. However, we must accelerate the pace of this transformation to fully realize its potential.

Climate Change

Trinidad and Tobago, like other Caribbean islands, faces the brunt of climate change's impact more intensely than many other regions. Our vulnerability underscores the urgent need for mitigation, adaptation and response strategies. Why can't Trinidad and Tobago assess its current actions, review past efforts in terms of maintenance and follow-up and develop a comprehensive, urgent plan for responsiveness, mitigation and adaptation across the nation? Such a plan, structured in phases and focusing on project-by-project execution, would enable the country to build the capacity needed to attract international funding based on commitments from COP 25 and COP 27. This approach could help Trinidad and Tobago leverage global support to safeguard its future in the face of escalating climate threats. Such an initiative properly done could harness resources from the University of the West Indies (UWI) and the University of Trinidad and Tobago (UTT), all the universities regionally and some internationally, as well as a range of selected international alliances with the people and people's organizations committed to saving the planet and dedicated to environmental and ecological sustainability. Such an approach could indeed position Trinidad and Tobago as a major global project, attracting international attention, collaboration and investment. A comprehensive initiative that addresses critical areas – coastal zones, swamps, forests, tree planting, rivers and streams – would not only tackle climate challenges but also elevate the country's profile as a sustainable tourism destination. By integrating climate action with the promotion of local agricultural production, Trinidad and Tobago could boost its culinary identity on the world stage, stimulating micro and small enterprises in the process. This holistic approach could also amplify the nation's cultural power, linking environmental sustainability with the vibrant annual cycle of festivals and cultural events.

The synergy between climate action and tourism offers tremendous potential. By meaningfully harnessing these sectors, Trinidad and Tobago could ensure widespread benefits for stakeholders while securing its future as both a sustainable and culturally rich destination.

The Next Decade

As has been previously articulated, every country's actions need to be informed by a guiding idea or principle. What is Trinidad and Tobago's guiding idea? What kind of people are the people of Trinidad and Tobago? What do citizens stand for, and what kind of nation are they seeking to build? After sixty years, the people of Trinidad and Tobago arrived at that point where there was something like a collective discussion. They shared an understanding of the answers to such questions needed to take place. There is a pervasive feeling that Trinidad and Tobago has lost its way. The divisive tendencies and polarizing currents in Trinidad and Tobago society have become too pronounced. There is an urgent need now to find common ground and something to believe in together. The stage has to be set for building on what other generations have built so far, and for learning from the mistakes that the country has made over time, to begin to craft Trinidad and Tobago's stairway to heaven as a nation, with a unity of purpose and a united resistance to failure.

We are living today in a world of fast-paced change, rapid and far-reaching technological innovations, the shifting of geopolitical positioning, boundary drawing and alliances, and political brinkmanship based on who will blink first in a stare-down contest of egos. At the same time, the tendencies are toward more authoritarianism and oligarchy and less democracy, greater inequity and larger disparities of income, resources and opportunities. Amidst all of these challenges, the planet faces severe threats largely due to centuries of human behaviour, particularly intensified by the rise of imperialism, colonialism, the Industrial Revolution and subsequent industrial development strategies. These historical forces have left the Earth in peril, driving entire populations to flee their communities and countries as a result of climate change. Humanity now stands at a crossroads: we must fundamentally change our ways, or we risk facing catastrophic consequences. The urgency of this moment demands global cooperation and transformative action to ensure the survival of both the planet and the human race. Political leaders and technocrats alike have to rethink development because of what science, statistical data, economic consequences and environmental degradation are revealing to us. New phenomena such as production and supply chain disruptions, the emergence of a more war-like global climate, food shortages, skyrocketing prices and rising poverty have created significant challenges. The number of hungry people is growing, prompting mass migrations in search of survival. Significant divides, such as disparities in technology, scientific advancement, health capacity and capability, along with the unequal distribution of vaccines, essential medicines and food, further deepen global inequalities. These are formidable issues in an increasingly lawless world, where arbitrary power is difficult to contain or restrain. Addressing these challenges requires urgent international cooperation, equitable policy solutions, and a strong commitment to justice and sustainability in a fragmented global landscape.

Trinidad and Tobago must change its ways and rethink the strategy required for its onward journey at this moment in human history. Given our ageing population and our severely declining birth rates, we may well have to consider a managed migration strategy. On this account, we can integrate more effectively the Venezuelan immigrants who have come here over the more difficult period of the Maduro regime. With these migrants comes a diverse workforce, including unskilled labour as well as more skilled talent, all bringing a strong willingness to work and contribute productively. Beyond this, we may wish to pursue a managed migration strategy linked to our national development priorities. That means, however, that as a country, clear priorities must be identified, and the nation must embark on a comprehensive, collaborative effort to achieve them. However, underscoring everything is a strategy for recovery, growth, restructuring and transformation, which can no longer be postponed within a framework of sustainable development.

At the heart of it all is the guiding idea of who the people aspire to be – both individually and collectively – as a nation within the broader community of nations. In a world growing more chaotic and unpredictable by the day, with the planet facing existential threats, the human race's only hope for sustainability and sustainable development lies in our ability to problem-solve, find solutions and continuously innovate.

Unifying Politics

Trinidad and Tobago needs more unifying politics; the country needs to put a collaborative governance model into practice. To be an enlightened and competitive country, Trinidad and Tobago need to insist on meritorious appointments so that the nation can benefit from the value of our best talent. Citizens need stakeholder democracy between elections, and the country needs an agreed national action agenda to achieve shared prosperity supported by national consensus, which can make partisan and sectoral politics containable and tolerable. If a country cannot get the small things right, it will be difficult to have success with the big things.

Macro strategies are crucial for aligning with global trends and broader development trajectories, but micro strategies tailored to local realities are equally essential. In the case of Trinidad and Tobago, addressing Tobago's unique circumstances and the specific regional challenges within Trinidad is both desirable and necessary. The chapter on Tobago by Vanus James et al. point to particular deficiencies between the two islands, worthy of serious consideration when looking at the issue of development and its impacts. Issues such as unexpected shocks to employment in Tobago's tourism sector, the over-reliance on state and government employment and the limited dynamism of the private sector deserve focused attention. Additionally, Tobago's relatively small contribution to national GDP highlights the need for strategic interventions to boost economic resourcefulness and resilience.

Sustainable development requires perpetual innovation. Islands and low-lying countries, such as those in the Caribbean, will be worst affected by climate change, sea level rise, coastal erosion and hurricanes. Development achievements are constantly threatened with reversal. The countries of the region must be capable of smart responses and innovative solutions and must build resilient systems to address these serious problems, which are likely to escalate.

Currently, and possibly well into 2028, Trinidad and Tobago will be living above its means because of revenue shortfalls. This will mean continuing deficit financing and borrowing if current levels of expenditure are maintained. Such a situation is unsustainable.

There are also positive signs of growing export earnings in the manufacturing sector, which earned US$100 million net in 2022 and 2023. However, bridging the shortfall in energy revenue still requires a long time.

Statistics on the services sector are difficult to source, but Statistica tells us that the services sector contributes 47.8 per cent to GDP in Trinidad and Tobago but also accounts for 70.3 per cent of employment. However, imports of services are three times the level of exports. In services, tourism is weak. Trinidad and Tobago needs a services export strategy to grow GDP, exports and jobs. Small and medium enterprises and family businesses are other areas to focus on in developing this strategy, as these small businesses contribute to local employment and generation of economic activity. As such, this sector needs to be supported. The government would be wise to enhance the entrepreneurial spirit as a long-term intervention to stem the flow of transfers and subsidies.

A notion of shared prosperity and economic participation is desirable for Trinidad and Tobago to have economic and social viability in the medium to long term. The current challenge, though, is that economic sustainability is some years away as the Dragon field in Venezuela is not likely to begin producing gas until 2027. And even more, to access the gas, a 17 km pipeline has to be established at an investment cost of US$1 billion. Loran-Manatee, another field, is a shared resource. Trinidad and Tobago's share is 26.25 per cent, but the services are substantial – 10.7 trillion cubic feet of natural gas. The government has done well in securing FAC licences from the United States, which seems to be relatively secure as we make firm arrangements with Venezuela for the monetization of natural gas resources. But time is of the essence. The times between start dates and the first gas in each instance are critical for the country's sustainability in the natural gas industry. There is the possibility that unpredictable geopolitical tensions could put these things in jeopardy

The present is extremely challenging, and while the medium-term outlook appears stable, there are no guarantees. Careful navigation over the next five to seven years is essential, along with meticulous, sensitive management in the immediate three-year period. Clear policy actions focused on diversifying export growth and promoting self-sustainability wherever possible are not just desirable – they are imperative. These strategies are crucial for ensuring long-term stability and resilience in the face of uncertainty, helping Trinidad and Tobago build a more sustainable and diversified economic future.

NOTES

1. OECD, "Food Supply Chains and COVID-19: Impacts and Policy Lessons."
2. Ministry of Finance: @MoFTT/Twitter.
3. See Budget Speech 2024, Minister of Finance.
4. ECLAC, "Development Paths in The Caribbean."
5. Ibid.
6. Ibid.
7. Ibid.

8. The highest number of murders in a single year (2022, 610 murders) and the highest murder rate for any month of January (2023, 62) were registered for the year of 2022 and 2023, respectively.
9. World Bank, "The World Bank in Trinidad and Tobago."
10. Ibid.
11. *Trinidad Express*, "SEA Scores Plunge."
12. Roshnie Doon, "Overeducation in Trinidad and Tobago's Labour Market: A Quantile Regression Approach."
13. CAF, "Development Bank of Latin America, Boosting Productivity and Innovation, key for Trinidad and Tobago's Long-Term Growth."
14. ECLAC, "Development Paths in The Caribbean."
15. Ibid.
16. Ibid.
17. Ibid.
18. Pew Research Center, "Experts Say the 'New Normal' in 2025 Will Be Far More Tech-Driven, Presenting More Big Challenges."
19. Ibid.
20. Ibid.
21. Security Service, MI5, Joint address by MI5 and FBI Heads.
22. ECLAC, "Structural Gaps in Latin America and the Caribbean, a Conceptual-Methodological Perspective."
23. Council on Foreign Relations, China's Growing Influence in Latin America.
24. ECLAC, "Development Paths in The Caribbean."
25. CARICOM, "Redesigning Strategy for Caribbean Success in the Age of Globalization."
26. CARICOM, "The Conference of Heads of Government of the Caribbean Community (Caricom)," 8–9 November 2004, Port of Spain, Trinidad and Tobago.
27. Anthony Klotz, *The Great Resignation Is Still Here, but Whether It Stays Is Up to Leaders.*
28. Ibid.
19. Ibid.
30. See for instance Jack Kelly's "What's Happening in the Tech and IT Services."
31. See, for instance, Rachael Hosie, "Barbados Visa for Remote Workers Could Be a Model for Tourism after the Pandemic – If It Is Done Right," *Business Insider*, 23 December 2020.
32. Ghamz E Ali Siyal, "Recovering from the Pandemic: South Asian Economies Need Greater Self-Sufficiency."
33. Ibid.
34. China passed a food security law in 2022. Lee Mei Mei Chu, "China Food

Security Law Comes into Force and Aims for Absolute Self-sufficiency," Reuters 1 June 2024. See also Mercator Institute for China's Studies, "Beijing Advances Technological Self Reliance by All Means," in *The Party Knows Best: Aligning Economic Actors with China's Strategic Goals*, especially chapter 4.

35. Countries pursuing self-sufficiency in addition to some already mentioned in this chapter, include Brazil, India, United States and Australia.
36. Fernando Funes et al., "Sustainable Agriculture and Resistance: Transforming Food Production in Cuba."
37. Josee Koch, "The Food Security Policy Context in South Africa."
38. Food and Agriculture Organization of the United Nations, FAO in India.
39. Charlie Reeve, "Agriculture and Horticulture Development Board, UK Beef Self-sufficiency and Impacts of Brexit."
40. *Trinidad Express*, "Only 37 per cent of SEA Pupils Scored More Than 50 percent: No Top Ranking Will Be Revealed," and *Trinidad Express*, "CAPE Grades Slightly Better."
41. Central Statistical Office, Ministry of Planning and Development, 2011 Census Data.
42. Ibid.
43. Ibid.
44. Transparency International, Corruption Perceptions Index 2021.
45. Legatum Prosperity Index, 2022.
46. World Bank, "Doing Business 2015."
47. World Bank, "Doing Business 2019."
48. World Economic Forum, "The Global Competitiveness Report 2019."
49. Ibid.
50. Ibid.
51. Ministry of Finance, Trinidad and Tobago Budget 2021.
52. Ibid.
53. Ministry of Finance, Trinidad and Tobago Budget 2021.
54. John Kenneth Galbraith, *Ambassador's Journal*.
55. The conflict between the minister of finance and the auditor general in 2024, now before the courts, make the matter an urgent necessity.
56. Trinidad and Tobago, The Human Development Atlas 2012.
57. Ibid.
58. Imperative of Adjustment, 1983, was prepared for the George Chambers administration.
59. Interview with V.S. Naipaul, writer and critical thinker, *Journal or West Indian Literature*, 2007.
60. Government of Iceland, Icelandic University of Agriculture, Food Security.
61. World Bank, GDP per capita 2020.

REFERENCES

CAF, Development Bank of Latin America. "Boosting Productivity and Innovation, Key for Trinidad and Tobago's Long-Term Growth." 2019. https://www.caf.com/en/currently/news/2019/11/boosting-productivity-and-innovation-key-for-trinidad-and-tobagos-longterm-growth/.

CARICOM. "The Conference of Heads of Government of the Caribbean Community (CARICOM)." 8–9 November 2004, Port of Spain, Trinidad and Tobago. https://caricom.org/welcoming-remarks-by-hon-patrick-manning-prime-minister-trinidad-and-tobago-to-the-tenth-special-meeting-of-the-conference-of-heads-of-government-of-the-caribbean-community-caricom-8-9-november-2/.

———. "Redesigning Strategy for Caribbean Success in the Age of Globalization by Dr Bhoendradatt Tewarie, Pro Vice-Chancellor and Campus Principal, St Augustine Campus, University of the West Indies." 17 September 2003. Belize Sixth Lecture of the Distinguished Lecture Series Celebrating the 30th Anniversary of the Caribbean Community. https://caricom.org/documents/4663/pres129_03.pdf.

Council on Foreign Relations. "China's Growing Influence in Latin America." Council on Foreign Relations, 2022. https://www.cfr.org/backgrounder/china-influence-latin-america-argentina-brazil-venezuela-security-energy-bri.

ECLAC. "Development Paths in the Caribbean." 2012. https://www.cepal.org/en/publications/38253-development-paths-caribbean.

———. "Structural Gaps in Latin America and the Caribbean: A Conceptual-Methodological Perspective." Cepal, 22 December 2020. https://www.cepal.org/en/news/new-document-eclac-examines-structural-gaps-characterize-region.

Funes, Fernando, Luis Garcia, Martin Bourque, Nilda Perez, and Peter Rosset. "Sustainable Agriculture and Resistance: Transforming Food Production in Cuba." Appropriate Technology 29, no. 2 (June 2002): 34.

Food and Agriculture Organization of the United Nations. "FAO in India." https://www.fao.org/india/fao-in-india/india-at-a-glance/en/#:~:text=In%20 2017%2D18%2C%20total%20food,of%20pulses%20in%20the%20world.

Galbraith, John Kenneth. *Ambassador's Journal: A Personal Account of the Kennedy Years*. Boston: Houghton Mifflin, 1969.

Ghamz E. Ali Siyal. "Recovering from the Pandemic: South Asian Economies Need Greater Self-Sufficiency." 9 May 2022. London School of Economics. https://blogs.lse.ac.uk/southasia/2022/05/09/recovering-from-the-pandemic-south-asian-economies-need-greater-self-sufficiency/.

Government of Iceland. "Icelandic University of Agriculture, Food Security." *Government of Iceland*, 11 February 2021. https://www.stjornarradid.is/efst-a-baugi/frettir/stok-frett/2021/02/11/Skyrslu-um-faeduoryggi-a-Islandi-skilad-/.

Josee Koch. "The Food Security Policy Context in South Africa." 2011. International

Policy Centre for Inclusive Growth, United Nations Development Programme. https://ipcig.org/pub/IPCCountryStudy21.pdf.

Klotz, Anthony. "The Great Resignation Is Still Here, but Whether It Stays Is up to Leaders." 2022. OECD. https://www.oecd-forum.org/posts/the-great-resignation-is-still-here-but-whether-it-stays-is-up-to-leaders.

Legatum Prosperity Index 2022. *World Population Review*. https://worldpopulationreview.com/country-rankings/legatum-prosperity-index.

Ministry of Planning and Development, Trinidad and Tobago. *The Human Development Atlas 2012*. Port of Spain: Ministry of Planning and Development, 2012.

MI5 Security Service. "Joint Address by MI5 and FBI Heads." 6 July 2022. https://www.mi5.gov.uk/news/speech-by-mi5-and-fbi.

OECD. "Food Supply Chains and COVID-19: Impacts and Policy Lessons." 2 June 2020. https://www.oecd.org/coronavirus/policy-responses/food-supply-chains-and-COVID-19-impacts-and-policy-lessons-71b57aea/.

Reeve, Charlie. "Agriculture and Horticulture Development Board, UK Beef Self-Sufficiency and Impacts of Brexit." *AHDB*, 6 November 2020. https://ahdb.org.uk/news/uk-beef-self-sufficiency-and-impacts-of-brexit.

Trinidad Express. "CAPE Grades Slightly Better." *Trinidad Express*, 6 September 2022. https://trinidadexpress.com/news/local/cape-grades-slightly-better/article_c02871c0-2d82-11ed-a1f0-eb73828f09c0.html.

———. "Only 37 Per Cent of SEA Pupils Scored More Than 50 Percent: No Top Ranking Will Be Revealed." *Trinidad Express*, 1 July 2022. https://trinidadexpress.com/newsextra/only-37-per-cent-of-sea-pupils-scored-more-than-50-percent-no-top-ranking/article_2ad54aee-f97f-11ec-b81d-67589659d849.html.

———. "SEA Scores Plunge." *Trinidad Express*, 2 July 2022. https://trinidadexpress.com/news/local/sea-scoresplunge/article_4d08e5f2-f9n3-11cc-9b3b-6b5905f75325.html.

Transparency International. "Corruption Perceptions Index 2021." *Transparency International*. https://www.transparency.org/en/cpi/2021.

World Bank. *Doing Business 2015: Going beyond Efficiency*. 12th ed. Washington, DC: World Bank, 2014. https://www.doingbusiness.org/content/dam/doingBusiness/media/Annual-Reports/English/DB15-Full-Report.pdf.

———. "GDP Per Capita 2020." *World Bank*. https://data.worldbank.org/indicator/NY.GDP.PCAP.CD?locations=KR.

———. "The World Bank in Trinidad and Tobago." *World Bank*. 2024. https://www.worldbank.org/en/country/trinidadandtobago.

Contributors

HAMISH ASMATH is a GIS officer at the Institute of Marine Affairs. He is focused on the Caribbean and works in the areas of spatial modelling and analysis, environmental remote sensing and GIS. His current position involves research, data management and operational support.

KENNETH BISSOON is a statistician and economist working out of Tobago.

CHERYLE BOWRIN-WILLIAMS is a senior instructor in curriculum studies, research methods and educational foundations. Her current focus is Teacher Professionalism in Trinidad and Tobago.

REGAN DEONANAN is a lecturer in the Department of Economics at UWI, St Augustine. His research specialties are applied economics and international finance, with an emphasis on long-run economic development of developing countries and small-island developing states.

JUDITH GOBIN is professor of marine biology and head of the Department of Life Sciences, UWI , St Augustine. One of her keen interests is Caribbean deep-sea biodiversity. She has published widely and collaborated extensively and has always been dedicated to public service and environmental activism.

REBECCA GOOKOOL-BOSLAND is president of the SURE Foundation, an NGO focused on food production and sustainability. She has lectured in economics at The University of the West Indies and is currently CEO of an NGO created by Atlantic LNG to support entrepreneurs and micro enterprises in the Southwestern peninsula of Trinidad. She has published articles and books on economic matters and has done research consulting as well as intervention-based projects.

CARLOS HAZEL is an economist and currently is a course instructor at the UWI's Global Campus, St Augustine Campus.

ROGER HOSEIN is professor of economics at The University of the West Indies and Head of the Trade and Development Unit at its St Augustine campus.

Professor Hosein has been a prolific writer and rigorous academic researcher producing a range of articles and books about economic issues in Trinidad and Tobago and the Caribbean region.

WENDY-ANN ISAAC is senior lecturer in crop science in the Department of Food Production, The University of the West Indies. Her research and teaching revolve around sustainable vegetable production, including protected agriculture and production in controlled environments.

VANUS JAMES is an economist from Tobago. He has been active in the consultancy business and has led projects for the UN as well as other multilateral agencies and government entities. He has written and spoken extensively on Tobago issues.

MICHAEL JOSEPH has been, for the last twenty years, an agriculture and environment consultant operating in most countries of the Caribbean. He is active in teaching, researching, consulting, writing and presenting papers in his area of expertise.

LA DAANA KANHAI studies marine ecosystems and their health and conservation. Her research interests are marine plastics pollution, especially in relation to SIDS, and anthropogenic threats posed to coastal and marine eco systems. She is strongly engaged in teaching and research at The University of the West Indies.

JEROME DE LISLE is professor and former director at the School of Education, UWI, St Augustine. He is currently chair of the campus ethics committee and chair of a Cabinet-appointed committee to resolve issues related to Secondary Entrance Assessment and the Concordat established with Denominational bodies in education. He has published extensively in his field.

TRACY LUCAS is a research fellow at the Research, Evaluation, and Outreach Unit of the School of Education, UWI, St Augustine. She is currently focused on the issue of student creativity in the Trinidad and Tobago secondary school system.

OMARDATH MAHARAJ is a lecturer in agricultural economics at The University of the West Indies, St Augustine. He has studied for short intense periods in India and China. He teaches agribusiness and entrepreneurship to undergraduates and has been an advocate for food security across the Caribbean.

KHESHAN RAMNARACE is a fourth-year medical student, School of Medicine, UWI St Augustine. He has gained valuable experience in internal medicine and surgery under the watchful eye of his mentors. He aspires to be a sound diagnostician and a top surgeon.

KEVIN RAMNARINE is a former minister of energy in the government of Trinidad and Tobago and now an international consultant, energy advisor and public commentator on energy matters.

MARK ROOPCHAN is a graduate student undertaking research at the Department of Economics at The University of the West Indies, St Augustine. His primary research area is Trade.

ANJANIE SHARMA has a focus on non-communicable diseases and has a special interest in health communications, including influencing change of behaviour. She was trained in the UK and besides her clinical practice in Trinidad, she works with the Ministry of Health on child obesity issues and the management of NCDs.

SURUJPAL TEELUCKSINGH is a specialist in internal medicine at Medical Associates Health Facility and professor of Medicine in the Faculty of Medical Sciences, UWI, St Augustine. His research interest is metabolic medicine and through his work on diabetes and its link to heart disease, he has become an advocate for public health medicine. Professor Teelucksingh is widely published.

BHOENDRADATT TEWARIE served as Principal of the Trinidad campus and Pro Vice-Chancellor for Planning and Development of The University of the West Indies. He also served as a minister of planning and development and minister of trade industry and enterprise. He has written several articles and books on developmental issues and is currently a columnist with the *Trinidad Guardian.*

NIGEL WILLIAMS is a professor of Project Management at University of Portsmouth, United Kingdom. He prides himself on linking education, research and professional practice. He is keen on social network analysis and systems thinking and incorporates sustainably into current practice in project management. He is well published.

Index

f indicates a figure; t *indicates a table;* T&T *stands for Trinidad and Tobago*